GERMANIC GENEALOGY

A Guide to Worldwide Sources

and Migration Patterns

Second Edition

Edward R. Brandt, Ph. D.

Mary Bellingham

Kent Cutkomp

Kermit Frye

Patricia A. Lowe

with a chapter on computer genealogy
by Paula Goblirsch and Ray Kleinow

and special thanks to George E. Arnstein, Ph. D.,
whose chapter on Jewish genealogy we have expanded

Germanic Genealogy Society
P.O. Box 16312
St. Paul, MN 55116

Published by the Germanic Genealogy Society, P.O. Box 16312, St. Paul, MN 55116.

Library of Congress Catalog Card Number: 97-72640.

Second edition, June 1997.

Cataloging-in-Publication Data.

Germanic genealogy: A guide to worldwide sources and migration patterns.
Second edition. / Edward R. Brandt <et al.>
  517p maps
  Bibliography: p.406-424.
  Includes index.

1. German-Americans—Genealogy. 2. Jews—Genealogy. 3. Jewish-Americans—Genealogy.
4. Germany—Genealogy—Sources. 5. Austria—Genealogy—Sources. 6. Switzerland—
Genealogy—Sources. 7. Germans—Foreign countries—Genealogy—Handbooks, manuals,
etc. 8. Germany—Immigration and Emigration—History—Sources. I. Brandt, Edward R.
929'.1072   97-72640

To order this book, send $32.00 plus $4.00 ($6.00 for surface delivery if outside the United States) shipping and handling to:

Germanic Genealogy Society, P.O. Box 16312, St. Paul, MN 55116.

Minnesota residents, add another $2.08 Minnesota sales tax.

TABLE OF CONTENTS

PREFACE v

INTRODUCTION vii

ACKNOWLEDGMENTS AND CREDITS viii

I. BEGINNING YOUR SEARCH 1

    A. Important Acronyms and Abbreviations 2

II. USING AMERICAN RECORDS TO FIND YOUR ANCESTOR'S PLACE OF ORIGIN 6

    A. Finding the Place of Origin 6
    B. Using the Records... 8
    C. Steps to Further Your Research 8
    D. Finding Professional Genealogists 9
    E. Checklist of Research Sources 10
        1. Family Sources 10
        2. Church and Other Private Records.. 10
        3. Newspapers and Other Publications.. 11
        4. Public Records 11

III. RESEARCHING GERMANIC ANCESTORS IN CANADA 19

IV. COMPUTERS AND GENEALOGY 30

    A. Genealogy Software 30
    B. Genealogy CD-ROMs 33
    C. On Line Services 33

V. FAMILY HISTORY LIBRARY AND ITS CENTERS 40

VI. PASSENGER DEPARTURE AND ARRIVAL LISTS 48

VII. PERSONAL NAMES 54

    A. German Surnames and Anglicized Versions 54
    B. German Given Names... 59
    C. Anglicization of German Given Names 60

VIII. PLACE NAMES 63

    A. Finding the Locality.. 63
    B. Misspelled Place Names 66
    C. List of Gazetteers and Atlases for Europe 67

IX. POLITICAL AND PHYSICAL GEOGRAPHY.. 74

    A. The Changing Political Geography of Ancestral Homelands... 74
    B. Physical Geography and Historic Designations 78
    C. Geographic Outline of Areas of Germanic Settlement in Europe 82

X. HISTORY OF GERMAN-SPEAKING PEOPLE IN EUROPE 86

    A. The German Empire of 1871 to 1919 86
    B. The Austro-Hungarian Empire of 1867 to 1919.. 91
    C. The Russian Empire of 1815 to 1917.. 98
    D. Switzerland.. 104
    E. Grand Duchy of Luxembourg 105
    F. Principality of Liechtenstein 106
    G. The Ottoman Turkish Empire.. 106

XI. HISTORY, MIGRATION AND GENEALOGY OF VARIOUS RELIGIOUS DENOMINATIONS 111

A. THE MEDIEVAL CHURCH AND DISSIDENT GROUPS 112
B. EARLY REFORMATION/COUNTER-REFORMATION ERA, 1517-1648 112
C. PERSECUTION, FLIGHT AND EMIGRATION AFTER 1648 115
    1. Flight and Emigration To and Within Germanic Europe 115
    2. Flight and Emigration From Germanic Europe 116
D. RELIGIOUS DEMOGRAPHY OF GERMANIC COUNTRIES IN 1900 118
E. RELIGIOUS DEMOGRAPHY OF GERMAN-AMERICANS IN 1906 119
F. EVOLUTION OF CHURCHES TO WHICH GERMAN-AMERICANS AND GERMAN-CANADIANS BELONGED 122
G. GENEALOGICAL RESOURCES FOR PARTICULAR DENOMINATIONS 125
    1. Roman Catholics 126
    2. Churches of Lutheran Or Reformed Origin 126
    3. Churches Which Practice Adult Baptism 131
    4. Churches Which Do Not Perform Baptisms 136
    5. Other Churches Of German Immigrants 137

XII. HISTORY AND DEMOGRAPHY OF GERMAN-SPEAKING JEWS 145

A. OVERVIEW OF THE HISTORY OF GERMANIC JEWS 145
B. EARLY JEWISH SETTLEMENTS 145
C. THE ERA OF MASSIVE EXPULSIONS AND EXTREME PERSECUTION 146
D. THE PERIOD BETWEEN EXPULSION AND EMANCIPATION 147
E. EMANCIPATION AND ANTI-SEMITIC REACTION 147
F. THE END OF GERMANIC JEWRY 148
G. OTHER JEWS WITH HISTORIC ROOTS IN GERMANIC EUROPE 149
    1. The Yiddish Language 149
    2. The Jews in the Eastern Parts of the Austro-Hungarian Empire 150
    3. Jews in the Russian Empire 151
    4. Demography 152

XIII. GENEALOGICAL RESOURCES FOR GERMAN JEWISH ANCESTRY 161

A. JEWISH NAMES 161
B. COMMUNAL RECORDS 161
C. CEMETERY RECORDS 163
D. FAMILY HISTORIES 164
E. GENEALOGICAL SOCIETIES AND PERIODICALS 164
F. COMPUTER GENEALOGY 166
G. YIZKOR BOOKS 168
H. HOLOCAUST RESEARCH 169
I. REVIVAL OF HISTORIC INTEREST IN JUDAICA LIBRARIES AND ARCHIVES 170
J. RESEARCH IN SOUTHWESTERN GERMANIC AREAS 172

XIV. GERMANIC MIGRATION TO NON-EUROPEAN COUNTRIES 182

A. REASONS FOR GERMANIC EMIGRATION 182
B. GERMANIC MIGRATION TO THE UNITED STATES 184
C. GERMANIC MIGRATION TO CANADA 190
D. GERMANIC MIGRATION TO LATIN AMERICA 192
E. GERMANIC MIGRATION TO THE SOUTHWEST PACIFIC 202
F. GERMANIC MIGRATION TO AFRICA 212
G. GERMANIC MIGRATION TO ASIA 221

XV. RESEARCHING GERMANIC ANCESTORS OUTSIDE THE UNITED STATES AND CANADA 238

A. LATIN AMERICA 238
B. THE SOUTHWEST PACIFIC 243
    1. Australia 243
    2. New Zealand 249
    3. Former German Colonies and Protectorates 252

C. AFRICA...252
    1. South Africa...252
    2. Former German Colonies and Protectorates...................................255
    3. North Africa 256
D. ASIA..257

XVI. GENEALOGICAL RECORDS RELATING TO GERMAN-SPEAKING ANCESTORS IN EUROPE 261

XVII. RESEARCHING GERMANIC ANCESTORS IN THE GERMAN-SPEAKING COUNTRIES 264

A. GERMANY...264
    1. Postal Codes and Forms of Address 264
    2. Church Records in Germany...265
    3. Public Records in Germany 265
    4. Genealogical Societies for Research in Germany............................273
    5. Researching Ancestors from Specific Areas in Germany.................277
    6. Tracing Illegal Emigrants 280
    7. Genealogical Resource Centers for Eastern Europe 280
    8. Other Specialized Genealogical Resource Centers.........................286
B. AUSTRIA..288
C. SWITZERLAND...298
D. LUXEMBOURG...300
E. LIECHTENSTEIN...302

XVIII. RESEARCHING GERMANIC ANCESTORS IN EAST AND SOUTH EUROPEAN COUNTRIES 306

A. THE SOVIET UNION - SUCCESSOR STATES 309
    1. The Baltic Countries (Estonia, Latvia, Lithuania) 321
    2. Commonwealth of Independent States 323
B. BULGARIA...329
C. CZECHOSLOVAKIA - SUCCESSOR STATES 329
    1. The Czech Republic..331
    2. The Slovak Republic...334
D. HUNGARY..335
E. ITALY 337
F. POLAND...338
G. ROMANIA 346
H. TURKEY...347
I. YUGOSLAVIA - SUCCESSOR STATES 348
J. MISCELLANEOUS OTHER COUNTRIES 351

XIX. RESEARCHING GERMANIC ANCESTORS IN WEST AND NORTH EUROPEAN COUNTRIES 356

A. BELGIUM...356
B. DENMARK 357
C. FINLAND..358
D. FRANCE...359
E. IRELAND..361
F. THE NETHERLANDS 361
G. NORWAY 363
H. SPAIN 367
I. SWEDEN 367
J. THE UNITED KINGDOM OF GREAT BRITAIN AND NORTHERN IRELAND.......372

XX. CORRESPONDING WITH EUROPEAN SOURCES 377

A. LANGUAGE OF CORRESPONDENCE 377
B. SENDING MONEY TO FOREIGN COUNTRIES 378
C. WRITING LETTERS TO GERMANY 378
D. SAMPLE LETTERS 379
E. TRANSLATIONS..384
F. FAMILY AND ANCESTOR CHARTS 384

XXI. READING THE RECORDS 391

    A. The Gothic Script 391
    B. German Language Notes 393
    C. German Vocabulary Related to Genealogy 395
    D. Records in Other Languages 401
    E. Calendars and Date Problems 401

XXII. ANNOTATED BIBLIOGRAPHY 406

    A. Books 406
    B. Periodicals and Indexes to Periodicals 425

XXIII. USEFUL ADDRESSES 427

    A. Publishers and Booksellers 427
    B. Map Sources 431
    C. Libraries and Information Centers 432
    D. Lending Libraries 434
    E. Special Resources In And Near Minnesota 435
    F. Genealogy-Related Germanic Societies 439
    G. Multi-Ethnic and Non-Germanic Societies of Importance to Germanic Research 441

APPENDIX A. DATELINE OF GERMANIC HISTORY 442

APPENDIX B. MAPS 451

INDEX 479

TABLES

Table 1: Soundex Coding Guide 15
Table 2: Germanic Microfilm Collection at the Family History Library 41
Table 3: Germans Outside Europe and the Soviet Union, 1927 182
Table 4: Germanic migration to Argentina 193
Table 5: German-born Residents in Australia, 1891 203
Table 6: Civil Registers in Latin American Countries 239
Table 7: Present Location of Former Austro-Hungarian Territories 289
Table 8: Germanic Population in Non-Germanic Europe, 1920s 306
Table 9: Germanic Population in the Russian Empire, 1897 319
Table 10: Official Languages of Selected European Countries 377
Table 11: Languages Used on Documents and Records 402
Table 12: Comparison of Julian and Gregorian Calendars 402
Table 13: Modern German, Old German and Dutch Month Names 403
Table 14: French Revolutionary Calendar 403

PREFACE

Perspective of This Guide

James N. Bade, in his book, *The German Connection: New Zealand and German-Speaking Europe in the Nineteenth Century*, concluded that "the basic criterion for the term 'German' should be that the person or people in question be German-speaking." This guide is based on the same premise. The bond shared by all humankind is the summit of civilization. The family, where the sense of linkage is much deeper, is its foundation.

Between these two, however, are intermediate levels of kinship. What is it that causes people to identify more closely with some of their fellow human beings than with others, beyond the degree of consanguinity? What makes them feel they share a tradition?

The notion of race has, of course, been proven to be totally incompatible with historical fact. The strongest ties are likely to be based on religion, a common homeland, territorial proximity, or language.

For our German-speaking immigrant ancestors, it could not have been religion, because nowhere else in contemporary Europe (with the exception of Bosnia) do you see such an even denominational cleavage as in Germany and Switzerland. Our ancestors were even more diverse, because members of small denominations emigrated in disproportionately large numbers, often because of religious intolerance.

Nor could the feeling of sharing be based on a common homeland. Today there are five German-speaking countries in Europe, although two have more than one official language. Before 1871 the number of sovereign entities was much larger.

There never has been a united "Germany" which included nearly all German-speakers and few other people. The closest parallel was Ludwig the German's ninth-century Austrasia, but this included Slovenia, which did not have a German majority. Furthermore, the northeastern half of what became the German Empire (roughly east of the Elbe River) was not a part of this "Germany," although it became "German" in the next few centuries. The Holy Roman Empire of the German Nation always included a lot of non-German territory and it never included East and West Prussia.

Nor can it be explained by proximity, since German-speaking people were scattered throughout most of Europe long before they became trans-oceanic migrants. Having been neighbors historically can explain a lot of migration patterns of different ethnic groups from the same general area. It can explain the affinity which Germans and Slavs often (though certainly not always) had for each other before the virus of nationalism hit the world and increasingly among their descendants into the post-nationalistic era ushered in by the incredible horrors of World War II. It can not explain, however, why certain groups of subjects of so many different countries shared a feeling that they were all part of "Our People" — a concept which has its identical equivalent, in terminology and importance, among a great many other peoples.

Thus the only thing our ancestors had in common was a language. We have used the term "Germanic" to denote this and to distinguish it from any particular former or present political entity.

We are well aware that linguists use the term, "Germanic," to apply to a much broader family of related languages, including English, Dutch, and the Scandinavian languages. We consider a second, narrower definition of the term to apply only to the German language as appropriate and necessary for genealogical purposes.

The reason is that no genealogist is likely to think that a book on "Germanic" genealogy will include researching English or other ancestors. However, there are a lot of genealogists who think of researching German-speaking ancestors as coming from what is or was Germany or, at most, the German-speaking countries. In absolute numbers, a large majority of German-Americans do have ancestors from this area.

However, in proportion to their numbers, the Germans from countries where they constituted a small proportion of the population provided a much greater number of immigrants. For example, the number of North Americans with one or more German ancestors who came from the former Russian Empire, excluding Russian Poland, is estimated at anywhere from 1.5 to 5 million people and the number is rapidly increasing in view of the ever growing number of inter-ethnic marriages. Many records, including naturalization certificates, falsely show them as being from Germany. In other cases, they are identified as Russians. This is a very serious problem for beginners, because relatives will often vigorously insist that an erroneous identity is, in fact, true.

While it is easy to exaggerate the relationship between a common language and a common culture, an important connection exists nevertheless. A shared language is certainly by far the greatest facilitator of communication. This makes a common culture possible, although the various sub-cultures (national, regional, religious) often had a more profound impact on people than the common culture.

Does this have any relevance for the scores of millions of descendants scattered throughout the world, most of whom have lost all knowledge of the ancestral mother tongue and become almost fully assimilated into the cultures of their respective countries of residence?

It certainly does. They have a common heritage. And heritage matters. As Hodding Carter put it, there are only two lasting bequests which parents can give to their children: roots and wings.

The molding effect of the past has an impact on everyone. The difference between genealogists and most non-genealogists is simply that the former tend to be more conscious of their heritage and more inquisitive about it.

This consciousness is, of course, shared by other historians, whether professionals or amateurs — "other," because family history is but a branch of history, even though it often does not get proper academic recognition.

These are the reasons why this guide has expanded so greatly in scope, not merely in the number of pages (which has increased by about 140 pages).

The more significant changes are listed in the Introduction.

Because this book deals primarily with research on Germans, we have used the German *Umlaut* mark (*ä, ö, ü*) throughout the book. However, in the case of the many varying diacritical marks in other languages, we have generally shown them only in the case of actual addresses, but not in the text, with such exceptions as seemed appropriate.

June 1997

Edward R. Brandt
Mary Bellingham
Kent Cutkomp
Kermit Frye
Patricia A. Lowe

INTRODUCTION

Germanic Genealogy: A Guide to Worldwide Sources and Migration Patterns is intended as a guide to help beginning and advanced genealogists search for their German-speaking ancestors throughout the world. Its emphasis is on the records of the countries of origin, although we have covered the records of immigrant countries briefly. Many of the records generated in Europe have, however, been microfilmed by the Family History Library and are thus available in the United States and other immigrant countries. Addresses of other important repositories in the United States and Canada are listed in the text.

A careful review of the table of contents or the index, for subjects of interest to you, will give you a clear idea of our coverage and where to find specific kinds of information.

The second edition of this guide is approximately one-third larger than the first edition. Major additions and updates in the second edition include:

(1) Completely revised and greatly expanded information about Jewish history and genealogy, now in two chapters, the nucleus of which was Dr. George Arnstein's chapter in our first edition.

(2) Completely revised chapter on Christian denominations to which German-Americans historically belonged, including changes such as mergers, and now including all denominations we have been able to identify as having had German-speaking congregations in the United States and Canada.

(3) Major expansion of genealogical records and resources for tracing German-speaking ancestors in Germany, Austria, Luxembourg, Poland, Sweden, Finland and Bosnia, and lesser but significant additions for Canada, the Commonwealth of Independent States, the Czech Republic, Italy and the United Kingdom.

(4) A new chapter on computers and genealogy.

(5) Substantial expansion of material on the migration of German-speakers to various countries.

(6) Updated information about the resources of the Family History Library. Records which are of the most direct genealogical value have been microfilmed and are available worldwide through the many Family History Centers.

(7) A large number of updated and additional bibliographic entries.

(8) A list of commonly used acronyms and abbreviations.

(9) Many new addresses.

(10) A number of new or revised maps.

(11) Added information about special resources for Minnesotans.

The more we know, the more we know what we do not know. We have striven for greater comprehensiveness and balance, but we are aware that some topics deserve more coverage than we have been able to provide, since there are always limitations as to expertise and time for further research on our part.

We welcome any correction of the inevitable errors or inaccuracies in a book of such a wide scope. We are also grateful for any suggestions as to future improvements.

Good luck with your ancestor-hunting. We hope that you will find this guide to be a worthwhile aid to your research.

ACKNOWLEDGMENTS AND CREDITS

This book could not have been as comprehensive or up-to-date without the assistance of many other individuals and institutions. We especially thank the following for providing substantive information or making it available to us:

Ken V. André of the **South African-German Cultural Association** (German immigration to South Africa, and genealogy).

Sharon Anno of *Historic Harmony* (history and settlements of the Harmonists).

David Armstrong of the **European Interest Group of the Western Australian Genealogical Society** (donated a book on the Germans in that state and helped in obtaining the leading Australian genealogical guide).

Dr. George E. Arnstein, contacted through *Avotaynu*, who generously contributed the chapter on Jewish genealogy for the first edition, which we have expanded in the second edition.

Ted Becker of the **Germans from Russia Heritage Society** (up-to-date information about compiling records for individual German villages in the Russian Empire and researching Germans in the Dobrogea).

Roy Bernard and **Peter Towey** of the **Anglo-German Family History Society** (German immigration to England).

Jan Christensen of Skien, Norway (Germans in Norway).

Jessie L. Daraska of the **Balzekas Museum of Lithuanian Culture** (Lithuania).

Dr. Victor G. Doerksen (Temple Society in various countries).

Patricia A. Eames of the **National Archives Volunteer Association** and editor of the *RAGAS Newsletter* (**Russian-American Genealogical Archival Service**).

Irmgard Hein Ellingson of the **Bukovina Society of the Americas** (Bukovina German history, bibliography and German sources).

Jean Ensch of the **Luxembourg National Library** (Luxembourg: updates, corrections, maps, American resource centers).

The **European Interest Group of the New Zealand Society of Genealogists** (donated a book on German-speaking immigrants to that country).

Dr. Peter G. Fast and **Dr. Peter J. Klassen** of the **Center for Mennonite Brethren Studies** in Fresno (contents of the Prussian State Privy Archives and Mennonite records, respectively).

Phil Fox of the **Finnish Genealogy Group of the Minnesota Genealogical Society** and **Duane Wiita** of FGG (Germans in Finland).

Karen Franklin and **Frank Mecklenburger** of the Leo Baeck Institute and **Fruma Mohrer** of the YIVO Institute (the holdings of these two major Jewish archives).

Dr. Duncan B. Gardiner of the **Czechoslovak Genealogical Society International** (contributed nearly all of the historical and genealogical information on the Germans in Slovakia and most of that on the Czech Republic, in addition to proofreading and correcting our drafts).

Paula Goblirsch and **Ray Kleinow** of GGS (chapter on computer genealogy).

Prof. Ayrton Gonçalves Celestino of Brazil, contacted through the **Bukovina Society of the Americas** (donated a manuscript on the Bukovina Germans in Brazil).

Steve Granger and Patrick Anzelc of the Archives of the Archdiocese of St. Paul and Minneapolis (German-American Catholic publications and resources, including repositories for Luxembourg).

Felix Gundacker, executive director of the Institut für Historische Familienforschung in Vienna (sources in and records of former Austro-Hungarian Empire and its successor states).

Dr. Wilmer Harms of the American Historical Society of Germans from Russia (latest information on Soviet German refugees in Harbin en route to the Americas).

Sir Rodney Hartwell of The Augustan Society and Joe Garonzik of the Genealogical Publishing Co. (status of publications).

Marianne Hauser (review and revision of the German form letters).

Sonia Nippgen Holz and Per-Olof Widing of Sweden (Sudeten Germans in Sweden and S_____ _genealogical re__

A__
m__ ation formed by Sandoz in Switzerland (Swiss

V__
In__ issues of *Die Zeitung*, published by the German
p__ __ty of Queensland, informing us of new books, __lition).

J__
B__ e University of St. Thomas (Luxembourgiana

N__
hi__ Santa Catarina, Brazil (donated a booklet on the

D__
T__ the Mennonite Heritage Centre (Mennonites, __o fled to the Americas via Harbin, sources in North America and the Commonwealth of Independent States, recent publications, Peter J. Braun Collection), and along with Henry N. Fast (1835 Russian Molochna Mennonite revision list).

Dr. David H. Koss of Illinois College (German-American Protestant denominations).

Dr. Ortfried Kotzian of the Bukowina Institute in Stuttgart and his daughter, Ruth Maria Kotzian (Bukovina Germans and their emigration).

Jo Ann Kuhr and Richard Rye of the American Historical Society of Germans from Russia (updates on the Commonwealth of Independent States).

Joseph Lamers (information and books about Germans in Bosnia), Michael Jaros (alerting us to this source) and Richard Lamers (facilitating communication).

Betty Lang of the American Historical Society of Germans from Russia (Baptist repositories and Canadian homesteading records).

Brian J. Lenius of the East European Genealogical Society (genealogical resources in Western Canada, Poland and Ukraine).

Virginia Less of the Northern Illinois Chapter of the American Historical Society of Germans from Russia (archival records on the Soviet German Lutheran refugees quartered in Harbin, China, pending travel to Latin America).

Glen Linscheid, editor of the *Galician Grapevine* (Mennonites in Galicia and Volhynia).

Dr. Edward A. Luft and indirectly Henry Wellisch (alerted us to publications and Polish, American, and Canadian collections of periodicals concerning Jewish genealogy in the Czech and Slovak Republics, Poland, the Germanic countries [especially the eastern states of present-day Germany], and elsewhere).

Dr. Roger Minert (reviewed section on Austria and provided helpful suggestions).

Zella Mirick of **GGS** and its branch, the **Ostfriesland Genealogical Society of Minnesota** (patronymic naming practices, resources for Ostfriesland, proofreading, citations, and bibliography).

Victoria M. Nied (Germans in Carpatho-Ukraine).

Glenn Offerman of the **Buenger Memorial Library of Concordia College** and **Paul Daniels** of the **District Archives of the Evangelical Lutheran Church of America** at **Luther Seminary** in St. Paul (publications for the Lutheran Church-Missouri Synod and the Evangelical Lutheran Church of America, respectively).

Robert J. Paulson of the **German-Bohemian Heritage Society** (records and publications for Germans from Bohemia).

Georgina Pinette of Winnipeg (Canadian records and publications).

Jill Robinson of Reefton, New Zealand (list of German pioneers on the west coast of South Island; help in getting a free copy of a book on the New Zealand Germans).

David F. Schmidt (Volga German research, organizational arrangement of collections in the Russian archives, and his experiences with various channels for genealogical research in the Commonwealth of Independent States).

Donnette Sonnenfeld of the **American Historical Society of Germans from Russia** and the **Germans from Russia Heritage Society**, **Paul Hile** of **AHSGR** and **Rachel Schmidt** of **GRHS** (sources for Pietists and Congregationalists).

Henryk Skrzypinski of Poland (German parishes in Poland and Polish archives).

Vladislav Y. Soshnikov, formerly of the **Archives of Russia Society, Ltd.**, and founder of the **Genealogy and Family History Society, Moscow** (current overview of the records of the former Russian Empire, supplementing information previously available here).

Liz Twigden of the **South Australian Genealogical and Historical Society** (South Australian resources and recent Australian books).

Miriam G. Weiner of the **Miriam Weiner Roots to Routes Foundation** (Jews in Ukraine, Moldova and Poland).

Karen Whitmer of **GGS**, who played a major role in the preparation of our first book, *Beginning Research in Germany*, out of which this guide eventually developed.

Judith Williams of Puhoi, New Zealand, identified through the *AGoFF-Wegweiser* (copy of the local *Homeland News* for the New Zealand members of the *Bohemian Association Originating in Puhoi - Ohaupo*).

Suzan Wynne of **Gesher Galicia** and **Wolfgang Ribbe** of the **Free University of Berlin** (acknowledging correspondence and correcting or confirming information about their respective areas of expertise).

The staff of the **Family History Library** was most helpful in reviewing our drafts and providing additional information and corrections where needed: **Kahlile B. Mehr** (Commonwealth of Independent States, Jewish sources), **Thomas Kent Edlund** (German records and German Lutherans in the Russian Empire), **Daniel Schlyter** (Jewish records and gazetteers), retired staffer **Eva T. Liptak** (Hungary), volunteer **Gwen B. Pritzkau** (Black Sea Germans), and **Tab Thompson** and **Tom Daniels** (Family History Library resources).

Help with bibliographical information, annotation and library research was received from **Margaret Freeman** of the **Glückstal Colonies Research Association** (Germans in the Lower Danubian region, some of whom migrated onward to the Russian Empire), **Jan Frye** (citations, proofreading, and publication data), **Carol O'Brien** and **Stephanie Frame** (German-language books), **Horst A. Reschke**, *Heritage Quest* columnist (Jews), and **Sophia Stalzer Wyant**, editor of *The Gottscheer Connection*, published by the

Gottscheer Research and Genealogy Association (history of the Gottschee Germans in Slovenia).

We appreciate the assistance in translating titles or letters by **Korkut Gurkanlar** (Turkish); **W. Kornel Kondy** and **Bernie Szymczak** of the **Polish Genealogical Society of Minnesota, Chester Rog** (*Pol-Am Newsletter*) and **Roma Kehne** (Polish); and **Linda Watson** of the **Immigration History Research Center** (Italian).

This is a better book because of the work of **Michael Haase, Douglas Lowe, Jan Frye** and **Candace Noot** (proofreading and editing); **Ginger Hamer** and **John Hamer** (cover design); **Charles Bellingham** and **Christopher Whitmer** (map-making), and **Bruce Brandt** (communications, word processing).

We obtained important addresses from **Myron Gruenwald**, editor of *Die Pommerschen Leute*, and **Maxwell O. Andrae** (for South Africa and Brazil); **Gail Hermann** (for New Zealand); **Michael Krannaweitter**, and **Carlos Windler** (Argentina); and **Ewald Wuschke**, editor of *Wandering Volhynians* (for Brazil).

The list of institutional or societal connections is obviously incomplete, since many of these genealogists belong to numerous societies.

SOCIETIES, AUTHORS, EDITORS, PUBLISHERS, SPEAKERS, LIBRARIANS AND PASTORS

Much of our information, of course, comes from numerous books, articles, periodicals and conference presentations. We have tried to give proper credit to these authors, editors and speakers in the text.

Although we relied heavily on numerous German-oriented sources, periodicals of various **other ethnic and multi-ethnic societies** which focus on non-Germanic countries where Germans lived were a very useful supplement. Genealogists with ancestors from countries where German-speakers constituted a minority of the population would be well advised to examine what such societies have to offer.

The multi-continental **Federation of East European Family History Societies (FEEFHS)** deserves special mention. It enabled us to establish connections with genealogists of many other ethnic groups, which made it possible for us to tap their expertise with respect to genealogical resources pertaining to non-Germanic countries where Germans lived. More than a dozen of the individuals mentioned above have spoken without reimbursement at FEEFHS conventions, or were contacted as a result of membership in FEEFHS. The names of other Germanic experts who gave presentations resemble a "Who's Who in Germanic Genealogy."

Librarians and staff members (other than those listed above), including those at the **University of Minnesota, Concordia College (St. Paul)**, local **Family History Centers**, the **North Star Chapter of the American Historical Society of Germans from Russia**, the **University of St. Thomas**, and the **Germans from Russia Heritage Collection at the North Dakota Institute for Regional Studies, North Dakota State University**, facilitated the preparation of this book.

The pastors of local **Seventh-day Adventist, Unitarian-Universalist** and **Salvation Army** congregations, or their spouses, clarified and confirmed some of our information.

ARCHIVES AND DIPLOMATIC ESTABLISHMENTS

Valuable information was received, often on very short notice, from the **Manitoba Provincial Archives (Ken Reddig)**, the **National Archives of New Zealand (Vicky Fabian)**, the **State Archives and Heraldic Services of South Africa (Letitia Coetzee and others)**, the **Ottoman Archives (Necati Gültepe)**, and the **National Archives of Canada**, for the first or second editions.

We have continued to use information provided for our 1991 guide by the **Hungarian National Archives (Dr. Imre Ress and others)**, the **Polish National Archives**, the

Romanian National Archives, the **Yugoslavian National Archives**, the **Austrian National Archives (Dr. Kammerhofer)**, the **German Central Office for Genealogy in Leipzig**, the **Tyrolean State Archives, Innsbruck**, and the **German Cultural Archives in Bozen, Italy**.

The **embassies** of **Belarus** and **Poland** provided new information for the second edition. The **Czechoslovakian, Yugoslavian, German and Brazilian embassies**, and the **Consulate General of the Netherlands, Chicago (Olga Burgerhout Tipton)**, sent us information for our first edition or previous book, which we have continued to use.

The following societies and institutions provided us with information in 1991: the **Society for Genealogy and Heraldry in Poznan, Poland (Rafal T. Prinke)**; the **Mennonite Historical Library in Goshen, Indiana (John D. Roth)**; and the **Max Kade Institute for German-American Studies in Madison, Wisconsin**.

Dozens of other **societies and individuals** contributed to the genealogical education of the authors and thus indirectly to the book.

FAMILIES

Especially, we want to express our personal thanks to our respective spouses and children, who provided tangible and intangible support for our efforts in many ways.

Minneapolis, Minnesota
June 1997

Edward R. Brandt
Mary Bellingham
Kent Cutkomp
Kermit Frye
Patricia A. Lowe

About the Authors

Germanic Genealogy: A Guide to Worldwide Sources and Migration Patterns is the co-operative endeavor of five members of the Germanic Genealogy Society, who have volunteered their time and pooled their knowledge to produce this guide. Cumulatively, they have over 150 years of experience in Germanic genealogical research. We are thankful for the many outside experts listed in our acknowledgments who have generously provided important supplementary information for the 1995 global edition.

Of the five primary authors, four are charter members of the Germanic Genealogy Society, founded as the German Interest Group in December 1979, or joined it in its first year; three had been active in its parent society, the Minnesota Genealogical Society, prior to that; four have served GGS as president; and four have served as research chair or research project director.

The authors have done personal or professional research in, or relating to, the United States, Canada, Germany, Luxembourg, Switzerland, Austria, France, Poland, Ukraine, England, Norway and Sweden. Their publications also pertain to Hungary and the successor states to the Soviet Union in particular, and to Eastern Europe in general. Organizations to which they belong are also concerned with Germans in the Czech and Slovak Republics, Slovenia, Romania and, peripherally, Latin America, Ireland, Croatia and Yugoslavia. In addition, they have relatives or ancestral roots in the Netherlands, Belgium, Mexico, and Belize.

Their experience includes deciphering and translating the Gothic script, on-site European research, cartography, working as a Family History Center director, hunting lost relatives for the probate process, giving genealogical seminars, working as an accredited genealogist, teaching history, and an active role in non-Germanic societies.

About the Publisher

The Germanic Genealogy Society is a non-profit organization. Proceeds from the sale of this guide and other publications are used exclusively to fund further publications relating to Germanic genealogy, broadly defined, to expand library resources, and for closely related genealogical purposes. Authors seeking a publisher are welcome to contact GGS to discuss contractual arrangements.

Chapter I

BEGINNING YOUR SEARCH

This chapter provides some suggestions for beginning your genealogical research. Some basic considerations are: questioning family members and relatives; following good rules of organization; using proper research procedures; visiting libraries, court houses and archives; finding original source material; and getting the most out of each record. Also included are some basic acronyms and abbreviations you will frequently encounter when doing Germanic research.

Begin with your family sources. Gather as much information as possible from your memory and by questioning your parents and relatives. Ask about full names, dates and places of birth, marriage and death. Don't forget to ask about interesting stories and family traditions as to where relatives came from. Ask for names and addresses of other relatives who may help. Ask to see old photos, the family Bible, old letters and passports.

Now it is time to get organized. Make use of available forms to help organize your information. These include ancestor charts, family group sheets, individual ancestor data sheets, and correspondence and research logs. These forms are available through many genealogical societies and book distributors. You should maintain a careful record-keeping system. Some elements of that system are:

- Keep all notes on paper of consistent size (8½ by 11 inch paper is recommended).

- Photocopy original documents for use and leave the originals at home in a file.

- Create a separate 3-ring binder for each major surname you are searching. This should contain all known details about that surname as it pertains to your family.

- Number each page and file it by surname. Create indexes as needed.

- Create a small traveling notebook of duplicate copies and blank forms.

William Dollarhide has developed a record keeping system that works well. See his book entitled *Managing a Genealogical Project*.

Follow good research techniques:

- Trace one generation back at a time. Do not attempt to jump generations.

- Keep a full citation of where each piece of information was found.

- When photocopying pages from a book, always copy the title page to remind you where you found the information.

- Record all information found for each record. This can save time if you need to re-examine the information in the record at a later time.

- Record information on a separate page for each surname. This makes it easier when you file your notes.

Record sources can be divided into two general categories: primary sources and secondary sources. **Primary sources** are original documents pertaining to a particular event: for example, birth certificates, census records, family Bible entries or passenger lists. They are primary sources only for that specific event. **Secondary sources** include any other sources, such as indexes to files, extracts of original documents, or a book written about your family. Many sources contain both primary and secondary information. For example, a census record is primary for the place of residence on a specific date, but secondary for peoples' ages. Some sources may be primary or secondary depending upon when the information was written. For example, family information in a family Bible may be considered primary if it appears to be written on or near the date of an event, but should be considered secondary if entered at a much later date. Primary sources are generally considered to be more reliable, although not always.

Federal, state and local census records (available on microfilm) and various vital records (births, marriages and deaths) recorded at county court houses are among the most helpful types of records. Chapter II contains more about these and other records. You can access public records at libraries, state historical libraries, county court houses or archives; each place might have some records but not others. You can rent census records at public libraries. Regional libraries or genealogical libraries contain many genealogical reference works. You can access microfilm copies of original records from around the world by visiting any of the Church of Jesus Christ of Latter-day Saints (LDS) Family History Centers. You can also visit the main LDS library, known as the Family History Library, in Salt Lake City, UT. Chapter V contains additional information about the Family History Library and Family History Centers.

Use a variety of sources to find out information about each generation. This is important to verify the information you have and to fill in missing details about names, events, dates, or places. Inevitably there will be inconsistencies in the data, and you must evaluate the accuracy and reliability of each source to decide which is most probable. Periodically go through your research notes to see if information on older documents has new meaning when compared with more recently acquired information.

For additional help and ideas, look in Chapter II, join a genealogy society, and read the following references or other beginning genealogy books.

IMPORTANT ACRONYMS AND ABBREVIATIONS

You will find that certain acronyms and abbreviations are used in this book or in other genealogical publications. Some of the key ones are:

WHAT EVERY GENEALOGIST MUST KNOW

SASE — Self-addressed, stamped envelope. You should always include one with any query as a courtesy to the recipient, unless you know that you will be billed.

IRC/IPRC — International (Postal) Reply Coupon. Such coupons are used in lieu of a stamped envelope when writing to foreign countries, since they can be used to buy stamps used in the country to which you are writing. They are available in every American post office and there should be similar access in the postal systems of every country. Junior post employees in post offices where there is little demand for them may not know that they have them in stock, but the supervisor always will. You should enclose two International Reply Coupons whenever you expect an answer to your letter to another country. If you have reason to believe that there may be some enclosures with the letter of response, you should enclose three.

SALT LAKE CITY

LDS — Church of Jesus Christ of Latter-day Saints, also known as Mormons, who have collected an enormous amount of genealogical data.

FHL — The huge Family History Library in Salt City, operated by the LDS Church, which is by far the largest genealogical repository (microfilms, books, periodicals, computer databases) in the world.

FHC — Family History Center. These are the branch or stake libraries of the FHL which exist throughout the United States, Canada, Germany, and in many other countries. Anyone can borrow microfilms from Salt Lake City at these centers, except for unfilmed books or periodicals, although many centers have a modest collection of books and periodicals.

| GSU | Genealogical Society of Utah, the microfilming arm of the LDS Church. It should not be confused with the Utah Genealogical Association, which is similar to other state genealogical societies. We have used the acronym, FHL, instead of the more accurate GSU, because the FHL is where the microfilms are housed. |

GERMANY

| DAGV | *Deutsche Arbeitsgemeinschaft genealogischer Verbände* [German Federation of Genealogical Societies], which is the national umbrella group to which dozens of societies (but few local societies) belong. |

| AGoFF | *Arbeitsgemeinschaft ostdeutscher Familienforscher* [Association of East German Family History Researchers]. This is the umbrella organization for the many research centers for tracing ancestors from east of present-day Germany and Austria. There is a separate society for East and West Prussia, as well as for the Baltic countries, and there are additional societies specializing in certain specific areas, e.g., the Sudetenland. |

| DZG | *Deutsche Zentralstelle für Genealogie* [German Central Office for Genealogy]. This office has the largest collection of genealogical materials in Germany, with extensive holdings for areas which are not, or never were, part of Germany. It is now a division of the State Archives of Saxony in Leipzig. |

| EZA | *Evangelisches Zentralarchiv* [Evangelical Central Archives]. This archive in Berlin has a very large number of parish registers for the merged Lutheran-Reformed Church, known as the Evangelical Church. Its holdings include many registers, or films of registers, from the area east of the present German boundary, but which once belonged to the German Empire. |

| GStA | *Geheimes Staatsarchiv preussischer Kulturbesitz* [Prussian State Privy Archives]. This Berlin archive has a vast amount of material, mostly in the nature of governmental records, which is of genealogical value. It does not have parish registers. Its collections include records from all parts of the former Prussian Empire and also some for the whole of Germany or the former German Empire. |

OTHER COUNTRIES

Many societies in varies countries use the initials of their name as acronyms. Examples:

| GGS | Germanic Genealogy Society (publisher of this guide) |

| EEGS | East European Genealogical Society (Canada) |

| AGFHS | Anglo-German Family History Society (England) |

| AFFHO | Australasian Federation of Family History Organizations (Australia-New Zealand) |

| AHSGR | American Historical Society of Germans from Russia (United-States-Canada; covers the entire former Russian Empire, except for the Baltic countries) |

| GRHS | Germans from Russia Heritage Society (United States-Canada; concentrates on Germans from the western Black Sea area, most of whom originally settled in the Dakotas. |

| JGS | Jewish Genealogical Society. A generic name when referring to any or all such organizations. |

| SIG | Special Interest Group, e.g., a group which focuses on researching a specific ethnic background or a specific area or topic. Some are sub-groups of a larger society; some are independent. |

GENEALOGICAL TERMINOLOGY (BOOKS, ETC.)

Meyers   *Meyers Orts- und Verkehrs-Lexikon des Deutschen Reichs [Meyer's Directory of Places and Commerce in the German Empire].* This is by far the most widely known and used gazetteer for locating places (even tiny hamlets and forestry stations) in the former German Empire.

HETRINA   *Hessische Truppen im amerikanischen Unabhängigkeitskrieg [Hessian Troops in the American War of Independence].* This is a large project, with many volumes of information about the Germans who fought for Britain in the American Revolution (not only Hessians) compiled by Eckhart G. Franz.

Glenzdorfs   *Glenzdorfs Internationales Genealogen-Lexikon [Glenzdorf's International Directory of Genealogists].* This is a 3-volume set of books which lists a large number of genealogists, mostly from Germany but including many from other countries who are researching German-speaking ancestors. The specific areas of interest of each are given. Since the volumes were published in 1977-1984, quite a few of those who are listed will have died or moved by now.

AGRIGA   *American Genealogical Resources in German Archives: A Handbook.* Lists various kinds of records, including published emigration lists. A major pioneering work, but no longer complete, since it was published in 1977.

RELIGIOUS ABBREVIATIONS

A.C.   Augsburg Confession. The Lutheran creed, sometimes used in mixed parish registers to identify Lutherans.

H.C.   Helvetic Confession. The Reformed creed, sometimes used in mixed parish registers to identify members of the Reformed faith.

CE   Common Era. The Jewish term for A.D.

BCE   Before Common Era. The Jewish term for B.C.

ADDRESS ABBREVIATIONS AND POSTAL DESIGNATIONS

In the United States, Canada and Brazil, there is a standard postal abbreviation, consisting of two capital letters for each state or province. In England the old abbreviations for the various shires, consisting of varying numbers of letters, are still used. In Australia, each state has an abbreviation consisting of two or three letters, which may or may not all be in capital letters.

In continental Europe, each country has a one or two-letter postal prefix, followed by a varying number of digits in each country, but frequently five for the larger ones (six in Russia, Ukraine and Belarus) and four for the smaller ones, with two letters following the digits in the Netherlands. (There may be a few other variations of which we are not aware.). However, sub-units, such as states, provinces or cantons, are only rarely used in addresses.

They are occasionally used in Poland, especially to distinguish between two localities with the same name. In Germany or Austria, such distinctions are often made by adding the name of the river on which they are located, e.g., Frankfurt an der Oder (Frankfurt a. d. Oder or Frankfurt/Oder) versus Frankfurt am Main (Frankfurt a. M. or Frankfurt/Main. Where appropriate, a different identifying feature, such as a forest or a historic geographic area, may be used. Where small villages are involved, they are often identified as being close to a larger city, e.g., "bei Wismar."

The postal prefix is frequently omitted from the address, especially in larger countries, just as many Americans still use only the old five-digit ZIP code, instead of the more precise nine-digit code, as a suffix.

In Canada the postal codes consist of two sets of three alternating letters and numbers, e.g., T2A 3B6, used as a suffix. Britain uses two sets of letters and numbers, with the letters constituting the first two and last two parts of the code. However, the numbers are sometimes double digits, e.g., EA11 8BL. Australia, New Zealand and South Africa use four-digit postal suffixes.

The difference between the continental European countries and the Anglo-Saxon countries is that the former always use postal prefixes before the name of the locality, whereas the latter use suffixes after the name of the locality.

BIBLIOGRAPHY (See ANNOTATED BIBLIOGRAPHY for full citations if not shown)

Fredrick H. Barth and Kenneth F. Thomsen, comps. *The Beginner's Guide to German Genealogical Research*. Bountiful, UT: Thomsen's Genealogical Center. 1988. 34 pp.
> Good short, simple starter for genealogical newcomers.

William Dollarhide. *Managing a Genealogical Project: A Complete Manual for the Management and Organization of Genealogical Materials*. Baltimore: Genealogical Publishing Co. 1988. 80 pp.
> A carefully presented system to organize your family research materials. Contains helpful terms and excellent discussion of their usage.

Family History Library. *Research Outline: Germany*. Salt Lake City: Family History Library. 1994.

F. Wilbur Helmbold. Edited by Karen Phillips. *Tracing Your Ancestry: A Step-by-step Guide to Researching Your Family History*. Birmingham, AL: Oxmoor House. 1976. 210 pp.
> Guide to beginning genealogy.

Richard S. Lackey. *Cite Your Sources: A Manual for Documenting Family Histories and Genealogical Records*. Jackson, MS: University Press of Mississippi. 1980. 94 pp. Indexed.

National Archives and Records Administration. *Getting Started: Beginning Your Research in the United States Archives in Washington*. Washington: National Archives and Records Administration. 1987. 22 pp.
> Mentions census (1900-1910), military (1865-1898), land (in 30 public land states) and passenger arrival (1820-1850, with gaps) records.

Diane J. Wandler and Prairie Heritage Chapter members. *Handbook for Researching Family Roots: With Emphasis on German-Russian Heritage*. B.H.G., Inc., P.O. Box 309, Garrison, ND 58540. 1992. 250 pp.
> One part of the book is a beginners' guide, with tips on how to interview relatives and other older people to obtain the maximum amount of genealogical information, as one example of a topic often not included in other guides.

Chapter II

USING AMERICAN RECORDS TO FIND YOUR ANCESTOR'S PLACE OF ORIGIN

Are you *really* ready to "cross the ocean" with your German research?

If you can't answer "yes" to all of the following questions, you aren't fully prepared to start German research from German sources, and you will probably end up wasting a lot of time, effort and money . . . unless you get lucky.

- Do you know which town or village your immigrant came from in Germany? Be aware there are some towns with the same name as a larger district, province or state. Also, there are often many towns with the same name, even in the same province. The great majority of people who immigrated came from small towns or villages. Have you located your German town or village on a map? If your information shows the place of origin as "Prussia," this generally means very little, since Prussia at one time covered about two thirds of Germany. See Chapters VIII and IX for further information.

- Have you prepared a list of family members with pertinent vital record data (called a family group sheet) for the family of your immigrant? Is it complete regarding events that took place in the United States? This includes all children in the family, whether they were born in Germany, the United States, or elsewhere. Sometimes tracing a sibling helps in gathering information about your ancestor. See Chapter XX for more information.

- Do you have dates or fairly narrow time periods so you can place some reasonable limits on your search?

- Do you know the political jurisdictions in which your German town is located? See Chapter IX for more information.

- Do you know the religion of your German ancestor? This is very important in German research. See Chapter XI for more information.

- Are you sure you have the German name of your immigrant, keeping in mind there may be more than one "correct" spelling? Name changes often occurred, particularly spelling changes and Anglicizing of names. You may have to look under more than one spelling or version of a name. See Chapter VII for more information.

FINDING THE PLACE OF ORIGIN

If you do not know the origin or place of birth of your ancestor, documents showing this can probably be found, but the key is to know where to begin looking. Remember that German immigration was very often a group effort. Friends and family left a German town or area, traveled together, and settled together in the United States. It is important to look carefully at the community situation and see if there is an old-world connection between your ancestor and others in the area.

If you can learn the origin of some of the others in the community, it may serve as a clue to the locale from which your ancestor originated. Look also for family ties among community members.

You may want to use some lesser-known sources like coroner or mortician files, medical records, or school and university records to see if your ancestor's origin is given in any of them. Look for local membership records of German-American immigrants who belonged to athletic clubs, musical societies, trade and benevolent groups, and mutual aid or church societies, which may give information on your ancestor. A visit to the area where your ancestor lived may also turn up more information.

If you cannot find any connection with the local people and area, you may want to investigate some of the following sources to see if you can find your ancestor's name.

FAMILY SURNAME ASSOCIATIONS

Family associations will be another place to look for origins. Many groups collect data on all people with the same surname and may publish newsletters, etc. This can be helpful for all but the most common names.

QUERIES IN GERMAN GENEALOGICAL PUBLICATIONS

There are two major German genealogical periodicals that are widely read in Germany and run queries. One is the *Familienkundliche Nachrichten* [*Genealogical News*], known as *FaNa*. The other is *Praktische Forschungshilfe* [*Practical Research Help*], known as *PraFo*, which is a quarterly supplement to the *Archiv für Sippenforschung* [*Archive for Genealogical Research*]. American sources are likely to identify them as FANA and PRAFO.

The German Genealogical Society of America has published the surnames listed in both of these publications in its *GGSA Bulletin*. It has complete indexed files of both, dating back to 1956. You can obtain entries relating to the surname(s) you are researching for a modest sum by sending a self-addressed, stamped envelope to GGSA, but you must know the date, volume, and number of the issue in which the entry appears. You may also wish to send your own query for publication.

FaNa is published by:	*PraFo* is published by:
Verlag Degener & Co.	C. A. Starke Verlag
Postfach 1360	Postfach 1310
D-91403 Neustadt/Aisch	D-65549 Limburg/Lahn
Germany	Germany

You may submit your query in English and ask the publisher to translate it. The cost depends on the length of the query, but a $20-$30 fee is common.

PUBLICATIONS LISTING NAMES BEING RESEARCHED BY VARIOUS GENEALOGISTS

Glenzdorfs Internationales Genealogen-Lexikon [*Glenzdorf's International Directory of Genealogists*] (3 vols.) lists genealogists throughout the world, but especially in German-speaking countries, who are researching specific ancestral names in specific areas, mostly in Europe. However, the fact that it was published in 1977-84 means that this detailed directory is losing some of its value as people die or move.

The *Genealogical Research Directory* is an annual worldwide multi-ethnic guide to names being researched by individuals who pay to have their interests inserted. Because entries are not always repeated, it may be worthwhile to check several editions.

Most German-American genealogical societies have lists of names, places and often time periods for each which their members are researching. Some of these may have been published; most are computerized.

LIBRARIES, GENEALOGICAL SOCIETIES, AND EMIGRATION LISTS

Some larger public libraries and libraries of genealogical and historical societies in the United States may have German phone books, German-language newspapers, books about emigrants to America, and published emigration lists. Check the indexes for your surname. Also look at newsletters and publications of societies that are located near your ancestor's residence.

The most substantial English-language emigration books are listed in the ANNOTATED BIBLIOGRAPHY. Hundreds of monographs and articles have also been published, many in English, but substantially more in German. The number is constantly increasing.

German genealogical societies publish periodicals that contain various queries and surname exchange information. There are many ethnic genealogical societies in the United States that publish similar information. See Chapter XXIII for addresses of some of them.

The Family History Library has many German lineage books and family histories, guild records and population lists, biographies and town histories. While generally arranged by German area, you may want to take a look at some of these to see if any contain your family name. Don't overlook the resources at the Family History Library discussed in Chapter V and the related books by Jensen, Dearden, and Hall mentioned and listed in the bibliography because there is no other comparably comprehensive genealogical resource in the world.

USING THE RECORDS

Develop a strategy for completing your research. Has someone else already done the research? There probably is someone who is researching the same family line. All you have to do is find them. Place a query in a genealogical periodical published by a United States or German genealogical society. The *Genealogical Helper* is a popular genealogical periodical published in the United States. Its German equivalent is *Familienkundliche Nachrichten* (see above). Another similar German publication is the *Praktische Forschungshilfe* (see above). You may also find another genealogist researching your surname or town in *Glenzdorfs Internationales Genealogen-Lexikon* (see above). Also check the Family History Library indexes for your surname. The independent *German Genealogical Digest* and the periodicals of German-oriented genealogical societies in immigrant countries also publish queries.

Contact relatives here and in Germany. Find possible relatives there by using a query in a German genealogical periodical, by looking in Glenzdorfs, or by checking in German phone books, which are available in some major libraries. You may also purchase specific phone books from AT&T and German post offices. The detailed Shell maps list even the tiniest hamlet existing today, even though it may belong to another municipality and not have its own post office.

Possibly there has been a village lineage book (*Dorfsippenbuch* or *Ortssippenbuch*) written about your village or a family history (*Familiengeschichte*) written about your family, or maybe someone can share family group sheets or ancestor charts with you. Also, the *Deutsche Geschlechterbücher* is a collection of over 200 volumes containing family genealogies for prominent German families and nobility.

Further information about *Ortssippenbücher* and *Geschlechterbücher* may be found in Wolfgang Ribbe and Eckart Henning's *Taschenbuch für Familiengeschichtsforschung* [*Handbook for Family History Research*]. *Bibliographie der Ortssippenbücher in Deutschland* [*Bibliography of Village Histories in Germany*], by Franz Heinzmann, lists more than 6,000 of these books. Also, see Chapter XVII under **Public Records in Germany** for more information about these resources and where they may be found in the United States.

STEPS TO FURTHER YOUR RESEARCH

To find the person, place and date, you need the immigrant's name with the correct spelling, specific place of origin, and a date associated with an event such as a birth, marriage or death that occurred there. Finding the place of origin has been covered on the preceding page. For spelling possibilities and information about names see Chapter VII on Personal Names and Chapter VIII on Place Names.

Once you know the exact location your ancestors came from, you will want to locate it on a map. Try using *Der Grosse Shell Atlas* [*The Large Shell Atlas*] if the town is not extremely small. You can find helpful information about specific contemporary German towns by using the gazetteer, *Müllers Grosses Deutsches Ortsbuch* [*Mueller's Large Gazetteer of German Places*]. It shows the nearest government offices, archives, churches, and the

German postal code of your ancestor's town. *Meyers Orts- und Verkehrs-Lexikon des Deutschen Reichs* [*Meyer's Dictionary of Places and Commerce in the German Empire*] has similar information about each town, no matter how small, for the period from 1871 until World War I. *Meyers Orts* is very complete but is in Gothic typescript. Both of these books are in German.

The purpose of checking these gazetteers is to help you determine where to find public and church records related to your ancestors. If you know the state or province, you may wish to consult a regional gazetteer first. You will find it helpful to use a guide to abbreviations for these two gazetteers.

Fay Dearden and Douglas Dearden, in *The German Researcher: How to Get the Most Out of an LDS Family History Center*, do a superb job of listing abbreviations commonly found in *Meyers Orts* and have instructions on how to read the entries.

Which parish church might your family have attended? Many communities were too small to have their own church. These gazetteers tell whether a place had its own church or churches, where the local court house (*Amtsgericht*) and local civil registrar (*Standesamt*) were, as well as help determine which city archive (*Stadtarchiv*) and which regional archive (*Staatsarchiv*) may have the relevant records. Larry O. Jensen's *Genealogical Handbook for German Research* is particularly good in describing how to conduct area searches for information.

FINDING PROFESSIONAL GENEALOGISTS

Most likely you will prefer to do your own research, because doing it is half the fun. But at some point you may want to get the assistance of a professional genealogist in North America or Europe.

There are two major organizations through which an American genealogist can establish professional credentials. One is the Board for Certification of Genealogists, P.O. Box 19165, Washington, DC 20036. Through it, a person with proven credentials can become a Certified Genealogical Record Specialist (C.G.R.S.) or a Certified Genealogist (C.G.). The difference is that the latter must have additional expertise in helping to solve difficult research problems. You should be able to obtain a list of people with these qualifications from your state genealogical society.

The other organization is the Accreditations Committee, Family History Library, 35 North West Temple St., Salt Lake City, UT 84150. Those who pass its examination are known as Accredited Genealogists (A.G.). These examinations are based on specialization in a given country or area, and require a good knowledge of a foreign language, where applicable. A list of genealogists who have qualified is available at any Family History Center or it may be ordered from the Family History Library in Salt Lake City. This list includes some European genealogists with a knowledge of English.

Many German-American genealogical societies publish such information in their newsletters from time to time. Palatines to America is one good source. In addition, there is a genealogical association of English-speaking researchers in Europe. See **OTHER SPECIALIZED GENEALOGICAL RESOURCE CENTERS** under **GERMANY** in Chapter XVII for more information.

Two major sources identifying experienced genealogists are the *Directory of Professional Genealogists*, published by the Association of Professional Genealogists, and *Who's Who in Genealogy and Heraldry*, edited by Mary Keysor Meyer and P. William Filby.

For a modest fee, many genealogical organizations provide record-searching and other specified research services that are not necessarily limited to members. They generally do not function as professional genealogists with respect to problem-solving. An organization with particularly extensive services is the Immigrant Genealogical Society, which has large German-oriented holdings. See **GENEALOGY-RELATED GERMANIC SOCIETIES** in Chapter XXIII.

The *FEEFHS Resource Guide to East European Genealogy* lists a large number of professional genealogists for East and Central Europe, including Germany and Austria.

CHECKLIST OF RESEARCH SOURCES

The following is a checklist of the most promising sources for further research in the United States (or, with a few variations, in other immigrant countries). Please feel free to use it if you are not yet ready for research in German records. Refer to standard genealogical books if you need ideas for other sources. Some of these books are listed in the references for this chapter and Chapter I, and others in the accompanying bibliography in Chapter XXII. Your local public library is likely to have books to help you get started.

FAMILY SOURCES

Relatives. Maybe you haven't yet contacted the person who can help you or you haven't jogged the memory of someone you have contacted. Give them time to think about your questions and contact them again. Ask about old papers or letters that might be stored away somewhere. Be careful to note dates and places of events. Try advertisements in newspapers when seeking current but unknown relatives.

Family Bibles, prayer books and funeral cards. These and other family papers may give pertinent information about various family members. Note the information given and try to determine if it was recorded near the time of the event or if it was recorded at a later time. Information recorded at or near the time of the event is almost always more reliable.

CHURCH AND OTHER PRIVATE RECORDS

Church records, especially the first church your immigrant ancestor joined after coming to the United States, will have information concerning baptisms, confirmations, marriages, funerals, communicants, members, and church histories. Note names of baptismal sponsors since they are probably related to the child being baptized. Don't overlook records of children born or married in the United States; sometimes church records give valuable information about their parents. These records may give the previous place of residence or place of birth of your ancestor. Occasionally, a baptismal record of a child will even give information about the place of birth of the parents or the location the parents lived before they emigrated to the United States.

Mortuary records contain information about death and burial dates and place of burial. They may also contain information about relatives, church membership, and place of residence. They also often have an obituary of the deceased person.

Tombstones carry inscriptions that may include birth and death dates, place of origin, immigration date, and family relationships. Tombstones in many cemeteries have been recorded by historical or genealogical societies and some of this information is available in published form.

Cemetery associations have record books with burial dates, and may also have birth and death dates, church membership, and family relationships. These records may be especially helpful for unmarked burials. Cemeteries can be either public or privately owned. Public cemeteries are usually administered by the township that contains the cemetery, and record books are kept by a township official. Sometimes townships are incorporated into cities and their records are transferred to city administration. Private cemeteries are owned by churches or private cemetery associations. Records should be maintained by the owning organization. Some cemeteries have been abandoned or destroyed and records may be difficult or impossible to find.

Private school records give information about student records and alumni of the school.

Lodge records have names of lodge members and can help establish new or old residences.

Professional associations have names and addresses of people in particular professions, such as nurses, doctors, teachers, ministers, priests and nuns.

Orphanage records have varied contents but may give the child's name, the time period the child was at the orphanage, where and when the child went to school, personal information such as physical description and attitude, and placement information. There were also numerous state schools for boys and private schools (for example, Father Flanagan's Boys Town in Nebraska).

From about 1854-1929 there were about 150,000 immigrant and other orphans who were taken from various institutions (especially the New York Children's Aid Society) and transported by trains to homes throughout the rural Midwest and Upper Midwest. The Orphan Train Heritage Society of America, Route 4, Box 565, Springdale, AZ 72764, seeks information about orphan train riders and their descendants.

NEWSPAPERS AND OTHER PUBLICATIONS

City directories will give the address of a person living within a specified city or suburban area. Usually only the head of household of a family is listed, but a spouse, the occupation of the head of household, and any boarders may also be shown. The older directories may give a date of death for a previously listed individual or a new address if the person moved out of the area covered by the directory. More current directories have three categories: alphabetical name, street address, and telephone listing. These later categories can be reversed to find the name of the owner of the property. City directories can be found at many libraries, genealogical societies, and some local historical societies. They may also be available as books or on microfilm.

County atlases, county plat books, and insurance maps. These maps help identify the location where a family was living if they were property owners. Brief sketches of residents are also sometimes included. Check census records to see if a person owned the property.

Newspapers, especially obituaries, anniversary articles, vital records listings, and local news columns, may give information about your ancestor's family. Many newspapers have been microfilmed and are available at many state and local historical societies and genealogical societies, and at some libraries.

German-language newspapers in the United States contained information about people in the area in which they were published, as well as those areas in which they were sold, both in the United States and abroad. Many of these newspapers have been microfilmed and are available at many state and local historical societies and genealogical societies, and at some libraries. See Karl J. R. Arndt and May E. Olson, *German-American Newspapers and Periodicals, 1732-1955*, for more information about German-American newspapers.

Printed genealogies and family histories should be helpful in case you haven't already tried them. Many of these are available, both privately and in libraries. They can be extremely helpful if well written and documented, but the quality of research varies.

Local histories, especially if they contain biographical information, may have helpful information. These are usually county and town histories. Look for them at historical societies, genealogical societies and local libraries.

Genealogical magazines, such as the *German Genealogical Digest*, contain many articles of general genealogical interest, book advertisements, genealogical information exchange columns, and other information such as how to hire researchers. Chapters XXII and XXIII contain short lists of periodicals.

PUBLIC RECORDS

Civil court records include probate records and related records such as conservatorships, guardianships and commitments. These records are kept by the county courts and are usually found at the county courthouses. It is important to know that different counties may have differing terminology for these records and may keep them in different county offices. Ask at the county offices in order to find out where the records are kept in that county.

Probate records are filed by the name of the deceased person, and consist of testate and intestate proceedings. **Testate proceedings** include the deceased person's will, which lists the devisees. Heirs may be listed. **Intestate proceedings** have no associated will, but all the heirs to the decedent are listed, along with their relationship to the decedent, and their addresses. Older wills may be found in books located at the probate office. The probate file may also contain the real estate description of property the decedent owned (which may be where the person lived), birth date and place, death date and place, and address of decedent. Occasionally other records can be found in the file, such as birth and death certificates for the decedent, birth (and sometimes, death) certificates of the heirs, and references to other files.

A **Conservator** is appointed to make decisions for a legally incapacitated person and a **Guardian** is appointed to make decisions for a legally incompetent person. In both of these files, the commencing petition is the document that will provide you with the most family history information. You will find the age, date of birth and last address of the proposed conservatee or ward; along with names, addresses and maybe the ages of the known family members; and the name, address and occupation of the proposed conservator or guardian. A guardianship or Conservatorship of the estate will provide you with an Inventory of the assets, personal property and real estate, owned by the conservatee or ward on the date the conservator or guardian was appointed.

Commitments consist of the confinement of an incapacitated person. This may be due to such things as inebriation, drugs, mental deficiency, senility, etc. Commitments may also be voluntary or involuntary. The file contains personal information such as date and place of birth, parents, spouse, family members, length of time residing in county or state, church membership, schooling and occupation.

Other records that may be found at county offices are adoptions, divorce files (including the divorce decree), judgments regarding what a person may owe to others, lawsuits in civil disagreements, paternity actions, name changes and naturalizations. Note that adoption records are generally not available to the public.

Criminal court records consist mainly of criminal cases. Some paternity actions are also found here.

Land records are usually kept at the county courthouses. In order to search land records, one should have the legal description of the property, although this is not necessary. Land records are of two types: abstract and Torrens. For **abstract property**, an abstract (or history) of the title to a particular tract of land summarizes all material parts of recorded legal instruments affecting the title of the property. The abstract provides a lengthy history of the real estate, usually in one bound document. It contains a record of previous owners, together with a report of all judgments, mortgages and similar claims against the property that have been recorded. For **Torrens property**, or registered property as it is sometimes called, there is a certificate of title documenting transactions during a particular ownership period. Registration creates a judicial determination of the status of the title at the time of the registration. Abstract property can be converted into Torrens property through the registration process. Access to these records can be gained through use of the tract index, which is a consecutive listing of the owners of a particular piece of property.

Land records contain the document number of the property, the names of the buyer and seller, and may also contain references to births, marriages, deaths and other court proceedings. Name changes, divorces, satisfactions, mortgages, taxes levied, and liens may also be included. When heirs sell property owned by a decedent, the file can be quite extensive.

Land records for land issued by the United States government are also found at the county offices. This includes so-called **homestead property** (which was given to a person by the United States government per the Morrill Act of 1862) and **bounty land property** (given to a person by the government for some service to the government, such as military service in a war). These records are the same as other land transactions, except that the government is the grantor of the property.

Some counties have **grantor and grantee indexes** to assist in finding the property if only the name of the person owning the land is known. These indexes are usually organized alphabetically by first letter of the surname. Other systems are also in use. Ask at the county office as to how the records are organized and what finding aids are available.

Tax records can be used to trace ownership of land. Older tax records can sometimes be used in lieu of census and other records to show a person resided in a given area.

Vital records. Births, marriages, and deaths are recorded at county court houses. Older birth and death records are also usually available through state agencies. Privacy laws exist in most states that limit access to these records. These laws vary widely and usually make exceptions for family members.

Civil registration was introduced at an early time but was not mandatory until 1850-1930 depending on the state. Even when it was made mandatory, events were not well-recorded for some time after that, even for years. As for all records, there are also errors in vital records, and in certified and non-certified copies of those records (even if the original was accurate). See *The Handy Book for Genealogists* by Everton Publishers for information about dates of introduction of vital registration in counties, names and organization dates of counties and whether they were formed from other counties, and other information of use when looking for vital records. This is especially true of older records and records for counties that no longer exist.

Birth records give the name, date and place of birth of the child, the name, age and residence of the mother and usually the name, age, residence and occupation of the father. Delayed birth records occasionally occur if the birth was not recorded near the time of birth; many times this happens when a person approaches retirement age and wants to file for Social Security benefits, but discovers that his or her birth was not recorded. The county requires other proofs of birth for a person to obtain a delayed registration of birth.

Marriage records consist of marriage banns, marriage applications, marriage licenses, and certificates of marriage. Marriage banns were public announcements of an upcoming marriage and were still in use in the early 1800s, especially in the New England states. They are no longer in use today. A marriage application is recorded when the future bride and groom apply for a marriage license. A marriage license is issued to the couple being married and is usually kept by them. The certificate of marriage is recorded after the marriage occurs. Occasionally a marriage application is recorded without a corresponding certificate of marriage. A marriage application by itself is not proof that the marriage occurred. Marriage records give the names of the bride and groom, their places of residence, the date and place of marriage, the name and residence of the person who married them, names of witnesses to the marriage, and sometimes the names of the parents of the bride and groom and the religions of the bride and groom.

Death records give the name, date and place of death of the decedent and the cause of death. Also usually included are the residence, age at death, and name of spouse. Sometimes the place of birth and names of parents are also given. Check the name of the informant for the record to get a clue as to the reliability of the information given on the record. Information for death records was sometimes given by children, relatives or friends who may not have had a first-hand knowledge of the event or were confused while giving the information, or the record keeper did not correctly understand them.

The information was sometimes passed down orally over a span of time before being recorded. Occasionally the record keeper did not ask all of the questions required to fill out the record, even though the informant knew the information.

Military records give a record of military service for a person. These records include information pertinent to the person's tour of duty, including such things as dates and places of service, battles, regiments, honors awarded, etc. A physical description of the person is also included in many cases, and information about the person's death is included if killed in service. Draft records also list vital data for those who did not serve.

Military pension files give information about the person after military service has ended and covers the time period when a pension is awarded. This usually continues until the person dies. The person's residence and occupation are shown, as well as any disabilities pertinent to the pension. These records can sometimes have information of surprising genealogical value, especially when the person dies and the spouse claims a pension continuation, since proof of relationship is required in this case.

Passenger departure lists for ports of embarkation may provide information about a town of origin or an emigrant destination. See Chapter VI for more information.

Ship arrival lists for ports in United States (and other immigrant countries as well) may help find previous residences if you know when your immigrant arrived in that country. See Chapter VI for more information.

Border crossing lists are valuable for those whose ancestors landed at Canadian ports, but with the United States as their destination. This was particularly true for early immigrants, so the records listed by Zaleski are of the greatest relevance for the eastern parts of the United States. Moreover, in most cases such records were not kept at western border points until a later date. The most extensive and most well-known of these records are for St. Alban's, Vermont, but similar ones are available for Detroit.

Naturalization records give information about an immigrant who wishes to become a United States citizen. The **Declaration of Intention** to become a citizen (sometimes called the "first paper"), is generally the most important record for genealogists, and is commonly filed in the county where your immigrant first settled in the United States, but might be in any county through which your immigrant traveled. Naturalizations could and did occur in any jurisdiction, whether it be county, state or federal. After a waiting period, usually about five years, the person could then petition to complete the naturalization process. The place where this occurred may or may not have been the place where the Declaration of Intention was obtained. Once the court decreed the person to become a citizen, a **naturalization paper** (sometimes call the "second paper") was issued to the person and the event was recorded by the court. In many states, naturalization records have been transferred from the counties to a central state archives or historical society. Contents of naturalization records vary greatly from time to time and place to place.

Federal census records are used for locating where people lived in the United States and who was living within each family unit. Federal censuses have been taken every ten years starting in 1790. Before 1850, only the heads of household are named, along with a tally of the number of people of various age groups and gender living in the same household. Beginning with the 1850 census, all household members are named. Places of birth are shown beginning with the 1880 census. The 1890 federal census was almost completely destroyed by fire but a very small number of schedules still exist. The year of immigration to the United States was first indicated in the 1900 federal census. The 1910 and 1920 federal census records are also currently available for use. Soundex indexes exist for the 1880, 1900 and later federal censuses. A special 1885 Federal census was taken by some states.

Mortality schedules listing deaths of persons in the twelve months immediately preceding the census were taken along with the census during the 1850-1885 time period. Revolutionary War pensioners were also recorded in the 1840 census.

A special 1890 census of Union veterans of the Civil War and widows of Union veterans exists, which is arranged alphabetically by state beginning with part of Kentucky and continuing through the remainder of the alphabet of states existing in 1890, and also including Washington, DC. The remaining schedules were destroyed in the same fire that destroyed the 1890 population census.

Other kinds of Federal census schedules also exist, such as agricultural schedules and Indian censuses.

Soundex index to federal census records was designed to assist in finding an individual name among the millions listed in the 1880, 1900, 1910 and 1920 census records and some passenger list records. The 1880 Soundex index only shows households in which there were children of age ten years or younger. The Soundex is a coded surname index based on the way a surname sounds rather than the way it is spelled, so surnames that sound alike but are spelled differently—like Schmidt, Schmied, Smith, and Smythe—have the same Soundex code and are filed together. The Soundex was developed so you can find a surname even though it may have been recorded under different spellings.

To search for a particular surname in the Soundex, you must first work out its Soundex code. Every Soundex code consists of a letter followed by three numbers (e.g., S650). The letter is always the first letter of the surname. The numbers are assigned to the remaining letters of the surname according to the following Soundex coding guide.

Table 1: Soundex Coding Guide

The number:	Represents the letters:
1	B, P, F, V
2	C, S, K, G, J, Q, X, Z
3	D, T
4	L
5	M, N
6	R
Disregard the letters A, E, I, O, U, W, Y and H.	

Most surnames can be coded using the following five steps.

1. Write out the surname you are coding.

2. Save the first letter of the surname as the letter part of the Soundex code for the surname.

3. For the remaining letters, cross out all letters A, E, I, O, U, W, Y, and H.

4. Assign numbers from the above Soundex coding guide to the letters still remaining.

   If the surname originally had any side-by-side letters with the same number code, these letters should be treated as one letter, e.g., in the surname Pfennig, the F should be crossed out since P and F both have 1 as their code number - also in Jackson, the C, K, and S all have code number 2 so the K and S should be crossed out. As a special case of this rule, if the surname has any doubled letters, they should be treated as a single letter, e.g., in the surname Lloyd, the second L should be crossed out.

5. If you now have three numbers, they are the ones to use in the Soundex code for the surname, e.g., Brandt = B653. If you have less than three numbers, add enough zeros at the right end so there are three numbers, e.g., Frye = F600. If you have more than three numbers, just use the leftmost three numbers and ignore the rest, e.g., Bellingham = B452 and Cutkomp = C325.

If your surname of interest has a prefix - like Van, Von, De, Di or Le - you should code it both with the prefix and without the prefix because it might be listed under either code. For example, the surname Von Grossman should be coded both as V526 and as G625. Mac and Mc are not considered to be prefixes. If your surname could have its first letter misspelled, you should code the surname other ways, e.g., Cutkomp (coded C325) could also be spelled Kutcomp (coded as K325). Catholic nuns are usually indexed as "Sister" being the surname. The side-by-side rule can sometimes be confusing, e.g., the surname Suess is indexed as S200 rather than S000 since the last two S's are doubled but are not next to the first one. Also be aware of possible misspellings in original documents and look-alike letters that may be incorrectly coded, e.g., Pfennig may be misspelled as Fennig, and Sanders may be mistaken for Landers. Surname coding errors do occasionally occur in the Soundex. So if you cannot find the name you are seeking, be creative in how the surname might have been coded.

Once you have coded your ancestor's name, you are ready to use the microfilmed Soundex card indexes. They are organized by state, then by Soundex code, and then alphabetically by first name or initial.

Some states, such as Minnesota, incorporate Soundex coding into automobile drivers license numbers, so you may be able to check the coding of your own surname by looking at your drivers license number.

State census records are similar to federal census records, except state censuses were authorized by individual state governments. State censuses were usually collected midway between federal censuses, or in special situations such as a territory preparing for statehood. State census records generally give the names of persons in a household and the county and township where the household was, and may give other information as well, such as age and occupation. Check for the state censuses that may exist for a particular state. See *The Source* for more information about state census records.

Alien registrations. All non-United States citizens are required to register their residence annually. These records are maintained by the counties. Alien registration was required from 1802 to 1828 and was again made mandatory in 1929 and continues to the present. A Special Alien Registration and Declaration of Holdings was required of all—particularly new—alien residents in the state of Minnesota in February 1918 by the State Commission of Public Safety. This record gives extensive and valuable information about each alien registration, such as full name, address, length of residence, age, data and place of birth, data of arrival in the United States and port of entry, occupation, names and ages of all living children, names of male relatives involved in World War I, date of "first papers," legal description of land holdings, etc. These records are organized by county and then by city or township. This registration may also have been required in other states as well.

Border crossing records. Check Chapter III for records pertaining to late immigrants and others who crossed the Canadian-American border because the port of arrival was not in the country which was their destination or because they later moved.

Miscellaneous public records. These records include such things as voter registrations, military draft registrations, drivers license registrations, Social Security registrations, public school records (student records and names of alumni), licenses (justices of the peace, ministers, school teachers, morticians, steam fitters, etc.), and building permits. Also included are bond and oath records of officials of state and local governments, burial records for state hospitals, correctional facilities records, and coroner's records.

BIBLIOGRAPHY (See ANNOTATED BIBLIOGRAPHY for full citations if not shown)

Karl J. R. Arndt and May E. Olson. *German-American Newspapers and Periodicals, 1732-1955*.

Elizabeth Petty Bentley. *County Courthouse Book*. 2nd ed. Baltimore: Genealogical Publishing Co. 1995. 416 pp.

Elizabeth Petty Bentley. *Directory of Family History Associations.* Baltimore: Genealogical Publishing Co. 1993. 318 pp.

Elizabeth Petty Bentley. *Genealogist's Address Book.* 3rd ed.

Johni Cerny and Arlene Eakle. *Ancestry's Guide to Research: Case Studies in American Genealogy.* Salt Lake City, UT: Ancestry, Inc. 1985. 364 pp.
> This is a companion to the original 1984 book, *The Source*, edited by the same authors. Provides many problem-solving examples of how to trace your ancestors, including a section on tracing a German immigrant family.

Meredith B. Colket, Jr. and Frank E. Bridgers. *Guide to Genealogical Records in the National Archives.* Washington: National Archives and Records Service. 1964. 145 pp.
> Contains some details not found in the 1983 book on records in the National Archives.

Directory of Professional Genealogists. Washington: Association of Professional Genealogists. 1995. 110 pp.
> Lists some specialists for Germanic and other European countries, as well as Australia and Israel.

Alice Eichholz, ed. *Ancestry's Red Book: American State, County and Town Sources.* Rev. ed. With maps by William Dollarhide. Salt Lake City, UT: Ancestry Publishing Co. 1992. 858 pp.

George B. Everton, Sr., ed. *The Handy Book for Genealogists.* Logan, UT: Everton Publishers, Inc. 8th ed. 1991. 382 pp. maps.
> Illustrated with outline maps of each state of the United States, showing boundaries and history of each county and the location of the county seat. Gives location of important reference sources, location of archives, libraries, historical and genealogical societies and other information for each state. Also contains some information about European countries.

Family History Library. *Tracing Immigrant Origins.* #34111. 31 pp.

P. William Filby. *A Bibliography of American County Histories.* Baltimore: Genealogical Publishing Co. 1985. Reprinted 1987. 449 pp.
> Standard work on U.S. county histories, often helpful for tracing immigrants and ancestors.

Johann Glenzdorf. *Glenzdorfs Internationales Genealogen-Lexikon.*

Val D. Greenwood. *The Researcher's Guide to American Genealogy.* 2nd ed. Baltimore: Genealogical Publishing Co., Inc. 1990. 623 pp. Revised 1992. 568 pp.
> Official textbook for correspondence course of the National Genealogical Society. Comprehensive guide to American research, especially land and probate records.

Guide to Genealogical Research in the National Archives. Washington, DC: National Archives and Records Service. 1983. 304 pp.
> A highly acclaimed and easy to use genealogical overview of the holdings of the National Archives. Gives inventory and ordering information to obtain photocopies of records, etc. Describes 20 different kinds of records in some detail.

Estelle M. Guzik, ed. *Genealogical Resources in the New York Metropolitan Area.* NY: Jewish Genealogical Society, Inc. P.O. Box 6398, NY, NY 10128. 1989. 404 pp.

Marian Hoffman, comp. and ed. *Genealogical and Local History Books in Print.* Vol. 1: *Family History Volume* (477 pp.); Vol. 2: *General Reference and World Resources Volume* (375 pp.). Baltimore: Genealogical Publishing Co. 1996, 1997.

Keith A. Johnson and Malcolm R. Sainty, eds. *Genealogical Research Directory: National and International.* Annual. North Sydney, Australia: Authors.

Marion Kaminkow, ed. *United States Local Histories in the Library of Congress: A Bibliography.* Baltimore: Magna Carta Book Co. 1975. 5 volumes.

Thomas Jay Kemp. *International Records Handbook.* 3rd ed. Baltimore: Genealogical Publishing Co. 1994. 417 pp.

> Contains addresses for civil records in every country in the world, with forms used to request birth, marriage and death records for English-speaking and some other countries.

Lucille L. Kirkeby. *Holdings of Genealogical Value in Minnesota County Museums.* Brainerd, MN (2103 Graydon Ave., Brainerd, MN 56401): Self published. 1985.

> This book lists addresses and available holdings of interest to genealogists, and other available resources within each library.

E. Kay Kirkham. *The Handwriting of American Records for a Period of 300 Years.* Logan, UT: Everton Publishers. 1973. 108 pp.

> Examines a variety of handwriting in American records at various times in history. Heavily illustrated.

Ann S. Lainhart. *State Census Records.* Baltimore: Genealogical Publishing Co. 1992; reprinted 1997. 116 pp.

> Comprehensive list of records of state census , which were often conducted midway between federal censuses or preparatory to statehood. Especially helpful for answers who moved soon after they originally settled in the United States.

Mary K. Meyer, ed. *Meyer's Directory of Genealogical Societies in the U.S.A. and Canada,* 11th ed. Mt. Airy, MD: Libra/Pipe Creek Publications. 1996. 135 pp.

> Also lists special interest organizations (ethnic, religious, geographic, adoptees).

Mary Keysor Meyer and P. William Filby, eds. *Who's Who in Genealogy and Heraldry, 1990.* Savage, MD: Who's Who in Genealogy and Heraldry. 1990. 331 pp.

Kory Meyerink. *Printed Sources: A Guide to Published Genealogical Records.* Salt Lake City, UT: Ancestry, Inc. 1997. 800 pp.

> This companion volume to the newly updated book, *The Source,* discusses published genealogical sources, including CD-ROMs. Describes nearly all published sources used by genealogists, including their benefits and shortcomings. Focuses on published literature, whereas *The Source* concentrates on original records.

Christina K. Schaefer. *Guide to Naturalization Records of the United States.* Baltimore: Genealogical Publishing Co. 1997. 406 pp.

Juliana Szucs Smith. *Ancestry's Address Book: A Comprehensive List of Addresses of Local, State, and Federal Agencies and Institutions.* Salt Lake City, UT: Ancestry, Inc. 1997. 600 pp.

Loretto D. Szucs and Sandra Luebking. *The Archives: A Guide to the National Archives Field Branches.* Salt Lake City: Ancestry. 1988. 340 pp.

> Describes records of various government agencies. Lists many printed sources and microfilms available in the 11 branch offices.

Loretto Dennis Szucs and Sandra Hargreaves Luebking, eds. *The Source: A Guidebook of American Genealogy,* Revised Edition. Salt Lake City, UT: Ancestry Inc. 1997. 846 pp.

> This collection, written by many of the nation's top genealogists, covers every phase of American genealogy, from colonial times to the present. It shows how to locate records and how to use them, and covers questions a genealogist might have on all levels of genealogical research. This is an updated edition of the book originally published in 1984 with Arlene Eakle and Johni Cerny, editors.

Jan Steven Zaleski. *Guide to Records of Border Crossings between the United States and Canada, 1895-1954.* Detroit: Author. 1993. 39 pp.

Chapter III

RESEARCHING GERMANIC ANCESTORS IN CANADA

Researching in Canada is much like researching in the United States. Most types of records found in the United States also exist in Canada. Canada has national repositories that can be compared to the United States National Archives and Library of Congress. Each province, county or rural municipality, and local area also maintains its own designated records. Those of genealogical importance include births, baptisms, marriages, deaths, census records, church records, court records, land records, immigration and naturalization records, military records, newspapers, etc.

After compiling information from your family members and learning that your ancestors immigrated to Canada, you are ready to begin researching Canadian records. First you need to locate the place in Canada where your ancestors lived. Next determine the county or rural municipality, the town or township, and the time period they were at that locale. Keep in mind that many place names have changed over the years, especially in Ontario. Questions regarding this will be answered by the Archives of Ontario. See Chapter XIV for more information about immigration to Canada.

If your ancestors came to Canada between 1764 and 1867, a unique index is available to help you locate where they lived: the "Computerized Land Records Index." See under **PROVINCIAL ARCHIVES** later in this chapter for land records of Ontario. Since the Canadian government advertised for settlers to come to eastern Canada and land was offered free until 1826 to those willing to improve the property, most settlers of this time period owned land. After 1826, land was purchased at a minimal cost. This index summarizes the original land grants from the Crown (government) dating from the earliest settlement in Upper Canada/Canada West/Ontario (1791-1867), and Lower Canada/ Canada East/Quebec (1764-1841). The index is alphabetized by surname of the applicant and/or by township name and is available on microfiche through Family History Centers. When using the index, remember to search every spelling variation of your surname. Data on the index includes: surname, given name, town or township, lot number, concession number, date identity code, issue date, transaction type, type of free grant, type of lease/sale, and archival reference (registry, series, volume and page number). Based on information from this index, photocopies of the actual records can be obtained. For more complete information, see *Genealogy in Ontario: Searching the Records*, by Brenda Dougall Merriman and Families (Vol. 25, No. 2, 1986) published by the Ontario Genealogical Society.

Once you have located the exact place of residence, many city and county directories from the 1840s to the present are available. See Dorothy E. Ryder's *Checklist of Canadian Directories, 1790-1950* (National Library of Canada, 1979).

Another unique aid to locating your Canadian ancestor is the useful *Directory of Canada of 1857*. This directory includes people from all parts of Canada although it does not list every household. Land owners and business people are most likely to be found. The Ontario section of this directory has been alphabetized and reprinted in *Directory of the Province of Ontario, 1857, with a Gazetteer*, by Thomas B. Wilson and Emily S. Wilson (1987), published by the Ontario Genealogical Society.

CHURCH RECORDS

Since registration of vital events did not begin in Canada until 1869, church registers should be consulted for baptisms, marriages, deaths or burials prior to this time. Many churches have their own cemetery and keep their own burial and sexton records. Additional records found in church registers may include communicants, membership and confirmation lists. Many churches kept records of arrival of church members as well as removal of members to other congregations. Vestry records can include lists of donors to the church, sometimes biographical material on members, records of orphans, illegitimate births, and lists of the poor.

Churches kept their own individual registers, but over time some churches merged, separated or disbanded. Census records can be used to determine a family's religious affiliation. The location of some church records can be a problem since many baptisms were performed in the "nearest" church, regardless of religious affiliation, and during particular periods of history only certain denominations were allowed to perform marriages. This means that marriages of various denominations can be found within one register. Some records were kept by circuit (traveling) ministers, and may be found miles from the area of the event, or were lost entirely. The following short dateline can help explain why it may be difficult to locate your ancestor's marriage record in Canada:

1754-1793	Only Anglican and Roman Catholic clergy could perform marriages.
1793-1798	District clerks were allowed to perform marriages if the couple lived more than 18 miles from an Anglican minister. Anglican and Roman Catholic clergy also performed marriages.
1798-1831	Anglican, Roman Catholic, Calvinists, Church of Scotland and Lutheran clergy could perform marriages.
1831-1858	All above denominations as well as Baptists, Methodists and Presbyterians were allowed to perform marriages. Marriage registers were required to be kept by law.

1858-Present All denominations can perform marriages.

Individual church archives can help in locating where the records are for a particular congregation. Before writing to Canada, check with a Family History Center to see if microfilming has been done in the area. Many church registers have also been published. The following are useful addresses pertaining to research in Canadian records. See the *Yearbook of American and Canadian Churches* (referenced in Chapter XI) for more addresses.

Organization: Address	Holdings
• Amish Historical Library RR 4 Aylmer, ON N5H 2R3	Has older order Amish records. Records of other Amish sects are kept at the University of Waterloo.
• Anglican Church of Canada General Synod Archives 600 Jarvis St. Toronto, ON M4Y 9Z9	Can help you locate which diocesan archives to contact for names and addresses of Anglican churches in the area your family lived. Records are kept in the local churches.
• Archdiocese of Toronto 355 Church St. Toronto, ON M5B 1Z8	Has Roman Catholic records. All records are in local churches. You can contact your local archdiocese or diocese to locate individual churches, diocese or archdiocese in Canada.
• Canadian Baptist Archives McMaster Divinity College Hamilton, ON L8S 4K1	The Baptist denomination has its roots in the Anabaptist movement.
• Canadian Jewish Congress Central Region Archives 150 Beverly St. Toronto, ON M5T 1Y6	May be helpful with questions concerning ancestry of Canadian Jews.

- Evangelical Lutheran Church
  in Canada
  114 Seminary Crescent
  Saskatoon, SK S7N 0X3

Church headquarters.

- Kitchener Public Library
  Grace Schmidt Room of Local History
  85 Queen St. N.
  Kitchener, ON N2H 2H1

Has extensive newspaper indexes and family histories in a heavily German area.

- Leo Baeck Institute
  129 E. 73rd St.
  New York, NY 10021

May be helpful for German Jewish genealogical research in both Canada and the United States.

- Lutheran Historical Institute
  7100 Ada Blvd.
  Edmonton, AB T5B 4E4

- Mennonite Archives of Ontario
  Conrad Grebel College
  University of Waterloo
  Waterloo, ON N2L 3G6

This is the central repository for Mennonite church records in Ontario.

- United Church of Canada Archives
  Birge Carnegie Library
  Victoria University
  73 Queen's Park Crescent East
  Toronto, ON M5S 1K7

This is a unity of the Congregationalists, Methodists, and some Presbyterians, including the United Brethren in Christ and German Methodists.

- Waterloo Lutheran Seminary
  75 University Ave. W.
  Waterloo, ON N2L 3C6

Records are kept in congregations. Some records are shared with synod archives at seminaries. German language is predominant in early Lutheran records.

CENSUS RECORDS

The 1901 census is the latest one which is available for genealogical research.

There seems to be a question as to whether later census records will be made public at all. Of course, statistical data for all censuses have been published, so that it is possible to identify changes with respect to where the largest concentration of people of Germanic ancestry are, since both urbanization and new immigration have certainly altered the patterns found in Lehmann's book.

GENEALOGICAL SOCIETIES

Genealogical societies can provide a variety of help in locating the records you need, but do not expect them to do your research for you. Many organizations have extensive indexes, obituary files, printed genealogies and local histories that they will check for you. See also Chapter XIV for more information.

Alberta Family History Societies
P.O. Box 30270, Sta. B
Calgary, AB T2M 4P1

Alberta Genealogical Society
Prince of Wales Armouries Heritage
    Centre #116
10440 - 108 Avenue
Edmonton, AB T5H 3Z9

Genealogical Association of Nova Scotia
P.O. Box 641, Station "M"
Halifax, NS B3J 2T3

Ontario Genealogical Society
40 Orchard View Blvd., Suite 253
Toronto, ON M4R 1B9

Manitoba Genealogical Society
885 Notre Dame Ave.
Winnipeg, MB R3E 0M4

East European Genealogical Society
P.O. Box 2536
Winnipeg, MB R3C 4A7
(*has much information on Germans
from Eastern Europe, especially
Galicia and Volhynia.*)

British Columbia Genealogical Society
P.O. Box 88054
Richmond, BC V6X 3T6

Saskatchewan Genealogical Society
P.O. Box 1894
Regina, SK S4P 3E1
(*library at 1870 Lorne St.*)

Waterloo-Wellington Branch of
   Ontario Genealogical Society (OGS)
Eastwood Square, P.O. box 43030
Kitchener, ON N2H 6S9
(*center of German settlement*)

The Ontario Genealogical Society is the largest genealogical society in Canada with 27 branches and over 6,000 members. OGS is recording all cemeteries in Ontario and is indexing the 1871 census for the Province of Ontario. It offers an extensive list of publications.

The Saskatchewan Genealogical Society has many branches. Since Germans (mostly from Eastern Europe) were widely scattered throughout the province, almost all of them are relevant for Germanic research. Contact SGS to get the name of the branch responsible for the area you are researching.

The Alberta Genealogical Society and the Manitoba Genealogical Society also have quite a few branches, while independent regional societies exist in British Columbia and Nova Scotia.

HOMESTEADING AND LAND RECORDS IN THE PRAIRIE PROVINCES

Homestead records and land purchase records of various kinds are available in the provincial archives of the western provinces. Homesteading was available there much later than in the United States, which is a major reason why many German-Americans migrated onward to Western Canada. In Manitoba, homesteading occurred in the 1870-1930 period. In northern British Columbia, it is still continuing on a small-scale basis.

Betty Lang provided the following information regarding repositories for homestead and land records.

Those for southern Alberta are at the:

Southern Alberta Land Registration
   District
P.O. Box 575, Stn. M
Calgary, AB T2P 2R4

Those for northern Alberta are at the:

Northern Alberta Land Registration
   District
P.O. Box 2380
Edmonton, AB T5J 2T3

Records for 1880-1930, when the heaviest homesteading occurred, are also available at the Provincial Archives of Alberta (address above) and at the:

Glenbow Archives
130 - 9 Ave. S.E.
Calgary, AB T2G 0P3

The Saskatchewan records are at the Saskatchewan Archives Board, with the same addresses as those of the two provincial archives.

Those for Manitoba are at:

Crown Lands Branch
Department of Mines, Resources &
   Environmental Management
600 Westrow Industrial Mall
1495 St. James St.
Winnipeg, MB R3H 0W9

Registrar
Land Titles Office
405 Broadway Ave.
Winnipeg, MB R3C 1T5

SPECIAL COLLECTIONS

The Li-Ra-Ma Collection at the National Archives of Canada consists of the records of Czarist consuls from about 1900 until 1922, when Canada recognized the Soviet Union. The title consists of the first two letters of the names of the three Russian consuls in Canada.

These records contain over 100,000 names of immigrants from the Russian Empire until such time as they had been naturalized, often long after their arrival. Canceled passports, other travel documents, birth certificates, identity cards, military service records, school records, wills, estate records, certificates of nationality, Russian police reports, family histories, immigration records and details as to place of origin are among the items of greatest interest to genealogists.

The records in Canada, like those in the United States, have been cataloged, indexed and microfilmed. Unfortunately, there is no publication similar to the Sack and Wynne book available for Canada. However, a brief but informative description can be found in Angus Baxter's *In Search of Your European Roots*.

For specific information, write to the Ethnic Branch of the Manuscript Division of the National Archives of Canada.

The Wanka Collection consists mostly of European books and other materials about ethnic Germans. It deals primarily with Germans from Eastern Europe, with particularly strong holdings for the Germans from the Czech Republic. It is located at:

> University of Winnipeg Library
> 515 Portage Ave.
> Winnipeg, MB R3B 2E9

The Henry Meyer Collection, which focuses on the Germans from Galicia, Bessarabia and Bukovina, is an important part of the Saskatchewan Genealogical Society's extensive Germanic holdings.

The Regina Public Library is noted for its collection of local histories for the three Prairie Provinces.

NATIONAL ARCHIVES AND LIBRARY

Canada's national record repository collects and preserves records of national importance. This includes all national government records and sizable collections of provincial, local and private records from all of Canada. This national collection includes census records, vital statistics, Crown Land records, wills and estate records, some early marriage bonds, military records and immigration records. The staff is permitted to provide limited photocopying of original documents and copies from microfilm. The archive is open for private research but an appointment should be arranged in advance. The archive has an inexpensive booklet, *Tracing Your Ancestors in Canada*, as a brief guide to using the archive for genealogical research. The National Library of Canada can be compared to the U.S. Library of Congress. Write to:

> National Archives of Canada   National Library of Canada
> 395 Wellington St.   395 Wellington St.
> Ottawa, ON K1A 0N3   Ottawa, ON K1A 0N3

Many of the above records, including census records, have been microfilmed by the Family History Library (FHL) in Salt Lake City and are available at local Family History Centers.

Estate records may include wills, inventories of property, petitions for and letters of administration, trusteeships and guardianships, as well as miscellaneous correspondence. These are located at the local court in which the estate was probated. Many of these documents have been microfilmed by the FHL.

Newspapers, school records, and military records are also found at the National Archives of Canada, and many have been microfilmed. These can be ordered through Family History Centers (see Chapter V).

DEPARTMENT OF CITIZENSHIP AND IMMIGRATION

The Department of Citizenship and Immigration has the post-1918 immigration records, a nominal card index to the naturalization records of 1854-1917 (the originals have been destroyed) and the genealogically more valuable post-1917 naturalization records.

Each application must be submitted on an "Access of Information Form" by a citizen or resident of Canada, with a check for $5 made out to the Receiver General for Canada, and sent to:

Citizenship and Immigration Canada
Public Rights Administration
300 Slater St.
3rd Floor, Section D
Ottawa, ON K1A 1L1

Each request must be accompanied by a signed consent from the person concerned or proof that s/he has been deceased for twenty years. Certain specific information, including the full name at the time of immigration or naturalization and date of birth must be provided.

From 1763 through 1946, immigrants from Great Britain and the Commonwealth (earlier Empire) who were British subjects by virtue of birth did not have to be naturalized.

PROVINCIAL ARCHIVES

The **Ontario Provincial Archives** has recently made many of its records available through inter-library loan. These records include some vital events before 1869, court records, and pre-1900 publications on microfilm. Births from 1869-96, marriages from 1869-1911 and deaths from 1819-1921 have been transferred to the archives and are being microfilmed. District marriage registers dating from 1831 (a few dating back to the early 1800s) of the minority denominations (i.e., other than Catholic and Anglican) are indexed and available on microfilm. Copies of the county marriage registers from 1858-69 have been microfilmed.

Among the most genealogically important holdings are the applications or petitions for **land grants**. The Ontario abstract records (1764-1867) were filmed by the FHL. A copy was given to the archives and can be borrowed. An index by surname provides an easy search for the appropriate petition. The **computerized land records index** mentioned earlier in this chapter is available through the FHL. This is an index for the Crown Land, Canada Company, and Peter Robinson papers (companies providing land settlement) and also to the land grants of the United Empire Loyalists and veterans of the South African War.

They also have a **card index** of 43,000 personal names from 1780-1869 extracted from family histories, marriages, land records, wills and cemetery records. This index has been microfilmed by the FHL.

The **Manitoba Provincial Archives** also has the records listed below, according to information received from archivist Ken Reddig and Brian Lenius of the Manitoba Genealogical Society. It is likely that similar records exist in most other provincial archives.

- Tax assessment and collectors rolls
- Probate (formerly surrogate) and estate records (beginning in 1871 in Winnipeg; later elsewhere)
- Many Canadian passenger arrival lists (microfilm copies)
- Census records (microfilm copies)

- Voters or electors lists (in Canada, as in most other countries, the government prepares a list of eligible voters, so these lists include almost all adults)
- Semi-annual school attendance reports, listing the name of the teacher and the names, ages, grades and attendance of students (beginning in 1915)

Selected Manitoba Government Records: Family & Community History, published by the provincial archives, lists court records (estate, divorce and other files), land records (including index to people who obtained crown land through homesteading, purchase or grant), school records (with full details on each student), township plans and municipal records available at the archives or other repositories.

Tracing Your Ancestors in Alberta, by Victoria Lemieux and David Leonard, is available from the Provincial Archives of Alberta. *Exploring Local History in Saskatchewan* can be obtained from the Saskatchewan Provincial Archives.

The following provincial archives contain material of particular importance for Germanic research:

Provincial Archives of Alberta
12845 - 102nd Avenue
Edmonton, Alberta T5N 0M6

British Columbia Archives and
    Records Service
655 Belleville St.
Victoria, BC V8V 1X4

Manitoba Provincial Archives
200 Vaughan St.
Winnipeg, MB R3C 1T5

Public Archives of Nova Scotia
6016 University Ave.
Halifax, NS B3H 1W4

Archives of Ontario
77 Grenville St.
Toronto, ON M7A 2R9

Saskatchewan Provincial Archives
Murray Memorial Building
3 Campus Drive
University of Saskatchewan
Saskatoon, SK S7N 0W0

Saskatchewan Provincial Archives
3303 Hillsdale Street
University of Regina
Regina, SK S4S 0A2

Addresses of provincial archives are also listed in other sources, including Thomas Jay Kemp, *International Vital Records Handbook*, 3rd ed. (Baltimore: Genealogical Publishing Co., 1994).

PROVINCIAL LIBRARIES

Published materials, including many family, local and church histories, can be found in the provincial libraries. Some provinces have requirements that a copy of each copyrighted book published in that province must be deposited with the provincial or legislative library on request. The addresses of these and other libraries can be found in Lynn Fraser (managing ed.), *Directory of Libraries in Canada*, published annually by Micromedia, Ltd., in Toronto. Alternatively, you can call 800-387-2689 to get the address you want.

State and local libraries house vast amounts of genealogical information and have formed local archive sections. See Angus Baxter, *In Search of Your Canadian Roots*, for a list of some of these libraries and a synopsis of their genealogical collections.

CIVIL RECORDS

There are ten Canadian provinces (similar to states in the U.S.), as well as the Yukon Territory and the Northwest Territories. The latter territories are in a state of transition. Previously they have consisted of Mackenzie, Keewatin and Franklin districts, but this administrative subdivision had no real significance. The eastern part of the Northwest Territories is to become Nunavut, a self-governing territory for the Inuit (previously known as Eskimos), who speak Inuktitut. Few Caucasians live there permanently, although quite a few work there for a while as government officials, business representatives, teachers, etc.

Each province and territory has the responsibility to collect and record events within its own jurisdiction. However, all past vital records for the Northwest Territories are in Yellowknife. No equivalent archive has as yet been set up in what will become Nunavut.

These records include births, marriages, deaths, civil and criminal court records, probate records, wills, guardianships, etc. Each province began civil registration at a different time period. Services and fees to obtain searches and copies of these records vary considerably from one province to another.

Alberta
Complete records from 1898, with some birth records from 1853 and some death records from 1893.

Division of Vital Statistics
Dept. of Social Services and
    Community Health
10405 - 100th Ave., 4th Floor
Edmonton, AB T5J 0A6

British Columbia
Civil registrations began in 1872 but early records are incomplete.

Division of Vital Statistics
Ministry of Health
655 Belleville St.
Victoria, BC V8V 1X4

Manitoba
Almost complete records since 1882 and also some incomplete church records prior to 1882.

Office for Vital Statistics
Dept. of Community Services and
    Corrections
254 Portage Ave.
Winnipeg, MB R3C 0B6

New Brunswick
Incomplete records from 1888-1920 and complete records from 1920.

The Registrar General
Vital Statistics Division
PO Box 6000
Fredericton, NB E3B 5H1

Newfoundland
Began civil registration in 1892.

Registrar General
Vital Statistics Division
Department of Health
Confederation Building
St. John's, NF A1C 5I7

Newfoundland (continued)

The Provincial Archives of Newfoundland has numerous church records for the period 1860-1891.

Provincial Archives of Newfoundland
and Labrador
Colonial Building
Military Road
St. John's, NF A1C 5T7

Northwest Territories
Complete records from 1925.

Registrar of Vital Statistics
P.O. Box 1320
Yellowknife, NT X1A 2L9

Nova Scotia
Records of births and deaths from 1865-1908 and marriages from the late 1700s.

Public Archives of Nova Scotia
6016 University Ave.
Halifax, NS B3H 1W4

Records of births and deaths after 1 Oct. 1908 and marriages after 1907-1918:

Deputy Registrar General
Department of Health
PO Box 157
Halifax, NS B3J 2M9

Ontario
Civil registration began 1 July 1869. (Some records are available through the Ontario Provincial Archives.)

Deputy Registrar General
MacDonald Block
Queen's Park
Toronto, ON M7A 1Y5

Prince Edward Island
Civil registration began in 1906, but some marriage records date back to 1787.

Director, Division of Vital Statistics
Dept. of Health and Social Services
PO Box 3000
Charlottetown, PE C1A 7P1

Quebec

Church records have been kept since 1621 by the priests of the Catholic Church. A duplicate of the church registry was sent to the office of one of the 34 district protonotaries. These are deposited in 9 regional offices of the Archives nationales du Quebec.

Archives nationales du Quebec
PO Box 10450
Sainte-Foy, PQ G1V 4N1

Write to this archive to obtain addresses of the regional offices. Extracts can also be made directly from the parish records. Many of the parish records have been indexed and printed as well as filmed by the Family History Library.

Saskatchewan

Complete records since 1920 and incomplete records for 1878-1920.

Vital Statistics, Dept. of Health
1919 Rose St.
Regina, SK S4P 3V7

Yukon Territory

Some birth records for 1898, an index of births about 1900-24 and complete records from 1924.

Vital Statistics
Government of the Yukon Territory
PO Box 2703
Whitehorse, YT Y1A 2C6

As of September 1, 1994, you must apply to **private registry offices** in Alberta for birth, marriage and death certificates; certified copies of registrations; or genealogical copies of registrations. For a list of authorized Alberta registries, phone (403)422-2362 in Edmonton, (403)297-890 in Calgary, or (800)465-5009 for registries elsewhere. The 800 number may be valid only for Canada.

COURT AND PROBATE RECORDS

These are available for the three Prairie Provinces at:

Alberta Attorney General	Surrogate Court	Surrogate Clerk
Madison Bldg.	Court of Queens Bench	Regina Court House
9833 109 St.	405 York Ave.	2428 Victoria Ave.
Edmonton, AB T5K 2E8	Winnipeg, MB R3C 0P9	Regina, SK S4P 3V7

BORDER CROSSING RECORDS

The Canadian-American border has always been very porous, with many families migrating in both directions, often more than once. However, the fact that there was still plenty of free land available in Western Canada after the frontier had been closed in the United States led to a huge migration, mostly from the Great Plains and western Midwest states to the Canadian Prairie Provinces. One estimate is that more than one million Americans, most of them probably with a Germanic background, moved north across the forty-ninth parallel in the late nineteenth and early twentieth centuries. For more information about pertinent records, see the articles by Aitken and Kinney.

Land was not the only reason for migration. Many were motivated by family and religious concerns; others moved, in both directions, because of their attitudes toward wars. After the American Revolution, those who had remained loyal to the British king went to Eastern Canada. During those years in the World Wars when Canada was at war and the United States was not, there was two-way migration. Some of this was temporary, but others remained permanently in their new home.

The National Archives has a list of immigrants arriving across the border and at certain ports for 1908-1918. However, these records date back to 1908 only in the east. Such records were not kept in the west until later. No record exists for any individual who crossed the border before such records were established at the place of entry, since people could move freely across the border.

BIBLIOGRAPHY (See ANNOTATED BIBLIOGRAPHY for full citations if not shown)

Kenneth G. Aitken, "When Our West Moved North: Canadian Border Entry Records for Great Plains Emigrants," in *Minnesota Genealogist*, Vol. 26, No. 3 (September 1995).

Angus Baxter. *In Search of Your Canadian Roots*. Baltimore, MD: Genealogical Publishing Co. 1994. 350 pp.
> Includes a 5-page bibliography. Books which appear to be most useful for German-Canadian and Jewish-Canadian genealogy are listed here. However, Baxter also lists a number of primarily historical books for some religious groups, especially Mennonites and Baptists. There are also a few books about passenger lists, which are noted in the bibliography for Chapter XV.

W. Bell. *Foreign Protestants and the Settlement of Nova Scotia*. Toronto. 1961.
> Germans represent a significant percentage of early foreign settlers.

P. Birkett. *Checklist of Parish Registers (NAC)*. Ottawa. 1987.

S. Burrow and F. Gaudet. *Checklist of Indexes to Canadian Newspapers (NAC)*. Ottawa. 1987.

Canadian Catholic Church Directory. Montreal: Publicite B.M. 1988.
> Includes addresses of all diocesan archives and much more information.

Virginia Easley DeMarce. *German Military Settlers in Canada after the American Revolution*. Sparta, WI: Joy Reisinger. 1984. 350 pp. Available from Joy Reisinger, 1020 Central Ave., Sparta, WI 54656.
> Roster of 2,000 men who remained in Canada after the American Revolution, with Anglicized and Gallicized names. Historical background on the formation of German mercenary units.

R. Fellows. *Researching Your Ancestors in New Brunswick*. Fredericton. 1979.
> Relevant for the small number of Germans who settled in this province, mostly after the American Revolution.

D'Arcy Hande. *Exploring Family History in Saskatchewan*. Saskatoon. 1986.
> Many Germans, mostly from Eastern Europe, came to this province.

T. A. Hillman. *Census Returns (NAC)*. Ottawa. 1987.

Eric Jonasson. *A Canadian Genealogical Handbook*. Winnipeg, Manitoba: Wheatfield Press. 1978. 352 pp.

Miles Kinney, "American Settlement in the Prairie West," in *Saskatchewan Genealogical Society Bulletin*, Vol. 11, No. 1 (February 1980).

W. M. Lorre. *Index to 1881 Census of Manitoba*. Vancouver. 1984.
> Most Mennonites, but relatively few other Germans, had arrived in Manitoba by 1881.

Janine Roy. *Tracing Your Ancestors in Canada*. 9th ed., revised 1987. Ottawa: National Archives of Canada. 1988. 47 pp.

Heinz Lehmann. *The German Canadians, 1750-1937*.

Brenda Dougall Merriman. *Genealogy in Ontario, Searching the Records*. Toronto, Ontario: Ontario Genealogical Society. 1988. 168 pp.

Mary Munk and Lorraine St. Louis-Harrison. *Tracing Your Ancestors in Canada*, 12th ed. Ottawa: National Archives of Canada. 1997.

Terrence Punch. *Genealogical Research in Nova Scotia*. Halifax. 1978.
> Includes ten of the twelve relevant passenger lists.

Provincial Archives of Manitoba. *Selected Manitoba Government Records: Family and Community History*. Winnipeg: Provincial Archives of Manitoba. 1996.

Leonard H. Smith, Jr., and Norma H. Smith. *Nova Scotia Immigrants to 1867*. Baltimore: Germealogical Publishing Co. 1992. 560 pp.
> Comprehensive index of immigrants, including many who came to the U.S., based on extensive research in Canadian, American, British and French archival sources.

K. R. Stokes. *Marriage and Death Notices from Manitoba Newspapers*. Winnipeg. 1986.

Lawrence F. Tapper. *Archival Sources: Canadian Jewry (NAC)*. Ottawa. 1987.
> Written by an archivist at the National Archives who is also a genealogist.

Ryan Taylor. *Family Research in Waterloo and Wellington Counties*. Kitchener, Ontario: Waterloo-Wellington Branch of Ontario Genealogical Society. 1986. 106 pp.
> Exceptionally well-done guide for the German areas of Ontario.

Chapter IV

COMPUTERS AND GENEALOGY

Computers can be a useful tool for organizing your data, finding the location of resources and exchanging information with other researchers. With your home computer and a good genealogy program you can organize, search, sort, and print out your family history. If you have CD-ROM capability with your computer, you can access information including general genealogy references, telephone directories, and surname databases. With access to the large Bulletin Board Systems or On Line services and/or the Internet, you can find additional help and information for your research from all over the world. A major reason to use a genealogy program is the genealogist usually needs to enter the data only once. The computer will then use the data, where needed, to create the report or chart requested. Equally important is the help a computer can give in quickly locating sources of genealogical information.

Genealogy Software

There are probably close to 100 genealogy programs available for computers but fewer than a dozen have become well-known. However, not one of these programs have all the features that genealogists want. Individual genealogists must decide what features they want and match them to the program fulfilling most of their needs. Some genealogists use two or more programs to fulfill their needs.

Most of the programs are for the IBM® type personal computer, but some are available for the Macintosh® as well. Some, such as Personal Ancestral File® from the LDS Church, Family Tree Maker® from Broderbund, and Reunion® from Leister Productions, are available on both computers. Most programs work with Windows® but a few run under DOS®.

A genealogy program may not require a large powerful computer, but to obtain the most help in your genealogy efforts, a computer with at least a 386 central processor, 4 megabytes of RAM, and a hard drive capacity of 100 megabytes or more, are recommended. The more you can exceed these minimums (or their equivalent), the better. The Family Tree Maker for the Macintosh requires a PowerMAC with 16 megabytes of RAM. A 4X speed CD-ROM drive and a 14.4 Kbyte modem are the recommended minimums for these add-ons if you wish to do research using CD-ROMs and/or the Internet as described later.

Genealogy programs are continuously being improved and updated. By the time you read this book, at least one, likely several, will have an updated, improved version available, and possibly a new one will have been introduced. Your best chance of getting up to date information is to join the computer interest group of your nearest genealogical society. If this is not practical, subscribe to a national newsletter such as *Genealogical Computing*. (Call 800-531-1790 for more information.) If you have an Internet connection, check the sites of the genealogy software suppliers for the latest information.

Some of the more common features a good genealogy program should have are discussed below.

- GEDCOM capability. This is a MUST HAVE feature. Without this feature the genealogist would likely have to re-enter data when switching to another program.

- How many people can be held in one database. As you add more of your collateral lines, it is not unusual to have thousands in your database. Most newer programs easily meet this requirement.

- Ease of use. The program must be easy to learn and use. Many programs use a Family Group Sheet; a Pedigree Chart; a Card File; or an Album metaphor, making it easy to relate to program actions. Most newer programs are easy to use, but a few have so many options they need large manuals for help.

- Easy browsing of the database contents. This is usually an alphabetical index of all the people in your database with much of the individual's vital statistics shown as you highlight their name. This makes it easy to find and identify the person you are looking for.

- Smart, editable place list. After entering the first few letters of the event "place", the program can show all the previous places entered, starting with those few letters. Then pick the one desired and it will be entered for you. Some programs will allow editing the list of places entered.

- Many event fields possible. Preferably as many as the genealogist wishes with the ability to create whatever title is needed. However, only those defined for that person should be maintained.

- Information and source recording. The basic rules in genealogy is to always document your information and cite the source of your information. A good genealogy program will make this task easy by having a good Notes Editor and allowing quick reference to all sources entered earlier, with easy connection of the selected sources to later material. An opinion of how "sure" the genealogist is of the accuracy of the source can be entered in a few programs. Most genealogists will be entering many notes and it can be very helpful to have a few of the basic editing features usually found in a word processor program such as word wrap, cut, paste, clear, undo, etc.

- Relationships. This makes it easy to understand relationships between people. Some programs will print a chart showing relationships between two people, from the first selected to the common ancestor then to the other selection. Special relationships, such as foster, step, half, adoption, and others, can be a problem with some programs.

- Find duplicates and merge. It is not unusual to find the same person entered twice, when working in large databases. Especially when one is entered as a spouse while documenting one line, then later as a child while documenting another, supposedly unrelated, line. This feature helps find possible duplicates and then selectively merge the two entries into one.

- Diacritics. The German language has characters (ä, ö, ü, ß) not found in the English alphabet. Most genealogy programs allow entry of these characters, with some having pop-up charts to pick the special characters.

- Reports and charts. Most programs will print the basic reports like the Family Group Sheet, Pedigree Charts, Individual Data Sheets, Descendants, Ancestors (*Ahnentafel*), and many types of search reports. Some programs will print Wall Charts and Tree Charts that are very helpful at family reunions. Some have reports that take the information from the database format and change it to a narrative format by adding words between the data. These Register, Modified Register, or Book reports read and look similar to a book. There may or may not be an index generated at the end. Some programs will send the information to a word processor program in its native format, making it easy to edit and set the format and style. These may become "camera ready" copies for publishing the genealogy work. Depending on the word processor program, it may include pictures, sound and video clips. Some of the newer programs also can generate a file ready to be placed on the Internet at your home page. These Internet-ready files may be able to include pictures, sound and video clips.

Some of the popular genealogy programs are discussed in the following paragraphs. This is only a summary evaluation since a full report would require many pages, and the information presented may also change as programs are updated and improved. The book, *Your Roots*, by Richard Eastman, covers some of the programs in more detail. However, this type of book usually becomes obsolete a year or two after being printed because the programs change and improve so rapidly.

- PERSONAL ANCESTRAL FILE® (PAF) by the LDS Church is a very easy to learn and use program. It has many of the basic features mentioned above such as good GEDCOM capabilities, easy to browse, find duplicates, merge records and has a good search feature. It is a DOS program available for the PC, but is not strong in taking notes, cannot handle diacritics, and the printouts are basic. A new PC version is due out in 1997 and may have improved these areas. There is also a MAC version available that has a better note editor, can handle diacritics, and has nice looking printouts. PAF costs about $35 and can be ordered by calling 800-537-5950.

- FAMILY TREE MAKER® (FTM) by Broderbund Software, Inc., also has many of the features mentioned above. It even includes a basic genealogy tutorial with the CD-ROM version. It uses the Album metaphor with tabs along the side to easily go to other people in the database. It has a nice feature called the Scrapbook where pictures, sound and video clips, etc. can be stored for later use. The Scrapbook Editor can set up multimedia shows which can be a hit at a family reunion. The printouts are some of the best available from genealogy programs. Documentation is very good, with a manual and the program helps. The cost is about $70 for the CD-ROM version, and is available in many large computer stores or call 800-474-8696. It is available for PCs running DOS or Windows. A Macintosh version is available but requires a PowerMAC with 16 megabytes of RAM. A new "Basic Edition" Family Tree Maker is available for the PC for about $20. It appears to be the earlier Version 3.02 for the PC repackaged with a brief 87-page manual.

- REUNION® by Leister Productions has many of the features above. It is very easy to learn and use. It uses a Card metaphor and is very intuitive. It does not have a merge feature but has one of the best looking chart outputs available. The charts can be easily modified to move boxes so they are not split between pages when multiple page outputs are required. Documentation is one of the best available with a easy to understand manual and good program helps. It costs about $100. It is available for PCs running Windows by calling 800-800-5555, or by calling 800-255-6227 for MACs.

- FAMILY ORIGINS® by Parsons Technology has most of the features mentioned above, yet it costs about $30, making it one of the best buys of the genealogy programs at the present time. It is easy to learn and use with most steps intuitive. An easy to understand Custom Reports section will help you create most of the usual reports a genealogist will want. The Modified Register report is normally not found in programs at this price. The Statistics and Problems reports are an added plus. Documentation is integrated with the program only. No manual is shipped with the package or available at extra cost. This may be a problem with genealogists not familiar with how to use program helps. It is available in many large computer stores or call 800-223-6925. It is only available for PCs running Windows.

- ROOTS IV® by CommSoft, Inc. This program runs under DOS on a PC but has many screen features similar to a program running under Windows. It has many of the desirable features mentioned above but will require study to make full use of them. The manual is about 500 pages. The program can handle multiple dates per event and can record a "surety" level of the data. Dates can be entered in many formats. The ability to define a report in almost any manner is one of the main features. Reports are very good looking and one of the main features of this program. Many users have published their efforts directly from this program. It has Projects to keep track of research on a particular person or line, a feature that is a help for the genealogist doing work for others. Call 800-327-6687 to order. Cost is about $130.

- THE MASTER GENEALOGIST® (TMG) by Wholly Genes Software. This program is easy to learn and use but is best for genealogists who are carefully recording all sources of information. The ability to record multiple entries for the same event supports real life problems. It has many formats to record dates. It also can record the "surety" level of the data, adding more reasons to have this program. It has a Research Log to keep track of research on a particular person or line, a feature that is a help for the genealogist doing work for others. The Custom Report Writer can show results on the screen, print, or save to a file, of anything the database has, in almost any way you want it. This report writer may require some study to use easily. Outputs can be sent to many word processors in their native format where the format, font and style can be controlled, making it easy to publish your genealogical efforts. A new reference manual is now available and said to be easy to use. Call 800-982-2103 to order. It is only available for the PC, under DOS at $100, or Windows at $130.

Many of the programs discussed above have a slide show demo or a working demo program available. The working demos will be limited in the number of people they can hold, or other ways, but will allow you to get the "touch and feel" of the program before buying. Check at the 800 numbers for more information or see information available at the company home pages on the Internet section following.

Genealogy CD-ROMs

Many CD-ROMs are available now with databases commonly searched by genealogists and more are becoming available almost every day. There are major efforts underway to put the contents of many databases onto CD-ROMs to sell to the public. However, as with most products, the CD-ROMs may have wide variation in content, functionality, price, and real value to the buyer. As with most products, try to buy from a reputable supplier that has a reasonable return policy if dissatisfied.

The content available on the CD-ROMs varies from copies of reference and source books, indexes of databases, the actual databases, data extracted from birth, marriage, death, and census records, family genealogical charts and records, and even images of the actual records. The latter usually having some contrast and brightness control and can be printed.

The most commonly used CD-ROMs are available at the nearest Family History Center. Their International Genealogical Index (IGI) has over 300 million names, obtained from their members and other genealogists around the world. They also have the Social Security Death Index and some military death indexes. The card catalog of the Family History Library is on a CD-ROM.

Another source of CD-ROMs containing genealogical information of possible help are the collection of about 50 CD-ROMs from the Banner Blue Division of Broderbund Software, Inc. Their Family Archive CDs have more than 115 million names from State Marriage and Land Records, the US Census and their World Family Tree collection. The World Family Tree consists of family trees collected from users of the Family Tree Maker genealogy program and other sources. The average size of a World Family Tree is about 500 individuals. The FamilyFinder® Index can quickly show which CD-ROM contains the information. The sources are grouped by record type, region, or time period. Contact a nearby Family Tree Maker dealer or the 800 number mentioned above for cost and availability. Also visit their web site at http://www.familytreemaker.com.

The cost of CD-ROM Writers are now within reach of many home computer users, making practical the publishing of your family histories on CD-ROMs. This allows the addition of audio and video clips with your pictures and family history, and may lower the cost of publishing. As the home multimedia computer becomes more common, this may become the choice of many relatives.

On Line Services

The fastest growing segment of genealogical resources is the worldwide availability of fast inexpensive communications, worldwide searching for the resource that may have the data you need, and the worldwide possibility of finding relatives. These resources are made possible by the ability of the average home computer to connect to these large or small Bulletin Board Systems. The larger ones are usually called On Line Services, such as America Online, CompuServe, and Prodigy, with the smaller ones being Delphi, Genie, etc. The larger services have excellent genealogical resources such as software libraries, newsletters, and even moderated forums where genealogists can ask and give assistance to others in their research. On America Online, use the Keyword "ROOTS"; and on CompuServe, use "GO ROOTS".

The largest resource by far is the worldwide interconnection of thousands of computers called the Internet. Standardized methods of communications have been agreed upon allowing easy transfer of documents, pictures, programs, etc. Access to the Internet is possible through the On Line Services mentioned above or by signing up with an Independent Service Provider (ISP), usually available in your area. All necessary software needed to connect is usually provided by the ISP or the On Line Service. You provide the computer and modem.

When successful access to the Internet has been established, you can find information about how to do genealogy, finding maps, locating libraries and archives, searching databases of information, and accessing other researchers. This information is available by e-mail, mailing lists and newsgroups, Telnet, or browsing or searching the web.

Keep in mind that information on the Internet is not static. Sites move, change, and disappear. Also, always remember that there is more than one way to find information. Be creative in the ways you use to locate this information.

E-MAIL

E-mail (short for electronic mail) is a way to send and receive messages from one computer to another. All you need is access to the Internet, an e-mail program and the e-mail address of the person you want to send mail to. With e-mail you can easily exchange information with family members, friends, and fellow researchers anywhere in the world. Many e-mail programs also allow you to send formatted files as an attachment. This allows you to include output from your genealogy program or word processor.

MAILING LISTS AND NEWSGROUPS

Mailing Lists are group discussions carried on through electronic mail. To post and receive messages from a mailing list you must first subscribe to it by sending an e-mail message to the list maintainer. You will receive a message back, verifying your subscription. Read and save this message. Once you have subscribed, you will receive a copy of every message posted to the mailing list and you will be able to post your own messages as well.

Newsgroups are similar to mailing lists, but messages are not sent by e-mail. You must have a stand-alone news reader program or a browser (like Netscape®) which can access newsgroups. In addition, your Internet access provider may not carry all newsgroups. To access a newsgroup you must subscribe to it. Then you will see all the messages posted to that group since you last accessed it. You can choose which messages to read.

There are some simple rules of etiquette you should follow when posting messages to mailing lists and newsgroups:

- Observe the mailing list or newsgroup activity for a while before posting your first message.

- Don't post messages pertaining to an unrelated subject.

- Don't post a message to numerous, unrelated discussion groups.

- Reply directly to the author of a message (rather than posting a reply to the discussion group) if the content of your reply won't interest the group as a whole.

There are many newsgroups and mailing lists related to genealogy available on the Internet, including groups for individual surnames, geographical areas, and how-to-do genealogy. In addition to the sites listed below there are web sites that have more complete listings:

> http://users.aol.com/johnf14246/gen_mail.html

> http://users.aol.com/johnf14246/gen_use.html

Mailing Lists

GEN-NEWBIE-L. A list for people new to computers and genealogy.

The mailing address for postings is gen-newbie-l@rootsweb.com.
To subscribe, send the following message to gen-newbie-l-request@rootsweb.com:
> subscribe

GEN-DE-L. A list for the discussion of German genealogy.

The mailing address for postings is gen-de-l@mail.eworld.com.
To subscribe, send the following message to listserv@mail.eworld.com:
> SUB GEN-DE-L yourfirstname yourlastname

JEWISHGEN. Discussions of Jewish genealogy. Gatewayed with the soc.genealogy.jewish newsgroup.

Mailing address for postings is jewishgen@mail.eWorld.com.
To subscribe, send the following message to listserv@mail.eWorld.com
> SUBSCRIBE JEWISHGEN yourfirstname yourlastname

ALSACE-LORRAINE. A mailing list for anyone with a genealogical or historical interest in Alsace-Lorraine.

The mailing address for postings is alsace-lorraine@rmgate.pop.indiana.edu.
To subscribe, send the following message to maiser@rmgate.pop.indiana.edu:
> SUB ALSACE-LORRAINE

AUSTRIA. A mailing list for anyone with a genealogical or historical interest in Austria including the German speaking lands annexed to Italy at the end of World War I.

The mailing address for postings is austria@rmgate.pop.indiana.edu.
To subscribe, send the following message to maiser@rmgate.pop.indiana.edu:
> SUB AUSTRIA

BADEN-WURTTEMBERG. A mailing list for anyone with a genealogical interest in Baden, Hohenzollern, and Württemberg.

The mailing address for postings is baden-wurttemberg@rmgate.pop.indiana.edu.
To subscribe, send the following message to maiser@rmgate.pop.indiana.edu:
> SUB BADEN-WURTTEMBERG

EW-PRUSSIA. A mailing list for anyone with a genealogical interest in East and West Prussia (not the Kingdom of Prussia) to 1945.

The mailing address for postings is ew-prussia@rmgate.pop.indiana.edu.
To subscribe, send the following message to maiser@rmgate.pop.indiana.edu:
> SUB EW-PRUSSIA

GER-BAVARIA. A mailing list for anyone with a genealogical interest in the Kingdom, province and state of Bavaria which includes the city of Munich.

The mailing address for postings is ger-bavaria@rmgate.pop.indiana.edu.
To subscribe, send the following message to maiser@rmgate.pop.indiana.edu:
> SUB GER-BAVARIA

GER-BRANDENBURG. A mailing list for anyone with a genealogical interest in Brandenburg which includes the city of Berlin.

The mailing address for postings is ger-brandenburg@rmgate.pop.indiana.edu.
To subscribe, send the following to maiser@rmgate.pop.indiana.edu:
    SUB GER-BRANDENBURG

GER-HANNOVER. A mailing list for anyone with a genealogical interest in the German province/state of Hanover which includes Brunswick (duchy of Braunschweig), Lippe, and the cities of Bremen and Hamburg.

The mailing address for postings is ger-hannover@rmgate.pop.indiana.edu.
To subscribe, send the following message to maiser@rmgate.pop.indiana.edu:
    SUB GER-HANNOVER

GER-HESSEN. A mailing list for anyone with a genealogical interest in the kingdoms, principalities, provinces, and state of Hesse (Hesse-Darmstadt, Hesse-Starkenburg, Hesse-Nassau, Waldeck, Rheinhessen) which includes the city of Frankfurt am Main.

The mailing address for postings is ger-hessen@rmgate.pop.indiana.edu.
To subscribe, send the following message to maiser@rmgate.pop.indiana.edu:
    SUB GER-HESSEN

GERMAN-BOHEMIAN-L. A discussion group for those interested in sharing information about the culture, genealogy and heritage of the German-speaking people of Bohemia and Moravia, now the Czech Republic.

The mailing address for postings is german-bohemian-l@rootsweb.com.
To subscribe, send the following message to german-bohemian-l-request@rootsweb.com:
    SUBSCRIBE

GER-OLDENBURG. A mailing list for anyone with a genealogical interest in Oldenburg which is west of the Hanover province/state.

The mailing address for postings is ger-oldenburg@rmgate.pop.indiana.edu.
To subscribe, send the following message to maiser@rmgate.pop.indiana.edu:
    SUB GER-OLDENBURG

GER-POSEN. A mailing list for anyone with a genealogical interest in Posen for the time period when it was under German rule to 1945.

The mailing address for postings is ger-posen@rmgate.pop.indiana.edu.
To subscribe, send the following message to maiser@rmgate.pop.indiana.edu:
    SUB GER-POSEN

GER-RUS2. A mailing list for general discussions of Germans from Russia genealogy and family research.

The mailing address for postings is ger-rus2@listserv.nodak.edu.
To subscribe, send the following message to listserv@listserv.nodak.edu:
    SUBSCRIBE GER-RUS2 firstname lastname

GER-SCHLESIEN. A mailing list for anyone with a genealogical interest in Silesia (Schlesien), including Upper Silesia (Ober-Schlesien) and Lower Silesia (Nieder-Schlesien), for the time period when it was under German rule. The German portion of this area is now in Poland.

The mailing address for postings is ger-schlesien@rmgate.pop.indiana.edu.
To subscribe, send the following message to maiser@rmgate.pop.indiana.edu:
    SUB GER-SCHLESIEN

GER-TRIER-ROOTS. A mailing list for anyone with a genealogical interest in the region known as the Trier Archdiocese of the Rhineland Province (South Rhineland/Saarland). This southwestern area of Germany borders France, Belgium, Luxembourg and the Netherlands. Parts of Luxembourg, Belgium and the Saarland flowed into one another at times. The Trier Archdiocese covers the counties (*Kreis*) of Bernkastel, Bitburg, Daun,

Merzig, Prum, Saarbrücken, Saarburg, Saarlouis, City of Trier, Land of Trier, Wendel and Wittlich, and includes the Saarland.

The mailing address for postings is ger-trier-roots@rmgate.pop.indiana.edu.
To subscribe, send the following message to maiser@rmgate.pop.indiana.edu:
    SUB GER-TRIER-ROOTS

MECKLENBURG-PROV. A mailing list for anyone with a genealogical interest in the Mecklenburg Province of Germany that covers the dukedoms of Mecklenburg-Schwerin and Mecklenburg-Strelitz.

The mailing address for postings is mecklenburg-prov@rmgate.pop.indiana.edu.
To subscribe, send the following message to maiser@rmgate.pop.indiana.edu:
    SUB MECKLENBURG-PROV

SACHSEN-SAXONY. A mailing list for anyone with a genealogical interest in Lower Saxony (Neider-Sachsen), Upper Saxony (Ober-Sachsen), Kingdom of Saxony (Sachsen Königreich), Province of Saxony (Sachsen Provinz), and the former Saxon principalities/duchies of Saxe-Coburg-Gotha, Saxe-Coburg-Alt, etc. (the entire region stretching from the North Sea to the east including Leipzig).

The mailing address for postings is sachsen-saxony@rmgate.pop.indiana.edu.
To subscribe, send the following message to maiser@rmgate.pop.indiana.edu:
    SUB SACHSEN-SAXONY

SCHLESWIG-HOLSTEIN. A mailing list for anyone with a genealogical interest in the German province/state of Schleswig-Holstein including the part formerly under Danish rule.

The mailing address for postings is schleswig-holstein@rmgate.pop.indiana.edu.
To subscribe, send the following message to maiser@rmgate.pop.indiana.edu:
    SUB SCHLESWIG-HOLSTEIN

THURINGEN. A mailing list for anyone with a genealogical interest in Thuringia (Thüringen) which includes the Reuss principalities.

The mailing address for postings is thuringen@rmgate.pop.indiana.edu.
To subscribe, send the following message to maiser@rmgate.pop.indiana.edu:
    SUB THURINGEN

Newsgroups

soc.genealogy.benelux (also see the GENBNL-L mailing list)

soc.genealogy.german (also see the GEN-DE-L mailing list)

soc.genealogy.jewish (also see the JEWISHGEN mailing list)

soc.genealogy.methods (genealogy methods and non-net resources) (also see the GENMTD-L mailing list)

soc.genealogy.misc (general genealogical discussions that don't fit within one of the other soc.genealogy.newsgroups) (also see the GENMSC-L mailing list)

soc.genealogy.surnames (surname queries and *tafels*) (also see the GENNAM-L mailing list)

LIBRARY CATALOGS

If you have a copy of a program called Telnet, which you can down load from many web sites for free, you have access to libraries all over the world. Telnet will let you connect to a library's on-line catalog and search for books and other resources. Library catalogs already on the Internet include those of universities, state and local libraries, historical societies and other research institutions.

CARL, Colorado Alliance of Research Libraries:
telnet://PAC.CARL.ORG

CASLIN Czech and Slovak Library Information Network:
telnet://login_visitor_Enter_your_Internet_address@alpha.nkp.cz:23/

Library Catalogs from Around the World (Hytelnet):
http://www.cc.ukans.edu/hytelnet_html/START.TXT.html

Library of Congress Catalog:
telnet://marvel.loc.gov/

LUMINA, University of Minnesota Libraries (can also access all Big Ten university libraries from here):
telnet://lumina.lib.umn.edu

MELVYL (Sutro Genealogy Library), University of California:
telnet://MELVYL.UCOP.EDU

PALS, Minnesota State Colleges and Universities (including MN Historical Society):
telnet://pals.msus.edu/

University of Wisconsin Libraries:
telnet://silo.adp.wisc.edu:5034/

THE WORLD-WIDE WEB

The World-Wide Web consists of information on computers all around the world that has been made available to users of the Internet. To access this information you need a connection to the Internet and a Web browser like Netscape® or Microsoft's Internet Explorer®. To go directly to a particular site, type that site's Web address, known as a URL (Uniform Resources Locator), into the URL window. Type URLs exactly as you see them written. To browse the Internet, you need to find a site with links to other sites. Then all you do is click on a link to go to that site.

General

Helm's Genealogy Tool Box:
http://genealogy.tbox.com/genealogy.html

Chris Gaunt and John Fuller's Genealogy Resources on the Internet:
http://www-personal.umich.edu/~cgaunt/gen_web.html

InfoBases, LDS Family History Network:
http://www.familyhistory.com/

Databases

ROOTS Location List Name Finder:
http://www.rand.org/cgi-bin/Genea/rll

ROOTS Surname List Name Finder:
http://www.rand.org/cgi-bin/Genea/rsl

Social Security Death Index, SSDI (Ancestry/Infobase):
http://www.ancestry.com/ssdi/main.htm

U.S. and World Resources

USGenWeb Project:
http://www.usgenweb.com/states.html

World Genealogy Web Project:
http://www.dsenter.com/worldgenweb/index.html

Germanic Resources

Germanic Genealogy Society:
http://www.mtn.org/mgs/branches/german.html

German Genealogy Home Page:
>   http://www.genealogy.com/gene/index.html

Internet Resources for German Genealogy:
>   http://www.bawue.de/~hanacek/info/edatbase.htm

Max Kade Institute for German-American Studies:
>   http://www.wisc.edu/mki/

Federation of Eastern European Family History Societies:
>   http://feefhs.org/

German-Bohemian Heritage Society:
>   http://www.rootsweb.com/~gbhs/

American Historical Society of Germans from Russia:
>   http://www.teleport.com/nonprofit/ahsgr/

Odessa - A German Russian Genealogical Library:
>   http://pixel.cs.vt.edu/library/odessa.html

Palatines to America:
>   http://genealogy.org/~palam/

Pomeranian data:
>   http://www.med.uni-giessen.de/~geneal/foko.html

Search Engines

Another good way to find information on the Web is to use a search engine. You type in the keywords you are searching for and the search engine will give you a list of all the sites that match your search criteria with the first item being the closest match.

Some of the most popular search engines are AltaVista, HotBot, WebCrawler and InfoSeek. One site, CNET, has brought all of these search engines and more into one place.

HotBot	http://www.hotbot.com
Alta Vista	http://www.altavista.com
WebCrawler	http://www.webcrawler.com/
InfoSeek	http://www.infoseek.com/
CNET	http://www.search.com

On-line Directories

Another good way to search the Web for surnames is to use an on-line directory. Some of these directories are general white pages and some contain information about just those who have subscribed to them. Switchboard is one of the most popular, containing general U.S. directories. Other countries also have directories on-line. Again, CNET brings many directories together in one place for your convenience. Some on-line directories are:

Switchboard	http://www.switchboard.com
International Telephone Directories	http://www.contractjobs.com/tel/
CNET Directories	http://www.search.com/Top/0,8,50082,00.html

BIBLIOGRAPHY (See ANNOTATED BIBLIOGRAPHY for full citations if not shown)

Elizabeth Powell Crowe. *Genealogy Online: Researching Your Roots*. New York: Windcrest/ McGraw-Hill, Inc. 1995. 280 pp.
>   How to access computer genealogy bulletin boards and library card catalogs online.

Richard Eastman. *Your Roots: Total Genealogy Planning on Your Computer*. Emeryville, CA: Ziff-Davis Press. 1995. 229 pp.
>   Includes a CD-ROM with free CompuServe genealogy software, shareware and demo programs, a list of genealogy resources, and more.

Chapter V

FAMILY HISTORY LIBRARY AND ITS CENTERS

Before you make any trip to Europe looking for your ancestors, you should take advantage of the world's largest genealogical library, the Family History Library in Salt Lake City, Utah. The Family History Library is affiliated with The Church of Jesus Christ of Latter-day Saints (Mormons). In this book we refer to it as the Family History Library (or FHL), but it is also popularly known as the LDS Library. It is free and open to the public, Monday 7:30am-6:00pm, Tuesday through Saturday 7:30am-10:00pm. Its address is 35 N. West Temple, Salt Lake City, UT 84150.

MAIN LIBRARY IS NEAR HISTORIC TEMPLE SQUARE

The Family History Library was organized in 1894 and has been characterized by a steady acquisition of family history material. This has necessitated two moves into larger facilities in its more than 100 year history. Its present site is located in downtown Salt Lake City, on the block west of historic Temple Square. This is a modern five story building, arranged geographically. Level one (main floor) and level two house the United States and Canada collection. Level B-1 is the British Isles collection. Level B-2 is the International collection which includes Europe. Each floor houses books, microfilm, and microfiche pertaining to that geographic location. There are hundreds of microfilm and microfiche readers on each floor, but be advised to get there early in the day to make sure you get one, since over 3,000 patrons use the library each day. Self-service copy centers on each floor have microfilm, microfiche, and paper copiers, and change machines. The copy centers also sell pamphlets, blank charts, and forms. The publications are designed to help you in using the collection more effectively. See end of this chapter for publications list and ordering information.

REFERENCE SERVICES AVAILABLE

Next to the collection itself, the best part of the library is the reference staff. The reference librarians are helpful and knowledgeable but will NOT do research for you. However, they know their collection well and will steer you to the most effective use of your time at the library. You need to prepare well and ask specific questions about the records you would like to use. Direct questions about the collection, not your specific ancestors, will get the best response. Most reference librarians can read the old handwriting and will assist you in learning to do it yourself. Ask for pamphlets of word lists and language helps. This reference service is also available by mail or by e-mail. E-mail specific questions about the FHL collection to: FHL@byu.edu.

AUTOMATED RESOURCE CENTER

In order to keep up with the latest in genealogy technology, a separate section located on the main floor of the library houses genealogy on CD-ROMs instead of the usual book, microfilm, or microfiche format. In this center you may also use a computer to access various genealogy-related resources of the Internet and on-line services such as CompuServe® and Prodigy®. Most of this collection will be useful for United States and Canadian research, but one of the CD-ROMs that could be particularly useful for Germanic genealogy is the German phone books. They are called Tele-Info. Since they are printed in German, they were moved to the B-2 level so the reference specialist there could help people read it.

MICROFILMING IS REASON FOR HUGE COLLECTION

Since the late 1930s the library has pursued an aggressive records preservation program, microfilming in over 150 countries of the world. Microfilming for the FHL is done under the auspices of the Genealogical Society of Utah. Presently the library operates 250 cameras in 46 countries to film birth, marriage, death, land, tax, probate, immigration, census, military, and many other types of records. The collection presently includes over 1.9 million reels of microfilm, 683,000 microfiche, and 270,000 books. Each year the library adds over

100 million new pages of microfilmed documents to its collection. This is approximately equivalent to 70,000 microfilm reels. The library also acquires some 25,000 microfiche and 12,000 books each year.

The Germanic collection itself is extensive, with over 114,000 microfilm reels preserving Catholic, Lutheran and Jewish registers and civil records of birth, marriage, death, and emigration records. There are over 42,000 additional microfilm reels for Austria and Switzerland. In recent years the library has also been able to microfilm in many areas of eastern Europe including the former East Germany, Poland, Hungary, Slovenia, Croatia, Yugoslavia, the Baltic states, Russia, Ukraine, and Belarus. The table below gives more detail about the size of the microfilm collection.

Table 2: Germanic Microfilm Collection at the Family History Library

Country	Number of Reels	Country	Number of Reels
Germany	122,000	Estonia	2,000
Austria	33,000	Croatia	1,600
Poland	24,000	Slovak Republic	1,200
Hungary	13,000	Bulgaria	300
Switzerland	13,000	Slovenia	185
Russia	6,650	Czech Republic	94

PLAN AHEAD FOR MICROFILM USE

Because of the huge and growing collection and limited space, the library has recently made some changes so a majority of their microfilms are stored off site. The library is arranged by geographic regions. Each geographical area determines which films are used heavily and forms a core collection that remains in the main library. The rest of the microfilms are stored off site, but are retrievable. The main floor and second floor contain the entire collection of the United States and Canada. However, this may change as space runs out. The other localities have already experienced this space crunch. Level B-1 is the International floor where the core collection of all continental European, Asian, and African materials is housed. Level B-2 holds the core collection of the British Isles, Australia and New Zealand.

To avoid delays in retrieving the films you need, consult the table below to determine if the films you need are at the main library or stored off site. If stored off site, you must request them ahead of time, preferably one month. Send a list of the requested films in NUMERICAL ORDER to the Film Attendant's Office, Floor B-1 (International). See address below. Be sure to include the date of your arrival and how long you will use the films. Three weeks are normally allotted for use. If only a few numbers are needed you may telephone the Film Attendant's office. Ask how long it will take to get the films to the main library. This call ahead process is also helpful for group visits. Guided tours are NOT provided, but orientation classes for groups of 15-60 people can be arranged by calling 801-240-2331, faxing 801-240-1919, or writing to the library in advance.

GERMANIC MICROFILMS USUALLY STORED AT MAIN LIBRARY

COUNTRIES	RECORD TYPES IN CORE COLLECTION
Germany, Luxembourg, Poland, Slovak Republic	Church, civil registration, Jewish records, emigration, census records
Belarus, Romania, Russia, Ukraine	Roman Catholic & Protestant church records (including those of many Russian Germans), civil registration, Jewish records, emigration and immigration records
Austria	Emigration records
Hungary	Jewish records, emigration records, census records. Also for Budapest: church records.

PERSONAL ANCESTRAL FILE

The Family History Library designed an easy to use and inexpensive ($37) software program in an effort to help members of the Church of Jesus Christ in their family history endeavors. It is called the Personal Ancestral File®, or PAF. It allows personal computer users to document their ancestry, print charts and forms and share this information with others. This ability to share data with others is a basic feature, called GEDCOM. The technology of GEDCOM was freely shared with other software programmers in private industry in order to make data sharing universal. By now almost all genealogy programs include GEDCOM as a standard feature. This means you can send your data to other genealogists on diskette, even if they use a different software program, if both have GEDCOM capability. This greatly facilitates sharing of information.

Another reason for making GEDCOM universally available, was also to make it easy to share your own genealogy with the Family History Library. They now have a huge database of shared genealogy called the Ancestral File. Your contributions are solicited. Ancestral File will be discussed in detail later in this chapter.

Personal Ancestral File is sold to anyone, not just church members. It is available in either MS-DOS or Macintosh format. Order by phone inside the US & Canada, at 800-537-5950 or outside US & Canada at 801-240-1174. To place an order by fax, use 801-240-3685. Send orders for computer materials (including PAF) or various publications listed in the bibliography to:

> Salt Lake Distribution Center
> Church of Jesus Christ of Latter-day Saints
> 1999 West 1700 South
> Salt Lake City, UT 84104-4233

FAMILY SEARCH CENTER

The Family History Library now has computers available on each floor to search the library's catalog, and other data files on an "umbrella" program called FamilySearch™. However, due to the enormous popularity of their FamilySearch computer data files, the library has opened the FamilySearch Center, located one block to the east in the Joseph Smith Memorial Building. The FamilySearch Center hours are 8:00am-10:00pm during the summer and 9:00am-9:00pm after the first weekend in September.

The FamilySearch Center is equipped with 133 computer terminals that are served by an on-line network. This center is staffed mainly by volunteers who have been trained to help beginners. Information from FamilySearch can be printed out on paper or down-loaded to diskette and taken with you.

Each data file contains millions of names of individuals and can be easily accessed in seconds. No previous computer experience is necessary. You don't even need to know how to type. If you can only hunt-and-peck, you can still use these computers to search millions of records. If you need more specialized help, you may go to the fourth floor of the Joseph Smith Memorial Building, where 60 additional computer workstations are located, or to the main library. The fourth floor also contains meeting rooms reserved for computer research by family groups or other organizations.

The FamilySearch computer program currently contains six different data files:

> Ancestral File™
> International Genealogical Index™
> Family History Library Catalog™
> U.S. Social Security Death Index
> Korean and Vietnam War Death Index
> Scottish Church Records Index (which will not be discussed further)

ANCESTRAL FILE

Ancestral File is a searchable database containing data on about 20 million individuals and their families. Individuals are linked together in a family group and pedigree format. It is easy to use and looks similar to the previously mentioned Personal Ancestral File.

Ancestral File links family members by pedigree charts and family group sheets with dates and places of birth/christening, marriage, death and burial. It also lists the names and addresses of submitters. You can then correspond with the submitter to learn documentation details. Any of the data found can be printed on paper or to a diskette. When data is downloaded to a diskette, it is put into GEDCOM format. This GEDCOM feature allows for data sharing with other software programs. This means that you can take the data on diskette, and look at it with your computer. You can then add it to your own files or make it a separate file, until you can determine whether it is correct or not.

Data from any software program with the GEDCOM feature can be saved onto a diskette and then mailed to the Family History Library for inclusion in the next version of Ancestral File. This sharing of data is the theme of the Library's centennial year celebrated in 1994. Write for the free pamphlet, *Submitting Names to Ancestral File*. Corrections to Ancestral File are also solicited. The method for submitting corrections is explained in another pamphlet, *Correcting Ancestral File*.

INTERNATIONAL GENEALOGICAL INDEX

The International Genealogical Index (IGI) is a large data file that contains over 200 million records worldwide. These records are organized by locality, then by name, then by birth/christening date or marriage date. The section for Germany contains over 25 million records and the section for Central Europe contains over 12 million records, so you can see the value of searching this huge database. Unfortunately, these names are not linked in relationships as in the Ancestral File. Usually a birth/christening entry of a child gives date and place, and names of parents. A typical marriage entry gives date and place, and names of spouses. Most German entries come from the indexing or extraction of early Lutheran or Catholic registers. This is due to the thousands of microfilms from Germanic areas of the world. So if you find an ancestor listed in the IGI, be sure to trace the source of the data, and the Family History Catalog entry for the microfilm involved. Or it could be that a member of the LDS Church submitted it and their name and address are available. Many details on the original records were not included in the IGI and extraction errors do occasionally occur, so always look at the microfilm source.

The IGI is also available in a microfiche version that is subdivided into geographical regions. It is available for sale for 15 cents per fiche through the Distribution Center listed above. Regional sets must be ordered together. Contact the Acquisitions Department for an order form.

FAMILY HISTORY LIBRARY CATALOG

Learning to use the Family History Library Catalog (FHLC) is the key to the collection's immense records. Here are some hints to help you find what you want.

There are two versions, CD-ROM and microfiche. Each format is updated at different times. Always check to see which format is the most current version. The version date will be included on the heading of each fiche and on each CD-ROM.

Your chances of finding what you want in the catalog will be improved if you understand the jurisdictions of your locality. You will need to use a gazetteer to learn more about your locality. (See Chapter VIII for a more complete discussion of using gazetteers).

Church records are listed in the catalog by the parish name. The parish may include other smaller villages nearby that are also listed by the parish name. It is necessary to determine if the locality you want is a parish. One quick way is to look at the beginning locality microfiche #1 of the country. An alphabetical listing of all entries used in that country is found there. If the place is a parish (and in the catalog), it will be listed there.

But if the place is not a parish itself or simply not in the catalog, this may not work. In this case you will need to find out more about your locality since it may be part of a larger place that is a parish.

The FHL's German collection is cataloged according to the 1871 through World War I boundaries used in *Meyers Orts- und Verkehrs-Lexikon des Deutschen Reichs*, a locality and business gazetteer. These jurisdictions include the states of Elsass-Lothringen (Alsace-Lorraine), Anhalt, Baden, Bayern (Bavaria), Braunschweig (Brunswick), Hessen (Hesse), Lippe, Mecklenburg, Oldenburg, Sachsen (Kingdom of Saxony), Waldeck, Württemberg, and Prussia. The cities of Hamburg, Bremen and Lübeck are cataloged individually.

Cataloging for Prussia is subdivided into the provinces of Brandenburg, Ostpreussen (East Prussia), Hannover (Hanover), Hessen-Nassau (Hesse-Nassau), Hohenzollern, Pommern (Pomerania), Posen, Rheinland (Rhineland), Sachsen (Saxony Province), Schlesien (Silesia), Schleswig-Holstein, Westfalen (Westphalia), and Westpreussen (West Prussia). The Pfalz (Palatinate) is cataloged as part of Bavaria, and Birkenfeld is cataloged as part of Oldenburg. However, the Palatine area around Mainz, still known as the government district of Rheinhessen, belonged to Hesse and would be cataloged thereunder.

However, Thüringen (Thuringia) is a confusing exception to the above rule of using *Meyers Orts* jurisdictions. *Meyers Orts* does not list Thüringen as a state, but the individual duchies and principalities within present Thüringen are listed. The FHL Catalog follows that format with a twist. It lists the localities in Thüringen separately, but the duchies and principalities of Sachsen-Altenburg, Sachsen-Coburg-Gotha, Sachsen-Meiningen, Sachsen-Weimar-Eisenach, Schwarzburg-Rudolstadt and Schwarzburg-Sondershausen are combined and listed alphabetically under Thüringen. And to confuse matters more, Thüringen is found as a separate jurisdiction on the FHL's International Genealogical Index. The IGI is discussed earlier in this chapter. See Chapter IX for more historical background on Thüringen.

Some of the records microfilmed in Poland in the late 1980s are listed under Poland. These include parish registers for primarily German-speaking congregations, military parish registers, land records (*Grundbücher*), and German-language publications. Some, perhaps most, of these are not cataloged under Germany.

You will have to find out the current Polish names of any localities which once had German names in order to use the locality index to find out which records fall into this category. For interwar German territory, this can easily be checked in Kaemmerer's book, which is still in print. For those areas which were ceded to Poland after World War I, you will have to use the Kredel and Thierfelder gazetteer, which has been microfilmed by the FHL.

The CD-ROM and Fiche formats of the FHL Catalog are accessed differently, so it is important to understand the differences. The CD-ROM format can be searched by surname or by microfilm number or by locality (then subject). You will probably use the locality search most. For example, if you are looking for the records of the village of Borgentreich, in the CD version you can simply type in, for example, Borgentreich, Germany; or even Borgentreich, and the computer will search for any town named Borgentreich in any country. This is pretty straight forward. A problem you might have is when you find more than one Borgentreich, one in Westphalia and one in Bayern, for example. Then you need to step back and use a gazetter to learn more about each location and determine which is the correct one.

However, the Palatinate is listed under Bavaria, without any intermediate reference to it (since it was treated as just another government district, not a province, by Bavaria) and the same is presumably true of the other non-Prussian territories in what is now Rhineland-Palatinate.

The microfiche version is separated into 4 sets: Surname, Author/Title, Subject, Locality (then topic). For example, in the fiche version, in order to find Borgentreich, you must first know the jurisdictions that cover it, i.e., country, (Germany), then the state (Preussen), and where applicable the province (Westphalia), and then the town (Borgentreich). You are going from the highest jurisdiction to the lowest. Read the pamphlet *Germany: Research Outline* by the Family History Library, for more detailed information about the Family History Library collection. See the bibliography at the end of this chapter for ordering details.

See Chapter VIII for an annotated list of gazetteers. Other books that are especially helpful are Larry Jensen's *A Genealogical Handbook of German Research*, Vol. I, and Fay Dearden's *The German Researcher: How to Get the Most Out of an LDS Family History Center*.

The FHL Catalog is also available for sale in microfiche format, for 15 cents per fiche, but regional sets must be sold together. Write to the FHL Acquisitions Department for an order form.

U.S. SOCIAL SECURITY DEATH INDEX

We mention this huge database here, not because it is Germanic, but because it is huge and covers a majority of the population of the United States. The United States Social Security Death Index includes some 39 million names of deceased individuals who received Social Security benefits, who died between 1938-1992. Most of the file is about deaths since 1962. Like the other data files it is searched easily by name. The typical information found is the deceased person's name, Social Security number, state of issue, birth date, death date and residence at death. Using information obtained from the index, you can write for a copy of the deceased person's original Social Security application, which will probably contain birth date and place, and parents' data. Unlike the death certificate, this data should have been supplied by the applicant and hopefully will be more accurate than a death certificate. Write to the following address or telephone 410-965-3962. The cost is $7.00 if a Social Security number is supplied, $16.50 otherwise.

Freedom of Information Officer
4HB Annex Bldg.
6401 Security Bl
Baltimore, MD 21235

KOREAN & VIETNAM WAR DEATH INDEX

The U.S. Military Death Index covers individuals who died or were declared dead in the Korean War from 1950 to 1957, or the Vietnam War from 1957 to 1975. This index can be searched by name. It contains birth and death dates, home residence, military rank, service number and branch of service, race, start date of tour of duty, religious affiliation and marital status, country where died (casualty locations include Cambodia, Communist China, Korea, Laos, North Vietnam, South Vietnam and Thailand).

FAMILY HISTORY CENTERS ARE WORLDWIDE

In an effort to make their vast collection more accessible to their members, the Family History Library operates over 2,000 branch libraries, called Family History Centers, in the United States and Canada and 62 other countries. Although they are geared for the members of their church, the Family History Centers are free and open to the public. They are usually located in Latter-day Saint church buildings. Check in your local telephone books under "Church of Jesus Christ of Latter-day Saints Family History Center" or Stake Center. A list of center locations and phone numbers is available upon request from the Family History Library in Salt Lake City. The mailing address of a Family History Center is not the building location. Call ahead before traveling long distances to reach them. Since each center is staffed by volunteers, hours of operation vary.

Family History Centers give local researchers access to practically the entire microfilm and microfiche collection of the FHL. Because each center is a branch of the main library you may, for a small fee, borrow any microfilm for 3 weeks, 6 months, or indefinitely. Borrowed microfilm/fiche must be used at the local center. Most centers are classroom size and are pressed for space, so they limit the number of microfilms kept on indefinite loan. Ask to speak to the director about the center's indefinite loan policy, which is set locally according to space and patron research needs. There may be some records the local center is trying to acquire, but hasn't yet, due to lack of funds. Generally a microfilm that has broad value to many people can be put on indefinite loan. Indexes to records generally qualify.

However, since microfiche take up so little space, generally anything you are willing to pay for can be borrowed and automatically becomes part of the local collection. The price is pennies per fiche, but the entire set must be borrowed. Check the FHL Catalog to determine the number of fiche in the set.

All centers are equipped with microfilm and microfiche readers and printers. Each has sets of reference books and microfiche. Usually they have some blank forms and charts for sale. Each center has the microfiche version of the Family History Library catalog and the International Genealogical Index. In addition, they may have compiled a catalog of their local holdings.

You may also obtain information in the unmicrofilmed books in the Family History Library collection. Ask for a free "Request to Microfilm" form. For a small copying fee the pages you need will be sent to you via mail.

Each center has the FamilySearch computer program discussed above. But because of heavy use, most centers may limit the time each patron may spend on the computer. If you phone ahead you may ask to make an appointment to use the computer. Each data file can be printed on paper or put onto diskette for a small charge. Also, most centers have diskettes for sale or you can bring your own.

The staff at Family History Centers are volunteers. Many have their own geographic area of expertise after years of personal research and volunteer service. However, if they are not equipped to answer your specific questions, they may telephone, e-mail, or fax questions to the Family History Library's reference staff. There is also a free "Reference Questionnaire" form that you may fill out and send to the Family History Library, but it will get the slowest response due to the heavy volume of mail.

If you need professional assistance beyond what the FHL staff and FHC volunteers are able to provide, see Chapter II for information.

BIBLIOGRAPHY (See ANNOTATED BIBLIOGRAPHY for full citations if not shown)

SELECTED LIST OF FAMILY HISTORY LIBRARY PUBLICATIONS

Ancestral File

Family History Library. *Contributing to Ancestral File.* #34029. 4 pp.*
Family History Library. *Correcting Ancestral File.* #34030. 4 pp.*
Family History Library. *Using Ancestral File Resource Guide.* #34113. 4 pp.*

Family History Centers

Family History Library. *FHC Address Lists: California.* #35260. 3 pp.*
Family History Library. *FHC Address Lists: Mountain States.* #35261. 2 pp.*
Family History Library. *FHC Address Lists: Nevada and Utah.* #35262. 2 pp.*
Family History Library. *FHC Address Lists: North Central States.* #35263. 2 pp.*
Family History Library. *FHC Address Lists: Northeastern States.* #35264. 2 pp.*
Family History Library. *FHC Address Lists: Northwestern States & Hawaii.* #35265. 2 pp.*
Family History Library. *FHC Address Lists: Southern States.* #35266. 2 pp.*
Family History Library. *FHC Address Lists: Southwestern States.* #35267. 2 pp.*
Family History Library. *FHC Address Lists: Canada.* #35268. 2 pp.*

Family History Library Catalog

Family History Library. *FHL Catalog on Compact Disc Guide.* #34052. 4 pp.*
Family History Library. *FHL Catalog on Microfiche Guide.* #30968. 4 pp.*
Family History Library. *How to Use the FHL Catalog.* #53191. Video.

Family History Research

Family History Library. *Discovering Your Family Tree.* #32543. 20 pp.
Family History Library. *Guide to Research.* #30971. 24 pp.
Family History Library. *Tracing Immigrant Origins Outline.* #34111. 31 pp.
Family History Library. *Where Do I Start?* #32916. 4 pp.*

FamilySearch

Family History Library. *FamilySearch Military Index Resource Guide.* #34540. 1 p.*
Family History Library. *FamilySearch Social Security Death Index.* #34446. 4 pp.*

International Genealogical Index

Family History Library. *Finding an IGI Source Resource Guide.* #31024. 4 pp.*
Family History Library. *IGI (on Compact Disc) Resource Guide.* #31025. 4 pp.*
Family History Library. *IGI (on Microfiche) Resource Guide.* #31026. 4 pp.*

Language Helps

Family History Library. *German Letter-Writing Guide.* #34066. 7 pp.

Personal Ancestral File

Family History Library. *PAF Brochure.* #30969. 2 pp. Includes 1 p. order form.*

Publications Lists

Family History Library. *Family History Publications List.* #34083. 4 pp.*
　　Additional publications can be found in the *Family History Publications List.*

Research Outlines

Family History Library. *Canada Research Outline.* #34545. 48 pp.
Family History Library. *Denmark Research Outline.* #34714. 28 pp.
Family History Library. *England Research Outline.* #34037. 52 pp.
Family History Library. *Germany Research Outline.* #34061. 52 pp.
Family History Library. *Hamburg Passenger Lists.* #34047. 4 pp.*
Family History Library. *Ireland Research Outline.* #34717. 48 pp.
Family History Library. *Latin America Research Outline.* #34075. 34 pp.
Family History Library. *Norway Research Outline.* #34090. 24 pp.
Family History Library. *Ontario Research Outline.* #31089. 7 pp.
Family History Library. *Sweden Research Outline.* #34716. 23 pp.
Family History Library. *United States (General).* #30972. 52 pp.
Family History Library. *United States (General), 50 States & D.C.* #34563. (package)
　　A *Research Outline* for each U.S. state may be purchased separately for a nominal fee.

Researchers

Family History Library. *Accredited Genealogists: International.* #32750. 3 pp.*
Family History Library. *Accredited Genealogists: U.S. and Canada.* #32749. 3 pp.*
Family History Library. *Hiring a Professional Genealogist.* #34548. 4 pp.*

The above FHL publications are available at a nominal charge (or free where indicated by an asterisk) and may be ordered from the Salt Lake Distribution Center at the address indicated earlier in this chapter. There is a service charge when ordering by phone unless all of the requested items are free.

OTHER PUBLICATIONS RELEVANT TO THE FAMILY HISTORY LIBRARY

Johni Cerny and Wendy Elliot. *The Library.* Salt Lake City, UT: Ancestry, Inc. 1988. 763 pp.
　　Reference to the Family History Library collection at Salt Lake City. Somewhat out of date but still very descriptive.

Fay Dearden and Douglas Dearden. *The German Researcher: How to Get the Most Out of an LDS Family History Center.* May be ordered from the authors at 8968 E. Gail Rd., Scottsdale, AZ 85260-6146.

Chapter VI

PASSENGER DEPARTURE AND ARRIVAL LISTS

Both departure and arrival lists usually include the names, ages and (for adults) the occupations of all passengers. Departure lists are more likely to include the specific place of origin.

DEPARTURE LISTS

A large majority of German-speaking trans-oceanic emigrants left from one of five ports: **Le Havre**, **Antwerp**, **Rotterdam**, **Bremen**, and **Hamburg**.

Those who left in the eighteenth century generally embarked at Le Havre (the shortest route) or sailed down the Rhine to Rotterdam. Later Antwerp, Bremen and then Hamburg became the leading points of departure. Only the Hamburg and Le Havre records are intact. The Hamburg records have been microfilmed by the Family History Library (FHL).

There are two Hamburg passenger lists: direct and indirect. The **direct list** covers those who sailed directly from Hamburg to an overseas port. The **indirect list** includes passengers on ships that (1) stopped at another European port (e.g., Southhampton) en route, or (2) sailed to Hull (or occasionally to a few other ports), then took the train across northern England and sailed to their destination from **Liverpool**, **Glasgow**, or other British ports. The indirect route was actually cheaper, so it was widely used by the poorer emigrants. The British passenger lists have not been preserved.

If attempting to read the FHL microfilms seems to be too much of an obstacle, you can get the Hamburg records searched for $60 per year by the:

> Historic Emigration Office
> Holstenwall 24
> D-20355 Hamburg
> Germany

This is the only place in Europe that will accept personal checks in United States dollars.

The Bremen records were routinely destroyed after a few years because of lack of space, although Clifford Neal Smith has published some monographs on the 1846-1850 departures. A number of passenger lists for specific voyages from Bremen have also appeared in *The Germanic Genealogist*. The lists are now being reconstructed, using United States port arrival lists, in the series, *German Immigrants: Lists of Passengers Bound from Bremen to New York, with Places of Origin*, begun by Gary J. Zimmerman and Marion Wolfert and now continued by the latter. But these include only the small minority of passengers for whom a specific place of origin is mentioned in the New York lists.

The Deutsches Auslands-Institut in Stuttgart, replaced after World War II by the Institut für Auslandsbeziehungen (address listed under **GERMANY** in Chapter XVII, Section 6), prepared an unpublished *Namenkartei aus den "Bremer Schiffslisten, 1904-1914"* [*Name Index Card File from the "Bremen Passenger Lists, 1904-1914"*]. The FHL has microfilmed these cards, which are alphabetized by province (or the equivalent) and then by surname.

Relatively few emigrants left Germany during that period, but this source may be quite helpful for emigrants from the Austro-Hungarian and Russian Empires.

Despite these numerous source, however, most of the Bremen records must be considered to be lost.

The Le Havre records have not been microfilmed. You can get information from them by writing to:

Archive nationale de France
60, rue des Frances-Bourgeois
F-75141 Paris
France

If you know the date of embarkation, the name of the ship and the name(s) of the passengers, Jacques de Guise, director of the Centre for Genealogical Research in Grand Saconnex, Switzerland, will search the Le Havre records for $90 per family and send you information (and evidence, whenever possible) from those records in English. It is also helpful to provide the following, if known: ages of passengers, place of origin or birth, destination, and any other significant information. Checks should be made payable to the Centre or to de Guise, but may be sent to 2845 North 72nd St., Milwaukee, WI 53210.

The FHL has microfilmed the 1817-66 typewritten in-transit records in Strasbourg for emigrants bound for Le Havre.

There are various other kinds of lists which supplement the Hamburg passenger lists. These include the names and occupations of male and female workers from outside of Hamburg (1843-90), the Hamburg passport records (1852-1929) and the indexes of transients in Hamburg (1868-89). All of these are available from the Family History Library. Many emigrants had to work in Hamburg for a while because they had not taken along enough money, their money had been stolen, they had been swindled by recruiting agents or others with whom they came into contact, or they became sick and could not leave when planned.

Except for fragments, the Antwerp and Rotterdam records were destroyed. Charles Hall has published a monograph on the Antwerp lists for 1855 and some for 1854.

Could your ancestor have left from another European port? Yes, although the chances are slim. For example, single young men might have worked for their passage on cargo ships, which sailed from a much larger number of ports.

A few passenger ships left from various minor ports, e.g, **Danzig** (Gdansk), **Stettin**, **Rostock**, **Riga** (Latvia), **Libau** (now Liepäja, Latvia), and others. The two Latvian ports are known to have had infrequent passenger service to England. We are not aware that records for any of these ports have been preserved, but with the collapse of Communism, it is conceivable that some records may yet surface.

Latvian ports were used mostly by the few thousand legal German emigrants from the former Soviet Union during the interwar period or by the Baltic Germans, few of whom migrated overseas.

Most Germans from the Russian Empire embarked at Hamburg or Bremen, with a few at Antwerp.

Chmelar states that quite a few emigrants from the southern part of the Austro-Hungarian Empire, especially those bound for South America but also some for North America, left from Adriatic ports, mainly **Trieste**. A few even left from Genoa and possibly other Mediterranean ports. No passenger records for these ports are known to have been preserved.

PASSENGER ARRIVAL LISTS

Port arrival lists are much more likely to provide only a general place of origin (e.g., France, Posen province, or Russian Poland) than the departure lists. However, the village of origin and/or the destination are sometimes recorded.

American Lists

The vast majority of German-speaking immigrants landed in **New York**. **New Orleans** was of secondary importance for the Mississippi River basin, including the Midwest, until 1860, since riverboat fares were very cheap. This was because the boats carried agricultural and other exports downriver to New Orleans, but had little cargo on the way back. Thus boat owners crammed the boats with passengers, charging a low fare, but also leading to tragedies in some cases, e.g., if a fire broke out.

Those who landed at New Orleans are most likely to have left from Le Havre, but they could have come from other ports as well. **Baltimore** had especially good connections with Bremen. **Galveston** was also used as a minor port of entry.

During the colonial era, New York was not in such a dominant position. **Philadelphia**, Baltimore and **Boston** were also important ports of arrival during the earlier period. An example of the numerous published books on these arrivals is Carl Boyer's 289-page, indexed *Ship Passenger Lists, Pennsylvania and Delaware (1641-1825)*, 3rd edition, 1980. Philadelphia and Baltimore continued to be important throughout the nineteenth century.

A major reference series for German immigration to the United States is the series being published by Ira A. Glazier and P. William Filby, called *Germans to America: Lists of Passengers Arriving at United States Ports, 1850-1893*. This work is still in progress and is a list of passenger arrivals at United States ports between 1850 and 1893, including all ports of embarkation. (For example, many people who arrived from Bremen are also in *Germans to America*.) So far, 54 volumes covering January 1850 to mid-1887 have been published. Information for the series is taken from original ship manifest schedules, or passenger lists, that were prepared by shipping agents and ship's officers, and filed by all vessels entering United States ports. These lists are now deposited at Temple-Balch Institute for Immigration Research in Philadelphia.

What makes this series such a great help is that the former place of residence is commonly included, as well as the name, age, sex and occupation of the passengers. One drawback is that the index for 1850-55 includes only ships that had 80% or more of their passengers with German surnames (all passengers on those ships are included in the index). From 1856 on, all passengers with Germanic surnames are included, regardless of the number on each ship, but non-Germans are not included in the index. However, many "German" passengers were actually from France, Switzerland and Luxembourg.

Since there is other information in the original records not included in the index, such as deaths on board, they should be consulted once you have determined the ship name and arrival date. Microfilms of the original passenger lists are available at the National Archives and for loan by various organizations, such as the American Genealogical Lending Library and Family History Centers.

Despite the enormous genealogical value of this series, many people are omitted from these published lists. For an explanation of omissions in this series, as well as the omissions in, *German Immigrants: Lists of Passengers Bound from Bremen to New York, with Places of Origin*, see Michael Palmer's critique, "Published Passenger Lists: A Review of *German Immigrants* and *Germans to America*" (*GGSA Bulletin*, May/August 1990). Fortunately, the Genealogical Research Association has found some missing passenger lists and is publishing them in *The German Connection*.

The National Archives has microfilms of passengers arriving at more than 60 Atlantic and Gulf of Mexico ports, but with many gaps and only a few records for most of the minor ports. Microfilmed indexes for Baltimore (1820-97), Boston (1848-1940), New Orleans (before 1850 to 1952), New York (1820-46, 1897-1902), and Philadelphia (1800-1906) are available from the National Archives or the FHL. For further information, see the *Guide to Genealogical Research in the National Archives*, which also describes many other records, or *Immigrant & Passenger Arrivals: A Select Catalog of National Archives Microfilm Publications*, both published by the National Archives and Records Administration.

Canadian Lists

The National Archives of Canada has passenger arrival lists for **Quebec City** (1865-1919), **Halifax** (1881-1919), **St. John** (1900-1918), **North Sydney** (1906-1919) and the Pacific ports of **Vancouver** and **Victoria** (1905-1919). These are microfilmed and can be borrowed through interlibrary loan. However, they are not indexed, so you must know the port and year of arrival. If you don't know the exact month, be prepared for a time-consuming search. The Genealogy Unit Immigration Records of the National Archives of Canada will undertake searches only if you provide all the specific details, including the month of arrival.

The National Archives of Canada also has filmed passenger lists for immigrants who arrived at New York (1906-1919) and various eastern American ports (1905-1921).

The archives has only a few scattered pre-1865 lists in its custody, mostly those relating to subsidized British emigration schemes in 1817-1831. There is a partial nominal index for the lists it does have.

Provincial archives also have copies of some of these records. A major problem is that the ink on many of these arrival lists has faded so badly as to be illegible or even invisible.

Both Canadian and American genealogists should be aware that at least prior to 1867, most passengers who landed in Canada headed for the United States, while most Canadian immigrants landed in New York.

Australian and New Zealand Lists

Nick Vine Hill, *Tracing Your Family History in Australia: A Guide to Sources*, has copious information about Australian passenger arrival lists. He indicates that some records can be found for nearly all European immigrants, despite gaps and faded pages, but many of the pre-1860 records appear to have sparse genealogical information. Many pre-1900 lists have been microfilmed.

The major ports were **Moreton Bay-Brisbane** (Queensland), **Sydney** and **Newcastle** (New South Wales), **Port Philip-Melbourne** (Victoria), **Port Adelaide** (South Australia) and later **Fremantle** (Western Australia).

There are numerous published and unpublished indexes and guides, but generally each one deals with only a certain port and a certain time period. In some cases, records for assisted passengers (whose fare was paid by others) are more detailed than for unassisted passengers.

The most valuable publication for Germanic research appears to be the 7-volume series, *Emigrants from Hamburg to Australia, 1860-69*, by Eric and Rosemary Kopittke (Indooroopilly: Queensland Family History Society, 1991-93).

Andrew G. Peake, *National Register of Shipping Arrivals: Australia and New Zealand* (Sydney: Australasian Federation of Family History Organizations, 3rd ed., 1992), covers both countries.

The 6-volume *M. Hodge Index* lists passenger traffic between South Australia and New Zealand, as well as with other Australian ports, for 1837-1859, which would include the Gold Rush years.

Olga K. Miller, *Migration, Emigration, Immigration*, lists quite a few publications on passenger lists and other immigrant and German emigrant records, including records for 1836-1918, with some gaps, for South Australia (mostly by the State Archives, Adelaide); Queensland (*Register of Overseas Arrivals in Queensland, 1848-1923*); Victoria (*German Emigrants to Victoria, 1849*); New South Wales (*Assisted Immigrants to Sydney, 1828-1890*); and Tasmania (*Lists of Free Arrivals, Tasmania, 1816-1871*). Some of these have been microfilmed by the Family History Library. She also lists a number of publications concerning immigrants who landed at **Canterbury** (1855-1871), **Christchurch** (1855-1864), **Otago** (1843-1950), and unspecified ports in New Zealand. **Auckland** and **Wellington** were also important.

South African and Namibian Lists

See R. T. J. Lombard, *Handbook for Genealogical Research in South Africa* (listed in Chapter XV), for information about records relating to South Africa and Namibia.

Most German immigrants to South Africa would have landed in **Cape Town or Port Elizabeth**. According to edition of *Meyers Kleines Konversations-Lexikon* [*Meyer's Small Encyclopedia of General Information*], Vol. 2 (listed in Chapter VIII), the chief German port in what used to be German South-West Africa was **Swakopmund**.

Latin American Lists

The principal immigration ports in Latin America were **Rio de Janeiro, Santos, Salvador, Buenos Aires** and **Valparaiso**. Relatively few Germans are likely to have landed at Salvador. **Porto Alegre**, **Montevideo** and **Ensenada** (La Plata) were also ports of entry. Port arrival records have been kept since the mid-nineteenth century. Check the Family History Library's *Research Outlines* and *Research Papers* for further details.

BIBLIOGRAPHY (See ANNOTATED BIBLIOGRAPHY for full citations if not shown)

Loretto Dennis Szucs and Sandra Hargreaves Luebking, eds. *The Source: A Guidebook of American Genealogy*, Revised Edition. Salt Lake City, UT: Ancestry Inc. 1997. 846 pp.
> See chapter 13 (Immigration: Finding Immigrant Origins) for references too numerous to mention here.

C. Boyer. *Ship Passenger Lists (USA)*. Newhall, CA. 1978.

Hans Chmelar. *Höhepunkte der österreichischen Auswanderung: Die Auswanderung aus den im Reichsrat vertretenen Königreichen und Ländern in den Jahren 1905-1914* [*The Peaks of Austrian Emigration: The Emigration from the Kingdoms and Lands Represented in the Imperial Council in 1905-1914*]. Vienna: Verlag der österreichischen Akademie der Wissenschaften. 1974. 187 pp.
> Detailed account of emigration from the Austrian part of the Austro-Hungarian Empire to various overseas countries. Lists areas of heavy emigration (Galicia, Bukovina, Dalmatia and Carinthia), although much emigration (especially from the Czech lands but also from other areas) occurred during the late nineteenth century. Specific information on ports of departure, numbers, and recruiting organizations.

Family History Library. *Hamburg Passenger Lists*. Order #34047. 4 pp.

Ira A. Glazier and P. William Filby. *Germans to America: Lists of Passengers Arriving at United States Ports, 1850-1893*.

A. H. Lancour. *Ship's Passenger Lists (1538-1825)*. New York. 1963.

National Archives Trust Fund Board. *Immigrant & Passengers Arrivals: A Select Catalog of National Archives Microfilm Publications*. Washington: National Archives Trust Fund Board. 1983.
> U.S. port arrival lists of the U.S. Customs Service (1820-ca. 1891) and the Immigration and Naturalization Service (1891-1954) for over 60 Atlantic, Gulf of Mexico and Great Lakes ports.

Michael H. Tepper. *American Passenger Arrival Records: A Guide to the Records of Immigrants Arriving at American Ports by Sail and Steam*. Baltimore: Genealogical Publishing Co. 1988. 134 pp. 8-page bibliography.

Michael Tepper, ed. *Emigrants to Pennsylvania: A Consolidation of Ship Passenger Lists from The Pennsylvania Magazine of History and Biography*. Baltimore: Genealogical Publishing Co. 1975; reprinted 1992. 302 pp.
> Information on some 6,000 (mostly British and German) immigrants who arrived at the port of Philadelphia, 1641-1819, transcribed from manuscripts in the Historical Society of Pennsylvania. Most of the names come from two extensive lists of indentured servants. Indexed. One of the few works to cover German immigration during the early post-colonial era.

Michael H. Tepper, gen. ed. *Passenger Arrivals at the Port of Baltimore, 1820-1834: From Customs Passenger Lists*. (transcribed by Elizabeth P. Bentley). Baltimore: Genealogical Publishing Co. 1982. 768 pp.

Details on all family members. About three-fourths of the 50,000 immigrants are estimated to have been Germans.

Michael H. Tepper, gen. ed. *Passenger Arrivals at the Port of Philadelphia, 1641-1819: The Philadelphia Baggage Lists*. (transcribed by Elizabeth P. Bentley). Baltimore: Genealogical Publishing Co. 1986. 913 pp.

United States. National Archives and Records Administration. *Immigrant & Passenger Arrivals: A Select Catalog of National Archives Microfilm Publications*, 2nd ed. Washington, DC: National Archives Trust Fund Board. 1991. 171 pp.

Gary J. Zimmerman and Marion Wolfert. *German Immigrants: Lists of Passengers Bound from Bremen to New York, with Places of Origin*.

Chapter VII

PERSONAL NAMES

Once you have identified your immigrant ancestor using records in the country of immigration, you need to determine what his or her name was in Germany or elsewhere in Europe. Both the given name and the surname may have been changed during migration or later. For example, one factor was the change in language when migrating to another country; another was the anti-German hysteria that occurred in the United States and other Allied countries during World War I. This chapter will give you clues about the possible German spelling of the name. It also describes different types of German names.

Spelling variations are common in German surnames since German spelling wasn't standardized until the 1800s after surnames had already been established. The local German spoken dialect also had an impact on what surnames were used and how they were spelled. When researching older records, consider all possible spelling variations for a given surname. Usually the different spellings will have the same pronunciation.

Sometimes the name may have an ending added to it to indicate the possessive (genitive) case. This ending might be *-s, -n, -en* or *-ens*.

In old records, vowels, but especially consonants, were often used interchangeably at the beginning or in the middle of a name, e.g., Plittersdorfer = Blittersdorfer, Reitenbach = Reidenbach

Common themes to look for in spelling variations are:

- *h* is a silent letter, unless it is the first letter of a syllable. It may be present in some names and missing in others. Standard spelling in the nineteenth century was *th* where only *t* would be used today.

- Some letters have the same sound and are interchangeable.

    i - y   *c - k*   *f - v*   *ei - ai*   *z - tz - ts*

- Other letters may have the same sound at the end of a word or syllable.

    d - t   *b - p*   *g - k*   *g - ch*

- Consonants may be single or double.

- Long vowels may be single or double, or they may be followed by an *h*.

- Short vowels may sound similar and may be interchanged.

    ä - e   *ü - i*   *ö - e*

GERMAN SURNAMES AND ANGLICIZED VERSIONS

German language surnames usually belong to one of four categories: patronymic, occupational, locational or descriptive. Surnames began to appear in parts of Switzerland in the 11th century. Their usage began around 1100 in Germany, first in the cities and then gradually spreading from southwestern German areas to the north and east. By 1600 surnames were in common usage throughout German speaking areas. However, many people continued to change their surnames from generation to generation, or even within their own lifetime. These surnames became permanent by decree between 1670 and the early 1800s depending on the German state. These decrees required surnames to be permanently attached to a family. The last regions to require permanent surnames were Schleswig-Holstein and Ostfriesland (East Frisia), where patronymic naming practices predominated, and Lippe.

PATRONYMIC AND MATRONYMIC NAMES

At one time patronymic naming practices were common in the northern and northwestern part of Germany. They continued in Schleswig-Holstein until the late 18th century and in the Ostfriesland (East Frisia) region until the early 19th century and in some cases as late as the middle part of that century.

Patronymic naming practices mean that the son or daughter derived his or her surname from the first name of the father, e.g.,

Father:	Friedrich Johannsen	Harm Simons	Fokke Hindriks
Son:	Karl Friedrichsen	Geerd Harms	Jan Fokken
Grandchild:	Hans Karlsen	Jeeljes Geerds	Udda Janssen

The most common surname endings are *s, es* and *(s)sen*. However, if the first name was Johan, the surname derived from that may be Johannsen or Janssen.

These patronymic names generally changed each generation. It became increasingly difficult for government agencies to fully identify individuals. This led to a decree outlawing the use of patronymics, first in Schleswig-Holstein (ca. 1770) and later in East Frisia (1811). However, many families delayed adopting a surname until well beyond these dates.

In some cases, the changes brought inconsistencies in the name that was used in the records. An example is Stientje Jeeljes Jacobs, the daughter of Jeeljes Geerds and Antje Abrams Janssen. At her birth in 1808, she was given the name of her maternal grandmother, Stientje Jacobs. Her marriage record in 1832 refers to her as Stientje Jacobs but later the same year she is called Stientje Jeeljes in the record for the birth of her first child. In subsequent records she is again called Stientje Jacobs. By her death in 1893 she was called Stientje Jeeljes Jacobs. The use of Jacobs is an example of the rare practice of matronymics.

In a few cases, to assure that a man's children were identified as his, all children (male or female) were given the father's first name as their middle name. As an example, between 1815 and 1850 Ede Reints Karsjens had 10 children. Nine of these children were given Eden as a middle name. The only exception was the first son who was named after the maternal grandfather and was called Ewe Mennen Karsjens. All ten of Ede's children were named after parents, grandparents and great grandparents. This can be important to keep in mind as you look for relationships and possible lineage in the patronymic system.

Although many surnames elsewhere in Germany had a patronymic derivation, it is unlikely that you will find generation-to-generation changes in other areas of Germany during the modern era.

SURNAMES DERIVED FROM OCCUPATIONS, LOCATIONS AND DESCRIPTIONS

Occupational surnames are very common in Germany. These evolved when people were named for the trade they performed. Later, when family members no longer performed these trades the surnames still remained. Examples of these can be found in the German vocabulary section of this book listing occupations (see Chapter XXI).

Many surnames are derived from locations. There are several different kinds of such names. Surnames from places might refer to a general area of origin, a specific village of origin, or some geographic aspect of the local place of residence.

Examples of those names referring to a general area of origin are:

Oesterreich	someone from Austria (Österreich)
Bayer	someone from from Bavaria (Bayern)
Weser	someone from the Weser river area
Schweitzer	someone from Switzerland
Hesse	someone from Hesse
Issel	someone from the Issel (lower Rhine) river area

Examples of a specific locality are:

Wiener	someone from Vienna (Wien)
Neukirch	someone from Neukirch
Bremer	someone from Bremen
Bessler, Bässler	someone from Basel
Kandel	someone from the village of Kandel
Frankfurter	someone from Frankfurt

Surnames from a small village usually meant that these people had originated in a nearby area, whereas those derived from a large city, state or region suggest the family may have come from relatively far away. For example, there were many Schweitzers in Alsace and the Palatinate, all usually stemming from one original migrant.

Examples based on local, non-place name features include:

Ambach, Bachmann	by the river
Bergmann, Amberg, Berger	on the mountain
Eichenhof, Eichhoff	oak farm

In a few areas, farms sometimes were, and still are, named after the man who initially established them. In earlier periods, when a son-in-law acquired a farm (or sometimes even when unrelated people bought them), the new owner might be referred to by either his surname at birth, or the name of the farm during his lifetime, or both. In some cases, the farm name became the permanent surname.

People moved for a variety of reasons. Residents of regions not greatly affected by the Thirty Years' War often moved to seriously devastated areas after 1648 to fill the vacant farms and repopulate the area. Journeymen often had to relocate if they wished to become masters of their trades, since the guilds strictly limited the number of master craftsmen in various localities (usually only one per village). Some people migrated for religious, personal or business reasons.

Such people were often known by the place from which they came. In fact, it is possible that their ancestors had moved several generations before the adoption of surnames, but oral history had preserved the place of origin.

Descriptive surnames are also prevalent in Germany. These may have originally described the person or may have been a nickname. Examples are:

short	Kurz	black	Schwarz, Schwartz
small	Klein	white	Weiss
tall	Lang, Lange	strong	Starke

Many such surnames reflected a temperamental or behavioral, rather than physical, characteristic. Examples: Wohlgemuth (good-natured), Esser (glutton), Schabbe (skinflint), Stolzmann (proud man). There are many names denoting drunkard or fighter.

Many surnames are in a particular dialect. This may help identify where the name originated. Germany has many dialects. The two major divisions are Low German, or *Plattdeutsch* (spoken in northern Germany where the altitude is low), and High German (actually a collection of dialects), spoken in the southern part of Germany and Austria. These dialects are very difficult for non-speakers of the dialect to understand, and contain many different pronunciations for the same words. Moreover, the Swiss dialect

(*Schwyzerdütsch*) is quite different from dialects in Germany. The official German language is often referred to as High German (although it is actually based on Middle German), but Germans are more likely to refer to it as *Schuldeutsch* (school German) or *Schriftdeutsch* (written German). The standardization of the German language began with Martin Luther and continued through the nineteenth century.

Dialects use different words to describe the same thing and have different spellings and pronunciations of the same words. Ernest Thode's *Atlas for Germanic Genealogy* contains maps that show the approximate location where certain German names originated. Jürgen Eichhoff's research, summarized by Kevin Tvedt in the January/February 1990 issue of the *GGSA Bulletin*, provides further detail. For example, a butcher might be called the following, in different areas:

Fleischer	Fleischhacker	Fleischhauer
Knochenhauer	Metzger	Schlachter

For researchers literate in German, Adolf Bach in *Deutsche Namenkunde* gives a thorough discussion of the origin and meaning of many given names, surnames and place names in the German language territory. The index alone comprises 457 pages.

Common diminutive endings of both first names and surnames (often a permanent part of the latter) had an l-form in the South, including Switzerland, e.g., *-l, -el, -le* and *-li* (the last being Swiss). In the north, the endings were *-ke(n)*, *-che(n)* and *-tje(n)*, the last reflecting Dutch influence. However, many Southern Germans migrated to the Northeast to lands under Prussian and Russian control, so ancestors of Southern origin may have come to America from the North. Dutch-Flemish, Oldenburg and Hannover migrants have also left name traces far to the east.

An *-in* or *-en* at the end of a surname usually referred to a woman, e.g., Mrs. Schmidt became Schmidtin. But occasionally this ending became a permanent part of the surname for both sexes, e.g., Eiselin.

The prefix *von* originally denoted a noble, e.g., Heinrich *von* (from) a particular castle. It again has that connotation in Germany today, but that was not always the case. When commoners first assumed surnames, they sometimes took the name of the noble at whose court they worked, so *von* is not proof of aristocratic lineage.

The Dutch-Flemish *van* and *ten*, as well as the French *de*, are the equivalent of *von*. They denote ethnic origin, but not necessarily of high status. However, many Huguenot refugees were nobles.

Many people from east of the Elbe River (which was occupied by Slavs in the early Middle Ages) have Slavic names or surnames with Slavic endings, even though most of them have been "German" for many centuries. This was the result of German eastward expansion and inter-ethnic marriages.

Other non-German surnames are of two types: German names that have been translated into Latin or Greek to make them sound special, or surnames from a foreign emigrant. The most common foreign names are Polish, Czech, Lithuanian or Slavic (from border areas), French (from Huguenot emigrants) or Italian (from traveling artists or tradesmen). The original foreign name may have been preserved or Germanicized or it may have been translated. For example, the Latin name Faber may have been translated to Schmidt, the German equivalent, or vice versa.

Two surnames for one person can be a challenge. These may have come about when a change in status or location occurred. Some examples: a man acquires a farm and becomes known by both his original name and the farm name, or he marries into a wealthier family (perhaps nobility) and takes the surname of the wife, or he moves to a new town and is referred to by the place name he came from. Some of these double surnames have been passed on as hyphenated names. Other times, either one of the two names may have been used only for a few years or during a person's lifetime. The use of two surnames is very rare and occurs almost exclusively in the Westfalian region.

GERMAN NAME CHANGES IN ENGLISH-SPEAKING COUNTRIES

While some families kept the original spelling of their German names, many names underwent some change when or after emigrating. German surnames had spelling changes to maintain approximately the same pronunciation in English or they may have been translated into the English equivalent meaning. Some names that are compound words may have only one part of the name translated. Others chose to change their name later, e.g., during World War I to camouflage the fact that they were of German heritage. Examples are:

German	English	Translated as:
Alsbach	Alspaugh	
Apfelbaum		Applebaum
Eisenhauer	Isenhower, Eisenhower	
Fink		Finch
Jäger	Yeger, Yaeger	Hunter
Müller	Muller, Mueller	Miller
Rahmöller		Rahmiller
Schleppi	Sleppy	
Schmidt		Smith
Schneider	Snyder	Taylor, Tailor

When *ö*, *eh* and *e* (all approximating the same vowel sound in the English "they" to the English ear) became Anglicized, they were often replaced by a "long a," e.g., Römer became Ramer. Various things happened to *Umlauts* in foreign lands, e.g., Schröder might become Schroeder, Schroder, Schrader, etc.

For more information on this subject see Arta Johnson's book, *A Guide to the Spelling and Pronunciation of German Names*.

FINDING THE NAME AND LOCATION IN EUROPE

The best way to find out whether the name is or was found in Germany or another Germanic country is to check the International Genealogical Index (IGI) at Family History Centers. Check all possible spelling variations. Because this index was compiled manually, there are occasional incorrect spellings. While it does not contain every surname that ever existed in Germanic Europe, the chances are very good that you will find the surnames of your immigrant ancestors in this enormous index. You will also find the names of many, though far from all, localities where the name was found.

If you know your ancestors spoke German, but you cannot find the name in the IGI files for Germany (which cover the entire German Empire of 1871-1919), try the less extensive files for other European countries.

Many German and German-American genealogical organizations have large surname index files. The German Research Association, with headquarters in San Diego, has recently published a particularly extensive one. See chapter XXIII for its address.

German names in Southeast Europe can be found in Wilhelm and Kallbrunner, *Quellen zur deutsche Siedlungsgeschichte in Südosteuropa* [*Sourcebook for Histories of German Settlements in Southeast Europe*]. The names in this work and numerous smaller books are indexed in Bruce Brandt and Edward Reimer Brandt, *Where To Look for Your Hard-to-find German-speaking Ancestors in Eastern Europe*.

For Swiss German names, see *Handy Guide to Swiss Genealogical Records* by Jared H. Suess.

Stumpp's book on the Germans in Russia, with comprehensive name lists, is also available in English translation for help in tracing Russian Germans.

MEANING OF NAMES

There are numerous German-language books that explain the meaning of surnames and where they were first recorded. The best known one is Hans Bahlow's *Deutsches Namen-Lexikon* [*Dictionary of German Names*].

There are also numerous specialized books of this nature. Some, including other books by Bahlow, deal more exhaustively with names in a given area, e.g., Silesia. Others deal with the names found in a given religious group, e.g., Mennonites or Jews.

If you are interested in what your surname means, see *German-American Names* by George F. Jones. This book also lists many Americanized German names, which are cross-referenced to the German originals. This may be valuable in connecting your name to those which appear in the other references mentioned above.

See Alexander Beider, *A Dictionary of Jewish Surnames from the Former Russian Empire*, and *A Dictionary of Jewish Surnames from the Kingdom of Poland*, and Rabbi Shmuel Gorr, *Jewish Personal Names: Their Origin, Derivation and Diminutive Forms*, for Jewish surnames.

GERMAN GIVEN NAMES

Once you know the German surname of your ancestor, given names are how you identify individuals. A brief discussion follows, which describes some of the different types of given names in use and some of the difficulties in making a positive identification of each individual.

German given names fall into one of the following categories: wish names, Christian names or heroes, and names of rulers. Wish names are some of the oldest Germanic names and describe a wish for strength of character, e.g., Bernhard (strong as a bear), Wolfgang (speedy as a wolf) or Conrad (wise counselor). Later the church's influence on names created new wish names, e.g., Gottlieb (love of God) and Gottlob (praise God).

With the increasing influence of the Christian church, Biblical names became prevalent: Adam, Josef, Maria, Johann, Margarethe. The strong rivalry between the Catholic church and the Protestants led both of them to encourage certain types of given names, e.g., the Catholic church encouraged the use of patron saint names.

Some names became extremely popular because they were German heroes or rulers: Friedrich or Wilhelm in Prussia, Heinrich in Saxony or Franz Josef in Austria.

A person might also be known by a nickname, e.g., Josef or Joseph may be called Peppi, Jupp, Sepp or Josel. There are also spelling variations of names: Anne or Anna; Johannes, Johann, Johan, Joann, Hannes or Hans. Other examples of common variations that might be baffling to Americans are: Dietrich, Diedrich, Dieter, Dirk and Richard (rare); Georg, Jörg, Jürgen and Gerhard; Heinrich, Henrich, Hendrich and Hendrick.

Abbreviations can also be puzzling, especially when they consist of only one letter. Common ones include: M. or Mar. for Maria; Marg. for Margaretha; A. for Anna; J. or Joh. for Johann; Jos. for Josef; Chr. or Christ. for Christian (in the north) or Christoph(er) (in the south). There may be some regional variations and exceptions. A rule of thumb is that when only one letter is used as an abbreviation and there are two names to which it could apply, it almost certainly refers to the one most common in the area in question. A straight line above the letter *m* or *n* meant that one should double the letter. For example, Aña means Anna. In Catholic records, an abbreviated form with a Latin ending may be used. For example, Jōes, with a tilde (wavy line) above the *o* denoting omitted letters, means Jo(hann)es.

Diminutives were used more often for women than men, at least in the north. They frequently included dropping the first syllable, as well as adding an ending. Examples are Trienke (Katharina), Stienke (Justine) and Lenke (Helena), which reflects a Dutch influence.

For more examples of spelling variations and nicknames see the chapter on "Vornamen" (Given Names) in Ribbe and Henning's *Taschenbuch für Familiengeschichtsforschung* [*Handbook for Family History Research*].

Often there were two or three or more given names for each child. Frequently one of the names was selected to honor a godparent, grandparent or other relative. When there were two or more given names, the person might be referred to by different names even in official records. This might occur by leaving out one of the given names or by reversing their sequence or perhaps due to a spelling variation.

Some given names were extremely popular. Those selected varied from place to place. It was not unusual for 50% of the boys or girls in a village to have only four to six different given names. Consequently many people were referred to by one of their other given names, usually the second name. Within a single family, five children might be named Anna or Johann. There might even be ten or more cousins with the same first and last name. Because of this duplication, often two people would have completely identical names, e.g., Johann Friedrich Kleinschmidt. Where this occurs one must be extremely careful to identify and trace the correct person as one's ancestor. If one notes each person's occupation or status, residence, parents, spouse and age along with the complete name, much (but not all) of this confusion can be avoided.

If a child died as an infant, the parents often gave the same name to another child. Because of the high infant mortality rate and the desire to preserve the first names of the parents, grandparents or other relatives, it was common in some groups for three or four children to be given the same name before one survived.

Names were often listed in two (or three, counting Latin) languages in border areas. Examples from other languages are:

- French: Jean (German: Johann), Henri (German: Heinrich), Pierre (German: Peter)
- Polish: Jan (German: Johann)
- Latin: Henricus (German: Heinrich).

ANGLICIZATION OF GERMAN GIVEN NAMES

When a German immigrant emigrated to the United States he often changed his first name to the English equivalent. This is also true in other English-speaking countries. However, if he actually went by his second given name in Europe, that name would probably be the one he would translate and use here, e.g., "Johann Heinrich" becomes "Henry." In this case it becomes more difficult to identify him in German records.

Translation of common German surnames can be done by using a large German-English dictionary. Some more common names are:

Friedrich	Fred, Frederick	Anna	Ann
Jakob	Jacob, James, Jack	Gertraud	Gertrude
Johann	John	Johanne	Joan, Joanne
Karl	Carl, Charles	Justine	Justina, Jessie
Ludwig	Louis	Katharine	Catherine
Wilhelm	William	Maria	Mary

BIBLIOGRAPHY (See ANNOTATED BIBLIOGRAPHY for full citations if not shown)

Adolf Bach. *Deutsche Namenbunde*. 3 vols. Heidelberg: Carl Winter. 1952-56.

Hans Bahlow. *Dictionary of German Names*. [translated edition of *Deutsches Namen-Lexikon*]. Frankfurt am Main, Germany. 3rd edition, 1977.
    A handbook about the origin of German names. (Bahlow also has German-language books concentrating on Silesian, Low German, and Mecklenburger surnames.)

Alexander Beider. *A Dictionary of Jewish Surnames from the Former Russian Empire.* Teaneck, NJ: Avotaynu. 1993. 782 pp.

> Compilation of 50,000 surnames from the Pale of Settlement, including Ukraine, Moldova, Belarus, Lithuania, and Latvia, including a liberal sprinkling of Germanic names from the Kingdom of Poland.

Alexander Beider. *A Dictionary of Jewish Surnames from the Kingdom of Poland.* Teaneck, NJ: Avotaynu. 1995.

Elizabeth Petty Bentley. *The Genealogist's Address Book*, 3rd ed.

> Sections on "Ethnic and Religious Organizations and Resource Centers" and numerous other valuable resources. Well-indexed. Has addresses of U.S. national and state archives.

Josef Karlmann Brechenmacher. *Deutsches Namenbuch.* [*Book of German Names*]. Stuttgart: Verlag von Adold Bonz & Comp. 1928. 388 pp.

> Describes first names and surnames based on the nature of their origin, e.g., pre-Christian German names, saints' names, foreign derivation, occupations, characteristics, etc. Difficult to use for those who do not know German, because of its extensive textual material.

Familiennamenbuch der Schweiz. [*Book of Family Names of Switzerland*] Polygraphischer Verlag. 1858-71. 6 vols.

> Contains an alphabetical list of surnames, showing the Swiss towns and villages where those names occur. This collection is available on microfilm from the Family History Library.

Albert Heintze. *Die deutschen Familien-Namen.* [*German Family Names*]. Halle a.S., Germany: Verlag der Buchhandlung des Waisenhauses. 1882. 227 pp.

> Strong on names of foreign and North German origin. By a Pomeranian teacher.

William F. Hoffman. *Polish Surnames: Origins and Meanings.* Chicago: Polish Genealogical Society of America. 1993. 295 pp.

> Contains quite a few German names and often a Polonized form.

Shmuel Gorr. *Jewish Personal Names: Their Origin, Derivation and Diminutive Forms.* Teaneck, NJ: Avotaynu, Inc. 124 pp.

Max Gottschald. *Deutsche Namenkunde*, 3rd ed. [*The Study of German Names*]. Berlin: Verlag Walter de Gruyter & Co. 1954. 630 pp.

> Deals with origin or meaning of German surnames. Strong on names of the pre-Christian era.

Heinrich W. and Eva H. Guggenheimer. *Jewish Family Names and Their Origins: An Etymological Dictionary.* Hoboken, NJ: KTVA Publishing House.

Institut grand-ducal, section de linguistique, de folklore et de toponomie. *Geschichte der Luxemburger Familiennamen* [*History of Luxembourger Family Names*]. Luxembourg: Imprimerie de Gasperich. 1989.

> Based on 1930 census. Indicates the number of bearers of each surname in Luxembourg and also in different towns and villages.

Arta Johnson. *A Guide to the Spelling and Pronunciation of German Names.*

George F. Jones. *German-American Names*, 2nd ed. Baltimore: Genealogical Publishing Co. 1995. 320 pp.

> Alphabetical list of surnames, including Americanized versions, explains the meaning. The long introductory section provides more detailed information about the derivation of many names. The paragraphs are numbered in parentheses; any parenthetical number for a name in the alphabetical material refers to this paragraph, not to a page.

Emil and Clothilde Meier, Fred Hänni, and Stephan and Claudia Mohr, eds. *Swiss Surnames: A Complete Register* (Commonly Known as the *Familennamenbuch der Schweiz*), 3 vols. First published by the Schweizerische Gesellschaft für Familienforschung in 1940, revised in 1982. Rockport, ME: Picton Press. 1995. 2,084 pp.

> Lists all 48,500 surnames of Swiss citizens in the Swiss communes in 1962, excluding those which have died out since 1800 (mostly Anabaptists) and individuals who appear only briefly in records where their surname does not usually connote citizenship.

Wolfgang Ribbe and Eckart Henning. *Taschenbuch für Familiengeschichtsforschung* [*Handbook for Family History Research*], 11th ed.

> Has a chapter on "Namenkunde" (Study of Names) and "Ältere Vornamenformen" (Old given names) with a lengthy list of old German first name variations. Lists *Ortssippenbücher* (village genealogies) and *Deutsche Geschlechterbücher* (prominent family genealogies).

Kenneth L. Smith. *German Church Books: Beyond the Basics.*

> Has a chapter on names.

Dr. Karl Stumpp. *The Emigration from Germany to Russia in the Years 1763-1862.*

Ernest Thode. *Atlas for Germanic Genealogy.*

Kevin Tvedt. "Using Surnames to Trace German Origin," in *GGSA Bulletin*, January/February 1990.

Chapter VIII

PLACE NAMES

This chapter gives references for many gazetteers that will help you find even the smallest German place. Many of these places are no longer within the boundaries of Germany, Austria or Switzerland. Also included are tips on how to decipher possible misspellings of place names.

FINDING LOCALITIES: GAZETTEERS AND OTHER SOURCES

If your ancestors came from a locality that is not now in a German-speaking country, you will need to obtain the current name of that place before you are likely to obtain genealogical information from the country in question. Conversely, many microfilmed records at the Family History Library in Salt Lake City may be indexed under the old German name. There are numerous sources for determining the place name.

To check whether the village was part of the German Empire of 1871-1919, consult *Meyers Orts- und Verkehrs-Lexikon des Deutschen Reichs* [*Meyer's Directory of Places and Commerce in the German Empire*], edited by E. Uetrecht, which is available on microfilm at Family History Centers and in book form at some libraries with a good selection of materials on Germanic genealogy. This will also enable you to identify where the village was located, in terms of pre-World War I jurisdictional units. If more than one locality had the same name, as was often the case, this source will provide you with the basic information needed to start finding the right one. *The German Researcher* by Fay and Douglas Dearden helps you to decipher the Gothic script and determine the meaning of many of the abbreviations in *Meyers Orts*. Ritter's gazetteer has less detailed information than *Meyers Orts*, but it is printed in the Roman script.

A more detailed gazetteer, with a separate volume for each Prussian province, is the *Gemeindelexikon für das Königreich Preussen* [*Gazetteer for the Kingdom of Prussia*], published by the Verlag des königlichen statistischen Landesamts in Berlin in 1907-1909.

An equally detailed gazetteer of the Austrian (but not Hungarian) provinces and crownlands, based on the 1900 census, is the 14-volume *Gemeindelexikon der im Reichsrate vertretenen Königreiche und Länder* [*Gazetteer of the Crownlands and States Represented in the Imperial Council*] (Vienna: K. u. k. Statistische Zentralkommission, 1903-1908).

These three gazetteers for the German Empire, the Prussian Empire (which encompassed most of North Germany before German unification, with those provinces still part of the kingdom of Prussia after unification), and the Austrian-ruled portion of the Austro-Hungarian Empire are all available on microfilm at Family History Centers.

If you wish to consult a gazetteer predating German unification as well as the establishment of the Austro-Hungarian Dual Monarchy, try H. Rudolf, *Vollständigstes geographisch-topographisch-statistisches Orts-Lexikon von Deutschland* [*Complete Geographical, Topographical and Statistical Place Name Gazetteer of Germany*], which also includes the non-German territories under the dominion of Austria and Prussia. It may well be the only gazetteer that provides information about all of the German-populated localities in Eastern Europe, except for those in Russia and under Turkish rule. While this gazetteer does not have as much detail about individual localities as *Meyers* does, it is ample for genealogical purposes. It was published by Karl Voigt, jun., Weimar, apparently in 1861 or 1862, although no date is shown.

Swiss place names may be in German, French, Italian or Romansh. It is unlikely that their names would have changed since your ancestor's departure. However, if you seek further information in this respect, Jared H. Suess, in his *Handy Guide to Swiss Genealogical Records*, lists the names of all the Swiss cantons in German, French and Italian and specifies the locally spoken language(s).

If the area was never under German rule, or ceased to be part of a German-speaking country in 1919, by far the most comprehensive reference work is *Deutsch-fremdsprachiges (fremdsprachig-deutsches) Ortsnamenverzeichnis* [*Gazetteer of Places, with German and Foreign Language Names*], by Otto Kredel and Franz Thierfelder. This book lists the post-World War I names of former (and often then still existing) German settlements in 24 European countries. This should be considered to be an authoritative source.

A number of area-specific sources are also available.

John M. Michels, in *Introduction to the Hungarian-Germans of North Dakota* (February 1988), published by the Germans from Russia Heritage Society in Bismarck, has a 6-page list of "Banat Village Names in the Different Languages," which includes the German, Hungarian and Romanian or Serbian place names. This area was part of Hungary until 1919, hence the designation. It was subsequently divided between Romania and Yugoslavia after World War I, except for three villages that remained in Hungary.

Jared Suess's *Handy Guide to Hungarian Genealogical Research* lists county and personal names, as well as the Hungarian, German Gothic, Russian, Serbian (Cyrillic) and Croatian (Latin) alphabets.

The *Genealogical Gazetteer of Galicia*, compiled by Brian J. Lenius and published by the author in 1993, identifies all of the villages in which Germans lived and lists the Polish and Ukrainian names for the various localities. Galicia was part of Poland before 1772 and during the interwar period and an Austrian crownland during the disappearance of Poland from the map. It is now divided between Ukraine and Poland, with most of the former German settlements in areas that are now part of Ukraine.

A very useful book for finding Danube Swabian localities is Anton Scherer, *Donauschwäbische Bibliographie, 1935-1955: das Schrifttum über die Donauschwaben in Ungarn, Rumänien, Jugoslavien und Bulgarie sowie — nach 1945 — in Deutschland, Österreich, Frankreich, USA, Canada, Argentinien und Brasilien* [*Danube Swabian Bibliography, 1935-1955: Literature about the Danube Swabians in Hungary, Romania, Yugoslavia and Bulgaria, as well as — after 1945 — in Germany, Austria, France, USA, Canada, Argentina and Brazil*] (Munich: Verlag des Südostdeutschen Kulturwerks, 1966), which cross-references town names in German, Serbian and Romanian.

Henryk Batowski's *Slownik Nazw Miejscowych Europy Srodkowej i Wschnodniej XIX i XX* [*Dictionary of Place Names in Central and Eastern Europe in the 19th and 20th Centuries*] (Warsaw: Panstwowe Wydawnictwo Naukowe, 1964) lists selected place names in East and Central Europe in 24 languages.

The most thorough gazetteer of Hungary, which is on FHL microfilm, is the *Magyarország Helységnévtára* [*Gazetteer of Hungary*] compiled by János Dvorzág (Budapest: "Havi Fäzetek," 1877).

Sophie A. Welisch, in *Bukovina Villages/Towns/Cities and Their Germans*, lists the Romanian, and in some cases Ukrainian, names of former German settlements in the text, but not in list form.

There are several excellent gazetteers for Poland. The most comprehensive one is by Filipa Sulimierskiego, Bronislawa Chlebowskiego et al, *Slownik Geograficzny Królestwa Polskiego i innych krajów slowianskich* [*Geographical Dictionary of the Kingdom of Poland and Other Slavic Countries*], 15 vols. (Warsaw: Sulimierski i Walewski, 1880-1902). This is on FHL microfiche. This gazetteer often gives more detailed entries of villages that were in Prussia (but are now in Poland) than does *Meyers Orts*. The entries are in Polish (with cross-reference citations of the German name of the village to the Polish name), but the introduction to this gazetteer gives a most helpful list of Polish terms and abbreviations with translations.

For those whose particular interest is the current Polish names of villages in Poland that had German names during the interwar period, there are two thorough German gazetteers: (1) M. Kaemmerer, *Ortsverzeichnis der Ortschaften jenseits von Oder und*

Neisse [*List of Names for Localities East of the Oder and Neisse (Rivers)*] (Leer: Verlag Gerhard Rautenberg, 1988), which is a 3rd edition of what used to be *Müllers Verzeichnis der jenseits der Oder-Neisse gelegenen, unter fremder Verwaltung stehenden Ortschaften* [*Mueller's Gazetteer of Localities Lying East of the Oder-Neisse Line, Which Are under Foreign Administration*], and (2) *Amtliches Gemeinde- und Ortsnamenverzeichnis der deutschen Ostgebiete unter fremder Verwaltung* [*Official Gazetteer for the Localities in the (Former) German East under Foreign Administration*], published by the (German) Bundesanstalt für Landeskunde.

Both of these provide the old German and new Polish names for all localities. However, since many communities carried the same name, you may need to find out the name of the current Polish county in which the place is located in order to distinguish between two or more places that may now have different names. This information is listed in *Spis Miejscowosci Polskiej Rzeczypospolitej Ludowej* [*List of Place Names in the People's Republic of Poland*], published in 1967 by Wydawnictwa Komunikacji i Lacznosci in Warsaw.

If trying to use German- and Polish-language gazetteers seems too difficult, Larry O. Jensen has a very thorough and detailed description about how to use these sources in Chapter 9 ("Determining the Present Name of Localities") of *A Genealogical Handbook of German Research*, Vol. I.

Jensen's book also includes numerous other useful items. Appendix E of his book gives the Lithuanian place and county names of former German settlements, primarily in the Memel River area (which came under Lithuanian control in 1923). He provides comparable information for the northern tip of old East Prussia, which has belonged to Russia since World War II. Elsewhere he provides the names of the French departments, as well as the Belgian and Danish counties, of the German-named villages ceded to those countries after World War I.

Finding the current names of villages in the Soviet Union that used to have German names is still a matter wrought with confusion. Kredel and Thierfelder list new names for most of those villages, but these differ from later sources in many cases. One reason for this is that many villages were destroyed during wartime, with new villages built more or less on the same sites, but quite often with new names.

A second reason is that the names of some of these villages may have been changed several times, being named for the currently fashionable Marxist hero, depending on Stalin's moods and those of subsequent rulers. Moreover, the alternatives to the original name may have been either in Russian or in Ukrainian (at least in the Black Sea region) or both. Many German place names were changed to Russian names as early as 1893.

To further complicate things, some villages were known locally and unofficially by one name, which might have found its way into print, yet had a different official name. (Compare "Minneapolis" with "Mill City," a term favored by some St. Paulites!)

Finally, in some cases the original German name was either translated literally into Russian or Ukrainian, or simply Slavicized with the appropriate ending.

There are two major post-1945 American sources of information concerning the current names of former German villages. One is the gazetteer for the Soviet Union (No. 42) published by the U.S. government as part of the series, *Official Names Approved by the United States Board of Geographic Names*. The 1970 edition is not complete and is often inaccurate in its list of cross-referenced former German village names.

A more promising approach is to obtain maps showing the location of the various former German settlements in the Soviet Union. The late Dr. Karl Stumpp prepared comprehensive and detailed maps of these settlements, which can be purchased from the American Historical Society of Germans from Russia (address in Chapter XXIII). These can then be compared with the U.S. Army maps of Eastern Europe, Series N501, which show comparable detail. While this can be a time-consuming process, it will pay off. Of course, there is a possibility that some of the villages shown on the maps may no longer exist, but it is unlikely that many of these localities ceased to exist after 1945.

For a very thorough discussion of maps and related materials that are useful in identifying ancestral locations in Eastern Europe, see Ron Neuman, "Maps and Your Family History," in *Journal of the American Historical Society of Germans from Russia*, Vol. 13, No. 4 (Winter 1990), pp. 31-38.

For detailed information comparing late nineteenth-century and contemporary political jurisdictions, see two articles by Dave Olinyk in the *East European Genealogist*: "Political Divisions of the Austro-Hungarian, German and Russian Empires: Eastern European Membership Interests" (March 1993) and "Modern East European Countries and Pre-World War I Regions" (June 1993).

If you are seeking a general orientation before searching for a specific village, Ernest Thode's maps in *Atlas for Germanic Genealogy* list the German and the Slavic (mostly Polish) names of some of the larger localities (apparently mostly former county seats) in Pomerania, Posen or Poznan, East and West Prussia, the former Kingdom of Saxony and Silesia. It also lists the French names of similar localities in Alsace-Lorraine.

MISSPELLED PLACE NAMES

In a great many instances, the notes left by an immigrant ancestor (and even more so, those recorded by descendants) concerning a place of birth or emigration cannot be found in any gazetteer or atlas because there is no place with a name spelled that way. If the village you are searching for cannot be found in *Meyers Orts* gazetteer, it is almost certain that the locality was outside the German Empire (dealt with above), the name of the locality changed, or the name is misspelled.

Many of our immigrant ancestors were barely literate, and some were completely illiterate. It should be no surprise that people with only a few winters of schooling had trouble spelling names. Moreover, many times these brief biographical notes were recorded in old age, decades after having left Germany, so what little had been learned could easily have been forgotten through lack of use. Even if the immigrants spoke German at home, they may have done very little writing in that language. In cases where a member of the second generation wrote down what he or she remembered of an oral communication with the parent, the problem was even greater. In many cases, members of a generation with no knowledge of the Gothic script incorrectly transcribed what was in the original, sometimes resulting in a distortion such as "Quiveriveide" for "Tiegerweide."

What can be done about this? If you have a reasonably precise idea of the region of origin, a thorough perusal of a detailed map for your misspelled town may solve the problem. If you have been able to identify the hometown of a spouse or relative, this should lead you to search the nearby area. If a couple was married in Germany, the odds are very good that they lived in nearby villages. Even if they were married in North America, such a search would be worthwhile, because it was very common for people from the same general area in Europe to settle in the same town in North America. Whether or not you have this kind of information, it is very helpful to know which letters in the town name were likely to be interchanged.

A great many spelling variations are possible for vowels, but the most likely to be interchanged, especially at the beginning of a name, would be *a* and *e*. Fortunately, a relatively small percentage of place names begin with vowels. The number of possibilities regarding erroneous use of vowels or double vowels in the middle of a word are so large that it is not practical to try to provide a complete list here.

Among consonants, *c* and *k* are identical sounds in German, as in English. You would be likely to find *ck* in the middle of a word or **name**, but never at the beginning. Letters or letter combinations, like *s*, *ss*, *ß* and *sch*, **were** often used interchangeably in old records. In the case of the *s* and *sch* sounds, such a transposition was particularly likely as a result of dialect variations and when illiterate people moved to a distant location.

Other identically pronounced letters include *v*, *f*, *ff* and *ph*. *Pf* could also have been used interchangeably with these by people with little education. Other consonant combinations that were quite likely to be used interchangeably in the past include *b* and *p*, as well as *k* and *g*. The following can also have the same sound: *d*, *t*, *dt* and *tt*. The double letters would never be used at the beginning of a word. *I* and *J* were written the same way and could also be interchanged with the rarely used *y*. Other letters or combinations that could have been used mistakenly or interchanged in an earlier era include *s*, *ss*, *sz*, *z*, *ts* and *tz*.

The English "sh" sound is always spelled *sch* in German, but English speakers in America could have written *sh*. Also, East European Jews used "sh," e.g., "*shtetl*" for "*Städtl*." Words beginning with *sp* or *st* have the *s* pronounced as "sh," but the pronunciation and spelling of *s* and *sch* were sometimes interchanged in olden days. The English "ch" sound is not found at the beginning of place names of German origin, but it is found in Slavic lands where Germans lived. The German spelling for this would be *tsch*, but the Slavic *cz* is quite likely to have been used instead in place names. However, when *cz* occurs at the end of a name, it has often become Germanicized as *tz*. The sound of a soft English *g* (as in "gem") is not found in German, but where this sound occurred as a result of foreign influences, it would be Germanicized as *dsch* (example: *Dobrudscha*).

In border areas, the spelling of a village name could easily follow the rules of the other language, e.g., French in Alsace-Lorraine. A particularly common linguistic alternative is *au* (German for "meadow") and *ow* in Eastern Europe at the end of a name.

The *j* in German is pronounced like the English *y*. Hence, the use of *y* instead of *j* could easily have occurred in writing among Germans in the United States, but not in Europe.

There is no English equivalent of either of the German "ch" sounds. These sounds could have been approximated by an *h* or *k* by a person writing in English. They could have been written as *g*, *k* or *ck* in Europe. A single *s* in German is pronounced like a *z* in English, except at the end of a word. Hence, an American-born descendant could easily have used a *z* in lieu of an *s*.

The German Umlaut letters (*ö*, *ä* and *ü*) are properly written as *oe*, *ae* and *ue*, when the *Umlaut* character is not practical, but in America the *e* as an equivalent was often dropped. German-Americans familiar with the spoken, but not the written, word might use *e* for *ö* or sometimes *ä*, and use *i* or *ie* for *ü*.

The German *h* is generally silent when used together with another consonant. The result is that *t* and *th*, *r* and *hr*, and *l* and *hl*, to cite a few of the more common examples, were often used interchangeably. Indeed, an old German dictionary often differs from a current one in this regard. Hence, wherever *h* appears together with another consonant, check for a spelling without an *h*. The other *h*-combinations are rare at the beginning of a word, but there are a few names that begin with *ch* and possibly *rh*. As for the other way around, a possibly silent *h* could occur after any vowel or vowel combination, but rarely when the same vowel is doubled. Hermann Lange, in *German Composition* (Oxford: Varendon Press, 3rd ed., 1900) gives a most helpful synopsis of the changes in German spelling revised to meet the requirements of the government regulations of 1880.

If you need additional help identifying a misspelled locality, consult an expert.

LIST OF GAZETTEERS AND ATLASES FOR EUROPE

BIBLIOGRAPHY (See ANNOTATED BIBLIOGRAPHY for full citations if not shown)

Allgemeines geographisches statistisches Lexikon aller österreichischen Staaten [*General Gazetteer of All Austrian Lands*]. Vienna: Franz Raffelsperger. 1845-53.

Amtliches Gemeinde- und Ortsnamenverzeichnis der deutschen Ostgebiete unter fremder Verwaltung [*Official Gazetteer for the Localities in the (Former) German East under Foreign Administration*]. Remagen: Bundesanstalt für Landeskunde. 1955.

> Lists name changes resulting from World War II.

Stephen Barthel. *Gazetteer of Parish and Civil Jurisdictions in East and West Prussia*. Salt Lake City: Church of Jesus Christ of Latter-day Saints. 1991. 314 pp.

> Based on 1905 and 1906 Prussian gazetteers. Lists province; district; Protestant and Lutheran parish; and civil registry office for each village.

Henryk Batowski. *Slownik Nazw Miejscowych Europy Srodkowej i Wschnodniej XIX i XX.* [*Dictionary of Place Names in Central and Eastern Europe in the 19th and 20th Centuries*]. Warsaw: Pañstwowe Wydawnictwo Naukowe. 1964. 85 pp.

> Lists selected place names in East and Central Europe in 24 languages.

Tadeusz Bystrzycki, ed. *Skorowidz miejscowosci rzeczypospolitiej. Przemysl: Nakladem Ksiaznicy Naukowej.* [*Index of Localities of the Polish Republic*]. 1923.

> Lists localities in interwar Poland.

Chester G. Cohen. *Shtetl Finder: Jewish Communities in the 19th and Early 20th Centuries in the Pale of Settlement of Russia and Poland, and in Lithuania, Latvia, Galicia, and Bukovina, With Names of Residents*. Bowie, MD: Heritage Books, Inc. 1989. 145 pp.

> Lists former Jewish communities in the Pale of Settlement, Lithuania, Latvia, Galicia, Bukovina, and a few from other parts of East Europe. Gives names of some documented inhabitants.

Christian Crusius. *Topographisches Post-Lexikon aller Ortschaften der k.k. Erbländer,* [*Topographical Postal Directory of All Localities in the Hereditary (Hapsburg) Imperial and Royal Lands*] 4 parts in 13 vols., plus 3 supplemental volumes and an index of the original volumes. Vienna. 1798-1828.

> Early gazetteer of all localities in the Hapsburg Empire.

Randy Daitch. *The Shtetl Atlas*. Venice, CA: Self-published. 1989.

> Maps and 40,000 names of towns and villages in Poland, Lithuania, Belarus and Ukraine, i.e., the Pale of Jewish Settlement in the Russian Empire. Index for old Poland.

F. A. Doubek. *Verzeichnis der Ortschaften mit deutscher Bevölkerung auf dem Gebiete des polnischen Staates.* [*Directory of Places with German Residents within the Country of (Interwar) Poland*]. Berlin: Publikationsstelle. 1939.

> Gazetteer of localities in interwar Poland with German residents.

János Dvorzág, comp. *Magyarország Helységnévtára* [*Gazetteer of Hungary*]. 2 vols. Budapest: "Havi Füzetek." 1877.

> Most thorough gazetteer on pre-World War I Hungary. Can be used without knowledge of Hungarian.

Duncan B. Gardiner. *German Towns in Slovakia & Upper Hungary: A Genealogical Gazetteer*, 3rd ed. Lakewood, OH: The Family Historian. 1991. Reprinted with addendum, 1993. 113 pp.

> Brief description of German towns in the Slovak Republic and Carpatho-Ukraine, with names in German, Hungarian and Slovak. Many detailed maps. Historical overview of German settlements in Eastern Europe. Addresses of Czech and Slovak archives, with instructions as to how to obtain data from them. Key terms in German, Latin, Hungarian, Slovak and Czech. Valuable bibliography.

Gazetteer of Central and Eastern Europe: Grid Sequence Charts. 6 microfiche. Teaneck, NJ: Avotaynu. 1995.

> Very useful in connection with *WOWW Companion* by Gary Mokotoff.

Gemeindelexikon für den Freistaat Preussen [*Gazetteer for the Free State of Prussia*, i.e., all parts of the post-1919 German Empire that were Prussian provinces] Berlin: Verlag des preussischen statistischen Landesamts. 1931-32. 14 vols. (one for each province)

Gemeindelexikon für das Königreich Preussen [*Gazetteer for the Kingdom of Prussia*, i.e., all parts of the pre-1919 German Empire that were Prussian provinces] Berlin: Verlag des königlichen statistischen Landesamts. 1907-1909. 14 vols. (one for each province)

Gemeindelexikon der im Reichsrate vertretenen Königreiche und Länder [*Gazetteer of the Crownlands and States Represented in the (Austrian) Imperial Council*] Vienna: K. u. k. Statistische Zentralkommission, 1903-1908. 14 vols. (one for each crownland or state)
> Gazetteer based on the 1900 census. Arranged by district, with both German and non-German names listed.

Martin Gilbert. *The Atlas of Jewish History*. Revised edition. New York: William Morrow and Co. 1993. 123 pp. plus 4-page bibliography.
> Contains 120 outline maps of Jewish history. Many maps are related to Germany and Europe. Thorough guide of Jewish history and migrations.

Der grosse Shell Atlas. [*The Large Shell Atlas*] Ostfildern, Germany: Mairs Geographischer Verlag. Yearly editions. About 500 pp. In German.
> Detailed modern-day road atlas of Germany and Europe, including city maps and county boundaries, with index. Some explanations are in English. Shell maps for individual areas (about 35) are on a more detailed scale (1:200,000 vs. 1:500,000 for the atlas) and even more detailed. They show every locality where anyone resides, including the tiniest hamlets and even forestry stations.

Charles M. Hall. *The Atlantic Bridge to Germany*.

Arthur Jacot. *Schweizerisches Ortslexikon* [*Swiss Gazetteer*]. Lucerne: C.G. Bucher.

Larry O. Jensen. *A Genealogical Handbook of German Research*, Vol. III.
> Includes brief history of each kingdom, province and duchy, with boundary and other changes. Excellent bibliography of German gazetteers and how to use them.

M. Kaemmerer. *Ortsverzeichnis der Ortschaften jenseits von Oder und Neisse* [*List of Names for Localities East of the Oder and Neisse (Rivers)*]. Leer: Verlag Gerhard Rautenberg. 1988. 230 pp.
> Third edition of what used to be *Müllers Verzeichnis der jenseits der Oder-Neisse gelegenen, unter fremder Verwaltung stehenden Ortschaften*. Lists German and Polish names of all places that were transferred from Germany to Poland after World War II.

Otto K. Kowallis and Vera N. Kowallis. *A Genealogical Guide and Atlas of Silesia*. Logan, UT: Everton Publishers, Inc. 1976. 442 pp. Presently out of print.
> Contains a cross reference of German place names in Silesia to their modern-day Polish names.

Wilfried Krallert, Walter Kuhn, and Ernst Schwarz. *Atlas zur Geschichte der deutschen Ostsiedlung*. [*Historical Atlas of the German East (European) Settlements*]. Bielefeld: Velhagen & Klasing. 1958. 32 pp.
> Contains historical maps showing German settlements throughout East Europe. At Borchert Map Library at the University of Minnesota.

Otto Kredel and Franz Thierfelder. *Deutsch-fremdsprachiges Ortsnamenverzeichnis*. [*Gazetteer of Places, with German and Foreign Language Names*]. Prepared on behalf of the Praktischen Abteilung der Deutschen Akademie. Berlin: Deutsche Verlagsgesellschaft G.m.b.H. 1931. 1173 pp.
> Gives post-World War I place names of localities outside the Germanic countries that formerly had German names. Very comprehensive guide to Germanic settlements, including all European countries.

Wolodymyr Kubijovic. *Ethnic Groups of Southwest Ukraine (Halychyna-Galicia)*. 1983. Distribution rights: Wiesbaden: Otto Harrassowitz.
> Breakdown of each village in eastern Galicia by ethnic group, including Germans.

Heinrich Kuhn (comp. for Sudetendeutsches Archiv). *Ortsverzeichnis der Tschechoslowakei: Deutsch, Tschechisch, Slowakisch, Ungarish, Stand 1957*. [*Gazetteer of Czechoslovakia: German, Czech, Slovak, Hungarian, as of 1957*]. Munich: Sekretariat des Sudetendeutsches Archiv. 1957.

Brian J. Lenius, comp. *Genealogical Gazetteer of Galicia*. Anola, Manitoba: Self-published. 1994.
> Identifies all villages in which Germans lived and lists the Polish and Ukrainian names for the various localities.

Marilyn Lind. *Researching and Finding Your German Heritage*. Cloquet, MN: The Linden Tree. Updated 1991. 150 pp.
> Small maps showing where each pre-World War I German state, province or principality was located.

Erich Dieter Linder and Günter Olzog. *Die deutschen Landkreise: Wappen, Geschichte, Struktur*. [*The German Counties: Their Coats-of-Arms, History and Structure*]. Munich: Günter Olzog Verlag. 1986. 280 pp.
> Maps showing current boundaries of all 237 West German counties and brief history of changes.

Edward David Luft. "Map Resources for the Genealogist at the U.S. Library of Congress." (3-part series in *Nase Rodina*, 1992-93)

Paul Robert Magocsi. *A Historical Atlas of East Central Europe*. Seattle: University of Washington Press. 1993. 218 pp.
> More than 50 maps from ca. 400 to 1992 extending from Odessa to Bavaria and from Greece to Lithuania, with accompanying text, including ethnolinguistic, political and other maps.

Colin McEvedy. *The Penguin Atlas of Modern History (1483-1815)*. Baltimore, MD: Penguin Books. Copyright 1972. 95 pp.
> Small nondetailed maps show European political units, population, religion, towns, trade and revenues. Has excellent associated text. Available in some local bookstores and from Genealogy Unlimited.

Colin McEvedy. *The Penguin Atlas of Recent History: Europe Since 1815*. New York: Penguin. 1982. 95 pp.

John M. Michels. *Introduction to the Hungarian-Germans of North Dakota*. Bismarck: Germans from Russia Heritage Society. 1988.
> Map showing former German settlements in the Banat.

Gary Mokotoff. *WOWW Companion - A Guide to Communities Surrounding Central and East European Towns*. Teaneck, NJ: Avotaynu Monograph. 1995.
> Shows how to locate small communities listed in *Where Once We Walked*, using grid maps.

Gary Mokotoff and Sallyann Amdur Sack. *Where Once We Walked: A Guide to the Jewish Communities Destroyed in the Holocaust*. Teaneck, NJ: Avotaynu, Inc. 1991. 514 pp.
> Documents more than 21,000 towns in Central and Eastern Europe where Jews lived before the Holocaust, lists more than 15,000 Yiddish and other alternate names, gives exact location, and population figures.

Friedrich Müller. *Müllers grosses deutsches Ortsbuch*. [*Muellers Large German Gazetteer*]. Wuppertal-Barmen, Germany: Post- und Ortsbuchverlag Postmeister a.d. Friedrich Müller. 1958. 18th edition 1974. 1988 edition has 941 pp.
> Lists 107,000 places in present-day Germany. Cross-references to the Shell atlas (see above). Useful for identifying present states of communities that belonged to different political entities before World War II.

Friedrich Müller. Ortsbuch für Eupen-Malmedy, Elsass-Lothringen und Luxemburg [Gazetteer for Eupen-Malmedy (Belgium), Alsace-Lorraine and Luxembourg]. Wuppertal-Nachstebreck: Post- und Ortsbuchverlag. 1942. 105 pp.

> Has only limited value for the 1940-44 period, when these areas were forcibly incorporated into Germany, the names Germanicized and their administrative subdivisions reorganized.

Dave Olinyk. "Political Divisions of the Austro-Hungarian, German and Russian Empires: Eastern European Membership Interests" and "Modern East European Countries and Pre-World War I Regions," in *East European Genealogist*, March and June 1993.

> Good cross-references between contemporary and pre-World War I jurisdictional units.

Österreichisches Statistisches Zentralamt. *Ortsverzeichnis von Österreich.* [*Directory of Austrian Place Names*]. Vienna:Verlag der Österreichischen Staatsdruckerei. 1965. 536 pp.

Ernst Pfohl. *Ortslexikon Sudetenland.* [*Sudetenland Gazetteer*]. Nuremberg: Hermut Preussler Verlag. 1932. Reprinted 1987. 698 pp.

> Despite its more limited title, this gazetteer lists the German and Czech or Slovak names of all pertinent places in the Czech and Slovak Republics.

Polska Atlas Drogowy [*Travel Atlas of Poland*]. Warsaw and various other cities: RV Verlag. 1997. 382 pp.

> Most detailed atlas available, with a scale of 1:200,000. 78 city maps of two different scales. General maps of Europe. Locality index.

Das Postleitzahlbuch: Alphabetisch geordnet. [*The (German) Postal Code Book, Arranged Alphabetically*]. Marburg: Bundespost, Postdienst. 1993. 986 pp.

> Shows the postal code for every small community and every street address in big cities under the new postal code system adopted in Germany in 1993. There is a separate book for post office box addresses, which are not always the same as those of the street addresses. Accompanying map available.

Postleitzahlenverzeichnis—Abc-Folge [*Postal Code Directory, in ABC Order*]. Bonn: Bundes-ministerium für das Post- und Fernmeldewesen. 1986. 447 pp.

> Lists the pre-1993 postal codes for localities in East and West Germany.

Isabella Regényi and Anton Scherer. *Donauschwäbisches Ortsnamenbuch.* [*Book of Danube Swabian Place Names*]. Darmstadt: Arbeitskreis donauschwäbischer Familienforscher (AKdFF). 1980.

> Cross-references Danube Swabian town names in German, Serbo-Croatian and Romanian. Brief historical introduction, bibliography and 12 detailed maps.

Gerhard Reichling, ed. *Gemeindeverzeichnis für die Hauptwohngebiete der Deutschen ausserhalb der Bundesrepublik Deutschland*, 2nd ed. [*Directory of Places for the Major Areas Where Germans Are Living Outside the Federal Republic of Germany*]. Frankfurt a.M., Germany: Verlag für Standesamtswesen. 1982. 508 pp.

> Government gazetteer of settlements of German-speakers outside Germany.

H. Rudolf. *Vollständigstes geographisch-topographisch-statistisches Orts-Lexikon von Deutschland.* [*Most Complete Geographic, Topographic and Statistical Gazetteer of Germany*]. Weimar: Karl Voigt, Jr. ca. 1861-62.

> Lists all places that were under Germanic rule at the time, including the Austrian Empire. This gazetteer has now been microfilmed by the Family History Society, according to Galizien German Descendants (Newsletter) (January 1997), and is also available on the FEEFHS Web site on the Internet.

Robert Sobotik. *Westschlesien (Tschechoslowakei): Eine anthropogeographische Studie mit einem Atlas.* [*West Silesia (Czechoslovakia): An Anthropological-Geographical Study, with an Atlas*]. Prague: Geographisches Institut der Deutschen Universität in Prag. 1930.

> Deals with what was known as Austrian Silesia (now northern Moravia), which was actually south, rather than west of the Prussian province of Silesia.

Spis Miejscowosci polskiej Rzeczypospolitej ludowej. [*List of Place Names in the People's Republic of Poland*]. Warsaw: Wydawnictwa Komunicacji i Lacznosci. 1967. 2 vols.

    Provides current Polish names for former German counties, which may be needed because of duplicate village names.

Statistisches Staatsamt. *Administratives Gemeindelexikon für Mähren, Schlesien, die Slowakei und Karpatorussland.* [*Administrative Gazetteer for Moravia, Silesia, Slovakia and Carpatho-Russia*]. Brünn (Brno): Verlag von Rudolf M. Rohrer. 1928. np.

Karl Stumpp. Series of individual maps relating to the Russian Germans: both settlements in Russia and places of origin. Lincoln, NE: American Historical Society of Germans from Russia.

Filip(a) Sulimierski(ego), Bronislaw(a) Chlebowski(ego), et. al. *Slownik Geograficzny Królestwa Polskiego i innych krajów slowianskich.* [*Geographical Dictionary of the Kingdom of Poland and Other Slavic Countries*]. 15 vols. Warsaw: Sulimierski i Walewski. 1880-1902.

    Most thorough gazetteer of localities in pre-partitioned Poland and associated areas. Use of this gazetteer is facilitated with the help of Helen Bienick, Cassie Bochinski and Christine Elia (transl.), "Volume Numbers and Abbreviations used in *Slownik Geograficzny* published in Poland in 1880-1902," in *Bulletin of the Polish Genealogical Society of California*, January 1995.

Ernest Thode. *Atlas for Germanic Genealogy*, 3rd rev. ed. Marietta, OH: E. Thode. 1988.

Ernest Thode. *Address Book for Germanic Genealogy*, 6th ed. Baltimore: Genealogical Publishing Co. 1996. 196 pp.

    Lists German and Slavic or French names for larger localities in the former German Empire.

Ernest Thode. *Genealogical Gazetteer of Alsace-Lorraine.* Indianapolis, IN: Heritage House. 1986. 137 pp.

    Most of the book consists of German and French names of larger towns, as well as geographic features such as rivers.

Finn A. Thomsen. *Atlas of the Austro-Hungarian Empire, 1892.* Bountiful, UT: Thomsen's Genealogical Center. 1990. 79 pp.

    Enlarged reproductions of map published by the Verlag des Bibliographischen Instituts, Leipzig and Vienna, 1892, with index.

Finn A. Thomsen. *Atlas of the German Empire, 1892.* Bountiful, UT: Thomsen's Genealogical Center. 1989. 110 pp.

    Enlarged reproductions of map published by the Verlag des Bibliographischen Instituts, Leipzig and Vienna, 1892, with index.

E. Uetrecht, editor. *Meyers Orts- und Verkehrs-Lexikon des Deutschen Reichs.* [*Meyer's Directory of Places and Commerce in the German Empire*]. Leipzig, Germany: Bibliographisches Institut. 5th ed. Vol. 1 (A-K): 1912, 1,092 pp. Vol. 2 (L-Z): 1913, 1,246 pp. plus 76 pp. appendices.

    Standard gazetteer for the pre-World War I German Empire, listing 210,000 localities. In Gothic print. Most of the German portion of the Family History Catalog at the Family History Library follows the organization presented in *Meyers Orts*.

U.S. Army. *Maps of Eastern Europe*, Series N501.

    Very thorough and detailed.

U.S. Board of Geographic Names. *Official Names Approved by the United States Board of Geographic Names.* Different volumes for various countries and dates.

    The one for the Soviet Union is very inferior for purposes of Germanic genealogy, since it is incomplete and inaccurate.

F. Vanderhalven. *Namensänderungen ehemals preussischer Gemeinden von 1850 bis 1942.* [*Name Changes of Former Prussian Communities from 1850 to 1942*]. Neustadt/Aisch, Germany: Verlag Degener. 1971. 139 pp.

> Quite a few places with Polish names were given German names during the late 1800s, changed back to Polish names (usually, but not always, the previous names) and changed again in a similar fashion during the Nazi occupation. This gazetteer is also helpful in locating villages or cities since the early years of the Industrial Revolution.

Max Vasmer. *Russisches geographisches Namenbuch.* [*Book of Russian Geographic Names*]. 12 vols. Wiesbaden: Otto Harrasowitz. 1964-89.

> Mostly Russian names, but some German and Polish ones, all arranged according to the Russian alphabet. Descriptive material in German.

Verzeichnis der Postleitzahlen. [*(Austrian) Postal Code Directory*]. Vienna, Austria. Published annually.

> Postal code directory for Austria.

Verzeichnis der Postleitzahlen. [*(Swiss) Postal Code Directory*]. Berne: Baubedarf AG. Published annually.

> Postal code directory for Switzerland and Liechtenstein.

Sophie A. Welisch. *Bukovina Villages / Towns / Cities and Their Germans.*

> Includes maps of German settlements in the Bukovina and places of origin of the settlers in Germany, Bohemia and the Slovak Republic.

Peter Wörster. *Das nördliche Ostpreussen nach 1945: deutsch-russisch und russisch-deutsches Ortsnamenverzeichnis mit einer Dokumentation der Demarkationslinie.* [*Northern East Prussia After 1945: German-Russian and Russian-German Locality Name Gazetteer with Documentation of the (Russian-Polish) Line of Demarcation*]. Marburg/Lahn, Germany: J. G. Herder-Institut. 1980. 96 pp.

> Only gazetteer that lists Russian names of localities in what was formerly the northern part of East Prussia.

Suzan F. Wynne. *Galician Towns and Administrative Districts.* Washington, DC: Jewish Genealogical Society of Greater Washington. 1990. 2 microfiche.

CHAPTER IX

POLITICAL AND PHYSICAL GEOGRAPHY

Did your "German" ancestors *really* come from Germany? If so, which Germany: today's Germany, the much larger German Empire put together by Bismarck, or Germany when it was only a geographic concept, not a political one? Perhaps they never lived in Germany, but in Austria. But which Austria: today's small, solidly German-speaking country or the much larger polyglot Austrian Empire of former centuries? Maybe they came from one of the many German "colonies"—meaning settlements in non-Germanic areas, often not German-ruled territory—which were scattered throughout most of Russia, East Central Europe and the Balkans.

THE CHANGING POLITICAL GEOGRAPHY
OF ANCESTRAL HOMELANDS

If you have a place of emigration listed on some old record or from an oral history by your ancestors, but can't find the place in any modern atlas or gazetteer, perhaps the outline presented later in this chapter will help you find it or at least give you a clue as to where to search. You may even be astonished to discover that your ancestors lived far from Berlin, Cologne, Munich, Vienna or Berne. Even if you know in which country or under which rulers your European ancestors lived, that information may be all wrong when applied to today's borders. The reason for this is that European boundaries were constantly changing. In fact, the birth or death of a country was not particularly unusual. However, the most significant changes which occurred, from the perspective of genealogical research on immigrant ancestors, were the following:

- the effect of the Napoleonic Wars and the settlement by the Congress of Vienna in 1815, which greatly reduced the number of sovereign territories on German soil (previously over 300), in spite of the fact that several dozen were left;

- the wars of German unification in 1864-71, which turned the previously independent states and Prussian provinces into sub-units of the German Empire;

- the redrawing of the map of Europe by the Treaty of Versailles with Germany (1919), the Treaty of St. Germain with Austria (1919) and the Treaty of Trianon with Hungary (1920), largely pursuant to President Wilson's principle of national self-determination, but with some exceptions at the expense of German-speaking countries; and

- the westward shift of Poland's location after World War II, as Russia took control of Eastern Poland, while Poland, in return, received the area west to the Oder-Neisse line, the current eastern border of Germany.

Many of the changes in the map of Germany are given in considerable detail in text and maps in the complete text of the Traité de Paix [Treaty of Peace] available from the federal government.

Since relatively few Germans emigrated to America before 1789, or even 1815, only those genealogists with colonial ancestors are likely to have to deal with the pre-Napoleonic hodge-podge of German mini-states at the outset of their research. Here, the German experts have problems too, and some of the German classics of genealogy are filled with errors as to places of origin as a result. If you don't know from which Germanic principality your colonial ancestor came, you are advised to seek the help of the best expert you can find, which often means the genealogist, historian or archivist living closest to the place in question.

Of course, if you know where the village is and you are searching parish registers, it may not matter whether you know to which principality the place belonged or how often this changed. But if you lose track of your lineage and wonder where to search for an earlier generation, it may matter.

However, sooner or later most German-American genealogists will encounter a problem with political jurisdictions. The reason is that if you can trace your ancestors back to Germany, you will almost certainly be able to trace them back to the pre-Napoleonic era, because Germans have earned their reputation of being meticulous record-keepers.

The units established in 1815 (which did not coincide with those of 1772-1806 in the east) continued to describe the various parts of Germany reasonably accurately, despite some minor changes, until World War II, with the exceptions mentioned below. After 1815, Eastern and much of Central and Western Germany belonged to Prussia, while Southern, Northwestern and parts of Central Germany were independent.

The 11 Prussian provinces were:

Brandenburg	Posen	Westphalia
East Prussia	Rhineland	West Prussia
Hohenzollern (2 states)	Province of Saxony	
Pomerania	Silesia	

The independent states that belonged to the loose German Confederation included:

Anhalt	Hanover	Nassau
Baden	Hesse-Cassel	Oldenburg
Bavaria[3]	Hesse-Darmstadt[3]	Kingdom of Saxony
Brunswick	Holstein	Thuringia
Bremen[1]	Lippe	(12 small states, later 8)[2]
Frankfurt[1]	Lübeck[1]	Waldeck
Hamburg[1]	Luxembourg	Württemberg
	Mecklenburg (2 states)	

[1] Denotes city-states.

[2] Also known as the Saxon duchies and the Reuss and Schwarzburg principalities.

[3] Most of the Palatinate belonged to Bavaria. The northeastern area around Mainz was part of the Grand Duchy of Hesse, also known as Hesse-Darmstadt.

The states in the Confederation that belonged to the Austrian Empire were:

Austria proper (Upper, Lower)	Carinthia	Salzburg
Austrian Silesia	Carniola	Styria
Bohemia	Moravia	Tyrol

Switzerland was outside the Confederation, as were Hungary, Slavonia, Galicia, Lombardy and Venetia, all predominantly non-German parts of the Austrian Empire.

The three easternmost Prussian provinces (East Prussia, West Prussia and Posen) were also outside the Confederation, an anomaly harking back to the Holy Roman Empire, which had been abolished in 1806.

In 1866-67 Hanover, Hesse-Nassau (Hesse-Cassel plus Nassau) and Schleswig-Holstein (Schleswig having been taken from Denmark) became Prussian provinces.

Alsace and part of Lorraine were taken from France in 1871 and became a state of the empire (*Reichsland*).

The tinier states were frequently involved with splintering, consolidation, boundary changes and name changes. This applied particularly to Anhalt, Birkenfeld, Hesse, Lippe, Schaumburg, Thuringia and Waldeck. Prior to 1815, it applied to many other areas as well. If you want to make sense out of this fluctuating world of mini-states, try chapter 13 of Marilyn Lind, *Researching and Finding Your German Heritage*, for a fairly detailed treatment.

Meanwhile, the now small country of Luxembourg was once much bigger. In 1839 it lost the territory that is now the Belgian province of Luxembourg. The people of the two Luxembourgs both represented the same German-French mixture, but in varying degrees, since the Belgian area was predominantly French-speaking. Their emigrants generally settled in the United States in or near communities of people from Germany, especially those from the adjacent Rhineland, part of which had also belonged to Luxembourg before 1815.

From 1871 to 1918 the following states, duchies and principalities comprised the German Empire:

Alsace-Lorraine (*Elsass-Lothringen*)	Lippe	Thuringia (*Thüringen*), comprising:
Anhalt	Lübeck	Reuss-Gera[3]
Baden	Mecklenburg-Schwerin	Reuss-Greiz[3]
Bavaria (*Bayern*)	Mecklenburg-Strelitz	Saxony-Altenburg[3]
Brandenburg[1]	Oldenburg	Saxony-Coburg-Gotha[3]
Bremen	Palatinate (*Pfalz*)[2]	Saxony-Meiningen[3]
Brunswick (*Braunschweig*)	Pomerania (*Pommern*)[1]	Saxony-Weimar-Eisenach[3]
East Prussia (*Ostpreussen*)[1]	Posen[1]	Schwarzburg-Rudolstadt[3]
Hamburg	Rhineland (*Rheinland*)[1]	Schwarzburg-Sondershausen[3]
Hanover (*Hannover*)[1]	Kingdom of Saxony (*Sachsen*)	Silesia[1]
Hesse (*Hessen*)	Province of Saxony (*Sachsen*)[1]	Waldeck
Hesse-Nassau (*Hessen-Nassau*)[1]	Schaumburg-Lippe	Westphalia (*Westfalen*)[1]
Hohenzollern[1]	Schleswig-Holstein[1]	West Prussia (*Westpreussen*)[1] Württemberg

[1] Prussian province

[2] Most of the Palatinate belonged to Bavaria. Rheinhessen (near Mainz) belonged to Hesse, and Birkenfeld (a Rhenish enclave, close to the Palatine border) belonged to Oldenburg, as did the Eutin area (north of Lübeck). The Saarland was divided between the Prussian Rhineland and the Rhenish Palatinate.

[3] These 8 duchies and principalities of Saxony (*Sachsen*), except Coburg which joined Bavaria in 1920, became the state of Thuringia (*Thüringen*) in 1920.

It is important to make note of the provinces, because your "Prussian" or "Bavarian" ancestor may have come from west of the Rhine. A geographic outline of the European areas of Germanic settlement is in the next section.

In 1919-23 Germany lost the ethnically mixed territories to the recreated states of Poland and Lithuania, to a newly established Czechoslovakia, and to France, Denmark and Belgium.

In the case of Upper Silesia and East Prussia, plebiscites were held in the border regions to allow the populace to choose the national home. In both cases, smaller parts of the territory chose Poland, but the greater part of the areas in question chose to remain with Germany.

No plebiscite was held in West Prussia. The largest part went to Poland and constituted the Polish Corridor to the Baltic Sea, which meant the division of Germany into two non-contiguous territories. Parts of the province were attached to neighboring German provinces, while the overwhelmingly German-populated Vistula-Nogat delta area became the Free City of Danzig in order to safeguard Polish access to a major port on the Baltic Sea.

While the residents of the Free City had a locally chosen government, not a Polish one, the resentment caused by being severed involuntarily from Germany became fertile soil for Hitler's propaganda.

The changes in the Austro-Hungarian Empire were even greater. In 1914, the Austrian-ruled half consisted of Austria proper, Bohemia, Bosnia and Herzegovina, Bukovina, Carinthia, Carniola, Dalmatia, Galicia, Istria, Moravia, Salzburg, the Austrian part of

Silesia, Styria, Trent, Tyrol and Vorarlberg. Pre-World War I Hungary included Slovakia, Sub-Carpathian Rus', the Satu Mare area, the Banat, the Batschka and a small area in northeast Slovenia. It ruled Slavonia (as eastern Croatia was known, but which included the area in the Serbian Vojvodina south of the Danube) and Croatia (except for Dalmatia and Istria) and Transylvania as administratively separate entities. After World War I, Austria and Hungary each became a separate, small country. A part of the ethnically mixed Burgenland region, which hitherto had belonged to Hungary, became part of Austria pursuant to a plebiscite.

Changes of much greater consequence were:

- the creation of Czechoslovakia (Bohemia, Moravia, Austrian Silesia, Hungarian-ruled Slovakia) in the north;

- the establishment of Yugoslavia (meaning the land of the South Slavs), combining the previously independent nations of Serbia and Montenegro with parts of the old Austro-Hungarian Empire which became the republics of Slovenia, Croatia and Bosnia-Herzegovina, and the Vojvodina, now an autonomous Serbian province; and

- the expansion of Romania, so as to include the largest German settlements in historic Hungary, as well as Bessarabia, which it annexed when the Russian Empire collapsed.

A very small portion of the Banat was transferred from Romania to Yugoslavia a few years after the war.

These changes meant that most of the ethnic Germans living between the predominantly German-speaking areas in the west and Russian or Ukrainian-speaking areas in the east were now subjects of a different country than the one to which they had belonged before World War I.

Part 3 of the geographic outline identifies the country in which these islands of German settlement are now located, although in several cases, mostly along the Soviet borders, there were changes in boundaries as a result of World War II, modifying the post-World War I map so that this outline does not describe the jurisdictional boundaries between the two world wars.

The areas where the boundaries changed in 1945 are listed under part 2(a) of the geographic outline, viz., East and West Prussia (including Danzig), Eastern Pomerania, Eastern Brandenburg and Silesia, most of which became part of Poland and some of which became part of the Soviet Union. Also affected were some of the islands of settlement identified under part 3 of the outline, viz., the Baltic countries, Western Volhynia, East Galicia, Bessarabia, Northern Bukovina and Carpatho-Ukraine, all of which became part of the Soviet Union.

There were also many temporary boundary adjustments during the 1938-45 period, beginning with Hitler's annexation of Austria and the Sudetenland. For a description of these, see the *AGoFF Guide* (see **ANNOTATED BIBLIOGRAPHY** in Chapter XXII). The 1940 Romanian-Bulgarian boundary change has been permanent.

It may be possible to trace some so-called "Germanic" ancestors back to other countries where they lived before becoming assimilated into the Germanic culture.

Of course, there were some inter-ethnic marriages in the border areas and islands of German settlements listed in parts 2 and 3 of the outline, although they were not nearly as numerous as they have been in the American "melting pot."

In addition, people of Flemish, Dutch and Frisian stock were quite numerous among the "Germans" who migrated to Eastern Europe during the late Middle Ages and the early centuries of the modern era, as the "Holländereien" testify. "Holendry," or "Oledry" in Polish, is still part of the name of some communities settled by people of Dutch origin, and later also sometimes by those of German descent. Sooner or later, these people became assimilated into the ethnically kindred Germans.

The trading relationships between England, Scotland, Scandinavia and the continent, dating back to the Hanseatic League, led some English and Scottish families to settle in northern German areas and the reverse was true of Germans who settled in London and these countries.

Religious refugees from France, Belgium and the Netherlands fled to Germany in the sixteenth and seventeenth centuries to avoid religious persecution.

Sweden controlled significant parts of the German Baltic coast, particularly Pomerania, during the 1600s and early 1700s, which obviously led to some Swedish-German marriages. Some Swedish soldiers are known to have remained in German-populated areas after 1648. The Swedish, Danish and Spanish soldiers who fought in Germany during the Thirty Years' War, and the French soldiers who did so in many wars, had progeny through unofficial liaisons, as well as through legal marriages.

The centuries of conflict between the Ottoman Turks and the European Christian powers led to the capture of some young attendants in the Turkish camp, who were taken home by officers and raised as Germans.

In other instances, Swiss, Palatine, Hessian, Hanoverian and other Germanic migrants went to England and Ireland, as well as to the New World. Some of the migrants stayed in Britain for an interim period and then continued on to North America.

PHYSICAL GEOGRAPHY AND HISTORIC DESIGNATIONS

In many cases people may find it hard to identify the location of their ancestors because they are identified as coming from a particular mountain, river or forest region. Ernest Thode, *Atlas for Germanic Genealogy*, has maps showing many of these physical features, especially the various rivers. You can also find many of them in the *National Geographic Society Atlas* or in German-language encyclopedias (e.g., *Brockhaus*) with some hunting. For your convenience, we have identified some of the commonly used references to geographic regions or to historical areas that may be hard for non-Europeans to identify.

We have also included references to historic regions whose names are no longer commonly used and which may or may not have been political entities. Of course, boundaries changed in earlier centuries, as well as in this century, so the identified area may not be accurate for all periods.

Alb: (Swabian and Franconian): hilly uplands running from the south end of the Black Forest (Baden-Württemberg) along the north side of the Danube to Bayreuth (Bavaria).

Alpen: (Alps): highest, largest European mountain range, extending from the French-Italian border near the Mediterranean through most of Switzerland and Austria and crossing the border into northern Italy and southwestern Slovenia; many different modifiers are used to describe certain portions of the Alps.

Altmark (Old March): area around and north of Magdeburg (Saxony-Anhalt), earlier part of the Electorate of Brandenburg; area of early eastward expansion of the Saxons.

Banat: area around Timisoara, Romania, including the area east of the Tisza river in the Vojvodina and a few Hungarian villages near Szeged.

Batschka (Backa, Bácska): area between the Tisza and Danube rivers (northeastern Vojvodina next to Croatia and Hungary; sometimes used to include the adjacent area in Hungary).

Bayerisches Oberland (Bavarian Uplands): foothills of the Alps in southern Bavaria.

Bayerischer Wald (Bavarian Forest): east of Regensburg; parallel to the Danube river.

Böhmen (Bohemia): Bohemia proper was western part of Czech Republic. But Bohemia was also a kingdom which included Moravia and Silesia, with boundaries approximating those of the current Czech Republic since the 1740s. After 1526 the emperors of the Holy

Roman Empire were also kings of Bohemia; the Austrian emperor continued to serve as king of Bohemia until the end of World War I.

Böhmerwald (Bohemian Forest): mountainous area along the border between Bohemia (southwestern Czech Republic) and Bavaria.

Breisgau: region in southern Baden which includes the Rhine river plain and the western slopes of the Black Forest; Freiburg is the main city.

Cherson (Kherson): western Black Sea province of the former Russian Empire between Odessa and Kherson.

Dobrudscha (Dobruja, Dobrogea): eastern Romania between the Danube and the Black Sea, extending into the northeastern tip of Bulgaria.

Donauschwaben (Danube Swabians): Germans who settled near the Lower Danube in what was then southern Hungary (now western Romania, the Vojvodina and southern Hungary) after the territory was reclaimed from the Ottoman Turks; known as Hungarian Germans until the 1920s.

Dongebiet (Don River area): province of the former Russian Empire around and northeast of Rostov.

Eifel: mountains between the Rhine and Moselle rivers to the boundary with Luxembourg and Belgium, reaching north almost to Aachen; southwestern part of current state of Northrhine-Westphalia.

Ekaterinoslav/Jekaterinoslav: former province of the Russian Empire north of Taurida, around Dnepropetrovsk.

Ermland (Warmia): area southeast of Braunsberg (East Prussia), between Königsberg and Allenstein.

Erzgebirge (Ore Mountains): range along the border between northeast Bohemia (Czech Republic) and southwest Saxony.

Franken (Franconia): northern Bavaria; land of the Frankish tribe, from which the name France is also derived; the Ansbach-Bayreuth area is mostly Protestant.

Generalgouvernement: the part of Poland ruled but not annexed by Hitler, essentially the area around Warsaw, Cracow and Lwów (now Ukrainian: L'viv; Russian: L'vov; German: Lemberg).

Glatz: former principality in southern Lower Silesia.

Grosspolen (Great Poland): area around Posen (Poznan) and Gnesen (Gniezno), site of a prominent early Polish duchy.

Haardt: vineyard-rich uplands parallel to the Rhine from west of Worms into northeastern Alsace; mostly in Rhineland-Palatinate.

Harzgebirge: mountains where Lower Saxony, Saxony-Anhalt and Thuringia meet.

Hinterpommern (Further Pomerania): eastern Pomerania, approximately the area which is now northwestern Poland.

Hunsrück: hilly area between the Moselle and Nahe rivers, extending from northwest Saarland to west of Bingen; northern part of current state of Rhineland-Palatinate.

Ingermanland (Ingria): Russian area east of Estonia and northeastern Latvia from St. Petersburg to Lake Peipus.

Jura: low mountains from southeast of Geneva along the north side of the Danube through Württemberg to north of Nuremberg (*Nürnberg*) in northern Bavaria; subdivided into Swiss, Swabian and Franconian Jura.

Kleinpolen (Little Poland): south Poland; Galicia and the Cracow area; site of an early Polish duchy.

Kuban: former Russian province along the Kuban River, which flows into the Sea of Azov directly east of the Crimean peninsula (northwestern part of the North Caucasus).

Kujawien (Kuyavia): in the Thorn (Torun)-Plock area near the Vistula.

Kulmerland: between Kulm (Chelmno) and Thorn (Torun), extending eastward; southwest East Prussia.

Kur- (e.g., Kurhessen, Kurpfalz): *Kur* = Electorate; when duchies and principalities were subdivided (as happened frequently in some areas), the elder line had the right to vote for the Holy Roman Emperor.

Kurland (Courland): western and southern Latvia.

Ländl: Same as Salzkammergut; term commonly used by Protestant refugees from the archbishopric of Salzburg.

Lausitz (Lusatia): east Saxony and southeast Brandenburg, between the Elbe and Bober rivers; Slavic Sorbs (also called Wends), the largest native minority in Germany and still speaking their own language although becoming assimilated, live here.

Lettgallen (Latgalia): former Polish Livonia (southeastern Latvia).

Livland (Livonia): eastern Latvia and southern Estonia (east and northeast of Riga).

Lodomerien: seldom used part of the official name of the Austrian crownland of Galizien und Lodomerien, derived from a former Volhynian duchy.

Lüneburger Heide (Luneburg Heath): between the Elbe and Weser rivers, southeast of Lüneburg; northeastern Lower Saxony.

Mähren (Moravia): eastern part of the Czech Republic, which included the former Austro-Silesia until some years after World War I.

Masowien (Mazovia): central Poland, around Warsaw and Lodz.

Masurien (Mazuria): southern East Prussia and the adjoining part of interwar Poland.

Mittelmark: Brandenburg west of the Oder river.

Moldau (Moldavia): northeastern Romania and Moldova.

Narewgebiet (Narew River area): around Lomza, Poland, and Hrodna (Grodno), Belarus.

Neumark: Brandenburg east of the Oder river (now in Poland); often used to refer specifically to northeast Brandenburg along the Netze river.

Neu-Ostpreussen (New East Prussia): the area south and east of East Prussia, extending from Kaunas, Lithuania, to Warsaw, which was under Prussian rule in 1795-1806.

Neurussland (New Russia): term applied to Russian conquests from the Turks along the Black Sea; synonymous with Südrussland (South Russia).

Odenwald: forested area between the Main and Neckar rivers in south Hesse and north Baden-Württemberg.

Ostsee: Baltic Sea (literally East Sea to distinguish it from the North Sea).

Pannonien (Pannonia): a somewhat imprecise term referring to the large plain which includes the northeastern half of Croatia, Hungary, northern Yugoslavia and westernmost Romania; for purposes of Germanic research, it is the area where the Hungarian Germans (most of them Danube Swabians) settled.

Podlachien (Podlachia): area around Brest Litovsk (western Belarus and east central Poland).

Podolien (Podolia): area east of Galicia around Khmel'nyts'kyi, Ukraine.

Pommerellen (Pomerelia): frequently translated as Pomerania (it was the center of Pomerania 750 years ago), but roughly identical with the interwar Polish Corridor to the Baltic Sea and the Free City of Danzig.

Rheinhessen: area around Mainz on the west bank of the Rhine, which belonged to Hesse when the rest of the Palatinate belonged to Bavaria; still the name of a government district intermediate between a state and a county.

Salzkammergut: area east of Salzburg (Austria).

Samogitien (Samogitia/Zmudz): northwestern Lithuania.

Sauerland: area southeast of the Ruhr industrial complex, between the Ruhr river in the north and the Sieg and Fulda rivers in the south.

Schwaben (Swabia/Swabians): name derived from the Swabian, also known as the Alamanni, tribe; Württemberg and southeast Bavaria; often used as a synonym for Württemberg, which is surrounded by C-shaped Baden on the north, west and south; sometimes used as a generic term for Germans who settled in East Central Europe in the late 18th and early 19th centuries, especially those from southwestern Germanic areas, including Alsace; same German word is used for the tribe, the area, and the people.

Seenplatte: coastal plains; differentiated by Mecklenburg, Pomeranian and Prussian plains.

Semgallen (Zemgalia, Semigalia): area south of the Western Daugava (Dvina) River in Latvia next to its border with Lithuania and Belarus.

Semland (Zemgalia): area north of Königsberg, East Prussia (now Kaliningrad, Russia).

Siebenbürgen (Transylvania): historically, the German area of settlement in what is now central Romania, north of Sibiu (*Hermannstadt*) and Brasov (*Kronstadt*); but Transylvania is now often used to describe the northwestern third of Romania.

Spessart: between the Kinzig river and Franconian fork of the Saale river in northwest Bavaria, crossing slightly into Hesse.

Steigerwald: forested area between the Main and Aisch rivers, west of Bamberg, Bavaria.

Strasse or **-strasse** with a prefix: refers to the area along one of many roads that are well-known in Germany, for example, the Weinstrasse is parallel to and west of the Rhine (roughly equal to Haardt), while the Romantische Strasse refers to a road, mostly in northeastern Württemberg, where many towns have retained their medieval features; such a term may occasionally be used to distinguish one village from another by the same name.

Sudauen (Sudavia; Pol.: Suwalki): area next to east central East Prussia.

Sudetengebirge: Sudety mountains along the border of Silesia and the northeast Czech Republic.

Sudetenland: the C-shaped mountainous rim of the Czech Republic annexed by Hitler in 1938; not limited to the Sudeten mountain region; most of the area was populated chiefly by German-speakers, especially in the west and north.

Südpreussen (South Prussia): the area west of Warsaw that was under Prussian rule in 1795-1806; roughly equivalent to Great Poland or to the province of Posen without the Netze (Notec) river district in the north.

Südrussland (South Russia): the Black Sea areas won by Russia from the Turks under Catherine the Great; now roughly southern Ukraine.

Syrmien (Syrmia, Srem): area south of the Danube in the southeastern part of the Serbian Vojvodina (northwest of Belgrade).

Taunus: northeast of Wiesbaden in southwest Hesse.

Taurien (Taurida): eastern Black Sea province of the former Russian Empire (Crimea and northeast of it).

Terek: former Russian province along the Terek River, which flows into the Caspian Sea in southernmost European Russia (southeastern North Caucasus region); mostly in Dagestan, Chechnya and Ingushetia.

Teschen (Pol.: Cieszyn; Cz.: Tesin): former ethnically-mixed Silesian area, now split between the easternmost part of the Czech Republic and Poland.

Thüringerwald (Thuringian Forest): from Eisenach (Thuringia) to northeast of Coburg on the Bavarian border; parallels the Werra river on the northeast.

Transnistrien (Transnistria): area northeast of Odessa between the Dniester and the southern Bug rivers (mostly southwestern Ukraine, but including the present breakaway portion of eastern Moldova).

U(e)ckermark: region of the U(e)cker river in the northeastern part of the present German state of Brandenburg and the eastern part of Mecklenburg-Vorpommern.

Vogesen (Vosges): mountains in western Alsace, parallel to the Rhine.

Vogtland: southwest Saxony in the vicinity of Plauen.

Vorpommern (Hither Pomerania): western Pomerania, approximately the area in the northeastern corner of present-day Germany.

Warthegau: the Warta river region around Kolo and Konin, between Warsaw and the city of Posen, in the west central part of former Congress Poland or Russian Poland.

Walachei (Walachia): southern Romania.

Westerwald: forested area north of Koblenz, east of the Rhine, in the northeastern part of Rhineland-Palatinate, extending into Hesse.

Windisch Mark: roughly equivalent to Slovenia; southeastern corner of Charlemagne's empire; name derived from the Wends, one of several peoples who migrated to the area.

Note: Often the suffix "-*land*" is attached to the name of a river, and occasionally other geographic features, to describe the area in question.

The suffix "-*bruch*," following the name of a river, indicates a broad, low, swampy area, which was drained and cultivated at a relatively late date, e.g., Oderbruch (sometimes written Odenbruch) or Netzebruch. The area in question was known by this name.

GEOGRAPHIC OUTLINE OF AREAS OF GERMANIC SETTLEMENT IN EUROPE

OVERVIEW
1. The Germanic Heartland
2. Adjacent Ethnically Mixed Areas (the Rimland)
3. Scattered Settlements in Eastern Europe
4. Other Countries of Origin (or Transit) for Germanicized Ancestors

DETAILED OUTLINE

1. **The German Heartland**. Countries where German is now an official language.

    (a) **Germany**. The Federal Republic of Germany now includes the following *Länder*:

Baden-Württemberg	Hesse (*Hessen*)	Saarland
Bavaria (*Bayern*)	Lower Saxony (*Niedersachsen*)	Saxony (*Sachsen*)*
Berlin (unique status)	Mecklenburg-Vorpommern*	Saxony-Anhalt*
Brandenburg*	Northrhine-Westphalia	(*Sachsen-Anhalt*)
Bremen	(*Nordrhein-Westfalen*)	Schleswig-Holstein
Hamburg	Rhineland-Palatinate	Thuringia*
	(*Rheinland-Pfalz*)	(*Thüringen*)

The starred areas were part of the German Democratic Republic from 1949 to 1990. At that time they constituted the *Bezirke* (Districts) of:

Cottbus	Gera	Neubrandenburg
Dresden	Halle	Potsdam
East Berlin	Karl Marx-Stadt	Rostock
Erfurt	Leipzig	Schwerin
Frankfurt an der Oder	Magdeburg	Suhl

The city of Berlin was divided between the two former German republics from 1949 to 1990.

(b) **Austria**. Austria currently has the following states:

Burgenland	*Salzburg*	Upper Austria
Carinthia (*Kärnten*)	Styria (*Steiermark*)	(*Oberösterreich*)
Lower Austria	Tyrol (*Tirol*)	Vienna (*Wien*)
(*Niederösterreich*)		*Vorarlberg*

(c) **Switzerland**. At least 94% of the people had German as their mother tongue in 1920 in the following Swiss cantons:

Aargau	Lucerne (*Luzern*)	*Solothurn*
Appenzell-Ausser-Rhoden	*Nidwalden*	*Thurgau*
Appenzell-Inner-Rhoden	*Obwalden*	*Unterwalden*
Basel-Land	St. Gall (*St. Gallen*)	*Uri*
Basel-Stadt (Basel City)	*Schaffhausen*	*Zug*
Glarus	*Schwyz*	*Zürich*

Berne (*Bern*) canton was formerly 83% German. However, the French-speaking northwestern portion of this canton later became the canton of Jura, so the present Berne canton is also overwhelmingly German-speaking. *Graubünden* (Grisons), which was home to 91% of the Romansch-speakers in Switzerland, was nevertheless 51% German.

About 31% of the people had German as their primary language in the French cantons of *Freiburg* (Fribourg) and *Wallis* (Valais). They lived primarily in the eastern part of these cantons. The German-speakers accounted for 10-12% of the people in the cantons of *Waadt* (Vaud), *Genf* (Geneva) and *Neuenburg* (Neuchâtel). Only 6% of the residents of overwhelmingly Italian *Tessin* (Ticino) canton were native German-speakers. The percentage of German-speakers in Jura canton is unknown but small.

For maps of the above present or recent jurisdictional units, see Ernest Thode, *Atlas for Germanic Genealogy*.

(d) **Luxembourg**. Luxembourg has the following cantons:

Capellen	Grevenmacher	Remich
Clervaux	Luxembourg-Campagne	Vianden
Diekirch	Luxembourg-Ville	Wiltz
Echternach	Mersch	
Esch-sur-Alzette	Redange	

(e) **Liechtenstein**. Liechtenstein is too small to have any sub-units.

2. **The Germanic Rimlands**. Areas adjacent to the Germanic heartland that had a substantial German-speaking population during the nineteenth century.

(a) Formerly mostly German areas that were part of the Weimar Republic and the Free City of Danzig (now Gdansk in Poland), 1919-1945
   (i) East Prussia (now Poland and the Soviet Union)
   (ii) Free City of Danzig (formerly part of West Prussia, now Poland)
   (iii) Eastern Pomerania (Pomorze, now in Poland)
   (iv) Eastern Brandenburg (now Poland)
   (v) Nearly all of Silesia (Slask, now in Poland)

(b) Ethnically mixed areas that were part of the German Empire, 1871-1919
   (i) Transferred to Poland in 1919-21
       (1) Nearly all of *Posen* (Poznan)
       (2) The greater part of West Prussia (which ceased to exist as a province in 1919)
       (3) Eastern Upper Silesia (Slask)
       (4) The southern tip of East Prussia
   (ii) *Memelland* (now Lithuania)
   (iii) The *Hultschin* (Hlucín) region in Silesia (now the Czech Republic)
   (iv) Eupen-Malmedy (now Belgium)
   (v) Alsace-Lorraine (now France)
   (vi) North Schleswig (now Nord Slesvig in Denmark)

(c) Areas near interwar Austria and Germany that were part of the Austro-Hungarian Empire, 1867-1919
   (i) *Sudetenland* in Bohemia/Moravia/Austrian Silesia (now the Czech Republic)
   (ii) South Tyrol (now Alto Adige in Italy); also northeasternmost and northwestern Italy
   (iii) Eastern *Burgenland* (Hungary)
   (iv) The *Teschen* (Cieszyn) part of Austrian Silesia (now in Poland)

(d) Adjacent to Luxembourg: the Belgian province of Luxembourg

3. **Major Islands of Germanic Settlements**. Major German settlements in non-Germanic lands.

(a) Contemporary Poland
   (i) Lodz area
   (ii) Lipno-Rypin-Gostynin area on both sides of the Vistula (*Weichsel*, Wisla) River, east and south of *Thorn* (Torun)
   (iii) On both sides of the Warta (*Warthe*) River, north and south of Konin and Kolo
   (iv) Western Galicia (*Westgalizien*, Galicja)
   (v) Eastern Poland (around Chelm)

(b) The Baltic countries (Estonia, Latvia, Lithuania)
(c) Russia
   (i) The Volga (*Wolga*) settlements
   (ii) Perm-Orenburg (near the foot of the Urals)
   (iii) Siberia (along the Trans-Siberian Railway and along the border with Kazakhstan)
   (iv) Northern Caucasus (southernmost European Russia)
   (v) Near Rostov (northeast tip of Sea of Azov)

(d) Ukraine
   (i) The Black Sea settlements (nearly all in Ukraine)
   (ii) Volhynia (*Wolhynien*)
   (iii) South Bessarabia (*Süd-Bessarabien*)
   (iv) East Galicia (*Ostgalizien*, Halychyna)
   (v) North Bukovina (*Buchenland*, Bukowina)
   (vi) Carpatho-Ukraine (Subcarpathian Rus'; Karpato-Ukraine; *Karpatenland*; formerly eastern tip of Czechoslovakia)

(e) Moldova (Northern Bessarabia, most *Glückstal* villages)

(f) Georgia and Azerbaijan
   (i) South Caucasus (southern Georgia, northern Azerbaijan)
   (ii) North Caucasus (northern Georgia)

(g) Kazakhstan and other Muslim republics belonging to the CIS
(now the main center of Germans; only a few pre-1914 settlements)

(h) Contemporary Romania
    (i) Transylvania (*Siebenbürgen*)
    (ii) Eastern Banat
    (iii) Satu Mare (*Sathmar*) and the tiny settlement at Tirna Mare (*Groß Tarna*) just north of there
    (iv) Most of Dobruja (*Dobrudscha*, Dobrogea)
    (v) Southern Bukovina/Bukowina (*Buchenland*)

(i) Yugoslavia (Serbia-Montenegro; almost all in the Vojvodina)
    (i) Western Banat
    (ii) Southern *Batschka* (Backa, Bácska)
    (iii) Syrmia (*Syrmien*, Srem)

(j) Croatia
    (i) Southern Baranya (*Baranja*)
    (ii) Slavonia (*Slawonien*)

(k) Slovenia
    (i) *Gottschee* (Kocevje)
    (ii) Carniola (*Krain*, Krajnska): Maribor (*Marburg*), Ljubljana (*Laibach*), Cilli
    (iii) Gorizia (*Görz*) and Gradisca (*Gradiska*)

(l) Contemporary Hungary
    (i) Swabian Turkey (*Schwäbische Türkei*)
    (ii) Northern Bácska (*Batschka*, Backa)
    (iii) Central Highlands north of Lake Balaton (*Plattensee*), including Budapest

(m) Czech Republic
    (i) Bohemia (*Böhmen*): outer rim, Jihlava (*Iglau*) and smaller enclaves
    (ii) Moravia (*Mähren*): north and south, Hrebec (*Schönhengst*), Olomouc (*Olmütz*) and smaller enclaves
    (iii) Former Austrian Silesia (*Österreichisch-Schlesien*), now part of Moravia

(n) Slovak Republic
    (i) Bratislava (*Pressburg*) area
    (ii) Spis (*Zips*)
    (iii) Hauerland (*Kremnitz*/Kremnica, *Deutsch-Proben*/Nitrianske Pravno)

(o) Contemporary Bulgaria (Southern Dobruja/Dobrudza/*Dobrudscha*)

4. Other Relevant Lands. Other countries of origin (or transit) for Germanicized ancestors

(a) Belgium
(b) Bosnia-Herzegovina
(c) Finland
(d) France
(e) Great Britain
(f) Ireland
(g) Netherlands
(h) Norway
(i) Sweden
(j) Turkey

Chapter X

HISTORY OF GERMAN-SPEAKING PEOPLE IN EUROPE

Any classification of European political entities for purposes of tracing the history of the Germanic peoples is arbitrary to some extent, because the changes were so frequent and so drastic. In this instance, the material is presented on the basis of the boundaries between 1871 and 1919, when there was relatively little change. This was the period during which a large majority of German-speaking immigrants came to North America and some other New World countries, so this arrangement will simplify coordinating information regarding immigrant ancestors with the sovereign units that existed at that time.

If your ancestors ever lived under German-speaking rulers, they almost certainly did so during that period, when both the German Empire and the Austrian (Austro-Hungarian) Empire were at their largest. However, German-speakers were not a majority in all of the territory included in these empires. There was no independent Poland at the time and Germans were but one of many minorities in the Hapsburg Empire, which had no ethnic majority.

THE GERMAN EMPIRE OF 1871 TO 1919

THE EARLY AND MEDIEVAL ERAS

Although there were many Germanic tribes in northern Europe during the days of the Roman Empire (described by the Roman historian, Tacitus), they scattered throughout much of Europe and North Africa during the following *Völkerwanderung* (Great Barbarian Migrations).

The modern German identity can be traced back to 843, when Charlemagne's empire was divided among his grandsons, and Ludwig the German became king of the East Frankish Kingdom (roughly east of the Rhine), as contrasted with the West Frankish Kingdom, which became France, with the Middle Kingdom (Rhineland, Alsace-Lorraine, Low Countries, Burgundy, etc.) between them.

Early medieval "Germany" included only about half of the territory of the nineteenth-century German Empire. Its eastern boundary approximated the Elbe River, along a line extending from just east of Hamburg to the northwest corner of the Czech Republic. Slavic tribes occupied the area east of the line during the early centuries of the medieval era after it had been vacated by the Goths and related tribes. Germans began to move into this area in the eleventh century as a result of overpopulation. In some instances they quietly settled in the uninhabited wooded or marshy areas between Slavic settlements. In other cases the eastward expansion was the result of military conflicts. The Teutonic Knights, the Hanseatic League, and the church were also driving forces, as concentrated Germanic settlement was extended to the Memel River.

Many of the people who became part of what German scholars refer to as the "new tribes" were actually Slavs who became Germanicized as a result of intermarriage, the policies of their rulers, the attractiveness of Western religions and technological influences, or sheerly because they were outnumbered by the incoming Germans. Thus in reality many of those easterners who identified themselves as Germans during the modern era had a mixed German-Slavic background. However, not all of the Slavs in Germanic territory became assimilated. The Slavs in Lusatia (Saxony) constitute an identifiable ethnic minority group in Germany to this day. Many Poles moved to the Rhine-Ruhr area to find jobs during the late decades of the Industrial Revolution. Some have retained a sense of their Polish heritage.

Nevertheless, by about 1350 the German-Polish linguistic border had come to approximate what it was until 1945, despite some relatively modest later changes along the entire line (but varying considerably in degree from one area to another). Bear in mind, that there was no clear-cut dividing line. There were substantial German minorities on the Polish side of the fuzzy border and, to a lesser extent, Poles on the German side.

In 962 Otto I, the Great, was crowned as emperor in Rome, reviving the empire established by Charlemagne (Karl der Grosse) in 800. The largest of the powerful duchies associated with this empire were those of Saxony, Bavaria, Franconia, Swabia and Lorraine.

This empire, established in 800 and re-established in 962, later came to be known as the "first" empire, and the one founded in 1870-71 as the "second" empire, hence Hitler's "Third Reich (Empire)."

The full name of this first empire came to be the Holy Roman Empire of the German Nation. Its territory was mostly Germanic. "Roman" signified the heritage it claimed and its religious connection with the pope in Rome, who crowned many of the early emperors.

After 1250, the emperor, who was chosen by 7 and later 9 electors, ceased to be a strong ruler except where he was the direct ruler and not just the overlord. After the Hapsburg dynasty took over the emperorship (initially in 1273, permanently from 1438 to 1806, with minor exceptions), the center of the empire shifted to Vienna, so it became more Austrian than German.

The Hapsburg Empire encompassed all of what is now Germany, Austria, Switzerland, the Czech and Slovak Republics, Hungary, the Netherlands, Belgium, Luxembourg, and Spain, as well as parts of Poland, Ukraine, Romania, the former Yugoslav federation, Italy and France, at some time during the sixteenth, seventeenth, or eighteenth centuries. Hence, even an emperor who was a weak overlord with respect to the many largely autonomous dukes and other local rulers was often a power to be reckoned with.

Other major developments of the Late Middle Ages included: the development of cities, beginning about 1070; the bubonic plague, known as the Black Death, which killed half the people in the mid-14th century and halted substantial Germanic eastward migration until the Protestant Reformation; the development of strong guilds and large-scale international trade and trade associations (*Hansas*) in the 14th and 15th centuries, with beginnings dating back to the 12th century; and the invention of movable type by Gutenberg in 1450, which rapidly changed the degree and significance of literacy.

THE REFORMATION ERA

The two primary initiators of the Protestant Reformation on the European continent were German-speakers: Luther and Zwingli. There were, however, many others who contributed to a proliferation of Protestant schools of thought, which developed into separate churches.

"Protestantism" actually predated Luther. Some Waldensians, originating with Peter Waldo in 1170, and the Moravian Brethren, stemming from the Hussite movement that gained strength after John Huss (Jan Hus) was burned for heresy in 1415, survived. Both groups later found refuge in Germany.

Protestantism (mostly Lutherans, but also Calvinists, with small pockets of Anabaptists) became the dominant religion in German areas in the first few decades after the Reformation, but the Counter-Reformation regained Catholic predominance in Bavaria and the Rhineland, as well as portions of southwestern Germanic areas and Westphalia. The Peasants' War of 1524-25, which was directed against oppression by secular authorities and feudal lords but inspired by Luther's "revolt" against the church, was squashed and left the peasants in a miserable and lethargic condition for several more centuries, especially in southern Germany.

The Catholic Counter-Reformation led to the re-Catholicizing of Poland, Bohemia, Moravia, and Hungary. Thereafter, assimilation tended to follow religious lines, particularly in Poland. German Catholics, especially in the more isolated settlements, tended to become Polonized, whereas the reverse was true for what was left of Polish Protestantism after the Counter-Reformation. But by no means did all members of the two religious minorities become assimilated in terms of their cultural identity. For example, in the Czech Republic and in Hungary the Germans became more solidly Catholic than the Slavs or Magyars.

The Reformation caused a relatively substantial flight of Protestants, especially Dutch, Flemish and Frisian Mennonites, from the then Spanish-ruled Netherlands to what later became known as West Prussia. Calvinists from the Spanish-ruled area also fled eastward, with those speaking Dutch or Flemish going mostly to West Prussia, then under tolerant Polish rule, and the French-speaking ones, known as Walloons, going to German principalities with Reformed rulers, especially the Palatinate and Hesse. Calvinists from some Lutheran-ruled states, like Mecklenburg, also joined the stream of eastward-bound refugees.

The religious wars in the early Reformation period, interspersed with battles against the Turks on the Hungarian frontier, ended with the Peace of Augsburg in 1555. This required people to accept the religion of their ruler, but it applied only to Catholics and Lutherans. Not until 1648 did the Reformed (Calvinist) Church achieve parity.

The Thirty Years' War (1618-48) was the most devastating war ever fought on Germanic and Czech territory. It started as a war to suppress Protestantism in Bohemia, a goal quickly achieved, but continued, with a few truces, as a war that at one time or another involved most of the countries in Europe, with Sweden, Denmark, and France helping the Protestant princes break the power of the Holy Roman Emperor and the Spanish forces on the other side. After 1635, when Catholic France, rather than the Protestant duchies, became the main opponent of its imperial arch-rival, the war lost its religious significance.

Historians estimate that one third or more of the German and Czech people died, many from famine. Many villages were destroyed, survivors were forced to flee, farmland was left uncultivated and commerce virtually ceased. But the amount of devastation was much greater in some areas than in others. As part of the postwar reconstruction, there was a major migration of people from areas that had been spared, more or less, to those which suffered the most. This took nearly a century.

In particular, large numbers of people from the Alpine Swiss and Tyrolean area moved northward to Württemberg, Thuringia, the Palatinate, Alsace and neighboring areas. This helps explain why the Schweitzer surname occurs in so many villages in these regions. The west central and northwestern Germanic areas also suffered relatively little, so Flemings and Walloons (today's Belgians), as well as people from the Holstein area, were well represented among those who moved eastward and southeastward to repopulate almost empty villages.

Mecklenburg, Pomerania, Northern Brandenburg and Saxony-Anhalt were also areas that suffered heavily, but the northeasternmost German lands, including Prussia, escaped serious destruction. Mecklenburg and Western Pomerania never fully recovered from the deaths of two-thirds of their residents.

The Peace of Westphalia in 1648 recognized the independence of Switzerland and the Netherlands and gave the hundreds of German rulers almost complete independence from the emperor in Vienna, who technically remained their overlord until the empire was formally abolished in 1806.

The Hapsburgs continued to dominate the lands they ruled directly, i.e., what came to be the Austrian (after 1867, Austro-Hungarian) Empire, but they ceased to matter in the political affairs of Germany proper after 1648, except as an outside power seeking to influence events.

Most of Alsace became part of France in 1648, after the war, although it had previously belonged to the Holy Roman Empire. Lorraine had a distinct history, becoming a part of France in 1766. Alsace and the northeastern fifth of Lorraine (so-called "German Lorraine") were part of the German Empire from 1871 to 1919.

Several groups of religious refugees settled in Germany after 1648. The Huguenots, most of whom were well-educated (including quite a few nobles), left France after the revocation of the Edict of Nantes in 1685 and settled in areas with Reformed rulers. The largest number went to Brandenburg. Wolfgang Ribbe states that at one time one-third of all Berliners were Huguenots. The Huguenot impact upon Saxony-Anhalt, especially Magdeburg, was also very substantial. Other settlements were in the Palatinate and other areas near the Rhine (including Alsace), the Frankfurt/Main-Hanau area, Hesse-Kassel, Franconia, cities in northwestern Germany and East Prussia. (Incidentally, a smaller number of Huguenot refugees had fled to Germany earlier as a result of the nine Huguenot Wars between 1562 and 1625.)

Many of the Huguenots from southern France originally fled to Geneva and then to Berne and Basel. Because of French pressure, they were forced to leave Switzerland, with most of them going to Germany.

Waldensians, whose original stronghold had been in mountainous southeastern France, were expelled from the duchy of Savoy (now northwestern Italy) in 1688. They developed a close connection with the Huguenots in Germany.

Another French-speaking group were the Orangeois, expelled from the duchy of Orange (Oranien) in the Burgundian part of eastern France in 1704.

Finally, some 20,000 Lutherans were expelled from the archbishopric of Salzburg (Austria) in the 1730s. About 14,000 settled in East Prussia. Others went to Franconia, Swabia and Lithuania, as well as to the United States (state of Georgia).

THE LATE MODERN ERA

Soon after the Thirty Years' War, a new German power began to arise in the northeast. In 1701 the Berlin-centered Mark of Brandenburg became the Kingdom of Prussia, taking its name from the Balto-Slavic tribe that the Teutonic Knights had largely annihilated. In 1740 it wrested almost all of Silesia from Austria. When Poland was partitioned in 1772-95, Prussia gained control over more than three-fourths of what constitutes Poland today, excluding only the southeastern area, roughly east of a line from Cracow to Warsaw. However, Central Poland, around Warsaw and Lodz, became the Duchy of Warsaw created by Napoleon and fell under Russian control after 1815. The eastern and western parts of Pomerelia (West Prussia) acquired by Prussia in the first two partitions were predominantly German-speaking, with a substantial German minority in Posen, central West Prussia, and the Netze River district, which belonged to Posen in the nineteenth century but constituted a distinct administrative entity during certain periods of history. Most of the Netze River area had a German majority in 1918. Prussian rule led to a heavy influx of Germans into Posen, and to a lesser but still quite significant degree, into Central Poland.

Meanwhile, Napoleon ruled many of the small independent German states much of the time from 1792 to 1815. There were many and frequent border changes, but the end result was the consolidation of over 300 existing principalities into 39 medium-sized ones. He also instituted civil registration of births, marriages and deaths in Hanover, Hesse, Baden and the areas to the west of them.

French nationalism led to German counter-nationalism, which led to the Wars of Liberation of 1813-15 and the liberal revolutions of 1830 and 1848 that sought a free and united Germany. After those events were suppressed, the German Empire was established under Otto von Bismarck's leadership as a result of the wars of 1864-71 against Denmark, Austria and France, respectively.

German nationalism, and especially Prussian policies seeking to Germanicize the Poles by coercion, in turn led to Polish nationalism. This produced the migration of many Germans in Central Poland to Eastern Poland, which had a substantial Ukrainian population and to a heavily Ukrainian Volhynia. The powerful wave of nationalism did not reach Russia and Ukraine until the 1870s, when it sparked German emigrations from there to the Americas.

Prussia controlled most of the northern half of Germany after 1815. Thus immigrants who renounced allegiance to the Prussian king upon naturalization as American citizens may have come from as far away from Prussia proper as the province of Rhineland.

The German Customs Union, established in 1833-36, and the building of a railroad system that bound the entire country together by the late 1850s, stimulated trade and facilitated travel. This made it much easier for a would-be emigrant from inland areas not close to navigable rivers to reach the ocean ports of Bremen, Antwerp, and especially Hamburg.

Karl Marx issued the *Communist Manifesto* in 1848. It was at about this time that the Industrial Revolution in Germany, begun in the 1840s, started to accelerate. Over the next several decades, mass production eliminated the cottage industries on which many small farmers depended for the supplemental income needed to survive.

The slums, which housed the early farm migrants turned factory workers, were probably one of the reasons why many villagers who were forced to relocate decided it might be better to go overseas (primarily to the United States) as farmers than to enter the industrial jungle. Bismarck instituted major social welfare programs in the 1880s in order to undercut the political appeal of the growing socialist party. The adoption of these measures was soon followed by the end of large-scale German emigration.

The wars of unification also contributed significantly to emigration, because many Germans did not care to serve in the armed forces of an empire dominated by Prussia, which had already long been regarded as a militaristic state. Those who fought in these wars often left in order to spare their sons that experience.

It is noteworthy, however, that many emigrants who had left Germany because of their antipathy to the authorities began to develop a sense of identification with German nationalism after Bismarck's many successes led to growing international respect for Germany as a major world power.

The end of World War I saw the reestablishment of an independent Poland, which included almost all of Posen, central West Prussia and eastern Silesia; and an independent Lithuania, which acquired the Memel territory, formerly belonging to East Prussia, in 1923. Germany also lost Alsace-Lorraine (which it had acquired in 1871) to France, the Eupen-Malmedy region to Belgium, and North Schleswig to Denmark. All of these, especially Alsace, were ethnically mixed areas from which a significant number of German-speaking emigrants went to both Eastern Europe and to the New World.

Bohemia and Moravia, which became part of Czechoslovakia, had belonged to the Austrian (not the German) Empire before 1918-19. But after World War I, these Germans began to identify more with a strong Germany than with a weak Austria. This area constituted the Sudetenland, which Hitler annexed in 1938.

In 1944-45 an estimated 5 million Germans fled westward from the areas east of the Oder-Neisse line in fear of the advancing Soviet armies. The Allies decided at the Potsdam Conference in 1945 to put this area under Polish administration, at least tacitly to compensate Poland for the loss of its eastern territories to the Soviet Union. Most of the Germans who had remained in the area (over 3 million) were expelled in or shortly after 1945. Most of those who were left (several hundred thousand, most of them married to Poles or otherwise largely assimilated into the Polish population) "resettled" in West Germany after both the Gorbachev "thaw" and the somewhat earlier and faster thaw in Poland made this possible. This area, eventually recognized *de jure* as part of Poland, included the former German states of East and West Prussia, most of Silesia, the eastern parts of Pomerania and Brandenburg, and a tiny corner of southeast Saxony.

The rest of Germany was divided into Soviet, American, British and French occupation zones, with four analogous sectors in Berlin. In 1949 the three Western zones were transformed into the Federal Republic of Germany, with a substantial rearrangement of the former states into what soon became 11 new states (*Länder*), including West Berlin, which had a special status, and the Saar, which remained under French control for a few years. The other states were Baden-Württemberg (3 states until 1952), Bavaria, Bremen, Hamburg, Hesse, Lower Saxony, Northrhine-Westphalia, Rhineland-Palatinate and Schleswig-Holstein. Lower Saxony, Northrhine-Westphalia and Rhineland-Palatinate were new political entities, not based on historic precedent. Hesse was a combination of several former states, as was Baden-Württemberg. Only Bavaria, Schleswig-Holstein and the city-states of Hamburg and Bremen represented continuity with the past.

The German Democratic Republic, a Communist state despite its name, was created by the Soviet Union as a response to an independent West Germany. Here the state boundaries were also changed, indeed twice, with the end result being 15 districts (*Bezirke*), which were deliberately drawn so as to represent a maximum break with the past.

In 1989-90, change overtook East Germany with lightning speed. Free elections were held when the Communist colossus collapsed very suddenly, following political liberalization in Poland, the Soviet Union, Hungary and Czechoslovakia and the mass flight of East Germans to the West through Hungary and Czechoslovakia. Within months Germany was reunited, and the "5 new states" of Saxony, Thuringia, Saxony-Anhalt, Brandenburg, and Mecklenburg-Vorpommern (a 1990 reestablishment of states that existed for a brief period after World War II) were technically admitted into the Federal Republic of Germany.

Now, perhaps for the first time in history, there is no dispute by national governments as to what constitutes Germany. But a large number of New World residents have German-speaking ancestors who immigrated from areas outside contemporary Germany. Their common heritage is language and culture, not necessarily identification with any past or present political entity.

THE AUSTRO-HUNGARIAN EMPIRE OF 1867 TO 1919

During the last two decades of the nineteenth century, when the largest number of German-speaking immigrants came to America, the second largest population of ethnic Germans was in the Austro-Hungarian Empire.

Roughly the western half of this empire had belonged to the Holy Roman Empire of the German Nation prior to its abolition by Napoleon in 1806. This area could be divided into what had been the archduchy of Austria from 1359 to 1804 (and a duchy, or sometimes more than one duchy, since 1156) and what had been the kingdom of Bohemia since 1158.

The eastern half was the kingdom of Hungary (dating back to A.D. 1000), which had also elected the Hapsburg emperor to be king in 1526 when the Ottoman Turks defeated the Hungarians. It had remained under Hapsburg control thereafter, but never was a part of the Holy Roman Empire.

The German word for Austria, "Österreich," means "eastern kingdom or empire." This was the easternmost part of the empire of Karl der Grosse, better known to us as "Charlemagne," and came under his control about the time he was crowned "Emperor of the Romans" (A.D. 800). Known initially as the "Ostmark," or "Eastern March," it has had a continuous existence since the tenth century, when it began as a margravate of Bavaria.

In 843, Louis the German received the lands east of the Rhine in the tripartite division of Charlemagne's empire. This marks the beginning of the separate development of French and German ethnic or linguistic identities, both originating from the same Frank tribe (although other Germanic tribes lived in both areas). The area became increasingly disunited until 962, when Otto I (the Great), the Saxon king of what was then the northern Germanic area, established the Holy Roman Empire, or, in a sense, re-established the united empire of Charles the Great.

In 1273, Rudolph I of Hapsburg ("Rudolf von Habsburg" in German) was elected both king of Germany (a largely honorific title, since most power was in the hands of the legally subordinate dukes) and Holy Roman Emperor. Although the "Habsburg" (hawk's castle) was in Switzerland and the dynasty originated in Alsace, the Count of Hapsburg soon established control over Austria and Styria by defeating the local ruler. This remained the core of the Hapsburg dominions, and the area that they actually ruled directly (in contrast to the much larger imperial area over which they had only nominal control).

To their holdings, the Hapsburgs added Carinthia and Carniola (*Kärnten* and *Krain*) in 1335, Tyrol (*Tirol*) in 1363, Istria (*Istrien*) in 1374, what was to become Vorarlberg in and after 1375, Trieste in 1382, Gorizia in 1500 and other Friuli (*Friaul*) districts in 1511.

Hence, even though the emperorship itself was a weak office after 1250, the extensive holdings of the Hapsburgs made them a power to be reckoned with throughout Europe. Thus the fact that the Hapsburgs served almost continuously as Holy Roman Emperors from 1438 to 1806 has led quite properly to historical references to "the Hapsburg Empire" as a major factor in great power politics.

Since the Reformation and the Counter-Reformation are very significant events for the purpose of explaining subsequent migration within and from Europe, it is noteworthy that from 1519 to 1556 (i.e., during the infancy of Protestantism), the Hapsburg dynasty, as a result of marriages, also ruled Spain, Burgundy, the Netherlands, most of Belgium, Luxembourg, much of Italy, and the Spanish possessions in the Americas. In 1526, Hungary and Bohemia were added. Therefore, they had an extraordinary concentration of power in Europe at that time, despite the limits of imperial authority.

On the other hand, the Ottoman Turks reached the gates of Vienna in 1529 before being turned back. For nearly two centuries, they ruled most of the Balkans and forced the Austrian ruler to pay for the privilege of ruling the remaining sliver of Western Hungary and Northern or Upper Hungary, i.e., today's Slovak Republic and Carpatho-Ukraine. In 1683, the Turks again approached Vienna and were repelled. But this time their retreat led to the reconquest of nearly all of Old Hungary (which then included large parts of what later became Romania and Yugoslavia) by 1688 (officially recognized by treaty in 1699), and additional gains (the Banat) in 1718.

Meanwhile, Protestantism had made significant strides, especially in Bohemia. In fact, John Huss had preceded Luther as a "Protestant" by a century. The initially splintered Hussites dominated Bohemia and Moravia for two centuries.

The Thirty Years' War (actually a series of wars, with brief truces) broke out in 1618 as a Catholic-Protestant conflict. The Protestant forces in Bohemia were squelched in 1620, but what had begun as a religious war gradually turned into a political war—fully so in 1635, when the Catholic French king intervened on the side of the Protestants in order to check his Hapsburg rival.

In 1648 an utterly exhausted Europe finally agreed to the Peace of Westphalia. Although it took more than another century before religious toleration became the policy in the Hapsburg lands, the days when dissident Christians were put to death for their beliefs were over. Swiss and Dutch independence, long a fact, was officially recognized.

For further information concerning the Hapsburg Empire, particularly as it relates to events of the Reformation era, see the previous section on **THE GERMAN EMPIRE**, since the Reformation had a greater impact on German history than on Austrian history.

The last 65 years of the Holy Roman Empire saw numerous changes in territorial control. In 1742, the Hapsburgs lost the greater part of tri-national Silesia (German, Czech, Polish) to Prussia and failed in the effort to gain it back in the Seven Years' War (1756-63). In the first partition of Poland in 1772, Austria gained the kingdoms of Galicia and Lodomeria. Adjacent territory to the north gained in 1795 was lost in 1809. The Bukovina (also known as "Buchenland") was obtained in 1775 from the Turkish-ruled principality of Moldavia in return for Austria's mediation in the Russo-Turkish Peace.

During the Napoleonic Wars (specifically in 1797, 1803-05 and 1809) numerous territorial changes took place, with most being Austrian losses. These included Tyrol and Salzburg. But when the wars were over in 1815, the Hapsburgs were left with full control over modern-day Austria, Czechoslovakia, Hungary, much of northern Italy, and significant portions of Yugoslavia, Romania and Poland, although they had lost Belgium and some Polish territory.

In 1859 and 1866, Austria lost most of its Italian territories in the Italian Wars of Unification. But the joint Austro-Hungarian government also expanded its territory by occupying Bosnia and Herzegovina in 1878 and annexing this area in 1908.

Defeat by the Prussians in the Seven Weeks' War (1866) eliminated Austria as a political force in the lands that formed the German Empire in 1871. This weakening of the Hapsburg authorities also led to the Compromise of 1867, which produced the Austro-Hungarian Empire, a Dual Monarchy under the Hapsburgs, but with separate governments and separate policies in the Austrian-ruled and the Hungarian-ruled portions. The "Austrian" part of the empire was often referred to as Cis-Leithania, the Leitha being the small river separating Austria from Hungary.

The Slavs, unlike the Magyars (Hungarians), were not able to assert their authority. While there were more Slavs than Germans or Magyars in the empire, they were divided into numerous linguistic groups. In the north were the Czechs, Slovaks, Poles and Rusins (Ruthenians, closely related to the Ukrainians). In the south were the Slovenes, Serbs and Croats (the latter two with one language, but separate alphabets and different religions). In addition, there were the Romanians, Italians, Jews, Gypsies, and several small groups, which did not belong to any of the three big categories.

The arrangement from the Compromise of 1867 led to quite different language policies in the two halves. The Hungarians made strong efforts to "Magyarize" the non-Hungarians under their jurisdiction, resulting in a decline in those who spoke German, especially in the cities. Meanwhile, the Austrians sought to hold their monarchy together by de-emphasizing the importance of the German language. This led to Germans living in linguistic enclaves in predominantly non-German areas (Slovenia, for example) feeling pressure to adopt another language and it led to friction in Bohemia and Moravia, where there were large numbers of both Germans and Czechs. These policies may have been a factor in some emigration decisions. American and Hungarian statistics indicate that Germans accounted for 15-20% of the immigrants from Hungary in 1898-1913, a much higher emigration rate than that of the Magyars, although well below that of the Slovaks.

Incidentally, while the American "melting pot" never mirrored the pattern in Europe (where various ethnic groups lived side by side), there were probably more cases of assimilation than we may think. Germanicization, Polonization, Magyarization and absorption by other ethnic groups were a significant part of European history, although the process often took longer than it usually has in the New World.

Who absorbed whom? The answer can usually be found in one of two criteria: either the larger number swallowed the minority in its midst or those of higher status (be it authority or economic development) incorporated the others into their culture. Where these were at odds (e.g., a high-status minority within a low-status majority), separate identities sometimes continued to coexist for many centuries.

According to C. A. Macartney, in *The Habsburg Empire, 1790-1918*, there were about 2.8 million ethnic Germans in the Austrian hereditary and crown lands in 1780, about 1.6 million in the Bohemian crown lands and nearly 1 million in the Hungarian crown lands, accounting for about one quarter of the empire's total population. By 1900, these figures would have approximately doubled. Boundary changes would not have affected the figures greatly, for there were no large numbers of Germans living in the affected territories.

If we want to trace the distinct history of each major ethnic German group that belonged to the Austro-Hungarian Empire at the time of the major emigrations to North America, we can distinguish between the relatively solid Germanic core in and near Austria proper and the various islands of Germanic settlements elsewhere in the empire.

From 962 to 1438 (the chief era of Germanic eastward expansion), the emperors came mostly from present-day western Germany (or Luxembourg), with frequent conflicts for the imperial crown. From 1438 until the abolition of the empire in 1806, the Hapsburgs served as emperors (except for 3 years), thus effectively turning a German empire into an Austrian one (even though the Hapsburgs had roots in the west).

In the former Hapsburg Empire, the dividing line between areas where most people spoke German until the twentieth century and where they spoke other languages changed very little for 600 years or so. Besides what is now Austria, German-speakers predominated in a relatively large area in what is now the Czech Republic and a quite small area in what is now Italy. Of course, along both of these boundaries, as well as those with Hungary (Burgenland) and Slovenia (Styria), there were some ethnically mixed areas.

BOHEMIA AND MORAVIA

Since the Germans actually represented a majority of the population in those parts of the Czech Republic that bordered on Germany and Austria, and the Kingdom of Bohemia (which included this area) was a distinct entity for centuries, this sub-unit of the Austro-Hungarian Empire will be dealt with separately.

Relatively large-scale Germanic migration to the Czech Republic (Bohemia and Moravia, including the small part of Silesia that remained under Austrian control after the 1740s and was incorporated into Moravia in the 1920s) occurred during the twelfth and especially the thirteenth and fourteenth centuries, although there are traces of a German presence much earlier. The Hussite wars of the fifteenth century, which had ethnic overtones, resulted in a modest retreat in the area of German settlement. But the forcible re-Catholicization policies of the Hapsburg authorities also led to the expulsion of many Protestant Germans in the seventeenth century.

Renewed Germanic immigration occurred during the modern era, especially as a result of the Thirty Years' War (1618-48), which devastated the Kingdom of Bohemia. Bob Ullman states that (mostly German) Catholics were awarded the estates of the (mostly Czech) Protestants during the 1624-37 period after the decisive Battle of White Mountain in 1620 (*German Genealogical Society of America Newsletter*, August 1994). There was a heavy influx of Catholics, most of them Germans, during the century after 1648.

However, the Germans in the Czech Republic never were a cohesive group until after World War I, when the term, "Sudeten Germans" (which is geographically accurate only for those in northeastern Bohemia, northern Moravia and Austrian Silesia), came into being. The whole area became a part of the Hapsburg Empire in 1620, although members of the Hapsburg dynasty ruled Bohemia and Moravia most of the time after 1526.

Basically, the Germans settled along the mountainous outer rimland of Bohemia, Moravia and Austrian Silesia (now the Czech Republic), with each group coming mostly from the adjacent Germanic or Germanicized area. Counter-clockwise and starting from the northeastern tip of the C-shaped area, this meant they were a spillover from Silesia (populated mostly by Germanicized Slavs), Saxony, Franconia (now Northern Bavaria, but with distinct tribal roots), Bavaria and Austria. Of course, there were ethnically mixed regions between the overwhelmingly German and the overwhelmingly Czech areas, especially in the south and in northern Moravia. There was a mixed Czech-Polish-German population in Eastern Austrian Silesia, with the area from Cieszyn (*Teschen*) east becoming part of Poland, and the area to the west now part of the Czech Republic. The mostly Germanic Czech rimland area became known as the Sudetenland and was annexed by Hitler, pursuant to the Munich Agreement of 1938.

As elsewhere in Eastern Europe, there were also many German urbanites, especially in Prague. Moreover, there were islands of German settlements in the interior or outside the Germanic core area. The largest one, which was not sharply separated from the German rimland, was the *Schönhengst* (Hrebec) area around *Mährisch-Trübau* (Moravská Trebová) and *Zwittau* (Svitavy). Others were at *Iglau* (Jihlava), *Brünn* (Brno), *Olmütz* (Olomouc), *Mährisch-Ostrau* (Ostrava), *Wischau* (Vysov) and *Budweis* (Cesky Budejovice).

Many Bohemian Germans moved farther eastward, especially between 1750 and 1850. They accounted for a large percentage of those who migrated to the Bukovina after 1775 and a small percentage of the so-called "Danube Swabians" in the last half of the eighteenth century. Bohemian weavers also were among those who settled along the southern and western borders of Posen, from where some of them migrated onward to Russian Poland.

Many migrated to the United States, Brazil, and New Zealand, beginning in the 1850s, but peaking in the 1880s and 1890s.

GERMAN ENCLAVES IN NON-GERMANIC PARTS OF THE HAPSBURG EMPIRE

After World War I, the eastern parts of the Hapsburg Empire, from which most German emigrants came, except during the Nazi era, were fragmented into countries whose borders were roughly along ethnic lines, but with sizable German and other minorities in all of them.

South Tyrol: On the Italian boundary, even after the unification of Italy, Austria continued to rule over an Italian-speaking area around *Trent* (Trient/Trento). In 1910 what was then the Austrian province of Tyrol had a ratio of about 4:3 in German and Italian speakers, respectively. After World War I, this was remedied by giving South Tyrol to Italy. But there was a small overcorrection, putting German-speaking *Bozen* (Bolzano) and *Meran* (Merano) in Italy, so that the boundary would be at the strategic Brenner Pass. This led to a German revanchist movement, which seems to have quieted down in recent decades, after the Italian government liberalized its policies toward identification with a Germanic heritage.

With respect to the German islands in the non-German areas, these can be divided into those dating back to the Middle Ages and those resulting from colonization efforts during the modern era, mostly in the eighteenth century.

Transylvanian Saxons: The Transylvanian Saxons are probably the most well known of the medieval settlers. They were invited to settle in the eastern border area of Hungary by its king in the twelfth century. In reality, they were mostly Franks, not Saxons, but since the Saxons lived next to the Hungarians, the latter may have thought of all Germans as Saxons. They seem to have come from a broad belt, reaching from Flanders (northern Belgium) on the Atlantic to easternmost Franconia (now northeastern Bavaria) on the Czech border. However, language patterns indicate that the largest number came from the Rhine-Moselle area in what is now Luxembourg and close to the present boundary between Northrhine-Westphalia and Rhineland-Palatinate.

These settlers in the *Siebenbürgen* (Erdély) area were under Turkish rule for about a century and a half, but they retained some local autonomy as a vassal state and suffered much less than those areas closer to the battlefront. There are several remarkable things about this group. Firstly, they lived as free and relatively equal people, never experiencing the feudal system. Secondly, they maintained their German identity very strongly a long time. Thirdly, they all became Lutherans while under Turkish rule, which in effect protected them from any pressures by Catholic secular or church authorities.

German-speakers from Saxony, the Rhineland, Flanders, Bavaria and Austria settled in Slovakia (especially in the *Zips* region), beginning in the early 1100s, more or less simultaneously with the Transylvanian Saxons and for the same defensive purposes. Some of these *Zips* residents migrated to northern Transylvania, where they became known as the *Nösner Zipser*. They lived in the area around Bistrita (*Bistritz*).

In 1241 the Mongols destroyed many of these settlements, but they were again rebuilt by Germans, especially during the period up to 1270, with significant immigration continuing until 1346, when the bubonic plague (Black Death) largely halted Germanic eastward migration. By then, there were several hundreds of thousands of Germans in what was known as Upper Hungary at the time. They dominated the political and commercial life of the towns. Compared with other Germanic settlements, an unusually high percentage of these Germans earned their living from non-agricultural pursuits, such as mining, commerce and various crafts.

Slovakia: The Turkish conquest of much of Hungary in the sixteenth and seventeenth centuries resulted in a large influx of Hungarians from the south. As a result, the influence of Magyars and Slovaks increased, with German-majority areas reduced to several enclaves.

These included the *Hauerland* in central Slovakia, Bratislava (*Pressburg*) and the surrounding area on the Austrian border, and the Spis (*Zips*) region in eastern Slovakia. Each of the three enclaves (each one actually consisting of proximate, but not adjoining, clusters of villages) in Slovakia had about 40,000-50,000 Germans in 1930.

The *Hauerland* (the term derives from *hauen*, which means "hew," in this case referring to mining, rather than clearing forests) actually consists of two twin enclaves centered around *Deutsch-Proben* (Nitrianske Pravno) and *Kremnitz* (Kremnica).

The *Zips* towns are somewhat farther apart, but also divided into two major enclaves, mostly in or near the Poprad and Hornad-Hnilec river valleys. The Upper *Zips* settlement, somewhat 8-shaped, is around Kezmarok (*Käsmark*) and Levoca (*Leutschau*). These towns formed the *Zipser Bund* (Zips League), which served to foster their commerce, and obtained local autonomy at an early date.

The Lower *Zips* area, west of Kosice (*Kaschau*), had a flourishing metalworking industry until the 1860s, when it was severely hurt by the Industrial Revolution. As a result, many of these Germans emigrated to larger industrial centers in Europe or to the United States.

The best treatment of this group is in Duncan B. Gardiner, *German Towns in Slovakia and Upper Hungary*.

Subcarpathian Rus': For information on the Germans in this area (also known as Carpatho-Ukraine), who were transferred from Czechoslovakia to the Soviet Union as a result of World War II, see Victoria Nied, "My Heritage in the Sub-Carpathian Ukraine," in the summer 1993 issue of *Nase Rodina* (the newsletter of the Czechoslovak Genealogical Society International). She refers to a book, *Deutsch Mokrá-Königsfeld: Eine deutsche Siedlung in den Waldkarpaten*. Some 200 people from Upper Austria moved here in 1775, with others following for at least four decades. She has also published a second article, "From Mokra to the Melting Pot," which deals with emigration from this area to Romania, Argentina, the United States and Canada, in the Summer 1996 issue of the *Journal of the American Historical Society of Germans from Russia*.

Slovenia: Germans also lived in various localities in northern Slovenia, particularly around Ljubljana (*Laibach*) and Maribor (*Marburg*) as early as the twelfth century and began settling around *Gottschee* (now Kocevje) in the south, beginning about 1310. The first wave of settlers apparently came from Carniola. Later waves of settlers are believed to have come mostly from eastern Tyrol. The more cohesive *Gottschee* group is of special interest to American genealogists because of massive emigration to the United States. Their story is told by L. Edward Skender in *A Short History of the Duchy of Carniola and Gottschee County*.

Danube Swabians: By far the most numerous among the modern German settlers are the Danube Swabians, formerly known as Hungarian Germans. However, the largest number came from Lorraine, with only a minority of them coming from Swabia (Württemberg). But they were called Swabians because they embarked at Ulm in Swabia and sailed down the Danube River to the many settlements in what was then Hungary. These areas had been won back from the Turks in 1699 and 1718. Most of the migrants arrived in 1765-72 and 1784-88, after an earlier wave of settlers in 1722-29 had been virtually annihilated in the 1737-39 Turkish War.

The largest of these settlements was in the Banat, the area around Timisoara (*Temeschwar* or *Temeschburg*) and southwest to Belgrade. The eastern Banat is now in Romania and the western part in Serbian Vojvodina, with the northwestern tip reaching toward Szeged in

Hungary. A second major colony was in the Bácska (*Batschka*), northwest of Belgrade and overlapping Serbian Vojvodina and present-day Hungary, with a smaller settlement in Syrmia (*Syrmien*) squeezed between Belgrade and the Bácska.

Still farther west was the Baranya (*Baranja*) settlement, along with other villages in Eastern Croatia (Slavonia) and the adjacent parts of Bosnia. Many Germans in Bosnia were government officials and entrepreneurs, who arrived after Austria took over this area in 1878, or people from the Banat, the Bácska and Syrmia migrating one step farther southwestward in the second half of the 1880s.

Some Germans, especially Catholics, settled in the Banja Luka area in north central Bosnia, partly as a result of Bismarck's anti-Catholic *Kulturkampf* in the 1870s, which left many parishes without priests.

Swabian Turkey is in today's Hungary, in the area near Pécs (*Fünfkirchen*). There were also German settlements in the Central Highlands near Budapest. Most of these Germans also settled there after the reconquest of most of Hungary, although there had been Germans in the area well before the Ottoman takeover. In fact, three-fourths of the residents of Budapest 1848 were German-speakers. This percentage, however, included such a substantial number of Jews that the city was sometimes referred to derogatorily as "Judapest." But Budapest became Magyarized very rapidly after 1867, so that by 1905, 85% of the residents were Hungarians (which category now included the 23% who were Jewish), with only 9% Germans.

Satu Mare: Germans in the Satu Mare (*Sathmar*) region, in what is now the northwesternmost corner of Romania, arrived from "Swabia" between 1712 and 1815, so they are kin to the Danube Swabians in terms of origin and period of immigration, although far away from the Danube. The most thorough account of this group can be found in Jacob Steigerwald, *Tracing Romania's Heterogeneous German Minority from Its Origins to the Diaspora.*

Galicia: A relatively large number of Germans were settled in Galicia, primarily in East Galicia, in 1782-85, after this fell into Austrian hands. There had been Germans in Western Galicia in the Middle Ages, but they had been thoroughly Polonized by the time the new stream arrived.

These German immigrants came mostly from the southwest Germanic area, with the largest number coming from what is now the state of Rhineland-Palatinate.

The Bukovina: It is estimated that 1,750-2,000 German-speakers immigrated to the Bukovina: 350-400 from Swabia; 1,100-1,300 from Bohemia; and an additional 3,000-4,000 from other parts of the Austrian Empire, including Galicia. See Sophie A. Welisch, "The Bukovina-Germans during the Habsburg Period: Settlement, Interaction, Contributions," in *Immigrants and Minorities*, Vol. 5, No. 1 (March 1986).

The first Danube Swabians migrated from the Banat to the Bukovina in 1782 without government sponsorship. Most of their ancestors had come from the Mannheim-Mainz areas.

In 1787, after the Bukovina had been annexed to Galicia, Galician authorities settled 74 mostly Protestant families in eight existing communities on a line between *Czernowitz* (Cernauti, now Chernivtsi, Ukraine) and *Sutschawa* (Suceava). Over two-thirds of these families had their roots in Württemberg, the Rhine Palatinate, Baden, and Nassau (Hesse-Nassau). About the same time, Germanic families came from the *Zips* district to work in a mine at Jakobeny on the Bistritz River, with other Zipsers arriving in 1797, and went to work at a new silver mine in Kirlibaba. A third group of Germans were Catholics of Bohemian origin who settled in the Bukovina in 1793. Beginning in 1843, farm families began arriving from the *Pilsen* (Plzen) and Prachatitz districts in Bohemia.

The Hungarians made distinctions among the "Saxons" in Transylvania; the "Swabians" along the Danube or its tributaries; and the "Germans," a term they applied only to the residents of cities (merchants, officials, etc.).

Religion: One important event should be borne in mind in researching German immigration to the eastern parts of the Hapsburg Empire. In 1781, the *Toleranzpatent* guaranteeing religious liberty was issued. This means that the modern immigrants prior to 1781 were exclusively Catholics, whereas the later immigrants represented a religious mix, with the Protestants (who were a combination of Lutherans and Reformed, with a tiny Mennonite minority) dominant at least in Galicia. Austrian Protestant refugees fled eastward, mostly to Transylvania, where they were given a haven by its German Lutherans, prior to 1781. Jews far outnumbered German Christians in Galicia and the Bukovina.

Population in Germanic Enclaves: Relying on *The Ethnic German Refugee in Austria, 1945 to 1954*, by Tony Radspieler, and other sources, the number of Germans in each group outside present-day Austria must have been approximately as follows prior to 1938: Sudeten Germans, 3-4 million; Danube Swabians, over 1 million; Transylvanian Saxons, 250,000; the Bukovina, Galicia and Satu Mare, each 50,000-100,000; Slovenia, Bosnia-Herzegovina and South Tyrol, each 15,000-25,000. Galicia and the Bukovina had about 100,000 Jews each, many of whom later moved to Vienna. Since they were sometimes classified as Germans in the censuses and sometimes not, this explains widely differing figures from different sources.

Repatriation, Expulsion and Emigration: Under the Hitler-Stalin Pact of 1939 and similar agreements with Romania (1940), Italy (1941) and Croatia (1942), ethnic Germans were given the opportunity for repatriation to a *Reich* that their ancestors had left more than five generations earlier. Actually they were sent mostly to the Warthegau, or Warta River region in Poland. Over 400,000 Germans, including many from former Austro-Hungarian areas (the Bukovina, the Dobruja and Yugoslavia) made that "choice." The first two groups came from what had been designated as Stalin's "sphere of influence" (but not from within the then existing Soviet borders).

In 1945-48, after the Hitler era, most Germans were expelled from the non-Austrian countries formerly part of the Hapsburg Empire. This was true to the greatest extent in Yugoslavia and Czechoslovakia, and least likely in Romania. While they went to Germany and Austria initially, many of these expellees were soon scattered throughout the Americas, Australasia and other areas. Many Romanian Germans followed them overseas in the 1980s, when the conditions for emigration were eased.

THE RUSSIAN EMPIRE of 1815 TO 1917

The third great continental European empire that included many German-speaking residents during the years of peak immigration to North America was the Russian Empire. This will be dealt with in three sub-sections: the Baltic countries, Central Poland and the rest of what was then Russia.

THE BALTIC COUNTRIES (ESTONIA, LATVIA AND LITHUANIA)

The oldest German settlements in the Russian Empire were those in the Baltic countries, especially Latvia and Estonia. Latvia and Southern Estonia were known for centuries as Livonia (eastern part) and Courland (western part). These settlements date back to the late twelfth century, when Germans and Danes sought to Christianize the local tribes. Germans founded the city of Riga ca. 1200.

In 1226, the Polish Duke of Masovia invited the Teutonic Knights to come to the Baltic to convert the neighboring peoples. This Order, originally founded to provide a hospital for the Crusaders in Palestine, soon absorbed the earlier knights, and by 1280 its sword had finished the task of "Christianizing" Livonia (*Livland*), Courland (*Kurland*) and Estonia (*Estland*), as well as (East) Prussia (*Preussen*). The original Prussians (*Borussians*) were a non-Germanic tribe that vanished as a result of decimation, with the survivors assimilating into the conquerors who now took over their name.

In 1385, the grand duke of Lithuania (*Litauen*) married the queen of Poland (*Polen*) to form a personal union of the two countries. Since this act was accompanied by the acceptance of Christianity by the Lithuanians, the original mission of the Teutonic Knights had now been fulfilled. However, the Knights had been authorized by the pope to rule the previously heathen lands they conquered. They continued to govern the entire Prussian-Baltic area, and rather harshly.

In 1410, the Knights suffered a crushing defeat by the Poles at the Battle of Tannenberg (German) or Grunwald (Polish). By 1466, the combined forces of the German cities near the Baltic Sea, who chafed under the rigid rule of the Knights, and Poland had ended the days of the Knights as a major power. The cities were now under the Polish crown, but had a great deal of local autonomy, unlike their status under the Knights. The Knights moved their headquarters from *Marienburg* (now Malbork) to *Königsberg* (now Kaliningrad) and had to accept Polish overlordship with respect to the territory they still ruled. In 1525, the Order of Teutonic Knights accepted Lutheranism, possibly stimulated by the lack of imperial and papal support for their interests.

Livonia and Courland fell under Polish rule in 1561, while Estonia became Swedish. That was the end of the Order of Teutonic Knights in the Baltic East, although it retained scattered possessions in western Germany until it was finally abolished in 1809.

Poland and Lithuania were officially united as one country, rather than two countries with the same monarch, in 1569. For a time, this large empire was the major power in the Baltic. However, Sweden expanded its holdings in the Baltic, step by step, and dominated the coastal regions throughout much of the seventeenth century.

The Great Nordic War of 1700-21 ended Swedish hegemony and substituted that of Peter the Great of Russia. The third, final partition of Poland in 1795 completed Russian acquisition of the Baltic area, except for a Lithuanian-Polish area, which belonged to Prussia from 1795 to 1806 and was known as New East Prussia at the time.

The Baltic German barons became one of the principal sources of administrative, military and diplomatic leaders for the Russian Czars for nearly two centuries. Since Germans owned most of the large estates in the Baltic and constituted the core of the urban mercantile and educational elite, they were in a dominant economic position until after World War I, when the newly independent countries nationalized their estates.

In 1897, there were somewhat more than 200,000 Germans in the Baltic lands, about half of them in Livonia, where they constituted about 8% of the population. In the key city of Riga, however, Germans represented 18% of the residents.

CENTRAL POLAND

The top expert on the Germans in Central Poland is Dr. Oskar Kossmann. His book, *Die Deutschen in Polen seit der Reformation*, is the most detailed history of this group and lists well over 1,000 communities in which Germans lived.

The strongly Polish-populated area under Russian control after 1815 was known as "Congress Poland" from 1815 to 1830, when the First Polish Revolt caused the Czar to terminate the relatively liberal and autonomous constitutional monarchy and place Poland directly under his autocratic personal control. This area continued to be called "Mittelpolen" (Central Poland) by Germans. In 1795, this area had been divided between Prussia (north and west of Warsaw) and Austria (southeast). In 1807, it formed the Grand Duchy of Warsaw, created by Napoleon. At the Congress of Vienna in 1815, it was given to Russia.

The most significant German immigration into this area in the early modern period took the form of "Holländereien." The term originally applied to the farms of the Dutch Mennonite religious refugees in the Danzig-Elbing area. In time, it came to mean their kind of agriculture, i.e., farming based on draining marshy lowlands and emphasizing dairy cattle. Though the very first *Holländereien* in Central Poland probably were the creation of these Dutch people, a heavy majority of those to whom this term later applied were German immigrants. These lowland farms initially were found along the Vistula, but a mixture of lowlands and uplands farms (the latter "Hauländereien," based on Pomeranian experience) developed in the areas east of *Thorn* (Torun) and north of *Kalisch* (Kalisz).

The large number of German settlements along the Vistula River consisted mostly of people who came up the river from West Prussia, although there were some South Germans there.

There were also a few Silesian weavers who came to the Lodz area in the sixteenth and seventeenth centuries. There they served as a magnet for the tremendous influx of both tradesmen and peasants into Poland in general, and the Lodz area in particular, beginning in the 1780s. The religious toleration decreed by the Polish Diet in 1768, and the increasing land rents in German areas as they developed, probably contributed to this wave of immigration.

Most of the immigrants were peasants from the Netze River region and neighboring parts of Pomerania, West Prussia, and the Neumark, with a second major influx from Swabia and other areas in southwest Germany in 1795-1806, when Prussia ruled the area. There was a huge class distinction between the two, with the terms "Kashubs" and "Schwabs" used in a highly pejorative sense. The term "Schwabs" was an abbreviation of "Swabians." The Kashubians are actually a tribe closely related to the Poles, but the Germans from the northwest came from the general vicinity of the medieval Duchy of Cassubia (bounded approximately by the Oder, Netze and Vistula rivers).

The Lodz area was the primary beneficiary of German immigration in the 1819-34 period, when the Lutheran population of Central Poland, an approximation of the German population, increased 50%. This was even more the case thereafter, when Lodz grew at what Kossmann calls an "American tempo," and was the only part of Central Poland with a strong inflow of German immigrants. Tradesmen, particularly weavers, moved to Lodz in huge numbers after 1815, especially from Posen and Silesia. The reason was access to the Eastern markets for cloth and clothing, since this location put them within the Russian customs zone instead of having to pay heavy duties to export their products. In its heyday, Lodz was one of the foremost textile centers in the world.

Notwithstanding that, a large majority of the Germans lived in rural areas and pursued farming. The crowded conditions that developed in the areas west and north of Warsaw led many to move farther east, where there had been few Germans previously. The Second Polish Revolt in 1863 and the freeing of the serfs in the Russian Empire in 1864, which changed both the political and the economic climate, led many Germans to migrate to Volhynia. A smaller number settled in the Chelm area west of the Bug River, thus remaining within Central Poland.

The principal concentrations of Germans in Central Poland prior to 1944-45 could be found along the Vistula River, from Thorn to slightly south of Warsaw, in the area between the Vistula and Drewenz Rivers east of Thorn; along both sides of the Netze and Warta Rivers, as well as between them and south of the latter almost to Kalisz; and in the area around Lodz. In 1865, 80% of the people in Lodz, including many Jews, spoke German. By 1905, after an influx of Polish factory workers, 40% of the residents were identified as Germans and 25% as Jews.

There were over 400,000 Germans in Central Poland in 1897. Although this number declined somewhat over the next 40 years, the main exodus occurred in 1944-45, when the Germans either fled before the advancing Soviet armies or were expelled pursuant to the Potsdam Agreement. Most of those who were left (who tended to be Polonized) emigrated to West Germany after liberalized Polish policies and the advent of *glasnost* in 1987 made this possible.

RUSSIA, UKRAINE, BELARUS, THE CAUCASUS, MOLDOVA AND ASIA

If we look at German immigration to what our ancestors considered to be "Russia" at the time, it all began with Catherine the Great's Manifesto of 1763.

To be sure, there was a prologue. A "German Suburb" of Moscow, which had isolated foreigners since the sixteenth century, stimulated Peter the Great's "Westernization" in the first quarter of the 1700s. He had won Russia's window on the Baltic and built St. Petersburg there.

Moreover, small groups of Germans had settled in the region between the Narew and Bug Rivers. Most of these settlements were west of Bialystok and thus in present-day Poland. However, there was a smaller string of settlements due east of Bialystok in what is now Belarussian territory. There were also a handful of villages along the Bug River north of Brest, as well as on the north side of the Prypec River and along its tributary, the Horyn, which flows from Ukraine northward into Belarus. But these settlers are not normally thought of as Germans from Russia, because they started migrating to this area in the sixteenth century when it was not yet under Russian rule and most of it was part of interwar Poland.

Thus it was Catherine the Great who stimulated the first large-scale German migration to what was generally considered to be Russia. She recognized Russia's backwardness and immediately set out to do something about it. Her first manifesto in 1762 was a dud, but the famous second one was spectacularly successful in attracting foreign settlers. By far the majority of these were Germans, but there were also a few from elsewhere.

A primary reason for the effectiveness of this invitation is that it was accompanied by a propaganda and recruitment campaign of Madison Avenue proportions. Another reason why it was so effective is that German peasants had suffered severely from the just ended Seven Years' War (1756-63). This, in addition to their heavy feudal obligations and religious persecution, put them in a mood to listen.

What they heard must have sounded as appealing as the "gold-paved streets" of America did to later generations. They were promised an impressive array of freedoms: free land and freedom to settle where they wanted to (with no feudal overlord), freedom from military service, freedom of religion, freedom to practice any trade, free transportation, interest-free loans for ten years, freedom from taxation for a period of years, freedom to choose their own local government, an assurance of these freedoms to their descendants in perpetuity, and freedom to leave Russia if they did not like it. Small wonder that the Germans in Russia saw this as their "Magna Carta!"

Reality turned out to be less attractive when they found out how undeveloped Russia was. But except for the freedom to locate where they wanted, which was not granted to the first group, these freedoms were honored — for over a hundred years.

The first huge wave of settlers came in 1764-67 before being stopped by German rulers alarmed at the population loss. Most of these newcomers were directed to the hinterlands near the Volga River, where they suffered from robbers, Cossack rebels and Kirghiz nomads who sold their captives into slavery. But the pioneers turned their ill fate around in 20 years and by 1800 they had indeed achieved remarkable prosperity.

A very small percentage of the first immigrants were allowed to settle in scattered locations in the west, particularly near St. Petersburg and Riga.

The Russo-Turkish Wars of 1768-74 and 1787-91 resulted in Russia acquiring approximately the southern half of Ukraine. Since this area had nomads, but few permanent residents, developing what was first known as New Russia, and then as South Russia, became the next colonization objective.

Immigration of Germans to the Black Sea area began with a few Lutherans and a larger group of Mennonites in 1787-89, the first large colony being Chortitza, near Alexandrovsk (now Zaporozhye). A second, larger migration to the Black Sea area occurred in 1803-10.

Prussian Lutherans and Mennonites settled in Eastern Ukraine, primarily in the Molotschna and Prischib colonies near Molochansk, northwest of the Sea of Azov.

During the same period there was a large migration from southwestern Germanic regions, particularly Württemberg, Baden, Bavaria, Hesse, Alsace and the Palatinate, to the area north of Odessa. These settlers included a much higher percentage of Catholics than found in Eastern Ukraine. The Liebental, Kutschurgan, Glückstal and Beresan colonies were the largest early settlements in this area. Some of these Swiss and Württemberger immigrants also founded the first colonies on the Crimean peninsula in 1804-05. There was a larger minority of Reformed church members (Calvinists) in this group than in most others.

In 1806-12, there was another Russo-Turkish War, which led to Russian acquisition of Bessarabia, west of Odessa (now divided between Ukraine and Moldova). Napoleon's crushing of Prussia in 1806-07, his establishment of the Grand Duchy of Warsaw in 1807 and his ultimately disastrous march on Moscow in 1812 created conditions that served as a strong incentive for Germans from Poland and Prussia to move on. This was especially true of the South Germans, known as Swabians, who had been settled in predominantly Polish-speaking areas by the Prussian government in 1795-1806, when Prussia ruled the greater part of Central Poland, as well as the Polish-majority areas in most of Posen and central West Prussia that remained under Prussian, later German, rule until 1918. Many went to Bessarabia in 1814-16.

Another important motivation for eastward migration was the large number of Württembergers forced to serve in armed forces allied with Napoleon and the very tiny percentage who survived and returned at the end of these wars.

This was followed by the emigration of religious dissidents from Württemberg in 1816-20. While some went to America, a larger number went eastward and dispersed themselves in settlements from Hungary in the west, to Bessarabia in the middle, and the Caucasus region between the Black and Caspian Seas in the east. They founded the Hoffnungstal colony in Western Ukraine and the Berdyansk colony in Eastern Ukraine, as well as the first settlements in the Southern Caucasus region near *Tiflis* (Tbilisi).

The post-Napoleonic depression and the 1816 crop failure, which produced famine in Western Europe, induced further immigration to Western Ukraine until about 1822. Bessarabia continued to draw immigrants until 1842. There was also another stream of migrants to Eastern Ukraine, chiefly in the 1818-24 period, but periodic wavelets continued until about 1848. Some of these came from West Prussia and farther south along the Vistula, while others came from southwestern Germanic areas, including Alsace and Switzerland. The largest group of new colonies was the one northwest of *Mariupol* (Zhdanov). There are also scattered references to Hungarian Germans, especially from the *Batschka*, migrating to the Russian Empire in the early nineteenth century.

The last group immigration of Prussian German settlers went to the *Samara* (Kuybyshev) region on the Volga River, north of the early settlements near Saratov. This occurred in the third quarter of the nineteenth century. With this one exception, nearly all of the new colonies founded by Germans after 1848 (and a few before then) represented daughter colonies for the surplus population in the original settlement areas. How striking this was is indicated by the fact that by the mid-1860s the number of landless Germans outnumbered the landowners in every colony, often by a substantial margin. Between the end of the Crimean War (1856) and 1890, a huge number of daughter colonies were established, wherever possible in areas near the older colonies, as well as in the Northern Caucasus (between Krasnodar and the Caspian Sea) and in the Don River region north and west of Rostov.

After 1890, large quantities of land could be obtained only in the areas near the Ural Mountains, such as Orenburg and Ufa, or in Asia. Many of the new colonies were along the Trans-Siberian Railway and on both sides of the border between Siberia and Kazakhstan, with a few farther south. How vast Russia's equivalent of the American "Wild West" was is indicated by the fact that these colonies extended from Orenburg, just west of the Urals, to

Semipalatinsk in the east, a distance that is greater than that between Orenburg and St. Petersburg (i.e., the entire width of European Russia).

German immigration to Volhynia, which is now the northwestern part of Ukraine, was an entirely different phenomenon. It consisted chiefly of individual families moving to Volhynia upon invitation from private landowners, in contrast to group immigrations, often with governmental sponsorship or support, which characterized the German migrants to other areas. This has made genealogical research for descendants of the Volhynian Germans more difficult.

Although there were a few Germans in Volhynia before 1800, there was little immigration prior to 1830-31, when the First Polish Uprising against Russia stimulated some Germans in Poland to move farther east and others to return to Prussian-ruled areas. The bulk of the immigration, however, occurred between 1863-64, when the Second Polish Uprising against Russia was accompanied by strong anti-German sentiment as a result of Prussia's policy of coerced Germanicization of Poles, and 1900, by which time German immigration to other parts of Russia had virtually ceased. A lesser flow of German immigration continued for another decade.

The Germans in this region also had different experiences in other ways. Volhynia was the only Russian area where there was a significant amount of emigration (to North America and to the Baltic lands) and immigration (mostly from Poland) at the same time. These Germans also were deported to the east in 1915, an experience not widely shared by other Germans until World War II.

Meanwhile, the end of the promised "forever" came in 1871, when the colonists' special privileges were ended. Growing nationalism led to the Russification programs of 1881-1905, which sought to turn people who spoke little Russian into people who spoke primarily Russian.

This led to large-scale emigration to North and South America, beginning in 1873-74, but in growing numbers after 1883. The American Great Plains and the Canadian Prairie Provinces, as the last frontiers of settlement, absorbed large numbers of these people. In western Canada, North Dakota and certain counties in all the intervening states as far south as Oklahoma, including Colorado, Germans from Russia outnumbered Germans from Germany. A large number also went to Argentina.

For those who remained in Russia, the Bolshevik Revolution and the following Civil War induced many to leave in the 1920s, most of them going to Canada or Latin America rather than the United States. But the New Economic Policy (1921-28), which reversed agricultural collectivization, as well as catering to non-Russian nationalities, exemplified by the creation of the Volga German Republic in 1924, persuaded many that things would not be so bad after all.

Then came the decade of disaster. In 1928-30 the more prosperous farmers ("kulaks") were liquidated and their families deported, as collectivization was re-instituted with a vengeance. Ruthless government requisitioning of farm products after the crop failures of 1932 and 1933 led to a "man-made" famine in the heart of what had been the "granary of Europe." In 1929-37 all pastors were arrested and religious services suppressed. Next came the Great Purge of 1936-38, which sent millions to their deaths, and millions more to slave labor camps. The rise of Hitler fanned anti-German sentiment in the mid-1930s. Because the Germans tended to be relatively well-to-do, they suffered disproportionately from some of these tragedies.

Under the 1939 Hitler-Stalin Pact, 400,000 Germans, most of them from the Baltic countries, Western Volhynia, East Central Poland and Bessarabia (all of which had once been ruled by the Russian Czar), were returned to the *Reich* (really to West Central Poland), since their home areas had been designated as Stalin's "sphere of influence."

But Hitler's invasion of the Soviet Union produced a dramatic change for the worse, as could be expected. Perhaps two-thirds of a million Germans, mostly from the Volga and

Ukrainian areas east of the Dnieper River were deported. When the smoke had cleared after 1955, the new "German heartland" turned out to be Kazakhstan, rimmed by other Islamic republics to the south and Siberia on the north. Many Germans had been in slave labor camps in the northeasternmost corner of European Russia.

However, several hundred thousand Germans, mostly from west of the Dnieper River, managed to escape deportation because the German armies advanced so rapidly that these plans could not be carried out. When the tide of battle turned at Stalingrad in 1943, most of them moved west. Many were settled in the Varta River region in Poland, in homes expropriated from their Polish owners. In January 1945 the Soviet armies advanced toward this area so rapidly that these people had to flee on extremely short notice, in the worst of winter weather. Many made it to West Germany; many did not.

The Soviet government insisted that these were Soviet citizens who had to be returned to the Soviet Union. In the early months after the war, when Westerners still thought of the Soviet Union principally as an ally, the Western powers cooperated in returning many of these people. Others "at large" did what they could to hide their identity.

In the Soviet Union itself, conditions for Germans did not improve until after German Chancellor Adenauer's 1955 visit, which led to the restoration of personal freedom for the Germans in the Soviet Union, but still banned them from returning to their old homes.

After *glasnost* began in 1987, large numbers of German "*Aussiedler*" (resettlers) emigrated to Germany. The fear that anti-Russian nationalism in the Central Asian republics may not distinguish between the two European ethnic groups is an unsettling factor for those Germans who might otherwise choose to remain in what they consider to be their homeland.

In late 1991, after the failed coup, the Soviet Union broke apart, as many component republics declared their independence. Except for the Baltic countries, most of these soon joined the Commonwealth of Independent States, a very loose federation.

Many people of German origin continued to emigrate to Germany. However, the German government has provided extensive aid to German communities in Siberia and the Muslim republics in order to dissuade people from leaving, because the growing resentment against foreigners during the German recession has also created hostile attitudes toward these people of Germanic origin.

SWITZERLAND

The Germanic population of Switzerland originated with the Alamanni and Burgundian tribes invading what had been Roman territory. The Burgundians have become assimilated French since then. The Alamanni, strongly opposed to central rule, have had a dominant influence on the political, economic and social development of Switzerland, with its emphasis on cantonal rather than national government.

The Swiss Confederation dates back to 1291, when three very mountainous cantons (including Schwyz, from which the country's name comes) asserted their independence from the Holy Roman Empire. By 1499, when the Confederation had quintupled in size but was still less than half the size of Switzerland today, the country had won its complete independence. However, its independence was not officially recognized until 1648.

By 1513, the confederation had expanded to 13 cantons. Soon thereafter, it adopted a policy of permanent neutrality, which was violated by Napoleon. The Congress of Vienna expanded the country to its present size, adding three cantons previously ruled by France. However, most of the German-speaking population already belonged to Switzerland before that. Today German is the primary language of 75% of the people, with other languages dominant in the southern and western areas, although many people are bilingual. See Swiss map in **Appendix B** for details on the growth of Switzerland.

Switzerland was the cradle of the Reformed religion, begun by Zwingli, and given its form by Calvin in Geneva. This branch of Protestantism was strong in various parts of Germany, especially the Palatinate, Hesse and Brandenburg, prior to the Lutheran-Reformed merger. It was dominant among the French Huguenots, many of whom fled to Germany. The Netherlands and Scotland also favored this form of Protestantism, known as Presbyterianism in Scotland and among the descendants of the Scots.

However, Switzerland was split right down the middle into the Reformed Protestant and the Roman Catholic camps. Four religious wars, the last in 1712, changed little. But post-1945 population movements (guest workers, refugees, immigrants, etc.) and other factors characteristic of the times have done so. The number of residents listed as neither Protestant nor Catholic quadrupled from 2% to 8% in 1970-80. Moreover, the Protestant majority (previously about 5:4) has recently shifted to a small Catholic plurality.

One wing of the Anabaptist movement, out of which the Mennonite church developed, also had its birth in Switzerland. But its adherents were persecuted and had to flee for their lives, just as they had in their other birthplace, the then Spanish-ruled Netherlands. Mennonite refugees, long known as "Brethren," went down the Rhine, settling on both the French and German sides of the border, as far north as the Palatinate, after being expelled, primarily from the canton of Berne.

Despite its religious strife, Switzerland managed to stay out of the Thirty Years' War. As a result, it was the source of many post-1648 immigrants to areas that had been badly devastated, particularly the Palatinate and Alsace.

Switzerland also experienced the revolutionary turmoil of 1830 and 1848, which affected much of the rest of Europe. A struggle between pro- and anti-reform forces led to a brief civil war in 1847. The end result, however, was the triumph of democracy, contrary to what happened in Germany. Switzerland was the only European country with a federal system similar to that in the United States until Germany adopted such a model in 1949. Industrialization in Switzerland, unlike the rest of continental Europe, preceded that in England.

Swiss immigration to North America seems to have been heaviest during three periods: 1816-17, when Europe suffered crop failures similar to the more severe ones of 1846-47; the 1840s; and the 1880s. However, a significant number of German-speaking colonial immigrants came from Switzerland. Swiss have also migrated to many other countries (South America, New Zealand, Australia, South Africa) in noticeable numbers.

GRAND DUCHY OF LUXEMBOURG

Luxembourg is both a very old and a very new country. It established a separate identity in 963 when a castle was built on the site of the present-day Luxembourg City. Its ruling dynasty provided several Holy Roman Emperors in the Middle Ages, prior to the Hapsburg era. However, it was ruled by Burgundy, Spain, Austria, France or the Netherlands throughout most of modern history.

At the 1815 Vienna Congress, the former Duchy of Luxembourg, which had been the French Département des Forêts during the French Revolution, became the Grand Duchy of Luxembourg. The king of the Netherlands was named the grand duke of Luxembourg. Luxembourg and the Netherlands were supposed to be two entities, with the same sovereign, but governed separately. However, the king decided to impose Dutch law and Dutch administration in Luxembourg, which was then governed like any other province of the Netherlands. This explains partly why Luxembourg took part in the 1830-39 uprising known as the Belgian Revolution. It then became largely self-governing, although its independence was not recognized internationally until 1867 and the Dutch king remained the sovereign until 1890. It was also part of the German Confederation from 1815 to 1866.

But while the country was gaining greater autonomy, it was also losing territory. It had already lost some of its southern territory to France in 1659. In 1815 it lost the territory east of the Moselle and Our Rivers to the Prussian province of Rhineland. In 1839 it ceded its western half to Belgium. Today this is the Belgian province of Luxembourg.

These changes left a definite impact on the migration patterns and the family ties of the Luxembourgers. Many American families can trace their ties back to ancestors living in close proximity on both sides of the rivers now forming the eastern border of the country. But until 1815, or about a generation before large-scale emigration to America, these people had been countrymen. Immigration from Luxembourg to the United States was truly "large-scale," if measured as a percentage of the country's population.

The same ties of culture and kinship exist between the people of the two Luxembourgs, i.e., the grand duchy and the Belgian province. Again, one finds overlapping patterns of emigration and settlement in this country.

The Luxembourgian language, or *Letzeburgesch*, is a German dialect. German and French are both official languages. At the time of immigration to the United States, which coincided pretty well with that from Germany, the affinity of Luxembourgers was mostly for Germans, as indicated by demographic patterns and parish allegiances in this country. However, the country's occupation by German forces in both World Wars has brought about a reorientation.

Luxembourgers are overwhelmingly Catholic, as is the case with the border residents in all the adjacent countries.

PRINCIPALITY OF LIECHTENSTEIN

Unlike other European mini-states, independent Liechtenstein is only a modern creation, although its identity goes back to the Middle Ages and its boundaries have remained constant for longer than nearly all other countries on the continent. It became a principality in 1719, but like so many other German-speaking areas, it belonged to the Holy Roman Empire and later to the German Confederation. In 1866 it became independent. Its external affairs are handled by Switzerland, which lies just across the Rhine River to the west.

THE OTTOMAN TURKISH EMPIRE

Hardly any ethnic Germans ever emigrated to North America from the Ottoman Turkish Empire, yet there were immigrants from territories that were formerly Turkish-ruled.

Historically, the most significant experience was that of the Transylvanian Saxons in the *Siebenbürgen* region of what is now Romania. These settlements, which date back to the Middle Ages, had been under Ottoman control for about a century and a half before they were "liberated" in 1688. But they retained some autonomy as a vassal state. Under Islamic overlordship, these Germans opted for Protestantism without any of the religious troubles that brewed in "Christian Europe."

A more recent experience with Turkish rule was that of the Germans in the Dobruja. Most of this Black Sea coastland is now part of Romania, but the southern portion belongs to Bulgaria. Germans from the Odessa region and Bessarabia settled in this territory in the 1840s and 1850s, when it was still under Turkish rule. Following the Russo-Turkish War the Dobruja became part of Romania in 1878, when that country achieved complete independence. However, the southern tip of the Dobruja, which had only a few Germans, went to the new country of Bulgaria. The new Christian rulers turned out to be less accommodating than the Moslems, leading to emigration to Western Canada and North Dakota within a few years.

Not all German settlers fared well in the hands of the Turks. Those who were settled on the Austrian Military Border in 1718-37, on land recently won from the Turks, were largely wiped out in later Turkish raids on the area. However, the conflict was military, not religious.

One other intriguing "Turkish connection" should be mentioned. Michael Palmer's article, "Moorish and Turkish Blood in German Families" (*GGSA Bulletin*, September 1987), has a 14-item bibliography of documented cases of Germanicized Turks, mostly captured during the 1683-99 war with Turkey, or Moors. The latter term was used to describe people from both North Africa and sub-Saharan Africa, including blacks in the Americas.

Genealogical research has revealed that there were young boys in the Turkish army, whose job was similar to what we would have called "stable boys" in the pre-auto era. A few of these boys were captured by German nobles/officers and taken home, where they were raised and assimilated as Germans. If you can go back several centuries in your research, there could be a Turkish ancestor in your past.

BIBLIOGRAPHY (See ANNOTATED BIBLIOGRAPHY for full citations if not shown)

Wilhelm Baum. *Deutsche und Slowenen in Krain: Eine historische Betrachtung.* [*A Historical View of Germans and Slovenians in Carniola*]. Klagenfurt, Austria: Carinthia Verlag. 1981. 247 pp.

Eugen Bellon. *Scattered to All the Winds, 1685-1720: Migrations of the Dauphine French Huguenots into Italy, Switzerland and Germany.* West Lafayette, IN: Belle Publications, 1983. Translation. 267 pp.

Edgar Bonjour. *A Short History of Switzerland.* Westport, CT: Greenwood Press, 1985 reprint of 1952 book. 388 pp.

Irma Bornemann. *The Bukovina Germans.* Sophie A. Welisch, trans. Ellis, KS: Bukovina Society of the Americas. English translation of 1986 German original. 1990. 21 pp.
> History, geography, politics, culture and 1940 repatriation of Germans, including places of origin (southern Germany, Bohemia, Slovakia).

Hans Fehlinger. *Deutsche in der Fremde: Eine Übersicht nach Abschluss des Weltkrieges.* [*Germans in Foreign Lands: An Overview after the Conclusion of World War I*]. Leipzig: Dieterich'sche Verlagsbuchhandlung. 1920. 48 pp.

John Foisel. *Saxons Through Seventeen Centuries: A History of the Transylvanian Saxons.* Cleveland: Central Alliance of Transylvanian Saxons. 1936. 348 pp.
> History of the Germans who migrated to Eastern Hungary (now Romania) in the twelfth century, with an introductory chapter on the earlier history of the Saxons.

Adam Giesinger. *From Catherine to Khrushchev: The Story of Russia's Germans.*

Peter Grassl. *Geschichte der deutsch-böhmischen Ansiedlungen Banat.* [*History of the German-Bohemian Settlements in the Banat*]. Prag: J. G. Calve'sche K.u.K. Hof- u. Universitats-Buchhandlung (J. Koch). 1904. 125 pp.
> Early account of the Bohemian Germans who settled in what was then southern Hungary in the late 1700s.

Hugo Grothe. *Grothes Kleines Handwörterbuch des Grenz- und Ausland-Deutschtums,* multiple volumes. [*Grothe's Small Encyclopedia of Germans in Border Areas and Abroad*]. München and Berlin: R. Oldenburg. 1932. 400 pp.
> The most complete book on the Germans in border areas and in foreign lands.

Otto Heike. *Schwabensiedlungen in Polen, 1795-1945.* [*Swabian Settlements in Poland, 1795-1945*]. Leverkusen, Germany: self published. 1979 and 1981. 364 pp.
> Account of the settlement of Swabians and other South Germans in Polish territory.

Jörg K. Hoensch. *Geschichte Böhmens von der slavischen Landesaufnahme bis ins 20. Jahrhundert.* [*History of Bohemia from Its Settlement by Slavs into the Twentieth Century*]. Munich: C. H. Beck. 1992. 380 pp.
> History of the lands of the kingdom of Bohemia, including Moravia and Silesia, until 1914, with considerable attention paid to the German settlers, as well as the Holy Roman Emperors and the large landowners (the church and the nobility), often of German origin.

Larry O. Jensen. *A Genealogical Handbook of German Research*, Vol. III.

Robert A. Kann. *The Multinational Empire: Nationalism and Reform in the Habsburg Monarchy, 1848-1918*. New York: Octagon Books, Vol. II. 1964. np.

A. Karasek and K. Lück. *Die deutschen Siedlungen in Wolhynien*. [*The German Settlements in Volhynia*]. Plauen: G. Wolff. 1931. 132 pp.
> Brief but good book on the Germans who migrated to Volhynia (now northwest Ukraine), mostly between 1860 and 1910.

Viktor Kauder. *Das Deutschtum in Ostpolen*. [*The Germans in East Poland*]. 1939.
> Deals with Germans who settled in the Cholm-Lublin area, mostly after 1860.

W. Kessler. *Ost- und südostdeutsche Heimatbücher und Ortsmonographien nach 1945: Eine Bibliographie zur historischen Landeskunde der Vertreibungsgebiete*. [*East and Southeast Local History Books and Locality Monographs Since 1945: A Bibliography of Local Histories for the Regions Where Germans Were Expelled*]. Munich. 1979.
> Bibliography of local histories of German villages in east and southeast Europe.

Manfred Klaube. *Deutschböhmische Siedlungen im Karpatenraum*. [*German Bohemian Settlements in the Carpathian Area*]. Marburg/Lahn: J. G. Herder-Institut. 1984. 168 pp.
> Bohemian German settlements in the area transferred from Czechoslovakia to the Soviet Union as a result of World War II.

Rolf Kosiek. *Jenseits der Grenzen: 1000 Jahre Volks- und Auslandsdeutschen*. [*Beyond the (German) Borders: 1000 Years of Ethnic Germans in Foreign Lands*]. Tübingen: Grabert-Verlag. 1987. 240 pp.

Oskar Kossmann. *Die Deutschen in Polen seit der Reformation: historisch-geographische Skizzen*. [*Germans in Poland Since the Reformation: Historical and Geographical Sketches*] Marburg/Lahn: J. G. Herder-Institut. 1978. 420 pp.

C. A. Macartney. *The Habsburg Empire, 1790-1918*. London: Weidenfeld and Nicolson, 1968. 886 pp. 6 maps.

William O. McCagg, Jr. *A History of the Habsburg Jews, 1670-1918*. Bloomington, IN: Indiana University Press. 1989, 1992. 289 pp.
> Deals mostly with the 1800-1918 period. Specific chapters or sections on Vienna, Bohemia, Hungary, Galicia, Bukovina and Trieste.

Richard Meyer. *Das Memelland*. [*The Memel Territory*]. Kitzingen/Main: Holzner Verlag. 1961. 27 pp.
> Deals with the former East Prussian border area transferred from German to Lithuanian control in the early 1920s.

John M. Michels. *Introduction to the Hungarian-Germans of North Dakota*. Bismarck, ND: Germans from Russia Heritage Society, February 1988.

Sepp Müller. *Von der Ansiedlung bis zur Umsiedlung: Das Deutschtum Galiziens, insbesondere Lembergs, 1772-1940*. [*Ethnic Germans in Galicia and Especially Lemberg, 1772-1940: From Early Settlement to Emigration (Repatriation back to Germany)*]. Marburg/Lahn: J. G. Herder-Institut. 1961. 256 pp.

James Newcomer. *The Grand Duchy of Luxembourg: The Evolution of Nationhood, 963 A.D. to 1983*. Lanham, MD: The University Press of America. 1984. 343 pp.

Victoria M. Nied, "From Mokra to the Melting Pot," in the *Journal of the American Historical Society of Germans from Russia*. Summer 1996.

Victoria M. Nied, "My Heritage in the Sub-Carpathian Ukraine," in *Nase Rodina*. Summer 1993. (Also in the *German Connection*, July 1993.)

Valentin Oberkirch. *Die Deutschen in Syrmien, Slawonien, Kroatien und Bosnien* [*The Germans in Syrmia (Srem), Slavonia, Croatia and Bosnia*]. Munich. 1989. 611 pp.

Géza C. Paikert. *The Danube Swabians: German Populations in Hungary, Rumania and Yugoslavia and Hitler's Impact on Their Patterns*. The Hague: Martinus Nijhoff. 1967.

Edward A. Peckwas. A *Historical Bibliography of Polish Towns, Villages, and Regions (except Warsaw and Krakow)*. Chicago: Polish Genealogical Society of America. 1990 reprint of 1971 bibliography compiled by Wiktor Kazmierczak. 104 pp.
>   Lists almost 1,000 local histories, nearly half of them German.

Carl Petersen and Otto Scheel, *Handwörterbuch des Grenz- und Auslanddeutschtums.* [*Encyclopedia of Germans in Border Areas and Abroad*]. Breslau: Ferdinand Hirt. 1933. np.
>   This book is one of the two comprehensive multi-volume works on German-speakers in non-Germanic areas of Europe.

Tony Radspieler. *The Ethnic German Refugee in Austria, 1945 to 1954*. The Hague: Martinus Nijhoff. 1955. 197 pp.

Wilhelm Rohmeder. *Das Deutschtum in Südtirol*. [*Ethnic Germans (Austrians) in South Tyrol*] Berlin: Verein für das Deutschtum im Ausland. 1919. 49 pp. 2 maps.

Georg Wilhelm Sante, ed. *Geschichte der deutschen Länder: "Territorien-Ploetz."* [*History of German Countries, or "Ploetz-Territories"*]. 2 vols. Würzburg: A. G. Ploetz Verlag. The second title is the publisher's abbreviated title.

Hermann Schreiber. *Teuton and Slav: The Struggle for Central Europe*. London: Constable. 1965. 392 pp. English translation by James Cleugh.

Klaus-Dieter Schulz-Vobach. *Die Deutschen im Osten: Vom Balkan bis Sibirien.* [*The Germans in the East: From the Balkans to Siberia*]. Hamburg: Goldman. 1989. 382 pp.

Ernst Schwarz. *Handbuch der Sudetendeutschen Kulturgeschichte.* [*Handbook of Sudeten German Cultural History*]. 4 volumes. München: R. Lerche. 1961-1966.
>   Authoritative work on the Germans in Bohemia and Moravia.

J. V. Senz. *Geschichte der Donauschwaben.* [*The History of the Danube Swabians*]. Straubingen-Sindelfingen, Germany. 1987. 277 pp.

L. Edward Skender. *A Short History of the Duchy of Carniola and Gottschee County.* Sonora, CA: Gottscheer Research and Genealogy Association. 1994. 29 pp.
>   History of this Slovenian area since Celtic times, with emphasis on the German connection.
>   Many detailed maps, including one on Germans in northeastern Italy.

Jacob Steigerwald. *Tracing Romania's Heterogeneous German Minority from Its Origins to the Diaspora*.

Karl Stumpp. *The Emigration from Germany to Russia in the Years 1763-1862*.

Anton Tafferner, Josef Schmidt and Josef Volkmar Senz. *The Danube Swabians in the Pannonia Basin: A New German Ethnic Group*. Milwaukee: Danube Swabian Asssociation. 1982. 24 pp.
>   Historical overview and maps of Danube Swabian settlements.

Mario Toscano. *Alto Adige, South Tyrol: Italy's Frontier with the German World*. Baltimore: Johns Hopkins University Press, 1975; translation. 283 pp.

Paul Traeger. *The Germans in the Dobrudscha (Dobrogea)*. English translation serialized in *Heritage Review*. Bismarck: Germans from Russia Heritage Society. 1985-88. German translation 222 pp.
>   Authoritative account of the German settlements near the Black Sea coast of Romania, extending slightly into Bulgaria.

Edward von der Porten. "The Hanseatic League: Europe's First Common Market," in *National Geographic*, Oct. 1994.

Ernst Wagner, et. al. *The Transylvanian Saxons: Historical Highlights*. Cleveland: Alliance of Transylvanian Saxons. 1982. 142 pp.

    History and maps pertaining to the Transylvanian Saxons in Europe and North America.

Johann Weidlein. *Die Deutschen in der Schwäbischen Türkei. [Germans in Swabian Turkey (South Hungary)]*. Wurzburg/Main: Holzner Verlag. 1956. 30 pp.

    One of the few books about the Germans in the southern part of contemporary Hungary.

Sophie A. Welisch. *Bukovina Villages / Towns / Cities and Their Germans*.

Franz Wilhelm and Josef Kallbrunner. *Quellen zur deutschen Siedlungsgeschichte in Südosteuropa. [Sourcebook for Histories of German Settlements in Southeast Europe]*. München: E. Reinhardt. 1832, 1935. 416 pp.

Chapter XI

HISTORY, MIGRATION AND GENEALOGY OF VARIOUS RELIGIOUS DENOMINATIONS

This chapter was previously devoted largely to the various small religious groups on the assumption that almost everything in the guide was valid for the major denominations, except for such things as the pertinent European addresses of religious archives. However, many of the more important genealogical resources we mentioned were not very useful for small groups, so we realized that mention of specific denominational resources was needed.

While this guide focuses on records in or from Europe, we began to realize that the standard works on American genealogy might not be adequate for tracing ancestors back to Europe, at least as far as the records of historically German parishes in North America are concerned. Thus we have broadened the scope of this chapter to include all churches in North America known to have had any German-speaking congregations.

There is still an emphasis on small groups, since the members of many of these frequently emigrated for religious reasons. A disproportionately large percentage of these belonged to the Anabaptist wing of the Reformation. Moreover, there are specific societies and genealogical specialists for many small denominations, but we have not come across any such resources focused on larger denominations in North America, although there is a Catholic Family History Society in Britain, where Catholics are a small minority, both in the total population and among Anglo-Germans. These factors explain the number of pages devoted to these churches.

Members of mainstream denominations rarely had to emigrate to overseas countries to worship in accordance with their beliefs. At worst, they had to migrate to another Germanic principality.

The churches to which Americans and Canadians of Germanic descent belong or belonged can be divided into five categories:

(1) churches that were established in or before the sixteenth century and had Germanic congregations during that time (covered by sections A and B)

(2) churches which were established in Germanic Europe at a later date, but prior to the emigration of its members to North America (covered by section C)

(3) churches of non-Germanic origin which took root among European Germans prior to emigration (also covered by section C)

(4) churches founded by German-Americans or German-Canadians (covered by section F)

(5) non-Germanic churches with German-speaking congregations established by immigrants or their descendants (also covered by section F)

Section G on genealogy is relevant in all cases, but it has more supplementary information for the last two groups. Some churches, of course, were hybrids.

To summarize the first three categories briefly, those in the first group include Roman Catholics, Lutherans, Reformed, Mennonites, Hutterites, and the Schwenkfelder fellowship (which became an organized church in America). Those in the second category include the Amish, German Baptist Brethren, the Pietistic Inspirationists movement (which eventually became the Amana Society in America), the Temple Society (Templers), and the Evangelical Church resulting from the merger of Lutherans and Reformed in Germany. Those in the third group include a small number of Quakers (Religious Society of Friends), the Methodists and Baptists (both hybrids), probably the Seventh-day Adventists and possibly a few Pentecostals. The last two categories are too complicated to summarize.

THE MEDIEVAL CHURCH AND DISSIDENT GROUPS

What is now the Catholic Church was, by and large, the Christian church for a thousand years, when it split into the Roman Catholic and Orthodox churches. The word, "catholic," means "universal." There had, of course, been many previous dissident groups, including the Arians (not to be confused with Hitler's ridiculous notion that the prehistoric Aryans, shrouded in mystery, have any relevance today). The Gothic tribes of the Roman days belonged to the Arians, but these had no direct lasting effect on Christianity, least of all in modern Germanic areas. The Orthodox church has no relevance for Germanic genealogy, except for rare instances of Germans in the Russian Empire, and later the Soviet Union, marrying Russians or Ukrainians, in which case they might have become converts or, more likely, their descendants might have grown up in the Orthodox church. Very few among this small number migrated.

With respect to researching German-speaking ancestors, the major schism, with much subsequent splintering, started with Martin Luther. However, there were actually two earlier "Protestant" churches which are pertinent, although both of them originated outside Germany.

The first one was the reform movement begun by Peter Waldo (Waldus) of Lyons in southern France in about 1170. The authorities never succeeded in totally obliterating this group, since small remnants survived in the Franco-Italian Alpine area. These fled to the German states, where they were closely associated with the Huguenots, well after the start of the Lutheran Reformation.

The second one was an offshoot of the Hussite movement, which was inspired by the teachings of John Wycliffe but developed in the Czech Republic. After the martyrdom of John Huss, the Hussite movement quickly enveloped the Czech lands, where it was dominant during most of the fifteenth and sixteenth centuries, although the Unity of Brethren [*Unitas Fratrum, Herrnhuter,* Moravian Church or Moravian Brethren] were a distinct group, established in 1457, with formal separation from the Catholic church about a decade later.

During the first half of the seventeenth century, Protestantism was virtually wiped out in Bohemia and Moravia, leaving its adherents with the choice of re-Catholicization or exile. But a small number of members of the Unity of Brethren survived in Moravia and eventually found a refuge in Germany.

Both the Waldensians and the Moravian Brethren became assimilated and can thus be seen as part of German Protestantism, although this was not the case until long after Martin Luther.

EARLY REFORMATION/COUNTER-REFORMATION ERA, 1517-1648

The early years of the Reformation gave birth to three wings of Protestantism on Germanic soil. The first and largest one developed into the Lutheran church.

David Koss states that all Protestants are in some way the children of Luther, although many of them are not Lutherans. This is because Luther's challenge to the Catholic church in posting the 95 Theses in 1517 stimulated other protests against Catholicism, and soon also against Lutheranism and Calvinism. This resulted in the formation of other Protestant denominations, in considerable measure because many of Luther's original supporters came to differ with him on important points before long.

The second most significant group was begun by Ulrich Zwingli, a Swiss German. But he was killed in battle within a few years, so it was French-born John Calvin of Geneva who molded it to a large extent. Hence, this stream of religious thought is usually referred to as Calvinism, although it was called the Reformed church in continental Europe. It soon became and remained the dominant Protestant church in Switzerland, as well as in France, the Netherlands and Scotland.

The third, most diverse and least known was the Anabaptist, or "radical," wing initiated by Conrad Grebel, originally a Swiss follower of Zwingli, in 1525. The name means "re-baptizers" and was initially applied to the group by outsiders. This group shared a belief in adult baptism, which meant that its earliest members, who had been baptized as infants in the Catholic church, were baptized again as adults. It does not mean a practice of being baptized twice, because the group rejects infant baptism as invalid.

These beliefs spread quickly to the Netherlands, Flanders and adjacent German areas (Rhineland, East Frisia). At first it was an amorphous movement, with many individual leaders preaching very different ideas. One group captured the city of Münster, where it established a bizarre dictatorship, in 1534. The city was recaptured in 1535, but the Münsterites frightened the authorities and gave the movement a reputation totally inconsistent with its subsequent development.

The "Calvin" of Anabaptism was Menno Simons, a former Frisian priest, and consequently the members of this non-violent church became known as Mennonites (originally Mennists or Mennonists). The Swiss-South German wing referred to itself as Brethren for a long time, but it later accepted the term, Mennonites.

According to John Hostetler, the Hutterites (or Hutterian Brethren) originated in South Tyrol, Carinthia and southern Germany in the 1520s. But they were only loosely associated with the Swiss Brethren. They believe in communal property and are often still included with the Mennonites, although the history of their persecution and flight from one refuge to another is quite different.

The Schwenkfelders also date back to the early days, with their original stronghold in Central Germany. They trace their origins to Caspar Schwenkfeld, who was influenced by the ideas of Hus and Luther, breaking with the latter over several issues, including baptism. He did not even attempt to start a church. Nevertheless, his followers were a distinct fellowship and eventually organized a church. They have had an almost entirely separate history from that of the other continental Anabaptists.

Religious persecution and coerced conversion among Christians was the rule, rather than the exception, in Germanic areas until the end of the Thirty Years' War (1618-48). Even expulsion, execution and torture were common in the sixteenth century. The large Protestant churches were often just as intolerant of smaller sects as the Catholics were of Protestantism.

The Peasants' War of 1524-25, based on the perception that socio-economic liberation was the logical sequel to Luther's "liberation" from an oppressive church, affected many parts of southern and central Germany. But the brutal suppression of the uprising effectively quashed Protestantism in southern Bavaria. Luther, who was a very conservative purifier and generally supported state authorities, strongly criticized the peasants although he later expressed some criticism of the behavior of the states' forces as well.

Inquisitions predated the Reformation and were instituted in most Catholic countries during the Reformation era, but the Spanish Inquisition was the most brutal. As background, Spain had driven the last Muslim rulers out of southern Spain in 1492 and promptly proceeded to homogenize the population by forcibly converting the Jews and Muslims who had helped to make Spain such a glorious civilization in the Middle Ages. Thus they reacted to the Reformation with a similar state of mind.

At the time of the Reformation, the Spanish Hapsburgs ruled the Low Countries, where the Mennonite, and somewhat later the Reformed, denominations spread rapidly. They were completely successful in stamping out Protestantism in Belgium, close to the provincial capital of Brussels, in the sixteenth century.

The Walloons (French-speaking Reformed from eastern and southern Belgium) fled mostly to Germanic principalities with Reformed rulers, including the Palatinate, Hesse, and eastern and central Franconia (now northeastern Bavaria), mostly in 1568, when Spanish persecution was at its worst.

The Anabaptists, who have believed in separation of church and state ever since the first few chaotic and tumultuous years (when there was no consensus on anything except adult baptism), had no rulers of their faith to protect them. Flemish Anabaptists initially fled to Friesland, a second major center of northern Anabaptism and one where the arm of the law was not quite as effective, although numerous executions were carried out there, too.

Before long, the majority of the Mennonites had fled eastward, mostly to West Prussia, a predominantly German-speaking area that was under Polish rule, but with local autonomy until 1569. Some sought refuge in Emden (Ostfriesland), where the rulers believed in tolerance, but were pressured by rulers of adjacent more powerful states to expel them. A few found a more permanent refuge in Holstein, especially on the estates of sympathetic noblemen who appreciated their skills in draining marshlands. The area was ruled by a comparatively tolerant Danish king.

However, the Commonwealth of Poland and Lithuania was the only Christian country which granted complete religious freedom to all groups during the latter half of the Middle Ages and the early Reformation period.

Moravia, Hungary (Transylvania) and Wallachia (both of the latter now part of Romania) served as temporary refuges at times, especially for the Hutterites. Some German cities (e.g., Strasbourg and Krefeld) also represented islands of tolerance (as did some small southern Italian principalities, but these have no relevance for Germans).

Protestantism made great strides in East Central Europe during the Reformation. Most of the Hungarians and Poles were Calvinists, although some were Socinians, a group of Italian origin whose ideas were similar to those of the Unitarians of a later day. The Hussite movement had, of course, already become dominant in the lands of the Bohemian crown in the fifteenth century. But the Catholic Counter-Reformation, beginning in the 1560s, largely eliminated Protestantism east of the Germanic areas, although it had little effect on German Protestants in Poland and Hungary/Romania.

The northern Dutch provinces, however, rebelled against Spain's autocratic rule. By the 1580s, the Netherlands had achieved de facto independence, although Spain did not recognize it as such until 1648, when an independent Switzerland also gained recognition. Independence marked the end of religious persecution, although not all discrimination, in the Netherlands.

Meanwhile, the Peace of Augsburg in 1555 provided that Catholic and Lutheran rulers could require their subjects to be of the same religion. But this peace was by no means always honored. Not until 1648 were Reformed rulers granted equal status. This meant frequent changes in the religion imposed on the people by successive rulers of different creeds, as in the Palatinate. It is no accident that the Palatinate still has a more mixed Lutheran-Reformed-Catholic population than most other areas.

The sheer exhaustiveness of the Thirty Years' War, which is estimated to have killed one-third or more of the German and Czech people, led to an alleviation of the harsh treatment of religious minorities, but discrimination continued to exist in German areas until the latter half of the nineteenth century in some cases.

The war left no Germanic areas untouched, except for Switzerland, and East and West Prussia. Among the areas which suffered most were southwestern Germany, Bohemia, Mecklenburg and Pomerania (which was the most purely Lutheran state or province at that time).

This resulted in large-scale Swiss migration down the Rhine to settle in depopulated southwest Germanic areas on both sides of the Rhine after 1648 and a small number of Dutch and northwest Germans moving up the Rhine.

PERSECUTION, FLIGHT AND EMIGRATION AFTER 1648

There was hardly any overseas emigration for religious reasons prior to 1648. But we sometimes overlook the fact that there was substantial intra-European flight or emigration for religious reasons. This was not a phenomenon unique to inter-continental immigration even after 1648.

FLIGHT AND EMIGRATION TO AND WITHIN GERMANIC EUROPE

Persecution and expulsion did not end with the Thirty Years' War. For example, while the Dutch Mennonites found security in the independent Netherlands, their counterparts in Switzerland were hunted down and expelled from the German Reformed cantons. Most of them went down the Rhine, both before and after 1648, settling in Alsace, the Palatinate, Württemberg, southern Hesse and the French Montbéliard region next to southern Alsace. A few of these later migrated eastward to what had been Polish areas (including Galicia, Volhynia and the Vistula River area).

In 1693 the Amish (or Amish Mennonites) were founded by Jacob Ammann, who withdrew from the South Germanic wing of the Mennonites. They became an ultra-conservative group. By then, persecution was no longer a serious problem in this area.

Furthermore France, which had seen the Thirty Years' War more as a struggle against the Austrian Empire for hegemony than as a religious war (as indicated by its choice of allies), had enunciated the Edict of Nantes, which guaranteed religious tolerance, in 1598, after the same kind of religious strife as had existed in Germany. However, after the renunciation of this edict in 1685, most of the Huguenots (French Reformed) scattered throughout the world, with quite a few fleeing to Switzerland, Brandenburg, Saxony-Anhalt, and the areas around Bremen and Frankfurt. (Some had already left after the St. Bartholomew's Day Massacre in 1572.) Waldensians joined the Huguenot emigration and the two groups established close ties.

Both the French and the Belgian Reformed (as well as the Flemish Mennonites) were relatively well-educated middle class people, with quite a few high nobles among the Huguenots. As a result, the more numerous Huguenots had a major impact on the development of Berlin and Magdeburg. They kept the French language for a considerable period of time. The Huguenots often had separate French churches and have retained a strong sense of a special identity, combining the purely religious identity of the Jews and the Mennonites, whose identities are based on persecution, with the prestige-based concepts of organizations such as the Mayflower Descendants, Sons and Daughters of the American Revolution or the United Empire Loyalists in Canada.

In 1722 the few Moravian Brethren who had survived forced re-Catholicization were given refuge on the estate of a pietistic Lutheran nobleman in Herrnhut in southeastern Saxony, whence they derived the name *Herrnhuter*, and soon became Germanicized. They, like the Huguenots, scattered to the four quarters of the globe, but in this case as a result of their emphasis on missionary work.

The Austrian Empire and the Archbishopric of Salzburg also banned Protestantism for a long time. The Transylvanian Saxons had become Lutherans while under Ottoman Turkish rule. The Hapsburg emperors were pragmatic enough not to attempt to forcibly re-Catholicize them after the area had been regained from the Turks. Transylvania thus also became a refuge for some Austrian Protestants, since Protestantism was generally not tolerated elsewhere by the Hapsburgs until 1781.

The Archbishop of Salzburg expelled some 20,000 Lutherans, mostly from the *Salzkammergut* or *Ländl* east of Salzburg, in the 1730s. These Salzburger refugees (*Exulanten* in German) found homes in many places, especially in East Prussia, where the Prussian king actively sought to colonize sparsely populated areas in the east and south. Others went to Brandenburg and to eastern and central Franconia (now northeastern Bavaria).

FLIGHT AND EMIGRATION FROM GERMANIC EUROPE

This section seeks to deal with two overlapping, but not identical, subjects. One is the continuation of discrimination which caused many members of dissident groups to migrate to Eastern Europe or to cross the Atlantic. The other is the emigration of dissident or unique groups, especially to North America, even though religious discrimination was not always their reason for doing so.

As far as emigration to Eastern Europe is concerned, the following groups are worthy of mention.

Mennonites from West Prussia migrated to the Russian Empire (eastern Ukraine), mostly in 1789-1806, but with a last small wave (which went to the Upper Volga area) in the 1850s. This was due primarily to restrictions on landownership imposed by the Prussian king after Poland lost the area in 1772 and 1793, since the Mennonites, as conscientious objectors, did not provide the soldiers which the land was supposed to produce. The Hutterites also found refuge there, but they had fled from one European country to another before the survivors found safety under the czars.

Württemberg Separatists, including many millenialists, who were dissatisfied with the laxity of the Lutheran state church at home, migrated to the Odessa and Berdyansk areas and Bessarabia (all near the western Black Sea), as well as to the southern Caucasus around Tiflis (now Tbilisi, the capital of Georgia), in 1816-19, with later daughter settlements in the Crimea.

Bismarck's anti-Catholic *Kulturkampf* (1871-78) caused some Catholic emigration from the Rhineland and certain other areas, with some accepting the invitation of a convent to settle in the Banja Luka area of north central Bosnia in order to produce food for the nuns.

A comparison of the religious composition of the people in Germanic Europe and the denominations found among German emigrants to the New World and their descendants shows a marked contrast.

The Evangelical Church resulting from a merger of the Lutheran and Reformed churches in Germany is often equated with, or even translated as, Protestant, so that religious affiliation is often seen as bipolar. Although there are other churches in Germany, such a small percentage of the German people belong to them that they are rarely mentioned, except in passing, when religion is discussed.

On the other hand, the denominational affiliation of people of German descent in non-Germanic countries is much more diverse and the heterogeneity is probably the greatest in the United States, despite the fact that Lutherans and Catholics far outnumber any other individual denomination. In that sense, our focus on non-mainstream religious groups can be seen as part of the religious portrait of German-Americans.

Krefeld Mennonites and Palatine Quakers represented the first German group migration to America in 1683-85, attracted by the religious tolerance of William Penn's colony, although most of the Quakers were Mennonite converts. (The two denominations are similar in many ways, although they differ on baptism.) Penn's colony soon became a haven for others seeking freedom of religion.

The German Baptist Brethren (*Täufer*, Tunkers, Dunkers, Dunkards) were founded by Alexander Mack in 1708. Unlike other pietists, they were not averse to establishing a new church organization. Almost all of them emigrated to the American colonies in 1719-35, according to John Humphrey.

Among the Protestant refugees expelled from Salzburg, some emigrated to the American state of Georgia in the 1730s. Silesian-Saxon Schwenkfelders settled in Pennsylvania in 1742, while Moravian Brethren went to both Pennsylvania and North Carolina during the half-century ending in 1753. So did migrants directly from Switzerland and also those of Swiss origin who had already feld down the Rhine.

In 1785 Father George Rapp established a group dedicated to total community of property, even with regard to marital ties. In 1804 this group came from Germany and settled in Harmony, Pennsylvania. Ten years later they founded New Harmony, Indiana, but after another decade they returned to Pennsylvania, specifically to Old Economy. In 1905 when membership had already dwindled greatly, the Harmonists were dissolved. John Duss then took the belongings to Florida, but the Harmonists do not consider this to be a valid continuation of the group.

Some Huguenots who had lived in Germanic areas for a while later emigrated overseas, especially to South Africa. However, if religion played any role in this, it was more likely the attractiveness of living in a country dominated by Dutch Reformed, rather than because of persecution in Germany or Switzerland.

Old Lutherans who rejected the Lutheran-Reformed merger imposed by the king of Prussia in 1817 were severely persecuted, so they migrated to Australia, Canada and the United States in 1837-54 to escape suppression. In *Nineteenth-Century Emigration of "Old Lutherans" from Eastern Germany (Mainly Pomerania and Lower Silesia)*, Clifford Neal Smith lists a large number of the emigrants to these three countries.

Despite the fact that most Germanic emigration to overseas countries occurred after this merger, it had relatively little effect in the immigrant countries where there were many Lutheran churches, with the Reformed minority joining one of the various Calvinist churches, although not always the German Reformed church. Only toward the end of large-scale German emigration to the United States did the German merged church have any significant counterpart here. There was no similar merger outside the states which became Germany.

A small group of dissidents who migrated across the Atlantic in the nineteenth century were the Labadists, a mystic and pietistic splinter within the German Reformed church.

The Temple Society (German Temple, Templers) was founded in 1861 in a village north of Stuttgart, where the pietistic Friends of Jerusalem, drawn mostly from Protestant circles, but including a few Catholics, had established a rural settlement. According to Josef Vondra, *German-Speaking Settlers in Australia*, the Templers started moving to Palestine, by arrangement with the Turkish government, in 1867. However, some scattered in other directions, since Templers in the Russian Empire split away from the Mennonites in 1863, although many Lutherans and some Catholics were also drawn to the group. The Templers founded settlements in the northern Caucasus, according to Adam Giesinger. Cornelius Dyck reports that Mennonite Templers also migrated to Palestine around 1870. Some Templers lived in the United States prior to World War I, although it is not known whether they came from Germany or Russia. The American Templers were advised to cut their ties to Germany in the 1930s and to join the Unitarian church, whose only similarity appears to be the lack of any formal creed. There seems to be no comprehensive account of the small group of Templers who lived in so many different countries (involuntarily during and after World War II).

The most significant splits in Europe often represented movements (pietists, mystics, millenialists, evangelists) which did not necessarily result in an entirely new church body, although it often resulted in separate fellowships or congregations and even new sub-denominations. Many dissident groups can trace their origins to such movements.

George J. Eisenach focuses on pietistic influences on the Lutherans and Reformed in the Russian Empire, where it remained a stream of thought, not a separate church. They required their adherents to be members of a church and saw themselves as a "church within a church." When they settled in the Dakotas, some joined the Lutheran or Reformed congregations, but many felt they lacked a natural home and concluded that the Congregational church was one in which they would be comfortable, because it was based on the concept of local self-government by each parish.

Wilhelm Peterson led a group of pietists to Pennsylvania in 1741 already. There he maintained contact with other like-minded groups, which led to the formation and growth of the Universalist church. For further information on this group, check the Miller book and the Irwin thesis listed in the bibliography.

The Methodists in Germany and Switzerland, one of many churches and groups which felt that a reform of the state churches with their lax standards was needed, encountered harsh social intimidation and lack of protection, when this church was established in those countries in the 1830s (at about the same time as German-American Methodist churches were founded) so a disproportionate number emigrated to the United States.

The first Baptist church was established in Germany in 1834 and quickly spread to Switzerland and Austria. The first Baptist church in the Russian Empire, founded in 1869, had increased to 20,000 members in 1897 as a result of converts from other German (and even non-German) churches, but especially from among the Lutheran Separatists. Quite a few of these came to Western Canada and the Great Plains states.

Somewhat earlier, Baptists from Ostfriesland came to the United States, settling mostly in Iowa and the Dakotas.

A Church of God, which appears to have been of Germanic origin and not an offshoot of the Winebrenner church, also existed in Germany, Switzerland, and Germanic settlements in the Russian Empire, Poland and the Balkans. German and Swiss preachers stimulated the founding of this church in western Volhynia (formerly in Poland, now in Ukraine) before World War I and re-established it there in 1925, after their work had been interrupted by the deportation of the Volhynian Germans to Siberia during the war. For a specific account, see Edmund Krebs's article.

World War I caused the church to spread throughout the distant eastern part of the Soviet Union, while many were able to emigrate to Argentina, Brazil and Canada. After World War II, members of the church emigrated to the United States and Canada, while others chose to remain in Germany.

Many of the Germans who emigrated from the Russian Empire in the last generation of the nineteenth century and again from the Soviet Union after each of the two World Wars left at least partly for religious reasons. This was especially true for the Mennonites (who had splintered into many groups by 1870) and the Hutterites, who began coming to the United States and Canada in 1874; they felt threatened by the demand for universal military service, which was contrary to their pacifist beliefs, although this decree was soon modified. It was likewise true for the legal and illegal refugees from Communism, regardless of religion. Those who left during the interwar period settled mostly in Canada and Latin America, because the United States had adopted very restrictive immigration laws in the early 1920s.

But quite a few post-World War II displaced persons or DPs (including many East European Germans) were allowed to enter the United States, although more apparently went to Canada and other New World countries.

Most of the post-*glasnost* Germans from the Soviet Union and Poland went to, and stayed in, Germany. But many of those from the Balkans crossed the ocean.

RELIGIOUS DEMOGRAPHY OF GERMANIC COUNTRIES IN 1900

Much of our information on this subject comes from *Meyers Kleines Konversations-Lexikon* [*Meyer's Small Encyclopedia of General Information*]. Although the detailed data are mostly for Germany, the religious distribution in the other Germanic countries is simpler to depict.

The religious demography of the major churches in the German-speaking countries has remained relatively constant since after it was stabilized by the rather substantial migration to repopulate areas devastated by the Thirty Years' War.

Internal migrations since the beginning of the Industrial Revolution modified the picture somewhat, although these changes were relatively minor and largely restricted to a few big cities. The mass flight and expulsion of Germans from Eastern Europe in 1944-45 changed the demographic map more drastically. Today all-Catholic or all-Protestant villages are rarities, but at the time our ancestors emigrated, they were not uncommon. But this has not had a great deal of effect as to which areas have a Protestant majority and which ones a Catholic majority.

To begin the sketch, Luxembourg, largely unaffected by recent migrations, remains 97% Catholic.

Austria still is 85% Catholic, despite an influx of post-World War II refugees and the transfer of part of the Burgenland (which had a comparatively large Protestant minority) from Hungary to Austria after World War I.

Until recent decades, there were slightly more Protestants (almost all Reformed) than Catholics among German-speakers in Switzerland. But there are slightly more Catholics than Protestants in Switzerland now and this is also probably also true of the German-speaking cantons. The Alpine core is staunchly Catholic, while most but not all of the northern and eastern cantons are predominantly Protestant, especially in and around Berne, Zurich and Basel.

What used to be West Germany has about an equal number of Catholics and Protestants. Bavaria (except for the northeastern part), the Saarland and the Rhineland are heavily Catholic. The northern states are heavily Protestant. Westphalia and the central and southwestern parts of West Germany (Hesse, Rhineland-Palatinate, Baden-Württemberg) have a more mixed population. Catholics constitute only a very small minority in the new eastern states, formerly under Communist rule.

The other areas of the pre-World War I German Empire were primarily Protestant. Catholics were dominant only in eastern and central Silesia and in the central part of East Prussia historically called Warmia. Areas in Posen and West Prussia which were transferred to Poland by the Treaty of Versailles had a Catholic majority, but religious affiliation tended to fall along ethnic lines. There were smaller pockets of Catholics elsewhere, mostly near the German-Polish linguistic border.

Before the Evangelical merger, Reformed Church members were concentrated mostly in Brandenburg, Hesse, Franconia, the Palatinate and some northwest German areas. The considerably more numerous Lutherans were a substantial part of the population in these areas and a large majority of Protestants elsewhere. Incidentally, the merger which took place in other areas, often voluntarily, never created the reaction caused in areas under Prussian rule, even though German Reformed churches continue to exist in some places.

In what is now France, the German-speakers in Lorraine were heavily Catholic. Alsace had a Reformed majority in areas around and north-northeast of Strasbourg, as well as in a much smaller belt near Colmar. Many emigrants to both the Russian Empire and to overseas countries came from northern Alsace. "German-speaking" did not mean the same thing as "German" in Alsace-Lorraine. Many of those who used German as their primary language were of mixed German-French ancestry and politically considered themselves to be French, although the other French did not always view them that way, especially when they were evacuated to southern France at the beginning of the World War II.

The Germans in the Sudetenland (Czech Republic) were nearly all Catholics, with the few Protestants mostly along the northern border.

RELIGIOUS DEMOGRAPHY OF GERMAN-AMERICANS IN 1906

According to the comprehensive *Encyclopedia of German-American Research* by Clifford Neal Smith and Anna Piszczan-Czaja Smith (which unfortunately is out of print), German-Americans belonged to what were specifically, or had historically been, German-speaking congregations, at the time of the special 1906 federal census, as listed on the next page. In some cases, we have taken the most specific figures, i.e., the state-by-state lists. The number of churches in each "family" is listed in parentheses, although there is some room for differences in interpreting the data, e.g., with respect to conferences of independent churches.

There were fewer than five German-speaking congregations in each of the following denominations: Christian Catholic Church in Zion, Temple Society, Disciples of Christ, Adventist Christian Church, Hephzibah Faith Missionary Association, and Church of Christ.

Where the number of communicants is not listed (NL), this is because these churches were not considered to be of Germanic or German-American origin. However, a majority of the congregations of the Missionary Church Association were German-speaking. See the section on the evolution of German-American and German-Canadian churches for an explanation.

Table 3: German-American Congregations in 1906

Church Bodies	Number of German-Americans	
	Congregations	Communicants
Lutherans (11)	9,363	1,683,754
Catholics	2,051*	1,519,978
United Brethren (2)	4,304	296,050
German Evangelical Synod	1,205	293,139
German Reformed	1,728	292,654
(Albright) Evangelicals (2)	2,678	174,690
German Baptist Brethren (5)	1,097	97,504
Methodists (4)	903	NL
Mennonites (14)	604	54,798
German Evangelical Protestants (2)	67	34,704
Churches of God	518	24,356
Baptists (2)	203	NL
Congregationalists	158	NL
Presbyterians (2)	146	NL
Moravian Brethren	117	17,155
River Brethren (3)	111	4,569
Seventh-day Adventists	85	NL
Apostolic Christian Church	42	4,558
Missionary Church Association	19	NL
Spiritualists	19	NL
Christian Reformed Church	15	NL
Protestant Episcopal	15	NL
Christian Reformed Church	15	NL
New Apostolic Church	13	2,020
Nonsectarian (Bible Faith)	13	NL
Swedenborgians	11	NL
Salvation Army	11	NL
Amana Society	8	1,756
Schwenkfelders	8	725
Latter-day Saints (2)	8	NL

* In 1906 there were 2,051 Catholic parishes which still used German as their only foreign language. The number of historically German parishes is not known, but if the ratio of historically German parishes to parishes which still used German in 1906 is the same as for Lutherans, there would have been about 3,465 historically German Catholic parishes.

The Smiths indicate that 11 of the 24 different Lutheran synods or other church bodies consisted mostly of Germans. However, the Germans apparently constituted a substantial majority of all the American Lutherans. Part of the reason is that there were so many ethnically distinct churches for immigrants from the various Scandinavian and Baltic countries, as well as Slovakia.

However, only three of the 11 Lutheran groups had more than 1,000 congregations: the Evangelical Lutheran Synodical Conference of America, the General Council of the Evangelical Lutheran Church of America, and the General Synod of the Evangelical Lutheran Church in the United States of America. Regionally focused synods for Iowa, Ohio, and the South had over 400 congregations. None of the others had more than 55.

The Smiths show the time periods when various German Baptist Brethren congregations were established; this shows a vast and progressive multiplication of churches from the eighteenth century until the quarter century preceding 1906. In 1906 they were split into five different churches, including the Seventh-day Baptists.

In 1906 specifically German-American Protestant churches with more than 10,000 communicants were broken down by area as shown below. No similar data are available for Catholics.

Table 4: German-American Protestant Congregations in 1906, By Region

Churches	Northeast	Midwest	South	West
Lutherans	2503	5592	914	354
United Brethren	1045	2869	272	142
German Evangelical Synod	109	976	97	23
German Reformed	1009	611	97	9
(Albright) Evangelicals	942	1439	41	150
German Baptist Brethren	262	639	169	42
Mennonites	195	337	57	18
German Evangelical Protestants	13	46	6	1
Churches of God	229	239	43	7
Moravian Brethren	34	56	24	3

Note that only the Reformed church was concentrated in the Northeast, with its offspring, the Churches of God, almost equally numerous in the Midwest and the Northeast. The Moravian Brethren were the most widely scattered, but with a solid plurality in the Midwest. There was a Midwestern majority, often a strong one, in the other seven churches.

However, if we look at the German churches in terms of clusters of adjoining states, and the ratio of the number of the churches to the total population of states at that time, a somewhat different pattern emerges.

With respect to German-American settlement and onward migration patterns, Oklahoma and Colorado clearly belong to the Midwest. Every single one of the states in this enlarged Midwest had a large number of German-speaking congregations. Of course, there is some difference between the East Central states, which had a lot of migrants the Eastern states and those farther west, which were populated mostly by nineteenth-century immigrants, but there is no clearcut dividing line.

A second cluster consists of the Mid-Atlantic states from New York to Virginia (including West Virginia, which was part of Virginia until the Civil War), but excluding Delaware and New Jersey. However, Pennsylvania overwhelmingly dominated this area in terms of German-American churches and had more congregations than any other state in quite a few cases. Although there were many in New York, the number was below the national average in relationship to the total population.

The third cluster, which the raw figures do not reflect, consists of the states on the Pacific rim and the northern Rockies (Idaho, Wyoming). The frontier may have been officially declared closed in 1890, but these states were still sparsely populated, so the German-American church-to-population ratio was quite high. The population of these states has multiplied much more rapidly during the twentieth century than that of the other states.

EVOLUTION OF CHURCHES TO WHICH GERMAN-AMERICANS AND GERMAN-CANADIANS BELONGED

The history of churches with German-speaking congregations was long characterized by increasing fragmentation, although the changes moved in the direction of mergers in the twentieth century, especially during the latter part of it.

The accompanying chart of the development of German-American churches by Dr. David Koss provides us with a good overview of the more significant splits and mergers.

The Smiths' *Encyclopedia* is a more detailed snapshot of German-American churches in 1906. For a brief history of the development of each church up to 1906, we recommend that you read the *Encyclopedia*.

For later developments, or the history of churches not covered by the Smiths or not covered in detail (i.e., those not founded by Germans or German-Americans and all Canadian churches), check the latest edition (and earlier ones, if need be) of the annual *Yearbook of American and Canadian Churches*.

We cannot possibly provide all the details, but we will attempt to sketch a generalized picture of the historical tendencies of some important church bodies.

The fragmentation within the original Anabaptist movement preceded the establishment of a specific church organization and it has continued throughout the centuries, despite rare moves toward greater unity. You will find more inter-church and interdenominational cooperation today, but few signs of any mergers.

The Smiths' list of 14 Mennonite church bodies includes two Amish and one Hutterite, groups which are often viewed as distinct entities. The vast majority belonged either to the Mennonite Church, comprised largely of the descendants of Swiss and South German immigrants of the colonial era, and the General Conference of Mennonites of North America, in which the Russian Mennonite immigrants since 1874 and their descendants were very numerous. The latter is not a church, but an organization to which dozens of individual denominations belong. These two are still among the larger groups, but the Amish and the Hutterites have increased very rapidly, the latter particularly in Canada, where the General Conference is also very strong.

The Lutheran church did not splinter the same way in Europe. However, each established state church in Germany was independent and the churches in various states differed substantially in their perspectives, despite a common creed. For example, Koss points out that the church in Luther's home state of Germany became ideologically dogmatic, whereas the Hessian church became so ecumenical that its "Lutheranism" was questioned by the orthodox. He sees this as the root of the formal splintering in North America. The story of the twentieth-century Lutheran mergers is a complex one, but only the Evangelical Lutheran Church of America (ELCA) and the Lutheran Church - Missouri Synod have a large membership today, since most of the larger Lutheran groups have merged into the ELCA. While the German Reformed church has not been subdivided to quite the same degree in North America, researching German Reformed immigrant ancestors is complicated by the fact that there are so many other Calvinist churches and other churches whose creed is considered quite compatible with Calvinism. German Reformed immigrants or descendants could well have joined one of these other churches upon arrival or later.

The Methodists, Baptists and Presbyterians, which have a considerable number of historically German churches, are likewise comprised of many separate churches, with far more Baptist churches today than shown in the 1906 census.

The German Methodists in North America represent the most complex hybrid, as far as origin is concerned. Many German-speaking Methodists emigrated soon after that church was established in Germany and Switzerland (early 1830s) because of the hostile environment. The first German Methodist congregations in the United States were established about the same time by German-Americans.

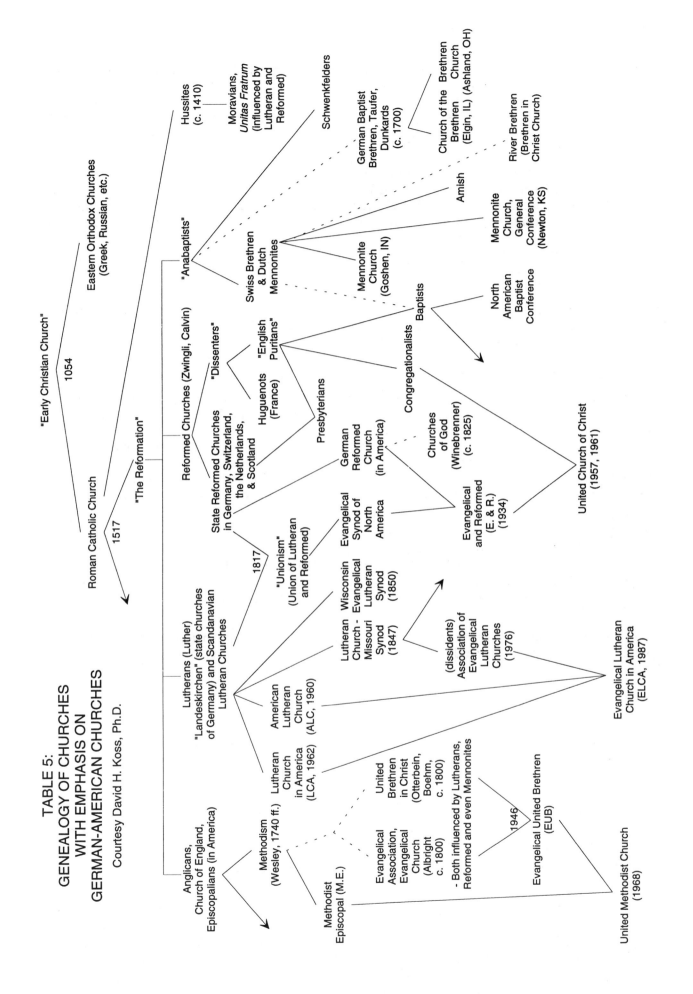

TABLE 5:
GENEALOGY OF CHURCHES
WITH EMPHASIS ON
GERMAN-AMERICAN CHURCHES

Courtesy David H. Koss, Ph.D.

"Early Christian Church"

Eastern Orthodox Churches (Greek, Russian, etc.)

1054

Roman Catholic Church

1517

"The Reformation"

Hussites (c. 1410)

Moravians, *Unitas Fratrum* (influenced by Lutheran and Reformed)

Schwenkfelders

German Baptist Brethren, Taufer, Dunkards (c. 1700)

Church of the Brethren (Elgin, IL)

Brethren Church (Ashland, OH)

River Brethren (Brethren in Christ Church)

"Anabaptists"

Swiss Brethren & Dutch Mennonites

Amish

Mennonite Church (Goshen, IN)

Mennonite Church, General Conference (Newton, KS)

Reformed Churches (Zwingli, Calvin)

"Dissenters"

"English Puritans"

Baptists

North American Baptist Conference

Huguenots (France)

Presbyterians

Congregationalists

State Reformed Churches in Germany, Switzerland, the Netherlands, & Scotland

German Reformed Church (in America)

Churches of God (Winebrenner) (c. 1825)

United Church of Christ (1957, 1961)

Evangelical Synod of North America

Evangelical and Reformed (E. & R.) (1934)

Lutherans (Luther) "Landeskirchen" (state churches of Germany) and Scandanavian Lutheran Churches

1817

"Unionism" (Union of Lutheran and Reformed)

Wisconsin Evangelical Lutheran Synod (1850)

Lutheran Church - Missouri Synod (1847)

(dissidents) Association of Evangelical Lutheran Churches (1976)

American Lutheran Church (ALC, 1960)

Evangelical Lutheran Church in America (ELCA, 1987)

Anglicans, Church of England, Episcopalians (in America)

Lutheran Church in America (LCA, 1962)

Methodism (Wesley, 1740 ff.)

United Brethren in Christ (Otterbein, Boehm, c. 1800)

Methodist Episcopal (M.E.)

Evangelical Association, Evangelical Church (Albright c. 1800)

- Both influenced by Lutherans, Reformed and even Mennonites

1946

Evangelical United Brethren (EUB)

United Methodist Church (1968)

Germanic Genealogy: A Guide to Worldwide Sources and Migration Patterns

Other immigrants who did not have a church representing their denomination near where they settled, or had no strong attachment to it, joined the Methodists because of their strong outreach efforts toward the immigrants, constituting a kind of "Welcome Wagon." But the Methodist church as a whole was not interested in linguistically distinct congregations, so these converts may not have belonged to predominately German-speaking congregations.

This lack of interest in promoting foreign-language worship services was one of the reasons why Albright, a former German Reformed minister, soon left the Methodist Church he had joined. However, according to the 1997 church yearbook, the Evangelical Church he helped found (after splitting and reuniting to form the Evangelical United Brethren Church) merged with the Methodist Church to become the United Methodist Church in 1968. Thus there was a reunion of the like-minded after the language issue ceased to hold them apart. While there are many Methodist church bodies in North America, the United Methodist Church is by far the largest one.

Splintering has not been quite as common among the German Baptist Brethren, but here, too, one finds various churches with the same roots. The Seventh-day Baptists are erroneously listed in the 1997 church yearbook as part of the Baptist family, but they may well be considered a body which is no longer part of the German Baptist Brethren family, just as the River Brethren are viewed as independent of their Mennonite origin.

The Seventh-day Baptist church was founded by Johann Konrad Beissel, who had been influenced by the mystical Inspirationists, came to Boston in 1720, joined the German Baptist Brethren in 1724, but withdrew from membership in 1728. In 1732 he and his followers founded the celibate Ephrata Society or Cloister, which originally was based on the concept of communal ownership of property. By the 1760s, the celibate membership had dwindled sharply before the creation of their church. Just when they organized under their present name is unknown to us, but they are often regarded as a separate group.

Germanic churches established in North America, often the result of groups splitting away from the parent church or the impact of revivalism, included the United Protestant Ministers' Association and Conference (which the Smiths list as "German American Protestant bodies"), the Evangelical Association and the United Evangelical Church (listed as "Evangelical bodies"), the Apostolic Christian Church, and the revivalist "United Brethren bodies," comprised of the Church of the United Brethren in Christ and its later "Old Order" offshoot.

Non-Germanic churches which immigrants on this side of the Atlantic joined, as German-speaking congregations, include the Presbyterians, the Congregationalists, the Christian Reformed Church of North America, the Universalists, the Salvation Army, the Swedenborgians (General Convention of the New Jerusalem in the USA), and some Methodists and Baptists (who both split into numerous sub-denominations).

The New Apostolic Church (which the Smiths list under "Catholic Apostolic Churches," along with a like-minded English-speaking church by that name) had contacts with the same church in Germany prior to World War I, but the German and German-American churches may have developed independently (as the Methodists did in part).

Most of the other churches have undergone changes as a result of mergers, or sometimes name changes. Furthermore, some churches have total congregational autonomy, rather than any hierarchical structure, so that it may be hard to find records even if there has been no formal division within the church.

Only the Catholics and some comparatively small Protestant denominations have remained constant and unified.

The most significant difference between Canada and the United States is the formation in 1925 of the United Church of Canada, representing a merger of the Methodists, the Congregationalists, the Council of Local Union Churches and about 70% of the Presbyterians. Nevertheless some small Methodist denominations and a small Congregational church still exist. Otherwise, the pattern is generally similar. For example, there are many Baptist and Mennonite churches in Canada, with somewhat fewer distinct Lutheran and Reformed churches.

Although most Canadian churches are autonomous national entities, they are nevertheless almost identical counterparts to American churches in many cases. In other cases, it is not clear whether a slight variation of the name represents a unique church or not, because so many churches bear rather similar names, although they may not be related.

We have attempted to identify the denominations which are relevant for researching the parish records of churches in North America to which people of Germanic origin belong in the section on genealogical resources. This is a very complicated, time-consuming and sometimes confusing task. But if you are interested in tracing the roots of only one denomination, the task should not be quite so overwhelming.

GENEALOGICAL RESOURCES FOR PARTICULAR DENOMINATIONS

In the absence of more specifically genealogical sources, we have listed those church archives in the United States and Canada which seem to be the most likely to have information about the churches of German-speaking immigrants and their descendants.

When writing to archives, you should always enclose either a self-addressed, stamp envelope or postage, since some of them may prefer to use their own stationery. It is quite possible that they may enclose a published brochure, so it would be best to enclose two stamps with your query.

Such archives rarely have the staff to do genealogical research for you, but they should be able to tell you whether they have church records pertinent to your personal research or where else these might be located. You can always ask whether the archives staff can recommend someone who is willing to do such research, unless you are planning to go there in person, in which case you should request information about access, the hours when the archives is open, whether any particular restrictions apply, etc.

If the archives has pertinent records but is not in a position to recommend a researcher, check Ernest Thode's *Address Book for Germanic Genealogy*, which includes the addresses of many genealogists both in North America and in Europe.

If you find no genealogist who lives in the area, but would like to save the cost of having to pay for travel time and other expenses, you can write the local or nearest genealogical society to see whether some of their members are willing to undertake research. If you are searching old parish registers, they could have been written in the German Gothic script, so you may need to ask whether anyone is available who can decipher and read such material.

A description of more than 2,600 genealogical societies, including ethnic and special interest organizations, can be found in the 11th edition of *Meyer's Directory of Genealogical Societies in the U.S.A. and Canada*. Elizabeth Petty Bentley's directory also includes other resources, like historical societies, but it is restricted to the United States.

Most of the addresses not otherwise previously known to us are from *1997 Yearbook of American and Canadian Churches*, edited by Kenneth B. Bedell, or from the 6th edition of Ernest Thode's *Address Book for Germanic Genealogy*.

Other sources which were checked for relevant information include: (1) Clifford Neal Smith and Anna Piszczan-Czaja Smith, *Encyclopedia of German-American Genealogical Research*, (2) Arta F. Johnson, *Bibliography and Source Materials for German-American Research*, Vol. 1; and (3) David Koss, "Unscrambling the German-American Churches," an update of an article originally published in *The Palatine Immigrant* in Vol. IX, No. 3 (Winter 1984).

ROMAN CATHOLICS

Catholic records in the United States are highly decentralized. There appears to be no nationwide publication indicating which churches were predominantly German-American, as there is for historically Polish-American parishes. However, the various diocesan and other archives can probably provide you with information as to where records are located and possibly which churches were historically German, which is especially useful if you are searching for ancestors in a known locality which had more than one Catholic parish.

The annual church yearbook lists many addresses. A more detailed book which lists the hours when many archives are open and whether a prior appointment is required is the *Membership and Repository Directory of the Association of Catholic Diocesan Archivists*. This book can be obtained from:

> Rev. George C. Michalek, Vice Chancellor
> Catholic Diocese of Lansing Archives
> 1500 E. Saginaw St., Suite 2
> Lansing, MI 48906-5550

Ernest Thode lists the following archives as having the most important and most extensive collection of materials on German Catholics in the United States, including information about parishes, but not parish registers:

> Archives of the Roman Catholic Central-Verein
> 3855 Westminster Place
> St. Louis, MO 63103

If you are researching Catholic ancestors in Canada, Kenneth E. Rowe's chapter on "Directories of Church History Material" in the church yearbook, indicates that you can request guides to many Canadian Catholic diocesan and institutional archives from:

> Rev. Pierre Hurtubise, O.M.I., Director
> Research Center on Religious History in Canada
> St. Paul University
> 223 Main St.
> Ottawa, ON K1S 1C4
> Canada

The Old Catholics in Germany and Austria rejected the concept of papal infallibility, but we have no information indicating that any of these ever emigrated.

CHURCHES OF LUTHERAN OR REFORMED ORIGIN

Although most immigrants continued to belong to Lutheran and Reformed churches long after the two had been merged in Germany, a German Evangelical Church was eventually established in the United States. Moreover, some of the churches established in the United States drew members from both the Lutheran and Reformed churches, which makes a clear distinction difficult. Some of these new churches, of course, had an even broader basis, attracting Mennonites or people belonging to churches of British origin as well.

Addresses of archives for different Lutheran synods are:

> Evangelical Lutheran Church of
> America Archives
> 8765 West Higgins Rd.
> Chicago, IL 60631-2818

> Department of Archives and History
> Lutheran Church - Missouri Synod
> 801 De Mun Ave.
> St. Louis, MO 63105-3188

> Wisconsin Lutheran Seminary Archives
> 11831 N. Seminary Dr., 651
> Mequon, WI 53092

In many cases, the regional ELCA archives may be able to provide more specific information about historically German parishes and the location of any church records then the national archives. These are:

Mortveldt Library
Pacific Lutheran University
Tacoma WA 98447
(for Alaska, Idaho, Montana, Oregon and Washington)

Pacific Lutheran Theological Seminary
2770 Marin Ave.
Berkeley, CA 94708
(for Arizona, California, Colorado, Hawaii, New Mexico, Nevada, Utah and Wyoming)

Region 3 Archives, ELCA
2481 Como Ave. W.
St. Paul, MN 55108-1445
(for Minnesota, North Dakota, and South Dakota)

Wentz Library
Lutheran Theological Seminary
66 Confederate Ave.
Gettysburg, PA 17325
(for Central Pennsylvania, Delaware, Eastern Maryland and the District of Columbia)

Region 7 Archives, ELCA
7301 Germantown Ave.
Philadelphia, PA 19119
(for New York, New Jersey, Eastern Pennsylvania, and New England)

Thiel College
Greenville, PA 16125
(for Delaware, Maryland, Central and Western Pennsylvania, West Virginia, and the District of Columbia)

Region 5 Archives, ELCA
333 Wartburg Place
Dubuque, IA 52001
(for Illinois, Iowa, Wisconsin, and Upper Michigan)

Lutheran Theological Southern Seminary
4201 N. Main St.
Columbia, SC 29203-5898
(for Alabama, North and South Carolina, Florida, Mississippi, Virginia, and the Caribbean Synod)

No archives have been established yet in two regions. Thode states that letters concerning these other states should be sent to the national office in Chicago.

However, it appears that many of the Old Lutherans who emigrated because of persecution may have joined the Wisconsin synod, the Missouri synod or the former Buffalo synod.

As a result of various mergers, the ELCA is the largest Lutheran church in the United States. The 673-page *1997 Yearbook: Evangelical Lutheran Church in America*, prepared by the Office of the General Secretary of the ELCA and published by the Augsburg Fortress Publishing Co. in Minneapolis, has more information on the various church bodies of the past are now a part of ELCA.

The *Lutheran Annual* is a periodical for the Missouri Synod which is comparable to the ELCA yearbook in terms of providing addresses of parishes. However, if you need more than this, you will probably find the quarterly of the Concordia Historical Institute at the central archives in St. Louis more helpful.

These sources should provide you with the addresses of district archives. District archives have valuable historical material which is relevant for genealogy. For example, most parishes publish a jubilee booklet on the 25th, 50th, 75th, or 100th anniversary of their existence, or on later occasions. These congregational histories can usually be found at the district archives. Moreover, the district archivist is more likely to be able to identify historically German-speaking parishes.

All of these resources should help you identify the past affiliations of various synods, which changed so much over the course of time.

Thode states that the typed transcripts of Lutheran parish registers in Pennsylvania, formerly at the Abdel Wentz Library of the Lutheran Theological Seminary in Gettysburg, are now in the custody of:

> Adams County Historical Society
> Old Dorm
> Seminary Campus
> Drawer A
> Gettysburg, PA 17325

Archives for Canadian Lutheran churches are at:

> Concordia Lutheran Archives
> 7100 Ada Blvd.
> Edmonton, AB T5B 4E4
> Canada
>
> Evangelical Lutheran Church in Canada
> 1512 St. James St.
> Winnipeg, MB R3H 0L2
> Canada

> Evangelical Lutheran Church in
>   Canada, Eastern Synod
> Wilfred Laurier University
> Waterloo, ON N2L 3C5
> Canada

Genealogical information about the Salzburgers, Lutheran refugees from the Archbishopric of Salzburg who went to Georgia, can be found in the newsletter of the following society:

> The Georgia Salzburger Society
> P.O. Box 478-B
> Rincon, GA 31326

The German Reformed Church is now part of the United Church of Christ, with its archives at:

> Archives of the United Church of Christ
> Philip Schaff Library
> Lancaster Theological Seminary
> 555 W. James St.
> Lancaster, PA 17603

The United Church of Christ also includes the former Evangelical and Reformed Church (which included the German Evangelical Synod of North America, initially the German Evangelical Church Society in the West, consisting of immigrants of the merged church in Germany) and the Congregational Christian Church. Thode also reports that German-language records of the former Evangelical Synod and the "German Evangelical Protestant" churches are at the address listed below. There were numerous Evangelical Synods in the United States in 1906, but presumably the reference is to the Evangelical Synodical Conference of America, since the other synods using this name were concentrated in a specific state.

> United Church of Christ
> Eden Archives and Library
> 475 E. Lockwood Ave.
> Webster Groves, MO 63119

However, a substantial number of German-Americans joined the Churches of God in North America, with the first founded in 1829 by John Winebrenner, with a General Eldership (now General Conference) formed in 1830. Winebrenner had been a minister in the German Reformed Church, then joined the Methodist Church, and soon concluded that neither church met the needs of those German-Americans who shared his views. Its archives are at:

> Shafer Library
> University of Findlay
> 1000 N. Main St.
> Findlay, OH 45840-3695

It is not clear whether immigrants who belonged to the Church of God in Europe, mentioned in Wuschke's translation of Krebs's article, have their roots in the Winebrenner church.

The church yearbook also lists the above repository for the Evangelical and Reformed Church, which now belongs to the United Church of Christ.

Nineteenth-century German Reformed immigrants, especially in the Midwest, also joined what was originally the Reformed Protestant Dutch Church, which still exists as the Reformed Church in America. Canadian congregations also belong to this church. The church headquarters are at:

> Reformed Church in America
> 475 Riverside Drive
> New York, NY 10015

The Canadian churches of this denomination have their headquarters at:

> Council of the Reformed Church in Canada
> Reformed Church Centre
> R. R. # 4
> Cambridge, ON N1R 5S5
> Canada

The Christian Reformed Church in North America appears to be of predominantly Dutch origin, but may well include some German Reformed. It has head offices in Kalamazoo, Michigan, and Burlington, Ontario. See the *1997 Yearbook of American and Canadian Churches* for addresses.

Many German Reformed also joined the Presbyterian Church, which had the same Reformed origin and creed, even though it was mostly Scottish. There are a number of Presbyterian church repositories in the United States, but its official archives are at:

> Historical Center
> Presbyterian Church in America
> 12330 Conway Rd.
> St. Louis, MO 63141

Thode lists the following archives as of genealogical value for German Presbyterians and Reformed:

> Presbyterian and Reformed Church Historical Foundation
> Assembly Drive
> Montreat, NC 28757

For Germans who belonged to the churches which formed the United Church of Canada (Methodists, Presbyterians, Congregationalists, Evangelical United Brethren), write to the following to get information:

> Central Archives
> Victoria University
> Toronto, ON M5S 1K7
> Canada

For Presbyterians who did not join the United Church of Canada, write to:

> Presbyterian Archives
> 59 St. George St.
> Toronto, ON M5S 2E6
> Canada

The United Church of Christ includes the former Congregational Church, which is not known to have existed in continental Europe but which a significant number of German-

Americans joined. The following repository may be particularly helpful for those researching Congregational ancestors:

Congregational Library
14 Beacon St.
Boston, MA 02108

However, evangelicals within the Congregational Christian Churches established the still existing Conservative Congregational Christian Conference, which includes churches that previously belonged to other congregations. Among these are the Community or Bible Churches, which could mean or include those referred to by the Smiths as Nonsectarian Churches of the Bible Faith. The church headquarters are located at:

Conservative Congregational Christian Conference
7582 Currell Blvd., Suite 108
St. Paul, MN 55125

The Congregational Christian Churches in Canada trace their origin to denominations in the eastern and northern American states, with the first church established in Canada in 1821. The early congregations called themselves simply Christians. The headquarters of these churches in Canada is:

Congregational Christian Churches in Canada
222 Fairview Dr., Suite 202
Brantford, ON N3T 2W9
Canada

According to Thode, the following archive formerly held the records of the largely German-American Evangelical Association and the United Brethren in Christ, both predominantly German churches with a Lutheran or Reformed background:

Historical Society
United Theological Library
1810 Harvard Building
Dayton, OH 45406

This society may still be able to provide information about members of these former churches. The fact that Thode lists this address under Methodists suggests the possibility that many members of the former German-language churches may have joined the Methodists.

However, Thode also has an address for the archives of the Evangelical Congregational Church, which he identifies as the former Evangelical Association and an offshoot, presumably the United Evangelical Church:

Evangelical School of Theology
121 S. College St.
Myerstown, PA 17067

The Huguenots are a distinct Calvinist group, but they do not constitute a separate church. German Huguenot publications are available at the Family History Library or can be viewed by making an appointment to visit the:

National Huguenot Society
9033 Lyndale Ave. S., Suite 108
Bloomington, MN 55420-3535

The Waldensians started off as a movement and developed into a church, but to the best of our knowledge, they do not constitute a separate Reformed church in terms of creed. Pertinent information may be available from the:

Museum of Waldensian Heritage
Rodoret St.
Valdese, NC 28690

CHURCHES WHICH PRACTICE ADULT BAPTISM

Most of these originated within the initially highly amorphous Anabaptist wing of the Reformation. However, a number of German and English churches which shared the same belief were established at a significantly later date.

We have lumped all of these together, regardless of origin, because in these churches baptism occurs only when people who are old enough to personally attest to their faith join the church. This usually occurred during the teens or early twenties as a rule, although the churches differ somewhat in terms of what age a person must be to be considered an adult. With respect to the difference between the date of birth and the date of baptism, this is more like confirmations, rather than baptisms, in most other churches.

There are no baptismal records for those who never joined the church. On the other hand, some people may join the church at a ripe age and some from other denominations may convert to one of these churches at a later time. In both cases, baptismal records are likely to be available, although the churches may differ somewhat with regard to the circumstances under which a new baptism is required in the case of interdenominational church transfers.

The Mennonites are extraordinarily active in genealogy and have published a huge number of family histories, many of which can be found at the archives and libraries listed below. The resource centers east of the Mississippi tend to focus on the Swiss-South German Mennonites who arrived during the colonial period, with some of them migrating to Ontario after the American Revolution.

Those west of the Mississippi tend to focus on the North European (Dutch-Prussian-Russian) wing of the Mennonites. These Russian Mennonites, together with a few who had remained in Prussia, came to the Americas, beginning in 1873-74.

For those reasons the repositories are listed approximately in east-to-west order, since there are no significant distinctions between the United States and Canada:

Lancaster County Mennonite
 Historical Society
2215 Mainstream Road
Lancaster, PA 17602-1499

Mennonite Historical Library and
Archives of Eastern Pennsylvania
1000 Forty Foot Rd.
Lansdale, PA 19446

Menno Simons Historical Library
 and Archives
Eastern Mennonite College
Harrisonburg, VA 22801

Mennonite Archives of Ontario
Conrad Grebel College
Waterloo, ON N2L 3G6
Canada

Mennonite Historical Library
Bluffton College
Bluffton, OH 45817

Mennonite Historical Library
Goshen College
1700 South Main St.
Goshen, IN 46526-4724

Illinois Mennonite Historical and
 Genealogical Society
P.O. Box 819
Metamora, IL 6158

Mennonite Heritage Centre
600 Shaftesbury Blvd.
Winnipeg, MB R3P 0M4
Canada
(has many Mexican church books)

Hanover Steinbach Historical Society
P.O. Box 1980
Steinbach, MB R0A 2A0
Canada

Mennonite Library and Archives
Bethel College
300 East 27th
North Newton, KS 46526-9989

Mennonite Brethren archives are at:

Centre for Mennonite Brethren Studies
   Archives
1-168 Riverton Ave.
Winnipeg, MB R2L 2E5
Canada
(*also the address for the Manitoba*
Mennonite Historical Society)

Center for Mennonite Brethren Archives
Tabor College
Hillsboro, KS 67063-1799

Library and Archives
Center for Mennonite Brethren Studies
4824 E. Butler Ave.
Fresno, CA 93727-5097
(*also the address for the California*
Mennonite Historical Society)

There are numerous other archives for specific Mennonite churches or for Mennonites in specific areas. Check Thode's *Address Book* for additional addresses.

More than 150,000 genealogical cards about Prussian and Russian Mennonites are at:

Mennonite Genealogy, Inc.
P.O. Box 393
Winnipeg, MB R3C 2H6
Canada

Although this resource center usually will respond to queries, expect a long wait because of the small staff of volunteers.

The following independent genealogical quarterly originally focused on the Mennonites who went to Pennsylvania and adjoining states, but by now it has published a considerable number of articles on the North European Mennonites, as well as on related groups like the Amish and the Brethren:

Mennonite Family History
P.O. Box 171
Elverson, PA 19520-0171

Winnipeg now has more Mennonites than any other city in the world, so it is probably the leading genealogical resource center in North America. The two institutions jointly publish the *Mennonite Historian*, which has extensive genealogical information about the Mennonites in and from West Prussia, the Russian Empire, Western Canada, Nebraska-Kansas, and Latin America. The Manitoba Mennonite Historical Society has extensive genealogical records of Mennonite forebears in Russia and Prussia on its web site (http://www.mmhs.org/mmhs.mmhs.htm), much of it compiled by Adalbert Goertz, a Prussian-born Pennsylvanian, who has been very prolific in writing articles in both English and German, with the German ones appearing mostly in *Altpreussische Geschlechterkunde* and *Ostdeutsche Familienkunde*, the latter published by AGoFF.

The societies in California, Manitoba, Pennsylvania, Illinois and possibly others also publish journals or newsletters which include substantial genealogical material. So does the Manitoba Mennonite Historical Society.

The Genealogy Project Committee of the society in Fresno is developing a database with the goal of eventually including data on all of the North European Mennonites, but particularly those who went to the Russian Empire and later to the Americas. Volume 1 of the GRANDMA database (GVM1) is now available on CD-ROM and includes more than 135,000 names organized into family groups. These include Mennonites in the United States, Canada, the Russian and Prussian Empires, and Latin America, primarily people born before 1930. But most of them pertain to families who can trace their ancestry through the American Midwest back to Russia.

Volume 2 (GVM2), which includes more Canadian names and more people born after 1930, may also be available already. For details, see the December 1996 issue of the *Manitoba Mennonite Historical Society Newsletter*. Later information may be available in *The Mennonite Genealogist*, published in Fresno.

Delbert Plett, founder of the Steinbach society, has published *The Mennonite Kleine Gemeinde Historical Series*, with a lot of genealogical information in most of the 6 volumes. John P. Dyck has written a book on the Bergthaler Mennonites.

For a more complete list of resources pertinent to Mennonite genealogy, see Lawrence Klippenstein and Jim Suderman, eds., *Directory of Mennonite Archives and Libraries*, English-German-French 3rd edition (Winnipeg: Mennonite Heritage Centre, 1990). It lists resources centers in Australia, Brazil, Canada, France, Germany, the Netherlands, Paraguay, Switzerland, the United Kingdom, the United States, and Uruguay, as well as for three Asian countries whose Mennonites are not of Germanic origin.

Mennonite Family History and other Pennsylvania Mennonite periodicals often include information about the Amish, but this is less true of those in western North America.

The outstanding expert on the Amish is John A. Hostetler, who published an *Annotated Bibliography on the Amish* in 1951. Arta Johnson reports, in her *Annotated Bibliography*, that a list of all available printed Amish genealogies was published in the Autumn 1969 issue of *Pennsylvania Folklife*.

According to Thode's *Address Book*, there are many Amish genealogies and settlement histories at:

> Amish Historical Society
> c/o David Luty
> Route 4
> Aylmer, ON N5H 2R3
> Canada

Betty Miller, *The Amish in Switzerland and Other European Countries* (Berlin, OH: Author, 1984) and J. Virgil Miller, "The Swiss Family Origins of the Amish-Mennonite Migration to America" in *Mennonite Family History*, 1993, deal with the group's roots in Switzerland and their flight down the Rhine in the seventeenth and eighteenth century.

The most comprehensive history of the Hutterites is John Horsch's *Hutterite Brethren, 1528-1931*. A great deal of genealogical information is included in *Hutterite Society* by John Hostetler and *Russia Record: Hutterite Family Records, 1700-1874*, by Tony Waldner. For further information, see John D. Movius and Evan Eichler, "Hutterite Genealogy Pages on the FEEFHS Web Site," in the *FEEFHS Newsletter* (March 1997). Eichler, of the Lawrence Livermore National Laboratories in California, is the leading Hutterite genealogist.

The following archive and the archives at Goshen College, listed above, include Hutterite records, as well as records for Mennonites who came to America from several different places:

> Freeman Junior College Library
> 748 Main St.
> Freeman, SD 57209

The principal genealogical book for the Schwenkfelders is Samuel Brecht, *The Genealogical Record of the Schwenkfelder Families, Seekers of Religious Liberty Who Fled from Silesia to Saxony and Then to Pennsylvania in the Years 1731 to 1737*.

The archives of the Schwenkfelder church are at:

> Schwenkfelder Historical Society Library
> Carnegie Library Building
> Perkiomensa School
> 1 Seminary Ave.
> Pennsburg, PA 18073

The Missionary Church Association of northern Indiana, which had a majority of German-speaking congregations in 1906, merged with a similar Canadian church, which had been renamed the United Missionary Church in 1947, to form the Missionary Church in 1969. The Canadian churches had their roots in the mission-minded Allianz congregations established by the Mennonite Brethren in Russia. Since there are many Mennonites in northern Indiana, it is reasonable to assume that the American church also included many members of Mennonite and possibly other German origin, as the names of some of its former officers indicates. The *1989 Yearbook of American & Canadian Churches*, edited by Constant H. Jacquet, Jr., gives a clearer picture of this and lists a substantial number officers bearing German names. Current addresses:

The Missionary Church
3811 Vanguard Drive
P.O. Box 9127
Ft. Wayne, IN 46899-9127
(*headquarters*)

Bethel Publishing Co.
1819 S. Main St.
Elkhart, IN 56516
(*publishing headquarters*)

The so-called River Brethren separated from the Mennonites in Pennsylvania in 1778. Their official name since 1863 has been the Brethren in Christ Church, with the United Zion Church organized in 1855 as a separate entity. Like many other churches founded in North America, its membership is drawn from other denominations as well, since it was also influenced by Methodism, and by the pietistic and evangelical movements.

The church's repository is at:

Murray Learning Resources Center
Messiah College
Grantham, PA 17027-9990

The largest of the various congregations of German Baptist Brethren is now known as the Church of the Brethren. All of the four groups are now Brethren bodies. Brethren archives are at:

Brethren Historical Library and
Archives
1451 Dundee Ave.
Elgin, IL 60120-1694

L. A. Beeghley Library
Juniata College
18th & Moore
Huntingdon, PA 16652

Thode lists several other archives for smaller sub-denominations within the Church of the Brethren or concerned with Brethren in specific areas.

The Fellowship of Brethren Genealogists, at the same Elgin address, publishes a newsletter.

Arta Johnson's *Bibliography* lists publications on the history of the German Baptist Brethren, including obituaries and family history data.

Dr. Emmett Bettinger, R. # 3, Box 116, Bridgewater, VA 22812, is a retired church historian. Mennonite Family History has published a number of his articles on Brethren genealogy.

Seventh Day Baptist congregations, historically affiliated with the German Baptist Brethren, not the Baptist church, are located in the United States and Canada. In 1906 the American congregations were all in Pennsylvania, but this must have changed, since the current address of the archives is:

Seventh Day Baptist Historical Society Archives
P.O. Box 1678
Janesville, WI 53547-1678

Thode states that the Apostolic Christian Church was an Anabaptist church of Swiss descent. Its national headquarters are at:

Apostolic Christian Church
P.O. Box 151
Tremont, IL 61568

Pentecostals originated in various countries as a movement, which developed into churches. The German Pentecostal movement began in Hesse-Kassel as a result of preaching by females in 1907. The third largest number of Pentecostals in Europe are in Germany, with 40,000 each belonging to the Assemblies of God, the Mulheim Association of Christian Assemblies, and other groups. There are far more in the Commonwealth of Independent States, but it is not clear whether this includes Germans.

There are quite a few Pentecostal churches founded by people of Germanic descent. However, it seems likely that nearly all of the Pentecostals among Germans in North America are descendants of immigrants who converted to Pentecostalism, not people who brought this religion with them from Germany. For a more authoritative account, see Walter J. Hollenweger's book.

The headquarters of the Pentecostals (formerly the Assemblies of God) in Canada is:

The Pentecostal Assemblies of Canada
6745 Century Ave.
Mississauga, ON L5N 6P7
Canada

The 1997 church yearbook lists 29 Pentecostal churches in the United States. Unless you know the specific Pentecostal church to which your ancestor belonged, it would be difficult to determine whether any of the three Pentecostal repositories would have any relevant information. Since most Germans in North America appear to have joined the church at a recent date, this church may have only limited relevance for Germanic genealogical research.

Two churches of English origin which share the belief in adult baptism are the Baptists and the Salvation Army. However, the Baptists established congregations in Germanic Europe, which the immigrants brought with them, while the small number of Germans in the Salvation Army appear to have joined that church after emigrating.

The Baptists, who already been discussed, had a similar history of spreading throughout Germanic Europe, where they numbered nearly half a million. Some, but not all, of the German Baptists in immigrant countries thus had adopted that religion in continental Europe already.

Because of the large number of Baptist churches and the relatively small percentage of Baptists who were of Germanic origin, it is somewhat difficult to identify the most relevant archives. However, the following are known to have records for German Baptists:

American Baptist Archives Center
P.O. Box 851
Valley Forge, PA 19482-0851

Southern Baptist Historical Library
    and Archives
901 Commerce St.
Nashville, TN 37203-3620

North American Baptist Seminary
1525 S. Grange St.
Sioux Falls, SD 57105

Canadian Baptist Archives
McMaster Divinity College
Hamilton, ON L8S 4K1
Canada

North American Baptist College Archives
11525 - 23 Ave.
Edmonton, AB T6J 4T3
Canada

The archives center in Pennsylvania is for the former Northern Baptist Conference, which included many German-American churches, according to the Smiths. The archives in Tennessee are for the former Southern Baptist Conference, which included a modest number of originally German-speaking congregations. The Ontario archives has material relating to Eastern Canada, which would include most of the early Baptist immigrants to Canada, whether from the United States or from Europe.

The South Dakota and Alberta archives are twin repositories which would be especially helpful for the German-speaking Baptists from the Russian Empire.

The headquarters of a church founded specifically for German Baptists in the United States and Canada by Konrad Fleischmann in 1843 could provide information about its parishes:

North American Baptist Conference
18210 Summit Ave.
Oakbrook Terrace, IL 60181

The Salvation Army, which likewise originated in England, shares the belief in adult baptism, but it had only a few German-American congregations. Its headquarters are at:

The Salvation Army
615 Slaters Lane
Alexandria, VA 22313

The Seventh-day Adventists grew out of a worldwide revival movement in the 1840s and established a church in the United States in 1863. They began sending missionaries to Europe in 1874. Its North American headquarters are at:

North American Division of Seventh-day Adventists
12501 Old Columbia Pike
Silver Spring, MD 20904-6600

There are also Canadian and various regional American offices, whose addresses are listed in the church yearbook.

CHURCHES WHICH DO NOT PERFORM BAPTISMS

The Religious Society of Friends (Quakers) and the Universalists both believe in the concept of universal salvation and therefore do not baptize members. However, the Universalist Church has a policy of congregational autonomy. Therefore, according to a Universalist minister, it is possible that some early German Universalist congregations might have performed baptisms.

The Unitarians, who are even more liberal than the Universalists with whom they merged, would not have any baptismal records either. Templers were encouraged to join the Unitarians. Whether there would be baptismal records for them is uncertain. The European Templers did not reject baptism, but they emphasized internal conversion more than baptism or creed.

The Friends also have congregational autonomy. They never had many Germanic congregations, but since German Quakers were in the first German group settlement in the United States in 1683, these few were probably of German origin. There are two associations which concentrate on planning annual meetings in the United States and Canada, as well as elsewhere, and related religious activities:

Friends General Conference
1216 Arch St., 2B
Philadelphia, PA 19107

Friends United Meeting
101 Quaker Hill
Richmond, IN 47374-1980

For further information about Quakers of Germanic ancestry, see William Hull, *William Penn and the Dutch Quaker Immigration in Pennsylvania*.

You might be able to get information about the few German Universalists and Unitarians of German-American origin from:

Unitarian Universalist Association
    of Congregations Archives
25 Beacon St.
Boston, MA 02108

Unitarian Universalist Historical Society
Universalist Unitarian Church
Haverhill, MA 01630-3032

OTHER CHURCHES OF GERMAN IMMIGRANTS

Much of our information about Moravian Brethren genealogical resources comes from Arta F. Johnson's bibliography.

The major Moravian archives are at:

The Archives of the Moravian Church
41 W. Locust St.
Bethlehem, PA 18018

Moravian Archives, Southern Province
of the Moravian Church
4 East Bank St.
Winston-Salem, NC 27101

The former has published the *Transactions of the Moravian Historical Society*. The latter also publishes a periodical.

Much pertinent information has been published by:

Moravian Historical Society
Whitefield House
214 E. Center St.
Nazareth, PA 18064

Moravian history and genealogy are also emphasized by the:

Tuscarawas County Genealogical Society, Inc.
P.O. Box 141
New Philadelphia, OH 44663-0141

There is also a Moravian community in North Dakota and probably in some other states.

Information about the Moravians in the Canadian Prairie Provinces is available from:

Canadian Moravian Historical Society, Edmonton Chapter
4204 - 16 St.
Edmonton, AB T5N 0M4
Canada

The Palatine Immigrant, published by the Palatines to America, has carried a number of articles relating to Moravian genealogy.

The Methodist Church was established by members of the Church of England who sought to purify it. It played the same role later in Germany. Therefore, it appears that many of the German Methodists either immigrated from Germany and Switzerland or were among those who formed German Methodist congregations in the United States at about the same time.

For published information which may be relevant for German Methodists, see Arta F. Johnson, *Bibliography and Source Materials for German-American Research*, and Kenneth E. Rose's multi-volume *Methodist Union Catalog: Pre-1976 Imprints*, which deals with the contents of major Methodist research collections in the United States and Europe.

Although most Methodist records are kept at the local parish, Thode states that general denominational information is available from:

General Commission on Archives and History of the Methodist Church
Drew University
P.O. Box 127
Madison, NJ 07940

Church records of the Amana Society (formerly the Ebenezer Society) are now at the relatively large colony in Iowa:

Amana Heritage Society
P.O. Box 81
Amana, IA 52203-0081

The Temple Society, originally the Friends of Jerusalem, had two congregations in the United States in 1906 (in New York and Kansas, respectively). There are no known congregations which still exist, although there is a group in Chicago that still identifies with the Templer movement, is in touch with the Temple Society in Germany, and participates in its tours of Palestine.

Many of the Templers in Canada (and possibly also in Kansas) returned to the Mennonite church, in which they had their roots.

Templers also have gravitated to the Free Christians, who do not constitute a formal church. Rather, they represent a movement of like-minded individuals.

The North American expert on the Templers is:

> Dr. Victor G. Doerksen
> 4920 West Ridge Dr.
> Kelowna, BC V1W 3B4
> Canada

The Swedenborgian church (originally known as the Church of the New Jerusalem) was founded in North America in 1792. It was of Swedish origin, but it had some German-speaking congregations. Its headquarters are at:

> The Swedenborgian Church
> 48 Sargent Ave.
> Newton, MA 02158

The key source of information for Harmony Society or Rappists is Karl J. R. Arndt, *George Rapp's Disciples, Pioneers and Heirs*.

An organization dealing with the German communal Harmonists from 1785 to 1905, when they were dissolved, is:

> Harmony Associates
> Old Economy Village
> 14 & Church Sts.
> Ambridge, PA 15003

The following museum serves as the archives of the former Harmony Society in Pennsylvania and Indiana (1805-1905) and publishes a newsletter devoted not only to the Harmony Society, but also to the Mennonites who populated the area later in the nineteenth century:

> Historic Harmony/Marmony Museum
> 218 Mercer St.
> P.O. Box 524
> Harmony, PA 16037

The obvious place to start researching the small number of German-American congregations of the Church of Jesus Christ of Latter-day Saints is the Family History Library in Salt Lake City.

BIBLIOGRAPHY (See ANNOTATED BIBLIOGRAPHY for full citations if not shown)

For books relating to more than one religious group, see the ANNOTATED BIBLIOGRAPHY.

Walser H. Allen. *Who Are The Moravians? The Story of the Moravian Church: A World-Wide Fellowship*, 8th ed. Bethlehem, PA: Department of Publications, Moravian Church. 1981. 91 pp.
    Authoritative history of the Moravian Brethren, including the church's founding (inspired by John Huss), its almost complete obliteration, its revival in Saxony and its establishment of congregations in many countries, with mission stations in many others.

Karl J. R. Arndt. *George Rapp's Disciples, Pioneers and Heirs: A Register of the Harmonists in America*. Edited by Donald E. Pitzer and Leigh Ann Chamness. 1992. 234 pp. Available from Michael Goelzhauser, University of Southern Indiana Bookstore, 8600 University Blvd., Evansville, IN 47712.

Association of Catholic Diocesan Archivists. *Membership and Repository Directory*. Annually. Available from Rev. George C. Michalek, Catholic Diocese of Lansing Archives, 1500 E. Saginaw St., Suite 2, Lansing, MI 48906-5550.
> Lists addresses and telephone numbers of archives and diocesan offices, names of archivists and diocesan officers, hours when archives are open, restrictions on access, and other details.

Roland H. Bainton. *The Age of the Reformation*. Princeton: D. Van Nostrand Co. 1956.
> One of the best accounts of the Reformation.

Kenneth B. Bedell, ed. *Yearbook of American and Canadian Churches: 1997*. (Earlier editions by Constant H. Jacquet, Jr., and others.) Nashville: Abingdon Press. 1997.
> Comprehensive list of denominations, addresses of their headquarters and repositories, brief historical descriptions, and more.

Harold S. Bender and C. Henry Smith, ed. *The Mennonite Encyclopedia*, 4 vols. Scottdale, PA: Herald Press. 1955-59.
> Most comprehensive source for Mennonite history, biography and other subjects.

Elizabeth Petty Bentley. *The Genealogist's Address Book*, 3rd ed.
> Lists addresses for genealogical and historical societies, with sections on specific ethnic and religious groups, and archives in the United States.

Samuel Brecht. *The Genealogical Record of the Schwenkfelder Families, Seekers of Religious Liberty Who Fled from Silesia to Saxony and Then to Pennsylvania in the Years 1731 to 1737*. New York: Rand McNally. 1923.

Martin G. Brumbaugh. *A History of the German Baptist Brethren in Europe and America*. Mount Morris, IL: Brethren Publishing House. 1899. 559 pp.

John M. Byler. *Amish Immigrants of Waldeck and Hesse*. Bowie, MD: Heritage Books. 1993. 231 pp.
> Specific genealogical records of Amish immigrants and their descendants up to 1865.

Damals in Palästina [*In Palestine at That Time*]. Stuttgart. 1990.
> Personal accounts of 46 Templers who returned from Palestine to Germany, including genealogical information.

Donald F. Durnbaugh. *The Believers' Church: The History and Character of Radical Protestantism*.
> Defines the various schools of thought within what was originally a variegated movement, leading to the establishment of various churches.

Cornelius J. Dyck. *An Introduction to Mennonite History*, 3rd ed. Scottdale, PA/Waterloo, ON: Herald Press. 1993. 452 pp.
> Standard, comprehensive text on Mennonite history.

Thomas K. Edlund, "Origins of the Russian Lutheran Church," in *Heritage Review*, Vol. 26, No. 4 (December 1996).
> Comprehensive history of this predominantly German church, with an emphasis on the Baltic countries. Estonia and Latvia became predominantly Lutheran early in the Reformation. Lists all the consistories and the areas each included.

George J. Eisenach. *Pietism and the German-Russians* (first published in English in 1948 under the title, *Pietism and the Russian-Germans in the United States*), translated and abridged by Arnold H. Marzolf. Bismarck, ND: Germans from Russia Heritage Society. 1991. 100 pp.

>Deals with seven sources of pietism among the Germans in Russia. Its 13 chapters include a four-chapter part on the pietistic background in Russia, a four-chapter part on its transplantation to the United States (including one chapter on Congregationalism) and five chapters on the religious practices of the pietistic "Brotherhood."

Mercia Eliade, ed. *The Encyclopedia of Religion*, 16 vols. New York: Macmillan. 1987.

>A useful place to begin research on churches, with key bibliographic entries.

Irmgard Hein Ellingson. *The Bukovina Germans in Kansas: A 200 Year History of the Lutheran Swabians*. Fort Hays, KS: Fort State University. 1987. 107 pp.

>Deals with one of the largest Bukovina Lutheran groups who emigrated to North America.

H. Frank Eshleman. *Historic Background and Annuals of Swiss and German Pioneer Settlers of Southeastern Pennsylvania, and of Their Remote Ancestors, from the Middle of the Dark Ages, Down to the Time of the Revolutionary War*. Lancaster, PA. 1917. Reprinted by the Genealogical Publishing Co. 1969, 1982, 1991. 386 pp.

>Fascinating account of the Mennonites and related groups, as well as those whom he sees as their predecessors, including the Waldensians and the Hussites, but full of misspellings, careless usage of words concerning related groups and other mistakes. However, essential for genealogists with Pennsylvania Mennonite ancestors because he lists many specific personal names, places of origin, years first mentioned, excerpts from passenger lists of the colonial era, and other documents.

Gerhard Florey. *Geschichte der Salzburger Protestanten und ihre Emigration 1731/32*. [*History of the Salzburg Protestants and Their Emigration in 1731-32*]. Vienna, Cologne, Graz: Verlag H. Bohlau. 1977, 2nd ed. 1986. 276 pp.

Charles M. Franklin. *Huguenot Genealogical Research*. Indianapolis, IN: Self-published. 1985. 58 pp.

>Lists specific records in Germany and Switzerland for Huguenots who fled from France between 1520 and 1787. Also lists some church records for Walloons (French-speaking Belgians) who fled from what was then the Spanish Netherlands, mostly in 1568.

Adam Giesinger. *From Catherine to Khrushchev*: The Story of Russia's Germans.

Hugh F. Gingerich and Rachel W. Kreider. *Amish and Amish Mennonite Genealogies*. Gordonville, PA: Pequea Publishers. 1986. 858 pp.

>Comprehensive encyclopedia of Amish families up to 1850, including all known early settlements.

Der Gottesacker zu Herrnhutt, Herrnhut 1822. [*The Cemetery in Herrnhut in 1822*]. Herrnhut, Germany.

>Contains information about 2,500 Moravian Brethren who were buried in Herrnhut in 1722-1822.

Hermann Guth. *Amish Mennonites in Germany: Their Congregations, the Estates Where They Lived, Their Families*. Morgantown, PA: Masthof Press. c1995. 350 pp.

Walter J. Hollenweger. *The Pentecostals*. Minneapolis. 1972.

>Most comprehensive treatment of Pentecostals throughout the world.

John Horsch. *Hutterite Brethren, 1528-1931*. Goshen, IN: Mennonite Historical Society. 1931.

John A. Hostetler. *Annotated Bibliography on the Amish*. Scottdale, PA: Herald Press. 1951.

John A. Hostetler. *Hutterite Society*. Baltimore: Johns Hopkins University Press. 1974, 1997.

Winthrop S. Hudson. *Religion in America: A Historical Account of the Development of American Religious Life*, 2nd ed. New York: Charles Scribner's Sons. 1973. 463 pp.
> Comprehensive account of various Protestant, Catholic, Jewish and Orthodox groups and the changes which have occurred.

William I. Hull. *William Penn and the Dutch Quaker Migration in Pennsylvania*. Originally published 1935. Reprinted by the Clearfield Co., Baltimore, 1990.
> Lists names of all German Quakers who settled in Germantown, PA, 1683-1709, with places of origin.

John T. Humphrey. *Understanding and Using Baptismal Records*. Washington, DC: Humphrey Publications. 1996. 166 pp.
> Refers to many churches, primarily but not exclusively focusing on Britain and the United States, especially Colonial America.

Charlotte Irwin. "Pietist Origins of American Universalism." Master's thesis. Tufts University, 1966.
> Provides description of the European background of this Universalist church.

Arta F. Johnson. *Bibliography and Source Materials for German-American Research*. Volume 1.

George F. Jones. *The Salzburger Saga: Religious Exiles and Other Germans Along the Savannah*. Athens, GA: University of Georgia Press. 1984. 209 pp.
> Key work on the Germans in the American state of Georgia.

J. Kaps. *Handbuch über die katholischen Kirchenbücher in der ostdeutschen Kirchenprovinz östlich der Oder und Neisse und dem Bistum Danzig. [Handbook of Catholic Parish Registers in the East German Archbishopric East of the Oder and Neisse (Rivers) and the Bishopric of Danzig]*. Munich: Katholisches Kirchenbuchamt und Archiv. 1962. 159 pp.
> Deals with Catholic parish registers of the former German eastern provinces.

Gerhard Kessler. *Die Familiennamen der ostpreussischen Salzburger. [Surnames of the Salzburgers in East Prussia]*. Königsberg: Wichern Buchhandlung. 1937. 124 pp.
> Presumably based on Schütz's earlier compilation.

Lawrence Klippenstein and Jim Suderman, eds. *Directory of Mennonite Archives and Libraries*, 3rd English-French-German ed. Winnipeg: Mennonite Heritage Centre. 1990.
> Lists resource centers in 14 countries in Europe, North and South America, Australia and Asia. All but the Asian repositories are of significant value for researching Dutch/Swiss/German/Russian Mennonites.

Eduard Kneifel. *Die evangelisch-augsburgischen Gemeinde Polen, 1555-1939. [The Evangelical Church (Augsburg Creed) in Poland, 1555-1939]*. Vierkirchen, Germany: Indersoderfestr. 1971. 358 pp.
> History of the Lutheran congregations in Poland. "Augsburger" refers to the Religious Peace of Augsburg in 1555, which allowed each ruler to determine the religion in his own land. This resulted in many people fleeing to Poland and other places to seek religious freedom.

David H. Koss, "Unscrambling the German American Churches," an update of an article originally published in *The Palatine Immigrant*, Vol. IX, No. 3 (Winter 1984).
> Best succinct treatment of the splits and mergers of German-American churches, with some historical background.

David H. Koss, Kenneth Smith and Arta F. Johnson. *Pages from the Past*. No. 6 in "Publications Plus" series. Columbus, OH: Palatines to America. 1994.
> Articles on German-American churches and German church records by three leading authorities: Dr. David H. Koss, Kenneth Smith and Dr. Arta F. Johnson.

Paul N. Kraybill. *Mennonite World Handbook*. Lombard, IL. 1978.
> Country-by-country study of Mennonites throughout the world.

Edmund Krebs. "The German Church of God, in Volhynia and Poland." Originally published in German in the *Evangeliums Posaune*. Translated by Ewald Wuschke and published in *Wandering Volhynians* (December 1996).

Margrit B. Krewson, *The German-Speaking Countries of Europe: A Selective Bibliography*.
Has information about more books dealing with religion among German-speaking peoples.

Rev. Reuben Kriebel. *Genealogical Record of the Descendants of the Schwenkfelders Who Arrived in Pennsylvania in 1733, 1734, 1736, 1737 (from the German of Rev. Balthasar Heebner and from Other Sources)*. 1879. Baltimore: Clearfield Co. Reprinted 1993. 371 pp.
Vital records of about 10,000 individuals descended from 140 families who fled from Silesia. Descendants today number hundreds of thousands.

Gary Land, ed. *Adventism in America*. 1985.
Chronological treatment of the church by six historians.

The Lutheran Annual of The Lutheran Church-Missouri Synod. St. Louis: Concordia Publishing House. 552 pp. Published annually.
Contains addresses of member congregations, pastors, teachers, districts, and publications.

Carl Mauelshausen. *The Salzburg Lutheran Expulsion and Its Impact*. Bowie, MD: Heritage Books. Reprinted 1962. 167 pp.
Background of Salzburgers who migrated to the U.S. state of Georgia and elsewhere.

Mary Meyer. *Meyer's Directory of Genealogical Societies in the United States and Canada, 11th ed. 1996*.
Description of more than 2,600 American and Canadian genealogical societies, including ethnic and other special interest groups.

Meyers Kleines Konversations-Lexikon [*Meyer's Small Encyclopedia of General Information*], 7th ed., 6 vols. Leipzig/Vienna: Bibliographisches Institut. 1908-09.

Betty Miller. *The Amish in Switzerland and Other European Countries*. Berlin, OH: Author. 1984.

J. Virgil Miller, "The Swiss Family Origins of the Amish-Mennonite Migration to America," in *Mennonite Family History* (1993).

Russell E. Miller. *The Larger Hope*. Vol. 1: *The First Century of the Universalist Church in America, 1770-1870*; Vol. 2: *The Second Century of the Universalist Church in America, 1870-1970*. Boston. 1980, 1986.
Considered the most authoritative account of this church.

Felix Moeschler. *Alte Herrnhuter Familien: Die mährischen, böhmischen und österreichisch-schlesischen Exulanten*. [*Old Moravian Brethren Families: The Moravian, Bohemian and Austro-Silesian Emigrés*], 2 vols. Herrnhut: Commissionsverlag der Missionsbuchhandlung. 1922-24.

John D. Movius and Evan Eichler, "Hutterite Genealogy Pages on the FEEFHS Web Site," in *FEEFHS Newsletter* (March 1997).

Don F. Neufeld, ed. *Seventh-day Adventist Encyclopedia*, rev. ed. Washington, DC. 1976.
Full of historical data.

Office of the General Secretary. *Yearbook: Evangelical Lutheran Church of America*. Minneapolis: Augsburg Fortress Publishing Co. 1997. 673 pp. Published annually.
Addresses and other details concerning ELCA churches, including information on various former Lutheran churches and synods which are now a part of ELCA.

Edward A. Peckwas. *Register of Vital Records: Roman Catholic Parishes from the Region Beyond the Bug River*. Chicago: Polish Genealogical Society of America. 1984. 44 pp.
Coverage includes German Catholic parish registers from East Galicia and West Volhynia.

Horst Penner. *Die ost- und westpreussischen Mennoniten.* [*The East and West Prussian Mennonites*]. Vol. I (1562-1772); Weierhof, Germany: Mennonitischer Geschichtsverein. 1978. Vol. II (since 1772); Kirchheimbolanden, Germany: Author. 1987.

> Lists the Mennonites in the 1776 rural census in the area taken from Poland by Prussia in the First Partition in 1772, i.e., all except those in the territory belonging to Danzig and those along the Vistula from Thorn (Torun) upwards, areas which were still under Polish rule at the time, but which included only a small percentage of the rural Mennonites.

Delbert F. Plett. *The Mennonite Kleine Gemeinde Historical Series*, 6 vols. Steinbach, MB: DFP (later Crossway) Publications. 1982-93. 166-932 pp. ea.

> Enormous amount of genealogical and biographical information about this specific Mennonite denomination, whose members settled in southeastern Manitoba and southeastern Nebraska in and shortly after 1874.

G. Elmore Reaman. *The Trail of the Huguenots in Europe, the United States, South Africa and Canada.* Baltimore: Genealogical Publishing Co. 1963; reprinted 1993. 318 pp.

> Indexed record of Huguenots who left France after 1685, many of them going to Germany, from where many of their descendants migrated to North America.

Wolfgang Ribbe and Eckart Henning. *Taschenbuch für Familiengeschichtsforschung.* [*Handbook for Family History Research*], 11th ed.

> Wolfgang Ribbe provides a significant amount of historical and bibliographical information about the Huguenots and other French-speaking refugees, Moravian Brethren, Anabaptists (Mennonites, Hutterites) and the Salzburgers which is helpful to genealogists.

Kenneth E. Rose. *Methodist Union Catalog: Pre-1976 Imprints.*

Paul Sauer. *The Holy Land Called.* Melbourne: Temple Society. 1991. 368 pp.

> Focuses on the Templers who migrated directly from Germany to Palestine, with minimal attention to those of Russian Mennonite origin.

Heinrich Sawatzky. *Mennonite Templers*, translated by Victor G. Doerksen. Winnipeg: Echo Verlag. 1990.

> Includes a selected bibliography.

Martin Schmidt. *Das Zeitalter des Pietismus* [*The Age of Pietism*], edited by Wilhelm Jannasch. Bremen. 1965.

Fritz Schütz. *Hauptregister von den sämtlichen nach Preussen gekommenen Salzburgischen-Emigranten sowie selbige in den von des Tit. Herrn Gemeinen Rath Osten angefertigten Rechnung sich befinden (1756 Aug. 20).* [*Main Register of All the Salzburger Emigrants Who Came to Prussia, as well as Those Found in the Account (1756 Aug. 20) Prepared by Titled Public Counselor Osten*]. Gumbinnen, East Prussia: Duplicated, typed manuscript. 1913.

> Lists 9,600 persons of the 20,000 who were expelled by the Archbishop of Salzburg and the 14,000 who settled in (East) Prussia, based on Prussian records and the results of an investigation by a commission sent to Salzburg in 1756 for the purpose of ascertaining the amount of property which had been confiscated. Village of origin recorded for most.

Richard W. Schwarz. *Light Bearers to the Remnant.* Mountain View, CA. 1979.

> College text about the Seventh-day Adventists.

Clifford Neal Smith. *Nineteenth-Century Emigration of "Old Lutherans" from Eastern Germany (Mainly Pomerania and Lower Silesia) to Australia, Canada and the United States.* McNeal, AZ: Westland Publications. 1980. 93 pp.

> Translation of 1943 German book by Wilhelm Iwan.

Clifford Neal Smith and Anna Piszczan-Czaja Smith. *Encyclopedia of German-American Genealogical Research.*

> An especially helpful chapter, "German Ethnic Religious Bodies in America," discusses each religious denomination and shows the location of German-speaking congregations in the United States. Another helpful chapter is "Jews in Southwestern Germany."

Christa Stache. *Verzeichnis der Kirchenbücher im Evangelischen Zentral Archiv in Berlin* [*Inventory of Parish Registers in the Evangelical Central Archive in Berlin*]; Part I, *Die östlichen Kirchenprovinzen der evangelischen Kirche in der altpreussischen Union* [*The Eastern Church Provinces of the Evangelical Church in the Old Prussian Union*], 2nd ed., 297 pp.; 1987); Part II, Berlin. Berlin: Evangelisches Zentralarchiv.

> Lists and dates of Protestant records for particular parishes in the former German eastern provinces in Vol. I. Vol. II includes Old Lutherans, French and other Reformed, and Moravian Brethren, with a few entries for Jews. A few records from the 1600s, most from 1700s or 1800s. Easy to use without knowledge of German.

F. Ernest Stoeffer. *German Pietism During the Nineteenth Century*. Leiden, Netherlands. 1973.

Philip Strobel. *The Salzburgers and Their Descendants*. Athens, GA. Reprinted 1953. c318 pp.

Solomon Stucky. *The Heritage of the Swiss Volhynian Mennonites*. Waterloo, ON: Conrad Press. 1981. 223 pp.

> Includes chart of the many migrations of this small group, map of relevant localities in Ukraine and Poland, mostly Mennonite bibliography, photos and genealogy of one family.

Templer Handbuch [*Templer Handbook*].

> New source of general information, including genealogy.

Ernest Thode. *Address Book for Germanic Genealogy*.

Benjamin Heinrich Unruh. *Die niederländisch-niederdeutschen Hintergründe der mennonitischen Ostwanderungen im 16., 18. und 19. Jahrhundert.* [*The Netherlandish-Low German Background of the Mennonite Eastward Migrations in the 16th, 18th and 19th Centuries*]. Karlsruhe: Author. 1955. 432 pp.

> The most comprehensive listing of Mennonite migrants from Prussia to the Russian Empire (Ukraine), with historical information on the Mennonite flight from the Spanish Netherlands to Polish Prussia during the Reformation era.

Josef Vondra. *German-Speaking Settlers in Australia*.

Tony Waldner. *Russia Record: Hutterite Family Records, 1700-1874*. 1996.

> Includes extensive details from various primary sources.

George H. Williams. *The Radical Reformation*. Philadelphia. 1962.

> Massive volume on the third wing of the Reformation, i.e., those who did not follow the teaching of Luther or Zwingli and Calvin. Most of these were Anabaptists.

Oren Windholz. *Bohemian Germans in Kansas: A Catholic Community from Bukovina*. 1993. Hays, KS: author. 50 pp.

> History of the Bohemian Germans who moved to the Bukovina and later to Kansas.

Ewald Wuschke. *Protestant Church Records on Microfilm for the Former Congress Poland (1815-1915) and Volhynia*. Vancouver: self-published. 1992. 42 pp.

> Covers Lutheran, Reformed, Mennonite and Baptist church records and includes references to some parish registers that either have not been microfilmed or are not known to have survived World War II.

Chapter XII

HISTORY AND DEMOGRAPHY OF GERMAN-SPEAKING JEWS

The history of German Christians and their pagan ancestors is frequently separated from that of the German-speaking Jews. One reason is that until the late eighteenth century, the Jews were considered to be a separate nation (*Volk*), both by themselves and by others. Many Jews and gentiles continued to think of the Jews as constituting a separate people, not merely a distinct religious group.

Almost all American Jews have Ashkenazic ancestors. These settled in northern Europe, initially in Gaul (now France) but later mostly in Germany, as contrasted with the Sephardim of southern Europe, North Africa and the Middle East.

OVERVIEW OF THE HISTORY OF GERMANIC JEWS

Our initial focus will be on the history of the Jews who were indisputably German-speakers during the modern era, i.e., those in the pre-World War I German Empire (including Alsace and Posen), Switzerland, Austria proper and the kingdom of Bohemia, which included Moravia and Austro-Silesia. The word "kingdom" does not imply independence. The Hapsburg emperors were also the kings of Bohemia for all but a few years after 1526. Any local autonomy which had existed previously was squashed at the beginning of the Thirty Years' War. Less than ½% of Luxembourgers were Jews.

Lest any doubt remain as to their "Germanness," the Jews of Posen at one time suggested that all Jews, at least in East Central Europe, should become Germans in a linguistic-cultural sense. This idea was not popular in eastern regions of the Austro-Hungarian Empire. Moreover, the Jews from Prussian Poland emigrated to the United States during the German waves between 1840 and the early 1890s, not during the period of heavy Jewish emigration from the Russian Empire and the eastern parts of the Austro-Hungarian Empire which began in the 1880s and ended with World War I.

Almost all the Ashkenazic Jews in France lived in Alsace, adjacent to German territory, but remote from the 20% of French Jews of Sephardic origin who lived in southern France. They hailed Napoleon as the great emancipator, but they were certainly a part of Germanic Jewry prior to that, even though Alsace was under French rule from the seventeenth century until 1871. Most Jews, as well as Christians (many of mixed German-French ancestry), continued to think of themselves as German-speaking French until the two World Wars, even when Alsace was part of the German Empire.

EARLY JEWISH SETTLEMENTS

Meyers Kleines Konversations-Lexikon [*Meyer's Small Encyclopedia of General Information*], written in 1908-09, indicates that the first Jews documented on German soil came from Gaul to the Cologne area in 321 CE, when both were still part of the Roman Empire. (This was about the same time that Christianity came to be tolerated in that empire and more than 450 years before the last German tribe, the Saxons, became Christians.) In *The Atlas of Jewish History*, Gilbert also shows a smaller but significant Jewish settlement at Regensburg (Ratisbon) in Bavaria dating back to the days of the Roman Empire. The map refers to "100-300 AD," but this is either a rounded off approximation or else Gilbert had discovered earlier records by 1939, when his book was first published.

Most of the early sizeable Jewish settlements in Germany (Mainz, Worms and Speyer in the Rhenish Palatinate; Regensburg; Trier; and Magdeburg) had a documented existence dating back to the ninth, tenth and eleventh centuries, according to Meyer.

Gilbert shows additional pre-1000 settlements in Frankfurt, Würzburg, Merseburg and Augsburg, as well as in Prague, Metz and Verdun, which were part of the Carolingian Empire until 943. This date marked the beginning of the Frankish tribe developing distinct languages and ethnic identities: French in the west; German in the east. There were also some in Marseilles and Avignon near the Mediterranean, from where they migrated to Lorraine. Most of the others crossed the Alps from the cities in central and northern Italy. Many towns in the valleys of various rivers, especially the Rhine, but also the Main, Moselle, Danube, Elbe and smaller tributaries, had small Jewish communities.

Jews arrived in Prague in 927, according to the jubilee book published by the B'nai B'rith lodge in Prague a thousand years later. They also settled in smaller Bohemian and Moravian market towns at an early date.

Gilbert also shows Swiss Jewish communities in Berne, St. Gall(en), Wintherthur, Schaffhausen and Lucerne by the late thirteenth century, Zürich and Aargau by 1500, and refugees from Bavaria and Alsace fleeing to Basel, Solothurn and Neuchâtel in the 1330s.

He mentions no Jewish communities in Austria by 1000 CE, but they must have arrived soon after that.

By the time of the First Crusade in 1096 (which was primarily Germanic, unlike many of the later ones), there were significant Jewish communities in most of the major cities in the new eastern states of the Federal Republic and south of a Berlin-Magdeburg line. Until then, the Jews had been able to lead a free and unencumbered life — in Germany usually as traders, initially as slave traders according to Gilbert.

THE ERA OF MASSIVE EXPULSIONS AND EXTREME PERSECUTION

The Jews were expelled from almost all of western and central Europe between 1000 and 1500 CE. However, because Germany, like Italy, was so fragmented, the expulsions never obliterated them as in most other countries. There were no Jews lawfully resident in Britain, Spain, France, Scandinavia or Muscovy at the time of the Protestant Reformation. Jews expelled from one German principality could often find another one where the ruler needed them at the time. They were sometimes readmitted later, often on a selective basis, and then expelled again.

Germany also represented a place of refuge for a few Jews from other countries during the expulsion period, as was also true in Switzerland and France. A small number of Portuguese Jews found a haven in Hamburg. Later a larger group fled from Provence (Mediterranean France) to Germany, according to Gilbert.

However, the vast majority of Germanic Jews fled eastward toward Poland, later the Commonwealth of Poland and Lithuania, where they were not only tolerated but welcomed, although the first serious anti-Semitic incident occurred in 1399. These expulsions began in the terrible year of 1096 and largely ended by 1400, although there were some later expulsions from Austria, the Rhineland, Berlin, and Bohemia.

The expulsion of the Ashkenazim in western Europe, especially Germany, had three basic causes:

(1) the fanaticism generated by the Crusades, which began as a temporarily successful effort to liberate Palestine from the Muslim "infidels," but which resulted in a massive slaughter of Muslims, Jews and Christians alike

(2) false accusations that Jews were murdering Christian children for Passover ritual (the so-called "Blood libels"), which occurred in the Western countries, as well as in Posen and Cracow, between 1144 and 1407, and spread to other Polish areas after 1566

(3) the accusation that the Jews were responsible for all manner of disasters, but especially the great bubonic plague ("Black Death") of 1348-50 and subsequent recurrences during the latter half of the fourteenth century

Jews were expelled from Austria in 1421, although a Jewish ghetto was established in 1570. Medieval Jews from Vienna and Budapest also found a refuge in Poland, although some Viennese Jews fled to Prague.

The expellees from Britain and France were also Ashkenazi, but they generally fled southward, rather than eastward, so any connection with the German Jews is remote.

THE PERIOD BETWEEN EXPULSION AND EMANCIPATION

The centuries after the expulsion of nearly all German and Austrian Jews were marked by many ups and downs for the Jewish community. Martin Luther expected the Jews to join his reformed church. When they failed to do so, he became vitriolic in his anti-Semitic diatribes. However, his words did not lead to any deeds of cruelty toward Jews.

Cyclical expulsion from particular principalities, followed by (often selective) readmission, continued to be a common pattern, at least in the fifteenth, sixteenth and seventeenth centuries, but there was no emigration from Germany which even remotely resembled the 1100-1400 period or the 1930s, in terms of the percentage of the Jews who left.

Despite isolated instances of executions, the early modern era saw less severe persecution of Jews in Germanic Europe than that which was directed against Christian dissidents during the pre-1648 era and even later in some cases. Severe persecution of Jews was after all sporadic, as Salo Wittmayer Baron, a former professor of Jewish history, literature and institutions at Columbia University, put it. (Early Swiss and Austrian Anabaptists were hunted down mercilessly and many were tortured to death.)

But official discrimination — sometimes more harsh, sometimes less harsh — continued until emancipation, which marked a major turning point for Jews in Austria, Germany and eventually Switzerland.

The first official Jewish ghetto on German soil was decreed in 1560 (Frankfurt), although ghettos existed in Italy before that. In other places, there was a Jewish quarter, either by force or by choice. Ghetto life was wretched, but at least it provided for communal self-government.

The requirement that Jews wear distinctive clothing was more objectionable to some Jews than the ghetto.

EMANCIPATION AND ANTI-SEMITIC REACTION

Emancipation was sparked partly by the Age of Enlightenment, when Jewish intellectuals and professionals, were welcomed into high-level circles on a basis of equality. However, for most Jews it was the French Revolution, based on egalitarian principles, which produced a real change.

Emancipation was often a drawn-out process, which might take up to 30-50 years (and longer in Austria) to complete. The first step was usually a law requiring that Jews adopt permanent surnames. This official liberating process began at different times in different jurisdictions, as shown in the table on the next page.

As George Arnstein points out, the differing dates of Jewish emancipation in various Germanic political entities make an understanding of history essential, particularly local or regional history.

The nineteenth century saw serious setbacks, as well as improvements, for Jewish life. Nevertheless, the overall outcome was the "transformation of rural peddlers, traders and craftsmen into a German Jewish bourgeoisie," in Arnstein's words.

Ironically, Bismarck, the "Iron Chancellor," was seen as sympathetic toward the Jews, in sharp contrast to Luther, the "reformer."

Despite this great progress, however, some Jews still found the social discrimination intolerable. For example, the Austrian writer, Theodor Herzl, was a strong assimilationist, but eventually concluded that Jews would never be fully accepted into German society — not even if they converted to Christianity.

Table 6: Laws Mandating Jewish Family Names

Austria	23 Jul. 1787
South Prussia and New East Prussia (formerly Polish)	17 Apr. 1797
City of Frankfurt (Main)	30 Nov. 1807
French possessions on the Rhine and in NW Germany	20 Jul. 1808 12 Jan. 1813
Kingdom of Westphalia	31 Mar. 1808 04 Jul. 1811
Oberhessen-Starkenburg	15 Dec. 1808
Baden	13 Jan. 1809
Lippe	16 Dec. 1809
Sachsen-Altenburg	20 Jun. 1811
Prussia proper (East of the Elbe)	11 Mar. 1811
Mecklenburg-Schwerin	22 Feb. 1813
Bavaria, Vorarlberg, Tyrol, & Salzburg	16 Jun. 1813
Schleswig-Holstein (Danish)	29 Mar. 1814
Mecklenburg-Strelitz	01 Jun. 1814
Anhalt-Dessau	1822
Sachsen-Weimar	1823
Kingdom of Württemberg	1828
Grand Duchy of Posen (Prussian)	1833
Sachsen (Saxonia)	1834
Oldenburg	1852

Anti-Semitism increased as a counter-reaction to Jewish progress. This anti-Semitism gave birth to Zionism. A Zion Society was formed in Frankfurt/Oder in 1861. However, while Zionist Congresses were held in Austria, the Czech Republic and Switzerland, such a conference never took place in Germany. Anti-Semitic parties were established in Germany and Austria twenty years later. An anti-Semite was elected mayor of Vienna before the turn of the century.

Nevertheless, this bigotry did not become especially harsh and widespread until after World War I. Then the old scapegoat mentality came to the fore again. Democrats in general, and socialists in particular, were blamed for the civilian "stab in the back" of a military force which was seen as not having been defeated. Both the prominent role of the Jews in the Socialist Party and the universal populist resentment against people in high finance, one of the fields in which Jews had been allowed to be active (in fact needed by rulers) in the Middle Ages already, caused them to be a particular target of those who believed in conspiratorial theories. The most striking example of this was the assassination of the Jewish foreign minister in the first post-World War I cabinet and the campaign of mass hatred which preceded it. His "fault" was simply that he was a realist, aware of what Germany could and could not do at that time.

Thus the groundwork had already been laid before Hitler was able to mobilize this sentiment as a result of the suffering and high unemployment during the Great Depression.

THE END OF GERMANIC JEWRY

Hitler's barbaric genocide, unparalleled in European history, produced the end of any significant Jewish population in Germany and Austria, even though Jews sent from Germany to concentration camps accounted for only about 2% of the Holocaust victims.

Apart from the fact that most European Jews lived in the East, the passage of harsh anti-Semitic laws soon after Hitler came to power created a significant exodus. For those who remained, the violence of the *Kristallnacht* [Night of the Shattered Glass] in 1938 served as a stark warning. The term is derived from the massive damage done to synagogues that night, but people were hurt too, and many were killed.

As a result, more than half of Germany's Jews had already emigrated or escaped by 1939. Many of those who had fled to France, Belgium and the Netherlands shared the fate of those who had remained in Germany after these countries came under Hitler's dominance.

Practically all of those Jews in Germany and Austria who survived the Holocaust emigrated almost immediately after the war, with many going to Israel and many others to the United States and other New World countries. There were about 40,000 to 50,000 Jews in Germany and Austria in 1991, but almost all of them were Displaced Persons (DPs) who chose not to return to their Communist homeland and their descendants, not Jews whose families had lived in those countries (often for centuries) before World War II.

OTHER JEWS WITH HISTORIC ROOTS IN GERMANIC EUROPE

This guide is intended to serve all genealogists whose ancestors spoke German or for whom German-language records are available, but it is difficult to determine which European Jews perceived themselves as being Germanic in this sense.

Our emphasis on German-speaking Jews, but also our attention to others, is partially due to this ambiguity. Because of limitations of time and expertise, we have relied heavily on *The Atlas of Jewish History* by Martin Gilbert, supplemented by a number of other sources, such as *A History of Habsburg Jews, 1670-1918*, by William O. McCagg, Jr., a *Historical Atlas of East Central Europe* by Paul Robert Magocsi, a 1908-09 edition of *Meyers Kleines Konversations-Lexikon* [*Meyer's Small Encyclopedia of General Information*] published simultaneously in Leipzig (long known as a center of German liberalism) and Vienna (which became the undisputed center of Germanic Jewry in the nineteenth century, despite the Hapsburgs' hostility toward all non-Catholics for centuries) and articles by Jewish scholars in an old edition of the *Encyclopedia Americana*.

At least four factors have to be taken into consideration in trying to determine which groups fall within the category which this book is designed to cover:

    (1) language of speech versus language of records
    (2) place of residence
    (3) time period
    (4) the relationship between Yiddish and German

THE YIDDISH LANGUAGE

Yiddish (from the German *jüdisch*, meaning Jewish), the primary language for nearly all Jews from the Russian Empire (including Russian Poland), was derived from the German which the Jews spoke at the time of their expulsion from Germany, chiefly between 1096 and about 1400.

Edward Luft states that 70% of Yiddish is similar to German and that most of the other words are intelligible to a German-speaker. A. A. Roback specifically identifies 65.5% of Yiddish words as of German origin. By this criterion, almost all of the East European Jews (except for those who settled in the Caucasus and near the Black Sea at a very early period) could be classified as German-speakers in a historical sense.

Yiddish can be viewed as a German dialect in the sense that its differentiation from standard German is certainly no greater than the differences between North and South German dialects (let alone Swiss German, which few Germans understand). The difference is that Yiddish became a written language, using the Hebrew script, whereas Low German, spoken in northern Germany, ceased to be a written language by about 1500 and other dialects never developed into distinct, widely used written languages.

The Jews in the Eastern Parts of the Austro-Hungarian Empire

Hungary (which included Slovakia, known as Upper Hungary at the time), Galicia, and the Bukovina are among the areas where the linguistic "Germanness," according to the above criteria, is unclear.

Although the imperial administrators in Galicia were mostly Germans, the relatively numerous and influential Polish gentry were given considerable autonomy by the Hapsburgs. This explains why the land cadasters were in both Polish and German, according to articles in the *East European Genealogist* (Winnipeg).

McCagg leaves little doubt that the Jewish elite in eastern (Ukrainian) Galicia, where three-fourths of the Jews lived, spoke German and sought to promote stronger linguistic and political ties with Vienna. This was particularly true in Brody and Lemberg (Lwów, L'viv).

The Hapsburgs established German-language Jewish schools, with many teachers recruited from among the Bohemian Jews. Later Jews were admitted to Christian schools. But Jews who attended German-language schools clearly represented a modest minority of the Jewish population, partly because of extreme poverty. Moreover, the period of instruction was brief (1-3 years). On the other hand, the first eruption of Polish anti-Semitism in Galicia in 1859 could have served as an incentive for Jews to become "more German."

McCagg draws a sharp distinction between the Jews in Galicia and the Bukovina, including differences of perspective regarding their relationship with German gentiles and the German language, even though these two areas were a single administrative unit from Austria's acquisition of the Bukovina in 1775 until 1848.

He says there were hardly any Jews in the Bukovina in 1775, since it had not been part of Poland. However, the Jewish population grew immensely, particularly after 1848. Most of the Jewish immigrants came from Galicia or the Pale. The percentage of the population which was Jewish in 1900 was higher in the Bukovina than in any other part of the Hapsburg Empire.

A Jewish-gentile German cultural-political alliance was obvious in the Bukovina, according to McCagg, in contrast to the more ambiguous situation in Galicia and Hungary. One of the reasons for this was the establishment of a German-language university in Czernowitz (Cernauti, Chernivtsi), as contrasted with a Polish-language university in Lemberg. This led to a relatively large well-educated German-speaking Jewish elite.

Meyer's census data clearly imply that there was a lower intra-imperial and/or inter-national emigration rate from the Bukovina than from Galicia.

When Austria acquired Galicia in 1772, this more than doubled its Jewish population, which had previously been split almost evenly between Hungary-Slovakia and Bohemia-Moravia, with a very small number elsewhere, chiefly in Trieste. But the migration of Galician Jews in the nineteenth century changed this distribution rather drastically. A large number of Galician Jews migrated to northeastern Hungary and Budapest.

Many also went to Vienna, either directly or after having lived in Hungary. Peter Trawnicek's article on "Vienna as a Magnet for Austro-Hungarian Jews" (*Avotaynu*, Winter 1996) indicates that 61% of the intra-imperial migrants to Vienna from Galicia were Jewish, compared with 44.5% from Hungary-Slovakia, 34.5% from the Bukovina, 14% from Moravia and 5.5% from Bohemia. This compares with data in Paul Robert Magocsi's *Historical Atlas of East Central Europe* which show that Jews constituted 11.1% of the population in Galicia, 13.2% in the Bukovina, 1.8% in Moravia and 1.5% in Bohemia.

None of the sources we checked provide detailed data for Jews in the Hungarian part of the Dual Monarchy. However, Jews represented more than 30% of the population of three medium-sized cities in northeastern Hungary, all of them now in Carpatho-Ukraine (easternmost interwar Czechoslovakia) or Romania. More than 10% of the residents were

Jewish in 13 other cities in what was then Hungary. Except for Budapest, they are all outside the borders of present-day Hungary or in the northeasternmost part of the country. The few rural areas where at least 10% of the people were Jewish are near these cities, but not many Jews lived in peasant villages.

Budapest, Pressburg (now Bratislava, Slovak Republic) and most of the other Slovakian cities had a large German-speaking population, at least until the 1848 Revolution, and later in most cases. McCagg says that the Hungarian Jewish migrants to Vienna were known as "German Jews."

By 1848 Hungary had almost as many Jews as Galicia. The Hungarian Jewish population multiplied from 83,000 in 1787 to 625,000 in 1880, much of it attributable to immigration from Galicia. By that time, Galician Jewish migration to Hungary had slowed down, with most of those leaving Galicia later going to Vienna or overseas.

Whether the Jews in northeastern Old Hungary were as Germanized as those farther west is uncertain. However, McCagg reports that both the modernizers and the conservatives among the Hungarian Jewish rabbis sought to Germanize the Hungarian Jews after the 1781 Patent of Tolerance, even if for different reasons. He states that this was also true elsewhere in East Central Europe, although the history of Galician Jewry shows that it was not universal.

One other group of Hungarian Jews deserves some attention, viz., the numerous Jewish communities in the Burgenland, with its mixed German-Hungarian population belonging to Hungary until after World War I, when a plebiscite split it between Austria and Hungary.

Burgenland was unique in several respects. It had a much larger number of Protestants than the rest of Austria and its Germans provided a very high percentage of the Austrians who emigrated, at least until 1938.

Both of these phenomena can be explained by the fact that the area historically belonged to Hungary. The Hungarians, like the Turks, had shown much greater religious tolerance than the Austrians, at least until 1781. This also explains the comparatively large Jewish population, most of whom appear to have been German-speakers, with Eisenstadt, now the provincial capital of Austrian Burgenland, as the largest Jewish center.

But the post-1867 Magyarization policies had a much different effect on the Germans than on the Jews in Hungary. The Jews readily accepted Magyarization, since it offered greater opportunities and because they had no particular attachment to any language used for secular purposes. But the German Christians, who had lived in the Burgenland, Budapest, and Slovakia for almost a millennium, had a strong attachment to the German mother tongue, so Magyarization reinforced other factors leading to emigration, especially in the Burgenland and Bratislava. Many Jews probably spoke both German and Hungarian, because their proximity to the Viennese magnet provided strong commercial reasons for retaining a knowledge of German.

This largely explains the nineteenth-century linguistic identity of the Hungarian Jews: German (at least in the west) until 1867, Magyar soon thereafter.

In 1900, there were two million Jews in the Austro-Hungarian Empire, i.e., three times the number in the German Empire. However, less than 2% of them lived in Austria proper.

Pre-1867 figures as to the number of Germans in various parts of the empire sometimes included Jews and sometimes not. That is why you can find huge statistical disparities in different sources, the most extreme case being those for the easternmost areas.

JEWS IN THE RUSSIAN EMPIRE

With regard to Russian Poland, the Jews in the western part clearly spoke German, although there may be few German-language records available, since even the German Lutheran parish registers were generally kept in Polish until 1868, when Russian became mandatory.

This was particularly true in Lodz, where the textile industry, and hence the population, grew phenomenally during the nineteenth century. It was initially developed by German Christians and, after the Industrial Revolution turned workshops into factories, mostly by Jews, also chiefly from the German Empire. By the late nineteenth century, Polish Catholics represented a minority of the population.

The picture in other parts of Russian Poland is unclear, but it seems likely that many Jews spoke both German and Polish. After all, this is where Ludwik Samenhof, a Jewish physician, developed Esperanto (based on Western European languages) as a means of facilitating communication because of the multiplicity of languages in the area.

But Jewish and other scholars differ as to the extent and significance of the Jews who arrived in the Black Sea area from the Middle East. Martin Gilbert, in *The Atlas of Jewish History*, emphasizes the Khazar kingdom established in about 700 CE by converts to Judaism influenced by Jews from Persia. He shows it as covering all of Ukraine and extending beyond it in every direction, even eastward beyond the Caspian Sea. However, he adds that the Russians drove the Khazars back to the Crimean Peninsula in 970 and destroyed the kingdom in 1016, i.e., before any Central European Jews fled to the pre-Partition Commonwealth of Poland and Lithuania, whose eastern border was approximately the same as that of the post-Partition Pale of Settlement.

Magocsi and others refer to Jews as having been among the Hellenistic settlers all around the Black Sea, centuries before Christ. It seems pretty clear, however, that most of the Jews in the Russian Empire were expellees, primarily from Germany, but including some from Austria and Hungary, whom Russia inherited when Poland was partitioned.

DEMOGRAPHY

In 1905, Jews constituted about 1% of the population of the German Empire. Nearly 100,000 of the 600,000 Jews lived in Berlin, with about 55,000 each in the Rhineland and Bavaria.

When we look at the Jews as a percentage of the regional population, an entirely different picture emerges. In Hamburg, Hesse and Hesse-Nassau, at least 2% of the inhabitants were Jewish. Other states or provinces with an above average percentage of Jews included Alsace-Lorraine, Posen and Baden. The percentage was especially high in Lower (northern) Alsace and in the Mannheim district (northern Baden). The Jewish population was above the national average in the Rhenish Palatinate, which belonged to Bavaria, but much lower in present-day Bavaria.

Except for Posen (part of Poland until 1772 and again after 1919) and parts of Hesse, most Jews were concentrated in modern commercial centers (Berlin and Hamburg) or near those market towns and cities where they had settled at an early date.

Very few Jews had been allowed to live in Austria prior to the late eighteenth century. At one time, the only Jewish community was in Hohenems in Vorarlberg, although there were some privileged few "court Jews" in Vienna. However, both the total population and the Jewish population of Vienna increased many fold during the nineteenth century. But even in 1900, there were hardly any Jews in Austria proper, except in Vienna and the surrounding area, i.e., eastern Lower Austria, according to Magocsi.

The Jews from the eastern part of the Austro-Hungarian Empire unquestionably became German-speakers after they cam to Vienna and a considerable number of them had become Germanicized linguistically even before their arrival.

The Jews in the Czech Republic (Bohemia, Moravia and Austro-Silesia) also identified themselves with the Germans prior to the establishment of Czechoslovakia. This was especially true of the large Jewish community in Prague, although it may not have applied to all of those who lived in small communities in areas where there were few Germans. But many of the latter moved to Prague after they were freed from residential restrictions.

In Switzerland, most Jews lived in the area north of the Alps, especially in the bigger cities.

Local history books nearly always have at least some genealogical value, but they differ a lot in terms of how much genealogical detail they offer. The titles often shed little light on this. Therefore, we have included all the titles mentioned by George Arnstein, that were in his chapter on Jewish genealogy in the first edition, in the chapter on Jewish genealogy, even though many of them are local history books.

BIBLIOGRAPHY (See ANNOTATED BIBLIOGRAPHY for full citations if not shown)

The following list is derived largely from the books available at the University of Minnesota Libraries. We have deliberately omitted most books published during the Nazi period, because the history of the Jews under Hitler is well known and any books dealing with prior history must be considered ideologically suspect, although some scholars who sought objectivity paid only as much lip service to Hitler as they considered necessary.

LOCAL AND STATE HISTORIES OF JEWISH COMMUNITIES

Hellmut Andics. *Die Juden in Wien* [*The Jews in Vienna*]. 132 illustrations based on documents, historical descriptions and photographs. Munich: Bucher. 1988. 416 pp.

Paul Arnsberg, for the Kuratorium für Jüdische Geschichte e.V. Frankfurt am Main, revised and completed by Hans-Otto Schembs. *Die Geschichte der Frankfurter Juden seit der Französischen Revolution* [*The History of the Frankfurt Jews Since the French Revolution*], 3rd ed. Darmstadt: E. Roether. 1983.

Ruth Beckermann, ed. *Die Mazzesinsel: Juden in der Wiener Leopoldstadt, 1918-1938* [*The Mazz Island in the Viennese Leopoldstadt, 1918-1938*], with a historical essay. Vienna: Locker. 1984. 142 pp.

Steven Beller. *Vienna and the Jews, 1867-1938: A Cultural History*. Cambridge/New York: Cambridge University Press. 1989. 271 pp.

Dieter Blinn. *Juden in Homburg: Geschichte einer jüdischen Lebenswelt, 1330-1945* [*Jews in Homburg: History of the Life in the Jewish World, 1330-1945*]. Homburg-Saarpfalz: Ermer. 1993. 222 pp.

Jutta Bohnke-Kollwitz. *Juden in Köln von der Römerzeit bis ins 20. Jahrhundert: Foto-Dokumentation* [*Jews in Cologne from the Roman Period into the Twentieth Century: Photo Documentation*], with photo selection from the Rheinisches Bildarchiv and accompanying text by Liesel Franzheim. Cologne: Kölnisches Stadtmuseum. 1984. 353 pp.

H. Breimesser. *Ursprung, Entwicklung und Schicksal der jüdischen Gemeinde Hechingen* [*Origin, Development and Fate of the Jewish Community of Hechingen*]. Schwäbisch Gmünd: Pädagogische Hochschule Schwäbisch Gmünd. 1981. Thesis.

Vicki Caron. *Between France and Germany: The Jews of Alsace-Lorraine, 1871-1918*. Stanford, CA: Stanford University Press. 1988. 278 pp.

Gerhard Robert Walter von Coeckelberghe-Dutzele. *Die Juden und die Judenstadt in Wien: Fragmente von Realis* [*The Jews and the Jewish City in Vienna: Fragments of Realism*]. Vienna: Lechners Universitäts-Buchhandlung. 1846. 94 pp.

Collegium Carolinum (Munich, Germany). *Tagung (1981): Bad Wiessee: Die Juden in den böhmischen Ländern: Vorträge der Tagung des Collegium Carolinum in Bad Wiessee vom 27. bis 29. November 1981* [*1981 Conference at Bad Wiessee (Germany): The Jews in the Bohemian Lands: Lectures at the Conference of the Collegium Carolinum in Bad Wiessee, November 27-29, 1981*]. Munich: R. Oldenbourg. 1983. 368 pp.

Adolf Diamant. *Chronik der Juden in Chemnitz* [*Chronicle of the Jews in Chemnitz*]. Frankfurt a. M.: W. Weidlich. 1970. 103 pp.

Adolf Diamant. *Chronik der Juden in Leipzig* [*Chronicle of the Jews in Leipzig*]. Chemnitz-Leipzig: Verlag Heimatland Sachsen. 1993. 836 pp.

Ulrich Eisenbach, Hartmut Heinemann und Susanne Walther, comps. *Bibliographie zur Geschichte der Juden in Hessen* [*Bibliography for the History of the Jews in Hesse*]. Wiesbaden: Kommission fur die Geschichte der Juden in Hessen. 1992. 341 pp.

David Harry Ellenson. *Modernization and the Jews of Nineteenth Century Frankfurt and Berlin: A Portrait of Communities in Transition*. Minneapolis, MN: Dworsky Center for Jewish Studies, University of Minnesota. 1988. 23 pp.

Stefanie Endlich, in cooperation with Thomas Lutz. *Gedenken und Lernen an historischen Orten: ein Wegweiser zu Gedenkstätten für die Opfer des Nationalsozialismus in Berlin* [*Remembering and Learning at Memorials in Historical Places: A Guide to the Memorials for the Victims of National Socialism in Berlin*]. Berlin: Edition Hentrich. 1995. 173 pp.

Ludwig Geiger, with a foreword by Hermann Simon. *Geschichte der Juden in Berlin: Festschrift zur zweiten Säkular-Feier: Anmerkungen, Ausführungen, urkundliche Beilagen und zwei Nächtrage (1871-1890)* [*History of the Jews in Berlin: Commemorative Publication for the Second Secular Ceremony: Notes, Lectures, Documentary Supplementation and Two Appendices (1870-1890)*]. Berlin: Arani. 1988.

Karlheinz Geppert. "Vom Schutzjuden zum Bürger" ["From Protected Jew to Citizen"], in *Der Sülchgau*, Vol. 23.

Geschichte der Juden in Speyer [*History of the Jews in Speyer*]. Speyer: Die Bezirksgruppe Speyer des Historischen Vereins der Pfalz. 1981.

Norbert Giovannini, Johannes Bauer, Hans-Martin Mumm, with contributions by Heike Baader, et. al., a foreword by the publisher and greetings from Land Rabbi Nathan Peter Levinson. *Jüdisches Leben in Heidelberg: Studien zu einer unterbrochenen Geschichte* [*Jewish Life in Heidelberg: Studies of an Interrupted History*]. Heidelberg: Wunderhorn. 1992. 334 pp.

Hugo Gold. *Geschichte der Juden in Wien* [*History of the Jews in Vienna*]. Tel Aviv: House Olamenu. 1966. 158 pp.

Max Grunwald. *Geschichte der Wiener Juden bis 1914, der Schuljugend erzählt von Max Grunwald im Anschlusse an die Jahrhundertfeier des Tempels der Inneren Stadt gewidmet vom Vorstande der Israelitischen Kultusgemeinde Wien* [*History of the Viennese Jews Prior to 1914 Related to Students by Max Grunwald at the Centennial Celebration of the Temple in the Inner City of Vienna, Dedicated by the Board of the Israelite Cultural Community of Vienna*]. Vienna: Israelitischen Kultusgemeinde. 1926. 80 pp.

James F. Harris. *The People Speak! Anti-Semitism and Emancipation in Nineteenth-Century Bavaria*. Ann Arbor: University of Michigan Press. 1994. 290 pp.

Johannes Georg Hartenstein. *Die Juden in der Geschichte Leipzigs von der Entstehung der Stadt an bis zur Mitte des 19. Jahrhunderts* [*The Jews in the History of Leipzig from the Establishment of the City up to the Middle of the Nineteenth Century*]. (The pictures are based on the originals in the City Historical Museum.). Berlin. 1938. 142 pp.

Wolfgang Hausler. *Das galizische Judentum in der Habsburgermonarchie im Lichte der zeitgenössischen Publizistik und Reiseliteratur von 1772-1848* [*The Galician Jewry in the Hapsburg Monarchy, as Viewed in the Publicity and Travel Literature of 1772-1848*]. Munich: R. Oldenbourg Verlag. 1979. 89 pp.

Werner Heise. *Die Juden in der Mark Brandenburg bis zum Jahre 1571* [*The Jews in the March of Brandenburg up to 1571*]. Berlin: Verlag Dr. Emil Ebering. 1932. 367 pp.

Rachel Heuberger, and Helga Krohn. *Hinaus aus dem Ghetto: Juden in Frankfurt am Main, 1800-1950* [*Out of the Ghetto: Jews in Frankfurt on the Main, 1800-1950*]. Frankfurt am Main: Fischer. 1988. 215 pp.

Klaus Hodl. *Als Bettler in die Leopoldstadt: galizische Juden auf dem Weg nach Wien* [*As Beggars in the Leopoldstadt* (A District in Vienna): *Galician Jews on the Way to Vienna*]. Vienna: Böhlau. 1994. 331 pp.

Franz Hundsnurscher and Gerhard Taddy. *Die jüdischen Gemeinden in Baden* [*Jewish Communities in Baden*]. Stuttgart: Kohlhammer. 1968. 329 pp.

Wilma Abeles Iggers, ed. *The Jews of Bohemia and Moravia: A Historical Reader*, translated by Wilma Abeles Iggers, Kaca Polackova-Henley, and Kathrine Talbot. Detroit: Wayne State University Press. 1992.

Stefi Jersch-Wenzel and Barbara John, eds., with contributions by Eckart Birnstiel, et al. *Von Zuwanderern zu Einheimischen: Hugenotten, Juden, Böhmen, Polen in Berlin* [*From Immigrants to Natives: Huguenots, Jews, Bohemians and Poles in Berlin*]. Berlin: Nicolai. 1990. 804 pp.

The Jews of Czechoslovakia: Historical Studies and Surveys, 2 vols. Philadelphia: Jewish Publication Society of America. 1968.

Ruth Kestenberg-Gladstein. *Neuere Geschichte der Juden in den böhmischen Ländern* [*Recent History of the Jews in the Lands of the Bohemian Crown*]. Tübingen: Mohr. 1969. Vol. 1 of series: *Schriftenreihe wissenschaftlicher Abhandlungen des Leo Baeck Instituts 18.*

Hillel J. Kieval. *The Making of Czech Jewry: National Conflict and Jewish Society in Bohemia, 1870-1918.* New York: Oxford University Press. 1988. 279 pp.

Guido Kisch. *Judentaufen: eine historisch-biographisch-psychologisch-soziologische Studie besonders für Berlin und Königsberg* [*Baptisms of Jews: A Historical-Biographical-Psychological-Sociological Study, Especially for Berlin and Königsberg*]. Berlin: Colloquium Verlag. 1973. 134 pp.

Helga Krohn. *Die Juden in Hamburg 1800-1850: Ihre soziale, kulturelle und politische Entwicklung während der Emanzipationszeit* [*The Jews in Hamburg, 1800-1850: Their Social, Cultural and Political Development During the Period of Emancipation*]. Thesis. Frankfurt a. M.: Europäische Verlagsanstalt. 1967.

Karl Kuhling. *Die Juden in Osnabrück* [*The Jews in Osnabrück*], published by the City of Osnabrück on the occasion of the dedication of the new synagogue on 1 June 1969. Osnabrück: Wenner. 1969. 110 pp.

Maren Kuhn-Rehfus. "Das Verhältnis von Mehrheit zu Minderheit am Beispiel der Juden von Hohenzollern" ["The Relationship of the Majority to the Minority by Example of the Jews of Hohenzollern"], in *Zeitschrift für Hohenzollern Geschichte*, Vol. 14 (1978).

Bernd-Lutz Lange. *Jüdische Spuren in Leipzig* [*Jewish Traces in Leipzig*]. Photos by Gudrun Vogel and Bertram Kober. Leipzig: Forum. 1993. 101 pp.

Ina Susanne Lorenz. *Die Juden in Hamburg zur Zeit der Weimarer Republik: Eine Dokumentation* [*The Jews in Hamburg During the Time of the Weimar Republic: A Documentation*]. Hamburg: H. Christians. 1987. 1,550 pp.

Steven M. Lowenstein. *The Berlin Jewish Community: Enlightenment, Family, and Crisis, 1770-1830.* New York: Oxford University Press. 1993. 300 pp.

Sigmund Mayer. *Die Wiener Juden: Kommerz, Kultur, Politik, 1700-1900* [*The Viennese Jews: Commerce, Culture, Politics, 1700-1900*], 2nd ed. Vienna/Berlin: R. Lowit. 1918. 531 pp.

Ulrike Minor and Peter Ruf. *Juden in Ludwigshafen* [*Jews in Ludwigshafen*]. Ludwigshafen am Rhein: Stadtarchiv. 1992. 189 pp.

Bernhard Post. *Jüdische Geschichte in Hessen erforschen: ein Wegweiser zu Archiven, Forschungsstätten und Hilfsmitteln* [*Researching Jewish History in Hesse: A Guide to Archives, Research Centers and Finding Aids*]. Wiesbaden: Kommission für die Geschichte der Juden in Hessen. 1994. 78 pp.

Alfred Francis Pribram. *Urkunden und Akten zur Geschichte der Juden in Wien* [*Documents and Records for the History of the Jews in Vienna*]. Vienna/Leipzig, W. Braumuller. 1918. Multiple vols.

Marsha L. Rozenblit. *The Jews of Vienna, 1867-1914: Assimilation and Identity*. Albany, NY: State University of New York Press. 1983. 284 pp.

Reinhard Rürup, ed. *Jüdische Geschichte in Berlin* [*Jewish History in Berlin*]. 2 vols. Vol. 1: *Bilder und Dokumente* [*Pictures and Documents*]. Vol. 2: *Essays und Studien* [*Essays and Studies*]. Berlin: Hentrich. 1995.

Paul Sauer. *Die jüdischen Gemeinden in Württemberg und Hohenzollern* [*Jewish Communities in Württemberg and Hohenzollern*]. Stuttgart: Kohlhammer. 1966.

Carl Anton Schaab. *Diplomatische Geschichte der Juden zu Mainz und dessen Umgebung, mit Berücksichtigung ihres Rechtszustandes in den verschiedenen Epochen, aus grösstentheils ungedruckten Urkunden* [*Diplomatic History of the Jews in Mainz and Its Surroundings, with Consideration of Their Legal Status in Various Eras, Mostly from Unpublished Documents*]. Unchanged 1995 reprint of 1855 edition. Wiesbaden, M. Sandig. 1969. 480 pp.

Ursula Schnorbus. *Quellen zur Geschichte der Juden in Westfalen: Spezialinventar zu den Akten des Nordrhein-Westfälischen Staatsarchivs Münster* [*Sources for the History of the Jews in Westphalia: Special Inventory of the Records of the Northrhine-Westphalian State Archives in Münster*]. Münster: Selbstverlag des Nordrhein-Westfälischen Staatsarchivs Munster. 1983. 352 pp.

Kurt Schubert, ed., with contributions by Ursula Schubert, et. al. *Judentum im Mittelalter: 4. Mai-26. Okt. 1978, Ausstellung im Schloss Halbturn: Katalog* [*Jewry in the Middle Ages: Catalog for the Exhibit in Halbturn Castle, May 4-Oct. 26, 1978*]. Sponsored by the Kulturabteilung des Amtes der Burgenland Landesregierung. Eisenstadt, Austria: Kulturabteilung des Amtes der Burgenland Landesregierung. 1978. 268 pp.

Stefan Schwarz. *Die Juden in Bayern im Wandel der Zeiten* [*The Jews in Bavaria During the Course of Time*]. Munich. G. Olzog. 1963. 368 pp.

Samuel Steinherz, ed. *Die Juden in Prag: Bilder aus ihrer tausendjährigen Geschichte: Festgabe der Loge Praga des Ordens B'nai B'rith zum Gedenktage ihres 25 jährigen Bestandes* [*Jews in Prague: Pictures from Their Thousand-Year History: Jubilee Celebration of the Prague Lodge of the B'nai B'rith Order on the Occasion of Its Twenty-fifth Year of Existence*]. Prague: Loge Praga des Ordens B'nai B'rith. 1927. 247 pp.

Hans Tietze. *Die Juden Wiens: Geschichte—Wirtschaft—Kultur* [*The Jews of Vienna: History—Economy—Culture*]. With 30 tables, pictures, and plans. Leipzig/Vienna: E.P. Tal & Co. 1933. 301 pp.

Isadore Twersky, ed. *Danzig, between East and West: Aspects of Modern Jewish History*. Cambridge, MA: Harvard University, Center for Jewish Studies. Distributed by Harvard University Press. 1985. 172 pp.

Peter Wilhelm. *Die jüdische Gemeinde in der Stadt Göttingen von den Anfangen bis zur Emanzipation* [*The Jewish Community in the City of Göttingen from Its Beginnings until the Emancipation*]. Göttingen: Vandenhoeck und Ruprecht. 1973. 143 pp.

Robert S. Wistrich. *The Jews of Vienna in the Age of Franz Joseph*. Oxford/New York: Published for the Littman Library by Oxford University Press. 1989. 696 pp.

Rudolf M. Wlaschek. *Juden in Böhmen: Beiträge zur Geschichte des europäischen Judentums im 19. und 20. Jahrhundert* [*Jews in Bohemia: Contributions to the History of European Jewry in the Nineteenth and Twentieth Centuries*]. Munich: R. Oldenbourg. 1990. 236 pp.

Gerson Wolf. *Die Juden in der Leopoldstadt ("unterer Werd") im 17. Jahrhundert in Wien* [*The Jews in Leopoldstadt ("Lower Island") in the Seventeenth Century in Vienna*]. Vienna: Herzfeld & Bauer. 1864. 109 pp.

HISTORIES OF JEWS IN GERMANIC LANDS

H. G. Adler. *The Jews in Germany from the Enlightenment until National Socialism.* Original German book published in Munich (Kosel, 1960). Notre Dame, IN: Notre Dame Press. 1969. 152 pp.

Julius Aronius. *Regesten zur Geschichte der Juden im fränkischen und deutschen Reiche bis zum Jahre 1273* [*Records for the History of the Jews in the Frankish (Carolingian) and German Empire Until 1273*]. Hildesheim: G. Olms. 1970. 370 pp.

Rena R. Auerbach, ed. *The "Jewish Question" in German-Speaking Countries, 1848-1914: A Bibliography.* New York: Garland. 1994. 385 pp.

Ruth Beckermann. *Unzugehörig: Österreicher und Juden nach 1945* [*Not Belonging (Together): Austrians and Jews After 1945*]. Vienna: Loecker. 1989. 140 pp.

Dietz Bering. *Kampf um Namen: Bernhard Weiss gegen Joseph Goebbels* [*Battle About Names: Bernhard Weiss vs. Joseph Goebbels*]. Stuttgart: Klett-Cotta. 1991. 527 pp.

David Bronsen, ed. *Jews and Germans from 1860 to 1933: The Problematic Symbiosis.* Heidelberg: Winter. 1979. 383 pp.

Ignatz Bubis. *Ich bin ein deutscher Staatsburger jüdischen Glaubens: ein autobiographisches Gespräch mit Edith Kohn* [*I am a German Citizen of the Jewish Faith: An Autobiographical Conversation with Edith Kohn*]. Cologne: Kiepenheuer & Witsch. 1993. 180 pp.

Werner Jacob Cahnman. *German Jewry: Its History and Sociology: Selected Essays, with an introduction by Joseph B. Maier, Judith Marcus, and Zoltan Tarr.* New Brunswick, NJ: Transaction Publishers. 1989. 256 pp.

Michael Cohn. *The Jews in Germany, 1945-1993: The Building of a Minority.* Westport, CT: Praeger. 1994. 128 pp.

Yehuda Don, and Victor Karady, eds. *A Social and Economic History of Central European Jewry.* New Brunswick, NJ: Transaction Publishers. 1990. 262 pp.

Anna M. Drabek, Mordechai Eliov and Gerald Stourzh. *Prag-Czernowitz-Jerusalem: der österreichische Staat und die Juden vom Zeitalter des Absolutismus bis zum Ende der Monarchie* [*Prague-Czernowitz-Jerusalem: The Austrian State and the Jews from the Absolutist Period until the End of the Monarchy*]. Eisenstadt, Austria: Roetzer. 1984. 117 pp.

Heinz Ganther. *Die Juden in Deutschland, 1951/52. Ein Almanach* [*The Jews in Germany, 1951-52: An Almanac*]. Frankfurt a. M.: Neuzeit Verlag. 1953. 376 pp.

Ruth Gay, with an introduction by Peter Gay. *The Jews of Germany: A Historical Portrait.* New Haven: Yale University Press. 1992. 297 pp.

Nachum T. Gidal (Tim Gidal). *Die Juden in Deutschland von der Römerzeit bis zur Weimarer Republik* [*The Jews in Germany from the Roman Period until the Weimar Republic*], with a foreword by Marion, Gräfin Dönhoff. Gütersloh: Bertelsmann Lexikon Verlag. 1988. 440 pp.

Martin Gilbert. *The Atlas of Jewish History*, rev. ed. New York: William Morrow and Co., Inc. 1993. 123 pp. plus bibliography.

William W. Hagen. *Germans, Poles, and Jews: The Nationality Conflict in the Prussian East, 1772-1914.* Chicago: University of Chicago Press. 1980. 406 pp.

Kathy Harms, Lutz R. Reuter and Volker Durr, ed. *Coping with the Past: Germany and Austria After 1945.* Madison, WI: University of Wisconsin Press. 1990. 269 pp.

Joseph Alexander, Freiherr von Helfert,. *Die confessionale Frage in Österreich, 1848: zugleich ein Beitrag zur Tages- und Flugschriften-Literatur jener Zeit* [*The Question of Faiths or Denominations in Austria, 1848: Simultaneously a Contribution to the Daily and Pamphlet Literature of That Time*]. Vienna: L. Mayer. 1882. 8 vols.

Walter Homolka, with a foreword by Albert H. Friedlander and an epilogue by Esther Seidel. *Jewish Identity in Modern Times: Leo Baeck and German Protestantism.* Providence: Berghahn Books. 1995. 143 pp.

R. Po-chia Hsia, and Hartmut Lehmann, eds. *In and Out of the Ghetto: Jewish-Gentile Relations in Late Medieval and Early Modern Germany.* Washington, DC: German Historical Institute; Cambridge: Cambridge University Press. 1995. 330 pp.

Heinrich Jaques. *Denkschrift über die Stellung der Juden in Österreich* [*Commemorative Publication Regarding the Position of the Jews in Austria*], 4th ed. Vienna: C. Gerolds Sohn. 1859. 51 pp.

Walter Jens. *Juden und Christen in Deutschland: drei Reden* [*Jews and Christians in Germany: Three Lectures*]. Stuttgart: Radius-Verlag. 1989. 119 pp.

Juden in Deutschland: Zur Geschichte einer Hoffnung: historische Langsschnitte und Einzelstudien [*Jews in Germany: Concerning the History of a Hope: Historical Overviews and Individual Studies*]. Berlin: Institut Kirche und Judentum. 1980. 224 pp.

Wanda Kampmann. *Deutsche und Juden: die Geschichte der Juden in Deutschland vom Mittelalter bis zum Beginn des ersten Weltkrieges* [*Germans and Jews: The History of the Jews in Germany from the Middle Ages until the Beginning of the First World War*]. Frankfurt am Main: Fischer Taschenbuch. 1963. 1979. 449 pp.

Alphonse Kannengieser. *Juden und Katholiken in Österreich-Ungarn* [*Jews and Catholics in Austria-Hungary*], transl. from French. Trier, Germany: Verlag der Paulinus-Druckerei. 1896. 308 pp.

Marion A. Kaplan. *The Making of the Jewish Middle Class: Women, Family, and Identity in Imperial Germany.* New York: Oxford University Press. 1991. 351 pp.

Dagmar C. G. Lorenz and Gabriele Weinberger, eds. *Insiders and Outsiders: Jewish and Gentile Culture in Germany and Austria.* Detroit, MI: Wayne State University Press. 1994. 365 pp.

Charles S. Maier. *Die Gegenwart der Vergangenheit: Geschichte und die nationale Identität der Deutschen* [*The Presence of the Past: History and the National Identity of the Germans*]. Translated from English by Udo Rennert. Frankfurt/Main; New York: Campus Verlag. 1992. 257 pp.

Trude Maurer. *Die Entwicklung der jüdischen Minderheit in Deutschland (1780-1933): neuere Forschungen und offene Fragen* [*The Development of a Jewish Minority in Germany (1780-1933): Recent Research and Open Questions*]. Tübingen: M. Niemeyer. 1992. 195 pp.

William O. McCagg. *A History of Habsburg Jews, 1670-1918.* Bloomington: Indiana University Press. 1989. 289 pp.

Michael A. Meyer, ed., and Michael Brenner, asst. ed. *German-Jewish History in Modern Times.* New York: Columbia University Press. Series starting 1996. Vol. 1: Mordechai Breuer and Michael Graetz, translated by William Templer. *Tradition and Enlightenment: 1600-1780.* 1996.

Werner E. Mosse, in cooperation with Arnold Paucker, eds. *Deutsches Judentum in Krieg und Revolution 1916-1923; ein Sammelband* [*Germanic Jewry in War and Revolution, 1916-1923: A Collective Compilation*]. Tübingen: J. C. B. Mohr. 1971. 704 pp.

Robin Ostow. *Jews in Contemporary East Germany: The Children of Moses in the Land of Marx.* New York: St. Martin's Press. 1989. 169 pp.

Peter G. J. Pulzer. *Jews and the German State: The Political History of a Minority, 1848-1933*. Oxford, UK, and Cambridge, MA: Blackwell. 1992. 370 pp.

Monika Richarz, ed. *Jewish Lives in Germany: Memoirs of Three Generations*. English translation of *Bürger auf Widerruf 1785-1945* [*Citizenship Retracted, 1785-1945*]. Indiana University Press. 1991. 484 pp.

> Original three-volume German edition in 1976-82 had 126 autobiographical excerpts from the Leo Baeck Institute Archives. English translation is of an abridged 1989 German version, which was limited to 51 essays.

Reinhard Rürup. *Emanzipation und Antisemitismus: Studien zur Judenfrage der bürgerlichen Gesellschaft* [*Emancipation and Anti-Semitism: Studies of the Jewish Question by the Bourgeois Society*]. Göttingen: Vandenhoeck und Ruprecht. 1975. 28 pp.

Gertrude Schneider. *Exile and Destruction: The Fate of Austrian Jews, 1938-1945*. Westport, CT: Praeger. 1995. 234 pp.

Paul Senstius. *Die Stämme der Israeliten und Germanen* [*The Tribes of the Israelites and the Germans*]. Leipzig: Eduard Pfeiffer. 1931. 45 pp.

Rafael Seligmann. *Mit beschränkter Hoffnung: Juden, Deutsche, Israelis* [*With Limited Hopes: Jews, Germans and Israelis*]. Hamburg: Hoffmann und Campe. 1991. 315 pp.

Moses Avigdor Shulvass. *From East to West: The Westward Migration of Jews from Eastern Europe During the Seventeenth and Eighteenth Centuries*. Detroit, Wayne State University Press. 1971. 161 pp.

Alphons Silbermann, and Herbert Sallen. *Juden in Westdeutschland: Selbstbild und Fremdbild einer Minorität* [*Jews in West Germany: Self-Image and Images of Others of a Minority*]. Cologne: Verlag Wissenschaft und Politik. 1992. 114 pp.

David Jan Sorkin. *The Transformation of German Jewry, 1780-1840*. New York: Oxford University Press. 1987. 255 pp.

Augusta Steinberg. *Geschichte der Juden in der Schweiz vom 16. Jahrhundert bis nach der Emanzipation* [*History of the Jews in Switzerland from the Sixteenth Century until the Emancipation*]. Distributed by: AG für Verlag und Druckerei, Goldach: 1966.

Selma Stern. *The Court Jew: A Contribution to the History of the Period of Absolutism in Europe*, translated by Ralph Weiman, with a new introduction by Egon Mayer. New Brunswick, NJ: Transaction Books. 1985. 312 pp.

Otto Stobbe. *Die Juden in Deutschland während des Mittelalters in politischer, sozialer und rechtlicher Beziehung* [*The Jews in Germany During the Middle Ages with Respect to Their Political, Social and Legal Status*]. Braunschweig, C. A. Schwetschke und Sohn. 1866. 312 pp.

Uriel Tal. *Christians and Jews in Germany: Religion, Politics, and Ideology in the Second Reich, 1870-1914*, translated by Noah Jonathan Jacobs. Ithaca: Cornell University Press. 1975. 359 pp.

Enzo Traverso. *The Jews and Germany: From the "Judeo-German Symbiosis" to the Memory of Auschwitz*, translated by Daniel Weissbort. Lincoln: University of Nebraska Press. 1995. 215 pp.

Shulamit Volkov. *Die Juden in Deutschland 1780-1918* [*The Jews in Germany, 1780-1918*]. Munich: Oldenbourg. 1994. 165 pp.

Jack Wertheimer. *Unwelcome Strangers: East European Jews in Imperial Germany*. New York: Oxford University Press. 1987. 275 pp.

F. Wilder-Okladek. *The Return Movement of Jews to Austria After the Second World War, with Special Consideration of the Return from Israel*. The Hague: M. Nijhoff. 1969. 130 pp.

Robert S. Wistrich, ed. *Austrians and Jews in the Twentieth Century: From Franz Joseph to Waldheim*. New York, NY: St. Martin's Press. 1992. 280 pp.

SELECTED HISTORIES OF JEWS IN EUROPE

Robert Chazan. *European Jewry and the First Crusade*. Berkeley: University of California Press. 1987. 380 pp.

John Edwards, transl. and ed. *The Jews in Western Europe, 1400-1600*. Manchester: Manchester University Press; New York: Distributed exclusively in the USA and Canada by St. Martin's Press. 1994. 159 pp.

Saul Friedlander, et al. *The Jews in European History: Seven Lectures*, with an introduction by Christian Meier and edited by Wolfgang Beck. Original publication in German: Munich: C. H. Beck. 1992. Cincinnati: Hebrew Union College Press in association with the Leo Baeck Institute, New York. 1994. 146 pp.

Walter Grab and Julius H. Schoeps, eds. *Juden im Vormärz und in der Revolution von 1848*, [*Jews Before March (1848) and in the Revolution of 1848*] with contributions Michael Werner, et. al. Stuttgart: Burg Verlag. 1983. 400 pp.

SELECTED HISTORIES OF JEWS IN AMERICA

Max I. Dimont. *The Jews in America: The Roots and Destiny of American Jews*. New York: Simon and Schuster. 1978. 286 pp.

> Interesting, scholarly and sometimes iconoclastic interpretation of American Jewish history.

Chapter XIII

GENEALOGICAL RESOURCES FOR GERMAN JEWISH ANCESTRY

Following is a description of the kinds of records that are available and where they might be found now, as well as information about the many sources for Jewish genealogy.

JEWISH NAMES

The naming practices of the Jews are complicated, partly because of differing laws in the jurisdictions where they lived and the diversity of languages which they spoke. They are further complicated by the practice of using a legal name (language of residence), a Hebrew name (used in Jewish religious records) and sometimes a nickname used by the family or in the community. George Arnstein's article, "Names and Their Origins," in the Spring 1995 issue of *Avotaynu* points out the idiosyncrasies of Jewish naming practices. For a more detailed study of naming practices, see the reference works by Alexander Beider, Heinrich and Eva Guggenheimer, Benzion Kaganoff, Dan Rottenberg, and Robert Singerman listed in the bibliography at the end of this chapter.

The two surname books by Beider (Russian Empire, Kingdom of Poland) are indexed on the Internet home page of Avotaynu, Inc. Warren Blatt discusses this subject in "Frequently Asked Questions" on the JewishGen home page. An InfoFile by Joachim Mugdan of the University of Münster (Germany) Institute of General Linguistics is also available on that home page. Most Jews did not adopt permanently established surnames until about 1800 or later. See the table in the chapter on **JEWISH HISTORY AND DEMOGRAPHY** for the dates of the laws mandating the adoption of such names in various jurisdictions.

COMMUNAL RECORDS

These types of records should have remained in the local Jewish community, but because of the Holocaust's destruction and mass emigration, there are relatively few local Jews left in Germanic Europe (although somewhat more in Switzerland and Austria, in proportion to their population than in Germany). The 40,000 to 50,000 Jews in Germany today consist mostly of postwar émigrés from Eastern Europe.

Birth, Marriage and Death Registers (called *Gemeindebücher* or *Familienregister* in German; *Pinkassim* or *Pinchassim* in Hebrew) were recorded and kept by local synagogues or communities. However, at various times pastors of the official state church were the official civil registrars, so records of births (or circumcisions), marriages and deaths (or burials) are frequently recorded in either Evangelical (earlier Lutheran or Reformed) or Catholic registers.

Mohel **or Circumcision Registers** could have been kept in the private hands of the *mohel* himself and moved with him.

Gravestone Registers were kept by the local burial society or *Chevra Kaddish*. Since Jews were restricted as to the number and location of places where they could be buried, this may not be the actual place of residence.

Trying to locate the local records is usually not an advisable first step, because the vast majority of Jewish records that still exist, either as originals or microfilmed copies, have been collected by archives or libraries outside of Europe. After World War II various archives were established, mostly in Israel or the United States, for the purpose of documenting and collecting information not only about German-speaking Jews, but also about Jews throughout the world. Other major genealogical resource centers have microfilmed Jewish records as part of their acquisition of European genealogical records in general.

Here are a few libraries and archives with major collections of communal vital records (for addresses and more details, see the section on **Revival Of Historic Interest In Judaica Libraries And Archives** later in this chapter):

- The **Leo Baeck Institute (LBI) Archive and Library** in New York City. A fine example of a family register in the LBI Collection is the *Familienregister, Israeliten Gemeinde Buchau* [*Family Register of the Jewish Congregation in Buchau*]. It was begun by Max I. Mändle, secretary of the Buchau Jewish community in 1809 and ends in 1853. Many of the early records were almost certainly prepared by the local Catholic priest. Since these registers include the date of birth of husband and wife, plus names of their parents, some entries make it possible to trace a family as far back as 1740, according to George Arnstein. The same format was used by both Jewish and Christian congregations and is almost identical to modern family group sheets.

- The **Central Archives for the History of the Jewish People** in Jerusalem has an ongoing goal of collecting records of worldwide Jewry. It has records of over 1,400 Jewish communities, mostly from Germany and Austria, plus 200 inventories of records of Jewish interest held by other archives. This includes family histories and family papers. For a further description of the archival collection, see Dan Rottenberg, *Finding Our Fathers*, and Sallyann Amdur Sack, *A Guide to Jewish Genealogical Research in Israel*. The Sack book includes a helpful surname list of the family histories and genealogies of this archive in Jerusalem. These are mostly German names, but this could be changing since the opening up of East European archives.

- The **Family History Library** in Salt Lake City has been microfilming Jewish, as well as other, vital records worldwide for years. It has filmed or is currently filming records throughout almost all of Europe, with many recent acquisitions from countries formerly behind the Iron Curtain. It is wise to check the Family History Library Catalog regularly to determine whether the records you seek have been filmed yet. Also check the Christian records for the same area, since church records were the official civil records in many areas before, during and shortly after the Napoleonic period in various jurisdictions, particularly in the western Germanic states. Jewish records have been found in these registers, either in a separate section or interspersed with other records of birth, marriage, and death/burial. The Jewish records will, of course, refer to circumcision rather than to baptism.

A very valuable collection of German Jewish records filmed by the FHL was that of the Gesamtarchiv der Deutschen Juden [Complete Archives of German Jews] in Berlin. This central archive had the largest collection of Jewish communal records in the 1920s and 1930s. See Peter Lande, "Complete Archives of the German Jews," in *Avotaynu* (Spring 1993), for further information. His update, "On-Site Research in Germany" (*Avotaynu*, Fall 1996), describes the Jewish collections of various libraries and archives, some just recently opened to the public. He identifies which records have been microfilmed and may thus be accessible through Family History Centers or other repositories in various parts of the world.

An excellent article by Edward Luft, "On-Site Jewish Genealogical Research in the Czech and Slovak Republics," (also in *Avotaynu*, Fall 1996) states that most Jewish vital records in the regional archives in the Slovak Republic have been microfilmed by the FHL. As is the case with Christian records, none have been microfilmed in the Czech Republic and no future filming is foreseen. To locate the unmicrofilmed Czech records, see Claire Bruell, "Archives in Bohemia and Moravia" (same issue of *Avotaynu*). She lists the addresses of all public archives in Bohemia and Moravia. This is especially important because you must obtain the vital records (*matricky* in Czech) from the regional or district archives (*statni oblastni archivy*).

The FHL has microfilmed many Jewish communal records for communities within the present-day boundaries of Hungary. These generally go up to 1895, when civil registration was introduced. The FHL also has the 1848 Census of Hungarian Jews (FHL film

#7192328). This covers the area of the pre-World War I Hungarian portion of the Dual Monarchy, including Slovakia and Subcarpathian Rus' (now part of Ukraine).

Unfortunately, the same is not true of Galicia, the Polish territory which fell into Austrian hands during the First Partition of Poland in 1772, although eastern Galicia is now in Ukraine. Galician Jews were recording their births, deaths and marriages as early as 1787, although most records start in the 1830s or 1840s. The same is presumably true of the Bukovina, which was administratively part of Galicia from 1775 to 1848. Keep checking the FHL catalog to see where these have been filmed in the meantime. Also check *Gesher Galicia* and any other Special Interest Group which may cover the area of interest to you.

Many libraries and archives in Germany and elsewhere in Europe may have communal records. Check the holdings of the state archives, for example, the Landesarchiv Baden-Württemberg in Stuttgart, which has a few surviving original records and many filmed records among its holdings. This archive is of particular value because many Jews lived in that area and the Nazis were still filming records there in April 1945, just weeks before the end of the war. Other archives are mentioned later, but use your research skills, bearing in mind that relevant records have been scattered throughout the world and may show up in diverse places.

CEMETERY RECORDS

Tombstone inscriptions are an extremely important source for Jewish genealogists for two reasons. In certain localities, tombstones are the oldest records available. Moreover, when the name is recorded in Hebrew (as is usually the case), you automatically get the name of the deceased's father. This is because the Hebrew name is patronymic (as was also true of Christians in Schleswig-Holstein and Ostfriesland until a comparatively late date). The inscription will specify, for example, that the dead person was Abraham, son of Jakob.

The Hebrew inscriptions may also give details about the character of the individual and his or her life, information not usually found on tombstones for other groups. So it is very important, if you don't know Hebrew, to photograph the inscription for later translation. If you don't have a camera with you, or the inscription is too weather-worn to show up, make a rubbing or copy the letters carefully. Remember the Hebrew text reads from right to left.

There has recently been a revival of interest by Jewish and non-Jewish historians to protect and preserve cemetery records in Germany and elsewhere. There are still some 2,000 cemeteries left in Germany. Some of the printed records of these cemeteries are beautifully done, with photographs of the headstones. Most transcriptions of the Hebrew or German have also been translated into English, which is very helpful.

One such example is the *Memorbuch: Die jüdischen Friedhöfe Jebenhausen und Göppingen* [*Memorial book: The Jewish Cemeteries at Jebenhausen and Göppingen*] by Naftali Bar-Giora Bamberger.

Many of these types of memorials are now in the Leo Baeck Institute, which participates in the interlibrary loan program.

Another valuable project of cemetery documentation has been undertaken by:

> Dr. Peter Honigmann
> Jüdisches Zentralarchiv 5
> D-69117 Heidelberg
> Germany

It was begun in 1985 by Prof. Künzel of the Institute for Higher Jewish Studies, affiliated with Heidelberg University. The first goal was to photograph all the tombstones in Baden-Württemberg (except for Jebenhausen and Göppingen, which were already documented very well). This collection currently includes about 95,000 photographs of more than 50,000 tombstones, with both the back and the front of the gravestones photographed as a rule.

The second stage, still in progress, is to transcribe the data on each stone. However, you may write to Dr. Honigmann at the above address to inquire about a specific cemetery. For more information on this project, see "Report on Documentation of Jewish Tombstones in Baden-Württemberg" (*Avotaynu*, Winter 1994).

The Weissensee Cemetery in Berlin has 110,000 graves and is the largest Jewish cemetery in that city. You can get permission from cemetery officials to use the records. Other Jewish cemeteries in Berlin are also accessible, and some cemeteries outside Berlin may also be accessible. The Zentralrat der Juden in Deutschland [Central Office for the Jews in Germany] nearest to an area may be able to help you gain access to local cemeteries if you plan to travel to Germany. The local city hall or florist or funeral director may have the keys to the cemetery.

Arlene Sachs of the Jewish Genealogical Society of Greater Washington (DC) began a very important project in 1993. Its very ambitious goal is to document all Jewish cemeteries worldwide. Now under the auspices of the Association of Jewish Genealogical Societies, the cooperative efforts of many have produced a file of 200,000 burials throughout the world. It looks as if the goal of one million burial files by the summer of 1997 will be achieved. See more details under **Computer Genealogy** later in this chapter.

FAMILY HISTORIES

Despite the resurgence of interest in Jewish history, including family history, resulting in many family histories being published, it has often been difficult to determine whether anything has been published about a particular family. Even if you know the title, it may be a time-consuming task to find out which library or archive has it.

But some efforts have been made to make the task easier. It began with two small, but useful, bibliographies, *American Jewish Genealogies* and *American Jewish Genealogies Worldwide*, by Janice Regenstein, published in 1981.

By far the most comprehensive work has come from David Zubatsky and Irwin Berent. This bibliography covers published and unpublished family histories and genealogies of at least three generations in over 50 American and foreign repositories. It is alphabetized according to the principal surname, but the index lists other surnames for which there is significant coverage (primarily for women who took different surnames upon marriage and their descendants).

In 1984, they co-edited Volume 1 of *Jewish Genealogy: A Sourcebook of Family Histories and Genealogies*. David Zubatsky added material from foreign repositories for volume 2, published in 1990. A third revision added thousands of new entries and now contains over 10,000 family names. This last edition was published by Avotaynu, Inc., and has also been released as part of the *Consolidated Jewish Surname Index (CJSI)*, which can be searched on the Internet.

GENEALOGICAL SOCIETIES AND PERIODICALS

Periodicals are of crucial importance in helping genealogists keep up-to-date in a rapidly changing world, especially with regards to discoveries, access and personal experiences with archival research. Limitations of time and local access have forced us to concentrate on *Avotaynu*, except insofar as we happened to hear about key articles in others.

Avotaynu, edited by Sally Sack and published by Gary Mokotoff, is widely regarded as the leading periodical. In fact, it is probably one of the best culturally distinct periodicals for any group anywhere in the world. Few periodicals have such an extensive worldwide network of associate or contributing editors. Its usefulness is not limited to Jewish genealogists, since other genealogists whose ancestors came from the same general area as is covered by particular articles are likely to find information which is also relevant for their research. In addition to informative articles, each issue carries some regular features:

- U.S. Update: This reads like a table of contents of the newsletters of many different genealogical societies and regional Special Interest Groups (not restricted to U.S. topics). This makes it easy to scan a newsletter to see whether you would like to subscribe or order specific issues.

- Ask the Experts: This column by Randy Daitch and Eileen Polakoff enables readers to ask questions and get free published answers which may be relevant for others.

- Family Finder: For a small fee, readers may place a query detailing their research interests in one issue. This is eventually included in the larger database of *Family Finder*, so your queries become widely circulated.

- Book Reviews: This gives readers an opportunity to read about recent publications by *Avotaynu* and others.

Most, perhaps all, Jewish genealogical societies in the United States and elsewhere belong to an umbrella group, the Association of Jewish Genealogical Societies (AJGS). AJGS has sponsored annual genealogical seminars which offer presentations of value for both beginning and advanced genealogists. Most of these are held in various American cities, but the seminars have also been held in Jerusalem and the 1997 seminar is in Paris. For the first time, mini-seminars will be held in East European locations, such as L'viv, Minsk, Vilnius and Warsaw, after the big annual seminar. In the year 2000, AJGS will meet in Salt Lake City for the second time. More information can be found on the Web at http//:jewishgen.org/ajgs/ or by writing to the:

Association of Jewish Genealogical Societies
P.O. Box 50245
Palo Alto, CA 94303

There are quite a few, and a growing number of, geographically-focused Special Interest Groups (SIGs) for various areas, including Germany, Galicia (Ukraine-Poland), Romania, Hrodna (Belarus), Hungary, Latvia, Lithuania, and Kielce, Radom and the Suwalk-Lomza area (the last three are in Poland). These SIGs are especially helpful due to the changing nature of genealogy and newly accessible records in Eastern Europe.

The various local societies hold meetings which may be especially helpful, because most of them are small, thus making a lot of individual help possible. As is the case with many non-Jewish societies, they often have information-sharing sessions and undertake special projects which require volunteers.

Many of these local societies or SIGs also publish a newsletter or journal. Those of American societies are listed in *The Genealogist's Address Book* by Elizabeth Petty Bentley.

A list of local genealogical societies and SIGs is published annually in the Spring issue of *Avotaynu*, together with information about meetings, e-mail addresses, phone numbers, and so forth. You can also get the latest information by sending an e-mail message to jgsaddr@jewishgen.org or sigaddr@jewishgen.org, as appropriate, or by sending a self-addressed, stamped envelope to AJGS. The Web address is http//:jewishgen.org; then look for the URL (link) for a list of societies and groups and click on that link.

The periodical, *Stammbaum* [*Family Tree*], focuses on Germanic Jewish genealogy, including Austria, Switzerland and Bohemia. It is edited by Bill Firestone, with guest editors for some issues, and currently published by the Baeck Institute. A table of contents, surname index and place name index is available on the *Stammbaum* home page. For more information, contact Firestone at 70401.1663@compuserv or the Baeck Institute.

Jüdische Familienforschung [*Jewish Family Research*] was a family history periodical published in Germany from 1924 to 1938. It contained many family and community histories. Copies can be found at the Baeck Institute and various other research libraries. A surname index has been compiled for the first 38 out of the 50 issues. It can be found in Rottenberg's guide. The extent of this list is illustrated by the fact that it comprises about two-thirds of the book.

There are dozens of Jewish genealogical societies in the United States and elsewhere. Most of them publish a newsletter or journal. Two of the better periodicals are considered to be *Dorot* and *Mishpocha*, published by the following societies, respectively:

Jewish Genealogical Society, Inc.
P.O. Box 6398
New York, NY 10128

Jewish Genealogical Society of
Greater Washington
P.O. Box 412
Vienna, VA 22183-0412

Bob Weiss, current president of the AJGS, also edits *Zichron Notes*. The first 13 volumes (1981-1993) are on FHL microfiche. You can also write to the following address or send an e-mail message to RWeissJGS@aol.com:

San Francisco Bay Area Jewish Genealogical Society
P.O. Box 471616
San Francisco, CA 94147

News of the Jewish Genealogical Society of Rochester has full-text articles on its home page. Look for the link off the JewishGen Web site already mentioned or contact the editor:

Bruce Kahn
265 Viennawood Drive
Rochester, NY 14618

Edward Luft made us aware of a very important collection of 68 Jewish periodicals at the Adam Mickiewicz University library, where they are now being indexed:

Biblioteka Uniwersytecka w Poznaniu
ul. Ratajczaka 38/40
PL 61-816 Poznan
Poland

These periodicals were published in 12 countries, but nearly all of the periodicals are relevant for Germanic Jews. Of these, 53 are in German, 5 in English, and 8 in Polish, Dutch or Italian. The Mickiewicz University library has about 20,000 Judaica titles, of which 2,000 came from the Jewish community in Berlin.

Many of these are available at the German Historical Institute in Washington, the New York Public Library, the Library of Congress, or Harvard University. Others can be found at the YIVO Institute, the American Jewish Periodical Center or Hebrew Union College (both in Cincinnati), the Leo Baeck Institute, various other university libraries (Princeton, Indiana, Stanford, Jerusalem) or the Jewish Genealogical Seminary for America.

Luft also passed on a message from Henry Wellisch, reporting that the Robarts Library at the University of Toronto has 31 rolls of microfilms of an equal number of German-language Jewish periodicals. These include at least 10 years of issues for 13 and 40 years for 4. Two, including *Die Wahrheit* [*The Truth*] (Vienna, 1885-1938), are also at Indiana University, Bloomington.

COMPUTER GENEALOGY

Computers have become very significant for finding out about genealogical resources and even for your own personal research. See Chapter IV for pertinent information. A very readable article by Gary Mokotoff, "Internet for Greenhorns," in *Avotaynu* (Fall 1996) explains in plain English just what this new communications channel is all about and how it can help you. Listed below are some key resources for Jewish genealogy.

World Wide Web (WWW): There are undoubtedly hundreds of Web sites for Jewish genealogy, but you can get almost anything you want by going to JewishGen (address above). It is a wonderful example of what can be accomplished through cooperative efforts. Susan King of Houston deserves credit for her determined efforts, over a ten-year-period, to share genealogical information on a not-for-profit basis. The result is that JewishGen is the major jumping-off place for information about worldwide Jewish genealogy. It deserves its title of "The Official Home of Jewish Genealogy." Over 100 volunteers make it happen.

A very helpful section for beginners is "Frequently Asked Questions," edited by Warren Blatt. There are InfoFiles, like a Jewish genealogical mini-encyclopedia, which cover each subject in more depth. An important section explains the Soundex system used by the U.S. Census Bureau, as well as the Daitch-Mokotoff Soundex system. This section also converts dates in the Hebrew calendar to modern calendar dates. Another group of volunteers will help you translate short documents without charge. If you need more help, you will find a list of professional translators. There are links to many other Jewish organizations and their home pages. This is what surfing the net means — going from one linked page to another.

Some of the most exciting developments is the recent creation of a large number of searchable databases. A few of the more outstanding ones are:

- **AJGS Cemetery Project:** Look for this link. This is a massive venture to collect Jewish burial information worldwide. Arlene Sachs began collecting this data in 1993, but now there are many volunteers working on it. It is a three-phase project. The first phase is to find out where Jews are buried. A list of 13,500 cemeteries in 85 counties and all American states has already been established. This is already searchable, but by no means complete, so contributions and information are solicited.

  The second phase is to include data on individuals buried in these cemeteries in a database, which already has 200,000 names from 1,500 cemeteries. The last phase is to make this information about individuals searchable. When 1 million burials have been listed, the information will be made available on CD-ROM. For details as to how to contribute, watch the Web site listed above or send an e-mail message to Sidney Sachs at Sachs@axsamer.org.

- **Yizkor Book Project:** This is discussed later in this chapter.

- **Russian Era Indexing of Poland Project:** This is a large database of indexed nineteenth-century Polish vital records. It is a tool to take advantage of the Jewish records at the Family History Library. Volunteers have indexed them so you can search by surname or by geographic region. You can narrow your search to a specific surname in a specific locality.

- **Shtetl Link Project:** Still getting underway, but the goal is to provide detailed information about the various *shtetlekh* or villages that were home to Jews throughout the world. Although *shtetl* is usually associated with Jews in the Pale of Settlement, this site offers information about other localities with significant Jewish populations, e.g., the East End of London, Maxwell Street in Chicago and the Lower East Side of New York City.

- **JewishGen Family Finder:** This is a database of more than 35,000 surnames places which are being researched by 2,500 Jewish genealogists throughout the world. Not only can you search by name or place, but you can also find the names and addresses of other genealogists with similar interests.

Avotaynu's home page at http//:www.avotaynu.com provides information about its publications and subscription. But its most remarkable feature is the Consolidated Jewish Surname Index. Its database includes some 200,000 Jewish surnames which appear in 23 different databases. They are all searched together by using the Daitch-Mokotoff Soundex system. If you find an entry of interest, check the individual publication. By now, many libraries have copies of the books or fiche. All AJGS member organizations have copies of the microfiche formats. You can also order any of the individual publications from Avotaynu.

The following databases have been included in the CJSI. This is the wave of the future for genealogical publishing and, as usual, Avotaynu leads the way.

1) *AJGS Cemetery Project Burials* (22,557 entries): 100,000 Jewish burials worldwide

2) *JewishGen Family Finder* (13,689 entries): described above

3) *Jewish Genealogical People Finder*

4) *A Dictionary of Jewish Surnames from the Russian Empire* (49,402 entries): surnames from the Pale of Settlement

5) *A Dictionary of Jewish Surnames from the Kingdom of Poland* (33,511 entries)

6) *Sourcebook for Jewish Genealogies and Family Histories* (10,257 entries): 25,000 surnames for which there is published information about family histories

7) *Index to the Russian Consular Records* (39,424 entries): 70,000 persons who did business with the Czarist consuls in the United States from about 1849 to 1926

8) *First American Jewish Families* (94,931 entries): 50,000 descendants of Jewish American families which arrived in America between 1654 and 1838

9) *Palestine Gazette* (16,325 entries): 28,000 persons, mostly Jews, who legally changed their names while living in Palestine during the British Mandate (1921-1948)

10) *Gedenkbuch* (10,247 entries): 128,000 German Jews murdered in the Holocaust

11) *Memorial to the Jews Deported from France* (26,524 entries): 70,000 Jews deported during the Holocaust

12) *National Registry of Jewish Holocaust Survivors* (14,806 entries): 35,000 Holocaust survivors in the United States and Canada

13) *Emergency Passports* (4,432 entries): 3,000 Jewish applicants for emergency U.S. passports in 1915-1924, processed by the State Department

14) *Index to State Department Records Found in the U.S. National Archives Containing Jewish Names in the Section on the Protection of Interests of U.S. Citizens in Russia* (3,142 entries): 5,000 records

15) *Index to State Department Records Found in the U.S. National Archives: A Registration of U.S. Citizens in Jerusalem, 1914-1918* (877 entries): 1,000 records

16) *Index to State Department Records Found in the U.S. National Archives: A List of Jewish Names in the Section on the Protection of U.S. Citizens in Austria-Hungary, 1910-1930* (1,602 entries): 2,000 records

17) *Refusniks* (2,490 entries): 7,000 Russian Jewish citizens refused emigration from the Soviet Union in 1985

18) *Jewish Surnames from Morocco* (4,644 entries): 4,644 different surnames

19) *Jewish Burials in Hartford County, Connecticut* (8,323 entries): 13,000 burials

20) *Jewish Surnames from Prague* (1,056 entries): Ashkenazic surnames from the fifteenth through eighteenth centuries

21) *Cleveland (Ohio), Burials* (1,413 entries)

22) *Obuda (Hungary), Census of 1850* (598 entries)

YIZKOR BOOKS

Yizkor or memorial books were written mostly after the Holocaust to memorialize families and friends in a specific community. They were written by individuals and/or immigrant groups, called *landsmanshaften* [German: *Landsmannschaften*], who came from a particular *shtetl* (village) or region. The regional books are particularly important for Baden-Württemberg, Bavaria, Hesse and Silesia (interwar Germany); Galicia (interwar Poland); Latvia; Lithuania; Karpatalja (Carpathia in interwar Czechoslovakia); Maramures, Salaj, Transylvania and Bessarabia (interwar Romania); Polesie (mostly Belarus), Crimea (Ukraine), and Volhynia (now in Ukraine, partly Polish before 1939).

These personal recollections about Jewish communities that no longer exist can be very genealogically and historically valuable. They often contain details like photos, town maps and personal accounts about town or community members from persons who knew them. Unfortunately, they are almost exclusively written in Hebrew or Yiddish. They were mostly privately published in limited editions and so are scattered over the world in homes and libraries and, until recently, difficult to locate and use. The *Yizkor* SIG (Special Interest Group) of the JewishGen newsgroup is trying to change that. Its goal is to facilitate access to and unlock the valuable information in *Yizkor* books. You can find them as a link from JewishGen, http://www.jewishgen.org. Or you may write and send a self-addressed stamped envelope to:

> Martin Kessel, Coordinator
> Yizkor Book SIG
> 43 Water St.
> Natick, MA 01760

Alternatively, send an e-mail to mkessel@jewishgen.org. This ongoing project allows you to search, by name of *shtetl* or region, all *Yizkor* books known to exist, and also to find out who has them. Because most will need translation into English, the names of genealogists who have a common interest in a specific *shtetl* and are interested in contributing funds or cooperating on the translation are listed.

A very long list of libraries which have *Yizkor* book collections of 25 or more is available. There is also a list of *Yizkor* book dealers and translators who may have the one you want for sale. Also included is a glossary of terms used in *Yizkor* books. To subscribe and learn more about *Yizkor* books, e-mail to listserv@jewishgen.org with the message: sub yizkor (to subscribe), unsub yizkor (to unsubscribe), sub yizkor_d (to subscribe in digest mode), unsub yizkor_d (to unsubscribe in digest mode).

HOLOCAUST RESEARCH

Since the end of World War II and the destruction of Jews by the Nazis, there have been efforts by historians to memorialize the Jews killed by the Holocaust. Many research libraries were established then to collect material, not only about Holocaust victims, but Jewry in general.

A very good resource specifically for Holocaust research is *How to Document Victims and Locate Survivors of the Holocaust*, by Gary Mokotoff, published by Avotaynu. It details many collections.

The United States Holocaust Memorial Museum and Archives in Washington, DC, is an excellent resource. It is designed to educate the public about the Holocaust and to document the victims and survivors. It maintains a museum as well as an archive and library. Its mailing address is:

> United States Holocaust Memorial Museum and Archives
> 100 Raoul Wallenburg Place SW
> Washington, DC 20024-2150

You can also check out their home page on the Internet. It tells about their many programs and also allows you to search several databases.

One database began as the registry at the American Gathering of Holocaust Survivors in 1981. It has been expanded to include all Holocaust survivors. It seeks to facilitate contact between survivors and assist families to contact their missing relatives.

The other searchable database allows you to find out what resources are in the archives and library. You may search by keyword, subject, author, place or person as subject. And from the home page, you may click to information about other Holocaust libraries such as Yad Vashem and the Simon Wiesenthal Center.

One of the more recent and major acquisitions by the U.S. Holocaust Memorial Archives has been the German Minority Census of 1939. This is significant because it gives us one last look at the German Jewish people before the Holocaust's destruction. This was filmed by the Family History Library at the Bundesarchiv in Potsdam, Germany, and will also be available there or in their centers worldwide. A very useful finding aid for this collection has been written by FHL librarian, Thomas Edlund. Since this collection is organized by census district, not community, Edlund's register helps you navigate the collection by town name. The census gives the following information: name, birth date, place of birth, and which of the person's four grandparents were Jewish. This register was published by Avotaynu.

Other books worth noting about Holocaust include the two-volume *Gedenkbuch* [*Memorial Book*], an incomplete list published by the German archives. It lists the name, sex, birth date, residence, and death date, and place of deaths of about 128,000 Holocaust victims. There was also an earlier regional book by Paul Sauer, called *Die Opfer der Judenverfolgung in Baden-Württemberg 1933-45: Ein Gedenkbuch* [*The Victims of the National Socialist (Nazi) Persecution in Baden-Württemberg 1933-45: A Memorial*].

REVIVAL OF HISTORIC INTEREST IN JUDAICA LIBRARIES AND ARCHIVES

Across the world where Jews have settled since the Holocaust, there has been a revival of interest in Judaica. This has resulted in the establishment of special libraries and archives in Jerusalem and America to memorialize Jewish communal life in Europe. There are also some established in Germany now. Since there are too many to be enumerated here, we list some of the ones with large collections which are particularly useful to genealogists.

The **Leo Baeck Institute**, Frank Mecklenburg, Archivist, and Karen Franklin, Genealogical Librarian (telephone 212-744-6400, e-mail LBI1@LBI1.com). Founded in 1955, its goal is to acquire material relating to German Jews. Holdings include communal records of over 500 communities, plus 6,000 archival collections, which include family histories and genealogies, family trees, collections of professional genealogists who have researched German Jewish families. For more information about their collection and publications, visit their Web site at: www.lbi.org or write:

> Leo Baeck Institute
> Library and Archives
> 129 East 73rd St.
> New York City, NY 10021

The catalog is not on-line, but will be searched for a specific topic or reference by mail. Some material may be used by interlibrary loan. Write to the Genealogical Librarian.

The 50-year anniversary of *Kristallnacht*, sparking a revival of interest among German historians in things Jewish, has resulted in the acquisition of some 1,000 publications about German Jewish communities before and during the Holocaust and tombstone inscriptions and *Memorbücher* [Memorial Books].

For 40 years the London branch of LBI has published a *Yearbook*, containing scholarly articles about German Jewry. The *Yearbook* will shortly be available on CD-ROM.

Another ambitious ongoing project, published in 1997 in 3 languages, is intended to become the complete history of German Jewry. The German and English titles are: *Deutsch jüdische Geschichten in der Neuzeit* and *German Jewish History in Modern Times*.

Leo Baeck Institute is moving in 1998 to a joint facility with three other institutions: YIVO, the American-Jewish Historical Society (of Waltham, MA), and Yeshiva University Museum. All four libraries, archives, and museum will be combined in a campus-like setting called Center for Jewish History. However, the catalogs of each will remain separate. The new address will be in Manhattan at 15 West 16th St.

Another recent emphasis is called the Austrian History Project, soliciting material such as photographs, memoirs, family trees, and family histories from Austrian emigrés.

YIVO (Yidisher Visnashaftlekher Institut), Zachary Baker, Librarian, and Marek Web, Archivist (telephone 212-246-6080, open M-Th 9:30-5:30), has temporary facilities until 1998 at:

> YIVO (Yidisher Visnashaftlekher Institut)
> 555 W. 57th St.
> New York City, NY 10019

YIVO was founded in 1925 in Vilna with the goal to preserve East European Jewish heritage. It has only a small staff who cannot do research for you, so it is best to visit yourself. Their extensive library collection includes 600 *Yizkor* books, many in Hebrew and Yiddish. Only microforms are available through interlibrary loan. Although the collection is strongly Eastern European, the library has several collections of Germanic material. For example, original communal records of the communities of Ostrowo, Posen, Krotoschin, Posen, and Briesen, West Prussia are in Record Group 13-15. Also check Record Groups 16 and 31. Use the Fruma Mohrer and Marek Web guide as a finding aid to their collection.

The **Central Archives for the History of the Jewish People** is located at:

> Central Archives for the History of the Jewish People
> Sprinzak Building
> Hebrew University - Givat Ram Campus
> P.O. Box 1149
> Jerusalem 91010
> Israel

Many city archives (*Stadtarchiv*) and regional and state archives (*Staatsarchiv*) in Germany today have Jewish collections. The trick it is to be able to find out what they have that might pertain to your family. The addresses for these archives are found in Chapter XVI. A guide for writing letters to archives is found in Chapter XIX. Another method is to check a German-language publication called *Quellen zur Geschichte der Juden in den Archiven der neuen Bundesländer* [*Sources for Jewish History in the Archives of the New (Eastern) Federal States*]. It gives up-to-date (1996) information on what each archive might contain for Jewish researchers. LBI has a copy.

Bavarian Jewish records can be found at:

> Landesverbund der Israelitischen Kultusgemeinde in Bayern
> Effernerstrasse 68
> D-81925 München
> Germany

See an article in *Avotaynu*, Spring 1992, by LBI archivist Frank Mecklenburg and Claus W. Hirsch, "More Jewish Holdings in East German Archives." Even though this article may be outdated by now, it is still a very readable analysis of where records may have been located.

There are also museums and archives that specialize in Jewish history. An example is the:

> Jüdisches Museum der Stadt Frankfurt am Main
> Unter Main Kai 14-15
> D-60311 Frankfurt am Main
> Germany

The papers of the noted German genealogist, Bernard Brilling, are located there. See the article in *Avotaynu* (Spring 1995), by Edward Luft and Peter Lande which describes this valuable collection and how to get access to it. It has not yet been properly cataloged, but a rudimentary inventory of its holdings is available at LBI and the library of the JGS of Greater Washington, DC. If you do not have easy access to these locations, you may write:

Peter Lande
3002 Ordway St. NW
Washington, DC 20008-3254

The city of Cologne, Germany, has a special library called **Germania Judaica**. It is supported by the city of Cologne and the state of Northrhine-Westphalia. According to its home page at www.stbib-koeln.derjudaica/, it specializes in books, primary sources, and academic research publications on all aspects of German-speaking Jewry from the 18th century onwards. The library has contacts with similar institutions worldwide and regularly publishes a directory of research projects relating to the history of German Jewry and anti-Semitism (the latest is Fall 1995). For further information or to order a copy of *Arbeitsinformationen* [*Directory of Research Projects Relating to the History of German Jewry, and Anti-Semitism*], 16th edition, please write to:

> Germania Judaica
> Josef Haubrich Hof 1
> D-50676 Köln
> Germany

Another place that could yield valuable information is the:

> Institut für Geschichte der deutschen Juden
> Rothenbaumchaussee 7
> D-20148 Hamburg
> Germany

It does not have genealogical material, *per se*, but is collecting Jewish community histories.

Another example of special libraries and archives devoted to collecting Jewish material is:

> Israelitisches Religionsgemeindeschaft Württemberg
> Hospitalstrasse 36
> D-70174 Stuttgart
> Germany

RESEARCH IN SOUTHWESTERN GERMANIC AREAS

We are indebted to George Arnstein, noted genealogist and author, for his permission to include the following article about community histories that he has found in his own research, which is focused on southwest Germany and nearby areas. This was where most of the early German Jews settled and, apart from those who settled in the big cities, it continued to have the heaviest concentration of German Jews until World War II.

Arnstein helpfully mentions where he found the publications. In some formerly Jewish communities in Europe there has been a revival, with some establishing Jewish museums, while others avoid memories of a difficult period. Historians are once again writing about and recording life in Jewish communities. Here is a small sampling of exhibits, memorials, books and articles in scholarly publications.

Nordstetten, in the Black Forest, commemorates Berthold Auerbach, a native son who became a celebrated secular German author, especially with his *Black Forest Stories*. He is the subject of a special issue of *Marbacher Magazin*, 36/1985, to accompany the permanent exhibit at the Auerbach Museum in Horb-Nordstetten. Relevant, as to lifestyle, are autobiographical "Childhood Memories from Nordstetten," translated into English by George Arnstein and published in *Mishpocha* (1991). Auerbach was born on 28 February 1812 as Moses Baruch Auerbacher; he earned his doctorate at Tübingen. He also illustrates the then common secularization of names: "I was born on Haman's feast, the night of Purim ..." See also H. Wagenpfeil, *Manuskripte zur Geschichte der Juden* [*Manuscripts of the History of Jews in Nordstetten*]. Typescript, before 1988.

Austria. Research services in Austria, the Czech Republic, and possibly other parts of the former Hapsburg Empire are available from the Institute for Historic Family Research (IHFF) (Phone/Fax 011/43/1/317-8806):

> IHFF Genealogie Gesellschaft mbH.
> Pantzergasse 30/8
> A-1190 Vienna

There are two Jewish museums in Austria:

Jewish Museum of the City of Vienna
Dorotheergasse 11
A-1010 Vienna
Austria
(*Phone: 011/43/1/535-0431*
Fax: 011/43/1/535-0424)

Jewish Museum Hohenems
Villa Heimann-Rosenthal
Schweizer Strasse 5
A-6845 Hohenems, Vorarlberg
Austria
(*Phone: (0043) 05576/3989*)

The Hohenems Jewish community began about 1631, suffered expulsion , returned, thrived and then declined after about 1900. The most famous local offspring was Salomon Sulzer, cantor, who became an honorary citizen of Vienna. Much genealogical information was compiled by Dr. Tänzer, the rabbi at the turn of the century, since updated by others.

- Aron Tänzer. *Geschichte der Juden in Tirol und Vorarlberg*. Teil 1 + 2: *Die Geschichte der Juden in Hohenems und im übrigen Vorarlberg* [*History of the Jews in Tyrol and Vorarlberg*, Parts 1 & 2: *History of the Jews in Hohenems and the Rest of Vorarlberg*]. Meran(o), 1905. He completed only the Hohenems portion of this book, reprinted in Bregenz in 1982 with additional material. Copies of the first edition are at the Leo Baeck Institute and the Library of Congress.

- Naftali Bar-Giora Bamberger. *Memorbuch: die jüdischen Friedhofe Jebenhausen und Göppingen* [*Memorial Book: The Jewish Cemeteries at Jebenhausen and Göppingen*].

Sulzbach-Rosenberg plans to convert the former synagogue into a city museum and documentation center for Jewish history in the Oberpfalz, a government district in Bavaria.

Haigerloch, formerly in Hohenzollern, has a memorial, has published three books dealing with their former Jewish citizens, and has inventoried them in a computerized database. All are available from the Stadtverwaltung, D-72394 Haigerloch, Germany.

- W. Schäfer. *Geschichte und Schicksal der Juden in Haigerloch* [*History and Fate of the Jews in Haigerloch*]. Thesis. Reutlingen: Pädagogische Hochschule Reutlingen. 1971.

Switzerland. Two Swiss villages on the Rhine between Basel and Lake Constance have had a Jewish community at least since the 17th century. A local association concerns itself with the cemeteries and in 1993 issued *Der Judenfriedhof Endingen-Lengnau* [*The Jewish Cemetery in Endingen-Lengnau*], some 400 pages in two volumes, published by:

> Menes Verlag
> Postfach 5070
> CH-5405 Baden
> Switzerland

For further information about Swiss Jewish genealogy, check the quarterly, *Majaan, Die Quelle* [*Majaan, The Source*], a German language quarterly published by the Swiss Society for Jewish Genealogy:

> Schweitzerische Gesellschaft für jüdische Familienforschung
> P.O. Box 876
> CH-8021 Zürich
> Switzerland

While it focuses on German-speaking Switzerland, it frequently publishes material about the ties of Swiss Jews to Alsace, southern Germany, Posen, and Austria.

For another look at Jewish life, there are monographs prepared in a variety of academic settings. Bernhard Purin, for example, received his master's degree at the University in Tübingen, based on a study of the short-lived Vorarlberg community in Sulz. This is the town where many of the Jews expelled from Hohenems sought refuge. Purin's study, which offers a marvelous slice of Jewish small town life, has been published:

- Bernhard Purin. *Die Juden von Sulz: eine jüdische Landgemeinde in Vorarlberg, 1676-1744* [*The Jews of Sulz: A Jewish Rural Community in Vorarlberg, 1676-1744*]. Bregenz, Austria: Autorengesellschaft. 1991.

The trick, of course, is to find some of these studies, including unpublished ones, complicated by the fact that Germany has nothing comparable to the American *Dissertation Abstracts*. However, there are valuable compilations like the massive bibliography by Angelika C. Ellman-Krüger, *Auswahlbibliographie zur jüdischen Familienforschung vom Anfang des 19. Jahrhunderts bis zur Gegenwart* [*Selected Bibliography of Jewish Family Research From the Beginning of the 19th Century to the Present*]. It contains more than 2,500 well organized citations, with a name and separate place index.

Other compilations seek to capture and list all residual Jewish evidences. Here are two:

- Israel Schwierz. *Steinerne Zeugnisse jüdischen Lebens in Bayern: eine Dokumentation* [*Harsh Testimonies of Jewish Life in Bavaria: A Compilation of Documents*]. Munich: Bayerische Landeszentrale für politische Bildungsarbeit. 1988.

- Joachim Hahn. *Erinnerungen und Zeugnisse jüdischer Geschichte in Baden-Württemberg* [*Memories and Testimonies of Jewish History in Baden-Württemberg*]. Thesis. Stuttgart. 1988.

Rev. Hahn's book has a detailed list, by town or village, of whatever traces remain of Jewish life in southwestern Germany. It cites many of the published and unpublished theses and honors papers listed here, courtesy of Dr. Arnstein.

- **Archshofen, Creglingen**: E. Bauer. *Die Geschichte der jüdischen Minderheit in Archshofen* [*History of the Jewish Minority in Archshofen*]. Senior thesis. Zulassungsarbeit zur Fachgruppenprüfung in Geschichte. 1964. Apparently published in 1985 - no details. Listed in Hahn's book.

- **Aufhausen (Bopfingen)**: U. Laurentzsch. *Zur Geschichte der Judengemeinde Aufhausen bei Bopfingen* [*History of the Jewish Community in Aufhausen near Bopfingen*]. Typescript thesis. Schwäbisch Gmünd: Pädagogische Hochschule Schwäbisch Gmünd. 1978.

- **Buchau**: Reinhold Adler. *Beiträge zu einer Geschichte der israelitischen Gemeinde Buchaus von den Anfängen bis zu Beginn des Hitlerreiches* [*Contributions to the History of the Jewish Community of Buchau from Its Beginnings to the Start of the Hitler Regime*]. Typescript thesis (copy at LBI, NYC, filed under G=Gemeinde, then B=Buchau). Weingarten: Pädagogische Hochschule Weingarten. 1973. (Kreisarchiv Biberach Nr. 961).

  J. Mohn. *Der Leidensweg unter dem Hakenkreuz,* [*The Path of Sorrow under the Swastika*], published in Buchau in 1970, lists all who suffered and/or died, ranging from Jews to Wehrmacht soldiers.

- **Bühl (Baden)**: H. Pieges. *Schicksale jüdischer Familien Bühls* [*Fate of the Jewish Families in Bühl*]. Thesis. Freiburg: Pädagogische Hochschule Freiburg. 1962/63.

- **Freiburg im Breisgau**: G. Blad. *Die Entstehung der israelitischen Gemeinde Freiburgs 1849-1941* [*The Origin of the Jewish Community of Freiburg, 1849-1941*]. Thesis. Freiburg: Freiburg University. 1985.

- **Göppingen, Jebenhausen**: J. Kühner. *Der Rabbiner Dr. Aron Tänzer und die jüdischen Gemeinde in Göppingen [Rabbi Dr. Aron Tänzer and the Jewish Community of Göppingen]*. Thesis. Schwäbisch Gmünd: Pädagogische Hochschule Schwäbisch Gmünd. 1981.

  G. Munz. *Die Geschichte der Juden in Jebenhausen. [History of the Jews in Jebenhausen]*. Thesis. Schwäbisch Gmünd: Pädagogische Hochschule Schwäbisch Gmünd. 1963.

  Aron Tänzer. *Geschichte der Juden in Jebenhausen und Göppingen [History of the Jews in Jebenhausen and Göppingen]*. Kohlhammer: 1927. Reprinted, with two additional chapters by Karl-Heinz Reuss. Göppingen: Standarchiv. (Volume 23 of series). Written by a rabbi who served there.

- **Görwihl, Oberwihl nr. Waldshut**: R. Fichtner and B. Wegemer. *Kinder einer Zukunft: von zwei Kinderheimen in der Weimarer Zeit [Children of One Future: From Two Children's Homes During the Time of the Weimar Republic]*. Thesis. Tübingen: Tübingen University, Erziehungswissenschaft. 1986. One of the children's homes was Jewish.

- **Heilbronn-Sontheim**: H. Gräf, in charge of the project of students of the Helene-Lang Real Schule and others: *Der jüdische Friedhof Heilbronn-Sontheim, eine Dokumentation [The Jewish Cemetery Heilbronn-Sontheim, A Documentation]*. Typescript. Processed 1987.

- **Hemsbach**: H. Hössler. *Juden in Hemsbach von 1660-1933 [Jews in Hemsbach from 1660 to 1933]*. Thesis. Heidelberg: Pädagogische Hochschule Heidelberg. 1984.

  Also a compendium by students of the Friedrich Schiller Hauptschule Hemsbach: Documentation "Traces and Recollections" in *Our Neighbors of the Jewish Faith*. 1984.

- **Laupheim**: Sybille Indlekofer. *Jüdisches Gemeindeschicksal aufgezeigt am Beispiel der Stadt Laupheim [Fate of the Jewish Community As Shown in the Example of the City of Laupheim]*. Lörrach/Baden: Pädagogische Hochschule Lörrach/Baden. 1970. (Kreisarchiv Biberach 431). Copy at LBI, NYC. 1965 thesis by Waltraut Kohl of the same teachers' training college is not mentioned, although it heavily overlaps the material on Laupheim in the Indlekofer thesis.

  Waltraut Kohl. *Die Geschichte der jüdischen Gemeinde in Laupheim [History of the Jewish Community in Laupheim]*. Typescript thesis. Weingarten: Pädagogische Hochschule Weingarten. 1965. (Kreisarchiv Biberach Nr. 365.) Copy at LBI, NYC (donated or arranged by John Bergman, Media, PA).

- **Ludwigsburg**: B. Gut. *Die Judenverfolgungen im Dritten Reich und deren Darstellung in der Ludwigsburger Zeitung [Persecution of Jews During the Third Reich and Its Portrayal in the Ludwigsburg Newspaper]*. Thesis. Schwäbisch Gmünd: Pädagogische Hochschule Schwäbisch Gmünd. 1971.

- **Oberdorf (am Ipf, Bopfingen)**: W. Kucher. *Die Geschichte der Oberdorfer Judengemeinde von der Gründung bis zur Emanzipation [History of the Jewish Community of Oberdorf From Its Origin to Its Emancipation]*. Thesis. Schwäbisch Gmünd: Pädagogische Hochschule Schwäbisch Gmünd. 1976.

- **Offenburg**: S. Möschle. *Das Schicksal der jüdischen Bevölkerung Offenburgs in der Zeit des Nationalsozialismus [The Fate of the Jewish Population of Offenburg during Nazi Times]*. Thesis. Freiburg: Freiburg University. 1977.

- **Rastatt**: O. Stiefvater. "Geschichte und Schicksal der Juden im Landkreis Rastatt" ["History and Fate of the Jews in the County of Rastatt"] in *Um Rhein und Murg*, Vol. 5 (1965), pp. 42-83.

- **Reutlingen**: Th. Schön. "Geschichte der Juden in Reutlingen" ["History of the Jews in Reutlingen"] in *Reutlinger Geschichtsblätter*, Vol. V (1894), pp. 36ff, 59-62; Vol. VI (1895), p. 64.

- **Schwäbisch Gmünd**: J. A. Grimm. *Zur Geschichte der Juden in Schwäbisch Gmünd [History of the Jews in Schwäbisch Gmünd]*. Thesis. Schwäbisch Gmünd: Pädagogische Hochschule Schwäbisch Gmünd. 1962.

- **Schwetzingen** and **Ketsch**: A. Lohrbächer and M. Rittmann. *Sie gehörten zu uns. Geschichte und Schicksale der Schwetzinger Juden [They Belonged to Us. History and Fate of the Schwetzingen Jews]*. Schwetzingen: Series of the Schwetzingen City Archives, Vol. 7. 1978.

- **Ulm**: A. Engel. *Juden in Ulm im 19. Jahrhundert: Anfänge und Entwicklung der jüdischen Gemeinde von 1803-1873 [Jews in Ulm in the 19th Century. Beginning and Development of the Jewish Community from 1803 to 1873]*. Masters thesis. Tübingen: Tübingen University. 1982.

BIBLIOGRAPHY (See ANNOTATED BIBLIOGRAPHY for full citations if not shown)

Most of the rare publications and all of the unpublished theses in this chapter are the result of the research of Dr. George E. Arnstein about Jewish life and community histories for southwestern Germany, Austria and Switzerland. These publications have already been cited in the **Research In Southwestern Germanic Areas** section of this chapter and are not repeated in the bibliography. Please refer to that section for details. The others are largely books available at the University of Minnesota libraries.

For information on Jewish genealogical research in New World countries other than the United States and Canada, please check the material on the countries in question.

Mary Antin. *From Plotzk to Boston*, with a new introduction by Pamela S. Nadell. New York: M. Wiener. 1986.

George E. Arnstein, "Names and Their Origins," in *Avotaynu* (Spring 1995).

George E. Arnstein, tr. "Childhood Memories from Neustetten," in *Mishpocha* (1991).

Zachary M. Baker, comp. *Bibliography of Eastern European Memorial (Yizkor) Books*. New York: Jewish Genealogical Society. 1992. 51 pp.
> Most complete list of memorial books found in six New York libraries.

Naftali Bar-Giora Bamberger. *Memorbuch: Die jüdischen Friedhöfe Jebenhausen und Göppingen [Memorial Book: The Jewish Cemeteries in Jebenhausen and Göppingen]*. Jerusalem; Göppingen, Germany: Bamberger Familien Archiv. 1990. 346 pp.
> For information, write to the Bamberger Family Archives, P.O. Box 627, Long Beach, NY 11561.

Franziska Becker. "Die nationalsozialistische Judenverfolgung in Baisingen" ["The National Socialist (Nazi) Persecution of Jews in Baisingen]," in *Der Sülchgau* (Vol. 23).
> Copy available at Harvard Library.

Alexander Beider. *A Dictionary of Jewish Surnames from the Kingdom of Poland*. Teaneck, NJ: Avotaynu. 1996. 608 pp.

Alexander Beider. *A Dictionary of Jewish Surnames from the Russian Empire*. Teaneck, NJ: Avotaynu. 1993. 760 pp.
> Contains 50,000 Jewish surnames from the Russian Pale of Settlement, excluding the Kingdom of Poland.

Alexander Beider. *Jewish Surnames from Prague (15th-18th Centuries)*. Teaneck, NJ: Avotaynu Inc. 1994. 46 pp.
> Identifies 700 surnames from the ancient city of Prague. Provides etymology of each name.

Elizabeth Petty Bentley. *The Genealogist's Address Book*, 3rd ed.
> Lists archives, historical societies, local or state genealogical societies, periodicals, and numerous other resources within the United States helpful for Jewish genealogy.

Claire Bruell. "Archives in Bohemia and Moravia," in *Avotaynu* (Spring 1993).

Chester G. Cohen. *Shtetl Finder—Gazetteer: Jewish Communities in the 19th and Early 20th Centuries in the Pale of Settlement of Russia and Poland, and in Lithuania, Latvia, Galicia, and Bukovina, with Names of Residents*. Los Angeles: Periday Co. 1980. 145 pp. Reprinted Bowie, MD: Heritage Books. 1989.

Kathinka Dittrich and Hans Wurzner, eds. *Die Niederlande und das deutsche Exil, 1933-1940* [*The Netherlands and German Exile, 1933 to 1940*]. Königstein/Taunus: Athenaum. 1982. 251 pp.

Paula Draper and Harold Troper, eds. *National Archives of Canada, Ottawa; Canadian Jewish Congress Archives, Montreal*. New York/London: Garland. 1991. 461 pp.

Thomas K. Edlund. *The German Minority Census of 1939, an Introduction and Register*. Avotaynu, Inc. 1996.

Petr Ehl, Arno Parík and Jirí Fiedler. *Old Bohemian and Moravian Cemeteries*. Translated by Sylvia Makousková and Zoja Joachimová. 1991. Prague: Paseka. 172 pp.
> Includes photographs, historical information and an alphabetical list of communities in which cemeteries are found.

Angelika C. Ellman-Krüger. *Auswahlbibliographie zur jüdischen Familienforschung vom Anfang des 19. Jahrhunderts bis zur Gegenwart* [*Selected Bibliography of Jewish Family Research From the Beginning of the 19th Century to the Present*]. Wiesbaden: Otto Harrassowitz. 1992. 202 pp.

Ludwig August Frankl. *Inschriften des alten jüdischen Friedhofes in Wien: Beitrag zur Alterthumskunde Österreichs* [*Inscriptions in the Old Jewish Cemetery in Vienna: A Contribution to the Archaeology of Austria*]. Vienna. 1855. 124 pp.

Ludwig August Frankl. *Zur Geschichte der Juden in Wien: der alte Friedhof, der Tempelhof* [*History of the Jews in Vienna: The Old Cemetery, the Temple Cemetery*]. Vienna. 1853. 78 pp.

Judith R. Frazin. *A Translation Guide to 19th Century Polish-Language Civil Registration Documents*, 2nd ed. Northbrook, IL: Jewish Genealogical Society of Illinois. 1989. 311 pp.
> Numerous examples of Jewish and non-Jewish documents. Extensive English-Polish and Polish-English vocabulary lists.

Henry Friedlander and Sybil Milton, eds. *Berlin Document Center*, 2 vols. New York: Garland Publishing Co. 1992.
> Most of the material deals with Jews or other Nazi records.

Geadelte jüdische Familien [*Ennobled Jewish Families*], 3rd ed. Vienna: Lesk und Schwidernoch; Salzburg: Verlag des "Kyffhauser." 1891. 112 pp.

Pierre Genee, in cooperation with Ruth Burstyn and Walter Lindner. *Wiener Synagogen 1825-1938* [*Viennese Synagogues, 1825-1938*]. Preface by Helmut Zilk und introduction by Kurt Schubert. Vienna: Locker. 1987. 117 pp.

Ira A. Glazier, ed. *Migration from the Russian Empire: Lists of Passengers Arriving at the Port of New York*. On-going series. Baltimore: Genealogical Publishing Co. 1995-. Vol. 1 (703 pp.), vol. 2 (631 pp.).
> Volumes 1 and 2, covering January 1875 through April 1886, have been published to date.

Hugo Gold. *Gedenkbuch der untergegangenen Judengemeinden des Burgenlandes* [*Memorial Book for the Extinct Jewish Communities of the Burgenland*]. Tel Aviv: Olamenu. 1970. 148 pp.

Fred Grubel, ed., in cooperation with Alan S. Divack, et. al. *Leo Baeck Institute: Catalog of the Archival Collections*. New York: Leo Baeck Institute; Tübingen: J.C.B. Mohr. 1990. 409 pp.

Heinrich W. Guggenheimer and Eva H. Guggenheimer. *Jewish Names and Their Origins: An Etymological Dictionary*. Hoboken, NJ. 1992. 882 pp.

Estelle M. Guzik. *Genealogical Resources in the New York Metropolitan Area*. New York: Jewish Genealogical Society. 1989. 404 pp.
> Describes the collection of major research facilities in the New York City area.

Handy Guide to Italian Genealogical Research. Logan, UT: Everton Publishers. 1978.
> Could be helpful for Jews in the Trieste area and other parts of Italy which were once under Hapsburg control.

Jan Herman. *Jewish Cemeteries in Bohemia and Moravia*. Prague: Council of Jewish Communities in the CSR. 1982. 32 pp. Chiefly illustrations, map.

Jewish Genealogical Society of Greater Washington, comp. *Jewish Genealogical Family Finder* (microform). Teaneck, NJ: Jewish Genealogical Society. Inc. 1993.

The Joseph Jacobs Directory of the Jewish Press in America, 3rd ed. New York: Joseph Jacobs Organization. 1990. 177 pp.

Jüdische Familienforschung [Jewish Family History Research].
> Periodical published in Germany from 1924 to 1938.

Jüdische Frontsoldaten aus Württemberg and Hohenzollern [Jewish Front-Line Soldiers from Württemberg and Hohenzollern]. Stuttgart: Zentralverein deutscher Staatsbürger jüdischen Glaubens. 1926.
> Lists Jewish soldiers who fought in World War I.

Joram Kagan. *Poland's Jewish Heritage*. New York: Hippocrene Books. 1992. 208 pp.
> Many details about Jewish communities and various other topics.

Benzion C. Kaganoff. *A Dictionary of Jewish Names and their History*. New York: Schocken Books. 1977. 250 pp.

Nathan M. Kaganoff. *Judaica Americana: An Annotated Bibliography of Publications from 1960 to 1990*, preface by Jonathan D. Sarna. Brooklyn, NY: Carlson Pub. 1995. 917 pp.

Arthur Kurzweil. *From Generation to Generation: How to Trace Your Jewish Genealogy and Family History*, rev. ed. New York: Harper Collins. 1994. 388 pp.
> Updated version of standard guidebook for tracing Jewish ancestry.

Arthur Kurzweil and Miriam Weiner, eds. *The Encyclopedia of Jewish Genealogy*. Vol. I: *Sources in the United States and Canada*. Northvale, NJ: Jason Aronson, Inc. 1991. 226 pp.
> A summary of North American record repositories and their holdings, with some useful appendices.

Peter Lande. "The Complete Archives of the German Jews," in *Avotaynu* (Spring 1993).

Peter Lande. "On-Site Research in Germany," in *Avotaynu* (Fall 1996).

Peter Lande and Edward Luft. "Brilling Archives in Frankfurt Museum," in *Avotaynu* (Spring 1995).

Daniel N. Lesson. *Index to the 1754 Census of the Jews of Alsace*.
> Documents about 20,000 Jews, with given names and surnames, including the maiden names of married women.

Edward David Luft. "The Complete Catalog of Jewish Communities in Bohemia and Moravia, Excluding That of Prague," in *Avotaynu* (Fall 1991).

Edward David Luft. "Jewish Genealogical Research in Czechoslovakia," in *Avotaynu* (Winter 1988).

Edward David Luft. "Genealogical Research in Czechoslovakia: An Update," in *Avotaynu* (Winter 1988).

Edward David Luft. "On-Site Jewish Genealogical Research in the Czech and Slovak Republics," in *Avotaynu* (Fall 1996).

Edward David Luft. "Slovakian State Archives," in *Avotaynu* (Spring 1993).

Edward David Luft. "An Update of Genealogical Research in Eastern Germany and Western Poland," in *Avotaynu* (Spring 1991).

Edward David Luft. "Twenty Miles of Prussian Archives," in *Avotaynu* (Spring 1992).

Edward David Luft. "Jewish Records Held in Leipzig Archives," in *Avotaynu* (Winter 1991).

Edward David Luft. "Jewish Genealogical Research in the German Democratic Republic," in *Avotaynu* (Summer 1990).

Max I. Mändle. *Familienregister, Israelitischen Gemeinde Buchau* [*Family Register of the Jewish Congregation in Buchau*].
> Covers the 1809-1853 period for what is now Bad Buchau, Baden-Württemberg. Original is at the Leo Baeck Institute.

Frank Mecklenburg and Claus W. Hirsch. "More Jewish Holdings in East German Archives," in *Avotaynu* (Spring 1992).

Michael Meyer and Michael Brenner, eds. *Deutsch jüdische Geschichten in der Neuzeit* [*German Jewish History in Modern Times*]. 2 vols. Beck: Munich. 1996. 1 vol. New York: Columbia University Press. 1996. 400 pp.

Mitteilungen zur jüdischen Volkskunde [*Newsletter for the Study of Jewish Folklore*] (Vienna, Austria) 1926- and *Jahrbuch für jüdische Volkskunde* [*Yearbook for the Study of Jewish Folklore*]. Vienna: J. Kauffmann. Annually.

Fruma Mohrer and Marek Web, eds. *Guide to the YIVO Archives*. M. E. Sharpe. 1997.

Gary Mokotoff, with foreword by Benjamin Meed. *How to Document Victims and Locate Survivors of the Holocaust*. Teaneck NJ: Avotaynu, Inc. 1995. 194 pp.

Gary Mokotoff. "Internet for Greenhorns." in *Avotaynu* (Fall 1996).

Gary Mokotoff. *WOWW Companion: A Guide to the Communities Surrounding Central and Eastern European Towns*. Teaneck, NJ: Avotaynu Inc. 1995. 197 pp.
> Identifies towns in the vicinity of any town listed in *Where Once We Walked*. Easy-to-use tables. See below and also Chapter VIII.

Gary Mokotoff and Sallyann Amdur Sack. *Where Once We Walked: A Guide to the Jewish Communities Destroyed in the Holocaust*. Teaneck, NJ: Avotaynu Press. 1991. 514 pages.
> A gazetteer of over 21,000 Central and Eastern European localities, arranged alphabetically and phonetically, with references for each locality. See also Chapter VIII.

Otto Muneles, in cooperation with M. Bohatec. *Bibliographical Survey of Jewish Prague*. Prague: Jewish State Museum. 1952. 562 pp.

Sylvia Prochazkova and Thomas R. Zahm. "Prague's Jewish Cemeteries," in *Nase Rodina*, Vol. 8, No. 3 (Sept. 1996).
> Written by a doctoral student in history at Charles University in Prague.

Dorothy Rabinowitz. *New Lives: Survivors of the Holocaust Living in America*. New York: Knopf; distributed by Random House. 1976. 242 pp.

Records of Russian Consulates, 1862-1922 (microform). Washington: National Archives and Records Administration. 1986. 180 microfilm reels.

Janice Mendenhall Regenstein. *American Jewish Genealogy: An Annotated Bibliography of Books of Jewish Local History and Other Subjects of Use to Genealogists*. Wichita, KS: (2751 Rivera, Wichita 67211): Family Heritage Institute. 1981. 27 pp.

Janice Mendenhall Regenstein. *American Jewish Genealogies Worldwide*. Wichita, KS: Family Heritage Institute. 1981.
> Represents a beginning in trying to identify in which repositories particular Jewish family histories are available. Archives and libraries in all countries are listed.

Harold Rhode. "What May Be Learned From 19th Century Czarist Jewish Birth Records and Revision Lists," in *Avotaynu* (Fall 1994).

Oded Roden, ed. *The Encyclopedia of Jewish Institutions: United States and Canada*. Tel Aviv, Israel: Mosadot Publications. 1983. 501 pp.

Dan Rottenberg. *Finding Our Fathers: A Guidebook to Jewish Genealogy*. New York: Random House. 1977. 401 pp. Reprinted, Baltimore:Genealogical Publishing Co. 1986.
> Chapter IV is a quick course in Judaica.

Sallyann Amdur Sack and the Israel Genealogical Society. *A Guide to Jewish Genealogical Research in Israel*. Teaneck, NJ: Avotaynu, Inc. 1995. 229 pp. (Update of Sallyann Amdur Sack. *A Guide to Jewish Genealogical Research in Israel*. Baltimore: Genealogical Publishing Co. 1987. 110 pp.)

Sallyann Amdur Sack and Suzan Fishl Wynne. *The Russian Consular Records Index and Catalog*. New York: Garland. 1987. 897 pp.

Paul Sauer. *Die Opfer des Nationalsozialismus: Ein Gedenkbuch* [*The Victims of the National Socialist (Nazi) persecution in Baden-Württemberg, 1933-45: A Memorial Book*]. Appendix to Volume 20 of the *Archival Series*. Stuggart: Stuttgart: Kohlhammer. 1969.

W. Schäfer. *Geschichte und Schicksal der Juden in Haigerloch* [*History and Fate of the Jews in Haigerloch*]. Reutlingen: Pädagogische Hochschule Reutlingen. 1971. Thesis.

Kurt Schubert, on behalf of the Verein Österreichisches Jüdisches Museum in Eisenstadt. *Der Wiener Stadttempel, 1826-1975* [*The Viennese City Temple, 1826-1975*]. Eisenstadt, Austria: Roetzer. 1978. 103 pp.

Jonathan D. Shea. *Russian Language Documents from Russian Poland: A Translation Manual for Genealogists*. Orem, UT: Genun Publishers. 1989.

Jonathan D. Shea and William F. Hoffman. *Following the Paper Trail: A Multilingual Guide*. New Milford, CT: Language and Lineage Press. 1991. 740 pp. Hardcover reprint: Teaneck, NJ: Avotaynu. 1994.
> Deals with genealogical documents in 13 languages, including nearly all languages which might have been used for records on Germans in Europe. Shows examples.

Robert Singerman. *Jewish and Hebrew Onomastics: A Bibliography*. New York: Garland. 1977. 132 pp.
> Subject listings of books and articles on Jewish names.

Clifford Neal Smith and Anna Piszczan-Czaja Smith. *Encyclopedia of German-American Genealogical Research*.
> Includes a chapter on Jews in southwestern Germany, showing the number for each locality, organized according to principality, for various dates from the late seventeenth century to 1840, with notes indicating which of these communities had no Jews in 1925-38.

Donald John Steel, and Mrs. A. E. F. Steel, eds. *National Index of Parish Registers*. London: Society of Genealogists; Baltimore: Magna Carta Book Co. 1967. Ongoing series. 12 volumes published to date.

Malcolm H. Stern. *First American Jewish Families, 1654-1988*, 3rd ed. Baltimore: Genealogical Publishing Co. 1991. 464 pp.
> Family trees of all Jews known to have come to America before 1840, which would not include many German Jews. Index to 50,000 persons.

Peter Strauss. *Familienforschung bei jüdischen Vorfahren aus Baden-Württemberg: Schwerpunkt Landkreis Hohenlohe*. [*Family Research for Jewish Ancestors from Baden-Wuerttemberg: Primarily Focused in Hohenlohe County*]. P.O. Box 0204, D-20307 Stuttgart, Germany: Privately published.
> About 540 localities that had Jewish communities.

Lawrence F. Tapper. *Biographical Dictionary of Canadian Jewry, 1909-1914*. 256 pp.
> Births, bar mitzvahs, marriages and deaths from *The Canadian Jewish Times*.

Lawrence F. Tapper. *Archival Sources for the Study of Canadian Jewry: National Ethnic Archives*. 2nd ed., rev. and expanded. Ottawa: National Archives of Canada. 1987. 102 pp.

Felix A. Theilhaber, comp. *Jüdische Flieger im Weltkrieg [Jewish Airmen in World War I]*. Berlin: Verlag der Schild. 1924. 124 pp.

Ernest Thode. *Address Book for Germanic Genealogy*, 6th ed. Baltimore: Genealogical Publishing Co. 1997. 196 pp.
> Lists addresses of public archives in most European countries; European Jewish and religious archives; genealogical and historical societies in numerous European countries; many genealogists on both sides of the ocean; and other resources.

Bernhard Wachstein. *Hebräische Grabsteine aus dem XIII.-XV. Jahrhundert in Wien und Umgebung [Hebrew Gravestones of the Thirteenth Through the Fifteenth Centuries in Vienna and Its Environs]*. Vienna: Commissioned by A. Holder. 1916. 22 pp.

H. Wagenpfeil. "Manuskripte zur Geschichte der Juden in Nordstetten" ["Manuscripts of the History of the Jews in Nordstetten"]. Before 1988. Typescript.

Miriam Weiner. *Bridging the Generations: Researching Your Jewish Roots*.

Miriam Weiner. *Jewish Roots in Poland: Pages from the Past and Archival Inventories*. Secaucus, NJ: Miriam Weiner Routes to Roots Foundation, Inc. 1997. ca. 425 pp.
> This book, resulting from a contract with the Polish State Archives, combines two inventories: one by repository and one by town. Both include data by town name, type of material, years covered, and the location of the material. In most cases, archival numbers are also listed. It covers Jewish records for 1,248 towns now in Poland, as well as 96 formerly Polish localities now in Ukraine and some documents for Lithuania and Belarus, which can be found in 75 Polish archives, 434 Polish civil registry offices, and the Jewish Historical Institute in Warsaw. Includes census lists, tax and voter lists, school and property records, notary and local government records, and hospital and immigration lists.

Thomas Welte. "Die Hohenemser Judengemeinde im 20. Jahrhundert" ["The Hohenems Jewish Community in the 20th Century"]. Innsbruck, Austria: Diploma thesis. 1990.

Manuel Werner. "Die Juden in Hechingen" ["The Jews in Hechingen"], in *Zeitschrift für Hohenzollern Geschichte [Journal of Hohenzollern History]* (Vol. 20, 1984).

Otto Werner. "Die jüdische Gemeinde in Hechingen bis 1933" ["The Jewish Community in Hechingen Until 1933"], in *1200 Jahre Hechingen*. Hechingen: 1200th Anniversary Jubliee Book. 1987.

Suzan Wynne. *Galician Towns and Administrative Districts* (microform). Washington, DC: Jewish Genealogical Society of Greater Washington. 1990.

Maria Zelzer. *Weg und Schicksal der Stuttgarter Juden: Ein Gedenkbuch [The Direction and Fate of the Jews of Stuttgart: A Memorial Book]*. Stuttgart: E. Klett. 1964. 588 pp.
> Contains long but not quite reliable lists, because it was compiled so soon after World War II.

David S. Zubatsky and Irwin M. Berent. *Sourcebook for Jewish Genealogies and Family Histories*. Teaneck, NJ: Avotaynu, Inc. 1996. Revised edition of David S. Zubatsky and Irwin M. Berent. *Jewish Genealogy: A Sourcebook of Family Histories and Genealogies*. New York: Garland Pub. Co. 1984. 422 pp. Vol. 2 by David S. Zubatsky. 1990. 452 pp.
> A guide to published and manuscript genealogies in archives and libraries, arranged by surname. Information in 1996 edition is also released as part of the *Consolidated Jewish Surname Index (CJSI)*, which can be searched on the Internet.

Chapter XIV

GERMANIC MIGRATION TO NON-EUROPEAN COUNTRIES

This chapter describes the migration patterns of Germans outside the European continent. First comes a description of the German migration to the United States; it includes when and why Germans came and where they settled. German migration to Canada is then described. Numerous Germans also went to South America, the Far East and Africa; these are described in Chapter XV.

Wilhelm Winkler, in *Statistisches Handbuch des gesamten Deutschtums* [*Statistical Handbook of All German Regions*], estimates (pp. 22-23) that there were 5,000 or more Germans in each of the following countries outside Europe and the Soviet Union:

Table 7: Germans Outside Europe and the Soviet Union, 1927

Country	Population	Country	Population
United States	10,000,000	New Zealand	18,000
Brazil	600,000	Egypt	11,000
Canada	300,000	Namibia (Southwest Africa)	10,000
Australia	141,000	Algeria	7,500
Argentina	130,000	Morocco	6,800
South Africa	57,000	Asian Turkey	5,500
French Foreign Legion	31,000	Mexico	5,000
Chile	30,000		

These figures almost certainly refer only to people who were born in Germany (or possibly other Germanic countries) or who had at least one German-born parent, since this is the kind of data usually available from censuses.

These data greatly understate the number of people of Germanic descent. For example, the 1990 census records 60 million Americans (certainly an undercount because of people who no longer know of their ancestry) who have German-speaking ancestors, considerably more than have ancestors from any other country, including England. They are almost as numerous as the current population of Germany.

To cite other examples, Argentina is estimated to have had a million residents in 1978 who had Volga German ancestors and James N. Bade estimates that several hundred thousand New Zealanders have Germanic ancestors, even though relatively few Germans emigrated to that country.

Moreover, large-scale Germanic immigration (including many displaced persons from Eastern Europe who crossed the seas after 1945) has occurred since 1925. Since the United States had comparatively restrictive immigration laws, a disproportionately large number went to Canada and to various Latin American countries. There has also been substantial migration within the western hemisphere, so that Mexico and Paraguay are estimated to each have at least 50,000 residents of Germanic origin (most of whom came from Canada and still speak German).

REASONS FOR GERMANIC EMIGRATION

Among the more important reasons for Germans to emigrate to the United States were:

Escape from economic hardship. The Thirty Years' War (1618-1648) devastated Germany. With the setbacks caused by several further wars, it took Germany 100 years to recover. The Seven Years' War (1756-1763) again created harsh conditions. The Palatinate, in particular, suffered from being the front-line battleground between French and German forces.

Religious freedom. This was particularly important for some of the earliest immigrants. It remained significant for non-mainstream groups, like the Mennonites, the Old Lutherans and dissident Catholics. Persecution was also a major factor for the Jews, but more so for those from Eastern Europe (who often spoke German or its derivative, Yiddish) than for those from Germany — until the 1930s, of course.

Abundant free or cheap farmland. The vast majority of immigrants came from rural villages, where there was insufficient farmland for all. German inheritance laws were of great importance in explaining emigration. Where one son inherited the entire farm, the others were effectively excluded from making a living off agriculture. Where the land was divided among all, the plots soon became too small for sustenance, which is why many peasants also practiced a trade. In areas east of the Elbe River there was often very little opportunity for land ownership, because much of the land was in the hands of a comparatively small number of owners of large estates. This was true especially in Mecklenburg and Pomerania, which had the highest rates of emigration in the 1870s, according to Mack Walker, *Germany and the Emigration, 1816-1885*. Hence, the opportunity for land ownership in America was very appealing. Most of the German immigrants, however, did not homestead on free land. Instead, for about $1.25 per acre they purchased land that others had already broken, whereupon the original pioneers moved one step farther west.

Freedom from compulsory military service. The frequency of wars and the expectation of more wars led many to emigrate. This was particularly true of those who lived under the militaristic Prussian Empire, which already ruled most of northern Germany before 1871, and which thereafter had the dominant voice in the new German Empire. Some emigrated to avoid the draft. In other cases, fathers who had served in the military left so that their sons would not have to do the same. Most of this emigration occurred during and after the German Wars of Unification. Many Germans also left Russia after 1873, when their previous exemption from military service was threatened and then abrogated. The Hessians who deserted from the British forces during the American Revolution also showed their distaste for the fighting that had been thrust upon them.

Political freedom. This was especially important for the refugees from the unsuccessful liberal democratic revolutions of 1830 and 1848, mostly the latter. These immigrants, though relatively few in number, had a strong impact upon the German-American community and American society in general, because these "Latin farmers" (so-called because of their education and lack of farming skills) included many intellectual and political leaders, like Carl Schurz. However, the ethnic Germans who came from the Soviet Union after the Bolshevik Revolution and after World War II also fled from severe political oppression, although they had never lived under an elected democratic government before then.

Hope for economic betterment in American cities. While most of the German immigrants (except perhaps the late ones) sought farms, a significant number also settled in the cities, where the streets were reputedly "paved with gold." When they discovered how misleading this was, some returned to Germany, but the vast majority stayed, either because they found opportunity anyway, or because they could not afford to return.

Nationalism and national policies. With respect to Germany itself, this factor applied only to the post-Napoleonic emigration to the Black Sea. However, this was an important factor in other areas. Most of the emigration from the Russian Empire was due to the removal of "eternal" special privileges of the Germans, and "Russification" policies soon thereafter as a result of the development of nationalistic attitudes. This was also a factor in areas ruled by Hungary after 1867, since its government also sought to force linguistic assimilation. In the areas ruled by Austria, nationalism affected Germans in a somewhat different way. Austria, unlike Prussia/Germany, Russia and Hungary, had very liberal policies in this respect, since the Hapsburgs realized that the only hope for saving their empire lay in an emphasis on its multilingual and multi-cultural nature. However, the result of this was that Germans living in predominantly Slavic areas experienced local pressures and felt that they had no government to protect them.

Personal and family reasons. Many came to join relatives or former neighbors who were already here. It was quite common for large numbers of German emigrants from the same village or neighboring villages to settle in the same American community. Of course, this would not have been an adequate reason unless some of the other reasons also applied.

Illegal emigration. A considerable number of people left Germanic lands without legal permission. This occurred most often for the sake of avoiding compulsory military service, but there were also other reasons: refusal of the lords of the feudal area to grant permission, government restrictions on emigration, or inability to meet the requirements for getting permission. Six professional German genealogists have now developed the "German Emigrants Register" for 1820-1918, which covers the entire former German Empire. It currently includes over a quarter of a million names of "missing people," culled from military, probate and other records. It is expected to include 800,000 persons eventually. You can obtain a form to request information from the register from the Immigrant Genealogical Society.

By and large, one or more of these reasons also applied to those who emigrated to other New World countries. Of course, some Germans (those poor enough to need public assistance, petty criminals, single mothers) were shipped off involuntarily by state and local authorities in the mid-nineteenth century, although criminals were deported even earlier.

German Jews who came to this country in the 1930s were much like the "Forty-Eighters," in that a relatively small number of professional people made a rather substantial contribution to education and science.

GERMANIC MIGRATION TO THE UNITED STATES

Individual Germans were on the first voyage of Columbus in 1492 and individual German soldiers were in St. Augustine about 1585. There is good evidence that some of the first colonists in Jamestown in 1607 were Germans. Other individual German immigrants were included in the Dutch settlement in New Netherlands (now New York), between 1624 and 1664.

The first group immigration of Germans to the New World was in 1683, when Mennonites from Krefeld emigrated to Germantown near Philadelphia. An estimated 65,000 to 70,000 Germans came to the American colonies, primarily to Pennsylvania, during the following half-century or so.

The next large wave came in 1709-11 via England. They were generally known as Palatines. Indeed, a large number came from the Palatinate, but others came from elsewhere close to the Rhine River, extending from Switzerland to the Netherlands, especially from the Middle and Upper Rhine regions. Many, but by no means all, of them settled in New York state. This group is well documented by numerous books, especially those by Hank Z. Jones, Jr. Another colonial wave appears to have crested in the 1750s. However, in sheer numbers, these colonial immigrants were dwarfed by nineteenth century immigration. Nevertheless, because their descendants have been on this side of the Atlantic for many generations, they constitute a significant percentage of German-Americans.

There are many publications on the colonial immigrants. The organization, Palatines to America, which has many state chapters in the eastern half of the country, focuses on them.

Those who came here during the colonial period settled mostly near what was then the frontier in New York, Maryland and Virginia, and especially in Pennsylvania, which had about half of the 225,000 Germans in America in 1776. About 10% settled in the Carolinas and Georgia. Those in Pennsylvania became known as the Pennsylvania Dutch — from the German word for German: *Deutsch*. A large percentage of them came from the southwestern parts of German-speaking Europe, particularly from the Palatinate, Württemberg, Baden, Alsace and Switzerland. Some of those of Swiss origin had migrated down the Rhine, especially after the Thirty Years' War, before their descendants went overseas.

Nearly 30,000 German soldiers, about two-thirds of them from Hesse, fought for the British in the American Revolution pursuant to contracts between their rulers and Britain. They were often referred to as mercenaries, troops paid to fight for foreign governments, but their rulers were the primary financial beneficiaries of this arrangement. Five thousand or more of these defected during the Revolutionary War and chose to stay in their new country.

There was very little German immigration to the United States prior to about 1830, as the bulk of German emigration was to Eastern Europe, but a modest flow began about 1818. A total of over seven million Germans immigrants have come to this country, most of them in three great waves between 1845 and 1895. If we add the German-speaking people from other countries (where the official immigration statistics do not show a breakdown by ethnicity) and those who went to Canada, the total is probably about 9 million.

The first big wave of Germans crossing the Atlantic lasted from 1846 to 1858. It began as a result of famine produced by the crop failures of 1846 and 1847, which affected most of Europe. Those who fled as a result of the unsuccessful liberal revolts of 1848, which occurred in nearly all of the many Germanic states, added to the flow. This wave peaked in 1854. Many Luxembourgers came in this wave.

The second wave occurred immediately after the American Civil War, lasting about a decade. Three factors were important in generating this stream: free or cheap land in the United States as a result of the homesteading provisions of the Morrill Act of 1862; the desire to escape from military service in the Prussian (after 1871, the German) army; and economic conditions, particularly the dislocations caused by the Industrial Revolution in Germany as the new factories squeezed the small peasants out of their supplemental earning opportunities as artisans.

The third and largest wave of German and Luxembourger immigrants occurred from 1879 to the early 1890s. Immigration from Germany reached an all-time peak in 1882. The closing of the American frontier in 1890 and the Panic (today we would say Depression) of 1893 halted this flow.

It is important, however, to remember that much of the "German" immigration was not from "Germany." For one thing, Germany did not exist until 1871. Before and after this, there was a second large "German" state, namely the Austrian Empire, which became the Austro-Hungarian Empire in 1867.

Moreover, a disproportionately large percentage of German-speaking immigrants came from Luxembourg and possibly also from Switzerland, which were independent countries throughout the period of German immigration. Dr. Karl Heinz Danner reports in the December 1995 issue of *The Palatine Immigrant* that over 70,000 Luxembourgers came to America between 1847 and 1914. He lists the numerous reasons for their emigration.

Many also came from the Russian Empire and these continued to come to North America in relatively large numbers even after immigration from Germany itself had almost stopped. Furthermore, German-speaking Jews came to North America not only from Germany, but also from Eastern Europe, most of the latter immigrants coming in 1903-14, with an afterflow in 1921-24.

A major portion of the third wave of German immigrants came from the northeastern provinces of East and West Prussia, Pomerania, Posen and Russian Poland. Almost all of Posen and, half of West Prussia and the eastern end of Silesia became part of the new

Poland when that country was re-established in 1919. The Germans living in German-Polish linguistic border areas, as well as in German settlements in heavily Polish areas, constituted a significant portion of the German immigrants to America.

The same is true of the Germans living in Bohemia and Moravia, in what later came to be known as the Sudetenland, which was part of the Hapsburg Empire and became a part of the newly established state of Czechoslovakia in 1919. According to Josef Reiter's "Ein Kirchspiel im südlichen Egerland" ["A Church Parish in Southern Egerland"], in the 1992 book, *Heimat auf den Laurenziberg [The Homeland at Laurenziberg]*, edited by Hertha Herzog, the first significant wave of emigration from this western Bohemian region occurred in the 1850s and 1860s, with a much larger wave in the 1890s. This is based on a translated excerpt on "Emigrants" by Kari Fangel in the June 1994 issue of the *German-Bohemian Heritage Society Newsletter*.

Another ethnically mixed area, which was part of "Germany" for less than half a century, but contributed large numbers of German-speaking immigrants to the United States, was Alsace-Lorraine in France.

Finally, even those areas east of the Oder-Neisse line (the boundary of contemporary Germany) that were overwhelmingly German in language and culture during the modern period of history, are now a part of Poland. While huge numbers of immigrants from this region came to America from "Germany," their ancestral lands are no longer part of any German nation.

Crossing the Atlantic by sailboat before 1840 was an arduous journey, which took 30-90 days, costing many lives and weakening others. The coming of the steamship in the 1840s reduced this to 2-3 weeks. This same decade saw the establishment of a large network of railways, which reduced emigrant dependence on river transportation. The chief ports of departure switched from Le Havre and Rotterdam, first to Bremen and Antwerp, and finally to Hamburg. This was, at least in part, a reflection of the changing origins of immigrants from southwestern to northwestern and then northeastern Germany, since most of those who emigrated chose the most accessible ports. Small numbers, however, came from various lesser ports. Many ships sailed directly to North American ports, but many immigrants took the indirect route via British ports. In particular, many went from Hamburg to Hull, crossed England by train and then sailed from Liverpool. This was a less expensive route, strange as it may seem to us today.

After 1840 the vast majority of immigrants landed at New York, being processed by the authorities first at Castle Garden and then, beginning in 1892, at Ellis Island. But there were some passenger arrivals at about 60 other ports, including about 15 of some significance. New Orleans was relatively popular for Germans coming to the Midwest, because boat fares up the Mississippi River were very inexpensive.

Quite a few ships went to the Canadian ports of Halifax, Quebec and Montreal. While most of their passengers stayed in Canada, a significant number also went to the United States, especially prior to the Civil War.

Many German-speaking immigrants came to North America and other New World countries from the Austro-Hungarian Empire, but few of them (at least prior to 1938) came from present-day Austria. Those who did came mostly from the Burgenland, which belonged to Hungary until after World War II and had a significantly larger Protestant minority than the rest of Austria.

The vast majority came from regions where they constituted ethnic minorities: Gottschee (Slovenia), the Lower Danube (so-called Swabians), Transylvania (so-called Saxons), Galicia, the Bukovina, Slovakia, and enclaves in modern-day Hungary. This pattern explains why there was a much larger percentage of Protestants among the immigrants than one would expect on the basis of the religious makeup of Austria.

The Germans from Bohemia and Moravia were a special case. These staunch Catholics came mostly from overwhelmingly German communities, but they represented a national minority, albeit a very large one, in what is now the Czech Republic and was historically a distinct political entity, although under Austrian rule for most of the modern era.

The immigrants from the Austrian heartland differ from other German-speaking immigrants in that a relatively large number came from Vienna. By contrast, German-speaking immigrants from elsewhere came overwhelmingly from rural areas.

The Jews who came to America from Germany had become fully acculturated, in most cases, before the crossed the Atlantic. Thus the time period when most of them came here did not differ from that of the main waves of German Christian immigration.

Max Dimont, *The Jews in America: The Roots and Destiny of American Jews*, has a chapter titled, "The Manifest Destiny (1840-1890): The Conquering German Jews." The significance of this is that a modest number of prior Jewish immigrants were Sephardic Jews, with origins in Portugal and Spain, with the few Ashkenazic Jewish immigrants coming mostly from England.

The German Jews preceded the Russian Jews who began to come to America by the millions after the 1880s, with enough arriving by 1890 for them to become the dominant group, although massive immigration continued until World War I, with a smaller wave right after the war before the United States passed very restrictive immigration laws in 1921 and 1924. (Actually, this group could more accurately be called the East European Jews, since a large number also came from Galicia and the Bukovina in easternmost Austria, but they were dwarfed in numbers by those from the Russian Empire.)

The Jewish refuges from Nazi domination (from Germany after 1933, from Austria and the Czech Republic after 1938) were, however, a distinct group, since few other Germans came to the United States during that period, although the Austrian immigrants also included a significant number of non-Jewish political opponents of Hitler's annexation of Austria.

Although the United States modified its restrictive laws somewhat to permit the entry of 157,000 Jews in the 1930s. The door was opened only a crack. Those allowed to come here constituted a significant part of the German intellectual elite.

But most Jewish refugees had to find a new home elsewhere, to the extent possible. However, most other countries also had restrictions on immigration at that time, so the Jewish refugees were widely scattered throughout much of the world.

Restrictions were waived again to allow the entry of 192,000 immigrants in 1944-45, but these included not only Jews but also various groups of stateless Displaced Persons from Eastern Europe, including Germans.

CONCENTRATIONS OF GERMANIC SETTLEMENTS IN THE UNITED STATES

At the time of the American Revolution, Pennsylvania was "the German state." Today Wisconsin has that reputation. The belt stretching from one to the other with a small balloon in the east to encompass the other mid-Atlantic states and a larger balloon in the west to include the entire Midwest, remains the heart of German-America today.

In the case of the settlements west of the Alleghenies, a significant percentage of Germans came from Pennsylvania and other seaboard states, rather than directly from Europe. Many families continued to hop-scotch westward to the Great Plains. The hop-scotching to the frontier of the nineteenth century has continued into the current era, so that there are now large numbers of Germans in the Pacific states.

The South is known as a region with limited German immigration, but there are some significant pockets of German settlements, especially in Texas, with smaller ones in Virginia, the Carolinas, Georgia and Louisiana.

Howard B. Furer, in *The Germans in America, 1607-1970*, provides the following population estimates of Germans in America in 1776.

Pennsylvania	110,000	Maryland-Delaware	20,500	North Carolina	8,000
New York	25,000	New Jersey	15,000	Georgia	5,000
Virginia	25,000	South Carolina	15,000	New England	1,500

Ernest Thode, in his *Atlas for Germanic Genealogy*, shows concentrations of German settlements in the following areas in 1880:

Philadelphia, Pennsylvania	Saginaw, Michigan	Saint Louis, Missouri
Buffalo, New York	Chicago, Illinois	Brenham, Texas
Cleveland, Ohio	Milwaukee, Wisconsin	San Antonio, Texas
Cincinnati, Ohio	Madison, Wisconsin	

Thode's map shows the number of German-born residents in 1930. It also shows counties with over 1,000 such residents in the following states in addition to those listed above. There was only one such county or cluster of adjacent counties in the states indicated by stars.

California	Indiana	Minnesota	Utah*
Connecticut	Iowa	Nebraska	Washington
Delaware	Maryland	New Jersey	
Florida*	Massachusetts	Oregon*	

A similar map by Thode for 1900 also lists significant concentrations of German-born residents in North Dakota, Kansas, Colorado and New Hampshire. Since these maps are based on numbers, not percentages, they do not fully reflect the importance of the German-American element in the more sparsely populated states, especially the Great Plains. Furthermore, these maps show only the German-born population.

Allen and Turner's *We the People: An Atlas of America's Ethnic Diversity* shows that counties with the highest percentage of residents of German ancestry were clustered in the Great Plains states, Minnesota, Wisconsin and Iowa in 1980, with a geographically smaller cluster in Pennsylvania. German-Americans comprised at least 10% of the population of most counties north of a shallow "V" from eastern Washington to northwestern Oklahoma to New York, but excluding New England.

Emigration from Switzerland to America began as early as 1710 when certain "undesirables" (people following minority religions, the poor and non-landowners) were encouraged to leave. These folk settled mainly in North Carolina, Pennsylvania and Virginia. By 1732 more came to South Carolina and Mississippi. The 18th century immigrants mostly arrived from Bern, Basel, Zürich, Schaffhausen, Aargau, Solothurn, Luzern and Graubünden cantons. By 1920, over 300,000 Swiss immigrants had entered the United States, many settling in the Midwest and California. In 1980 the largest number of Swiss-Americans were in Wisconsin, Indiana and Ohio, with lesser concentrations in southern New England, New York, Pennsylvania, New Jersey, Michigan, Illinois, Iowa, Kansas, and along the Pacific coast.

Luxembourgers tended to settle in Illinois, Wisconsin, Iowa and Minnesota. Many Bohemian Germans came to Wisconsin, Minnesota and Michigan's Upper Peninsula. Bukovina Germans went to Kansas and other midwestern states.

German-speaking Austrians, mostly Burgenlanders, are concentrated in Chicago, Detroit, the Cleveland-Washington-Boston triangle, and in the Sunbelt states of Florida and California.

There were relatively few German Jews in purely rural areas. But when compared to the Sephardic Jews which preceded them, and the East European Jews which followed them, they spread out widely throughout the country. They played an important role in the founding of many cities, but many also were important in the commerce of small towns. A considerable percentage went to the frontier and the percentage who settled in the South (about 20%) was much higher than it was among German Christians.

In 1980, German-born residents constituted 5-10% of the population of Philadelphia, Phoenix, Detroit, Washington, Chicago, San Antonio and Dallas. Those born in Austria constituted at least 1% of the population in Philadelphia, New York, Detroit and Chicago. The combined Germanic element was strongest (in terms of percentages) in Philadelphia, Phoenix, Detroit, Chicago, Washington, San Antonio, New York and Dallas, in that order, among the biggest metropolitan areas.

Almost all of these would have arrived here after the end of heavy emigration from Germany in 1893. The Sun Belt cities probably include a large number of retirees who may have come here during the following half-century. The figures for the northern cities probably reflect post-World War II and some Nazi-era immigration.

If we look at where Americans of German ancestry live today, rather than the areas to which they originally immigrated it is easier to answer the question, "Where don't they live?" than "Where do they live?"

The Germans are the largest ethnic group in the United States today. They are the largest ethnic group in each of the four geographic regions in the country and they represent the largest ethnic group in a majority of the states.

To be specific, they are the largest ethnic group in 29 states and the second largest ethnic group in another 9, plus the District of Columbia. They constitute a majority of the residents of five midwestern states. No other ethnic group has an actual majority anywhere, except for the Afro-Americans in Washington, DC.

The states where those of German ancestry are not the largest or second largest group include the six New England states, New Jersey (where they are third), four states in the Deep South (Alabama, Georgia, Louisiana, Mississippi) and Hawaii.

In contrast, the English are the largest group only in the three small northern states of New England and two sparsely populated mountain states. They outnumber the Germans in only six other states: three in New England and three in the Deep South.

If we look at what percentage of the population is of German ancestry, a somewhat different concentration become apparent, due to the fact that some states are far more heterogeneous in their population than others.

Using this criterion, we find that Wisconsin, South Dakota, North Dakota, Nebraska and Iowa are more than 50% German, while Minnesota is more than 45% German. Of course, in the Great Plains states, but especially in North Dakota, this is true only because of the large number of Germans from the Russian Empire.

Other states which are more than 30% German are Colorado, Indiana, Kansas, Missouri, Montana, Ohio, Oregon, Pennsylvania, and Wyoming. Viewed from that perspective, Germania is clearly strongest in the heartland of the country.

If, on the other hand, we look at the total number of Americans of German ancestry, state by state, reflecting both the population of the state and the percentage of Germans among them, the densely populated states have the largest number of Germans. For example, even though the Germans are only the second largest group in California, where they amount to less than 20% of the population, there are nevertheless more German-Americans there than in any other state.

The other states with a large total number of German-Americans are mostly in the mid-Atlantic states, the more densely populated, more urbanized states in the eastern half of the Midwest, and the largest, rapidly growing Sunbelt states. Following California, in order, we find Pennsylvania, Ohio, Illinois, Texas, New York, Michigan, Wisconsin, Florida and Indiana. The next ten are Minnesota, Missouri, New Jersey, Iowa, Washington, Maryland, Virginia, North Carolina, Colorado and Kansas.

No matter which way we look at it, however, except for the sparsely populated states west of the north-south line from North Dakota to Texas, the only areas where the Germans do not constitute a formidable presence are in the Deep South and New England. Even in the Deep South, however, there are significant German pockets. In both Georgia and Louisiana, German-Americans account for at least 12% of the residents.

The Great Plains states, including eastern Colorado, are also noteworthy for having a much larger percentage of Germans from the Russian Empire, as well as the eastern parts of the German and Austro-Hungarian Empires.

A map in Adam Giesinger's *From Catherine to Khruschev: The Story of Russia's Germans* shows that large settlements of Russian-born Germans were founded in North and South Dakota, Nebraska, Kansas and Colorado. Significant numbers moved on to Oklahoma, as well as to the Pacific Coast.

Many Danube Swabians, Transylvanian Saxons and Gottschee Germans, however, settled in Cleveland and other eastern cities.

GERMANIC MIGRATION TO CANADA

The best account of this subject can be founded in Heinz Lehmann, *The German Canadians, 1750-1937*, translated by Gerhard Bassler, which is our chief source.

German immigration to Canada was small compared to the number who went to the United States, but the earliest ones came in 1750-52. They settled in Nova Scotia, primarily in Lunenburg, with lesser numbers in Halifax. Terrence Punch's book on *Genealogical Research in Nova Scotia*, includes the passenger lists for most of the ships on which these Germans came.

After the American Revolution, about 2,500 Hessian and other German soldiers stayed in Canada, about one-third as many as in the United States. Most of them settled in Ontario, especially along the St. Lawrence River, but some went to Nova Scotia and New Brunswick.

More than a thousand Germans, especially from New York, were among the United Empire Loyalists who were expelled, or pressured to go, to Canada, because their land had been confiscated in 1779. Most of them were Lutherans, with some Reformed, who settled in Ontario, primarily west of Kingston and in the Niagara area, but also in Stormont and Dundas counties in the east. Most of the Lutherans in the Kingston area (which also included a few Moravians) became Methodists in the 1840s. There was little immigration from Germany to these areas and the German Loyalists soon became Anglicized. Some Loyalists also went to Nova Scotia, New Brunswick and southern Quebec.

But the first concentrated German settlements were established mostly by Pennsylvania Mennonites in the Niagara peninsula and elsewhere in southern Ontario, but especially around Kitchener (named Berlin until World War I) and Waterloo, beginning in 1786. A second wave of these immigrants began arriving in 1807, when more land was bought, and continued until the 1820s. Kitchener-Waterloo soon became by far the most significant German center in eastern Canada and has remained that ever since. In the 1870s it became a stopover point for many of the German-speaking emigrants who settled in Western Canada.

Immigrants from Germany began arriving there in 1817, but in much larger numbers after the 1846 famine and the failed Revolution of 1848. The 1848 census shows that about 25,000 people of German descent lived in southern Ontario, the vast majority in or near Waterloo County, and about 15,000 in eastern Ontario, along the shores of Lake Erie and the St. Lawrence River.

Many German immigrants arrived in Ontario in and after the 1830s. They came from Alsace-Lorraine, Baden, Bavaria, Hesse-Darmstadt, Holstein, Mecklenburg, the Palatinate, Rhineland and Württemberg, as well as from Latvia, Estonia and Lithuania. They were similarly heterogeneous with respect to religion, including Lutherans, Moravians, Baptists, Swedenborgians and, by the 1850s, Catholics.

During the 1850-57 period many German farmers and farm laborers immigrated to Waterloo and to the neighboring counties of Perth, Bruce and Grey to the west and north.

After 1857, when land had become scarcer and more expensive in southern Ontario, German Lutherans and Kashubian Catholics from the Neumark, Pomerania and West Prussia settled in Renfrew County, west of Ottawa, which has remained the chief German center in eastern Ontario, despite the fact that many disillusioned farmers left for the United States or Western Canada. Unlike the Germans elsewhere in eastern Canada, the Renfrew County Germans continued to provide instruction in German until 1914. Three different Lutheran synods had churches there in the 1930s, although some of the Germans had become Methodists or Presbyterians.

The net effect was that by 1871 nearly three times as many Germans were counted in southern Ontario as in the eastern part of the province.

Except for the early immigrants to Nova Scotia, who sailed mostly from Rotterdam to Halifax, nearly all German emigrants to Canada debarked at New York until 1846, when direct passenger service between Germany and Canada began, and a majority continued to come via American ports until about 1870, although the American Civil War had some effect on this pattern.

Most of the Germans who arrived at Quebec were very poor. This resulted from the fact that the indirect route from Hamburg via England and Scotland (mostly through Hull and Liverpool) was actually less expensive. But because there was more frequent passenger ship service to New York than to Canadian ports, a lot of migrants continued to take that route.

Western Canada has more ethnic Germans than eastern Canada. This immigration began in 1874 and continued until 1914, with peaks in 1874-76, 1901-03 and 1911-14. The Germans who came to western Canada came primarily from Eastern Europe. Lehmann estimates that 44% of the German-speaking pre-World War I immigrants came from the Russian Empire, 18% from the Austro-Hungarian Empire, and 6% from the Dobrogea (west coast of the Black Sea in Romania, going slightly into Bulgaria).

Those from the Russian Empire came mostly from present-day Ukraine, especially the Black Sea region, but also many from Volhynia. Only a small number came from the Volga region. Most of the Austro-Hungarian immigrants came from Galicia, but a significant number of Bukovina Germans and Banat Swabians settled in Saskatchewan.

Some 18% came from the United States, almost all from the Upper Midwest, especially the Dakotas. The vast majority originally came from the western Black Sea region and other East European areas, settling in the Prairie Provinces where free or very inexpensive land remained available much longer than in the United States.

Only 12% are estimated to have immigrated directly from Germany and only 2% from Switzerland. (80% of the Swiss immigrants were German-speakers.)

There was a relatively large stream of interwar immigrants, namely Mennonite refugees from the Russian Revolution who arrived mostly in 1923-26 to join their co-religionists who had come in the 1870s and a later, more diverse stream of immigrants in 1927-31, roughly half of whom were from Eastern Europe and one-quarter directly from Germany.

Among the German-Canadians, Lutherans are the largest group in Ontario (most of whom arrived before Canada became a Dominion in 1867) and Alberta.

Mennonites, the first sizable group of immigrants, are the largest group in Manitoba. In Saskatchewan, Catholics are the largest group. Baptists and Moravian Brethren were also among the immigrants.

Mennonites came mostly from East Ukraine and Catholics from the western Black Sea region, while Volhynians and Galicians represent a large share of the Lutherans.

In terms of numbers, the 1931 census reported the largest number of Germans in Ontario (174,000), followed by Saskatchewan (129,000), Alberta (74,000), Manitoba (38,000) and Nova Scotia (27,000). However, in the three Prairie Provinces the number who stated that German was their mother tongue exceeded those who identified themselves as of German origin. This discrepancy reflects the confusion regarding national origin among Germans from Eastern Europe. For example, Mennonites might describe their origin as Dutch (correct for the most part if one goes back to the sixteenth century), German (their mother tongue since the second half of the eighteenth century) or Russian (their citizenship at the time of immigration).

On the other hand, the number who reported German as their mother tongue was negligible in Nova Scotia, while only half of the Germans in Ontario made this claim, reflecting the longer time span since immigration.

The largest concentrations of German-speakers in the West were found in a belt in northern Saskatchewan, reaching from the Alberta border to east of Humboldt; in and south of Edmonton; and in and south of Winnipeg. There were also many Germans in and near Regina, especially between Regina and Yorkton; around and east of Swift Current, Saskatchewan; and along the South Saskatchewan River from southwest of Medicine Hat, but especially northeastward into Saskatchewan.

Lehmann has excellent maps of German settlements. For an updated map of ethnic and religious settlements, originally published in the *Atlas of Saskatchewan*, see Ethel A. Starbird's article on "The People Who Made Saskatchewan" in the May 1979 issue of the *National Geographic*. It is especially useful for its identification of Hutterite settlements in western, especially southwestern, Saskatchewan and northwest of Rosthern. All the more significant ones were founded in 1956-68. The map also is more specific than Lehmann's in defining a few settlements, especially the New Elsass Germanic Colony northwest of Regina. However, it is less useful for identifying German settlements in the areas where they did not, or now do not, constitute the dominant group, e.g., in the region between Regina and Yorkton.

One problem in tracing a German-Canadian connection is that virtually all of the pre-1846 and a large number of pre-1861 immigrants who went to Canada initially arrived at New York. This is relevant mostly for Ontario Germans. Conversely, over half of those who arrived in Quebec prior to 1870 appear to have gone to the United States. Furthermore, there has been extensive two-way migration of Germans between Canada and the United States, as evidenced by the fact that a majority of the authors of this guide have ancestors or collateral relatives in Canada.

There has also been substantial immigration since World War II. The Gottschee Germans and Danube Swabians among this group have settled mostly in Ontario. Urbanization has attracted many Germans of East European origin to Toronto and Vancouver, as well as to the larger cities in the Prairie Provinces (particularly Winnipeg, Regina, Edmonton, Calgary and Saskatoon).

GERMANIC MIGRATION TO LATIN AMERICA

Among the Latin American countries with a large number of German-speaking immigrants, those from the German Empire represent a majority only in Brazil and Chile.

ARGENTINA

The first wave of Germanic immigration began in 1878 when most of the Volga Germans who had begun arriving in Brazil in 1877 moved on to Argentina to find more favorable farming conditions. They settled in Buenos Aires province (south of the capital) and in Entre Rios province (directly west of Uruguay). These remained their chief centers.

Substantial immigration both directly from the Volga and indirectly via a brief stay in Brazil was heavy during the 1878-89 period. There seems to have been a lull in direct immigration from Europe in 1883-85. Onward migration from Brazil peaked in 1881-82, but continued throughout the 1880s.

From Buenos Aires province, some moved westward into La Pampa province. The Entre Rios Germans spread out even more: to Santa Fe and Cordoba to the west, as well as to Chaco and Formosa to the north. By the centennial year of 1978, Argentina had an estimated one million residents of Volga German descent.

Those in the southern provinces seem to have been mostly Catholics. In and around Entre Rios, both Catholics and Lutherans were numerous, although they rarely settled in the same village. There were also a few Baptists, Moravian Brethren, Reformed and Mennonites in Argentina. Other churches were established after immigration, usually due to North American missionary activity.

The small number of Mennonites are concentrated mostly in the Buenos Aires metropolitan area today. Volhynian Germans settled mostly in Misiones province and neighboring parts of Brazil and Paraguay. Germans from Romania settled in Entre Rios province in the 1980s.

Among the many English-language sources for the Volga Germans in southern South America, we relied most heavily on Adam Giesinger, *From Catherine to Khrushchev: The Story of Russia's Germans* and the *Journal of the American Historical Society of Germans from Russia* (especially the Winter 1978 issue, which was devoted largely to a tour of Argentina, Brazil and Paraguay in connection with the Volga German centennial celebration in Argentina). Ewald Wuschke provided information on the Volhynian Germans. The information on the Romanian Germans comes from Jacob Steigerwald's book.

Georg Hiller, *Einwanderung und Kolonisation in Argentinien* [*Immigration and Colonization in Argentina*], Vol. 1: *Einwanderung und Einwanderungspolitik* [*Immigration and Immigration Policies*], indicates that the heaviest period of Germanic immigration occurred in 1867-1911. The countries of origin were as follows:

Table 8: Germanic Migration to Argentina

Russia	115,827
Austria-Hungary	73,750
Germany	49,943
Switzerland	29,621

Unfortunately, this does not coincide with ethnicity. Those from Russia were almost exclusively German Christians and Jews. An unknown number of immigrants appear to have come from the western Black Sea area, according to Joseph S. Height, *Paradise on the Steppe: The Odyssey of a Pioneering People*, and other sources. Those from Austria-Hungary, on the other hand, appear to have included few German-speakers. The percentage of Swiss who were German speakers is also unknown, but they were numerous. The peak year for Swiss immigration was 1873, but the largest sustained wave occurred in 1883-89.

The peak years of immigration from the German Empire were 1882-90, 1895-96 and 1902-1911. The last period, which occurred after immigration to the United States had largely ceased, was by far the largest. The number of German-speaking immigrants was probably 2-3 times the number of immigrants from Germany, although no reliable statistics exist. Those from the German Empire settled mostly in Buenos Aires and other cities, but they included farmers in the provinces of Santa Fe, Entre Rios and Buenos Aires.

The total number of foreign-born in Argentina approximately doubled between 1895 and 1910. For Swiss, it went up less than that; for Germans, it tripled; for those directly from the Russian Empire, it increased more than fourfold.

BELIZE AND JAMAICA

Mack Walker, *Germany and the Emigration, 1816-1885*, mentions that after the emancipation of the slaves in the British possessions in the West Indies and Central America in 1833, planters sought German bond servants to provide labor. He estimates that thousands arrived at the Jamaica plantations and in the jungles of Central America (Belize, formerly British Honduras, and possibly British-dominated east Nicaragua).

There is currently a Moravian Brethren church in Kingston, Jamaica. To what extent its members are descendants of German-speaking missionaries and to what extent they may be Jamaican converts is unknown to us.

In 1958 several thousand Mexican Mennonites began settling in Belize. They were subsequently joined by Mennonites from Alberta, as well as some Amish and Old Order Mennonites from the United States. Their biggest settlements are at Shipyard, Orange Walk and Spanish Lookout, but there are quite a few other settlements. For further information, see Gerhard S. Koop's "Mennonite Families in Belize" in the January 1995 issue of *Mennonite Family History*.

BOLIVIA

Virtually all of the known German-speakers in Bolivia are Mennonites who began moving to the Santa Cruz area from the Paraguayan Gran Chaco in 1954. Later they were joined by immigrants from Canada, Mexico and Belize. Their ancestors were among the Russian German Mennonites who came to North America, mostly Canada.

BRAZIL

The story of German immigration to Brazil is very complex, despite the fact that the Germans are overwhelming concentrated in the southernmost states of Rio Grande do Sul, Santa Catarina, Parana and Sao Paulo, decreasing significantly in number as one goes north from the Uruguayan border.

The first settlers were convicts deported from Mecklenburg-Schwerin in the early 1800s or possibly already beginning in the late 1700s, according to *Hundert Jahre Deutschtum in Rio Grande do Sulm 1824-1924* [One *Hundred Years of German Culture in Rio Grande do Sul, 1824-1924*]. Quite a few Mecklenburgers followed later. Four German parishes were already established in this state in 1809.

Pre-1824 colonization efforts also included two German villages established in Bahia in 1818 and a Swiss settlement in the Rio de Janeiro area in 1818-20. Both floundered. Furthermore, there were German mercenaries in the Brazilian army before this. After they had revolted, they were settled in the interior of Santa Catarina state in the 1820s. But they soon fled to the coastal city of Florianopolis because of the hostility of the natives.

Heavy German immigration occurred in 1823-29, when Brazil was the favored destination of those who left Germany. Mack Walker estimates that 7,000 to 10,000 Germans took advantage of the opportunity of free passage in return for military service. This immigration came to an abrupt halt in 1830, because of the bad reputation that the German recruiting agent in the service of the Brazilian government got and because the Brazilian emperor instituted a policy of requiring immigrants to prove that they were self-sufficient.

The city of Sao Leopoldo in Rio Grande do Sul was founded in 1824. The first settlers were mostly Protestants from the Hamburg area. Nearly 5,000 came to this state in the 1820s. Eventually the Germans in this area came to be closely balanced between Lutherans (including some from the separate Missouri Synod) and Catholics, with a few Baptists, Seventh-day Adventists and Jews.

The majority of the immigrants appear to have come from the Hunsrück-Eifel uplands in the northern part of what is now Rhineland-Palatinate, with a significant number from the various Hessian duchies.

The Rio Grande do Sul centennial book indicates that nine colonies were founded in 1830-36, but these may have been daughter colonies.

In 1837 German immigrants bound for Australia (probably Old Lutherans) forced their continuously drunk captain to land in Brazil. There they founded Petropolis. For an account of this, see Hanzheinz Keller, *Neuer Beitrag zur Auswanderungsgeschichte unter besonderer Berücksichtigung der Gründung von Petropolis bei Rio de Janeiro* [*New Contribution to Emigration History with Particular Regard to the Establishment of Petropolis near Rio de Janeiro*].

Beginning in the mid-1840s Brazil again actively recruited German colonists, offering free passage or other assistance to many. This recruitment was aided by numerous "push" factors in Germany. Many government officials, the press and the elite had come to favor emigration as the answer to poverty. Some states and villages thought providing assistance for emigration would cost the public treasury less in the long run than paying for poorhouses. Thus the poor, single mothers and petty criminals were strongly encouraged, and sometimes virtually forced, to emigrate.

German colonization societies were also founded and very active in 1846-54. They were established partly for the purpose of preventing immigrants in foreign countries from being ripped off. But they also actively encouraged emigration — sometimes, but not always, with the ideal of creating a "New Germany" abroad.

Emigration was also stimulated by the failure of the 1848 Revolution for freedom and German unity, which stemmed from the impact of the French Revolution. Although the number of political refugees was not large, the environment they created undoubtedly influenced others to leave.

Moreover, the early years of the Industrial Revolution had the effect of depriving many rural residents of their livelihood. An example was the destruction of iron mining as a "cottage industry" in the Hunsrück area. Working conditions of industrial laborers in those years were as bad as Marx depicted them. Besides, Germans were always hungry for a piece of their own land. In Hesse, feudal obligations (although not serfdom) still imposed a heavy burden on the peasants. Therefore, overseas emigration often seemed more attractive than internal migration. Thus again the center of emigration was a broad belt that stretched approximately from Trier to Giessen, including the Hunsrück, Hesse and adjacent areas.

These push and pull factors contributed to large-scale emigration to Brazil in 1845-59. In 1858, the peak year, Brazil was the destination of 8% of German emigrants, a higher percentage than at any other time except the 1820s, when there was little emigration to the United States.

This wave seems to have started when the provincial government of Rio de Janeiro asked a French agent to recruit 600 laborers. He overfilled his quota by sending 2,500, but when the promise of free passage was withdrawn, many poor people were stranded in Dunkirk. Santa Izabel, in the state of Espirito Santo northwest of Rio de Janeiro, was founded in 1847. Preston E. James, *Brazil*, estimates that 35,000 Germans and Austrians settled in eastern Espirito Santo in 1840-50. A private landowner brought 400 Germans to the state of Sao Paulo in 1847.

But most of the Germans went to the three southernmost states. James reports that over 20,000 Germans settled on small farms in Rio Grande do Sul with government aid during the 1824-59 period. The Rio Grande do Sul centennial book shows that 50 colonies were established by the government, 27 by societies, and 187 privately, so the total influx was several times 20,000.

One of the most important German centers, Blumenau in eastern Santa Catarina state, was established in 1850 and named for its founder. The initial settlers were Pomeranians and they always remained the largest group. But by 1870 more than 6,000 immigrants had arrived from many parts of Germany. They were joined by Swiss and Austrians.

A number of very small Swiss settlements were founded in Sao Paulo in 1854-57, with the largest number from the canton of Glarus and the others primarily from Berne and Freiburg. Presumably the Zürich canton police chief, Dr. J. Christian Heusser, was sent out to investigate complaints that these colonists were being exploited in that their debts (for passage or land) increased, because the yearly interest exceeded the value of their crops. His account, *Die Schweizer auf den Kolonien in St. Paulo in Brasilien* [*The Swiss in the Colonies in Sao Paulo, Brazil*], was a graphically critical evaluation.

Similar complaints (or maybe even this specific one) caused the Prussian government to ban emigration to Brazil in 1859. This sharply reduced the number of immigrants, although its effectiveness seems to have declined over the years. For example, Mack Walker reports that during the heaviest period of German emigration (1871-85, by his classification), when 3.5% of the total German population emigrated, 95% went to the United States, but Brazil was still the second most popular destination, even though the ban was not lifted until the 1890s, by which time German emigration had dropped sharply.

Twentieth-century German authors acknowledge that there were a few cases in Sao Paulo of immigrants forced into virtual peonage, but they argue that this never happened in the three southern states where a large majority of the Germans lived. Their claims that the reports of abuse that led to the Prussian ban were greatly exaggerated are credible, since Dr. Heusser reported on only a few dozen families in small, isolated clusters.

Meanwhile, various groups of East European Germans began to come to Brazil. Volga Germans settled there in 1877-79. A majority of them soon left for Argentina, but some remained in Brazil, mostly in the Ponta Grossa in Parana. Dr. Mathias Hagin (*Journal of the AHSGR*, Fall 1984) mentions that at that time an estimated 17,000-18,000 Brazilians had Volga German ancestors.

Prof. Ayrton Gonçalves Celestino's manuscript, "Die Bukowiner von Rio Negro und Mafra, in Brasilien" ["The Bukoviners of Rio Negro and Mafra, in Brazil"], reports on a particular, but significant, group of Bukovina Germans, as well as Bohemian Germans, settling in Brazil. This group had its roots in the Bavarian Woods from whence it migrated to the Bohemian Forest. He lists Bavarian towns of origin, but has no information as to when they moved, except that it was long ago. He also gives a reason: lack of land for all sons because of inheritance laws.

Many Bohemian Germans had already moved to the Bukovina (under Austrian rule after 1775) in the late 1700s. The ancestors of the Brazilians, however, arrived in the predominantly Romanian southern Bukovina in 1835-40. Some immediately sold their land and migrated to the United States, Canada and Brazil. Bohemian Germans had already migrated to Brazil before that. Bohemians founded the city of Sao Bento do Sul in the Brazilian state of Santa Catarina.

Those who went to the Americas from the Bukovina and from Bohemia, the former home, settled in the same countries, often even in the same areas. Some Bukovina Germans arrived in 1877 and settled in Rio Negro, Parana, and Mafra, Santa Catarina (across the Parana River). Among their neighbors were Germans who had gone to the area in 1829. But some of the immigrants returned home because of a poor crop, massive flooding that year, a major epidemic, and complaints about the soil, the climate, the lack of wood and the Indians.

Gonçalves found the names of the 1887-88 immigrants from the Bukovina in the National Archives of Brazil and lists them, including all family members, identifying the returnees. He lists others mentioned by Ignatz Schelbauer in "Manuskripte eines der Pioniere" ["Manuscript of One of the Pioneers"], but at least one of these families had already come in 1877.

All of these Bohemian and Bukovina Germans were, of course, staunch Catholics. There were also Catholics from Germany in the area.

The Bukovina Germans immediately established new colonies, or moved to individual farms, in the two states as the population grew. According to Schelbauer's research, there were 3,687 persons of Bukovina German descent in 1837, when this group celebrated its 50th anniversary.

Gundacker reports that a significant number of Burgenlanders migrated to Brazil. Burgenland is in eastern Austria today, but it was part of Hungary until 1921. Most of the emigration appears have been in the late nineteenth and early twentieth centuries, when Hungary pursued forced Magyarization policies.

There are numerous brief references to a new wave of Brazilian immigration beginning in the late 1890s. Although Germans clearly represented a minority of the post-1890 immigrants, the closing of the American frontier in 1890 may have led to an increased percentage of the smaller number of German emigrants going to Brazil. Among the immigrants of this period are the Volhynian Germans who settled in the Santa Rosa area in northwestern Rio Grande do Sul.

According to the *Encyclopedia Americana*, German immigration to Brazil peaked in the 1920s, since American immigration laws had become so restrictive.

Later Germanic immigrants include thousands who left the Soviet Union legally or illegally. German Lutherans and Catholics settled mostly in Rio Grande do Sul in 1928-33, while Mennonites who fled from the Soviet Union via China settled in the interior jungle around 1930, but soon moved to Curitiba. Next came the political and racial refugees from Hitler-dominated areas who settled in Brazil, as in most other countries in the Americas, but how many of them became permanent Brazilian residents is another question. Finally, a significant number of Danube Swabian displaced persons must have settled at Entre Rios in Parana in 1951, since Jacob Steigerwald cites three books about them. (Note that place names like Entre Rios and Parana occur in both Brazil and Argentina. The latter, derived from the Parana River, is also relevant in Uruguay and Paraguay.) This group was only one among the numerous displaced, stateless East European Germans who migrated to many overseas countries after World War II.

Migration of Mennonite refugees to Brazil is chronicled in Peter Pauls, Jr., *Urwaldpioniere: persönliche Erlebnisse mennonitischer Siedler aus den ersten Jahren am Krauel und von Stolzplateau, S.C.* [Jungle Pioneers: Personal Experiences of Mennonite Settlers in the Early Years on the Krauel and from the Stolzplateau, Santa Catarina].

In any case, the founding of new colonies in Brazil after 1859 is primarily the story of internal expansion, not immigration. The German colonies in the eastern portions of both Rio Grande do Sul and Santa Catarina expanded westward and northward, overflowing into Parana state, as the population increased. For example, the Rio Grande do Sul centennial book lists 15 new colonies founded in 1846-64 (nearly all by 1858, i.e., toward the end of the period of heavy immigration), but a peak of 19 in 1872-78 before the number began declining, presumably due to urbanization, which led Blumenau to become a sizable Germanic city. Those who went to the metropolises later in the twentieth century went mostly to Sao Paulo, which has been gaining both internal migrants and immigrants from abroad. The Hitler-era refugees who contributed to this were mostly urbanites.

A map in James's 1942 book shows the whole area from northwest of Sao Paulo to the Uruguayan border, except for western Parana, was populated largely by post-1824 European immigrants and their descendants. Of course, these were by no means all Germans, but the farther south you go, the more Germanic the population becomes.

The Blumenau-Curitiba area is a primary example of Germanic influence because of its cohesiveness. As late as 1927, the census showed that 63% of the people in Blumenau, and 75% in the surrounding rural area, claimed German as their mother tongue. German was the language of instruction until 1938. Since then the Brazilian government has allowed it to be taught only as a foreign language, beginning in the fifth grade. Thus linguistic assimilation is undoubtedly occurring. Nevertheless, given the Germanic nature of the area and the introduction of German-language classes at the elementary school level, a substantial residue of the ancestral mother tongue remains.

Although German-speaking immigrants came from all parts of Germany, as well as from Austria, Switzerland and non-Germanic countries, the literature suggests that the majority came from:

- a broad belt extending roughly from Trier in the southwestern Rhineland to Giessen in Hesse (often referred to as the Hunsrück which is, however, only the major part of this region, not all of it)

- Pomerania and probably also the area to the west to around Hamburg, chiefly Mecklenburg-Schwerin

James estimates the number of Brazilians of German descent in the most Germanic states in 1942 as:

Rio Grande do Sul	520,000
Santa Catarina	275,000
Parana	126,000

Sparse earlier data suggest that 40-50% of the Germans lived in Rio Grande do Sul. If this was reasonably accurate, there would have been at least 1 million Brazilians with German ancestors at that time. That was more than 50 years ago. Thus it is safe to assume that there are at least several million German-Brazilians today. If inter-ethnic marriages have increased even almost as much as in North America, the actual figure could be in the 5-10 million range.

CENTRAL AMERICA AND THE CARIBBEAN (HISPANIC COUNTRIES)

There is abundant literature on an ill-fated colony at Santo Tomas in **Guatemala**. The Belgian Colonization Company recruited an estimated 1,000 Europeans, including Germans, to settle on the land it had bought in 1843 and 1845. Hundreds died in the jungle, while others became dispersed throughout the land.

Karl Sapper, in *Ansiedlung von Europäern in Mittelamerika [European Settlement in Central America]* in the volume published by the Verein für Sozialpolitik, reported that there were quite a few Guatemalans with German names and that this was the only Central American country where Germans were the most significant non-Hispanic, non-native element. This suggests that a significant number of Germans must nevertheless have survived and multiplied, since there is no report of any later colonization.

In 1846-48 some German princes sought emigrants to settle on the Mosquito Coast of **Nicaragua**. Clifford Neal Smith, in *Passenger Lists (and Fragments Thereof) from Hamburg and Bremen to Australia and the United States, 1846-49*, mentions both Nicaragua and **Honduras**.

Because of strongly adverse commentaries, generated at least partly by the Santo Tomas disaster, the project was aborted. But some East Prussians sailed there, unaware of the cancellation, according to Mack Walker. Since the British had established a *de facto* protectorate in the area, the British consul was left with the problem of what to do about the stranded Germans.

There are some brief references to immigrants going to **Cuba**. Gonçalves mentions this as one of the places to which Bukovina and Bohemian Germans went. Refugees from Hitler also went there.

Goldner writes that the **Dominican Republic** was especially helpful toward the refugees from Nazi-ruled countries. It seems doubtful, however, that many of these refugees regarded the country as more than a temporary haven.

Sapper reports that there were 137 Germans in **Panama** and about 20 German small landowners in **Honduras** at the time of the 1908 census. But Winkler estimates the total number of Germans in Central America and the West Indies in 1925 at only 2,000 (which appears to include only first- and second-generation immigrants), so this was not a significant area of settlement, especially considering that his designation apparently also includes the British and Dutch possessions.

In recent years, a few Dutch-Prussian-Russian-Canadian-Mexican-Belizean Mennonites have found yet another country: **Costa Rica**.

CHILE

This is the only Latin American country with a substantial number of residents of Germanic origin that has no documented German immigrants from Eastern Europe. It is also one of the few where Germans have been able to maintain their mother tongue as the language of instruction in the schools.

This account on the Chilean Germans is based on George F. W. Young, *Germans in Chile: Immigration and colonization, 1849-1914*. Because of inadequate data, the information is not always consistent.

Hamburg already had strong trade ties with Chile during the pre-immigration decades. It appears that almost all the German emigrants for Chile left from that port. Although there were comparatively few Germans, they were nevertheless the largest group of non-Mediterranean origin. Moreover, a disproportionately large number came from the Austro-Hungarian Empire and Switzerland. Of the Hapsburg subjects, about half came from Austria proper and half from the Czech Republic. What percentage of the immigrants from Bohemia, Moravia, and Switzerland were German-speakers is unknown.

Despite the small number of Germans in Chile, both in absolute numbers and relative to the United States, Canada, Brazil and Argentina, Young says that, with the possible exception of Paraguay, only in Chile did the concept of a "national colony" or "New Germany" succeed and survive. He finds this ironic in that the idea originated with the liberal democrats of the 1848 Revolution and yet the pro-German sentiment was obvious even during World War II, when the German government was the exact opposite of what the liberal democrats had envisioned.

The first German settlements were established in south central Chile, around Valdivia and, to a lesser extent, near Lake Llanquique in 1846-66, peaking in 1852 and 1856-57, with a smaller afterflow in 1872-75. These were agriculturalists and craftsmen with some means who sought economic independence. It was chiefly in this area that a sense of German identity was preserved. One reason for this may be that this area was effectively isolated from populous central Chile because it was occupied largely by the Araucanian Indians. Only after the 1880-82 uprising of the latter was defeated did this situation change.

This area, bordering Valdivia on the north, then became the province of La Frontera. A small number of Germans who had gone to this area in 1858-59 had quickly become assimilated. However, the Chilean government settled a substantial number of Germans here in 1882-89, with a small afterflow in 1900-02. These were poorer than the earlier immigrants so that the Chilean government had to pay for their passage against future repayment.

The poorest ones of all, including Swiss as well as Germans, were sent to Chiloé province, south of Valdivia, in 1895-97, but many later left this poor area with its unfavorable climate.

The province of Valdivia-Llanquique accounted for half the Germans in Chile in 1917. Together with neighboring La Frontera, they amounted to two-thirds. The overwhelming majority of the others lived in the cities of Santiago, Valparaiso, and Concepcion. These consisted mostly of industrial workers, professionals, and businessmen. However, the support of the more well-to-do urban element, and especially the German-language newspapers in Santiago and Valparaiso (1870-1943), did a lot to nurture the preservation of a German identity in south central Chile.

Young attributes most of the German immigration (especially the early immigration) to Chile to individual recruiting agents, especially Bernhard-Eunom Philippi, and to colonization promotion societies established in the 1840s. However, the first Germans arrived in 1846-47 primarily as a result of famine (caused by potato rot and poor harvests) and the industrial depression of those years, while recruited immigration did not begin until 1848 and did not pick up speed until the 1850s.

At first the Chilean government instructed Philippi to recruit only German Catholics. However, because Catholic bishops were disinclined to work with the Protestant Philippi, the Chilean government guaranteed freedom of religion in 1850. As a result, a considerable majority of the German immigrants were Protestants. Moreover, the German Catholics, who shared the religious beliefs of the native Chileans, were therefore more likely to become assimilated, as has been documented for La Frontera for example. Nevertheless, Catholics from Westphalia, Prussian and Austrian Silesia, and a few impoverished ones from Württemberg were among the immigrants. The Llanquique region had about an equal number of German Catholics and Protestants. In 1910, there were 9 Protestant schools, 2 Catholic schools and 21 non-denominational schools in Chile.

MEXICO

Almost all of the Germans in Mexico are Russian German Mennonites. Though mostly of Dutch-Flemish origin, they stress the importance of the German "mother tongue" their ancestors finally adopted after centuries in West Prussia.

In 1922-27 some 6,000 very traditional Mennonites left Saskatchewan and Manitoba (with a few from Kansas and Oklahoma) to settle in remote parts of Mexico, primarily because of fears about "worldly" influences and increased government regulation of their schools. Most of them settled in the state of Chihuahua, with a smaller number in Durango. In 1929-30 a small group of Soviet Mennonite refugees joined them.

In 1948 another 1,700 Manitoba Mennonites went to Chihuahua for the same reason as the earlier group. Since then, they have spread out, some returning to Canada or the United States, with others going on to new frontiers in Belize, Costa Rica, Paraguay and Bolivia.

The best accounts of the Mexican Mennonites can be found in:

- Harry Leonard Sawatzky, *They Chose a Country* (which also has a chapter on Belize)

- Walter Schmiedehaus, *Die Altkolonier-Mennoniten in Mexico* [*The Old Colonial Mennonites in Mexico*]

- William Schroeder and Helmut T. Huebert, *Mennonite Historical Atlas* (which is all-encompassing and has a text accompanying the maps)

PARAGUAY

George Young estimates that there were 30,000 Germans in Paraguay in 1914, although Winkler's 1925 estimate is only 4,000. Some are known to have come from Bohemia, the Bukovina and Volhynia. By the time Young published his book in 1974, a lot of Mennonites had migrated to Paraguay. However, when he parenthetically refers to Paraguay as possibly having become a "New Germany," this could only be true in a cultural-linguistic — not a political — sense, for the Mennonite immigrants were totally apolitical, in sharp contrast to the Chilean Germans as he saw them.

The first group of over 2,000 Mennonites came in 1926-27 at the same time as, for the same reasons as, and from the same area of emigration as the Mexican Mennonites. They settled in the Gran Chaco in western Paraguay. A fifth found the rigors too great and returned to Canada. There is a brief account of this by Irene Enns Kroeker in "Immigration (Paraguay)," found in *Preservings*, the newsletter of the Hanover/Steinbach (Manitoba) Historical Society (No. 4, July 1994).

Nearly 5,000 Soviet Mennonite refugees founded settlements in both eastern and western Paraguay in 1947-50. In 1948 another 2,000 Canadian Mennonites migrated to eastern Paraguay, with a larger percentage returning home (probably because they were better able to afford it than the immigrants of the 1920s). Beginning in 1969, some Mexican Mennonites, as well as some Old Order Mennonites from the United States, relocated in Mexico.

By 1954 the Paraguayan Mennonites had begun to migrate onward again, this time to Bolivia.

PERU

Mack Walker makes brief mention of "scandalous stories" from Peru, resulting from the activity of Peruvian agents in Austrian Tyrol in or about 1859. Whether the number of immigrants was as small as the few dozen Swiss in Brazil on whose condition Heusser made such an unfavorable report is not specified, but the lack of further information on the subject suggests that this may have been the case.

Winkler's estimate of 1,800 Peruvian Germans may have been a reference to missionaries or businessmen, since any descendants of survivors of the Austrians who apparently went there in 1859 would be likely to have been of the third generation already (i.e., not included in census data as Germans).

URUGUAY

According to Winkler's estimate, there were only about 1,500 Germans in Uruguay in 1925. If this is interpreted as "German-speaking" or "of German descent," the Russian Germans, who settled mostly in western Uruguay, may have accounted for the total number. However, Winkler's low estimates on the other non-European countries suggest that he may have meant 1,500 "German-born" residents.

VENEZUELA, SURINAM, CURACAO, COLOMBIA AND EQUADOR

Winkler estimated that there were 2,600 Germans in Venezuela in 1925. George Young refers to an 1846 article about Germans in Tovar, Venezuela. An up-to-date account of the still very German settlement at Kolonia Tovar on the highest mountain northwest of Caracas is Jim Keeble, "From the Black Forest to the Rain Forest," in *Mitteilungen* (June 1996), published in England. Over 75% of the villagers have ancestors among the more than 300 people from Baden who settled there in 1843. Gonçalves states that some Bohemian and Bukovina Germans went to Venezuela. Steigerwald mentions post-World War II Danube Swabian refugees going there.

On the other hand, attempts to settle Germans in Dutch Guiana (now Surinam), have been thoroughly chronicled by D. von Blom, in "Niederländisch-West-Indien" in *Die Ansiedlung von Europäern in den Tropen [European Settlement in the Tropics]* (Verein für Sozialpolitik, Vol. 147) even though all these efforts seem to have been a flop. The record: immigrants from the Palatinate and the Basel area, 1749; some arrivals in the 1840s, after the governments of Saxony and Prussia had inquired about sending criminals and poor people there; Württemberg immigrants, 1853-55; and a final colonization effort in 1896. Nearly all of these died, returned to Germany, or forsook farming and went to the capital, Paramaribo.

Von Blom makes only a passing reference to Europeans of many nationalities on the island of Curacao.

Winkler estimates that there were 1,400 Germans in Colombia and 1,100 in Ecuador in 1925. These may have been missionaries or businessmen, since we have seen no reference to actual immigrants.

GERMANIC MIGRATION TO THE SOUTHWEST PACIFIC

AUSTRALIA

Among the non-European countries, only the United States, Brazil, Canada and Argentina received more German-speaking immigrants than Australia.

A large majority of the Germans settled in South Australia, Victoria, New South Wales and Queensland. The number who went to Western Australia was much smaller and includes a disproportionately large percentage of post-1945 immigrants. There were a few thousand German immigrants scattered in various parts of Tasmania, especially around Hobart. The sparsely populated Northern Territory had only a few dozen.

Our coverage is based primarily on the books by Lyng, Borrie, Wegmann, Norst and McBride, Cohen and Davis, Vondra, and Harmstorf and Cigler, although we included some useful contemporary information by Liz Twigden of South Australia.

Both Lyng and Borrie have valuable maps of German settlements, and both also list the names of specific German communities, including some name changes.

South Australia had the first significant number of immigrants, whereas the bulk of the German immigrants to Queensland (which consistently had the largest percentage of German-born from 1881 until at least 1921) arrived later than in the other three states.

The names listed by Clifford Neal Smith in *German-American Genealogical Research Monograph*, Number 7, suggest that nearly one third of the "Old Lutherans" who emigrated in 1838-1854 because they objected to the forced merger of the Lutheran and Reformed Churches into the Evangelical Church went to Australia. They constituted the first large group of Germanic immigrants in South Australia.

While Queensland and South Australia clearly have the largest number of Australians concerned with researching German ancestry, there may be more residents of New South Wales and Victoria with at least one German ancestor. This is because of greater intermarriage among ethnic groups, related to the scattering of the Germans, the transitory presence of gold miners (especially in Victoria, but also in New South Wales) in the early decades of the second half of the nineteenth century, and the twentieth-century phenomenon of urbanization.

There can be a big difference between the place of immigration and the later residence of the immigrants and especially their descendants. Australia is a classic case of this. Victoria benefited the most from this internal migration of German-Australians during much of the nineteenth century, whereas New South Wales seems to have received the largest number of internal migrants since the late nineteenth century, based on inferences from the census statistics.

In 1921 there were over 36,000 German-born residents in Australia, with over 61,000 of the second generation. But the total number of Germanic descendants was much larger, because the Germanic population multiplied so rapidly, as documented by the fact that German-born wives had considerably more children (averaging 5.81) than those of other nationalities, based on Lyng's data.

The overwhelming majority of Germans were Lutherans. On the other hand, the overwhelming majority of Lutherans were Germans, although there was a significant Scandinavian minority in some areas.

The Lutheran Church, initially that of the "Old Lutherans," soon split into many synods, but by 1927 they had been combined into two. The number of pastors in each state, including both synods, for that year was: South Australia, 166; Queensland, 101; Victoria, 64; New South Wales, 39.

In 1914, when the two largest Lutheran groups had 99 parishes, these included 4 in Western Australia, 4 in New Zealand and 1 in Tasmania.

If we look at the proportion of all-German families, we find a clear distinction between South Australia and Queensland, on the one hand, and Victoria and New South Wales, on the other. In the former, the ratio of German-born males to females remained constant at about 1.5:1 during the censuses from 1881 through 1921. But in Victoria and New South Wales, the ratio was constantly higher than 2:1 from 1871 through 1933, wavering around 2.5:1 most of the time.

In 1861 the number of German-born residents in the more populous states was: Victoria, 10,400; South Australia, 8,900; New South Wales, 5,500; Queensland, 2,100.

The large in-migration to Victoria, especially of miners, explains the high German figures for that state. The number of South Australian Germans is reduced both by out-migration and the fact that there were a large number of Australian-born Germans in that state by that time. The percentage of Germans in Queensland, compared to other states, climbed constantly and sharply, at least during the half-century from 1871 to 1921.

In 1891 the number of German-born residents was:

Table 9: German-born Residents in Australia, 1891

Queensland	14,910
Victoria	10,772
New South Wales	9,565
South Australia	8,553
Western Australia	290
Tasmania	918
Northern Territory	3

With respect to the urban population, Borrie's maps show more Germans in the Greater Melbourne area than any place else in 1891, with the Greater Sydney area second. However, if we lump together the six centers in the general vicinity of Brisbane, southeast Queensland would have had the largest urban population.

Harmstorf and Cigler estimate that 135,000 Germans came to Australia in 1945-75. This figure includes German-born children of other nationalities, but does not include German children born elsewhere. The first ones were refugees and Displaced Persons, including not only those from pre-World War II eastern Germany, but also hundreds of German women who had married some of the 170,000 Displaced Persons, including a considerable number who came to Australia in 1948-51 after some years in Germany.

Tradesmen and laborers came to Australia because of job opportunities before Germany had recovered from its wartime destruction. Some prisoners of war also chose to remain permanently in Australia.

According to Jacob Steigerwald, *Tracing Romania's Heterogeneous German Minority from Its Origins to the Diaspora*, many Romanian Germans, especially Danube Swabians, who left for Germany after World War II soon went on to numerous other countries, with some settling in South Australia.

Cornelius J. Dyck, *An Introduction to Mennonite History*, states that some 2,000 Templer Mennonites, who went to Palestine in the 1870s, were deported to Victoria and New South Wales during World War II. He also indicates that a few thousand Dutch Mennonites emigrated to Australia in the 1960s and 1970s. They now live mostly in Sydney, Melbourne and Brisbane. However, while they have the same religious and ethnic roots as the Prussian and Russian Mennonites, they never underwent the process of "Germanicization" because they stayed in the Netherlands.

Immigrants who started coming to Australia in the 1960s were generally fairly well off. These included German business representatives who decided to stay in Australia rather than return home after their tours were over. Another group has been called the "atom bomb emigrants" who left out of fear of a nuclear war in Germany, together with other concerns such as pollution, overcrowding and a feeling of guilt about the war.

New South Wales

According to J. Lyng, the German element was stronger in New South Wales than in any other state, except Queensland. This appears to be based on the number of German-born residents, rather than the number of those of German descent. The overwhelming majority of Germans migrated to New South Wales from other states (or New Zealand), rather than directly from Europe, so this was the second or third, not the initial, home of most of the immigrants. However, most of them arrived at a rather late date, with the first sizable group coming from South Australia in the late 1860s. Thus they had had only two generations to multiply, not three as in South Australia. A small group of vine dressers had already arrived in 1838, at the same time that a larger group of Germans went to South Australia. But there was no connection between the two, since they came from different areas and for different reasons.

There was a steady stream of immigrant rural laborers from Germany to New South Wales from the 1840s until 1879, with some interruptions, according to Jenner in Carol Wardale and Margaret Jenner, *German Genealogy Directory*. But these immigrants appear to have been few in number for most of this period, compared to those who settled in South Australia. In any event, there was nothing resembling a concentrated German settlement until the 1860s. Even today, the Germans in New South Wales are more widely scattered than in South Australia, Queensland or even Victoria. Those who came directly from Germany (with no further specification of origin) settled northwest of the Newcastle area, according to Lyng. Those from Queensland established widely scattered settlements, mostly in the northeastern part of the state.

The first substantial internal migration (and probably the largest one), however, came from South Australia. Many of them trekked to the area north of Albury in the 1860s and farther north, around and beyond Temora, in the 1870s. In the 1880s many went up the Murray River and settled in the western part of the state, around and south of Broken Hill. Most were wheat farmers. Some of these were ex-miners (from Victoria as well as New South Wales). The largest number probably came from the Woomera district in western Victoria, where they had already pioneered in low-rainfall farming. Many of both groups had originally come from South Australia.

Lyng's map of the 1920s shows German settlements mostly northwest of Albury, two-thirds of the way to Queensland. Borrie's map of the 1950s shows more in the coastal area, primarily near Sydney and Newcastle, with more scattered settlements farther northeast. He also shows Broken Hill in the west as one of two urban centers. Although Sydney had the most Germans, Germans constituted a much larger percent of the population in the west around Broken Hill.

Queensland

A substantially larger number of Germans immigrated to Queensland than to any other state, but most came at a relatively late time. Between 1861 and 1891 the German-born population of South Australia and Victoria remained fairly constant. In New South Wales it went up by 70%, but in Queensland it jumped 700%.

Thus the recency of immigration is a big help in determining the origin of the Queensland Germans. A large majority of the early settlers came from Pomerania, West Prussia and Silesia, with quite a few from Württemberg. However, the Ueckermark, which is in eastern Mecklenburg-Vorpommern and northeastern Brandenburg, is mentioned most frequently as a place of origin by Queensland German genealogists. Later immigration came from all parts of Germany, but with the eastern areas apparently still dominant.

Apart from missionaries, the first Germans arrived in 1838-44. These were the only ones who had religious reasons for leaving Germany. By the time the Moreton Bay district of New South Wales became Queensland in 1861, there were already 2,000 Germans there, a significant percentage of the population. However, as a result of very active recruitment by the government of Queensland (offering free passage, i.e., to the so-called assisted settlers), the number of Germans had doubled by 1864 and increased to more than 12,000 in 1881.

Many of the early Germans went to the Toowoomba area (in the mountains west of Brisbane) to work on railroad construction. But a large majority went into farming. Borrie shows an overwhelming concentration to the south, west and north of Brisbane. Lyng also shows a concentration in the Darling Downs area farther west, on the other side of the Great Dividing Range, which hugs the east coast.

There is a much smaller, but still significant, number of Germans in the Maryborough-Bundaberg area, a good 100 miles north of Brisbane, with scattered settlements farther north along the coast (e.g., near Mackay), as well as in the interior.

South Australia

The first sizable group of German immigrants to Australia were "Old Lutherans," who arrived in 1838-39. Although a few seem to have gone to other parts of Australia, most of them settled just north (Klemzig) and east (Hahndorf) of Adelaide. In 1842 an important village was established at Lobethal (near Hahndorf). This migration continued through 1854, with the emigrants favoring the United States some years and Australia (mostly South Australia) in others, in a see-saw fashion. Clifford Neal Smith's lists indicate that Australia was favored in 1841-42, 1844-45, 1847-51, and 1854. Most of the immigrants came from the general vicinity of the Oder River and especially from the east of it (Silesia, Brandenburg and Posen, with fewer from Saxony and Pomerania).

Twigden states that according to the 1861 census, about 7% of South Australians were of German extraction. By 1891 this figure had risen to 9%, according to Lyng, despite the substantial out-migration from the colony.

In the late 1840s, a large number of immigrants came from the Harz mountains when the lead and silver mines there experienced economic difficulty. Furthermore, Sorbs from Lusatia began coming to South Australia in 1845 with steadily increasing numbers until 1860. They constitute the largest distinct ethnic minority group in modern Germany. But in South Australia they soon became integrated into the German Lutheran community. Moreover, Rhinelanders settled in the Barossa valley north of Adelaide, where they developed viticulture.

A larger percentage of Germans than any other immigrant group settled in rural areas, mostly east of Adelaide and in the Tanunda region north of Adelaide.

South Australia represented the mother colony for many German settlements in other states. Thousands of Germans went to the gold fields in Victoria after 1851. Some returned, whereas others stayed there or moved on to New South Wales. The small number of early German settlers in Western Australia also came mostly from South Australia.

After 1881, deaths and departures exceeded the number of new immigrants, according to Lyng. But by that time the German settlements were so well established that this became irrelevant. By 1900 over half of the German immigrants went to the city of Adelaide, but they were easily outnumbered by the descendants of the early immigrants, most of whom remained in the rural areas.

There were far more communities that had enough Germans to establish a Lutheran church than in any other colony. In part, this may have been due to the influence of the first immigrants who came for reasons of religious freedom. The Lutherans were all Germans, except for a Scandinavian minority that was distinctly smaller than in Queensland. Many of the later immigrants, especially those who went to Adelaide, either did not join or left the Lutheran church.

During World War I about 70 German place names were changed to English or aboriginal names, although some were changed back again later. This means that the problem of identifying the current name of a locality that originally bore a German name is greater than in most other countries.

The name lists in Borrie's book show that 39% of the Germans naturalized in this colony from 1836 to 1900 came from northeast Germany, 27% from central Germany, 24% from northeast Germany, and the rest from western and southern Germany.

Victoria

In the late 1840s and early 1850s immigrants who came directly from Germany settled in a semicircle around Melbourne, with the first group arriving in the Port Philip district. By 1849 there were Germans in Geelong and soon thereafter in Germantown (now Grovedale). The first large group apparently consisted of Moravian Brethren recruited by a Bremen agent in 1849.

Immigrants from Mecklenburg, Saxony and Silesia settled around Thomastown in 1850. In 1853, Germans (mostly Silesians) settled in the Duncaster and Berwick areas. But in the 1851-1861 decade, large numbers migrated from South Australia to central and western Victoria. Many came to dig for gold. Miners from South Island in New Zealand joined them. The gold fields were mainly around Ballarat, Bendigo and Castlemaine. In the 1857 and 1861 censuses a majority of German-born Australians were in the mining area.

Between 1861 and 1881 the Germanic population decreased significantly, primarily because many miners returned home after the gold rush petered out. However, ex-miners and other migrants from South Australia became wheat farmers, mostly in the Wimmera area around Horsham. Some of the Wimmera Germans moved to the Mallee district. The Wimmera region became the stronghold of Lutheranism in Victoria. Viticulture was introduced into Victoria by a few Swiss in Geelong, but it did not become significant until 1847 when Rhinelanders developed vineyards in the Barrabool Hills.

Many of the miners and later immigrants also went to Melbourne. By 1933 a slight majority of the Victorian Germans were urbanites.

Victoria never had the dense concentrations of Germans found in South Australia. But Borrie estimates that there were 20,000 first- and second-generation Germans in the colony by 1891. About half of that number had been born in Germany, but not all of these migrated directly from Germany to Victoria. The 1921 census counted nearly 100,000 first- and second-generation Germans. By then there must have been quite a few of the third generation already.

Western Australia

In 1947 the percentage of Western Australians who were German-born was only 0.7%, compared to 2% for the whole country. Due to post-World War II immigration, the respective figures for 1971 were 2.5% and 4.3%, respectively. Since immigration from Germany to Western Australia peaked in 1982-83, the percentage may have increased somewhat.

Furthermore, Swiss immigration has increased, so that in 1990-91 it was two-thirds of immigration from Germany. Moreover, the ratio of Austrian to German immigrants has been relatively high. In 1986 there were one-seventh as many Austrian-born as German-born in the five metropolitan local government areas with the largest number of residents from Germanic countries (Stirling, Wanneroo, Perth, Melville, and Gosnells).

In the 1986 census, fewer than 30,000 Western Australians claimed German ancestry. Of these, nearly 7,000 had been born in Germany and over 500 each in the United States and in England.

Nevertheless, this small number has been well documented by Mary Mennicken-Cooley in *The Germans in Western Australia: Innovators, Immigrants, Internees* (Mt. Lawley, Western Australia: Edith Cowan University, 1993), the sole source of our information on this Australian state. Because of the small numbers, however, it is possible only to list the places of origin of specific immigrants or small groups, rather than to offer broad generalization as to the chief places of origin. Among the places of origin that are listed are Bremen, Hamburg, Saxony, Lower Silesia, Baden, Hanover, East Friesland, Schleswig-Holstein, Pomerania, Magdeburg, and Bavaria, as well as Austria and Switzerland. Of the 1841-1903 naturalizations, Prussia is named as the previous place of residence for well over half of those for whom this information is listed (only a minority). But most of northern Germany belonged to Prussia at the time.

Despite the small numbers, there were more Germans naturalized in Western Australia in 1841-1903 than immigrants from any other country. Those who came from Britain were British subjects, so no naturalization was involved. The list of names published in Mennicken-Cooley's book shows that the overwhelming majority were naturalized between 1894 and 1903, with only a few before 1887.

The first few permanent German settlers arrived in the state in 1836 from England. The introduction of regular steamship service from Germany to Fremantle in the 1880s and especially the gold rush of 1884-92 led to a more significant number of immigrants of Germanic origin. However, many of the Germans (especially the miners and to some extent the "Old Lutherans") first settled in the eastern states and moved to Western Australia in the late 1800s and 1900s, while others came from England.

The early German pioneers were mostly farmers and tradesmen who settled throughout the state, especially in the Swan River district just northwest of Perth. When gold was discovered, the wheatbelt town of Katanning in the southwestern part of the state attracted Germans (many of them farmers) from South Australia. The turn-of-the-century immigrants from both the eastern states and Germany settled especially in the Fremantle-Perth area, the southern wheatbelt and around the gold fields (Coolgardie, Kalgoorlie, Kenawa) in the interior of the south central part of the state, with a small number in the northwest in the vicinity of Broome.

Very few immigrants came from Germany during the interwar period, due to the lingering anti-German sentiment, which caused not only German nationals, but also Australians of German descent, to be interned during both World Wars. There is an interesting reference to World War II internees receiving charitable packages from Brazil and Argentina, an indication that relatives and neighbors from Germany had settled on both continents and maintained contact. However, the post-World War II period produced by far the largest wave of German and Swiss immigrants.

The overwhelming majority of Germans were Lutherans, although Scandinavians, Estonians, and Latvians also belonged to this church. But there are isolated references to German Catholics, Baptists, and Moravian Brethren.

German-Speaking Swiss in Australia

In addition to the Germans from Germany, there were also other German-speaking immigrants in Australia.

Wegmann provides key information about the Swiss in Australia. Nineteenth century immigrants were primarily French- or Italian-speaking, but included several hundred German-speaking farmers, tradesmen and skilled workers who settled throughout the country, as well as ladies making butter in Camden near Sydney.

On the other hand, most twentieth-century Swiss immigrants were German-speakers. There was a small peak of German-Swiss immigration in 1924-28.

Wegmann's detailed linguistic map of Swiss in Victoria shows that by 1924 German-Swiss were concentrated in the Melbourne area, but that scattered German settlements outnumbered those where other languages were spoken in most of eastern Victoria, with the striking exception of the Swiss concentration at Rutherglen on the border with New South Wales. They represented a small minority in the mining areas around Ballarat, Daylesford and Bendigo and a large minority near Geelong, where viticulture was the prime occupation.

A majority of the Swiss in other states were German-speakers, but the number of Swiss outside Victoria was fairly modest until after World War II, with the largest number in New South Wales and Queensland. South Australia, which played such an important role in early migration from Germany, never had many Swiss settlers and ranks fifth today, with a much larger number of recent immigrants preferring Western Australia.

Swiss immigration skyrocketed after 1945, with New South Wales first equalling and then overtaking Victoria. From the 1960s to the early 1980s, Australia was the primary destination of Swiss emigrants. Australia did not adopt restrictive immigration laws until 1983. German-speakers accounted for 7/8 of the immigrants in the 1980s.

Australia was only seventh among the foreign countries in which Swiss lived, but the small percentage doubled from 1960 to 1980. Temporary, rather than permanent, emigration to foreign countries was the most common Swiss pattern, which explains why many returned to Switzerland.

The German-speaking Swiss who remained quickly became assimilated, with 75% marrying non-Swiss spouses. They had little rapport with the Germans, since they did not feel comfortable with standard German. Moreover, most of the Protestants, who represented two-thirds of the twentieth-century immigrants (in sharp contrast to the nineteenth century), joined the Presbyterian church, rather than the Lutheran church favored by the Germans. As a result, the German-speaking Swiss suffered very little discrimination during the two World Wars.

Today one-third of the Swiss live in Sydney and one-fourth in Melbourne. There was always a much smaller percentage of the German-speaking Swiss in rural areas than was true of the other linguistic groups. Few Swiss farmers went to Australia, with most of these going to Queensland.

German-Speaking Austrians in Australia

Norst and McBride, our principal source for Austrian-Australians, discuss quite a few prominent early German-speaking settlers from the Hapsburg Empire. Most came from Vienna, but others were from Bohemia, Moravia, Hungary, Slovenia, Trieste and Gorizia.

There was a minor peak in Austrian arrivals in 1902-08, but the first major wave consisted of refugees who came mostly in 1938-39 after the Nazi annexation (*Anschluss*) of Austria. According to Australian archival records, over 2,000 had arrived by 1942. This does not include those who first went to England and were then deported to Canada or Australia. These refugees were a highly diverse group, in terms of both their political orientation and their religion. Vondra states that a large percentage were Viennese Jews, but other authors stress heterogeneity.

However, all the previous wavelets of immigrants were dwarfed by the tens of thousands who arrived after World War II. If we include the post-1956 Hungarian refugees who listed Austria as their last place of residence, the number exceeded 100,000.

The first postwar group consisted of the "Shanghaiers," who were a closely-knit group in Sydney and Melbourne. As of 1988, they published their own newsletter.

In 1951 Australia agreed to accept 462,000 displaced persons (DPs), including 108,000 refugees. Almost 20,000 Austrians applied under the Assisted Passage Scheme in 1952-61 and a few came without assistance. But immigration declined after 1971.

The later immigrants differed greatly from the refugees and early immigrants who had, for the most part, been well-educated professionals, mostly from Vienna. Most of the late immigrants came from Austrian provinces, especially Styria. They were more likely to be tradesmen and farmers, and went to more widely scattered areas. The majority embarked at Trieste or Genoa, although some early post-1945 immigrants left from Bremen or Cuxhaven.

The largest number of Australians who declared themselves to be of Austrian ancestry in the 1986 census were in Sydney and Melbourne, but the most concentrated Austrian community seems to be in Canberra. A considerable number settled not only in other parts of New South Wales and Victoria, but also in Queensland, South Australia and West Australia. In proportion to the small population of those areas, they were rather numerous in Tasmania and the Northern Territory, with a large majority outside the capital cities, as was also true in Queensland.

The Austrians are increasingly being seen as different from the Germans, perhaps partly because of differences in dialect and religion. Christian German-speaking immigrants from Austria proper were almost all Catholics, in contrast to the strong Lutheran majority among those from Germany. Some 6.4% of Australians who considered themselves to be of Austrian ancestry in 1981 were Hebrews, while 25% identified themselves as neither Christians nor Jews.

German-Speaking Jews in Australia

The genealogical guide by Norst and McBride makes it clear that a significant number of Jews came to Australia from England, the United States, and the German, Austro-Hungarian and Russian Empires. There is no direct, and only a little indirect, information as to the significance of each country of previous residence with respect to total numbers, periods of immigration or location of settlements. It is clear, however, that quite a few of them spoke German or came from countries where German-language records for them exist.

Hebrew congregations were established in Sydney in 1826 and in Hobart, Melbourne, Western Australia and Adelaide in 1840-42. Evidence that German Jews emigrated to Australia in the 1840s and 1850s can be found in the indexed records for Germans on bounty ships for 1849-52 in New South Wales.

The largest number of Jews, including Jews with German-speaking ancestors, are in Sydney and Australia. Based on information about available genealogical records, there are also groups in Hobart, Adelaide, Brisbane and Ballarat.

Krauss's book indicates that Austrian Jews settled in Australia. To what extent these were refugees from, or survivors of, Nazi persecution is not known to us.

NEW ZEALAND

The total number of German-speakers who immigrated to New Zealand, which has a current population of less than 3.5 million, was small. This was even true in terms of percentages. Nevertheless, James N. Bade, ed., *The German Connection: New Zealand and German-speaking Europe in the Nineteenth Century*, states that they were the second largest group of immigrants. He estimates that several hundred thousand New Zealanders have Germanic ancestors.

Nearly all of the information in this section comes from this source. Particularly helpful are the articles by Marian Minson on "Trends in German Immigration to New Zealand," by Gertraut Maria Stoffel on "The Austrian Connection with New Zealand in the Nineteenth Century," and by Hans-Peter Stoffel on "Swiss Settlers in New Zealand."

For more details, see the articles by James N. Bade on the province of Nelson (the northernmost part of South Island), by Rolf E. Panny on the Lower (i.e., southern) North Island, by Judith Williams on the Bohemian Germans in Puhoi (in the northern part of the North Island) and by Pauline J. Morris on the settlements in the southernmost part of South Island.

The book is a model because of its careful distinction between "German" and "German-speaking." It is also a classic illustration of the importance of a multi-ethnic approach to Germanic genealogy in that it deals carefully with the immigrants from German Poland, Bohemia and Dalmatia (the Adriatic coast of southern Croatia).

The mixture of Germanic and Slavic names in the case of those from Poland and Bohemia show that neighbors belonging to different ethnic groups moved together and that many people with a Germanic (or Slavic) identity were the product of mixed marriages and/or assimilation, even though these events might have occurred centuries ago.

Minson states that the three major waves of Germanic immigration were in 1842-1845, 1861-67 and 1872-86. The first two waves were primarily the product of maritime traders from the Hanseatic League (Hamburg, Bremen), but also from the Austrian Adriatic ports.

These came mostly from Hamburg, Bremen, Hanover, Hesse, Saxony, Holstein and Prussia. The number from southern Germany, Austria and Switzerland was always comparatively small, although they were more important in certain particular areas.

It is interesting to compare these with the major waves in the United States. The first New Zealand wave occurred just before the first major American wave began in 1846. The other two New Zealand waves began about the time when the American Civil War and the Panic (Depression) of 1873 interrupted large-scale immigration to the United States.

The German-speaking migrants to New Zealand were overwhelmingly Lutheran, with two exceptions: the Bohemians in the extreme north and the Poles in the southern part of the South Island.

The first German group settlement was in the Nelson area, one contingent arriving from North Germany (Hamburg, Hanover, Holstein and the Rhineland) in 1843 and the second group from Mecklenburg in 1844. Additional shiploads arrived from 1850 to 1869.

The opening of gold fields in the northern part of Westland province on the west coast of South Island led to an influx of north Germans and Austrians in the 1860s and 1870s. Pomeranians settled in Jackson's Bay Special Settlement in southern Westland province between 1865 and 1880. All of the latter and many of the former group left before long.

More permanent settlements were established in Canterbury province on the east coast, particularly in the Christchurch area, but also in the southeasternmost part of the province. Many Germans arrived in the late 1860s and 1870s under the Assisted Immigration Scheme. The early immigrants came particularly from Hanover, Austria and East Prussia. Others came from Bavaria, Saxony, Moravia and German Poland.

German-speaking immigrants were first attracted to the Otago-Southland region in the 1860s to seek gold. But the first substantial number came in 1872 from German Poland. The overwhelming majority of them were identified as German Poles.

Many of them soon went to the Dunedin area to build the Southern Trunk Railway. By 1873 many had become farmers around Allanton (Greytown until 1895). Waibola Township, somewhat farther south, included a proportionately larger number of German names. The Otago-Southland German-speaking immigrants consisted mostly of nuclear and extended family groups.

German names were also common among immigrants who came to Otago in 1874 from the vicinity of Lunow near the Oder River and to Southland (where a Germantown was founded) in 1875. Settlers from Hanover and Austria were also significant in Canterbury.

While all of the above settlements are on South Island, most of the German-speakers eventually ended up on North Island, which has 2½ times as many residents. The first immigrants to North Island seem to have been Pomeranians, Brandenburgers and Rhinelanders who settled in the province of Hawkes Bay in the southeastern part of the island. Little trace of them has been left.

A more significant concentration was established in Taranaki province (on the west side) by immigrants from Switzerland, Pomerania, Prussia and German Poland. These early settlements have largely disappeared. Toward the end of the nineteenth century, Germans settled farther south in the same province.

The Rangitikei River region (around Marten) on the west coast of Wellington province attracted a large group of Germans. Many German Lutherans from the Neisse River region, who had settled in the Adelaide region in South Australia in 1838, arrived in 1860. Others arrived from Otago province.

The Bohemian Germans (many bearing Czech names) came to Puhoi, north of Auckland, in 1863. They were staunch Catholics from Mies county in the Pilsen district, who spoke the Egerland dialect. Three more groups of immigrants followed in 1866, 1872, and 1876.

Apart from the Bohemians, North Island settlers from the Austro-Hungarian Empire included male Moravians and Austrians who participated in the 1860s gold rush in the southern provinces, as well as families who settled in Canterbury province in the 1870s. However, the largest number of Austrians have always lived in populous Auckland province. But immigrants from the Austro-Hungarian Empire also included Dalmatian Croats, who did not identify themselves as German-speakers.

Most of the Swiss immigrants were German-speakers from southwestern Graubünden canton, close to its border with Ticino, but immigrants also included people who spoke French, Italian, or Romansch. The early arrivals came between 1850 and 1880. There was a very high ratio of males to females (which was also true of non-Swiss miners), which gradually decreased. There was a parallel migration of Swiss to the Australian state of Victoria in 1855-58 to work in the gold fields. Most of them spoke Italian or French. Some migrated onward to the gold fields in New Zealand's South Island. Others came directly from Europe. About half of the first naturalized Swiss in New Zealand seem to have been French or Italian.

The first permanent Swiss settlers, as contrasted with gold-seekers, came to the province of Taranaki (North Island). Those in the 1870s and 1880s were mostly German-speakers from Graubünden. Later ones came from Central Switzerland. In 1874 nearly 25% of the New Zealand Swiss lived in this province. In 1886 only 54% of the Swiss lived on North Island, but by 1916 this had increased to 89%. The decline on South Island must have been largely mining-related. On the other hand, almost 43% of the New Zealand Swiss lived in Taranaki province in 1916, with another 33% in Auckland and Wellington provinces, which contain the two largest cities (of the same name) in the country.

There was significant migration between New Zealand and Australia: mostly with Victoria in the case of miners, and mostly with South Australia in the case of farmers (especially from the Nelson area).

By the mid-1880s quite a few people of German ancestry lived in the major cities of Auckland (especially north Germans, but also Bavarians, Swiss, Saxons, and Austrians), Wellington (Swiss, north and northeast Germans), Christchurch (Bavarians, Moravians, Swiss, Austrians, "Poles," and north Germans) and Dunedin ("Poles" and northeast Germans). People from Hanover constituted a particularly significant component of the North Germans in most areas.

The largest percentage of urban residents who were of Germanic origin was found in the medium-sized city of Palmerston North in northern Wellington province.

A Hebrew congregation, which probably included Jews from German-speaking areas, was established in Auckland in 1843.

FORMER GERMAN COLONIES AND PROTECTORATES IN THE PACIFIC

Samoa

According to Bade, this was the only island where permanent German immigrants were numerous enough to have left a significant number of descendants, as evidenced by German names in the telephone books, even though the number of Germans was only 248 in 1908. Germany, Britain and the United States acquired contractual rights to ports in 1878-79, but not until 1899 did Germany finally obtain Western Samoa.

Papua New Guinea and the Western Pacific Islands

The German government established a protectorate over northeast New Guinea in the 1880s. The protectorate included the Bismarck Archipelago, Kaiser-Wilhelms-Land, the German Solomon Islands, the Mariana Islands (exclusive of Guam), the Caroline Islands and the Marshall Islands. This protectorate actually included the largest number of Germans in the South Seas, but there is little evidence of permanent immigration. Nevertheless, the hopes were reflected in such place names as Neu-Pommern and Neu-Mecklenburg.

However, there was a large enough settlement in Pohnpei (*Ponape*) to have a German church at one time.

The Solomon Islands are now independent, as is Belau (Palau), but most of the islands, excluding New Guinea, now belong to the Federation of Micronesia. Papua New Guinea is a combination of the former German and British possessions in the eastern half of this large island.

GERMANIC MIGRATION TO AFRICA

OVERVIEW

The overwhelming majority of German immigrants went to South Africa. The next largest number settled in Namibia, which was German South-West Africa for a generation before World War I. A modest number went to other former German colonies, primarily to German East Africa, now mainland Tanzania.

The Germans in Cameroon and Togo, which were pre-World War I West African German colonies, numbered only in the hundreds. Included were some plantation owners and livestock farmers in Cameroon. The northwestern part of former German Cameroon became a part of Nigeria in 1961.

A tiny handful of job-seekers or adventurers went from South Africa to Rhodesia (now Zimbabwe and Zambia) or British East Africa (now Kenya).

There is a record of some German immigrants to Algeria, which had an estimated 7,500 Germans in 1925. These may have been augmented by some German members of the French Foreign Legion who may have chosen to stay there after completion of their service. The number of Germans who served in Africa with the French Foreign Legion in the 1920s exceeded the total number of Germans in Africa who lived north of Namibia, according to data on pages 18-23 of Winkler's *Statistisches Handbuch des gesamten Deutschtums* [*Statistical Handbook for Germans Throughout the World*]. The fact that there were also an estimated 6,800 Germans in Morocco at the time strengthens the supposition. However, we have no explanation for the estimated 11,000 Germans in Egypt, nor do we have any knowledge of any permanent immigration to that country.

Most of the Germans in North Africa were probably there for business reasons and, in the case of Egypt, perhaps scholarly reasons. Such people may have lived in the country in question for a long period, so that pertinent vital records may exist. But it seems likely that only a small percentage stayed there permanently.

SOUTH AFRICA

Werner Schmidt-Pretoria, in his book, *Der Kulturalanteil des Deutschtums am Aufbau des Burenvolke* [*The Cultural Contributions of Germans to the Development of the Boer People*], argues that some 55-65% of the original Boer forefathers were Germans, almost all of them soldiers in the service of the Dutch East Indies Co. He acknowledges, however, that the male-female ratio among Germans who settled in South Africa in the early centuries was 20:1. Hence, there were few German foremothers. Those German veterans who got married almost always had wives of Dutch, or later Dutch-German mixed, descent. However, a few married Huguenots who had fled to Germany and lived there for several generations before going to South Africa.

But J. Hoge, in "Personalia of the Germans at the Cape, 1652-1806" in *Yearbook for South African History*, 1946, argues that the percentage of Germans in the service of the Dutch East Indies Co. was not as high as estimated (24% in 1716, 64% in 1767), because Schmidt-Pretoria's well-documented work was based on the incomplete and inaccurate data gathered by H. T. Colenbringer.

However, E. L. Schnell, in a recent book, *For Men and Women Must Work; An Account of German Immigration to the Cape with Special Reference to the German Military Settlers of 1857 and the German Immigrants of 1858*, cites statistics and estimates from various sources that suggest that slightly over a quarter of the Cape residents in 1807 were of German origin.

One problem is that because of inter-ethnic intermarriage in all immigrant countries (and especially so in pre-1857 South Africa), all figures that total 100% are misleading. The number of Caucasian Cape residents with at least one German ancestor clearly exceeds 50%. On the other hand, the number of those of predominantly German background is much smaller and the number of those who have retained a sense of Germanic identity still smaller.

Almost all the Lutherans in South Africa were Germans, although there was a Scandinavian minority. However, because of intermarriage and lack of permission to build a Lutheran church until 1779 according to Schnell, many Germans (or at least their mixed-descent children) joined the Reformed Church.

German immigration was heaviest in 1750-1800. A large majority came from the North German plains (from the Dutch-German borderland to East Prussia), where the Low German dialect (a cross between German and Dutch) is spoken, facilitating communication and assimilation. But there was also a Württemberg regiment (1786-1808) and there are some references to origins in Bavaria, Alsace, Bohemia, the Palatinate, Breslau and Leipzig.

Schmidt-Pretoria also cites H. T. Colenbringer's article (translated from the Dutch into German by Franz Thierfelder as "Die Herkunft der Buren" ["The Origins of the Boer People"]) as stating that 24% of the burghers in 1657-62 were Germans, according to the *Freibücher* [books of free men, who were property owners]. Incomplete records for 1718-91 show that about half were Germans.

According to Schnell's recent book, 63% of the deeds of burghership between 1817 and 1851 (thus spanning the bridge between the early assimilated Germans and the later ones who retained their sense of a German identity) were granted to Germans. Moreover, nearly 60% of the private teachers in South Africa in the nineteenth century were Germans. The data show that nearly all of them came from predominantly Protestant areas, but scattered from Latvia to Alsace to Switzerland. Another group he mentions are the Herrnhuter, or Moravian Brethren, missionaries (1737), a Germanicized denomination of Czech origin.

Colenbringer (Dutch original, "De Afkomst der Boeren," published by Het Nederlandsche Verbond) and George McCall Theal seem to be the leading authorities on the origins of South Africans. Theal's work was first published in two volumes in Cape Town in 1896 and later in three English volumes as *History and Ethnography of Africa South of the Zambesi, from the Settlement of the Portuguese at Sofala in September 1505 to the Conquest of Cape Colony by the British in September 1795*.

Schmidt-Pretoria also lists the following article on German Jews in South Africa in a footnote: S. A. Rochlin, "Die ersten deutschen Juden in Südafrika" ["The First German Jews in South Africa"], in *Jahrbuch der jüdisch-literarischen Gesellschaft* [*Yearbook of the Jewish Literary Society*], Vol. 21.

However, these early German settlers, whatever the percentage, have long since been totally assimilated, so that dealing with their family history would be tantamount to covering all of South African genealogy, which is far beyond our scope. The extent of assimilation is illustrated by the fact that not a single surname on the 1780 Lutheran congregation roll could be found in the 1860 list, as noted by Schnell.

The history of those South Africans who have retained a distinct ethnic identity begins in the 1850s. The most detailed treatment is Johannes Spanuth's "Britisch Kaffraria und seine deutsche Siedlungen" ["British Kaffraria and Its German Settlements"] in *Schriften des Vereins für Sozialpolitik* [*Publications of the Society for Social Betterment*], Vol. 147, Part 4. Briefer accounts are in English-language histories by T. R. H. Davenport and by Donald Denoon et al. Our information is based mostly on Spanuth. The more extensive work by Schnell was not available to us, except for short excerpts dealing mostly with the pre-1857 period.

The first settlers were soldiers of the (English) King's German Legion, which was dissolved before going into action, since the Crimean War ended. They were given the choice of being mustered out and transported to any place in the world.

Some 8,000 men were willing to settle in British Kaffraria (now the southeastern part of Cape Province) as military settlers. They agreed to bring their families or to get married. Despite mass marriages before departure, only 2,400 Legionnaires arrived in 1857. They brought only 330 wives and daughters with them, according to T. R. H. Davenport, *South Africa: A History*.

However, they were not farmers at heart. Most asked to go to India for military service and nearly half of them did. About one third of those sent to India later returned to the Cape Colony, but they scattered to the four winds. Thus this scheme had to be regarded as a failure and the military settlement in Ciskei, i.e., the area on this (west) side of the Kei River, was dissolved. Quite a few of their village names indicate origins from Brandenburg or northwest Germany, and there were also some from Hesse.

The government soon made arrangements to recruit German civilian settlers, providing them with free passage, to be repaid later. Some 2,700 arrived in 1858-59. Ken André reports that most of the 444 families who sailed from Hamburg to East London (South Africa) in 1858-59 came from Pomerania. Other sources indicate that 60-80 of them are believed to have moved to other parts of South Africa. Schnell also indicates an afterflow of German immigrants through 1862.

The largest percentage came because of the desire to own their own farms. This was impossible for most of them in Germany, especially in the areas where most of the land belonged to large estates. This was especially true of Mecklenburg and the Prussian provinces to the east of it. Smaller numbers came from such places as Hanover, Bavaria, Baden, and Silesia.

The census of December 31, 1859, listed 1,494 German civilians and 1,165 Legionnaires. According to Spanuth, those figures understate the total number of Germans, because they did not include those who resided east of the Keiskama River (Transkei), an area that was not part of Kaffraria at the time, nor those who went elsewhere to find work.

Few of the Legionnaires were farmers, but some were in middle-class urban occupations and others moved to other parts of South Africa.

After a rough start, the villages prospered, due to the discovery of gold in the 1860s (when Kaffraria also became a part of Cape Colony), which led to more demand for foodstuffs and other goods. Some farm villages remained entirely or largely German, while others (primarily administrative centers) soon had a mixed population. There was a significant German minority in the towns in eastern Cape Province.

After the Transkei region, between the original Kaffraria and Natal, was annexed, more Germans moved to trading stations or even native villages in that area.

By around 1880, isolated individual farms began to replace the European-style villages, a change that was still in progress in 1914, although the vast majority of farmers appear to have moved away from villages by then.

A few of the Kaffrarian Germans bought farms in the Orange Free State. An even smaller number migrated to German South-West Africa, Rhodesia or British East Africa.

In 1878-79 there was another wave of German settlers. Schnell identifies the later waves as occurring in 1877 and 1883. Many settled on the sandy plains near Cape Town, while others went to the vicinity of King William's Town in Kaffraria. There was a small afterflow in the immediately following years, but virtually no German immigration during the two decades before World War I.

The most concentrated Germanic settlement continues to be in a semi-circular area around East London, but especially to the northwest toward Stutterheim (ca. 50 miles away).

There may be an even larger number of residents of German descent in the Cape Town area. However, because they represent a more scattered minority in a more densely populated region, they are less likely to have retained a Germanic identity.

Ken V. André has written a 400-page work, *10 Generations, 1720-1990: Some Aspects of German Immigration to the Eastern Cape*. He has incidentally also done smaller studies based on visits to Australia, Chile and Wisconsin.

With respect to the much smaller number in other provinces, Maurice C. Evans (in an article on Natal, translated into German by G. von Poellnitz and published in 1913 in Part 3 of the *Schriften* already mentioned) refers to diverse missionary activity in Natal, including Trappist Catholics, Moravian Brethren, and Lutherans.

Lantern: Journal of Knowledge and Culture, published by the Foundation for Education, Science and Technology in Pretoria, published a special tri-lingual issue on "The German Contribution to the Development of S[outh] A[frica]," in February 1992. This German festival year indicates that events were scheduled for Stutterheim, King William's Town and East London in the Cape Province, the former Kaffraria, which seems to have had the largest concentration of Germans in South Africa; Cape Town (southwest), Port Elizabeth (south center) and Kimberley (northeast, adjacent to the Orange Free State) in the north) in other parts of Cape Province; Vryheid (north), Pietermaritzburg and Durban (south) in Natal; Piet Relief (southeast), Johannesburg and Pretoria (center) and Rustenburg and Potchefstroom (west) in Transvaal; and Bloemfontein in the Orange Free State.

Although the vast majority of Germans lived in rural settlements, these places indicate the location of these settlements or the cities nearest to them.

All the following references to articles, most of them written by South Africans of German descent, but with a liberal sprinkling of European scholars, refer to this special issue of *Lantern*, which includes several detailed maps of Germans in specific areas.

The broadest overview is provided by Heinz von Delft, "Der Anteil der Kirche und Mission an der deutschen Einwanderung" [The Role of the Church and Missions in the Immigration of Germans]. The title is aptly chosen, for apart from the soon assimilated members of the Dutch East Indies Co. and the Kaffrarians, who retained the German language to some extent until after World War II, most of the other settlements consisted of German artisans and farmers who accompanied the missionaries in order to provide them with support and sustenance.

He states that the first German Lutheran church was established in Cape Town in 1780, after greater freedom of religion had been granted, and some 120 years after the German settlers in the service of the Dutch East Indies Co., had arrived. (These seventeenth-century Germans were quickly absorbed into the Boer population, but their German surnames are still quite numerous.) He also points out that most German missionaries stayed in South Africa, instead of just serving there for a period of years as was true in many other parts of the world.

This church, supervised by the Evangelical church in Hanover, which had the same monarch as the United Kingdom, also presumably served the so-called Württemberg

Regiment, sold by Duke Karl Eugen to the Dutch East Indies Co. However, the latter's stay in South Africa was brief. Most were shipped to the East Indies, where they vanished.

"Die Kaffrariadeutschen" ["The Kaffrarian Germans"] by Rolf Grüner deals explicitly with the three waves of German settlement in this area. The first civilian settlers in 1858 came mostly from Pomerania, the Ueckermark and Lusatia, i.e., from the Oder-Neisse area. Some of their descendants moved farther inland because a shortage of land soon developed.

New Hermannsburg (now just Hermannsburg), north of Durban, was founded by the Hermannsburg Mission Society in Hermannsburg, Hanover. These missionaries had Ethiopia as their intended destination. However, since they were refused permission by the Imam of Gallaland (now Somalia) to transit through his territory, they returned to South Africa, where they began work in 1854. These settlers seem to be the only ones to have retained the German language for two reasons. The founder of the Mission Society insisted on the importance of maintaining German traditions and the German culture, although not political identification with Germany. Therefore, he sent a group of German brides-to-be to South Africa, instead of having the German immigrants marry native South Africans, which usually led to assimilation before long. Secondly, a German school was built and continues to function today. For details, see Arthur Leuschke, "The Hermannsburg Mission Society in Natal and Zululand."

Actually, these missionaries had been preceded by Jonas Bergtheil, a Bavarian Jew, who had already brought a group of immigrants from Osnabrück (after he failed to recruit settlers from southern Germany) to the same general area in 1848, with the intention of establishing cotton plantations in New Germany. This group is dealt with by Anneliese Peters in "The Bergtheil Settlers, 1847/48."

The Hermannsburg society also established more than 26 named missions along the western boundary with Botswana in 1857, extending eastward close to the Johannesburg-Pretoria line. This community was four times as large as the mission settlement in Natal. However, only Ramotswa (formerly Harmshope) retained its Hermannsburger character. See the article by Hinrich Pape, "Hermannsburger Missionsarbeit in Transvaal."

However, many of the settlers left Hermannsburg and, under the guidance of the Berlin Missionary Society, established a new community in Lüneburg, since they had all come from the Lüneburg area in Germany. Thekla Heineke writes about "Lüneburg."

She also has an article on "Vryheid und Umgebung" [Vryheid and the Surrounding Area], which tells the story of a large German settlement in northern Natal, but one established only in the late nineteenth century.

However, the earliest missionary settlements were those of the Moravian Brethren who came in 1737, only half a generation after they had fled from the Bohemian crownlands to Saxony. But while they were of Czech origin, many Germans must have flocked to this church very soon, because the names which are mentioned are German. These Moravians established mission stations in both the western and eastern parts of Cape Province, the first and best known one being at Gnadenthal (now Genadendal), which was 150 kilometers (about 95 miles) east of Cape Town. Georg Schmidt was soon forced to leave when the Reformed church declared that his activities were illegal.

However, Wolfgang Reith deals with the re-establishment of this mission station in "Die Neugründung der Missionsstation Genadendal, 1792." Again the mission ran into objections from the Boer farmers, but the British takeover of the Cape provided protection, so it built its first church in nearby Baviaanskloof in 1795. This community grew so rapidly that in 1802 it was the second largest community in the Cape.

The Berlin and Hermannsburg Missionary Societies also established settlements in Bloemfontein in the Orange Free State, Pretoria, the Witwatersrand and other parts of northern Transvaal.

The Hanover Lutheran Church and the Rhenish missionaries provided assistance for German communities in western Cape Province. One of the rural settlements was at Kap-Vlakte, but its proximity to Cape Town led to its absorption.

The London Missionary Society also brought German missionaries to the Orange Free State.

Gerhard Brunner has an article on "Deutsche katholische Einwanderer," which covers not only South Africa, but also the former German colonies in Africa. Catholic missionaries had served in these colonies since the mid-nineteenth century already, but after World War I, they were banned from these and other African areas. Hence they looked for new mission fields in South Africa.

Most of the missionaries came in the 1920s. Their origins were in Limburg, Bonn-Oberkassel, Mainz, Cologne, St. Ottilien near Augsburg, and Ellwangen/Jagst in Württemberg. They established themselves in Oudtshoorn, Queenstown, Aliwal North, Kimberley, Kroonstad, Bethlehem, Lydenburg/Witbank, Zululand, and Vryheid, which became a religious, educational and agricultural center.

Nuns from Tutzing, Schlehdorf in Upper Bavaria, Neustadt/Main, Mallersdorf, Pfaffendorf/Koblenz, Landshut, Altötting, Limburg and Vallendar/Rhein likewise served in southern Africa.

However, the most significant Catholic settlement goes back to the 1880s. In 1880 Bishop Riccards of Grahamstown/Port Elizabeth asked Trappist monks to come to South Africa, in order to teach the natives farming, as well as to do missionary work. The first group arrived in Dunbrody in 1880, but they soon found that the absence of rainfall and ground water made this area unsuitable for farming, so in 1882 they moved to Mariannhill, near Pinetown in Natal, where the greatest Trappist monastery in the world was established. In 1885 there were 22 priests and 68 laymen there. Mission Sisters also arrived that year in order to look after the needs of the women and children.

But it became increasingly clear that an order devoted to silence was not well suited for missionary work. Therefore, the Mariannhill monastery was separated from the Trappists in 1909. In 1920 Mariannhill was founded as an independent mission congregation. From here several other mission stations were founded. Today Mariannhill is a town of over 10,000 people, of whom only a few hundred are whites. Austrian and Swiss missionaries also contributed to its development.

In contrast to the mission stations, German immigrants settled in the Witwatersrand-Johannesburg-Pretoria region. They were mostly steelworkers from the Ruhr River region who arrived in the 1930s. When the doors were reopened to immigrants in 1948, many Germans came because of the shortage of housing and work at home.

By 1960, when the German-Speaking Catholic Community was formed, there were 1,200 German families in the Johannesburg area. In 1959 the first Catholic church in Pretoria-West, where the largest number of German Catholics lived, was dedicated. Thus it is clear that the German Catholic community in South Africa is of very recent vintage.

Erwin A. Schmidl writes about "Österreicher und Ungarn im Burenkrieg" ["Austrians and Hungarians in the Boer War"] in this issue of *Lantern*. He indicates that about 2,000 Austrians and Hungarians arrived around 1899-1902, with those in higher positions coming mostly from German-speaking areas.

Kurt Scheurer, co-author of the *History of the Swiss in South Africa*, editor of the *Swiss Review* and a member of the South African Genealogical Society wrote the *Lantern*'s article about "The Swiss in South Africa." Swiss soldiers serving the United Dutch East Indies Co. arrived as early as 1658. They were also utilized as artisans, married local women and quickly became assimilated. They are the founders (*Stamvaders*) of many Afrikaans families.

In 1783 a whole Swiss regiment arrived at the Cape. However, their stay was brief. They were soon shipped to Sri Lanka (Ceylon), switched allegiance and served the British in India and Canada.

The first Swiss missionaries arrived in 1872, with some serving in Morija in Basutoland, now Lesotho. The Elim Mission in northern Transvaal, started in 1879, soon became the center of Swiss activity. It expanded its field across the border into Mozambique. The missionaries were soon followed by laymen serving the Boer Republic and migratory workers in the gold fields. The Swiss missions extended their work to the Witwatersrand and later in the Orange Free State to serve their compatriots. They are still active there today.

The 1850-99 period brought many Swiss doctors, scientists, teachers and other prominent people to South Africa. They included people who served in Namibia and Botswana. However, artisans always constituted the core of the Swiss community. Both French-speakers and German-speakers are well represented among the Swiss in South Africa.

With the discovery of gold on the Witwatersrand, the third phase of Swiss immigration began, this time mostly businessmen.

L. A. Möller lists numerous examples of German place names in "Duitse Plekname in Suid-Afrika" ["German Place Names in South Africa"].

NAMIBIA

Most of our information about what was German South-West Africa from 1884 to World War I comes from two sources: (1) Donald Denoon with Balan Nyeko and the advice of J. B. Webster, *Southern Africa Since 1900*, and (2) Jan H. Hofmayr (with the 2nd rev. ed. prepared by J. P. Cope), *South Africa*.

South-West Africa became a German protectorate in 1884, although German missionaries had been active there since 1814.

The special issue of the *Lantern*, described more fully under **SOUTH AFRICA**, also refers to German missionaries, including some recruited by the London Mission Society, who settled in Namibia. These missionaries were generally accompanied by laymen in order to provide for their sustenance and to promote agricultural and economic development among the natives.

Heinz von Delft says the missionaries stayed in Namibia, instead of just serving there for a limited period of time. Gerhard Brunner talks about German Catholic missionaries starting to work there in the 1920s.

The Herrero and Nama tribes resisted the Germans, especially in 1890-94. After a significant number of German settlers had started arriving, there was a more serious uprising in 1903-05, which was ruthlessly crushed by the Germans. Small-scale local resistance began as early as 1896 and did not end until 1908.

The result was that South-West Africa was largely depopulated, except for the Ovambo territory in the north, which was unaffected by the Germans.

Apart from the civilian immigrants, many German soldiers decided to remain in the country. By 1914 there were about 15,000 Germans in the country, attracted mainly by the discovery of gold.

Many Germans left or were deported after World War I. Nevertheless, Winkler estimates that there were still 10,000 Germans in the country in 1925. Furthermore, German remained a language of instruction and one of the country's three official languages even in the 1920s, after the area had become a South African mandate.

LESOTHO

Kurt Scheurer, in his *Lantern* article, refers to Swiss missionaries in Basutoland, now Lesotho, a mountainous enclave within South Africa, by the 1780s.

ZIMBABWE

The large Mariannhill German Catholic mission established a station at Bulawayo in Zimbabwe (formerly Southern Rhodesia) in the early twentieth century, according to Brunner.

A few of the Kaffrarian German settlers in South Africa had gone north to Rhodesia (presumably Zimbabwe) in the nineteenth century already.

TANZANIA

There is an abundance of literature on the former German East Africa, despite its small European population. There were 4,107 Germans among 5,356 Europeans in the colony in 1913. Winkler estimates the number of Germans in 1925, when it had become a British mandate, at 2,000.

This colony represents a classic example of the conflict between commercial interests concerned with trade and those who sought colonies for the sake of settlement. Bismarck, who was not favorably inclined toward colonies, especially settler colonies, nevertheless declared what was known as Tanganyika until its union with Zanzibar in 1964 to be a German protectorate in 1884, when the domestic electoral advantage of doing so became apparent.

The pressure for the establishment of colonies came from the middle class, which desired colonies for settlers. Despite his contempt for this group, Bismarck immediately granted a charter to the Deutsche Ostafrika Gesellschaft [German East Africa Co.], or DOAG, to rule the area, as if to get the matter off his hands. The company proceeded with settlement forthwith, but in 1891 the German government reluctantly assumed responsibility for governing the area because of the DOAG's ruthless behavior and near-insolvency.

Settlement occurred first along the coastal area, then in the temperate northern highlands bordering Kenya, and thereafter in central and, to a lesser extent, southern German East Africa.

The propaganda arm of the DOAG had its strongest support in the kingdom of Saxony, according to Fritz Ferdinand Müller, *Deutschland-Zanzibar-Ostafrika: Geschichte einer Kolonialeroberung* [*Germany-Zanzibar-East Africa: History of a Colonial Conquest*]. It also had strong support in Bavaria, Brandenburg, Silesia, and Baden. It seems logical to suppose that most of the settlers would have come from the areas where the colonization scheme was promoted most actively.

The major conflict with the Hehe and Fiti tribes in 1891-98, due to German land-grabbing, may have stunted the growth of German population in central German East Africa. However, this area was also much less conducive to European settlement than the north, due to its climate.

The large-scale Maji Maji rebellion of 1905-07 against the hut tax, which resulted in forced labor as a practical matter, also occurred in this area and may have had an even greater effect on settlement potential.

The scorched earth policy of the German army in this war resulted in the appointment of the first civilian governor. He immediately instituted reforms greatly benefiting the Africans. These were opposed by the settlers, who eventually forced his resignation but could not reverse the reforms.

The revolt and the reaction to it also re-ignited the conflict between the settlers and the international traders, who favored an African small-holder peasant economy. The German government supported the latter.

But one cannot accurately describe the German population in Tanzania in these terms. There were two groups of settlers with differing interests: the plantation owners and those with more modest-sized farms.

Albert F. Calvert, in *German East Africa*, describes three plantation areas:

- the Usambara highlands in the north,
- along the central rail line leading to Lake Tanganyika and the Rufiji River somewhat to the south, and
- along the southern coast near the port of Lindi.

He mentions isolated plantations in other areas.

Although there were initially cotton, coffee, rubber, kapok and sisal plantations, H. H. Y. Kaniki, editor for the Historical Society of Tanzania, in *Tanzania under Colonial Rule*, states that by 1914 European agriculture consisted chiefly of sisal plantations and coffee grown by the smaller European landholders.

According to the German population map (plate 219 in Calvert's book), there were only seven districts with at least 100 Europeans: four along the Kenyan border, where 1,222 whites lived (the largest number in the Moshi district), two in the central area (with 803 Europeans, 618 of them in the Dar-es-Salaam district and the others in the Morogoro district immediately to the west); and one in the southeast near Lake Nyasa (with 118).

Only in the Moshi district and the coastal Dar-es-Salaam districts did Europeans constitute 5% of the population.

In terms of occupation, we find that only 25% were planters and farmers. The others were engineers, mechanics and laborers (20%), merchants and traders (15%), government officials (16%), missionaries, including Lutherans, Catholics and Moravian Brethren (14%), and military and civilian support personnel (5%). The engineers, mechanics and laborers worked on railroad construction and possibly also in mining.

This breakdown offers clues concerning the makeup of the German population in the various other German colonies, protectorates and even the North African countries that had never been under German domination, despite obvious and substantial differences among them.

During World War I, when there was prolonged military action in German East Africa, many settlers and missionaries abandoned the farms and plantations that had been destroyed. This reduced the European population by half during World War I.

Nevertheless, many Germans returned after the war. They were the dominant group of Europeans until World War II in what had become a British mandate. Even today, there are still a noticeable number of Germans in Dar-es-Salaam and the northern plantations.

Gerhard Brunner, in his article in the South African *Lantern*, refers briefly to the Catholic missionaries who served there from the mid-19th century until World War I.

KENYA

A tiny number of South African Germans left Kaffraria to seek jobs in British East Africa (now Kenya).

CAMEROON

There were a small number of German cacao and rubber plantation owners, as well as some cattle farmers, in Cameroon. Germans are known to have lived in Douala (Duala), Buea (*Buëa*), and Victoria. The stock farmers were mostly in the Adamowa (*Adamáua*) region straddling the current border between Cameroon and Nigeria. However, the total German population never quite rose to 1,000. There were also Catholic missionaries in Cameroon, according to Gerhard Brunner.

TOGO

Brunner reports that there were Catholic missions in Togo. No other reference to Germans in Togo has been found.

ALGERIA

In 1845 French agents were hired to recruit German immigrants for Brazil. However, the Germans kept arriving at Dunkirk long after the quota had been overfilled. In 1846 the French government provided free transportation to Algeria for 900 of the stranded, destitute Germans. Since many of those who went to Brazil came from the Hunsrück and Trier districts of the southern Rhineland, it is possible that some of those who ended up in Algeria may have also originated there.

EGYPT

Some Templer Mennonites of Germanic origin who had gone to Palestine in or about 1867 were interned in Egypt during World War II. After the war, they were sent to Cyprus for a short period.

GERMANIC MIGRATION TO ASIA

No country in Asia ever had a substantial number of German residents, but the largest number lived in Asian Turkey (Asia Minor) and China. Wilhelm Winkler estimates that in 1925, Palestine, Indonesia and the "British East Indies" (which included what are now India, Pakistan, Sri Lanka, Myanmar and possibly Hong Kong) each had about 2,000 Germans, with about 1,000 in Japan.

The number of Templers of German origin in Palestine, to which they had migrated in and after 1867 was probably greater than Winckler indicates, since many of them would have been born there already and thus would not be included in Winckler's estimate, except possibly if they had registered with the German consular authorities to retain their German citizenship, as many did. However, it is highly unlikely that the Templer Mennonites, who constituted a sizable portion of the group, would have fallen into either category.

The Germans counted by Winkler in other Asian countries were probably mostly people involved with commerce, possibly including some scholars and missionaries. The Moravian Brethren were engaged in worldwide missionary activities at an early date, but it is unlikely that the number of Moravian missionaries in any of these countries would have been large.

CHINA

In 1898-99 Germany obtained a 99-year lease over Jiaozhou (*Kiautschou*) in the southern part of the Shandong peninsula (eastern part of the state by that name). It asserted a sphere of influence over a larger area.

According to *Meyers Kleines Konversations-Lexikon* [*Meyer's Small Encyclopedia of General Information*], there were 3,298 Germans in this briefly held "German Hong Kong" in 1905. This territory had a Protestant and a Catholic church. Most of the Germans were engaged in commerce.

A second Chinese city that has indirect German connections is Harbin (*Charbin*) in Manchuria (now in Heilongjiang province). Thousands of Russian Germans fled across the Soviet-Chinese border in the late 1920s and stayed in Harbin for a while, until they could find a new homeland (mostly in Canada and Latin America).

A second group of 20,000 refugees fled from Nazi-dominated Europe and spent the Second World War in Shanghai, where they were interned in compounds after the Japanese invasion. Shanghai was the only port which did not require an entry permit. This included about 4,000 from Austria. After the war ended, many went back home, but others found new homes in the United States and Australia, according to Norst and McBride.

PALESTINE

Templers lived in Palestine from 1867 until World War II, when many were either conscripted into the German armed forces, deported by the Allies to Australia, or interned in Egypt. After the war those who had remained in Palestine were sent to a camp in Cyprus and given the choice to return to Germany or emigrate overseas. Most chose to go to Australia. Victor Doerksen estimates that there are about 300 Templers in Germany today.

The Templers in Palestine included both those who had come directly from Germany, where the Temple Society was founded, and from the German-speaking Templers of Russian Mennonite origin.

TURKEY (ASIA MINOR)

Some Russian Germans, particularly Templar Mennonites who were later deported to Australia, established temporary colonies in Asia Minor, with Palestine as their ultimate goal. However, the Germans who were there in the twentieth century were probably mostly commercial and professional personnel.

MISCELLANEOUS OTHER COUNTRIES

Some of the Germans and Swiss who served the Dutch East Indies Co. were sent from South Africa to Indonesia, Sri Lanka and subsequently India.

BIBLIOGRAPHY (See ANNOTATED BIBLIOGRAPHY for full citations if not shown)

GENERAL, EUROPEAN OR MULTI-CONTINENTAL REFERENCES:

Thomas Albrich. *Exodus durch Österreich: die jüdischen Flüchtlinge, 1945-1948* [*Exodus through Austria: The Jewish Refugees*]. Innsbruck: Haymon-Verlag. 1987.

Angus Baxter. *In Search of Your European Roots: A Complete Guide to Tracing Your Ancestors in Every Country in Europe*, 2nd ed. Baltimore, MD: Genealogical Publishing Co., Inc. 1994. 304 pp.
> Specifies the kinds of records available in every European country, which is useful because ethnic Germans lived throughout almost all of Europe.

Angus Baxter. *In Search of Your German Roots: A Complete Guide to Tracing Your Ancestors in the Germanic Areas of Europe*, 3rd ed. Baltimore, MD: Genealogical Publishing Co., Inc. 1994. 118 pp. Map.
> Expansion of material on Germany in the author's book on European roots, but with added material on Germans who lived outside Germany.

Christian Ludwig Becker. *Donauschwaben in Nordamerika, in Südamerika und in Australien.* [*Danube Swabians in North America, in South America and in Australia*]. Munich/Sindelfingen: Donauschwäbische Kulturstiftung. 1990. 231 pp.
> Oriented toward popular culture, but identifies many specific localities in which Danube Swabian immigrants settled.

Eva Beling. *Die gesellschaftliche Eingliederung der deutschen Einwanderer in Israel. Eine soziologische Untersuchung der Einwanderung aus Deutschland zwischen 1933 und 1945.* Frankfurt a. M.: Europäische Verlagsanstalt. 1967. 283 pp. Bibliography.

Wolfgang Benz, and Marion Reiss, eds. *Deutsch-jüdisches Exil, das Ende der Assimilation? Identitätsprobleme deutscher Juden in der Emigration* [*German-Jewish Exile: The End of the Assimilation? Identity Problems of German Jews in the Emigration*]. Berlin: Metropol. 1994.

Marion Berghahn. *German-Jewish Refugees in England: The Ambiguities of Assimilation.* New York: St. Martin's Press. 1984.

Christian Ludwig Brücker. *Donauschwaben in Nordamerika, in Südamerika und in Australien [Danube Swabians in North America, South America and Australia]*. Munich/Sindelfingen: Donauschwäbische Kulturstiftung. 1990. 231 pp.

> Detailed account of Danube Swabians in the New World, with various maps, charts, illustrations and photos, intended for the general public. Map of largest ethnic groups in various American states is no longer valid, since 1990 census data show Germans as the largest group in quite a few additional states.

Johann Christian Dressler. *Illischtie, a Rural Parish in Bukovina: Primary Source Records for Family History* [tr. by Irmgard Hein Ellingson]. Ossian, IA: translator. 1994. 517 pp.

> This compilation presents church, cemetery and school records; immigration lists; census and tax rolls; family letters; and personal interviews for 440 Bukovina families, covering the 1549-1949 period.

Cornelius J. Dyck, ed. *An Introduction to Mennonite History*, 3rd ed. Scottdale, PA/Kitchener, ON: Herald Press. 1993. 452 pp. Maps and diagram.

Daniel Judah Elazar, with Peter Meding. *Jewish Communities in Frontier Societies: Argentina, Australia, and South Africa*. New York: Holmes & Meier. 1983.

David Englander, ed. and comp. *A Documentary History of Jewish Immigrants in Britain, 1840-1920*. Leicester/New York: Leicester University Press; distributed exclusively in the USA and Canada by St. Martin's Press. 1994.

P. William Filby and Mary K. Meyer, eds. *Passenger and Immigration Lists Bibliography, 1538-1900*. Detroit, MI: Gale Research Co. 1981. 5 volumes, ongoing.

> A guide to published arrival records of about 500,000 passengers who came to the United States and Canada in the 17th, 18th and 19th centuries.

Eckhart G. Franz, compiler. *Hessische Truppen im amerikanischen Unabhängigkeitskrieg (HETRINA). [Hessian Troops in the American Revolution (HETRINA project)]*

Adam Giesinger. *From Catherine to Khrushchev: The Story of Russia's Germans*.

Montague S. Giuseppi. *Naturalization of Foreign Protestants in the American and West Indies Colonies*. Published by Huguenot Society of London, 1921; reprinted Baltimore: Genealogical Publishing Co., 1979. 196 pp.

> Records of 6,500 naturalizations (mostly of Germans), 1740-1722. Indexed.

Ira A. Glazier and P. William Filby. *Germans to America: Lists of Passengers Arriving at United States Ports*. Wilmington, DE: Scholarly Resources, Inc. 54 vol. covering January 1850 to mid-1887 published to date. Series is to continue through 1893.

> Information taken from the original ship manifests kept at Temple-Balch Institute for Immigration Research. Gives name, age, sex, occupation, date of arrival, and many times the former residence of each passenger. 1850-55 lists all passengers, but only on ships where at least 80% of the passengers were "German." 1856 and on includes all ships, but only passengers who called themselves Germans, including some from Switzerland, Luxembourg, and France. Includes some ships from Latin America and the Caribbean.

Franz Goldner. *Austrian Emigration, 1938 to 1945*. New York. Frederick Ungar Publishing Co. 1979. 212 pp.

Nicholas Gonner. *Luxembourgers in the New World*. Edited and translated into English by Jean Ensch, Jean-Claude Muller and Robert E. Owen. Esch-sur-Alzette, Luxembourg: Editions-Reliures Schortgen, 1889. New edition, 1987.

> Volume I contains Luxembourger emigration information between 1840-1890, Luxembourger settlements in the U.S. and aspects of the Luxembourger presence in the U.S. Volume II contains a personal and place-name index to the Luxemburger Gazette newspapers (1871-1918).

Felix Gundacker, "Research in the Former Austro-Hungarian Empire," multi-part series of articles in *Heritage Quest*, beginning in May/June 1996.

> Up-to-date information by the director of the Institut für historische Familienforschung Genealogie Gesellschaft in Vienna. Provides historical background and describes what kinds of records for what general periods are available where, and why it is difficult to get information from archives and parish offices. Based on May/June only.

Werner Hacker. *Eighteenth-Century Register of Emigrants from Southwestern Germany.* Apollo, PA: Closson Press. 516 pp.

Änder Hatz. *Emigrants et rémigrants luxembourgeois de 1876 à 1900: Etats-Unis d'Amerique, Argentine et pays extra-européens [Luxembourger Emigrants and Returnees from 1876 to 1900: The United States of America, Argentina and (Other) Non-European Countries].* Luxembourg: Archives Nationales. 1994. 232 pp.

> Contains a list of 7,135 "official emigrants" and returnees, with an alphabetical name and place index.

Joseph S. Height. *Homesteaders on the Steppe: The Odyssey of a Pioneering People.* Bismarck, ND: North Dakota Historical Society of Germans from Russia. 1975. 431 pp.

> Deals with the cultural history of Lutheran colonies near Odessa, 1804-1945.

Joseph S. Height. *Paradise on the Steppe: The Odyssey of a Pioneering People.* Bismarck, ND: North Dakota Historical Society of Germans from Russia. 1973. 411 pp.

> Deals with the cultural history of three clusters of Catholic villages near Odessa, 1804-1972.

Dirk Hoerder and Jörg Nagler, eds. *People in Transit: German Migrations in Comparative Perspective, 1829-1930.*

George Jabbour. *Settler Colonialism in Southern Africa and the Middle East.* Khartoum, University of Khartoum. 1970.

William Keel and Kurt Rein, eds. *German Emigration from Bukovina to the Americas.* Lawrence, KS: Max Kade Institute for German-American Studies, University of Kansas. 1996. 300 pp.

> Includes a chapter on genealogy and sections on Bukovina German settlements in five states, Canada and Brazil.

Miles Kinney, "American Settlement in the Prairie West," in *Saskatchewan Genealogical Society Bulletin*, Vol. 11, No. 1 (February 1980).

Thomas Koebner, et al, eds., on behalf of the Society for Exile Studies. *Das Jüdische Exil und andere Themen.* Munich: Text und Kritik. 1986.

Eugene Michel Kulischer. *Jewish Migrations: Past Experiences and Post-War Prospects.* New York, NY: The American Jewish committee. 1943.

Peter Marschalck. *Inventar der Quellen zur Geschichte der Wanderungen, besonders der Auswanderung, in Bremer Archiven. [Inventory of the Sources Related to the History of Migration and Especially Emigration Found in the Bremen Archives].* Bremen: Self-published. 1986. 879 pp. Part of series *Veröffentlichungen aus dem Staatsarchiv der Freien Hansestadt Bremen.*

Meyers Kleines Konversations-Lexikon, 7th ed. *[Meyer's Small Encyclopedia of General Information]*. 6 vols. Leipzig/Vienna: Bibliographisches Institut. 1908-09. (8th ed. 3 vols. 1931)

Victoria M. Nied, "From Mokra to the Melting Pot," in the *Journal of the American Historical Society of Germans from Russia*. Summer 1996.

Eberhard Reichmann, La Vern J. Rippley and Jörg Nagler, eds. *Emigration and Settlement Patterns of German Communities in North America.* Indianapolis: Max Kade German-American Center, Indiana University-Purdue University at Indianapolis. 1995. 380 pp.

> Includes good chapter by Donald F. Durnbaugh on "Radical Pietism as the Foundation of German-American Communitarian Settlements."

Herbert Rosenkranz. *Verfolgung und Selbstbehauptung: die Juden in Österreich, 1938-1945* [*Persecution and Self-maintenance: The Jews in Austria, 1938-1945*]. Vienna/Munich: Herold. 1978.

D. Schäfer. *Kolonialgeschichte.* [*Colonial History*]. Leipzig: G. J. Goschen. 1906. 151 pp.

Leo Schelbert. *Einführung in die Auswanderungsgeschichte in der Neuzeit.* [*Introduction to Emigration History During Modern Times*]. Zurich: Leeman. 1976. 443 pp.

Trudy Schenk, Ruth Froelke and Inge Bork. *The Wuerttemberg Emigration Index.* Salt Lake City, UT: Ancestry, Inc. 1986. 5 volumes, ongoing.

> Each volume extracts a small area of Württemberg from German emigration records. Gives name, place and date of birth and often the destination of each emigrant.

William Schroeder and Helmut T. Huebert. Mennonite *Historical Atlas.* Winnipeg: Springfield Publishers. 1990. 133 pp.

Cornelia Schrader-Muggenthaler. *The Alsace Emigration Book.* Vol. 1, 277 pp.; Vol. 2, 203 pp. Apollo, PA: Closson Press. 1989-1991.

> Vol. 1 provides detailed information, in alphabetized form, on 13,500 German and French emigrants who left Alsace in 1817-69. Vol. 2 adds over 8,000 18th and 19th century emigrants and includes a list of all villages in Upper and Lower Alsace.

Cornelia Schrader-Muggenthaler. *The Baden Emigration Book.* Apollo, PA: Closson Press. 1992. 193 pp.

> Lists emigants, including some from Alsace, found in Karlsruhe archives.

Cornelia Schrader-Muggenthaler, comp. *The Swiss Emigration Book*, Vol. 1. Apollo, PA: Closson Press. 1993. 216 pp.

> Lists 18th and 19th century emigrants who migrated from or through Switzerland to America. Vol. 1 lists ca. 7,000 emigrants, with origins in Switzerland, Germany, Italy and France, recorded in the cantons of Solothurn, Basel and Aargau.

Ari Joshua Sherman. *Island Refuge: Britain and Refugees from the Third Reich,1933-1939*, 2nd ed. Newbury Park, Ilford, England/Portland, OR: Frank Cass. 1994.

Jürgen Sielemann. "Lesser Known Records of Emigrants in the Hamburg State Archives," in *Avotaynu*, Vol. 7., No. 3.

Clifford Neal Smith. *German and Central European Emigration Monographs.*

Clifford Neal Smith. *German-American Genealogical Research Monographs.*

Clifford Neal Smith. *The Immigrant Ancestor: A Survey of Westland Monographs on Emigration from Germany, Great Britain, France, Switzerland and Eastern Europe.*

Gerald Sorin. *A Time for Building: The Third Migration, 1880-1920.* Baltimore: Johns Hopkins University Press. 1992. 306 pp.

Jacob Steigerwald. *Tracing Romania's Heterogeneous German Minority from Its Origins to the Diaspora.*

Verein für Sozialpolitik. *Schriftenreihe des Vereins für Sozialpolitik* [*Publications of the Society for Social Betterment*], Vol. 147; Part 1: *Deutsch-Ostafrika als Siedlungsgebiet für Europäer unter Berücksichtigung Britisch-Ostafrikas und Nyassalands* [*German East Africa as a Settlement Region Regarding British East Africa and Nyasaland*] (1912, 114 pp. plus map); Part 2: *Die Ansiedlung von Europäern in den Tropen* [*European Settlement in the Tropics*] (1912, 171 pp.); Part 3: *Die Ansiedlung von Europäern in den Tropen* [*European Settlement in the Tropics*] (1913, 162 pp.); Part 4: *Britisch-Kaffraria und seine deutschen Siedlungen* [*British Kaffraria and its German Settlements*] (1914, 82 pp. plus map); Part 5: *Die deutschen Kolonisten im brasilianischen Staate Espirito Santo* [*The German Colonists in the Brazilian State of Espirito Santo*] (1915, 149 pp. plus photos and maps). Munich/ Leipzig: Verlag von Duncker & Humblot.

> Part 2 covers settlement in Central America, Lesser Antilles, Dutch West Indies, Dutch East Indies. Part 3 covers settlement in Natal, Rhodesia, British East Africa and Uganda. Part 4 covers British Kaffraria, a region of the Cape Province of South Africa.

Ernst Wagner, et. al. *The Transylvanian Saxons: Historical Highlights. Cleveland: Alliance of Transylvanian Saxons.* 1982.

> History and maps pertaining to the Transylvanian Saxons in Europe and North America.

Mack Walker. *Germany and the Emigration, 1816-1885.* Cambridge, MA: Harvard University Press. 1964. 284 pp.

Wilhelm Winkler. *Statistisches Handbuch des gesamten Deutschtums.* [*Statistical Handbook for Germans Throughout the World*]. Berlin: Verlag Deutsche Rundschau G.m.b.H. 1927. 704 pp.

Jan Steven Zaleski. *Guide to Records of Border Crossings between the United States and Canada, 1895-1954.* Detroit: Author. 1993. 39 pp.

> Valuable because of the extensiveness of people either migrating from one country to the other, or landing at a port in one country, but with the other country as their destination. Concentrates mostly on crossings from Canada to the United States at St. Albans, Vermont.

UNITED STATES

Willi Paul Adams. *Die deutschsprachige Auswanderung in die Vereinigten Staaten: Berichte über Forschungsstand und Quellenbestände.* [*Emigration of German-Speakers to the United States: Report on Research and Sources*]. Berlin: John F. Kennedy Institut für Nordamerikastudien, Freie Universität Berlin. 1980. 235 pp.

James Paul Allen and Eugene James Turner. *We the People: An Atlas of America's Ethnic Diversity.* New York: Macmillan Publishing Co. 1988. 315 pp., maps, indexes, 11-pg. bibl.

> Huge atlas. Could be considered geographic counterpart to the history in the *Harvard Encyclopedia of America's Ethnic Groups.*

Bernard Bailyn. *From Protestant Peasants to Jewish Intellectuals: The Germans in the Peopling of America: Causes and Consequences of the German Catastrophe.* Heinrich August Winkler. Oxford ; New York: Berg, for the German Historical Institute,1988.

Avraham Barkai. *Branching Out: German-Jewish Immigration to the United States, 1820-1914.* New York: Holmes & Meier. 1994.

Reinhard Bendix. *From Berlin to Berkeley: German-Jewish Identities.* New Brunswick, NJ: Transaction Books. 1986.

Lucy Forney Bittinger. *The Germans in Colonial Times.* 1901. Reprinted by Heritage Books, Bowie, MD. 314 pp.

> Covers reasons for emigrating and lists most, if not all, colonial German settlements in the United States.

Annette K. Burgert, "Are Your Pennsylvania Dutch Ancestors Really Swiss?" and "Selected Bibliography for Swiss Research in German and French Territories," in *The German Connection* (1st quarter 1995).

Annette Kunselman Burgert. *18th Century Emigrants from German-Speaking Lands to North America*. Camden, ME: Picton Press.

    Vol. I: *The Northern Kraichgau* [area south of Heidelberg]. 1983. 485 pp.

    Vol. II: *The Western Palatinate*. 1985. 421 pp.

    Vol. III: *The Northern Alsace*. 1992. 714 pp.

    One of the classics on Pennsylvania German research by a leading expert on colonial-era immigration. Originally published by the Pennsylvania German Society in its *Proceedings*.

Bruce E. Burgoyne. *Waldeck (Germany) Soldiers of the American Revolutionary War*. Bowie, MD: Heritage Books. 1991. 182 pp.

    Contains brief biographies of every man who served in the 3rd British Waldeck Regiment, including date and place of birth, and who remained in America.

Eugene Camann. *Uprooted from Prussia—Transplanted in America*. Niagara Falls, NY: Self-published. 1992. 140 pp.

    Lists names and details about 800 "Old Lutherans" from the Uckermark who settled in Wheatfield, New York, in 1843.

Sanford Hoadley Cobb. *The Story of the Palatines: An Episode in Colonial History*. New York & London: G. P. Putnam's Sons. 1897. 319 pp. maps. Reprinted Bowie, MD: Heritage Books. 1988. 319 pp. maps.

    Covers Palatine communities along the Rhine River and migration in the early 1700s to the Carolinas, Virginia, New Jersey, Pennsylvania, and New York, with emphasis on New York.

Maurice Rea Davie. *The Refugees are Now Americans*. New York: Public Affairs Committee, Inc. 1945.

Frank Ried Diffenderffer. *The German Immigration into Pennsylvania Through the Port of Philadelphia, from 1700 to 1775, and the Redemptioners*. Lancaster, PA: Author. 1900. Reprinted Baltimore: Genealogical Publishing Co. 1988. 330 pp.

    Covers the background of colonial German, especially Palatine, immigration.

Ellen Eisenberg. *Jewish Agricultural Colonies in New Jersey, 1882-1920*. Syracuse, NY: Syracuse University Press. 1995.

Irmgard Hein Ellingson. *The Bukovina Germans in Kansas: A 200-Year History of the Lutheran Swabians*. Hays, KS: Fort Hays State University Ethnic Heritage Studies. 1987; reprinted 1993. 107 pp.

    Summarizes the history of German Lutheran settlement in the Bukovina and immigration to Kansas.

H. Frank Eschleman. *Swiss and German Pioneers of Southeast Pennsylvania*. 1919. Reprinted Baltimore: Clearfield Co. 1991. 338 pp.

    Devotes considerable attention to Mennonites, with other information about flight of Schenkfelders and Waldensians, including their history and emigration. Very detailed information, but also numerous historical inaccuracies.

Albert Bernhardt Faust. *The German Element in the United States, With Special Reference to its Political, Moral, Social, and Educational Influence*. 2 vols. New York: The Steuben Society of America (Kingsport, TN: Kingsport Press). 1927. Reprinted Baltimore: Clearfield Co. 1995. 605 and 730 pp.

    This is the classic work on German-Americans, with a long detailed bibliography and index. Vol. 1 covers immigration and early settlement.

Albert B. Faust and Gaius M. Brumbaugh. *List of Swiss Emigrants in the Eighteenth Century to the American Colonies*. 2 vols. in 1; reprint of 1920-25 work with corrections from the *National Genealogical Society Quarterly* (March 1972). Baltimore: Genealogical Publishing Co. 1991. 429 pp.

    Indexed, authoritative work on immigrants from the canton of Zürich (1734-1744) in Vol. I, and of Berne (1706-1795) and Basel (1734-1794) in Vol. II.

Gerhard Florey. *Geschichte der Salzburger Protestanten und ihre Emigration 1731/32.* [*History of the Salzburg Protestants and Their Emigration in 1731-32*]. Vienna, Cologne, Graz. 1977, 2nd ed. 1986.

Robert W. Frizzell. "Reticent Germans: The East Frisians of Illinois," in *Illinois Historical Journal*, Vol. 85 (Autumn 1992), pp. 161-174.

Howard B. Furer. *The Germans in America, 1607-1970.* Dobbs Ferry, NY: Oceana Publications. 1973.

German-Bohemian Heritage Society Newsletter. June 1994.

Ira A. Glazier, ed. *Migration from the Russian Empire.* Baltimore: Genealogical Publishing Co. Vol. 1 (703 pp.) and Vol. 2 (631 pp.). 1995. Ongoing series.
> Volumes published to date cover the period from January 1875-April 1886. The majority of emigrants were Jews or Germans.

Arthur A. Goren *The American Jews.* Cambridge, MA: Belknap Press of Harvard University Press. 1982.

B. Gornberg *On Jews, America, and Immigration: A Socialist Perspective*, translated and edited by Uri D. Herscher and Stanley F. Chyet. Cincinnati: American Jewish Archives. 1980.

Charles R. Haller. *Across the Atlantic and Beyond: The Migration of German and Swiss Immigrants to America.* Bowie, MD: Heritage Books. 1993. 324 pp.
> Deals with changes of personal and place names, reasons for emigration, number and period (mostly 1727-1775) of colonial immigrants, the postwar whereabouts of Revolutionary War German conscripts, the rise of Protestantism, and quadripartite dialectic divisions, with maps of the Rhine valley, from where most early immigrants came.

Uri D. Herscher, ed. *The East European Jewish experience in America: a century of memories, 1882-1982.* Cincinnati: American Jewish Archives. 1983.

John Higham. *Send These to Me: Jews and Other Immigrants in Urban America.* New York: Atheneum. 1975.

Edward W. Hocker. *Genealogical Data Relating to the German Settlers of Pennsylvania and Adjacent Territory: From Advertisements in Newspapers Published in Philadelphia and Germantown, 1743-1800.* Baltimore: Genealogical Publishing Co. 1989. 242 pp.

Klaus Hodl. *Vom Shtetl an die Lower East Side: galizische Juden in New York.* Vienna: Böhlau. 1991. 305 pp. Maps.

June Drenning Holmquist, ed. *They chose Minnesota: A Survey of the State's Ethnic Groups.* St. Paul: Minnesota Historical Society Press. 1991. 614 pp.
> Includes chapters on Germans (Hildegard Binder Johnson), Swiss (Louis de Gruyter), and Jews (Hyman Berman).

Edmund J. James, Oscar R.Flynn, J. R. Paulding, Mrs. Simon N. Patton (Charlotte Kimball) and Walter Scott Andrews. *The Immigrant Jew in America.* Issued by the Liberal immigration league, New York. New York: B. F. Buck & company. 1906.

Norbert Jansen. *Nach Amerika! Geschichte der liechtensteinischen Auswanderung nach den Vereinigten Staaten von Amerika.* [*To America! History of Emigration from Liechtenstein to the United States of America*]. Vaduz: Verlag des Historischen Vereins für das Fürstentum Liechtenstein. 1976.

Henry Z. Jones, Jr. *The Palatine Families of New York.* Camden, ME: Picton Press. 2 vols. 1985. 1,298 pp.
> Lists original Palatine families who came to New York state about 1710.

Henry Z. Jones, Jr. *More Palatine Families: Some Immigrants to the Middle Colonies, 1777-1776*. Universal City, CA: privately published. 1991. 592 pp.

> Majority of names listed are those who went to New Jersey. Every-name index.

Samuel Joseph. *Jewish Immigration to the United States from 1881 to 1910*. New York: Arno Press. 1914. 1969.

Abraham J. Karp *Golden Door to America: The Jewish Immigrant Experience*. Harmondsworth, England/New York: Penguin Books. 1977.

Walter A. Knittle. *Early Eighteenth Century Palatine Emigration*.

> Indexed list of about 12,000 Palatine immigrants to Pennsylvania, North Carolina and New York.

Ruth Maria Kotzian. *The Emigration of Bukovina-Germans to the United States of America (1880-1914)*. Augsburg: Author. 1993. 21 pp.

> A well-written senior honors paper by a Gymnasium graduate.

Margrit B. Krewson. *The German-Speaking Countries of Europe: A Selective Bibliography*, 2nd ed. Washington, DC: Library of Congress. 1989. 318 pp.

> A highly diverse sampling of books in the Library of Congress, including many dealing with genealogy and migration history. For sale by Supt. of Docs., U.S. Govt. Printing Office.

Margrit B. Krewson. *Hidden Research Resource in the German Collections of the Library of Congress*. Washington, DC: Library of Congress. 1992. 170 pp.

> A selective bibliography of reference works in the German collection at the Library of Congress. For sale by Supt. of Docs., U.S. Govt. Printing Office.

Oscar Kuhns. *The German and Swiss Settlements of Colonial Pennsylvania: A Study of the So-called Pennsylvania Dutch*. 1901. Reprinted by Heritage Books, Bowie, MD. 268 pp.

> Lists colonial German settlements and German surnames, with information about their origins, meanings and English equivalents.

Kate Everest Levi. *Geographical Origin of German Immigration to Wisconsin*. Originally published in *Collections of the State Historical Society of Wisconsin*, 1898. Reprinted Minneapolis: Edward R. Brandt. 1992. 28 pp.

> Detailed account of areas of origin of Germans who settled in various counties of Wisconsin.

Elaine Maas. *The Jews of Houston: An Ethnographic Study*. New York: AMS Press. 1989.

Jacob Rader Marcus, ed. *The Jew in the American World: A Source Book*. Detroit, MI: Wayne State University Press. 1996.

Bernard Marinbach. *Galveston, Ellis Island of the West*. Albany: State University of New York Press. 1983.

Milton Meltzer. *Taking Root: Jewish Immigrants in America*. New York: Farrar, Straus, and Giroux. 1976.

Ken Meter and Robert Paulson. *The Böhmisch (German-Bohemians) in America*. Minneapolis: Crossroads Resource Center, with the German-Bohemian Heritage Society, New Ulm. 1993. 32 pp.

> Packed with surnames of German immigrants from southwestern Bohemia to Wisconsin, Minnesota and Michigan's Upper peninsula.

Olga K. Miller. *Migration, Emigration, Immigration: Principally to the United States and in the United States*.

Jacob Ornstein-Galicia. *Jewish Farmer in America: The Unknown Chronicle*. Lewiston: Edwin Mellen Press. 1992.

Margaret Krug Palen. *Genealogical Guide to Tracing Ancestors in Germany*. Bowie, MD: Heritage Books. 1995. 159 pp.

> General guide on research in the United States and Germany, including what kinds of records are available in Germany, where to find them and how to access them.

Brian A. Podoll. *Prussian Netzelanders and Other German Immigrants in Green Lake, Marquette & Waushara Counties, Wisconsin*. Bowie, MD: Heritage Books. 1994. 241 pp.

> Primarily marriage, naturalization and death records of Germans in these counties. Brief history of the Netze River area. Maps of various counties in Posen, Pomerania, West Prussia and the Neumark (Northeast Brandenburg), as well as in Wisconsin (and Minnesota, to which the Netzelanders went).

George Rath. *The Black Sea Germans in the Dakotas*. Freeman, SD: Pine Hill Press. 1977. 435 pp.

Hertha Herzog. *Heimat auf den Laurenziberg*. [*The Homeland at Laurenziberg*]. 1992.

Eberhard Reichman, La Vern J. Rippley, and Jörg Nagler, eds. *Emigration and Settlement Patterns of German Communities in North America*. Indianapolis: Max Kade Center for German-American Studies. 1995. 380 pp.

La Vern J. Rippley. *The German-Americans*. Lanham, MD: University Press of America. 1984. 271 pp.

La Vern J. Rippley and Robert J. Paulson. *The German-Bohemians: The Quiet Immigrants*. New Ulm, MN: German-Bohemian Society. 1995. 246 pp.

> History of German-Bohemian immigration to southern Minnesota in the 1800s.

Israel Daniel Rupp. *A Collection of Upwards of 30,000 Names of German, Swiss, Dutch, French and Other Immigrants into Pennsylvania, 1727-1776*. Leipzig, 3rd ed., 1931. 2nd (English) rev. ed., with an index by Ernst Wecken from the Third Edition (1931) and added index to ships. Baltimore, MD: Genealogical Publishing Co. 1994. 583 pp.

> Passenger lists from 319 ships, giving name of ship and its origin arranged by date of arrival. Also included is a list of over 1,000 settlers who came to Pennsylvania from other states. Index to ships and surname index. Separately published index by Marvin Vastine Koger: *Index to the names of 30,000 Immigrants — German, Swiss, Dutch and French — into Pennsylvania, 1727-1776, Supplementing the I. Daniel Rupp, Ship Load Volume*, Pennington Gap, VA, 1935, 232 pp.

Richard Sallet. *Russian-German Settlements in the United States*. Translated by La Vern J. Rippley and Armand Bauer. Fargo: North Dakota Institute for Regional Studies. 1974. 207 pp. plus map.

Leo Schelbert. *Swiss Migration to America: the Swiss Mennonites*. New York: Arno Press. 1980. (German version: 1976. 443 pp.)

George Schnucker, tr. by Kenneth DeWall. *The East Friesens in Maerica: An Illustrated History of Their Colonies to the Present Time*. Originally published in German in 1917. Cleveland: Central Publishing House. Translation 1986, Topeka, KS: Jostens Printing and Publishing.

Karin Schulz, ed. *Hoffnung Amerika: Europäische Auswanderung in die Neu Welt*. [*The Hope of America: European Emigration to the New World*] Bremerhaven Nordwestdeutsche Verlaggesellschaft. 1944. 293 pp.

> Deals with emigration from Germany and Eastern Europe through German ports. Heavy emphasis on Jewish migration to the United States.

Herrmann Schuricht. *The German Element in Virginia*. Originally published in 1898-1900; reprinted by the Clearfield Co., 1989. 2 vols. in 1. 1,433 pp.

> Examines early German settlements in a number of counties and the eventual concentration of Germans in the Shenandoah valley.

Clifford Neal Smith. *Passenger Lists (and Fragments Thereof) from Hamburg and Bremen to Australia and the United States, 1846-49.* McNeal, AZ: Westland Publications. 1988. 27 pp. German-American Research Monograph Number 23.

Clifford Neal Smith and Anna Piszczan-Czaja Smith. *American Genealogical Resources in German Archives (AGRIGA): A Handbook.* New York, NY: R. R. Bowker Co. 1977. 336 pp.
> Has lists arranged alphabetically by village and individuals; also court records, emigration records, and other documents. Includes a bibliography of published emigration lists in German with English titles in brackets.

Gerald Sorin. *The Prophetic Minority: American Jewish Immigrant Radicals, 1880-1920.* Bloomington: Indiana University Press. 1985.

John M. Spalek. *Guide to the Archival Materials of the German-Speaking Emigration to the United States After 1933.* Charlottesville, VA: University Press for the Bibliographical Society of the University of Virginia. 1978. 1,133 pp.

Ralph B. Strassburger and William J. Hinke. *Pennsylvania German Pioneers, 1727-1808.* 3 volumes. Pennsylvania German Society, Norristown, PA. Baltimore, MD: Genealogical Publishing Co., Inc. 1934. Map. Reprinted in 2 volumes, 1966 and 1980.
> Has all of the original lists of early Germans coming to the port of Philadelphia from 1727-1808. Includes 29,837 names in the index.

Herbert A. Strauss, ed. *Jewish Immigrants of the Nazi Period in the USA.* New York: K. G. Saur. 1978.

Philip Strobel. *The Salzburgers and Their Descendants.* Athens, GA. Reprinted 1953. 309-318 pp. plus illus.

Stephan Thernstrom, ed. *Harvard Encyclopedia of American Ethnic Groups.* Cambridge: MA: Belknap Press. 1980. 1,076 pp.
> Broad coverage. One of the few books dealing explicitly with Austrian immigration.

Ernest Thode. *Atlas for Germanic Genealogy.*

Don Heinrich Tolzmann, ed. *The German-American Soldier in the Wars of the United States: J. G. Rosengarten's History.* 1890. Reprinted by Heritage Books, Bowie, MD, in 1996. 347 pp.
> Updated to cover the period from the Revolutionary War through the Gulf War.

Don Heinrich Tolzmann. *German-Americana in Europe: Two Guides to American History in the German, Austrian and Swiss Archives.* Bowie, MD: Heritage Books. 1997. 683 pp.
> Reprint of Dexter Learned Hand's *Guide to Manuscript Materials Relating to American History in the German State Archives* (1912) and Albert Bernhardt Faust's *Guide to the Materials for American History in the Swiss and Austrian Archives* (1916), with indexes. Very useful for immigration research. Arranged geographically.

Don Heinrich Tolzmann, ed. *The German Element in Virginia: Herrmann Schuricht's History.* Original published in 1898; edited, expanded reprint: Bowie, MD: Heritage Books. 1992. 426 pp.
> Documents the history of Germans in Virginia, 1607-1898.

Don Heinrich Tolzmann. *German Immigration in America: The First Wave.* Bowie, MD: Heritage Books. 1993. 352 pp.
> Focuses on reasons for the first German wave of emigration to North America, beginning in 1708. Uses *The German Exodus to England in 1709* by Frank Ried Diffenderffer and *The German Emigration to America, 1709-1740* by Henry E. Jacobs.

Don Heinrich Tolzmann, ed. *John Andrew Russell's History of the German Influence in the Making of Michigan.* 1927. Reprinted: Bowie, MD: Heritage Books, Inc. 1995. 415 pp.
> The key book for researching Germanic ancestors in Michigan, where 29% of the population was Germanic in 1927.

Don Heinrich Tolzmann, ed. *Maryland's German Heritage: Daniel Wunderlich Nead's History*. 1913. Reprinted by Heritage Books, Bowie, MD. 304 pp.
> Standard text on the history of the Germans in Maryland and their close relationship with those in Pennsylvania.

Don Heinrich Tolzmann. *Ohio Valley Biographical Index*. Bowie, MD: Heritage Books. 1992. 78 pp.
> Alphabetical index of 3,754 names of German settlers in the tri-state Greater Cincinnati area, including some who migrated onward to other states, e.g., Iowa and Minnesota.

John Tribbeko and George Ruperti. *Lists of Germans from the Palatinate Who Came to England in 1709*. Baltimore: Clearfield Co. 1965; reprinted 1994. 44 pp.
> Detailed information on nearly 2,000 families, most of whom continued on to America, found in the British Museum and the *New York Genealogical and Biographical Record*.

Maralyn A. Wellauer. *German Immigration to America in the Nineteenth Century: A Genealogist's Guide*. Milwaukee: Roots International. 1985. 87 pp.

Oren Windholz. *Bohemian Germans in Kansas: A Catholic Community from Bukovina*. Hays, KS: author. 1993. 50 pp.
> Illustrated history of the migration of Germans from the Bohemian Forest to the Bukovina and America.

Don Yoder, ed. *Pennsylvania German Immigrants, 1709-1786: Lists Consolidated from Yearbooks of the Pennsylvania German Folklore Society*. Baltimore: Genealogical Publishing Co. 1984, 1989. 394 pp.

Gary J. Zimmerman and Marion Wolfert. *German Immigrants: Lists of Passengers Bound from Bremen to New York, with Places of Origin*.

CANADA

Irving M. Abella, and Harold Troper. *None is Too Many: Canada and the Jews of Europe, 1933-1948*. Toronto: L. & O. Dennys. 1982.

Kenneth G. Aitken, "When Our West Moved North: Canadian Border Entry Records for Great Plains Emigrants," in *Minnesota Genealogist*, Vol. 26, No. 3 (September 1995).

Angus Baxter. *In Search of Your Canadian Roots*. Baltimore, MD: Genealogical Publishing Co. 1994. 350 pp.

Michael G. Brown. *Jew or Juif? Jews, French Canadians, and Anglo-Canadians, 1759-1914*. Philadelphia: Jewish Publication Society. 1987, 1986.

Robert J. Brym, William Shaffir and Morton Weinfeld, eds. *The Jews in Canada*. Don Mills, ON: Oxford University Press. 1993.

Raymond Arthur Davies. *Printed Jewish Canadiana, 1685-1900; tentative check list of books, pamphlets, pictures, magazine and newspaper articles and currency*. Montreal: L. Davies. 1955.

Richard Hordern, ed./tr. *St. John's Evangelical Lutheran Church, 1890-1990*. Balgonie, SK: St. John's Lutheran Church, c/o Barbara Siebert. 1990. 138 pp.
> Translates the the parish registers of 1890-1927, as well as records of the work of early pastors in the districts of Assiniboia and Saskatchewan (Northwest Territories), later the province of Saskatchewan.

Eric Jonasson. *A Canadian Genealogical Handbook*. Winnipeg, Manitoba: Wheatfield Press. 1978. 352 pp.

Heinz Lehmann. *The German Canadians*, 1750-1937.

Terrence Punch. *Genealogical Research in Nova Scotia*. Halifax. 1978.
> Includes ten of the twelve relevant passenger lists.

George Elmore Reaman. *The Trail of the Black Walnut*. Baltimore: Genealogical Publishing Co. 1957, 1993. 288 pp.

> Describes the role of Pennsylvania Germans, as well as Huguenots and Quakers, in the settlement of Ontario in the late eighteenth century.

G. Elmore Reaman. *The Trail of the Huguenots in Europe, the United States, South Africa and Canada*. Baltimore: Genealogical Publishing Co. 1963; reprinted 1993. 318 pp.

> Indexed record of Huguenots who left France after 1685, many of them going to Germany, from where many of their descendants migrated to North America.

S. B. Rohold. *The Jews in Canada*, 2nd ed. Toronto: Board of Home Missions, Presbyterian Church in Canada. 1913.

Louis Rosenberg. *Canada's Jews*. Montreal: Bureau of Social and Economic Research, Canadian Jewish Congress. 1939.

Louis Rosenberg. *The Jewish Community in Canada, 1931-1961*. Montreal: Bureau of Social and Economic Research, Canadian Jewish Congress. 1965.

Stuart E. Rosenberg *The Jewish Community in Canada*. Toronto: McClelland and Stewart. 1970.

Benjamin Gutelius Sack. *History of the Jews in Canada, from the Earliest Beginnings to the Present Day*. Montreal: Canadian Jewish Congress. 1945.

LATIN AMERICA

Haim Avni. *Mexico — Immigration and Refuge*. Washington, DC: Latin American Program, Woodrow Wilson International Center for Scholars. 1989.

Ayrton Gonçalves Celestino. *Die Bukowiner von Rio Negro und Mafra, in Brasilien*. [*The Bukoviners of Rio Negro and Mafra, in Brazil*].

Liga Chileno-Alemana, comp. *Los Alemanes en Chile en su primer centenario: resumen histórior de la colonización alemana de las provincias del sur Chile*. [*The Germans in Chile on Their First Centennial: Historical Summary of the German Colonization of the Southern Provinces of Chile*]. Santiago: Liga Chilano Alemana. 1950. 207 pp. Reprinted 1978.

Armin Clasen. "Deutsche Auswanderung nach Chile: 1850-52; 1853-56; 1857-1875" ["German Emigration to Chile: 1850-52; 1853-56; 1857-1875"], in *Niedersächsische Familienkunde*. Mar. 1957-Jan. 1959.

Alfred Funke. *Die Besiedlung des östlichen Südamerika mit besonderer Berücksichtigung des Deutschtums*. [*The Colonization of Eastern South America with Particular Attention to the Germans*]. Inaugural doctoral dissertation at Friedrich-Wilhelms Universität Halle-Wittenburg. Printed by Gebauer Schwetschke, Druckerei und Verlag m.b.H., Halle a.S., 1902. 48 pp.

Fred Heller. *Das Leben Beginnt noch Einmal, Schicksale der Emigration* [*Life Begins Again, The Fate of the Emigrants*]. Buenos Aires: Editorial Cosmopolita, Freier deutscher Buchverlag. 1945.

J. Christian Heusser. *Die Schweizer auf den Kolonien in St. Paulo in Brasilien*. [*The Swiss in the Colonies in Sao Paulo, Brazil*].

Georg Hiller. *Einwanderung und Kolonisation in Argentinien* [*Immigration and Colonization in Argentina*], Vol. 1: *Einwanderung und Einwanderungspolitik*. [*Immigration and Immigration Policy*]. Berlin: Dietrich Reimer (Ernst Vohsen) Verlagsbuchhandlung. 1912. 155 pp.

Hundert Jahre Deutschtum in Rio Grande do Sulm 1824-1924 [*One Hundred Years of German Culture in Rio Grande do Sul, 1824-1924*]. Porto Alegre: Verband deutscher Vereine. 1924. 568 pp.

Preston E. James. *Brazil*. New York: Odyssey Press. 1942, 1946. 262 pp.

Journal of the AHSGR. Winter 1978. Fall 1984.

K. Kaerger. *Landwirtschaft und Kolonisation im Spanischen Amerika* [*Agriculture and Colonization in Spanish America*], Vol. 1: *Die La Plata Staaten*. [*The States of La Plata*]. 2 vols. Leipzig: Dunker und Humbolt. 1907. (also on microfilm)

Hanzheinz Keller. *Neuer Beitrag zur Auswanderungsgeschichte unter besonderer Berücksichtigung der Gründung von Petropolis bei Rio de Janeiro*. [*New Contribution to Emigration History with Particular Regard to the Establishment of Petropolis near Rio de Janeiro*]. 1963.

Gerhard S. Koop. *Pioneer Years in Belize*. Translation by author of *Pionier Jahre in Britisch Honduras*. Belize City: author, 1991. 133 pp.

Irene Enns Kroeker. "Immigration (Paraguay)," in *Preservings*. No. 4, July 1994. Steinbach, Manitoba, Canada: Hanover/Steinbach Historical Society, Inc. Steinbach, MB, Canada K0A 2A0.

Hugo Kung. *Chile und die deutschen Colonien*. [*Chile and the German Colonies*]. Leipzig: Klinkhardt. 1891. 633 pp.

Henry Lange. *Süd-Brasilien*. [*South Brazil*]. Leipzig. 1886.

Jeff Lesser. *Welcoming the Undesirables: Brazil and the Jewish Question*. Berkeley: University of California Press. 1995.

Wilhelm Lütge, Werner Hoffmann and Karl Wilhelm Körner. *Geschichte des Deutschtums in Argentinien*. [*History of the Germans in Argentina*]. Buenos Aires: Deutscher Klub. 1955. 385 pp.

Michael George Mulhall. *Rio Grande do Sul and its German colonies*. London: Longmans, Green. 1873. 202 pp.

Peter Pauls, Jr. *Urwaldpioniere: persönliche Erlebnisse mennonitischer Siedler aus den ersten Jahren am Krauel und von Stolzplateau, S.C.* [*Jungle Pioneers: Personal Experiences of Mennonite Settlers in the Early Years on the Krauel and from the Stolzplateau, Santa Catarina*]. Published on behalf of the Festkommission der Jubiläumsfeier. Witmarsum. 1980.

Pomerode: sua história, sua cultura, suas tradições [*Pomerode: Its History, Its Culture, Its Traditions*], *Historical Series*, Volume 5. Pomerode, SC, Brazil: Prefeitura Municipal de Pomerode/Fundação Cultural de Pomerode. 1991. 60 pp.

Harry Leonard Sawatzky. *They Sought a Country: Mennonite Colonization in Mexico*. Berkeley: University of California Press. 1971.
     Includes a chapter on migration to Belize.

Ignatz Schelbauer. "Manuskripte eines der Pioniere" ["Manuscript of One of the Pioneers"].

Walter Schmiedehaus. *Die Altkolonier-Mennoniten in Mexico*. [*The Old Colonial Mennonites in Mexico*]. Winnipeg: CMBC Publications. 1982. 216 pp.

Ferdinand Schröder. *Die deutsche Einwanderung nach Süd-Brasilien bis zum Jahr 1859*. [*German Immigration to South Brazil up to the Year 1859*]. Berlin: Verlag ev. Hauptverein für deutsche Ansiedler und Auswanderer. 1931. 131 pp.

Fritz Sudhaus. *Deutschland und die Auswanderung nach Brazilien im 19. Jahrhundert*. [*Germany and the Emigration to Brazil in the 19th Century*]. Hamburg: J. Christians. 1940. 192 pp.

Johann Wappäus. *Handbuch der Geographie und Statistik des Kaiserreichs Brasilien*. [*Handbook of Geography and Statistics of the Brazilian Empire*]. Leipzig. 1871.

Carol Wardale and Margaret Jenner, comps. *German Research Directory*. 7th ed. Stones Corner: German Research Group, Genealogical Society of Queensland. 1988.

George F. W. Young. *Germans in Chile: Immigration and Colonization, 1849-1914*. New York: Center for Migration Studies. 1974. 234 pp.

Gordon Young. *Early Barossa Settlements, South Australia*. Adelaide: Australia Techsearch. 1978. 78 pp.

ASIA

Virginia Less. "The Story of the Harbin, China, Refugees," in *Wandering Volhynians*. Vol. 8, No. 3 (September 1995).

James Rodman Ross. *Escape to Shanghai: A Jewish Community in China*. New York: Free Press; Toronto: Maxwell Macmillan Canada; New York: Maxwell Macmillan International. 1994.

SOUTHWEST PACIFIC

James N. Bade, ed. *The German Connection: New Zealand and German-speaking Europe in the Nineteenth Century*. Auckland/Melbourne/New York/Toronto: Oxford University Press. 1993. 259 pp.

Michael Blakeney. *Australia and the Jewish Refugees, 1933-1948*. Sydney, NSW: Croom Helm Australia. 1985.

W. D. Borrie, assisted by D. R. G. Packer. *Italians and Germans in Australia: A Study of Assimilation*. Melbourne: F. W. Cheshire for The Australian National University. 1954. 236 pp.

A. H. Chote. *German Community in Western Australia*. Typescript in Battye Library, Perth. 1973.

Patricia Cloos and Jürgen Tampke. *Greetings from the Land Where Milk and Honey Flow: The German Immigration to New South Wales, 1838-1858*. Canberra: South Highland Publishers. 1993. 216 pp.

Harvey A. Cohen and Beverley Davis, comps. *A Guide to the Jewish Genealogical Records of Australia and New Zealand*. Melbourne: Australian Jewish Historical Society (Victoria). 1988. 9 pp.

> Includes bibliography of books, periodicals and congregational histories for Australian Jewish history.

Gerald. K. Conolly. *Die Einwanderung in der Geschichte Australiens, 1788-1903, unter besonderer Berücksichtigung des österreichischen Anteils*. [*Emigration in the History of Australia, 1788-1903, with Special Attention to the Austrian Portion*]. Vienna: Doctoral dissertation. 1955.

Europa Kurier Printing, Ltd. (ed.) *200 Jahre Geschichte der deutschsprachigen Gemeinschaft in Australien, 1788-1988*. [*200-Year History of the German-speaking Community in Australia, 1788-1988*]. Sydney: Europa Kurier. 1988.

Lester Firth and Murton Ptg, Ltd. *Barossa Valley Heritage Study*. Adelaide: Lutheran Publishing House. 1981. 163 pp.

John Foster. *Community of Fate: Memoirs of German Jews in Melbourne*. Sydney: Allen and Unwin. 1986. 174 pp.

Miriam Gilson and Jerzy Zubrzycki. *The Foreign Language Press in Australia, 1848-1964*. Canberra: Australian National University. 1967. 233 pp.

Goethe Institut. *The German Network in Australia*. Melbourne: Contemporary Press. 1992.

Max Gordon. *Jews in Van Diemen's Land*. Melbourne: Ponsford Newsman & Benson. 1965.

Ian Harmstorf and Michael Cigler. *The Germans in Australia*. Melbourne: AE Press. 1985. 182 pp.

> Volume in the *Australian Ethnic Heritage Series*. Identifies many German settlements. Strongest on South Australia. Bibliography includes publications on Germans in various specific areas of Australia.

Walter Krauss. *Austria to Australia: The Autobiography of an Austrian Jew from Birth to Emigration, 1904-1938*. Melbourne: University of Melbourne Politics Monograph. 1983. 125 pp.

Augustin Lodewyckx. *Die Deutschen in Australien*. [*Germans in Australia*]. Stuttgart: Ausland und Heimat Verlag. 1932. 272 pp.

J. Lyng. *Non-Britishers in Australia: Influence on Population and Progress*. Melbourne: Macmillan & Co. with Melbourne University Press. 1927. 242 pp.

Mary Mennicken-Cooley. *The Germans in Western Australia: Innovators, Immigrants, Internees*. Mt. Lawley, Western Australia: Edith Cowan University. 1993. 156 pp.

> Extensive research based on the national and state Australian Archives, reports of the Australian Bureau of Statistics, the Censuses of the Commonwealth of Australia for various years, publications of the Australian Department of Immigration, Local Government and Ethnic Affairs, newspapers, libraries, church records, and books.

Marlene J. Norst and Johanna McBride. *Austrians and Australia*. Potts Point, NSW, Australia: Athena Press. 1988. 207 pp. plus map.

> Devotes considerable attention to prominent Austrians who settled in Australia or were connected with it in other ways. But there is also good coverage of Austrian immigrants, with the first major wave during the 1930s and the second and larger one after World War II.

C. A. Price. *German Settlers in South Australia*. London: Melbourne University Press. 1945.

Charles Archibald Price, assisted by Lilian Wilson and Elizabeth Tyler. *Jewish Settlers in Australia*. Canberra, ACT: Australian National University. 1964.

Odeda Rosenthal. *Not Strictly Kosher: Pioneer Jews in New Zealand*. Wainscott, NY: Starchand Press. 1988.

Hilary L. Rubinstein. *Chosen: the Jews in Australia*. Sydney/Boston: Allen & Unwin. 1987.

Hilary L. Rubinstein. *The Jews in Victoria, 1835-1985*, with an appendix by W.D. Rubinstein. Sydney/Boston: Allen & Unwin. 1986.

Paul Sauer. *The Holy Land Called*. Melbourne: Templer Society. 1991. 368 pp.

> Focuses on the Templers who migrated directly from Germany to Palestine, with minimal attention to those of Russian Mennonite origin.

Isaac Nachman Steinberg. *Australia, the Unpromised Land: In Search of a Home*. London: V. Gollancz. 1948.

Jürgen Tampke and Colin Doxford. *Australia Willkommen: A History of the Germans in Australia*. Kensington, NSW: New South Wales University Press. 1990. 282 pp.

Berend von Tiesenhausen. *Deutsche in Australien*. [*Germans in Australia*]. Leipzig: Lahe & Co. 1938. 42 pp.

Liz Twigden. Letter of July 16, 1994. Torrensville, SA.

Josef Vondra. *German Speaking Settlers in Australia*. Melbourne: Cavalier Press Ptg. Ltd. 1981. 286 pp. plus 2 maps.

> Deals with all aspects of German-Australians, including some attention to Swiss and Austrians. Stresses post-1945 immigration and prominent individuals and organizations. Strongest on the Melbourne area. Excellent coverage of the history and migration of Templers who went directly from Germany to Palestine, but no mention of those of Russian Mennonite origin.

Susanne Wegmann. *The Swiss in Australia*. Grüsch, Switzerland: Verlag Rüegger. 1989. 144 pp.

AFRICA

Ken V. André. *1720-1990: Some Aspects of German Immigration to the Eastern Cape.*

Albert F. Calvert. *German East Africa*. Originally, London: T. Werner Laurie, Ltd., 1917. Reprinted, New York: Negro Universities Press. 1970. 122 pp. plus photos, diagrams and maps.

H. T. Colenbringer. "De Afkomst der Boeren." Het Nederlandsche Verbond.

T. R. H. Davenport, *South Africa: A History*. London: Macmillan. South Africa: A Modern Hx. Toronto & Buffalo: University of Toronto Press. 1977. 432 pp.

Donald Denoon with Balan Nyeko and the advice of J. B. Webster. *Southern Africa Since 1900*. New York: Praeger Publishers. 1973. 242 pp.

Ran Greenstein. *Genealogies of Conflict: Class, Identity, and State in Palestine/Israel and South Africa*. Hanover, NH: Wesleyan University Press, published by University Press of New England. 1995.

Joseph Herman Hertz. *The Jew in South Africa*. Johannesburg. 1905.

Jan H. Hofmayr (2nd rev. ed. prepared by J. P. Cope). *South Africa*. New York/Toronto: McGraw-Hill Book Co., Inc. 1952. 253 pp.

J. Hoge. *Personalia of the Germans at the Cape, 1652-1896.*

H. H. Y. Kaniki, ed. *Tanzania under Colonial Rule*. London: Longman Group, Ltd., for the Historical Society of Tanzania. 1980. 391 pp.

R. Lubetzky, "Sectoral Development and Stratification in Tanganyika, 1890-1914," mimeographed for the 1972 Universities Social Science Conference in Nairobi and frequently cited as a source on population matters.

Eduard Moritz. *Die Deutschen am Kap unter der holländischen Herrschaft, 1652-1806*. Weinar. [*The Germans at the Cape Under the Dutch Government, 1652-1806*]. Verlag Hermann Bohlaus Nachf. 1938. 336 pp.

Fritz Ferdinand Müller. *Deutschland-Zanzibar-Ostafrika: Geschichte einer Kolonial-eroberung*. [*Germany-Zanzibar-East Africa: History of a Colonial Conquest*]. Berlin: Rutten & Loening. 1959. 581 pp.

Gustav Saron. *The Jews in South Africa: A History*. Cape Town/New York: Oxford University Press. 1955.

Werner Schmidt-Pretoria. *Der Kulturanteil des Deutschtums am Aufbau des Burenvolkes*. [*The Cultural Contributions of Germans to the Development of the Boer People*]. Hanover: Hahnsche Verlagsbuchhandlung. 1938. 303 pp. plus map.

E. L. Schnell. *For Men and Women Must Work; An account of German immigration to the Cape with special reference to the German Military Settlers of 1857 and the German immigrants of 1858*. Cape Town: Maskew Miller Ltd.

Johannes Spanuth. "Britisch Kaffraria und seine deutsche Siedlungen" ["British Kaffraria and Its German Settlements"] in *Schriften des Vereins für Sozialpolitik* [*Publications of the Society for Social Betterment*], Vol. 147, Part 4.

Richard P. Stevens and Abdelwahab Elmessiri. *Israel and South Africa: the Progression of a Relationship*, rev. ed., with foreword by John Henrik Clarke. New York: North American. 1977.

George McCall Theal. *History and Ethnography of Africa South of the Zambesi, from the Settlement of the Portuguese at Sofala in September 1505 to the Conquest of Cape Colony by the British in September 1795*. London: George Allen & Unwin, Ltd. 1923. 3 English vols.

J. B. Webster. *Southern Africa Since 1900*. New York: Praeger Publishers. 1973. 242 pp.

Chapter XV

RESEARCHING GERMANIC ANCESTORS OUTSIDE THE UNITED STATES AND CANADA

LATIN AMERICA

The principal aids to genealogical research in Latin America are the *Research Outlines* published by the Family History Library (FHL), although they contain very few explicit references to Germans in those countries. The FHL has published Spanish-language *Research Outlines* for Argentina (1975), Chile (1974), Mexico (1970), Paraguay (1977) and Uruguay (1974).

In 1992 the FHL published an English-language *Research Outline: Latin America*, which is the main source for the information in this section. We have used Thomas Jay Kemp, *International Vital Records Handbook*, 3rd ed. (Baltimore: Genealogical Publishing Co., 1994) as a supplemental source. The FHL Research Outline contains many useful tips for beginners who have had no, or only limited, experience in researching their ancestors.

Addresses of some multi-purpose Germanic societies and useful genealogical contacts are listed at the end of this section.

Family History Library Holdings

The Family History Library has over 190,000 microfilm and microfiche records, including some from almost every Latin American country. The largest collections are for Mexico, Guatemala, Chile, Argentina and Brazil. The number of Germans in Guatemala was small, but nevertheless they were the largest non-Hispanic, non-native group. There are a large number of Germans in the other four mentioned countries.

The Family History Library has microfilm copies of records in government archives, church archives, and private collections, including:

- birth, baptism, marriage and death records
- census records
- notarial records
- Immigration records

The library's books also include family histories, as well as atlases, gazetteers, and national and local histories. Copies of some of these books are on microfilm.

Church and Cemetery Records

The original German immigrants included Catholics (apparently a majority in Argentina and possibly in Brazil, and minorities in other countries), Lutherans (apparently a majority in Chile and possibly in Brazil, with a sizable minority in Argentina and other countries), and Mennonites (a majority of Germans in Mexico and, at least among the unassimilated, in Paraguay, as well as several other countries with only a small number of Germans).

A small number of Seventh-day Adventists and Baptists appear to have been among the original immigrants. Various other denominations (e.g., Congregationalists and members of the United Church of Christ) are now represented, but this appears to be the result of later North American missionary activities.

Ernst Wagemann, in his article, "Die deutschen Kolonisten im brasilianischen Staate Espirito Santo" ["The German Colonists in the Brazilian State of Espirito Santo"] (in *Schriften des Vereins für Sozialpolitik* [*Publications of the Society for Social Betterment*], Vol. 147, Part 5 (Munich/Leipzig: Verlag von Duncker & Humblot, 1915), indicates that parish registers in this small state, northeast of Rio de Janeiro, date back to the 1850s. It seems likely that earlier registers can be found in southern Brazil, an area to which many

Germans had already immigrated in the 1820s. These registers include the same kind of data as in other countries.

To what extent any of these German parish records have been microfilmed is uncertain. However, if they are kept at the parish level, they probably have not been filmed. Those kept at the state, and possibly diocesan, archives are more likely to be on microfilm.

The Catholic Church took ecclesiastical censuses every 10-15 years or so. *Censo* or *padrón* is the Spanish word for "census"; *rol*, the Portuguese one. Presumably the censuses were universal and included the German Catholics. Furthermore, German Catholics were more likely to live in multi-ethnic parishes than the Lutherans were, not only because of their religious affinity with the long-time residents, but also because most of the other non-Iberian immigrants came from Catholic countries, especially Italy and Poland.

In case you visit the ancestral parish in person, you may find local cemetery records and gravestones to be useful.

Civil Registers

Civil registration was introduced in the following years in the various countries, but these records often are not complete. However, information is less likely to be missing for European immigrants and their descendants than for the native population.

Table 10: Civil Registers in Latin American Countries

Country	Year of Introduction
Argentina	1886
Belize	1881-1885
Bolivia	1898-1940*
Brazil	1870
Chile	1885
Costa Rica	1881
Guatemala	1877
Mexico	1859
Paraguay	1880
Uruguay	1879

* Civil registration was authorized in 1898, but modern civil records (which are incomplete) begin in 1940.

Civil registers are in the local towns in Brazil, Guatemala and Mexico. They are kept in the provincial civil registry offices in Argentina. For other countries, write to:

Registrar General
The General Registry
Judiciary Department
Court House Plaza
P.O. Box 87
Belize City
Belize, C.A.

Director
Oficina de Registro del Estado Civil
	de las Personas
Ministerio de Justicia y Trabajo
Herrera 875
Asunción
Paraguay

Director General del Servicio
	de Registro Civil e Identificacion
Ministerio de Justice
Hurfanos 1570
Santiago
Chile

Dirección General del Registro
	del Estado Civil
Ministerio de Educación y Cultura
Av. Uruguay 933
11.100 Montevideo
Uruguay

Dirección de Registro Civil y Notariado
Tribunal Supremo de Eleciones
AP 10218-1000
San Jose
Costa Rica

The *International Vital Records Handbook* includes copies of the forms for various countries.

Census Records

Public, as well as church, censuses began at an early date in most Latin American countries. The FHL has census records of eight Latin American countries, taken prior to the arrival of any Germanic immigrants. Those for Chile are only for 1777-1816, i.e., they end before the Germans arrived. The microfilmed censuses for Argentina include those for 1869, i.e., prior to the period of the heaviest Germanic immigration, and 1895, by which time a majority of the Germans had arrived. Only the 1930 census is listed for Mexico, but this would be useful because the first large Germanic immigrant wave occurred in the 1920s. No microfilmed census records are listed for Brazil, Paraguay, or Uruguay.

Emigration and Immigration Records

Except for early German immigrants to Brazil, nearly all Germans went to Latin America during the period for which the Hamburg passenger lists are available (and most sailed from Hamburg). Since Hamburg had strong connections with Latin America, these are likely to be valuable in most cases.

Clifford Neal Smith has also published a few monographs that include passengers whose destination was Latin America.

The Hunsrück region in what is now the northern part of the state of Rhineland-Palatinate was one of the centers of pre-1845 emigration to Brazil. It was also the primary source for the 1845 emigrants who founded the city of Petropolis. Therefore, it would be worthwhile to check the huge emigrant file at the Institut für pfälzische Geschichte und Volkskunde in Kaiserslautern. Most parish registers for this area are in Koblenz (for Protestants) or in Trier (for Catholics). The addresses are listed in Chapter XVII under **GERMANY**.

For the twentieth-century immigrants, passport records may be available. A large percentage of immigrants of Germanic stock went to Mexico, Belize, Costa Rica, Paraguay, and Bolivia during this period. The number of those who went to various other countries, especially in the temperate zones of South America, is substantial.

The post-1933 Jewish and political refugees from Austria also fit into this category, although what percentage remained in their country of refuge after 1945 is unknown. Ironically, the Dominican Republic, under the Trujillo dictatorship, was the most helpful, according to Franz Goldner, *Austrian Emigration, 1938 to 1945*. The English translation of this book was published by the Frederick Ungar Publishing Co., New York, in 1979.

Land Records

A variety of land records are available in Latin America. Since the overwhelming majority of Germanic immigrants were landowners (that desire being the main reason why many landless Germans migrated to Latin America), land grants are likely to be useful. Free land was often offered to induce immigration, especially to Brazil. Later immigrants had to pay a small price for farmland, often on a delayed basis. Land titles may be particularly valuable in such cases.

Probate and Notarial Records

These two types of records are lumped together inasmuch as they both include wills and probably guardianship records. Some wills may also appear in church death registers.

Notarial records also include mortgages and records of the sale and purchase of land or other property. These are especially likely to be helpful for urban dwellers. Some Germans settled in the cities. Many more later moved to large cities, such as Buenos Aires, Sao Paulo, Santiago, or medium-sized ones like Curitiba (southern Brazil), Concepcion (central Chile), or Rosario (northeast Argentina).

Military Records

Records of active service personnel are likely to be significant only in Brazil, which entered World War I in 1917 and World War II in 1942. Although Mexico also declared war in 1942, the overwhelming majority of Mexican Germans were Mennonite conscientious objectors, who would not have served in the military. Argentina, Paraguay and Uruguay declared war in 1945, when the war was almost over, so military records in these countries are not likely to be helpful.

Although there were quite a few nineteenth-century wars among Latin American countries, these occurred before there were large numbers of Germans in the affected countries.

However, some military records included all males eligible for service or even all civilians protected by a military outpost. These records are often kept in town or municipal archives. It may be worth checking whether such records existed for the country or area in question.

Published Records

As elsewhere, there are numerous family histories, biographies, compilations of pedigree charts, and articles in genealogical periodicals in Latin America. Many of the family and local histories are in German, although this is less likely to be the case for recent publications. These can probably be found in local libraries or church archives. Biographies of prominent persons are likely to be found in state, university, or large city libraries.

Many published materials, often printed in small quantities largely for local use, may be hard to find. Multi-purpose Germanic societies may have copies of some of these.

It may also be worth checking the *Revista Genealógica Latina* [*Latin American Genealogical Journal*], published by the Federacao dos Institutos Genealogicos Latinos in Sao Paulo since 1949, because it contains articles in six languages, including German. Some issues are on microfilm.

The pertinent chapter in the Ribbe and Henning *Taschenbuch*, written by Wolfgang Ribbe and Diana Schulle, lists the following periodical for German-Brazilians: *Familias Brasileiras de origem Germánica*, published by Subsidios genealógicos in Sao Paulo since 1962.

Wandering Volhynians (Vancouver, Canada) regularly carries a column on "News from Brazil," which provides information on where congregations of the Independent German Baptist Church in Brazil are located or where new ones are being founded. Its members appear to be mostly Germans from Volhynia.

Gazetteers, Maps and Atlases

The Family History Library has a good collection of gazetteers, maps and atlases, but few have been microfilmed. These would, of course, be available in many national, state, university, or possibly metropolitan libraries in the country in question. Researchers in other countries who are concerned with Latin America are most likely to find what they want at certain university libraries.

Language of Records

Records pertaining to Germans may be in German, Latin (mostly for Catholics), Spanish, Portuguese (Brazil), or English (Belize and some Caribbean countries).

Repositories

The Family History Library *Research Outline: Latin America* lists the addresses of nearly all the national archives and libraries in Latin America. The addresses for the national libraries of the six countries with the largest Germanic population are:

Biblioteca Nacional
México 564
1097 Buenos Aires
Argentina

Biblioteca Nacional
Av. Rio Branco 219-239
20042 Rio de Janeiro, RJ
Brazil

Biblioteca Nacional
Av. Bernardo O'Higgins 651
Santiago
Chile

Biblioteca y Archivo Nacionales
Mariscal Estigarribia 95
Asunción
Paraguay

Biblioteca Nacional de México
Instituto de Investigaciones
Bibliográficas
Universidad Nacional Autónoma
    de México
Centro Cultural, Ciudad Universitaria
Delegación Coyoacán
Apdo. 29-124
64150 México
Mexico

Biblioteca Nacional del Uruguay
Centro Nacional de Documentación
    Científica,
Técnica y Económica
18 de Julio 1790
Casilla 452
Montevideo
Uruguay

In Paraguay the archive is combined with the national library. The addresses of the other archives important for Germanic genealogy are:

Archivo General de la Nación
Av. Leandro N. Alem 246
1003 Buenos Aires
Argentina

Archivo General de la Nación
Tacuba 8, 2o. piso
Palacio Nacional
Apdo. 1999
México 1
Mexico

Arquivo Nacional
Rua Azeredo Coutinho 77
Centro
20230 Rio de Janeiro, RJ
Brazil

Archivo General de la Nación
Calle Convención 1474
Montevideo
Uruguay

Archivo Nacional
Miraflores 50
Santiago
Chile

For other countries, see the Family History Library *Research Outline*. The FHL has an unfilmed book describing the contents of these archives, viz., Roscoe R. Hill, *Los Archivos Nacionales de la América Latina* [*National Archives of Latin America*], published by the Archivo Nacional de Cuba in Havana in 1948.

There are both English and German-language guides to all major archives in the world. The English one is *The World of Learning*, which should be available in any university library. The German one is *Internationales Bibliotheks-Handbuch* [*World Guide to Libraries*], published by K. G. Saur, Munich, in 1986. Various other repositories have been mentioned elsewhere.

Writing to Latin America

The Family History Library recommends that in writing to Latin America, you should:

- enclose an International Reply Coupon (this is a universal expectation for foreign requests and it is better to enclose two)

- enclose $5 per search when requesting photocopy or search services (you may be billed for more later if any extensive research is required)

- have your letter translated into the language of the country (unless you know that the addressee has a knowledge of German or English)

Useful Addresses

Asociacion Argentina de los Alemanes
del Volga
Crespo, Entre Rios
Argentina
  (*The Volga German Society of Argentina*)

Centro Germano-Argentino de Entre Rios
Rivadava 1070
Crespo, Entre Rios
Argentina
  (*German-Argentinian Center of Entre Rios*)

Sudetendeutsche Landsmannschaft
Argentinien
Warnes 95
1602 Florida - Buenos Aires
Argentina
  (*Sudeten German homeland society*)

Prof. Ayrton Gonçalves Celestino
Associação Alema-Bucovina de Cultura
Rua Waldemar Kost, Vila Hauer
Curitiba, PR
Cep. 81.500-180 Brazil
  (*Bukovina Germans in Brazil*)

Conselho de Curadores da Fundação
Cultural de Pomerode
c/o Prefeitura Municipal de Pomerode
Rua 15 de Novembro, 525
Caiza Postal, 36
89107 Pomerode, Santa Catarina
Brazil
  (*genealogical-cultural organization in heavily Germanic area*)

Jason Epstein
c/o J. P. De Olivares
Rua Macedo Sobrinho No. 4/804
Humaita
22271 Rio de Janeiro
Brazil
  (*English-speaking professional genealogist*)

Instituto Hans Staden
Rua Sete de Abril, 59
CEP 01043 - 000
Sao Paulo, SP
Brazil
  (*Institute for German family history research*)

Pr. Vilson Wutzke
Caixa Postal 07
85930-000 Nova Santa Rosa, PR
Brazil
  (*Volhynian Germans in Brazil*)

Instituto Chileno de Investigaciones
Genealogicas
Casilla 1386
Santiago de Chile 1
Chile
  (*Chilean institute for genealogical research*)

THE SOUTHWEST PACIFIC

AUSTRALIA

Although there is a tremendous amount of information in Nick Vine Hill, *Tracing Your Family History in Australia: A Guide to Sources*, 2nd ed. (Albert Park, Australia: Scriptorum Family History Centre, 1994), very little of it pertains specifically to Germanic genealogy. However, most of the sources would be applicable to all ethnic groups. He also lists a number of publications that concentrate more directly on the history and genealogy of German-speaking immigrants to Australia and their descendants. These are listed in the bibliography at the end of the chapter.

Our account is based mostly on the Vine Hill, Mennicken-Cooley, Butler, and Wardale and Jenner books, *Die Zeitung* (published by the German Research Group of the Genealogical Society of Queensland), and a letter, with enclosures, from Liz Twigden of the South Australian Genealogy and Heraldry Society, all listed at the end of the chapter.

The "South Australiana Source Sheet No. 12" bibliography prepared by the State Library of South Australia lists numerous pertinent books, pamphlets, theses and newspaper articles. Those most valuable for genealogical research appear to be Harmstorf's thesis and Schubert's book on the early German settlers in South Australia.

Die Zeitung [*The Newspaper*], published by the German Research Group in Queensland, also mentions a book by Alan Corkhill, *Queensland and Germany: Ethnic, Socio-Cultural, Political and Trade Relations, 1838-1991*. A second book by Dr. Corkhill on the cultural and social history of German immigration and settlement throughout Australia is in preparation.

Corkhill has also written "The German Presence in Queensland Over the Last 150 Years," contained in the proceedings of an international symposium held August 24-26, 1987 at the University of Queensland, Brisbane (published by Department of German, University of Queensland, 1988).

Genealogical Societies

Australia's one specifically German-oriented genealogical organization is the:

> German Research Group
> Genealogical Society of Queensland, Inc.
> c/o Margaret Jenner
> 73 Plimsoll St.
> Greenslopes, Qld 4120
> Australia

It publishes a genealogical periodical, *Die Zeitung* [*The Newspaper*], edited by Valerie Dieckmann.

In Western Australia there is a European (i.e., continental, in contrast to British) Interest Group. This multi-ethnic group includes Germans and publishes the Western Ancestor quarterly. The address is:

> European Interest Group
> Western Australian Genealogical Society, Inc.
> Unit 5, 48 May St.
> Bayswater, WA 6053
> Australia

There is a lot of information on Germans (and not only in that state) available from the following society, which welcomes inquiries, according to Liz Twigden:

> South Australian Genealogy and Heraldry Society, Inc.
> GPO Box 592
> Adelaide, SA 5001
> Australia

New South Wales has at least 74 regional genealogical societies, with an umbrella group, the New South Wales Association of Family History Societies, which does not answer mail queries, according to Vine Hill. Regional societies that are readily identifiable as covering areas with a significant number of Germans (excluding those having a no-mail-queries policy) are:

> Albury Family History Group
> P.O. Box 822
> Albury, NSW
> Australia

> Broken Hill Family History Group
> P.O. Box 779
> Broken Hill, NSW 2880
> Australia

The two Victoria state genealogical societies, the Genealogical Society of Victoria and the Australian Institute of Genealogical Studies, Inc., do not respond to mail queries. However, the following regional societies in areas known to have Germans are believed to be willing to accept queries:

Bendigo Regional Genealogical Society, Inc.
P.O. Box 1049
Bendigo, Vic 3550
Australia

Hamilton Family History Centre
P.O. Box 179
Hamilton, Vic 3300
Australia

Wimmera Association for Genealogy
P.O. Box 880
Horsham, Vic 3402
Australia

The Genealogical Society of Tasmania has five branches, but the one in Hobart, where most of the few Germans live, does not answer queries. Neither does the Australian Jewish Genealogical Society (with an unknown number of Australians who had German-speaking immigrant ancestors). Nevertheless, there are quite a few publications that should provide clues about this number. The one appearing to have the greatest genealogical value is H. A. Cohen, *Resource Manual for Australian Jewish Genealogy* (Melbourne: Australian Jewish Historical Society, 1982). It is possible that the various state branches of the Australian Jewish Historical Society might answer queries.

Heather E. Garnsey and Martyn C. H. Killion have compiled two directories of genealogical societies, both published by the Australasian Federation of Family History Organisations in Sydney:

- *AFFHO Directory of Genealogical Organisations in Australasia* (1992)

- *AFFHO Directory of Member Organisations* (1993)

Civil Registers

Civil registers began early enough to include records on most of the Germanic immigrants, although they would not cover the earliest ones in New South Wales, Queensland and South Australia. The dates when civil registration went into effect in the various states and territories are as follows:

Australian Capital Territory	1911 (mandated 1930)	New South Wales	1856
Northern Territory	1876	Queensland	1856
South Australia	1842	Tasmania	1838
Victoria	1837 (mandated 1853)	Western Australia	1841

The registers for New South Wales, as well as those for 1911-1930 for the Australian Capital Territory and for 1855-59 for Queensland (then the Moreton Bay district of New South Wales) are at:

Registry of Births, Deaths and Marriages
191-199 Thomas St.
Haymarket, NSW 2000
Australia

The repositories for the other states and territories are:

Registry of Births, Deaths and Marriages
59 King William St.
Adelaide, SA 5000
Australia

The Registrar
Births, Deaths and Marriages
Department of Property and Services
295 Queen St.
Melbourne, Vic 3000
Australia

Queensland State Archives
435 Compton Road
Runcora, Qld 4113
Australia
(*for 1860-1890*)

Registry of Births, Deaths and Marriages
33 Herschel St.
Brisbane, Qld 3000
Australia
(*since 1891*)

Registry of Births, Deaths and Marriages
Westralia Square
141 St. George's Terrace
Perth, WA 6000
Australia

Archives of Tasmania
91 Murray St.
Hobart, Tas 7000
Australia
   (*19th century*)

Registry of Births, Deaths and Marriages
15 Murray St.
Hobart, Tas 7000
Australia
   (*20th century*)

Registry of Births, Deaths and Marriages
Building 3
ACT Administration Centre
London Circuit & Constitution Ave.
Civic, ACT 2600
Australia
   (*since 1930*)

Registry of Births, Deaths and Marriages
Cavanaugh & Bennett Sts.
Darwin, NT 0800
Australia

Parish Registers

Parish registers may be at:

- local churches
- church archives
- the offices for civil registers
- various other archives

Almost all of the pre-1914 German immigrants were Lutherans, with the small number of Catholics integrating with the Irish. The history of the various Lutheran synods in Australia is complex. The oldest large synod was the Evangelical Lutheran Church of Australia. In 1921 five other synods joined to form the United Evangelical Lutheran Church in Australia. Vondra states that these two big ones were united in 1966. Vine Hill provides the following archival address:

> Lutheran Church of Australia
> 101 Archer St.
> North Adelaide, SA 5006
> Australia

Vondra lists four Lutheran churches (one in New South Wales and three in Victoria) and one German Catholic church in Victoria among 60 German-speaking organizations in Australia. But he also provides the address for two church-affiliated German Catholic Centres in New South Wales under cultural organizations (Appendix I).

The addresses of various Baptist and Catholic archives are listed on pp. 480 and 482, respectively, in Vine Hill's book. *Die Zeitung* [*The Newspaper*] indicates that there were German Baptists in the Fassifern district, Marburg/Tallagala area and at Albion in Brisbane. The pertinent address is:

> Baptist Union Archives
> 26 Hall St.
> Alderley, Qld 4051
> Australia

The frequent and widespread migration of the Templers (or Templars), both voluntary and involuntary, only provides clues as to where pertinent records could be found: Württemberg and nearby areas (where they originated), the Ottoman Turkish archives and British archives for Palestine, the Czarist archives, records of those interned and/or deported during World War II or removed at the end of the war (which could possibly be found in Britain, Egypt or Cyprus), or the U.S. Unitarian church.

Vondra has the following addresses in New South Wales and Victoria, respectively, for the Australian Templers:

Germanic Genealogy Society

Temple Society of Australia
40 Adamson Ave.
Dundas 2117
Australia

Temple Society
152 Tucker Road
Bentleigh 3204
Australia

Besides Melbourne (the largest center) and Sydney, there are also Templers in Adelaide and a few in Brisbane, according to Dr. Victor G. Doerksen, an expert on the Templers. Dr. Doerksen reports that there are now about 1,100 Templers in Australia. This includes the descendants of both those who migrated directly from Germany to Palestine and the Mennonite Templers who moved there from the Russian Empire.

Two publications dealing with parish registers are:

- Nick Vine Hill, *Parish Registers in Australia*, 2nd ed. (Middle Park, Australia: author, 1990)

- Rev. H. F. W. Proeve, "Lutheran Records in Australia," in Andrew G. Peake, *Genealogical Papers—1990 Genealogy Congress (Supplement)* (Adelaide: South Australian Genealogy and Heraldry Society and Guild Books, 1981)

Marriage Records

When early parish registers cannot be found, marriage licenses (preceded by a marriage declaration) and marriage banns may prove especially helpful. They can sometimes be found in the same repositories as civil registers.

Banns were required to be read in the home parishes of both bride and groom, if different, which may provide clues for further research. Ministers were supposed to keep *Registers of Banns*, as well as marriage registers.

Passenger Lists

Since there was a strong Australian connection with Hamburg, the Hamburg passenger departure lists include many German-speaking people who emigrated to Australia. Bear in mind that many took the indirect route via Liverpool and Plymouth in England.

Eric and Rosemary Kopittke have published seven volumes of *Emigration from Hamburg to Australia for 1860-69*, one volume being the index. The series was published by the Queensland Family History Society, Inc., Indooroopilly, in 1991-93.

Many pre-1900 passenger arrival lists have been published and often filmed, or they are available in manuscript form. Newspapers also published such information. However, sometimes only the surnames are mentioned and even this is not always the case for passengers in steerage. In the early period, many Germans came to Australia as "assisted immigrants," i.e., they received free passage. There are many publications and some indexes relating to these.

Monographs by Clifford Neal Smith and Charles M. Hall list the names of passengers on those fragments of the Bremen and Antwerp records that have been preserved, including quite a few who went to Australia. They are especially useful for the "Old Lutherans" who constituted the first significant group of immigrants to Australia.

Another source with exquisite detail about the early immigration and settlements of the "Old Lutherans" is A. Brauer, *Under the Southern Cross—History of the Evangelical Lutheran Church of Australia* (Adelaide: Lutheran Publishing House, 1956). This book begins with the voyages of the first group of Lutherans, led by Pastor A.L.C. Kavel, to emigrate to South Australia in 1838 and 1839 aboard the ships *Prairie George, Bengalee, Zebra* and *Catharina*. About 500 "Old Lutherans" emigrated from the district of Zuellichau in East Brandenburg (just north of Silesia) and a neighboring area of Posen, boarded barges to Hamburg and then boarded ships to Port Adelaide via Plymouth. They initially settled near Adelaide in towns such as Hahndorf, Klemzig, Lobethal, Bethany and Hoffnungstal. They were employed as farmers, shepherds and sheepshearers. Later chapters cover settlements of Lutherans in other areas of Australia. This book indicates that passenger lists of many of the ships carrying Lutheran immigrants are available from archives of the Evangelical Lutheran Church of Australia.

Naturalization Records

A very high percentage of male German immigrants became naturalized, since this carried with it the right to own land. The documents relating to this process include the name, place of birth or residence prior to emigration, length of residence in Australia, age and occupation. The problem is that these are scattered among many archives. However, a review of the pertinent information in Vine Hill's book should lead you to the right depository.

Other Records

Among the Australian records that are significant for genealogists, the following deserve particular mention: biographical and genealogical dictionaries, cemetery records (for on-site research), personal name changes (which were common because of the strong anti-German sentiment during and after World War II), various kinds of directories (especially those listing residents, similar to U.S. city directories and county atlases), electoral rolls (voting is mandatory in Australia), published genealogies and genealogical directories, the records of hospitals and asylums (which were essentially poorhouses in earlier times), land records, and the published and unpublished material of local historical societies.

Newspapers

There were numerous German-language newspapers, which often merged in order to survive. W. D. Borrie lists the *Südaustralische Zeitung* [*The South Australian Newspaper*] (Adelaide), the *Australische Zeitung* [*The Australian Newspaper*] (Melbourne and Tanunda), and the Queenslander Herald as of lasting significance. In view of the rapid assimilation of many Germans and the scattered nature of Germanic settlements in many areas, local English-language newspapers may be equally valuable. *Newspapers in Australia: A Union Catalog*, with the 4th edition published by the National Library of Australia, Canberra, in 1985, may help identify where the various newspapers are stored.

The most comprehensive, although still brief, history of German-language newspapers can be found in Miriam Gilson and Jerzy Zubrzycki, *The Foreign Language Press in Australia*.

Gazetteers

A Geographical Dictionary or Gazetteer of the Australian Colonies, 1848 (facsimile edition by the Council of Libraries of New South Wales, Sydney, 1970; republished by the Library Council of Victoria, Melbourne, 1991, and available on microfiche) is valuable for the German settlements established during the first decade. Robert P. Whitoworth prepared a series, *Baillier's ... Gazetteer and Road Guide*, for each colony (Melbourne: F. F. Bailliere, 1865-77). *Gazetteer No. 40: Australia* (Washington: Department of the Interior, 1957) is a standard gazetteer of modern Australia. You will have to find the many place name changes elsewhere, for example, in the W. D. Borrie and J. Lyng books, which give quite a few examples, but are not comprehensive.

Record Repositories

The Australian Archives has its national headquarters in Canberra, but nineteenth-century materials will often be found in the branch archives in each state. Each state has its own state archives. There are also a large number of religious, local, university and specialized archives. Vine Hill has an extensive list of addresses. Published material (and possibly other records) can be found at the:

> National Library of Australia
> Parkes Place
> Canberra, ACT 2600
> Australia

A great deal of valuable material also exists in the various state libraries. The following library is of particular significance for German-Australians:

> Mortlock Library of South Australia
> State Library of South Australia
> Jervois Wing
> North Terrace
> Adelaide, SA 5000
> Australia

For further information on genealogical records and the addresses of repositories, check Nick Vine Hill's voluminous, detailed guide.

Ian Harmstorf, who was (and may still be) a history professor at the Adelaide College of Arts, helped found the Educational Council for the German-Speaking Communities in South Australia in 1978. Although this council is concerned with preserving or recapturing the Germanic heritage in a broader sense, it may nevertheless have important information concerning the nature and location of genealogical records.

NEW ZEALAND

Several books listed under Australia, particularly the following, also include information about New Zealand:

- Owen B. Mutzelburg, *How to Trace Your German Ancestors: A Guide for Australians and New Zealanders* (Sydney: Hale & Iremonger, 1989)

- Heather E. Garnsey and Martyn C. H. Killion, comps., *AFFHO Directory of Genealogical Organisations in Australasia* (Sydney: Australasian Federation of Family History Organisations, 1992)

- Heather E. Garnsey and Martyn C. H. Killion, comps., *AFFHO Directory of Member Organisations* (Sydney: Australasian Federation of Family History Organisations, 1993)

Genealogical Societies

For information relating specifically to the genealogy of continental (as contrasted to British) ancestors, contact:

> Graham Clark, Secretary
> European Interest Group
> 1/2 Islington St.
> Ponsonby
> Auckland 1002
> New Zealand

The addresses of the national society and its Canterbury (South Island) Group are:

> New Zealand Society of Genealogists
> P.O. Box 8795
> Auckland
> New Zealand

> New Zealand Society of Genealogists
> Canterbury Group
> c/o Miss M. Corsar
> 4/32 Elizabeth St.
> Christchurch
> New Zealand

Civil Registers

Birth and death records have been maintained since 1848 and marriage records since 1854. Information from civil registers can be obtained from:

Registrar-General
Births, Deaths and Marriages
P.O. Box 31115
Lower Hutt
New Zealand

Births, Deaths and Marriages
Auckland City Registry
Justice Departmental Building
Kingston St.
Auckland
New Zealand
(*for the city of Auckland*)

Passenger Lists

The Hamburg passenger lists are important, since many of the German-speaking emigrants embarked there. So, to some extent, are the Australian port arrival and departure records, considering the significant amount of migration between these countries, especially during the gold rushes of the mid-nineteenth century. New Zealand arrivals are covered under archival records.

Archives and Archival Records

The addresses of the National Archives and its regional offices are:

National Archives
10 Mulgrave St.
P.O. Box 12050
Wellington
New Zealand

Auckland Regional Office
B. J. Ball Building
Hardinge St.
P.O. Box 91220
Auckland 1
New Zealand

Christchurch Regional Office
90 Peterborough St.
P.O. Box 1308
Christchurch
New Zealand

Dunedin Regional Office
556 George St.
P.O. Box 6183
Dunedin
New Zealand

The National Archives has brochures on the *National Archives Record Groups* and on *Card Indexes at National Archives*. According to these, the records in Wellington include:

- shipping index (1840-ca. 1960s; incomplete after 1910), by ship
- assisted immigration index (ca. 1871-1888)—photocopies of lists of immigrants whose fare was paid by others
- records of the Immigration Department, 1870-1911
- notices of intention to marry, 1856-1956
- records of the Registrar-General of Births, Deaths and Marriages since 1856
- records of the Alien Registration Branch, 1915-77
- records of the Electoral Department since 1865
- records of the Social Security Department since 1883
- various archival records for Samoa that may be relevant for Germanic genealogical research in that former New Zealand mandate, 1879-1933
- private papers of a number of prominent New Zealanders bearing German names

A booklet on *Genealogical Sources at National Archives, Auckland* lists:

- Auckland ship arrivals (not indexed), 1909, 1915-65
- Port of Wellington entry records, 1856-87
- records for Puhoi or the "German settlement," 1863-66
- various indexed probate and intestate records, 1842-1973
- some old age pension records (1896-1910)
- widow's pension records (1916-17)
- school class lists (1879-1953), including private schools since 1903

A Brief Guide to Family History Sources at National Archives Christchurch Office as of 1 September 1993 indicates the non-current official records of the Canterbury and Westland regions there include:

- probate files (1855-1979)
- maternity records (1876-1981)
- shipping papers, including passenger lists, for Canterbury (1850-84)
- Canterbury school records, including names and ages of students (also for schools that have closed)

The National Archives also has a three-page list of "Addresses for Genealogical Research in New Zealand," which may be helpful, especially with respect to specific areas or specific groups of people.

The records mentioned above may be incomplete, because in some cases they cover only certain areas and in others, there are gaps. Moreover, we have combined some of the listings for related records.

Family History at National Archives (Allen & Unwin, NZ Ltd., 1990) and its successor, "Beyond the Book," provide more comprehensive information about the archives' holdings and are available from the archives.

The National Archives offers written research services at various levels, but with some restrictions on the number of requests for basic research and a fee for all overseas research. Prepayment is not required for basic research (for example, a duplicated copy of a specific entry in a census, register, etc.), but is required for more extensive research.

Other Records and Sources

Land records are housed at:

> Lands & Deeds Registry
> Price Waterhouse Centre
> 41 Federal St.
> Auckland
> New Zealand

Church records for Catholics are at:

> Catholic Archives
> c/o Records Pompalier Centre
> Auckland Catholic Diocese
> Private Bag
> Auckland
> New Zealand

> Roman Catholic Diocese of Christchurch
> Archives
> c/o Rev. K. Clark
> 42 Douglas St.
> Timaru
> New Zealand

We do not have an address for Lutheran archives in New Zealand, but presumably the European Interest Group of the New Zealand Society of Genealogists can provide information as to the whereabouts of any Lutheran archives or registers.

Published books and other publications. Information about or from published books and other publications is available from:

> National Library of New Zealand
> Reference Service
> P.O. Box 1467
> Wellington
> New Zealand

Judith Williams of Puhoi provided information about a multi-purpose group, the Bohemian Association Originating in Puhoi-Ohaupo, which publishes the *Homeland News* (which is mostly of a local nature). The editor is:

> Mrs. C. Krippner
> Te Rore RD 6
> Te Awamatu
> New Zealand

A list of early German settlers on the west coast of South Island, including places and dates of birth, is available from:

> Mrs. Jill Robinson
> P.O. Box 48
> Reefton 7853
> New Zealand

FORMER GERMAN COLONIES AND PROTECTORATES

The only former German possession where a substantial number of German descendants can be found is Samoa, where registration began prior to the German occupation. For civil records, write to:

> Registrar General
> Justice Department
> P.O. Box 49
> Apia
> Samoa

Prior to World War I, many Pacific islands, including (besides Samoa), the Solomon Islands, the Mariana Islands (except Guam), and the Marshall Islands, belonged to Germany. The German population was small. However, there was enough of a German settlement at one time to establish a German church in Pohnpei. It is not known whether any church records have survived. The Embassy of Micronesia might know of any archives or historical society that might have pertinent records. Alternatively, you could try writing to the office responsible for civil registration:

> Clerk of Courts
> State of Pohnpei, FSM
> P.O. Box 1449
> Kolonia, Pohnpei, ECI 96941
> Micronesia

New Guinea was divided among the Dutch, British and Germans prior to World War I. There were quite a few missionaries and related staff in the German portion, but we know of no permanent German settlement.

The former German and British protectorates now form Papua New Guinea. The German portion became an Australian mandate after World War I. Nick Vine Hill's book (see **AUSTRALIA**) lists a number of addresses and resources for this region, in case you should want to explore whether any records pertaining to Germans have been preserved.

AFRICA

SOUTH AFRICA

Our information comes from the *Guide to Genealogical Research in the State Archives* and other information provided by the Transvaal Archives Depot, State Archives and Heraldic Services, Department of Arts, Culture, Science and Technology, Private Bag X236, Pretoria 0001, South Africa. This also included the table of contents of R. T. J. Lombard, *Handbook for Genealogical Research in South Africa*, 2nd ed. (Pretoria: Human Sciences Research Council, 1990), as well as some addresses listed in it. Lombard's book also covers Namibia and Zimbabwe. The Transvaal Archives Depot is, in fact, also the national government archives, not only the archives for that province.

Parish Registers

These are housed at the various church archives and State Archives Depots. Lutheran registers are at:

The Secretary
United Lutheran Church
P.O. Box 873
Edenvale
1610
South Africa

Many of the early German settlers probably joined the Reformed church. There are Dutch Reformed Church (*Nederduitse Gereformeerde Kerk*) Archives Depots in Pretoria, Cape Town, Bloemfontein and Pietermaritzburg. The other branches of the Reformed church (which use no English name) have only one archive each. The addresses of the pertinent archives for the Cape Province are:

The Archivist
Nederduitse Gereformeerde Kerk
P.O. Box 3171
Cape Town
8000
South Africa
(*location: Church Centre, Gray's Pass*)

The Archivist
Nederduitse Hervormde Kerk
P.O. Box 2368
Pretoria
0001
South Africa
(*location: 224 Jacob Maré St.*)

The Archivist
Gereformeerde Kerk
P.O. Box 20004
Noordbrug
Potchefstroom
2520
South Africa

The address for the state archives for Cape Province is:

The Chief
Cape Archives Depot
Private Bag X9025
Cape Town
8000
South Africa

For information from microfilmed copies of pre-1900 church registers for Cape Colony, write to:

Section Genealogical Information
Human Science Research Council Library
Private Bag 41X
Pretoria
0001
South Africa

To view these in person, you have to make an advance appointment and pay a fee for the use of a microfilm reader.

The Transvaal Archives Depot also has the parish registers of the Dutch Reformed Church of the Cape Colony for 1665-1845.

Civil Registers

Birth registers (*Geboorteregisters*) are closed for a period of 100 years. Marriage registers (*Huweliksregisters*) are closed for 30 years. There is no restriction on access to death registers (*Sterfteregisters*). For information from civil registers, write to:

Registrar of Births, Marriages, and Deaths
Department of Home Affairs
Private Bag X114
Pretoria
0001
South Africa

Other Records

Lombard, in his chapter on "Repositories of Genealogical Sources," lists the following kind of records at the Cape Archives Depot that might be of genealogical value for Germanic research: Master of the Supreme Court (1673-1928), British Kaffraria, Immigration Board of Port Elizabeth (1858-1862), Immigration Board of Cape Town (1858-1861), and Immigration Agent of Cape Town (1878-1885), with the dates supplied by the state archives in Pretoria.

He also lists the following records for the national government archives in Pretoria: Orphan Master (1873-1974), Chief Immigration Officer (1907-1912), and European and Indian Immigration (1857-1911).

Immigration and naturalization records are housed at the State Archives Depots and at the:

Department of Home Affairs
Private Bag X114
Pretoria
0001
South Africa

Wills, probate and orphan records are in the custody of the various Masters of the Supreme Court. For the western Cape Province, this would be the Orphan Master, Private Bag X9018, Cape Town 8000. For the eastern Cape Province, this would be the Orphan Master, Private Bag X1010, Grahamstown 6140. However, such records are regularly transferred to the State Archives Depots, so the Cape Archives Depot (or others, for the few Germans who lived elsewhere) would have the older ones, which are generally more useful for genealogy.

Microfilmed copies of the pre-1919 Cape estate files are at the Transvaal Archives Depot. Some estate documents are also in the various Magistrates Archives.

Land records are in the custody of the various Deeds Offices: for the western Cape, the Registrar of Deeds, P.O. Box 703, Cape Town 8000; for eastern Cape Province, the Registrar of Deeds, Private Bag X7402, King William's Town 5600. Tax records are not accessible to the public.

Military records for after 1912 can be accessed through:

Director
Directorate Documentation Service
South African National Defence Force
Private Bag X289
Pretoria
0001
South Africa

However, the Transvaal Archives Depot has Red Cross and casualty records for the Anglo-Boer War.

A particularly relevant book for Germanic genealogy is J. Hoge, *Personalia of the Germans at the Cape, 1652-1896*. The overwhelming majority of the Germans lived in Cape Province.

Genealogical Societies and Services

No specifically Germanic society in South Africa has been identified. The address for the national society that we received in the letter from the South African archives is:

> The National Secretary
> Genealogical Society of South Africa
> P.O. Box 2119
> Houghton
> 2041
> South Africa

Presumably the addresses of any state or regional genealogical societies could be obtained from this source.

The German genealogy team of this society is starting a Web site for German migration to South Africa. Send e-mail to fred@k2nesoft.com or WebMaster@genealogy.net for more information.

Published books and records are available at:

> The State Library (legal deposit library)   South African Library
> P.O. Box 397   Queen Victoria St.
> Pretoria   Cape Town
> 0001   8001
> South Africa   South Africa

Non-genealogical institutions that might be able to provide helpful contacts for Germanic genealogy include:

> German Language and Cultural Institute   Huguenot Memorial Museum
> 93 Lynburn Road   P.O. Box 37
> Lynnwood Manor   Franschhoek
> 0081   7690
> South Africa   South Africa
>
> Kaffrarian Historical Society   South African-German Cultural
> P.O. Box 1434   Association
> King William's Town   P.O. Box 70944
> 5600   Die Wilgers, Pretoria
> South Africa   0041
>   South Africa
>   (*publishes journal titled* Brucka)

Ken V. André of the South African-German Cultural Association (who was our only non-archival source in South Africa) has written a 500-page genealogical study of about 250 Kaffrarian German families.

Key books for research in South Africa are included in the bibliography at the end of the chapter.

FORMER GERMAN COLONIES AND PROTECTORATES

For records pertaining to the former German South-West Africa, try writing to:

> Vital Registration Department
> Government House
> Windhoek
> Namibia

Lombard mentions that estate documents, newspapers, and military records are available in the Namibian archives.

For records pertaining to the former German East Africa, try writing to:

> Registrar General
> Ministry of Justice
> Office of the Administrator General
> P.O. Box 9183
> Dar-es-Salaam
> Tanzania

To get information about the location of any possible records in what became French mandates in West Africa after World War I, write to the Consular Section of the Embassy of the country in question. Alternatively, you could write to the offices in charge of civil registers (which did not exist at the time of German occupation, or began at the very end of it) in the hope that your letter would be forwarded to the appropriate archives or other offices. The addresses for these are:

Ministre de l'Administration Territoriale B.P. 7854 Yaounde Cameroon	Division des Affaires Politiques et Administratives Ministre de l'Interieur Lome Togo

NORTH AFRICA

Algeria began civil registration for the northern areas, where almost all German settlers would have lived, in 1882. Civil registers were established in the south, where Germans might have served in the French Foreign Legion, in 1905, but it is more likely that any pertinent records would be in France than in Algeria.

Vital records can be requested from:

> Service d'État Civil des Communes
> Ministre de l'Interieur
> Alger
> Algeria

Births and deaths have been recorded in Egypt since 1839, but marriages were exclusively the province of ecclesiastical authorities. Civil records may be requested from:

> Department of Civil Registration
> Ministry of Interior
> Abassia, Cairo
> Egypt

Published and other documentary materials can be found at:

> National Library and Archives
> Corniche El-Nil Street
> Boulac, Cairo
> Egypt

Civil registration of Europeans in Morocco began in 1915. For records of births and deaths, contact:

> Chef
> Division d'État Civil
> Ministre de l'Interieur
> Rabat
> Morocco

Marriage records were kept exclusively by ecclesiastical authorities.

However, unless you can get your letters translated into Arabic or French (except Egypt), you are more likely to receive a reply from the Consular Section of the pertinent Embassy.

ASIA

Only two Asian countries had significant German settlement. China and Turkey had several thousand Germans each. This, of course, excludes the Asian portions of what was first the Russian Empire, then the Soviet Union and now the Commonwealth of Independent States. (See the section on **EAST AND SOUTH EUROPE** for the latter.)

CHINA

There are hundreds of pages of material on the Soviet German Lutheran refugees who fled via Siberia to Harbin (German: *Charbin*), Manchuria, dealing with arranging their resettlement in the Americas, at:

> Evangelical Lutheran Church of America Archives
> 5400 Milton Parkway
> Rosemont, IL 60018

These records include the names of many of the refugees, as well as letters and articles from the Nansen International Office for Refugees, functioning under the auspices of the League of Nations in Geneva.

Also included are records pertaining to food drafts sent to the Black Sea and Volga areas in 1921-23, including the names of the recipients and senders (who were relatives in many cases).

The archives is not in a position to answer queries, but researchers are welcome to use the archives.

The Northern Illinois Chapter of the American Historical Society of Germans from Russia has copied the following records:

- Group RG-2: Boxes 3, 4, 7, 8, 12, 17, 19, 20, 22, 23
- Group 3A: Boxes 14, 19, 23, 28, 33, 35, 36, 38, 41, 42, 43, 45, 46, 47, 49, 50, 51, 65

The project of copying records is continuing. For an authoritative account of the Lutheran refugees, see Virginia Less, "The Story of the Harbin, China, Refugees," in Wandering Volhynians, Vol. 8, No. 3 (September 1995).

The material which has already been copied is now in the hands of the head office of AHSGR in Lincoln, Nebraska, which has a board member translating pertinent excerpts for publication.

A lot of research on the Mennonite refugees who were in Harbin is being done by:

> Dr. Wilmer Harms
> 2904-13 Ivy Drive
> North Newton, KS 67117

The Harbin refugees and their descendants (or at least those in North America) hold reunions every four years, so they constitute a tightly knit group. The contact person for the 1995 Harbin Reunion Committee is:

> Nick Friesen
> 296 E. Curtis Ave.
> Reedley, CA 93654

Isaak's book and Loewen's German-language book deal with this group.

Records for Catholic refugees are at the Russian archives in Saratov and Engels.

The Summer 1994 issue of *Avotaynu* carried an article by Dr. Jonathan Goldstein on "Consular Records in Shanghai about Jewish Refugees," based on visits with Polish, Russian and American consular officials.

Copies of the Polish consular log book for citizens who passed through Shanghai or Nanjing between 1934 and 1941 (mentioned by Goldstein) are now in the Library of Congress and at the Sino-Judaic Archives of the Hoover Institution at Stanford. Dr. Ristaino of the Library of Congress is preparing an article on the book's usefulness.

The following institute is dedicated to the study of Jews in China, which presumably also includes some German Jews who were involved with commerce in Jiaozhou (*Kiautschou*) during the period when Germany had a lease on it (1898-99 to World War I):

Prof. Albert Dien, President
Sino-Judaic Institute
2316 Blueridge Ave.
Menlo, Park, CA 94025

Prof. Dien estimates that there are several thousand unindexed names in the Polish register mentioned by Goldstein, which sometimes includes such notes as "emigrant from Russia."

The Russian vice-consul indicated that all pertinent records had been sent to the Russian Central Archives in Moscow. He recommended the following two Russian-language books:

(1) V. D. Jiganoff, *Russians in Shanghai* (Shanghai, ca. 1930); and
(2) Natalya Ilyana, *Roads to Return* (Moscow, ca. 1952), which deals with the refugees in Harbin.

Any pertinent Chinese records are likely to be at the city level, especially in Harbin and Shanghai. Contact the Consular Section of the Chinese Embassy for further information.

TURKEY (ASIA MINOR)

Look under **TURKEY** in the section on **EAST AND SOUTH EUROPE** for any pertinent information concerning possible records pertaining to Germans.

SOUTH ASIA, MALAY PENINSULA, MALAY ARCHIPELAGO (EAST INDIES OR EAST INDIA)

The Portuguese, Dutch, English (later British), Danes, French and Swedes all formed East India (or East Indies) Companies to engage in what later become European (mostly British and Dutch) colonies and protectorates in Asia. This was generally accompanied by military and political dominion, although the home governments assumed this non-commercial role in time.

Of greatest interest for Germanic genealogy is the Dutch East India Co., which had many Germans in its service. It was established in 1598, joined with other companies to form a monopoly in 1602, and colonized the Cape of Good Hope (**SOUTH AFRICA**) in 1650-70.

In the seventeenth century it became dominant in what is now **INDONESIA**, although it did not conquer Java until 1750 and some outlying islands until the nineteenth century.

From 1658 to 1796 it was in control of present-day **SRI LANKA** (earlier called **CEYLON**). In a struggle following a 1654 incident, England temporarily lost control of all of its East Indies possessions to the Dutch. In 1663 the Netherlands won control of the Malabar coast of **INDIA** (roughly Kerala state) from the Portuguese. It even held **TAIWAN** briefly (1658-61).

Although few Germans are likely to have remained in these Asian areas permanently, it is possible that there may be some genealogical information on Germans in the archival records of the Dutch East India Co., now kept at:

Rijksarchiefdienst
Prins Willem Alexanderhof 20
2595 BE The Hague
Netherlands
(*street location*)

Rijksarchiefdienst
P.O. Box 90520
2509 LM The Hague
Netherlands
(*mailing address*)

The British East India Co. became dominant in what later became British India, the Malay Peninsula and part of the Malay Archipelago of islands (chiefly Borneo) in the last half of the seventeenth century, although it lost its political power to the British government a century later. Brunei and parts of India were ruled by local princes, but were really British protectorates.

This area constitutes **INDIA**, **PAKISTAN**, **BANGLADESH**, **MYANMAR** (formerly **BURMA**), **MALAYSIA**, **SINGAPORE**, and **BRUNEI** today.

Since many of the soldiers discharged from the (English) King's German Legion after the Crimean War chose to serve in **INDIA**, at least for a while, in preference to settling down as farmers in **SOUTH AFRICA**, there may be some pertinent information on them in the records of the British Colonial Office at:

> Public Record Office
> Kew
> Richmond, Surrey
> England TW9 4DU

It is considerably less likely that Germans served in the Portuguese, French, Danish or Swedish East India Companies (of which only the French company had a prolonged and major effect on the area), but it is conceivable that there could be rare instances of such service. Anyone inclined to pursue this remote possibility should contact the National Archives of the respective countries.

BIBLIOGRAPHY (See ANNOTATED BIBLIOGRAPHY for full citations if not shown)

AUSTRALIA

Reg Butler. *A College in the Wattles: Hahndorf and Its Academy*. Hahndorf, SA: Hahndorf Academy. 1989.

Patricia Cloos and Jürgen Tampke. *Greetings from the Land Where Milk and Honey Flows: The German Immigration to New South Wales, 1838-1858*. Mawson, ACT, Australia: Southern Highland Publishers. 1993.

Alan Corkhill. *Queensland and Germany: Ethnic, Socio-Cultural, Political and Trade Relations, 1838-1991*. Forest Hill, Victoria, Australia: Academia Press. 1992.

Genealogical Society of Queensland (German Research Group). *Die Zeitung* [*The Newspaper*]. Periodical.

Ian Harmstorf. *German Migration, with Particular Reference to Hamburg, to South Australia, 1851-1884*. M.A. thesis. Adelaide: University of Adelaide. 1971.

Ian Harmstorf and Michael Cigler. *The Germans in Australia*. Melbourne: AE Press. 1985.

M. J. Horst and J. McBride. *Austrians and Australians*. Blackburn, Australia: Australasian Educa Press Pty Ltd. 1987.

Mary Mennicken-Cooley. *The Germans in Western Australia*. McLawley, WA, Australia: Edith Cowan University. 1993.

Owen B. Mutzelburg. *How to Trace Your German Ancestors: A Guide for Australians and New Zealanders*. Sydney: Hale & Iremonger. 1989.

David A. Schubert. *Kavel's People: Their Story of Migration from Prussia to South Australia for the Sake of Faith,...* Adelaide: Lutheran Publishing House. 1985.

Colin Gordon Sheehan. "Germans in Australia: A Guide to Sources," in *Generation*. Stones Corner: Genealogical Society of Queensland (Vol. 6, No. 4, 1984).

Clifford Neal Smith. *Nineteenth Century Emigration of "Old Lutherans" from Eastern Germany (Mainly Pomerania and Lower Silesia) to Australia, Canada and the United States)*. McNeal, AZ: Westland Publications. 1980.

Jürgen Tampke and Colin Doxford. *Australia, Willkommen: A History of the Germans in Australia*. Kensington: New South Wales University Press. 1990.

Jürgen Tampke, ed. *Wunderbar Country: Germans Look at Australia, 1850-1914*. Marrickville, NSW: Hale & Iremonger Pty Ltd. 1982.

Liz Twigden. A letter from Torrensville, SA (with enclosures) providing genealogical, historical and bibliographical information on Germans in South Australia.

Josef Vondra. *German-Speaking Settlers in Australia*. Richmond, Australia: Cavalier Press Pty Ltd. 1981.

Carol Wardale and Margaret Jenner, comps. *German Research Directory*, 7th ed. Stones Corner: German Research Group, Genealogical Society of Queensland. 1988.

Susanne Wegmann. *The Swiss in Australia*. Grusch, Switzerland: Verlag Ruegger. 1989.

200 Jahre Geschichte der deutschsprachigen Gemeinschaft in Australien, 1788-1988 [*200 Years of History of the German-Speaking Community in Australia, 1788-1988*]. Sydney: Europa Kurier Pty Ltd. 1988.

CHINA

H. P. Isaak. *Our Life Story and Escape: From Russia to China to Japan to America*. Dinuba, CA: Author. 1977. 181 pp.
> Report of the flight of one group of Mennonite refugees via Harbin, with names.

Abram J. Loewen. *Immer weiter nach Osten: Südrussland-China-Kanada* [*Ever Farther Eastwards: South Russia-China-Canada*]. Available from Mennonite Heritage Centre, Winnipeg.
> Story of those Soviet refugees, temporarily quartered in Harbin, who ended up in Canada.

SOUTH AFRICA

An Alphabetical Guide to Gravestones in Smaller Cemeteries in South Africa, 28 vols. Pretoria. 1989-1993.

C. C. De Villiers and C. Pama. *Genealogies of Old South African Families*, 2 parts. Cape Town. 1981.

J. A. Heese and R. T. J. Lombard. *South African Genealogies*, 4 parts (1986-1992). Continuing series.

J. Hoge. "Personalia of the Germans at the Cape, 1652-1806," in Coenraad Beyers et al (eds.), *Archives Year Book for South African History*, 9th year. Published by authority of the Minister of the Interior and printed by the Cape Times Ltd., Cape Town, for the Government Printer.

R. T. J. Lombard. *Handbook for Genealogical Research in South Africa*, 2nd ed. Pretoria: Human Sciences Research Council. 1990. 119 pp. plus bibliography.

Maureen Joan Stern. *South African Jewish Biography, 1900-1966*: A Bibliography. Cape Town: University of Cape Town Libraries. 1972. 28 pp.

L. Zöllner. *The Descendants of Rhenish Missionaries to South Africa*. Pretoria. 1991.

L. Zöllner and J. A. Heese. *The Berlin Missionaries in South Africa*. Pretoria. 1984.

Chapter XVI

GENEALOGICAL RECORDS RELATING TO GERMAN-SPEAKING ANCESTORS IN EUROPE

This chapter presents a brief introduction to the kinds of records available for genealogical research in German-speaking areas of Europe. Once you understand the kinds of records that are available, you can better utilize the next chapter, which contains more detailed information about the kinds of records and their location for each country of Europe. See Chapters II, V and VI regarding records available in the United States, and Chapters III, VI and XV for other immigrant countries.

How to Find My German Ancestors and Relatives by Dr. Heinz F. Friedrichs, one of the leading German authorities, presents a brief overview of the subject presented here. Although the records listed below refer particularly to Germany, similar records (sometimes using different terms) can be found in German-speaking countries and sometimes for the German-speaking enclaves in other countries.

KINDS OF RECORDS AVAILABLE

Many types of records helpful for your genealogical research can be found in Germany. Although some records were destroyed during various wars or by fires, the vast majority of records are intact and can be found mainly in the local and state archives or at the local parishes. Since Germany has no central index to its records, you must refer to the state archive that contains regional records of interest to you, as well as checking local and church archives. Church records are nearly always the most useful resource, at least for information prior to the 1870s. Civil registration and wills can also be very useful. These and other kinds of records are described in the following checklist. Some records are only found in a few regions. Larry Jensen mentions a few other, less common kinds of records in his handbooks.

Many of the records have been microfilmed by the Family History Library (FHL). Contact a local Family History Center to see what is available for localities where your German-speaking ancestors lived.

1. **Relatives of ancestors** who remained in Germany. You may learn of them from German genealogical societies, from the local parish church, from a local German phone book (available at FHL, Immigrant Genealogical Society, etc.) or *Glenzdorfs*. They may be able to provide you with a great deal of information.

2. **Church records** (*Kirchenbücher* or *Kirchenregister*). Earliest church records for a parish may date back to 1650, and as early as 1480 for a few churches. Catholic Church records were written in Latin, while Evangelical (Reformed, Lutheran) records were written in German. Gothic script was used until about 1920. The Evangelical Church was established by the formal union of the Reformed (Calvinist) and Lutheran Churches in 1817 in Prussia by a royal edict. The merger took place in the rest of Germany soon thereafter, mostly voluntarily. Some Lutherans protested and continue to worship as Old Lutherans (*Altlutheraner*).

   Members of other German religions included Jews (*Juden*), Mennonites (*Mennoniten*), Baptists, Brethren (*Brüdergemeinden*), Dunkards, Schwenkfelders and Moravians (*Herrnhuter*), Seventh-day Adventists (*Adventisten*), and Methodists. There are some cases where the records of one church (apart from the Lutheran-Reformed combination) included entries of members of other churches. This was most likely to happen in the early years when there were still strong restrictions on the privileges of the dissenting churches, or in cases where the religious minority was so small that it did not have its own church in the village or nearby.

Germanic Genealogy: A Guide to Worldwide Sources and Migration Patterns   261

Regional church archives now have many of the original parish registers or microfilms of them; but most of the originals can still be found at the parish church. The most valuable church records include:

- **Baptism register** (*Taufregister*) or sometimes birth register (*Geburtsregister*), that contains date of baptism and/or birth, name and legitimacy of the child, and names of the parents and godparents. Also usually included are the residence and occupation or status of the parents and godparents, the maiden name of the mother, the name of the clergyman, and notes.

- **Confirmation register** (*Konfirmationregister*), which contains the name and age of the confirmand, the date and place of confirmation. Also sometimes included are the name and occupation of the father and name of the mother.

- **Marriage register** (*Trauregister*), which contains name, age, residence and occupation of the bride and groom, marriage date and place, and often the names of their parents and the fathers' occupations. Information regarding consent to the marriage, place and time of the proclamation of banns, the name of the pastor, and remarks are also sometimes included.

- **Death register** (*Sterberegister*), which includes name, age, occupation, date and place of death and sometimes includes cause of death, date and place of burial and names of spouse and children.

- **Funeral sermon** (*Leichenpredigt*), which may list birth and death date and other information. These are not available in many areas.

Very helpful records that are sometimes available include family registers, lists of communicants, and church council records.

Many terms that are used in these records may be found in the **German Vocabulary** section of Chapter XXI. One of the best books describing how to get the most out of German church books is *German Church Books: Beyond the Basics* by Kenneth L. Smith.

3. **Civil registration** (*Zivilregister*) of births, deaths, and marriages was required after 1876. Baden and some regions west of the Rhine have records from the early 1800s when they were introduced by French occupation authorities. National civil registration was adopted for Switzerland in 1848. These records are kept at the town civil registry (*Standesamt*).

4. **Passenger lists** (*Passagierlisten*) give names, ages and occupations for all family members, and often the place of origin. Passenger lists are covered in Chapter VI.

5. **Tax lists** (*Steuerlisten*) beginning in the 14th and 15th century list taxpayer's name and address.

6. **Land records** are among the oldest records, some dating prior to the 8th century, but records of land deeds did not begin until the 1300s or 1400s for most regions. The number of landowners was greatly restricted during feudal times, which continued until the 1700s or 1800s. These records are found in the local courthouse (*Amtsgericht*).

7. **Emigration records** (*Auswandererlisten*) may be found in some state archives (*Staatsarchiv*) from the early 1800s. However, many people left without recording their intent to emigrate.

8. **Wills** (*Testamente*) may be found in Germany dating from about 1200. They list the heirs and their relationships to the deceased. They are found in local courthouses (*Amtsgerichte*).

9. **Court records** may also provide family relationships of those involved, and will be located at the court house (*Amtsgericht*).

10. **Census records** (*Volkszählungslisten, Bauernverzeichnisse, Einwohnerlisten*, etc.) exist in only a few cases, except for the regions listed below, because censuses were not conducted regularly, nor were they national in scope before 1871. The census records that do exist may be found in local and state archives (*Staatsarchiv*).

> Mecklenburg (tax and tithing records of the 16th through 19th century)
> Schleswig-Holstein (19th century)
> Württemberg (family registers of the 16th through 19th centuries)

There are also several censuses of Mennonites (and possibly other) farm households in Prussia, the most extensive one being the special "Consignation" of 1776, after the Vistula-Nogat delta area had been transferred from Polish to Prussian rule in 1772. These have been published in various books, including *Die ost- und westpreussischen Mennoniten*, Volume I (Weierhof, Germany: Mennonitischer Geschichtsverein, 1978), by Horst Penner.

The first Prussian census was conducted in 1719, although lists of the heads of household in rural West Prussia, then part of Poland, date back to 1675 for some villages.

11. **Family registers** (*Familienregister*) of Württemberg and other regions may be helpful.

12. **Burgher rolls** or **citizen records** (*Bürgerbücher*) were kept until about 1850 for prominent residents. They contain name, occupation, father's name and hometown. Many have been published. Others may be found in the city archives (*Stadtarchiv*).

13. **Police registers** (*Polizeiregister*) replaced the *Bürgerbücher* and kept track of name and address of every permanent resident. These registers are kept at the town office of registration (*Einwohnermeldeamt*).

14. **City directories** or **address books** (*Adressbücher*) date from the early 1800s, depending on the town. Ribbe and Henning's *Taschenbuch für Familiengeschichtsforschung* lists the years each town printed address books. The address books may be found in local archives.

15. **Apprentice** and **guild books** (*Gilderbücher*) from 1500-1900 list name, parents, occupation, residence and employer. They are scattered. Write to the local archive to see whether they have been preserved (since there are many gaps) and, if so, where.

16. **Military records** (*Kriegslisten* or *Militärakten*) are scattered throughout the country in local and state archives near where soldiers were stationed.

17. **University student lists** that are available are shown in Ribbe and Henning's *Taschenbuch für Familiengeschichtsforschung*.

18. **Printed family histories** (*Sippenbücher* or *Familiengeschichten*) may be available from German genealogical societies. Those published in genealogical journals have been indexed in *Der Schlüssel* [*The Key*], a multi-volume series. The first volumes of *Der Schlüssel* were originally published by the now defunct Hans Reise Verlag; the volumes have been reprinted and the series continued by Verlag Degener & Co.

19. **Local histories** show the genealogy of a village (*Dorfsippenbücher* or *Ortssippenbücher*). Thousands are listed in Franz Heinzmann's bibliography of such books. They are extremely helpful when they are available for a particular place.

20. **Pedigree charts** (*Ahnenpässe*) for each individual were required during the Nazi era. Despite some false data to hide Jewish ancestors, these are very valuable, but hard to find.

The August 1983 issue of *The German Connection*, published by the German Research Association (address in Chapter XXIII) carried a table showing what kind of records were available in Germany, Austria and Switzerland, and where they could be found. The data came from Robert Ward's *German-American Genealogical Workshop Bulletin*.

Chapter XVII

RESEARCHING GERMANIC ANCESTORS IN THE GERMAN-SPEAKING COUNTRIES

Apart from this guide and its predecessor, the *Research Guide to German-American Genealogy*, there are few comprehensive English-language guides which deal with all of the German-speaking countries, although there are quite a few on the former German Empire and a much smaller number for other German-speaking countries listed in the **ANNOTATED BIBLIOGRAPHY**. However, there are a number of more specialized books.

Ernest Thode's *Address Book for Germanic Genealogy* lists institutions and genealogists in the various German-speaking countries, as well as in some others.

Angus Baxter, *In Search of Your German Roots*, focuses on records in Germany, but includes some information on other countries.

For an overview of genealogical, historical and other literature, see Margrit B. Krewson, *The German-Speaking Countries of Europe: A Selective Bibliography*, which lists many other bibliographies, most of them in German.

John M. Spalek's *Guide to the Archival Materials of the German-Speaking Emigration to the United States After 1933* is helpful for refugees from Naziism and post-World War II immigrants.

The best source of information is Wolfgang Ribbe and Eckart Henning's comprehensive *Taschenbuch für Familiengeschichtsforschung* [*Handbook for Family History Research*]. Although its scope is worldwide, it is useful for Germanic research only in European countries.

A useful starting point for an overview of the literature concerning Germany, Austria, Switzerland and Liechtenstein is *The German-Speaking Countries of Europe: A Selective Bibliography* by Margrit B. Krewson. It lists a number of other bibliographies, most of which are in German, but including John M. Spalek's *Guide to the Archival Materials of the German-Speaking Emigration to the United States After 1933*.

GERMANY
(Deutschland)

In 1994 the Family History Library published a 52-page *Research Outline: Germany*. It provides comprehensive coverage of topics relating to research on the pre-World War I German Empire, with some limited information about East European Germans and individual German states. This booklet is an absolute must for beginners and includes information of value to more experienced genealogists as well. For more information on various aspects of Germanic genealogy than what is provided in this guide, see the books listed in the bibliographies, as well as Larry O. Jensen, *A Genealogical Handbook of German Research*, George K. Schweitzer, *German Genealogical Research*, and Shirley J. Riemer, *The German Research Companion*.

POSTAL CODES AND FORMS OF ADDRESS

The postal code (*Postleitzahl*) for all locations in the recently reunited Germany was changed in 1993 to D- followed by a five digit number. The city is no longer underlined in German mailing addresses, as was the case until recently. Instead, it is now customary to leave a blank line between the street or post office box and the city in typed or pre-printed addresses. We have not done so in this guide in order to conserve space.

CHURCH RECORDS IN GERMANY

Local Churches. You can write to the local church pastor using the following address format:

Roman Catholic:	**Evangelical (Lutheran):**
Das katholische Pfarramt	Das evangelische Pfarramt
D-*(postal code)* *(name of town)*	D-*(postal code)* *(name of town)*
Germany	Germany

If you write to the local church, you may have only limited success. Many young ministers are not able to read the old Gothic script. Most pastors in the new eastern states, as well as older pastors in the western states, have little or no knowledge of English, so you should write in German.

Church Archives. Duplicate copies of some church records can be found in regional church archives. Expect to pay a research fee when writing to an archive. Check the Family History Library microfilms before writing to Germany, since many parish registers have been microfilmed. If the records you want are not on film, you can find the addresses of all the major church archives in Thode's *Address Book*. Other sources of addresses are listed in the section on **RESEARCHING ANCESTORS FROM SPECIFIC AREAS IN GERMANY**.

The Family History Library has been unable to microfilm some German parish registers, including the Catholic and Lutheran registers in Bavaria and the Lutheran registers in Saxony, Thuringia and Hanover. "Microfilming in Germany, Poland, Bulgaria and Armenia" by John D. Movius (*FEEFHS Newsletter*, December 1994) provides an up-to-date report on alternative records being microfilmed. The current filming in Poland also includes areas where there were many Germans (Breslau, Posen, Danzig).

PUBLIC RECORDS IN GERMANY

Civil Registration was required in Prussia by 1874 and in all of Germany by 1876. But Hanover, Hesse, Baden and areas to the west of them have records predating 1815. Birth, marriage and death records are kept at the local civil registry office (*Standesamt*). Write to the *Standesamt* of the town in question. Check the *Postleitzahlenbuch* (postal code directory of Germany) for German postal code information. Write to:

> Standesamt
> *(street address if known, but not needed for small villages)*
> D-*(postal code)* *(name of town)*
> Germany

Military Records of the German, and previously Prussian, government reportedly were destroyed in World War II. However, Horst Reschke's *Germany Military Records as Genealogical Sources* covers the records of various German states which never were under Prussian rule, i.e., most of South Germany and some parts of North Germany. Furthermore, many military parish registers for units with bases in various parts of the former German Empire have been preserved. Those at three of the four largest repositories (Deutsche Zentralstelle für Genealogie, Leipzig, Evangelisches Zentralarchiv and Geheimes Staatsarchiv preussischer Kulturbesitz, both of Berlin) have been microfilmed.

The fourth major repository is:

> Kirchliches Archiv im Katholischen Militärbischofsamt
> Kaiserstr. 141
> D-53113 Bonn

There are also quite a few, though a lesser number, at:

Landeskirchliches Archiv
Altsädter Kirchplatz 5
D-33602 Bielefeld

Archiv der evangelischen Kirche im Rheinland
Archivstelle Koblenz
Karmeliterstr. 1-3
D-56068 Koblenz

Several hundred other repositories have a modest number of military parish registers.

Two books by Wolfgang Eger list over 6,000 original or microfilmed military parish registers, by regiment or other military unit and home base, according to the alphabetical order of the place where they are now located.

His *Verzeichnis der Militärkirchenbücher in der Bundesrepublik (nach dem Stand vom 30. September 1990)* [*Inventory of Military Parish Registers in the Federal Republic*], as of 30 September 1990] lists some 4,000 Evangelical military parish registers, although there are a very small number of references to other religious groups.

His *Verzeichnis der Militärkirchenbücher in der Bundesrepublik Deutschland (neue Bundesländer — Römisch-Katholische Kirche)* [*Inventory of Military Parish Registers in the Federal Republic of Germany (New States — Roman Catholic Church)*], published in 1996, ostensibly refers to the new eastern states of the Federal Republic and the Roman Catholic registers. In reality, it must be considered a general supplement to his 1993 publication, since there are also quite a few entries which fall into neither category.

Some registers may have been interdenominational. Both books are indexed, but the later one has a cumulative index for both of them. A few registers are in archives in Copenhagen or Antwerp.

Not all of the entries have a heading showing the state or province in which the military units were based. However, the largest number at the Prussian State Privy Archives are, in numerical order, for Brandenburg, Silesia, Pomerania, East Prussia, Posen and the Prussian province of Saxony. The largest number at the Evangelical Central Archives are for West Prussia. All of these are in currently German or Polish areas which were ruled by the Communists until the collapse of the Iron Curtain. These registers are especially useful if your immigrant ancestor came from areas such as Pomerania and Posen, for which many regular parish registers are missing or widely scattered.

Also included are some military registers for Luxembourg (1816-67, when it was part of the German Confederation), France (mostly during or shortly after the Franco-Prussian War), Belgium (World War I), Austria (mostly for 1938-44) and the Czech Republic (1938-45).

The oldest register dates back to at least 1711, but there are very few until the late eighteenth century.

If you know where your ancestor was stationed or to which regiment or garrison he belonged, Eger's books will tell you all you need to know in order to begin the search for vital data. Of course, a lot of registers remain at unidentified locations or are lost and the listed registers won't help you unless a marriage, birth or death occurred during your ancestor's period of military service.

In the absence of such information, you can hazard a guess that your ancestor joined a military unit stationed close to home and check those registers.

Guild Records can be very useful to genealogists with artisan ancestors. But such records are widely scattered and have many gaps. For the most comprehensive article on which of such records have been microfilmed by the Family History Library and the German state and city archives known to have some, see "Guild Records in Germany," an adaptation of a lecture given by Gerhard Jeske in the Winter 1994 issue of the *German Genealogical Digest*.

Burgher books may be of importance if your ancestor was a prominent local individual. In most German-speaking countries, "citizenship" denoted one's status in a city (which included what we might call towns, but rarely villages), rather than to a larger political unit, until about 1850. "Citizens" were comparable to the individuals whose biographies we might find in local histories in the United States. When someone, usually from elsewhere, became a "new citizen," this information was recorded in the *Bürgerbuch*. The sons of citizens would usually be entered when they attained the status of a citizen. Although citizenship was not automatically inherited, the sons of citizens certainly received preferential consideration.

Some of these burgher books go back to the Middle Ages, but only in the modern era do they become comprehensive enough to be of genealogical value. The application for citizenship included the name of the father (occasionally both parents), the applicant's home and trade, etc. "New citizens" had to present a letter of birth (*Geburtsbrief*) from their hometown to prove legitimacy. At first, property ownership was also required. Until a rather late date, the applicant had to have been born to Christian parents. There were also some honorary citizens recorded in *Ehrenbürgerbücher* which continued to be kept after 1850.

By now a considerable number of these burgher books have been published, mostly as articles in genealogical or historical periodicals. In the 11th edition of Ribbe and Henning's classic book (which emphasizes, but is not limited to, German genealogy), Eckart Henning lists over 600 localities for which such records have been published. These are not limited to Germany, Austria and Switzerland, since some books for France, the Netherlands, the Czech Republic and the Baltic countries are included. His chapter bibliography lists books devoted specifically to burgher books in East Prussia, Pomerania, Saxony, Mecklenburg, Westphalia and the Baltics.

These publications usually cover only a given time period. Many of them do not include such records from the time they were first kept until they ceased to be kept.

Censuses were conducted in Germany, the first one in 1871 after Germany was united, and every 5 years between 1880 and 1910. They took place in a number of German entities at irregular times before then. Baxter lists pre-unification censuses for Baden (4 for 1852-61), Bavaria (6 for 1846-61), Hamburg (1866), Württemberg (9 for 1821-61) and one for all members of the (North) German Customs Union (1855). Censuses were also conducted at the level of a county or individual town or city.

The Family History Library has a copy of the Mecklenburg-Schwerin census of 1819, which has been published and indexed by Franz Schubert in *Mecklenburg-Schwerin Volkszählung 1819: Register der Familiennamen [Mecklenburg-Schwerin Census of 1819: Register of Surnames]*, published in 5 volumes by the author in 1981-86 in Berlin, Göttingen, and Ditterich.

Information recorded in each census varies greatly. In some cases only the names of the heads of household are given, but in other cases each family member is named with date and place of birth plus additional information.

Privacy laws may prevent access to more recent census records (1890 and newer). These German privacy laws do not allow access to personal records for 110 years after birth if the person's death data is unknown, or for 30 years after death.

Some less significant censuses for various German principalities have also been micro-filmed by the FHL. It should be borne in mind that pre-unification censuses were usually conducted for purposes of taxation, sometimes for purposes of keeping track of individuals with future military obligations. Therefore, the term, "census," is often less accurate than tax registers, land registers, lists of residents, etc. Moreover, the FHL cautions that these records are generally less reliable than religious or civil registers with respect to such things as age.

Prussia conducted a peasant census of the territory it acquired in the First Partition in Poland in 1772, or at least in West Prussia. The names of Mennonite peasants have been published in various German-language books, but they list only the place, the head of the household, and the number of minor and adult females and males, as far as genealogically useful information is concerned. Whether similar records for non-Mennonites have been preserved is uncertain, but the dates of archival research by German authors suggest that they should be available, unless they were among the records destroyed by World War II. Prussia conducted nine regular censuses between 1831 and 1861.

In many cases, only the statistical data, not the information about specific individuals, has been preserved, so don't get your hopes up too high. The limited value of German censuses is indicated by the fact that the classic German work on genealogy (Ribbe and Henning's 11th edition) makes no reference to them. However, genealogists researching Germans who lived under Danish or French rule may fare better.

Schleswig-Holstein was under Danish rule until 1864. The first Danish census in 1769 contained much the same information as the 1772 Prussian census. Nine additional censuses between 1801 and 1860 contain details about each individual. The four held in 1845-1860 go even farther, listing the place of birth, the parish to which it belonged, and the length of residence at the current home. These censuses (in German, Danish or both) have been microfilmed, but not indexed by the FHL. According to Baxter, seven Danish censuses for 1787 to 1860 are available for inspection.

Baxter also states that France has held regular censuses at five-year intervals since 1836. These would include Alsace and Lorraine prior to 1871. Quite a bit of genealogical information is contained in these records, but not the place of birth. Some have been destroyed, but others can be found in the archives for each department or in the mayor's office.

Village lineage books (now called *Ortssippenbücher*, formerly *Ortsfamilienbücher* or, in Schleswig-Holstein, *Kirchspielsippenbücher*, i.e., parish lineage books) are being published in a rapidly increasing number. Diana Schulle, in Ribbe and Henning, says about 100 are being published each year. Those for the Saarland are almost complete. In addition, there are an estimated 1,500-2,000 unpublished or typewritten manuscripts. The German Central Office for Genealogy in Leipzig is attempting to compile a master list and already has about 700 volumes in its own collection.

About 30 such books were published in 1937-1940, with ambitious Nazi plans for 20,000-30,000 within 20-30 years, but only a tiny percentage were published prior to 1956.

Published village lineages include quite a few for former German communities outside Germany, e.g., the Czech Republic, Alsace, Yugoslavia and Romania.

In contrast to the burgher books, most of these lineage books are for individual villages, although there are some for larger towns and even a few for cities as large as Kaiserslautern.

At least 45 *Ortssippenbücher*, *Dorfsippenbücher* and *Familienbücher* have been published for Ostfriesland and are available in the United States at the Family History Library, George Public Library in George, Iowa, and many large universities. They are also available for some villages from other parts of Germany. New *Ortssippenbücher* continue to be published by German genealogists.

The *Deutsche Geschlechterbücher* is a collection of over 200 volumes containing family genealogies for prominent German families and nobility. The *Deutsche Geschlechterbücher* are available in the United States at Harvard University, Cornell University, Rice University (Fondern Library), Dallas Public Library, Easton Area Public Library (Easton, PA), Cleveland Public Library, University of Colorado at Boulder, Allen County Public Library, University of Missouri (Columbia), Saint Louis Public Library, Public Library of Cincinnati/Hamilton County, and the Family History Library, and at the University of Alberta in Canada.

Further information about *Ortssippenbücher* and *Geschlechterbücher* may be found in Wolfgang Ribbe and Eckart Henning's *Taschenbuch für Familiengeschichtsforschung* [*Handbook for Family History Research*]. *Bibliographie der Ortssippenbücher in Deutsch-*

land [*Bibliography of Village Histories in Germany*], by Franz Heinzmann, lists more than 6,000 of these books.

Closely related to these are the **card indexes** being prepared for many parishes (*Kirchenbuchverkartungen*), often in the form of family registers. Thousands of these were allegedly compiled before World War II, but few of these are known to have been preserved, according to Katja Münchow and Volkmar Weiss of the German Central Office for Genealogy (in Ribbe and Henning). In recent years a tendency has developed to make some of this information public only through electronic channels.

Münchow and Weiss estimate that published or unpublished lineage books have been compiled for some 3,000 parishes, including 1.7 million families, representing an estimated 5-10% of all such records in or for present or former German-speaking areas of Europe. The ultimate goal is a central database for all of Germanic Europe.

Address books, comparable to city directories (but occasionally prepared for an entire county), are especially important for researching ancestors from urban areas or tracing relatives who may have become urbanites rather than emigrants. Quite a few exist for modest-sized towns. However, they were published at rather irregular intervals, at least until recently, with the exception of a few major cities like Berlin. **Calendars**, the predecessors of these directories, date back to shortly after 1700, although many localities did not publish directories until after 1850 or even after 1900.

Christel Wegeleben has a 27-page list of localities with such directories, as well as the years in which they were published in Ribbe and Henning's *Taschenbuch*.

Records Pertaining to Royalty, the Nobility and Prominent Burghers. There are an ample number of German-language publications relating to the upper class. The most comprehensive one is *Siebmachers Wappenbücher*, which includes a huge number of volumes. However, little attention has been paid to this group in non-German countries, since very few of them emigrated. Most of the rare cases involve the illegitimate offspring of rulers, or children of nobles who were disinherited because of their misbehavior or disagreements with their father. A few wealthy German burghers emigrated for the sake of adventure and because they believed that America might offer even richer rewards.

The Germanic Genealogist, published by the Augustan Society, is the only American periodical which has carried quite a few articles on the nobility.

For information about university registers, see John D. Movius, "Snooping for Cousins in Germanic Universität Matrikel Registers," in Vol. 1, No. 2, of *FEEFHS: The Newsletter of the Federation of East European Family History Societies* (March 1993).

Local Court House (*Amtsgericht*) has records, deeds and other land records as early as the 7th century, municipal records and tax lists. Write to the *Amtsgericht* of the city in question using the *Postleitzahlenbuch* [*German Postal Code Directory*]. Write to:

> Amtsgericht
> (*street address if known*)
> D-(*postal code*) (*town name*)
> Germany

City Archives (*Stadtarchiv*) contain documents such as births, marriages and deaths since 1876, as well as city directories, some funeral sermons, apprentice and guild records, school and university records, house books, some census records and burgher rolls. Some date back to the Middle Ages. Lists of city archives are too numerous to mention here; please refer to the *Address Book for Germanic Genealogy* by Ernest Thode. Write to the *Stadtarchiv* of the city in question using the *Postleitzahlenbuch* [*German Postal Code Directory*]. Write to:

> Stadtarchiv
> (*street address if known*)
> D-(*postal code*) (*town name*)
> Germany

National Archives. Because of the fragmentation of Germany until 1871, the national archives are not at all comparable to those of most Western countries with respect to their significance for genealogical research. However, they do contain a few genealogical treasures, particularly with respect to the ethnic Germans in Eastern Europe who were "repatriated" during the Hitler era. There are extensive genealogical materials for the repatriates, since each one had to complete a genealogical questionnaire and there are lists of all the Germans who were residents in each of the affected villages. The address is:

> Bundesarchiv
> Potsdamer Strasse 1
> Postfach 320
> D-56075 Koblenz
> Germany

The voluminous records of the Berlin Document Center, which pertain to the Nazi period, will be transferred to the national archives, but not before being microfilmed by the United States government.

State Archives (*Staatsarchiv*). Each state or regional archive has different holdings; if you cannot locate the information needed, write to archives in the following list, asking the whereabouts of the information you need. They will refer you to the right source.

The following central state archive is the main archive of the former German Democratic Republic. It has official records of the former German Empire and the former German Democratic Republic. All materials formerly at the central archive in Merseburg have now been transferred to Potsdam.

Zentrales Staatsarchiv
Historische Abteilung I
Berliner Strasse 98-101
Postfach 42
D-14467 Potsdam
Germany

BADEN-WÜRTTEMBERG STATE ARCHIVES:

Generallandesarchiv
Nördliche Hildapromenade 2
D-76133 Karlsruhe
Germany

Baden
Staatsarchiv
Colombistrasse 4
Postfach 323
D-79098 Freiburg
Germany

Württemberg
Hauptstaatsarchiv
Konrad-Adenauer-Strasse 4
D-70173 Stuttgart
Germany

Württemberg
Staatsarchiv
Schloss Ludwigsburg
Schloss-Strasse 30
D-71634 Ludwigsburg
Germany

Hohenzollern
Staatsarchiv
Karlstrasse 3
Postfach 526
D-72488 Sigmaringen
Germany

BAYERN (BAVARIA) STATE ARCHIVES:

Bayerisches Hauptstaatsarchiv I
Arcisstrasse 12
Postfach 200507
D-80005 München
Germany

Coburg
Staatsarchiv
Schloss Ehrenburg
D-96450 Coburg
Germany

Mittelfranken
Staatsarchiv
Archivstrasse 17
D-90408 Nürnberg
Germany

Niederbayern
Staatsarchiv
Burg Trausnitz
D-84036 Landshut
Germany

Oberbayern
Staatsarchiv
Schönfeldstrasse 3
D-80539 München
Germany

Oberfranken
Staatsarchiv
Hainstrasse 39
Postfach 2668
D-96047 Bamberg
Germany

Oberpfalz
Staatsarchiv
Archivstrasse 3
D-92224 Amberg
Germany

Schwaben
Staatsarchiv
Salomon-Idler-Strasse 2
D-86159 Augsburg
Germany

Unterfranken
Staatsarchiv
Residenzplatz 2
D-97070 Würzburg
Germany

BRANDENBURG STATE ARCHIVES:

Brandenburgisches
    Landeshauptarchiv
Sanssouci-Orangerie
Postfach 48
D-14469 Potsdam
Germany

BREMEN STATE ARCHIVES:

Staatsarchiv
Am Staatsarchiv 1
D-28203 Bremen
Germany

HAMBURG STATE ARCHIVES:

Staatsarchiv
ABC-Strasse 19A
D-20354 Hamburg
Germany

HESSEN (HESSE) STATE ARCHIVES:

Nassau
Hauptstaatsarchiv
Mosbacher Strasse 55
D-65187 Wiesbaden
Germany

Hessen-Darmstadt
Staatsarchiv
Schloss
D-64283 Darmstadt
Germany

Hessen-Kassel
Staatsarchiv
Friedrichsplatz 15
Postfach 540
D-35037 Marburg
Germany

MECKLENBURG-VORPOMMERN STATE ARCHIVES:

Mecklenburg
Staatsarchiv
Graf-Schack-Allee 2
D-19053 Schwerin
Germany

Vorpommern
Staatsarchiv
Martin-Andersen-Nexö-Platz 1
D-17489 Greifswald
Germany

NIEDERSACHSEN (LOWER SAXONY) STATE ARCHIVES:

Hauptstaatsarchiv
Am Archiv 1
D-30169 Hannover
Germany

Braunschweig
Staatsarchiv
Forstweg 2
D-38302 Wolfenbüttel
Germany

Bückeburg
Staatsarchiv
Schloss
Postfach 1350
D-31675 Bückeburg
Germany

Oldenburg
Staatsarchiv
Damm 43
D-26135 Oldenburg
Germany

Osnabrück
Staatsarchiv
Schloss-Strasse 29
D-49074 Osnabrück
Germany

Ostfriesland
Staatsarchiv
Oldersumer Strasse 50
D-26603 Aurich
Germany

Stade
Staatsarchiv
Am Sande 4c
D-21682 Stade
Germany

NORDRHEIN-WESTFALEN (NORTHRHINE-WESTPHALIA) STATE ARCHIVES:

Hauptstaatsarchiv
Mauerstrasse 55
D-40476 Düsseldorf
Germany

Lippe
Staatsarchiv
Willi-Hofmann-Strasse 2
D-32756 Detmold
Germany

Rheinland
Nordrhein-Westfälisches
Personenstandsarchiv Rheinland
Schloss-Str. 12
D-50321 Brühl
Germany
*(devoted to the preservation of civil
and parish registers, especially for the
Rhineland; has a publication listing
the Rhenish civil registers; contains
the library of the Westdeutsche
Gesellschaft für Familienkunde)*

Westfalen
Staatsarchiv
Bohlweg 2
D-48147 Münster
Germany

RHEINLAND-PFALZ (RHINELAND-PALATINATE) STATE ARCHIVES:

Rheinland
Landeshauptarchiv
Karmeliterstrasse 1-3
D-56068 Koblenz
Germany

Pfalz
Staatsarchiv
Otto-Meyer-Strasse 9
Postfach 1608
D-67346 Speyer
Germany

SAAR (SAARLAND) STATE ARCHIVES:

Landesarchiv
Scheidter Strasse 114
Postfach 101010
D-66010 Saarbrücken
Germany

SACHSEN (SAXONY) STATE ARCHIVES:

Sächsisches Hauptstaatsarchiv
Dresden
Archivstrasse 14
D-01097 Dresden
Germany

Aussenstelle Bautzen des Sächsischen
Hauptstaatsarchivs
Schloss Ortenburg
D-02625 Bautzen
Germany

Aussenstelle Freiberg des Sächsischen
Hauptstaatsarchivs Dresden
(Bergarchiv)
Kirchgasse 11
D-09599 Freiberg
Germany

Sächsisches Staatsarchiv Leipzig
Georgi-Dimitroff-Platz 1
D-04107 Leipzig
Germany

SACHSEN-ANHALT (SAXONY-ANHALT) STATE ARCHIVES:

Landeshauptarchiv Sachsen-Anhalt
Hegelstrasse 25
Postfach 92
D-39104 Magdeburg
Germany

Aussenstelle Wernigerode
des Landeshauptarchivs
Sachsen-Anhalt
Orangerie
Leninalle
D-38855 Wernigerode
Germany

Aussenstelle Oranienbaum
des Landeshauptarchivs
Sachsen-Anhalt
Schloss
D-06785 Oranienbaum
Germany

SCHLESWIG-HOLSTEIN STATE ARCHIVES:

Landesarchiv
Schloss Gottorf
D-24837 Schleswig
Germany

THÜRINGEN (THURINGIA) STATE ARCHIVES:

Thüringisches Hauptstaatsarchiv
Weimar
Marstallstrasse 2
D-99423 Weimar
Germany

Reuss-Greiz
Aussenstelle Greiz des
Thüringischen Hauptstaatsarchivs
Oberes Schloss
D-07973 Greiz
Germany

Sachsen-Altenburg
Aussenstelle Altenburg des
Thüringischen Hauptstaatsarchivs
Schloss 2a
D-06429 Altenburg
Germany

Sachsen-Coburg-Gotha
Aussenstelle Gotha des
Thüringischen Hauptstaatsarchivs
Schloss Friedenstein
D-99867 Gotha
Germany

Sachsen-Meiningen
Thüringisches Staatsarchiv
Meiningen
Schloss Bibrabau
D-98617 Meiningen
Germany

Schwarzburg-Rudolstadt
Thüringisches Staatsarchiv
Rudolstadt
Schloss Heidecksburg
D-07407 Rudolstadt
Germany

GENEALOGICAL SOCIETIES FOR RESEARCH IN GERMANY

Religious archives are not listed here because many parish registers are still in the local parsonages and because the archives are so numerous. Addresses can be found in Thode's *Address Book* and the Immigrant Genealogical Society's *1993 Updated Addresses to German Repositories*, with less complete coverage in many other books.

NATIONAL GENEALOGICAL SOCIETIES

The Deutsche Arbeitsgemeinschaft genealogischer Verbände (DAGV) is an umbrella organization for 56 German genealogical associations representing 19,000 genealogical researchers, with its office at Schloss-Strasse 12, D-50321 Brühl, Germany. Its list of member organizations (*Mitgliederverzeichnis*) provides details concerning services and addresses. It is published by the Verlag Degener & Co., Postfach 1360, D-91403 Neustadt/ Aisch, Germany, as part of the series, *Aktuelle Themen zur Genealogie* [*Current Topics in Genealogy*].

The Zentralstelle für Personen- und Familiengeschichte, Birkenweg 13, D-61381 Friedrichsdorf, Germany, is a genealogical institute that was founded in Leipzig in 1904, not a genealogical society in the strict sense of the word. It is specifically concerned with providing information and research tips to genealogists throughout the world, in addition to registering *Ortssippenbücher* or *Dorfsippenbücher* (village genealogies) and publishing a genealogical yearbook.

The Verein zur Förderung der Zentralstelle für Personen- und Familiengeschichte e.V., Archivstrasse 12-14, D-14195 Berlin-Dahlem, Germany, is a membership organization devoted to the promotion of the above-mentioned genealogical institute. The HEROLD at the same address is a related society that emphasizes publications specifically about heraldry and diverse disciplines that have some relevance to heraldry and genealogy.

Another organization that is devoted to the dissemination of information about genealogical research is the Akademie für Genealogie, Heraldik und verwandte Wissenschaften e.V., Gutenbergstr. 12 B, D-38118 Braunschweig, Germany.

STATE AND REGIONAL SOCIETIES

Baden-Württemberg
Verein für Familien- und Wappenkunde
in Württemberg und Baden e.V.
Konrad-Adenauer-Strasse 8
Postfach 105441
D-70047 Stuttgart
Germany

Baden-Württemberg (Baden)
Landesverein Badische Heimat
Ausschuss für Familienforschung
Heilbronner Strasse 3
D-75015 Bretten
Germany

Bayern (Bavaria)
Bayerischer Landesverein
für Familienkunde e.V.
Hauptstaatsarchiv
Ludwigstrasse 14/I
D-80539 München
Germany

Bayern (Franken area)
Gesellschaft für Familienforschung
in Franken e.V.
Staatsarchiv
Archivstrasse 17
D-90408 Nürnberg
Germany

Bayern (Oberpfalz area)
Gesellschaft für Familienforschung
in der Oberpfalz e.V.
Pustetstr. 13
D-93155 Hemau
Germany

Berlin
Interessengemeinschaft Genealogie
Berlin
Heinrich-Heine-Str. 11
D-10179 Berlin
Germany

Bremen
"Die Maus"
Gesellschaft für Familienforschung e.V.
Staatsarchiv
Am Staatsarchiv 1/Fedelhören
D-28203 Bremen
Germany

Hamburg
Genealogische Gesellschaft e.V.
Alsterchaussee 11
Postfach 302042
D-20307 Hamburg
Germany

Hessen (Hessen-Darmstadt area)
Hessische Familiengeschichtliche
Vereinigung e.V.
Karolinenplatz 3 (Staatsarchiv)
D-64283 Darmstadt
Germany

Hessen (Kurhessen & Waldeck area)
Gesellschaft für Familienkunde
in Kurhessen und Waldeck e.V.
Postfach 101346
D-34013 Kassel
Germany

Hessen (Nassau & Frankfurt area)
Familienkundliche Gesellschaft
für Nassau und Frankfurt e.V.
Hessisches Hauptstaatsarchiv
Mosbacher Strasse 55
D-65187 Wiesbaden
Germany

Hessen (Fulda area)
Vereinigung für Familien- und
Wappenkunde zu Fulda
Taunusstrasse 4
D-36043 Fulda
Germany

Mecklenburg-Vorpommern
Arbeitsgemeinschaft Genealogie
und Heraldik
Zum Netzboden 14
D-23966 Wismar
Germany

Niedersachsen
Niedersächsischer Landesverein
für Familienkunde e.V.
Am Bokemahle 14-16 (Stadtarchiv)
D-39171 Hannover
Germany

Niedersachsen (Göttingen area)
Genealogisch-Heraldische Gesellschaft
Untere Karspüle 10
Postfach 2062
D-37010 Göttingen
Germany

Niedersachsen (Oldenburg area)
Oldenburgische Gesellschaft
    für Familienkunde
Lerigauweg 14
D-26131 Oldenburg
Germany

Niedersachsen (Ostfriesland area)
Upstalsboom-Gesellschaft für
    historische Personenforschung und
    Bevölkerungsgeschichte in
    Ostfriesland e.V.
Flotowweg 4
D-26386 Wilhelmshaven
Germany

Nordrhein-Westfalen (Aachen area)
Genealogie ohne Grenzen
Postbus 10
NL-6343 ZG Klimmen
The Netherlands
*(regional society for the tri-national area
around Aachen)*

Nordrhein-Westfalen (Berg area)
Bergischer Verein für Familienkunde e.V.
Zanellastr. 5
D-42287 Wuppertal
Germany

Nordrhein-Westfalen (Dortmund area)
Roland zu Dortmund e.V.
Hansastrasse 61
Postfach 103326
D-44033 Dortmund
Germany

Nordrhein-Westfalen (Kleve area)
Mosaik: Familienkundliche
    Vereinigung für das Klever
    Land e.V.
Mosaik-Archiv
"Christus-Königschule"
Lindenallee 54
D-47533 Kleve
Germany
*(half-German, half-Dutch society for this
area where political and linguistic
borders shifted)*

Nordrhein-Westfalen (Lippe area)
Lippischer Heimatbund
Bismarckstrasse 8
D-32756 Detmold
Germany

**Nordrhein-Westfalen
(Mark & Sauerland area)**
Arbeitskreis für Familienforschung
    im Hagener Heimatbund e.V.
Hochstr. 74
D-58095 Hagen
Germany

**Nordrhein-Westfalen
(former Rhein province area)**
Westdeutsche Gesellschaft für
    Familienkunde e.V.
Postfach 100822
D-51608 Gummersbach
Germany
*(branches in Aachen, Bonn, Düsseldorf,
Essen, Gummersbach, Kleve, Koblenz,
Köln, Krefeld, Mönchengladbach, Trier
and Wuppertal)*

Nordrhein-Westfalen (Westfalen area)
Westfälische Gesellschaft für
    Genealogie und Familienforschung
Warendorfer Strasse 25
Postfach 6125
D-48133 Münster
Germany

Rheinland-Pfalz
Arbeitsgemeinschaft für
    Pfälzisch-Rheinische
    Familienkunde e.V.
Staatsarchiv
Rottstrasse 17
D-67061 Ludwigshafen
Germany

Saarland
Arbeitsgemeinschaft für Saarländische
    Familienkunde e.V.
Hebbelstrasse 3
D-66346 Püttlingen
Germany

Sachsen (Annaberg-Buchholz area)
Arbeitsgemeinschaft Genealogie
Hauptstr. 118
D-09477 Arnsfeld
Germany

Sachsen (Auerbach area)
Arbeitsgemeinschaft Genealogie
Poststr. 4
D-08233 Treuen
Germany

Sachsen (Chemnitz area)
Arbeitsgemeinschaft Genealogie
Str. Usti nad Labem 23
D-09119 Chemnitz
Germany

Sachsen (Dresden area)
Arbeitsgemeinschaft Genealogie
Krenkelstr. 9
D-01309 Dresden
Germany

Sachsen (Leipzig area)
Leipziger Genealogische Gesellschaft e.V.
c/o Deutsche Zentralstelle für Genealogie
Postfach 274
D-04002 Leipzig
Germany

Sachsen (Plauen area)
Arbeitsgemeinschaft Genealogie
Weststr. 73
D-08523 Plauen
Germany

Sachsen-Anhalt (Halle area)
Genealogischer Abend "Ekkehard"
Halle e.V.
Otto-Hahn-Str. 2
D-06126 Halle-Neustadt
Germany

Sachsen-Anhalt (Magdeburg area)
Arbeitsgemeinschaft Genealogie
Magdeburg
Thiemstr. 7
D-39104 Magdeburg
Germany

Schleswig-Holstein
Schleswig-Holsteinische Gesellschaft
für Familienforschung
und Wappenkunde e.V.
Postfach 3809
D-24307 Kiel
Germany

Schleswig-Holstein (Lübeck area)
Arbeitskreis für Familienforschung e.V.
Mühlentorturm
Mühlentorplatz 2
D-23552 Lübeck
Germany

Thüringen
Arbeitsgemeinschaft Genealogie
Thüringen e.V.
Martin-Andersen-Nexö-Str. 62
D-99096 Erfurt
Germany

RESEARCHING ANCESTORS FROM SPECIFIC AREAS IN GERMANY

Many genealogists are more interested in information about researching the specific areas from which their ancestors came than about Germanic genealogy as a whole.

One complication in attempting to provide such information is the fact that not only the boundaries, but the entities themselves (kingdoms, duchies, principalities, archbishoprics and bishoprics with secular governing authority, provinces and states) changed so frequently. In addition, quite a few books, monographs and articles deal with geographic areas, rather than past or present political jurisdictions.

For pertinent background information, read Chapter IX. For more detail, try encyclopedias. Those in German will be most helpful, but the *Encyclopedia Britannica* is likely to provide more detailed information than encyclopedias published in the United States or other immigrant countries.

To find a place of origin, check the published and unpublished passenger lists (Chapter XV) and the numerous relevant books listed in Appendix A.

The geographic-historical pattern of migration may be helpful in some cases. For example, most colonial immigrants came from, or close to, the Rhine River valley, stretching from Switzerland to the Netherlands. These are often referred to as Palatines, since a large number came from the Palatinate, which at one time included territory east of the Rhine.

Books by Henry Z. Jones, Jr., Strassburger and Hinke, Don Yoder, Faust and Brumbaugh, Montague Giuseppi, Walter Knittle, and Israel Daniel Rupp, all listed in Appendix A are helpful researching these colonial immigrants.

The so-called "Hessian mercenaries," listed in Eckhart Franz's published *HETRINA* project, who fought for the British in the American Revolution were not really mercenaries, since their rulers were paid by Britain and the soldiers usually were not volunteers. Moreover, a significant minority came from outside Hesse, particularly small jurisdictions within what are now the states of Bavaria and Baden-Württemberg. Many deserters, prisoners of war, and other survivors chose to remain in the United States or Canada.

There is some anecdotal information to suggest that those "Hessians" who originally crossed the Atlantic involuntarily may have started a small chain migration of relatives and neighbors. Relatively little has been published about the early post-colonial immigrants, but the number may be larger than is generally thought to be the case, despite elusive documentation, although it is known that Brazil was the favorite destination of German emigrants in the early nineteenth century.

The much larger number of Germans who emigrated approximately during the second half of the nineteenth century came from all parts of the German Empire.

However, there is a clockwise pattern to this emigration. The largest number in the earliest large wave came from southwest Germanic areas, including Switzerland, Alsace, and Luxembourg. Most of those in the latest wave came from the northeastern Prussian provinces. The intermediate wave seems to have been the most diverse, in terms of place of origin, but emigrants from a belt stretching from northwestern Germany to Bohemia, i.e., roughly the area where the Saxon tribe had been dominant, were most likely to have come during this period.

We can also identify, even if rather imperfectly as yet, the areas which produced a disproportionately heavy percentage of immigrants. In general, these areas had a relatively limited percentage of land suitable for cultivation or land which was not very productive due to the soil.

The areas of heaviest emigration included the Eifel mountain region along the western border of Germany, the hilly Hunsrück region which approximates the ill-defined boundary between the Palatinate and the Rhineland, Württemberg with its hilly terrain, and Pomerania, where the land is relatively flat but not very productive.

Among the most useful books are the emigration books for Württemberg (Schenk et al), Baden and Alsace (Schrader-Muggenthaler) and Schleswig-Holstein (Blevins).

However, factors other than the land-to-population ratio were also of some consequence. The areas west of or close to the Rhine River suffered the most from the devastation of frequent wars near the Franco-German border. The large percentage of the land in at least some of Prussia's eastern provinces which was owned by a comparatively small number of large estate owners, who came to be known as *Junkers*, created a large landless class with limited hopes of being able to acquire land. Religious and political persecution caused a significant number to leave, with a rather varied but complicated pattern of geographic concentrations.

Volume III of *A Genealogical Handbook of German Research* by Larry O. Jensen is probably the best overview with its maps and one-page state histories, but it is out of print. The best booklets which are in print are R. Dienst, *The German States*, Parts I and II (Cookham, Berks., England: Anglo-German Family History Society, 1993). Marilyn Lind's *Researching and Finding Your German Heritage*, which has small maps showing the location of nineteenth-century entities and a modest amount of historical information about each, is a somewhat similar American publication.

Specialized publications for specific areas include the monographs and books by Clifford Neal Smith and Annette Kunselman Burgert; *The Atlantic Bridge to Germany* by Charles M. Hall; *A Genealogical Guide and Atlas of Silesia* and by Otto K. and Vera N. Kowallis, which area is not covered by Hall (out of print). Smith has now prepared an index of the Westland monographs for Germany and some other countries, according to the December 1996 issue of CO-PAL-AM, the newsletter of the Colorado Chapter of Palatines to America. A few examples of regionally-specific projects include:

(1) a project by Prof. Walter Kamphoefner, Department of History, Texas A & M University, College Station, TX 77840, to identify all the immigrants from Lippe-Detmold.

(2) Joan Lowrey's article, "Research Project: Lower Saxons in the USA," in *The Germanic Connection* (October 1992), mentions the establishment in 1986 of "The Research Center Lower Saxons in the USA" by American, German and Dutch universities and historical, heritage, or scholarly societies. The German scholars heading this project are Dr. Wolfgang Grams, Dr. Antonius Hiltman, and Rotraud Poehl. They can be reached at:

> Forschungsstelle Niedersächsische Auswanderer in den USA (NAUSA)
> Institut für Politikwissenschaft II
> Carl Ossietzky Universität
> Ammerländer Heerstr. 114-118
> Postfach 2503
> D-26129 Oldenburg
> Germany

The present state of Lower Saxony includes Oldenburg (without Birkenfeld), Ostfriesland, western Hanover, the duchy of Schaumburg in the Prussian province of Hesse-Nassau, Schaumburg-Lippe, northern Waldeck, and Cuxhaven and Neuwerk from the Free City of Hamburg.

(3) records for Mecklenburg (described in "Research Services in Germany" in the September 1996 issue of the *Newsletter of the Germanic Genealogy Society*), which will be researched by:

> Karl-Heinz Steinbruch
> Mecklenburgica - Archival Research Service
> Wittenberger Str. 6
> D-19063 Schwerin
> Germany

(4) The Ostfriesens (East Frisians) in North America, especially the Upper Midwest, are very active in genealogy and related matters. We have listed a number of societies and books in the pertinent portions of this guide. Village lineage books have been published for a large percentage of localities in this area.

Two Low German societies in northwestern Ohio and central Missouri are also devoted mostly to the dialect of people from or near Ostfriesland.

For further information, see the resources described by John Neill, "Ostfriesian Research," in the December 1996 issue of *The Palatine Immigrant*.

(5) Waldeck

(6) Schleswig-Holstein

The Locality Index in the *German Genealogical Digest Index, 1985-1988*, compiled by Laraine K. Ferguson and A. Les Kowallis, which lists entries for states or principalities, as well as a for a very large number of specific communities, makes it easy to identify issues of special interest to a particular genealogist. Many of its issues have featured specific present or former entities. The same area has often been featured in several issues. The periodical's index of its first ten volumes, which lists a very large number of specific places, makes it easy to identify the issues of special interest. Back issues are available in most cases.

The Germanic Genealogist, published by the Germanic Genealogy and Research Committee of the Augustan Society, also includes articles dealing with specific areas in Germany.

Public archives and genealogical societies are key sources of data. The addresses of the most important ones are in this chapter, For a larger number of institutions and other resources, including religious archives, see Thode's *Address Book for Germanic Genealogy*. Even more are listed in the Immigrant Genealogical Society's *1993 Updated Addresses to German Repositories*.

Many addresses in the former German Democratic Republic have changed recently (often because of renaming streets which formerly honored Communist heroes but also for other reasons. The latest information, as of now, can be found in the 3rd edition of Martina Wermes's *Important Addresses and Telephone Numbers for Genealogical Research in the Five New (Eastern) States of the Federal Republic of Germany and Berlin*, partially translated, supplemented and adapted for English-language users by Edward Reimer Brandt.

Supplementary information can also be found in the books by Schweitzer and Baxter.

With respect to German-language publications, Ribbe and Henning have many bibliographical entries for specific areas, although the substantive information in their guide is not organized by areas within Germany.

If you have an ancestor where a birth, marriage or death occurred during military service, check the section on **Military Records**. If your ancestor served in the army of a relatively small German principality, Reschke's *German Military Records as Genealogical Sources* may be quite useful even if you do not have further information about the unit in which he served. In other cases, it will be quite difficult to find the information unless you know either the regiment or the base at which he was stationed.

If you have already identified the specific place of origin, you are likely to find a treasure chest of genealogical and historical information. However, almost all of these locally-oriented publications are in German.

In 1808 all parishes in Württemberg were ordered to compile a family registry of every family to make it easier for the government to identify young men liable for military service, according to Trudy Schenk, as reported in the *Immigrant Genealogical Society Newsletter* (February 1996).

The Nordfriisk Institut in Bredstedt is establishing a central database, called the North Frisian Emigrant Archive, with records of 4,000 emigrants from North Friesland and the northwestern part of the former duchy of Schleswig, today part of Denmark, to be immediately incorporated. This information is being enlarged in order to include the histories of as many as possible of those who emigrated from this region. Their address is:

Nordfriisk Institut
Süderstr. 30
D-25821 Bräist/Bredstedt, NF
Germany

The following person is their U.S. representative:

Jens Jacobs
#9 Logan Hill Rd.
Northport, NY 11768-3429

TRACING ILLEGAL EMIGRANTS

Many people emigrated from Germany without registering their intent to depart, but if they did register, a helpful source (if you can find it) is the Emigrants' Lists (*Auswandererlisten*) kept by the various German State Archives (*Staatsarchiv*) and by the local church parishes. They usually give name of emigrant, date and place of birth, place of residence, occupation, country of destination, and given names of the wife and children. See Chapter XVII for the addresses of state archives in Germany and elsewhere in Europe.

A group of professional German genealogists has established a very large *Germanic Emigrants Register*, listing people who may have emigrated illegally. It consists of names in newspaper notices from 1870 to 1918 when the German government discovered that they were missing, often when it failed to find people who were to be called up for military service or they could not be located when they were heirs in a will that was to be probated. The dates are those when the people were discovered to be missing, which could be as much as 40-60 years after they left the country in probate cases.

This information is now on an indexed database which is checked twice a year in response to queries which have been received in the meantime. Send 2 International Reply Coupons to secure an acknowledgment of receipt of your request. There is no fee for submitting information about your ancestor to be checked against the database. The database will be checked again annually if no relevant information is found initially.

If the place of origin is discovered, the submitter will be notified and may request copies of maps or documents. The fee for successful searches is $250, which may be paid with a personal check. Write to:

Germanic Emigrants Register
Postfach 1720
D-49347 Diepholz
Germany

The book by Faust and Brumbaugh lists some illegal Swiss emigrants of the eighteenth century.

GENEALOGICAL RESOURCE CENTERS FOR EASTERN EUROPE

The former Zentralstelle für Genealogie in der Deutschen Demokratischen Republik, established in 1967, which served as the main archives for researching genealogy in former East Germany, will accept letters written in English requesting genealogical information. Its archives are open to visiting American genealogists without any restrictions or prior application procedures. It is now addressed as:

Deutsche Zentralstelle für Genealogie
Postfach 274
D-04002 Leipzig
Germany
(*located at: Käthe-Kollwitz-Strasse 82*)

Literally, the name means "German Central Office for Genealogy." But its actual nature is more complicated. It has records for all of the former German Empire that were gathered by various other institutions dating back to 1904, but it is not a repository where all German genealogical information is centralized. It served as the key genealogical contact with the current German eastern states during the Communist era. It has a large number of microfilms for the former German eastern territories, with a significant, but lesser, number of parish registers and other records for German linguistic enclaves in East European territory that was never under German rule.

It is now more likely that letters sent directly to local parish offices in the "five new states" of Germany (the current preferred terminology for the territory of the former East German state) will be answered, but writing in English may be a barrier in some cases.

The Zentralstelle, however, continues to have resources which are unique in their comprehensiveness regarding ancestors who lived in these eastern states, namely:

- a special library collection of about 20,000 items including all important genealogical periodicals, reference works, collections of material and monographs as well as several thousand diverse manuscripts and materials relating to seals, coats-of-arms, pictures, etc.

- the 5 million lineage cards (*Ahnenstammkartei*) that grew out of the former "Deutschenahnengemeinschaft," housed in Dresden until 1967. This integrates various lineages connected by marriage. Most of the data are for the 1650-1800 period. Members may send in lineages traced back at least until the middle of the eighteenth century (or otherwise, if all readily accessible sources have been exhausted). This information is periodically updated and circulated to members. This enormous collection of genealogical data on a large number of German families has been microfilmed by the Family History Library.

- an alphabetized catalog of writings relating to particular individuals (*Personal-schriftenkatalog*) begun by the "Roland" Society in Dresden in 1919 and constantly expanded since then. About 150,000 index cards identify the location of over 100,000 documents (funeral sermons and other written materials relating to prominent persons) that can be found in public archives, libraries and collections, including three collections from Sweden.

- various parish registers (some originals, some microfilms) from the former German eastern territories, but also some from non-Germanic countries. A two-volume inventory of indexed parish registers has now been published. However, the archive is reported to have many additional boxed, unindexed registers of Germans in foreign countries. These registers were acquired in World War II but are not currently accessible.

  There is a fee for any research that is done and an annual subscription of DM 25 for participation in the circulating *Ahnenstammkartei* network.

Register to the Ahnenstammkartei des deutschen Volkes [*Lineage Cards of the German People*], by Thomas Kent Edlund, published by the Germanic Genealogy Society in 1995, greatly facilitates access to the information in the *Ahnenstammkartei*. It is a detailed soundex guide to finding microfilms for the 2,700,000 names in the microfilmed lineage cards at the Zentralstelle.

There are also copies or microfilms of many Protestant parish registers in the former German eastern territories at the:

Evangelisches Zentralarchiv
Jebensstr. 3
D-10623 Berlin
Germany

Both the Leipzig and Berlin records have been microfilmed by the Family History Library. Each archive has published an easy-to-use inventory of its church records. Records for eastern Pomerania are widely scattered. A large number of East Pomeranian Lutheran registers are in various archives in Greifswald, including the Landesarchiv and the:

Pommersche Evangelische Kirche
Landeskirchliches Archiv
Bahnhofstr. 35/36
Postfach 187
D-17489 Greifswald
Germany

For a list of those in and near Naugard County, see the summer 1994 issue (Vol. 16) of *Die Pommerschen Leute*.

The following archive has many East European Catholic registers, especially for ex-German territories, but also for some other areas (including the 1780-1820 duplicate registers for the Egerland, i.e., the western tip of the Czech Republic, which belonged to the diocese of Regensburg at the time):

Bischöfliches Zentralarchiv
St. Peters-Weg 11-14
D-93047 Regensburg
Germany

If you are unable to find out whether the parish registers for which you are looking have been preserved or, if so, where, you can obtain the best available information for $30 from the former executive director of AGoFF, who is fluent in English:

Heike Brachwitz
Genealogischer Computerdienst
Am Mühlenhof 5
D-26180 Rastede
Germany

Many civil registers remained at the local civil registry offices in Poland. Those that were taken to Germany are at:

Standesamt I in Berlin
Rheinstr. 54
D-12161 Berlin
Germany

Some of the Transylvanian German Lutheran parish registers are believed to be at the:

Archiv des Landeskirchenamts der Evangelischen Kirche von Westfalen
Altstädter Kirchplatz 3
Postfach 2740
D-33603 Bielefeld
Germany

In the 3rd edition of *In Search of Your German Roots*, Angus Baxter indicates that a large number of microfilmed parish registers and other records pertaining to Germans in Estonia and Latvia are at the:

Johann-Gottfried-Herder-Institut
Gisonenweg 5-7
D-35037 Marburg/Lahn
Germany

The institute also has some records for the former eastern parts of Germany and the Sudetenland. The Herder-Institut has a very large library and will copy any books, parts of books, articles and other materials in its collection that are no longer in print. Its archives includes a substantial map collection. In addition, it is a publisher.

There are a great many government records for the former German eastern territories at the Prussian State Privy Archives (which are not secret, despite the title):

Geheimes Staatsarchiv Preussischer Kulturbesitz
Archivstr. 12-14
D-14195 Berlin
Germany

A two-volume inventory, *Übersicht über die Bestände des Geheimen Staatsarchivs in Berlin-Dahlem* [*Overview of the Contents of the Privy State Archives in Berlin-Dahlem*], was published in 1965-67, but many of the records are reportedly not indexed, which impedes access.

This archive has many land records (*Kontributionskataster*) for 1772-1808 for the area which came under Prussian control after the first and at least part of the second partition of Poland. Some of the records which are not in Berlin are at:

Staatsarchiv
Friedrichsplatz 15
Postfach 1540
D-35037 Marburg
Germany

The most detailed account of these records, their location, archival numbers and the history of the transfers of these records from archive to archive is given by Ruth Bliss, "Zur Überlieferung der Friderizianischen Landesaufnahme für Westpreussen und den Netzedistrikt in den Jahren 1772/73" ["About the Friderizian Land Transfer for West Prussia and the Netze District in 1772/73"], in *Preussenland: Mitteilungen der Historischen Kommission für Ost- und Westpreussische Landesforschung und aus den Archiven der Stiftung Preussischer Kulturbesitz* [*Prussia: News From the Historical Commission for East and West Prussian Land Research and From the Archives of the Prussian Cultural Foundation*], Vol. 6, No. 4 (1968).

The Prussian State Privy Archives also has a library at Potsdamer Str. 33, D-10785 Berlin, which participates in the international inter-library loan program.

The principal German society for researching German ancestors from Eastern Europe, including both former German and non-German areas, which is widely known by its acronym (**AGoFF**), is:

Arbeitsgemeinschaft ostdeutscher Familienforscher (AGoFF)
Detlef Kühn, Vorsitzender
Zum Block 1A
D-01561 Medessen
Germany

It has numerous regionalized research centers and subcenters, with the main ones listed below. Up-to-date addresses are published annually in the membership roster (*Mitgliederverzeichnis*) of the DAGV, the German genealogical federation or umbrella group. Many of these centers are staffed by older people who left Eastern Europe in 1945, so relatively frequent changes can be expected. They are all run by volunteers, often consisting of only one person, and vary greatly in the kind of information they can provide.

Some of the researchers know English, but many don't, so writing in German is advisable. Often they charge no fees for providing data from their files, beyond requesting reimbursement for postage and duplicating, but they welcome contributions to promote their research. In such cases it is appropriate appropriate to enclose 3 International Reply

Coupons with your request and to make a donation. Some of them will, however, do further research for a fee.

Heinz Ulbrich, Leiter
Forschungsstelle Mittelpolen und
    Polnisch Wolhynien der AGoFF
Sperberweg 6, Postfach 1039
D-92661 Altenstadt
(*for Central Poland and Volhynia*)

Dr. Martin Armgart, Leiter
Forschungsstelle Donauschwaben der
    AGoFF
Graitengraben 31
D-45326 Essen
(*for Danube Swabians*)

Elmar Bruhn, Leiter
Forschungsstelle Pommern der AGoFF
Lohkamp 13
D-22117 Hamburg
(*for Pomerania*)
(*Also publishes* SEDINA-Archiv.
Knows English)

Hilde Möller, Leiter
Forschungsstelle Posen der AGoFF
Oppenheimer Str. 50
D-60594 Frankfurt/Main
(*for Posen, except East Netze area*)

Otto Firchau, Leiter
Forschungsstelle Netzeland Ost der
    AGoFF
Nachtigallenweg 6
D-32105 Salzuflen
(*for East Netze area of Posen, Polish
territory after 1918 - extends east to
Bydgoszcz, formerly Bromberg*)

Neithard von Stein, Leiter
Forschungsstelle Schlesien der AGoFF
Talstr. 3
D-31707 Bad Eilsen
(*for Silesia*)

Rita Sydow, Leiter
Forschungsstelle Ostbrandenburg-
    Neumark der AGoFF
Veilchenweg 12, Hundsmühlen
D-26203 Wardenburg
(*for East Brandenburg, including
Neumark*)

Manfred Daum, Leiter
Forschungsstelle Galizien und
    Bukowina der AGoFF
Haferkamp 25
D-29525 Ülzen
(*for Galicia and Bukovina*)

Dr. Dieter Pohl, Leiter
Forschungsstelle Fgr. Grafschaft Glatz
    der AGoFF
Forststr. 3
D-64379 Modautal
(*for former Magistracy of Glatz, south
central Silesia*)

Kurt Michael Beckert, Leiter
Forschungsstelle Fgr. Kreis Lauban der
    AGoFF
Kiefelhorn 13
D-38154 Königslutter
(*for former Magistracy of Lauban
County, southwestern Silesia*)

Oswald Frötschl, Leiter
Forschungsstelle Sudetenland der
    AGoFF
Meraner Str. 5
D-86316 Friedberg/Bayern
(*for Sudeten area, now Czech Republic*)

Dr. Martin Armgart, Leiter
Forschungsstelle Südosteuropa der
    AGoFF
Graitengraben 31
D-45326 Essen
(*for Southeast Europe*)

Genealogical researchers for the various sub-centers (not all listed above) are included in the *AGoFF-Wegweiser*. The second German edition was published in 1994 by the Verlag Degener & Co. and the second edition, under the title, *Genealogical Guide to German Ancestors from East Germany and Eastern Europe*, in 1995. (East Germany means the former eastern German territories that are now a part of Poland or Russia.)

Other societies devoted to Eastern Europe include:

Baltics:

Deutsch-Baltische Genealogische Gesellschaft
Herdweg 79
 D-64285 Darmstadt
Germany

East and West Prussia:

Verein für Ost- und Westpreussen e.V.
Wilhelm Kranz
Wiedauweg 13B
D-21147 Hamburg
Germany

Reinhard Wenzel, Geschäftsführer
Verein für Familienforschung in Ost- und Westpreussen
An der Leegde 23
D-29223 Celle
Germany

Sudeten Germans:

Lore Schretzenmayr
Vereinigung Sudetendeutscher Familienforscher
    und Sudetendeutsches Genealogisches Archiv
Erikaweg 58
D-93053 Regensburg
Germany

Danube Swabians:

Arbeitskreis donauschwäbischer Familienforscher
Hohlweg 5
D-75181 Pforzheim
Germany

U.S. contact:
Michael Stoeckl
1420 W. Farragut
Chicago, IL 60640

Other Sources:

There is another multi-purpose organization concerned with East Central Europe that includes five genealogically-oriented study groups for Posen and Poland, Silesia, Central Poland and Volhynia, West Prussia and Pomerania, and Estonia. It consists of nominees, rather than general members. Contact:

Gesellschaft für ostmitteleuropäische Landeskunde und Kultur
Zum Nordhang 5
D-58313 Herdecke
Germany

There is an extremely large card index file of emigrants from the Palatinate to various countries, including the United States, as well as Ernst Hexel's voluminous Galician German data, at:

Institut für pfälzische Geschichte und Volkskunde
Benzinoring 6
D-67657 Kaiserslautern
Germany

Other important libraries and research centers devoted to the study of Germans in foreign countries are:

Institut für Auslandsbeziehungen
Charlottenplatz 17
D-70173 Stuttgart
Germany
(*specializes in Southeast Europe, and the Volga and Black Sea Germans*)

Heimatarchiv der Deutschen aus Mittelpolen und Wolhynien
Platz der Republik
D-41065 Mönchengladbach
Germany
(*archive for Germans from Central Poland and Volhynia*)

Landesarchiv
Scheidter Strasse 114
Postfach 101010
D-66010 Saarbrücken
Germany
(*has substantial records relating to Danube Swabians*)

Studienstelle ostdeutsche Genealogie der Forschungsstelle Ostmitteleuropa
Universität Dortmund
Emil-Figge-Strasse 50
D-44227 Dortmund
Germany
(*has large genealogical name index file for West Prussia, which can be accessed through Dieter God, Schorlemmerskamp 20, D-44536 Lünen, Germany*)

There is also a *Heimatortskartei* (a card file of German refugees and expellees) for every non-German country that was under Communist rule. The addresses for the various areas (not always coinciding with national borders) are listed in the *AGoFF Guide*. The information in these files is more likely to be helpful for finding relatives than ancestors, but it may provide useful genealogical contacts.

OTHER SPECIALIZED GENEALOGICAL RESOURCE CENTERS

Huguenots, Waldensians and Walloons

The German Huguenot Society has published a periodical devoted to history for over a century. The current title is *Der Deutsche Hugenott* [*The German Huguenot*]. Its publications are valuable for tracing Huguenot and other originally French-speaking ancestors. At least some of them have been microfilmed by the Family History Library. The society's address is:

> Deutsche-Hugenotten-Gesellschaft
> Deutsches Hugenottenzentrum
> Hafenplatz 9a
> D-34385 Bad Karlshofen
> Germany

The society's genealogical expert is:

> Frau Ute Bilshausen-Lasalle
> Fuhrberg
> An der Schale 14
> D-30938 Burgwedel
> Germany

The one for the Waldensians is:

> Dr. Theo Kiefner
> Lehengasse 5
> D-75365 Calw
> Germany

Records of assistance given to Huguenot refugees, which contain specific genealogical data, are in Frankfurt, which was a central location for many nearby Huguenot settlements in Hesse, the Palatinate and Franconia. Contact:

Stadtarchiv
Stadtverwaltung (Amt 41A)
Postfach 3882
Karmeliterkloster
Karmelitergasse 5
D-60311 Frankfurt am Main
Germany

American and Canadian Military Forces in Germany

This organization was founded to help defense personnel with their genealogical research. However, it also includes English-speaking German members and may thus be able to provide information concerning German genealogists who know English. It can be contacted by telephone (011-49-6227-51942), fax (011-49-6227-54008), or by mail at either of the following addresses:

Genealogical Association of English Speaking Researchers in Europe
HEADQUARTERS USAREUR
CMR 420, Box 142
APO AE 09063
(*United States APO mailing address*)

Genealogical Association of English Speaking Researchers in Europe
US Army Library, Sullivan Barracks
Benjamin Franklin Village, Building 252
D-68309 Mannheim (Kafertal)
Germany
(*library location, and for mail in Germany or international mail*)

Salzburger Protestant Emigrés

The organization listed below is devoted primarily to research relating to the Protestant refugees who left the archbishopric of Salzburg, mostly in the 1730s, and settled in East Prussia. It may, however, be a useful contact for the descendants of those Salzburgers who migrated to other areas, including the American state of Georgia.

Salzburger Verein e.V.
Memeler Str. 35 (Wohnstift Salzburg)
D-33605 Bielefeld
Germany

Germans of Dutch Descent

This Dutch society is devoted to promoting the research of amateur German genealogists with Dutch roots:

Werkgroep Genealogisch Onderzoek Duitsland
P. C. Hooftlaan 9
NL-3818 HG Amersfoort
The Netherlands

The following society, which has published a periodical intermittently since 1938, is concerned mostly with the predominantly Mennonite religious refugees from the former Spanish Netherlands and pre-1685 immigrants from the Netherlands and from Belgium or of Belgian descent:

Niederändische Ahnengemeinschaft
Ostersielzug
D-25840 Friedrichstadt
Germany

Lineage Societies

The following federation includes about 200 societies devoted to genealogy involving specific families:

> Bund der Familienverbände e.V.
> Kirchgasse 18
> D-98693 Ilmenau
> Germany

Nobility and Historic Upper (Governing) Class

The nobles of all Germanic countries are the concern of the following institution:

> Deutsches Adelsarchiv
> Schwanallee 21
> D-35037 Marburg
> Germany

The following institute is concerned with the historic elite, including prominent burghers or laypersons:

> Friedrich-Wilhelm-Euler-Gesellschaft für personengeschichtliche Forschung e.V.
> Ernst-Ludwigstr. 21
> D-64625 Bensheim
> Germany

The New Eastern States of the Federal Republic (ex-GDR)

The following association has been involved with research in this area (including Berlin) for over 30 years:

> Arbeitsgemeinschaft für mitteldeutsche Familienforschung e.V.
> Strasse der Freundschaft 2
> D-99706 Sondershausen
> Germany
> (archives in Hessisches Staatsarchiv, Marburg)

Templers

Information about this religious group can be obtained from the head of the Temple Society:

> Peter Lange
> Felix-Dahn Str. 39
> D-70597 Stuttgart
> Germany

AUSTRIA
(Österreich)

The Austro-Hungarian Empire existed from 1867 to 1918. Prior to 1867 it was the Austrian Empire. Vienna (Wien) was the imperial capital, but there was a Hungarian government headquarters in Budapest. The sub-units of this empire, not all of an identical nature in a jurisdictional sense, are listed in the table on the next page. All of these areas had a significant number of German-speaking people, with the possible exception of the areas along the Adriatic coast.

If your ancestors are said to have come from Austria, it is likely they came from some part of the empire that is not part of Austria today, unless you have specific information to the contrary. Those people whose ancestors had already migrated once were more likely to emigrate than those who had stayed in the original homeland. A disproportionately large percentage of immigrants from present-day Austria came from the Burgenland, which was part of Hungary until after World War I.

Table 11: Present Location of Former Austro-Hungarian Territories

German name	English name	Today located in:[8]
Banat	Banat	Romania, Serbia[7] & Hungary
Baranja	Baranya	Croatia & Hungary
Batschka	Backa, Bácska	Serbia[7] & Hungary
Böhmen	Bohemia	Czech Republic
Bosnien[1]	Bosnia	Bosnia-Herzegovina
Bukowina	Bukovina	Romania & Ukraine
Burgenland	Burgenland	Austria & Hungary
Dalmatien	Dalmatia	Croatia
Dobrudscha	Dobruja	Romania & Bulgaria
Fiume	Rijeka	Croatia
Galizien	Galicia	Ukraine, Poland & Romania
Görz & Gradiska	Gorizia & Gradisca	Slovenia & Italy
Herzegowina[1]	Herzegovina	Bosnia-Herzegovina
Istrien	Istria	Croatia & Slovenia
Kärnten	Carinthia	Austria
Karpato-Ukraine	Carpatho-Ukraine	Ukraine
Krain	Carniola	Slovenia
Kroatien	Croatia[5]	Croatia
Mähren	Moravia	Czech Republic
Österreich	Austria	Austria
Österreichisch-Schlesien	Austrian Silesia	Czech Republic
Salzburg	Salzburg	Austria
Sathmar	Satu Mare	Romania & Hungary
Schwäbische Türkei	Swabian Turkey	Hungary
Siebenbürgen[4]	Transylvania[5]	Romania
Slawonien[3]	Slavonia[5]	Croatia & Serbia[7]
Steiermark	Styria	Austria & Slovenia
Syrmien	Syrmia, Srem	Serbia[7]
Tirol	Tyrol	Austria & Italy
Trient	Trent	Italy
Triest[2]	Trieste	Italy
Ungarn[6]	Hungary	Hungary
Vorarlberg	Vorarlberg	Austria

[1] Bosnia and Herzegovina were one unit, not two.

[2] Trieste was part of Istria.

[3] Slovenia, which exists today, should not be confused with Slavonia, which used to exist. Slovenia was the northwesternmost republic of the former Yugoslav federation. The former Slavonia was east and southeast of present-day Slovenia and belongs to the present republic of Croatia and to the Vojvodina (Serbia).

[4] While Germans generally use "Siebenbürgen" as the equivalent of "Transylvania," the latter designation has sometimes been applied to a larger area than the old Siebenbürgen "Saxon" settlement.

[5] Hungary also ruled Transylvania, Croatia and Slavonia, although these were separate, semi-autonomous political entities.

[6] Parts of what was pre-1914 Hungary now belong to Austria, Croatia, Slovenia, Slovakia, Romania, Serbia and Ukraine.

[7] Virtually all of the German settlements in Serbia were in the formerly autonomous province of Vojvodina.

[8] Where more than one present-day country is listed, the first-named one has the largest portion of the area in question.

Some records concerning all of the areas that were once under Austrian rule are still in the Austrian archives, but check the sections on the various countries that now exist for further information regarding relevant records. Keep these facts in mind when researching ancestors from "Austria," since relatively few pre-1945 immigrants came from within the present borders of Austria.

Unlike emigrants from Germany, almost all of whom came from rural villages, a substantial percentage of Austrian emigrants came from Vienna. This was even more the case for those who came during or after the Nazi era.

Roger P. Minert states that the largest number of emigrants from what is now Austria came from Vorarlberg.

Austria today is a much smaller country than when it was the Austro-Hungarian Empire prior to 1919. Austria is made up of the following nine provinces:

Burgenland	Oberösterreich (Upper Austria)	Tirol (Tyrol)
Kärnten (Carinthia)	Salzburg	Vorarlberg
Niederösterreich (Lower Austria)	Steiermark (Styria)	Wien (Vienna)

The most detailed and up-to-date account of genealogical records in contemporary Austria can be found in the first three parts of an article by Felix Gundacker, executive director of the Institut für historische Familienforschung Genealogie Gesellschaft in Vienna, on "Research in the former Austro-Hungarian Empire," in three consecutive issues of *Heritage Quest*, beginning with the May/June 1996 issue. Parts IV and V cover records and repositories in other countries which belonged to the former Hapsburg Empire. He is the principal source for much of our information concerning the location, dates and filming of parish registers, as well as seignorial records, but Minert provided additional information.

Some of the addresses and other details come from the 6th edition of Ernest Thode's *Address Book for Germanic Genealogy*, which lists a much larger number of addresses of repositories, including some parenthetical notes about certain special holdings.

In order to do on-site research in Austria, you need to make an appointment in advance and do your homework prior to your trip, since little assistance is available and the number of books you can inspect each day is often quite limited. Furthermore, most archives are closed during Easter week and in August. In many cases, you have to secure a permit to check the records in church archives or get permission to do so in parish offices. Most archives will tell you where specific registers are deposited, but few will do research for you. You usually have to make appointments in advance, because of limited hours.

You may also have to prove your ancestral connection in order to obtain access to records which otherwise would be confidential under privacy laws, i.e., most 20th century records.

Roger Minert is an Accredited Genealogist with a specialty in Austrian research. He speaks and reads German fluently, travels to Europe several times a year and is familiar with the archives in several countries. He can be contacted by telephone at 801-298-1526 or fax 801-298-1651, or write to:

> Dr. Roger P. Minert
> 1001 S. 1020 West
> Woods Cross, UT 84087

GAZETTEERS

See Chapter VIII, section (c), for information on Austrian gazetteers.

CATHOLIC RECORDS

Most Austrian parish registers are still in the parish churches and have not been microfilmed. It is difficult to get responses to genealogical queries from them, because of the shortage of priests. Some have to take care of as many as three parishes, most of them do not know the Gothic script (called Kurrent in Austria) used from 1550 to 1930, and quite a few have been recruited from other countries so that their knowledge of German is not comparable to that of a native. You may also have to pay a fee for research.

The location, dates and amount of microfilming are listed for Vienna and each state, since there are some significant differences:

Vienna: Some records (St. Stephan's Church) go back to 1523, but relatively few predate the 1780s. Illegitimate births were usually registered at the parish of St. Marx, which was a hospital, until 1783 and at Alservorstadt thereafter. The father is rarely listed.

The population of Vienna increased ten-fold from 1800 (200,000) to 1910 (2,100,000), with most of the increase after 1860, when poor rural peasants from various parts of the Hapsburg Empire flocked to the city for work. The number of Catholic parishes also increased from 28 in 1784 to 81 by 1900. Therefore, it is important to know that the records of migrants from the west were usually recorded in the Schottenfeld parish and those from the east in the Erdberg parish.

Two very helpful indexes have been compiled for most Vienna districts. No Viennese Catholic records have been microfilmed.

The 5-volume *Index Nomimum Ex Libris Copulatorum Vindobonensibus*, compiled by Herbert A. Mansfeld and Hans Burgauer, has a complete list of marriages in five Vienna districts for 1542-1850. It is available in book form at the FHL, listed as the *Index to Vienna Register Marriages*, and is also available at the archives of the archbishopric in Vienna:

> Erzbistum Wien
> Diözesanarchiv
> Wollzeile 2
> A-1010 Wien
> Austria

The *Index IHFF Genealogie GmbH* has computer-stored data for Catholic marriages between 1542 and 1850-60. The bride is sometimes listed. This index has not been published. Requests for information should be sent to this genealogical research firm, which will also accept research assignments for any religious group in present-day Austria and other parts of the Hapsburg Empire:

> Institut für historische Familienforschung
>   Genealogie Gesellschaft (IHFF)
> Pantzergasse 30/8
> A-1190 Wien
> Austria

Lower Austria: About 50% of the pre-1900 registers in the western half of this province are in the central archives of the diocese in St. Pölten. The Family History Library has microfilmed some of these records, but many films are of poor quality.

For on-site research, the address is:

> Diözesanarchiv
> Domplatz 1
> A-3100 St. Pölten
> Austria

Records which begin in 1797 for the eastern half are still in the parishes. The duplicate registers in Vienna are not available for inspection.

Upper Austria: All registers are still in the parish churches, except that early records for parishes near the Inn River (*Inn Viertel*) are in the archives in Passau, because this area belonged to Bavaria until 1771. Some registers predate 1650 and even 1600 in a few cases. None have been filmed.

However, the *Heider Index* includes births, deaths and marriages prior to about 1784 for all parishes north of the Danube, as well as in the Salzkammergut in the southwestern part of the state.

To use parish records, you must get permission from the:

> Bistum Linz
> Ordinariatsarchiv
> Harrachstr. 7
> A-4020 Linz
> Austria

Salzburg: The registers for this state and part of northeastern Tyrol, which formerly belonged to the archdiocese, are in the archdiocesan and county archives in Salzburg. Unlike other archives, the Salzburg archive answers queries. The address of the church archive is:

> Erzbistum Salzburg
> Konsistorialarchiv
> Kapitelplatz 2
> A-5010 Salzburg
> Austria

Tyrol: The northeastern part of Tyrol was part of the archdiocese of Salzburg, where the records are kept. All registers in Tyrol have been microfilmed and indexed by the archives but they are not at the FHL. They can be inspected at the state archives, but the archives will not search the records for you:

> Tiroler Landesarchiv
> Michael-Gaismair-Str. 1
> A-6010 Innsbruck
> Austria

Vorarlberg: All registers are still in the parish. Some records go back to an early date. All registers have been microfilmed. They are available from the FHL and can also be inspected at the state archives:

> Vorarlberger Landesarchiv
> Kirchstr. 28
> A-6900 Bregenz
> Austria

Styria: Most of these records, belonging to the diocese of Graz-Seckau, are still in the parishes. For information as to their whereabouts, contact the:

> Bistum Graz-Seckau
> Diözesanarchiv
> Bischofsplatz 4
> A-8010 Graz
> Austria

Carinthia: About two-thirds of the records are in Klagenfurt in the archives of the diocese of Gurk. The archives will inform you as to where particular registers are. The address is:

> Bistum Gurk
> Archiv der Diözese
> Gurker Fürstbischöfliches Palais
> Mariannengasse 9
> A-9020 Klagenfurt
> Austria

Burgenland: Most records are in the diocesan archive in Eisenstadt, but some may be in the Hungarian language or in Budapest, because the Burgenland belonged to Hungary until 1921. The archive will answer queries as to whether it has the registers you seek or whether they are still in the parishes:

> Diözesanarchiv
> St. Rochusstr. 21
> A-7001Eisenstadt
> Austria

For an interesting and detailed account of an ancestor-hunting trip to this state, see Gerald J. Berghold, "Rooting Around in the Burgenland," in *Heritage Quest*, Sept.-Oct. 1995. The same author also wrote, "Burgenland Genealogy in Pennsylvania" (*Heritage Quest*, Nov.-Dec. 1995).

RECORDS FOR OLD CATHOLICS

There was a separate conservative minority group, known as the Old Catholics. For further information, contact:

> Alt-Katholische Kirche Österreichs
> Schottenring 17
> A-1010 Wien
> Austria

LUTHERAN RECORDS

All vital records for all religious groups are to be found in local Catholic parish registers up to 1781, when the Patent of Tolerance was issued.

Thode reports that the following archive has registers for all Lutheran parishes in the Austro-Hungarian Empire for 1878-1917:

> Archiv des evangelischen Oberkirchenrates
> Severin-Schreiber-Gasse 3 A
> A-1180 Wien
> Austria

Burgenland: This province belonged to Hungary, which had more Protestants and a longer tradition of policies of freedom of religion. Therefore, it has a large Lutheran minority, with most records going back to the 1780s. In Rust, they begin in 1647.

Burgenland is the only province where almost all Lutheran parishes were established before 1900. This small area has about two dozen Lutheran parishes.

Carinthia: The Reformation was more prominent here than in any other province which was Austrian before World War I, with 19 Lutheran parishes, most of which date back to the 1780s.

Quite a few parishes were established almost immediately after the Patent of Tolerance.

Upper Austria: Gundacker states that the Reformation affected this province relatively strongly and that Lutheranism held its ground even during the 1652-1782 period when Catholicism was the only religion allowed by law. However, while there are a number of parishes with records dating back to the late eighteenth century, none of the parish registers predate the 1781 Patent of Tolerance.

Lower Austria: Although there are some parishes with records dating back to the late eighteenth and early nineteenth centuries, the vast majority were established in the twentieth century.

Salzburg: This was fertile ground for Lutheranism, but the Lutherans were expelled; hence, Salzburgers have become a unique group. However, later records compiled as a result of a Prussian victory over Austria, which required that the expellees be compensated for the property that was confiscated, will enable many of the Lutherans whose ancestors came from this archbishopric to trace their ancestry back to Salzburg. The Landesarchiv in

Salzburg has records for the Protestant expellees for 1731-44, according to Thode. A Salzburger society is also listed under **GERMANY**.

Styria: There are few pre-1900 Lutheran records in this province, with pre-1781 records only in Graz.

Tyrol: The only pre-1900 parish register is in Innsbruck (1876).

Vorarlberg: Gundacker makes no reference to any Lutheran records here.

OTHER PROTESTANT RECORDS

Although members of the Reformed faith comprised a larger percentage of the population in the Austro-Hungarian Empire than the Lutherans, they almost all lived in Hungary and Slovakia, with some German Reformed in Galicia. Gundacker makes no reference to any Reformed church in present-day Austria.

Likewise, while some other Protestant groups, e.g., the Hutterites, had Tyrolean origins and found temporary refuge in Moravia, they appear to have become extinct in modern Austria almost immediately.

Look under **CIVIL RECORDS** for data for various small sects.

SEIGNORIAL PROTOCOLS

Gundacker considers these to be the second most important source of genealogical information. Some go back to 1650, but most do not begin until 1750. They include:

 (1) Marriage settlements
 (2) Sale and purchase of property
 (3) Inventories of property at time of death
 (4) Estate registers
 (5) Orphanage registers

The marriage records are especially important, since parental consent was required for all those under 24 until 1848. They list not only the bridal couple, but also their places of origin and the names of their parents. The inventories of the deceased frequently include the names of the spouse and children who inherited property.

Furthermore, ordinary subjects had to get permission to move from the local authorities (reigning lord, priest, municipal council) until 1848.

Although nobles were not required to hand these over to the government, quite a few can be found in the archives of the individual states. Gundacker especially mentions Vienna (for Lower Austria), Linz (Upper Austria), Klagenfurt (Carinthia), and Bregenz (Vorarlberg). He says that only a small number are in Eisenstadt (Burgenland) and makes no reference to Salzburg, Graz (Styria) or Tyrol (except for the archives in Bozen [Bolzano] and Trent [Trient/Trentino], which are now in Italy).

STATE ARCHIVES

The addresses of the state archives (*Landesarchiv*, in contrast to the national *Staatsarchiv*) are as follows:

Burgenländisches Landesarchiv
Freiheitsplatz 1
A-7001 Eisenstadt
Austria

Steiermärkisches Landesarchiv
Bürgergasse 2
A-8010 Graz
Austria

Kärntner Landesarchiv
Präsenzbibliothek
Landhaus
Herrengasse 14
A-9020 Klagenfurt
Austria

Tiroler Landesarchiv
Michael-Gaismair-Str. 1
A-6010 Innsbruck
Austria

Niederösterreichisches Landesarchiv
Regierungsviertel
A-3100 St. Pölten
Austria
(*has seignorial records*)

Oberösterreichisches
Landesarchiv
Anzengruberstr. 19
A-4020 Linz
Austria

Landesarchiv Salzburg
Michael-Pacherstr. 20
A-5020 Salzburg
Austria

Vorarlberger Landesarchiv
Kirchstr. 28
A-6900 Bregenz
Austria

Since the Lower Austrian state archives is moving from Vienna to St. Pölten, it will be closed until the end of 1997.

CIVIL RECORDS

The first census was held in 1754. In 1784 the government decreed that all parish registers were government property. But civil registers recorded by government officials did not begin until 1938, except for Wiener-Neustadt (a city south of Vienna) and Burgenland (1895, when it was under Hungarian rule). Few early records appear to have survived, but censuses for 1869-1981 are at the central statistical office:

> Statistisches Zentralamt
> Heldenplatz
> Neue Burg
> A-1010 Wien
> Austria

However, Thode reports that provincial censuses for Styria, going back as far as 1707, are in the state archives in Graz.

Burgenland would also have been included in the 1828 Hungarian land census, now being transcribed by Martha Remer Connor on a county-by-county basis.

A special civil registry for small dissident groups (Moravian Brethren, Mennonites, free-thinkers), as well as Muslims and other denominations which are not likely to have included German-speakers, was begun in 1870. These records are at the:

> Standesamt
> Währingerstr. 30
> A-1100 Wien-Alsergrund
> Austria

"Lehmann" city directories for homeowners in 1859 and 1872-1942 are in the Vienna City Library.

MILITARY RECORDS

After 1869, men had a lifelong obligation for military service in the Austro-Hungarian Empire, with exemptions for Catholic clergy, nobles and some government officials. There were separate military parish registers, as in Germany. The Family History Library has microfilmed many records of the Austrian War Archives. The military archive, one of four branches of the Austrian national archives, has records for the whole empire going back to 1740. Its address is:

> Österreichisches Staatsarchiv
> Kriegsarchiv
> Nottendorfergasse 2
> A-1030 Wien
> Austria

Either the original or microfilmed records for the affected areas can also be found in the national archives of countries created out of the former Hapsburg Empire, e.g., in Prague for the Czech Republic and in Bratislava for the Slovak Republic.

Steven W. Blodgett write a 10-page article, "Great-grandfather Was in the Imperial Cavalry: Using Austrian Military Records as an Aid to Writing Family History," published by the FHL in Vol. 7 of the presentations at the (1984) World Conference on Records. The gist of the article is that it is almost impossible to find your ancestor in these records unless you already have nearly all of the genealogical information you are seeking.

MISCELLANEOUS RECORDS

Other records, some going back to the sixteenth century, which are available for at least some places and time periods, include: city directories, emigration records, police registers, census lists, school and university records, house books, citizen registers, probate records, apprenticeship and guild records, land records, records pertaining to the nobility, tax records, orphan records, poorhouse records and court records. Of particular significance are the city archives of Vienna:

> Wiener Stadt- und Landesarchiv
> Neues Rathaus
> Felderstrasse 1
> A-1082 Wien
> Austria

Of the four branches of the Austrian national archives, the one with the most information of genealogical value for ancestors from Austria (it has emigration records from 1861-1919) is:

> Österreichisches Staatsarchiv
> Haus-, Hof- und Staatsarchiv
> Minoritenplatz 1
> A-1010 Wien
> Austria

Check Edward Reimer Brandt, "Consular Records on Austrian Emigration and Immigration at the Austrian State (National) Archives," in *Heritage Review*, vol. 23, no. 2 (1993) for details concerning the nature of these records and the archival file or box numbers. According to Norst and McBride (*Austrians and Australia*), many Austrian emigration records were destroyed in 1927 and more during World War II. Therefore, you certainly won't find anything resembling a complete list of overseas emigrants in them. They are more like the Czarist consular records in the United States and Canada, which have information about those people who had reason to contact the consulates.

However, records pertaining to the German settlers in the Banat, Galicia and Transylvania can be found at:

> Österreichisches Staatsarchiv
> Hofkammerarchiv
> Himmelpfortgasse 4-8
> A-1010 Wien
> Austria

The names and other details, often including the (sometimes misidentified) place of origin, of the German settlers in Galicia, the Banat and the Batschka were published by Franz Wilhelm and Josef Kallbrunner. They are listed in the Vienna archives as *Passregister* [*Passport Registers*] of the *Konskriptionsamt Wien*.

But Ludwig Schneider's later book is more accurate and more complete for Galicia. It also includes some post-immigration data. Both books are indexed, although there are a few unindexed pages in the Wilhelm and Kallbrunner volume. An English-language index of surnames for these and other books has been compiled by Edward Reimer Brandt. All three books are discussed under **POLAND** (although only Galicia ever belonged to Poland) and are listed in the bibliography for Chapter XVIII.

The FHL has microfilmed the *Ansiedlerakten* [*Card File and Documents Related to Settlers from Germany, Bohemia and Moravia to Galicia and the Bukovina*]. A separate FHL microfilm roll includes an alphabetized *Ansiedlerkartei* [*Card File Index of Settlers*].

The Banat Germans comprised the largest group among the Danube Swabians (known as Hungarian Germans until after World War I). They settled mostly in Romania and the Vojvodina (now northern Yugoslavia). Check the index for numerous references to this group.

The information listed under **CIVIL RECORDS** in the section on **POLAND** with respect to land cadasters (land survey and ownership records for tax puposes) and accompanying land maps is also applicable to other parts of the Hapsburg Empire. Karen Hobbs has extracted the 1654 tax rolls for two western Bohemian counties, so they may be available for other areas as well.

Since the Bozen-Südtirol area was under Austrian rule until 1919, documents concerning Germanic emigrants from there are more likely to be available from the Tiroler Landesarchiv. This archive indicates, however, that no centralized emigration records were kept, so the prospects of locating ancestors without knowing the village from which they came are slim.

For further details about Austrian records, see Ward's *German-American Genealogical Workshop Bulletin*, which contains a table that is reproduced in *The German Connection*, August 1983.

Dagmar Senekovic's *Handy Guide to Austrian Genealogical Records* deals with records from contemporary Austria.

The entire Hapsburg Empire is covered by Felix Gundacker, director of the Institute for Historical Family Research in Austria (address below), in his five-part article on "Research in the Austro-Hungarian Empire," published in five consecutive issues of *Heritage Quest*, beginning in the May/June 1996 issue. He lists the addresses of many archives in all of its successor states.

A German-language book, which includes a lot of statistics, especially regarding the numbers, areas of origin and ports of embarkation of emigrants from the Austrian part of the Dual Monarchy, is Hans Chmelar, *Höhepunkte der österreichischen Auswanderung: Die Auswanderung aus den im Reichsrat vertretenen Königreichen und Ländern in den Jahren 1905-1914* [*The Heydey of Austrian Emigration: The Emigration from the Kingdoms and Lands Represented in the Imperial Council in 1905-1914*]. However, much of the emigration from the northern areas (Bohemia, Moravia, Galicia and Bukovina) already occurred prior to 1905.

For further genealogical information about areas which are no longer part of Austria, look under the name of the country to which the area now belongs, the annotated bibliography and references at the end of various chapters dealing with gazetteers, emigration, history and religion.

The registers of passports issued in Vienna (for all of the Hapsburg Empire) for 1792-1901 have been filmed by the Family History Library. Look under "Wien Konskriptionsamt."

GENEALOGICAL SOCIETIES AND RESEARCH SERVICES

The principal Austrian genealogical societies are:

Heraldisch-genealogische
  Gesellschaft "Adler"
Haarhof 4a
A-1014 Wien
Austria

Arbeitsbund für österreichische
  Familienkunde
Bürgergasse 2A/1
A-1040 Wien
Austria

Austrian genealogical societies do not provide research services. However, the following institute provides such services:

Institut für historische Familienforschung Genealogie Gesellschaft
Pantzergasse 30/8
A-1190 Wien
Austria

Its specialties include eastern Austria (including Vienna), for which it has prepared a general index of all Catholic marriages since records began in 1542 until about 1850-1860 for some 80 parishes, i.e., about 800,000 records. Bohemia and Moravia constitute another area of in-depth expertise.

However, all queries will be answered. (Be sure to include two International Reply Coupons.) Churches in Austria were required to register all births, marriages and deaths until 1939. Therefore, it is important to mention the religion of your ancestors.

The staff also works directly with archives in the Czech and Slovak Republics, Hungary, Slovenia and northern Italy, i.e., much of the former Hapsburg Empire.

Thode lists the genealogical societies or branches for specific provinces, as well as the central archives for the Teutonic Knights (whose chief impact, interestingly, was in areas never part of the Holy Roman Empire). See under **GERMANY** for the address of a genealogical society for the Salzburger Protestants (*Exulanten*) expelled in the 1730s.

SWITZERLAND
(die Schweiz)

SEARCHING THE RECORDS

The most important factor in researching Swiss ancestry is to determine the place of origin or the community in which the person possessed rights of citizenship. All vital statistic information is recorded at the place of origin of the Swiss citizen. Most communities have records for three or four generations and some records date back to the 1600s.

Before undertaking research in the records of Switzerland, keep in mind the following facts:

1. Of the four national languages, French is spoken in the west, Italian in the south, Romansh in the southeast, and German in the rest of the country, as well as being interspersed with Romansh in the southeast.

2. Although the cantons are united to form one Confederation of Switzerland, each canton is politically independent with its own government and record keeping system. Access to the records differs from canton to canton. If you write to Swiss record offices, be sure to state that you are researching your own family line.

3. A Swiss person becomes a **citizen of the community of origin** and this automatically makes the person a citizen of that canton and of Switzerland (in contrast to the United States, where national citizenship makes a person a citizen of all states and local areas of the United States). Records of the citizen remain at the community of citizenship, even if the person moves from town to town (or even leaves Switzerland). Movements are often noted in these records. When women marry, they forfeit their native rights of citizenship and assume the rights of citizenship in the husband's community.

4. Most people are members of the Catholic or Reformed Church, but there are also members of smaller churches, especially Mennonites and Baptists. Many Huguenots passed through Switzerland on their flight from persecution.

CHURCH RECORDS

These records are extensive and are among the best kept in Europe. Some date as far back as 1490. Church or parish records include records of baptisms, confirmations, marriages and deaths. Confirmation books contain records of 15-year-old boys and girls preparing themselves for this event. Catholic records are kept in the local churches, while Protestant registers are either in the city or town archives, the state archives, or the civil registrar's office. Many have been microfilmed by the Family History Library in Salt Lake City. Always check these records before writing to Switzerland.

CIVIL AND MISCELLANEOUS RECORDS

Civil records for all of Switzerland began in 1848 at the church level and in 1876 at the federal level. Each municipality or community keeps all records for its citizens. Included in these papers are vital records, ecclesiastical records and family records (*Familienscheine*). **Family records** show names of parents (and often grandparents), their children and their marriages (naming the spouse). They give details regarding births, marriages, deaths, and mention religions and occupation. These cover 1820 to the present day (some go back to the 1600s), and are kept at the local registrar's office.

Other civil records include **wills**, often dating back to the 1600s, and census records starting in 1836-38 and continuing. These records are housed at the state and city archives. **Military records** dating from 1800 and **emigration records** from the early 17th century to 1848 are found in the state archives of the canton; after 1848 the records were kept by the Schweizer Bundesregierung, Bundeshaus, CH-3000 Bern. Sometimes the local registrar has **burgher rolls** (*Bevölkerungsverzeichnisse*) dating back to the 11th century. For additional details concerning the nature and location of various records, see Ward's *German-American Genealogical Workshop Bulletin*, referenced under Austria.

A unique reference source for locating a Swiss family's origin is the set of books called *Familiennamenbuch der Schweiz (Swiss Surname Book)*, published by Polygraphischer Verlag in Zürich. This collection lists every Swiss surname, in which town it is found, and the time period when the name first appeared in the records. The lists are compiled from the citizenship records in each town. This has now been published in English as *Swiss Surnames: A Complete Register*.

Another resource to locate a Swiss surname and family information is the data compiled between 1896 and 1950 by Swiss genealogist, Julius Billeter, who traced many Swiss lines. The information was obtained from parish and civil registers. It is arranged in family groups with entries dating from 1500-1900. Billeter's surname work and data on family groups has been microfilmed by the FHL. The *Handy Guide to Swiss Genealogical Records* by Jared Suess lists the kinds of records which are available, for what period, the type of information they contain, and where they are located, as well as the FHL film numbers. Also check *The Swiss Emigration Index* by Cornelia Schrader-Muggenthaler.

You can get a brief pamphlet, *A Genealogical How-To for Americans of Swiss Descent*, free from the Swiss National Tourist Office, 608 Fifth Ave., New York, NY 10020. This pamphlet describes the services and fees of the Schweitzerische Gesellschaft für Familien-forschung (Central Office for Genealogical Information) in Zürich, which is maintained by the Swiss Genealogical Society, or SGFF. The pamphlet also lists researchers for specific cantons, as well as several private Swiss and American services providing genealogical research assistance.

For further information, check the guides by Wellauer, Nielsen, and Steinach. *The Swiss Connection* has a history of a particular canton as a regular feature in each issue.

GENEALOGICAL SOCIETIES

For general genealogical information, you may write in English to:

Manuel Aicher, Manager
Central Office for Genealogical Information
Vogelaustrasse 34
CH-8953 Datikon
Switzerland

You must enclose a $20 fee with the inquiry for any name or place of interest. In your letter you should include available details on your family, especially its place of origin. Otherwise, more extensive research will need to be done, involving a higher fee. This office will send you information as to what kinds of archival, published and unpublished material are available. But you will have to hire a professional researcher to do specific research on your family.

The following is the Jewish Genealogical Society of Switzerland:

> Schweizerische Vereinigung für jüdische Genealogie
> c/o Rene Loeb
> P.O. Box 876
> CH-8021 Zürich
> Switzerland

LUXEMBOURG
(Luxemburg)

CHURCH RECORDS

The chief religion in Luxembourg is Roman Catholic. Church registers have been kept since the 1600s, with the majority written in Latin. Most of the records are still kept in the parish office, although the records of larger cities have been incorporated in the commune archives. The commune is a political division roughly similar to our township. The FHL has filmed many of these church records. You will have to know the name of the canton (county) in which the town is located before being able to use these films.

CIVIL REGISTRATION

The French occupied Luxembourg and introduced the system of civil registration in 1795. These vital statistics are referred to as *état civil*. By 1802, all communes were recording births, marriages, and deaths. Every ten years an index (*tables décennales*) was prepared for each commune. These name indexes are located at the respective commune archives, at the district courts (*tribunal d'arrondissement*) of Diekirch (for the north of the country) and Luxembourg (for the south and center of the country) and at the Luxembourg National Archives (for the whole country). They have also been microfilmed by the FHL. Individual registers for 1796 to 1894 have also been filmed by the FHL. Note that the tables décennales start only in 1802.

CENSUS RECORDS

The first census was taken in 1806. After that the National Archives have the censuses for 1843, 1846. 1847, 1849, 1851, 1852, 1855, 1858, 1861, 1864, 1867, 1871, 1875, 1880 and 1885. Generally speaking, census records which are older than 100 years are available for consultation. The censuses for 1843 to 1875 have been microfilmed and can be consulted in the National Archives in Luxembourg. There is no general index, so you have to know the name of the town in order to use them.

OTHER INSTITUTIONAL RESOURCES AND PUBLICATIONS

The key sources in Luxembourg are:

Luxembourg National Archives:

Archives Nationales
Plateau du St.-Esprit
Boîtes postale 6
L-2010 Luxembourg-Ville
Grand Duchy of Luxembourg

Luxembourg Genealogical Society:

Association Luxembourgeoise de
  Généalogie et d'Héraldique
Château de Mersch
Boîte postale 118
L-7502 Mersch
Grand Duchy of Luxembourg

The Luxembourg Genealogical Society published *de Familjefuerscher* [*The Family Researcher*], with articles in French (most), German, Luxemburgish or Letzeburgesch (popular with older people) and occasionally in other languages. It also publishes a yearbook (*Annuaire - Jahrbuch*), currently edited by Jean-Claude Muller, the head of the Luxembourg National Library.

The Luxembourg National Library (*Bibliotheque Nationale Luxembourg*) publishes annual volumes on Luxembourg bibliography (*Bibliographie Luxembourgeoise*). Presumably these are supplements to a book by the same name first published in Luxembourg City in 1902-32, with the revised 2-volume 2nd edition, edited by Martin Blum and completed by Carlo Hury, published in Munich in 1981.

The most comprehensive book for North American genealogists is Nicholas Gonner's two volumes on *Luxembourgers in the New World*, originally published in German in 1889. A new English-language edition, edited and translated by Jean Ensch, Jean-Claude Muller, and Robert E. Owen, was published in 1987. Although both were published in Luxembourg, the English-language book is readily available in the United States.

Camille Perbal's huge 1990 book, *Fragments Généalogique: Familles Luxembourgeoises* [*Genealogical Fragments: Luxembourg Families*] also includes information about the Belgian province of Luxembourg, which belonged to Luxembourg until 1839, but there were relatively few Germans there.

If the place of your ancestor's birth is unknown and you can't find it in either the index to *The Luxembourger Gazette* in Volume 2 of the Gonner book or Hatz's book, it may be worth checking the Luxembourg telephone directory, which is on the Internet on the home page of the editor: http://www.editus.lu.

NORTH AMERICAN RESOURCES

The Be-Ne-Lux Genealogist, published by the Augustan Society, has only a modest amount of information about Luxembourgers, but its bibliographic entries provide leads for further research.

The following unindexed monthly newsletter is not a genealogical publication, but it includes a lot of obituaries:

Luxembourg News of America
5204 Brown St.
Skokie, IL 60077

There are also Luxembourger societies in Wisconsin and Iowa which publish newsletters. They are not devoted to genealogy, but the one in Wisconsin in particular contains some genealogical material.

The University of St. Thomas library in St. Paul, Minnesota, has one of the largest collections of books, maps, periodicals, etc., which deal with every aspect of Luxembourg and Luxembourgers in North America. This collection, which includes some very rare items, currently has over 1,000 items, more than double the number two years ago, and is still growing rapidly. Most of these items are in the Luxembourgiana Bach-Dunn Collection (also known as the Biblioteca Luxembourgiana) in the:

Department of Special Collections
O'Shaughnessy-Frey Library
University of St. Thomas
2115 Summit Ave.
St. Paul, MN 55105-1096

Items of interest to genealogists include:

(1) volumes 1-43 of *de Familjefuerscher*
(2) many issues of the yearbook published by the genealogical society in Luxembourg
(3) all issues of the *Luxembourg News of America*

(4) Blum's two-volumes of Luxembourg bibliographies, as well as the annual issues published by the Luxembourg National Library, since 1944-45

(5) Perbal's book on the genealogy of families in Luxembourg and Belgian Luxembourg

(6) issues of *The Be-Ne-Lux Genealogist* for 1977-88

(7) newsletters of the Luxembourger societies in Wisconsin and Iowa

(8) many old maps

(9) Gonner's book *Luxembourgers in the New World*

The St. Paul Seminary library near St. Thomas has a set of 30 sheets of very detailed maps of Luxembourg (1 inch = 1 mile)

A list of many Luxembourgers in the United States is available for a fee. For details, send SASE to:

> Luxembourg Heritage
> 5675 Holyoke Ln.
> Columbus, OH 43231

A second major American repository for publications and other materials about Luxembourg is:

> Texas Christian University
> 2800 University Drive
> Ft. Worth, TX 76129

LIECHTENSTEIN

CHURCH RECORDS

Roman Catholicism is the chief religion. Church records for the period before 1878 remain in the local churches and often go back to 1640. For more information about birth, marriage and death records, write to the Catholic parish (*katholisches Pfarramt*) of the town in question.

CIVIL RECORDS

All records from 1878 forward are now kept in the Civil Registry Bureau in Vaduz, the capital of Liechtenstein. Wills are in the custody of the local courts in each district, with the earliest dated 1690. The Civil Registry Bureau will look up records for a fee (or sometimes free if staff is available and the records are easily located). Send inquiries to:

> Kanzlei der Regierung des Fürstentums Liechtenstein
> FL-9490 Vaduz
> Liechtenstein

You may also want to write to the archives if you need help with your Liechtenstein family:

> Liechtensteiner Landesarchiv
> Regierungsgebäude
> FL-9490 Vaduz
> Liechtenstein

BIBLIOGRAPHY (See ANNOTATED BIBLIOGRAPHY for full citations if not shown)

Albert Bartholdi, ed. *Prominent Americans of Swiss Origin*. New York: James T. White & Co. 1932.
> A compilation of numerous biographical sketches of prominent Swiss-Americans.

Angus Baxter. *In Search of Your European Roots: A Complete Guide to Tracing Your Ancestors in Every Country in Europe*.

Angus Baxter. *In Search of Your German Roots: A Complete Guide to Tracing Your Ancestors in the Germanic Areas of Europe.*

Scharlott Blevins. *Guide to Genealogical Research in Schleswig-Holstein, Germany.* Davenport, IA: self-published. 1994.
> Most comprehensive book for the Schleswig-Holstein area.

Steven W. Blodgett. *Germany: Genealogical Resource Guide.* Salt Lake City: Family History Library. 1989. 76 pp.

Steven W. Blodgett. "Great-grandfather Was in the Imperial Cavalry: Using Austrian Military Records as an Aid to Writing Family History," in Vol. 7 of *World Conference on Records.* 1984.

Martin Blum, ed. *Bibliographie Luxembourgeoise* [*Luxembourg Bibliography*], rev. ed. with a preface and completion of Volume 2 by Carlo Hury. Munich: Kraus International Publishers. 1981. Vol. 1: 755 pp.; Vol. 2: 700 pp. Original edition was published in Luxembourg City in 1902-32.
> In alphabetical order by author. Shows language in which each book or article was published. Has 70-page name-subject-place index.

Bibliographie Luxembourgeoise [*Luxembourg Bibliography*]. Luxembourg City: Bibliotheque Nationale Luxembourg. Annually.
> Presumably supplemental to the Blum book.

Deutsche Bundespost, Postdienst. *Das Postleitzahlenbuch.* [*The (German) Postal Code Book*].

Thomas Kent Edlund. *Register to the Ahnenstammkartei des deutschen Volkes* [*Lineage Cards of the German People*].

Familiennamenbuch der Schweiz. [*Register of Swiss Surnames*]. 3rd ed. 3 vols. Zurich: Polygraphischer Verlag. 1989. 2,082 pp.
> Official inventory of names of families which possessed Swiss citizenship in a Swiss community in 1962. Surnames are followed by cantons, arranged in alphabetical order, according to the official names of the places of citizenship; the year in which citizenship was granted (acquired before 1800; acquired in the nineteenth century; or acquired in 1901-62). Regulations governing the release of information and the large amount of data generated since 1962 have made an inventory of post-1962 surnames impossible. The 3rd edition incorporates the Jura Canton (previously part of Berne), which came into existence after the 6-volume 2nd edition was published in 1968-71 and also includes numerous other revisions and additions. Foreword, preface, instructions and index of abbreviations are printed in the four official Swiss languages, as well as English.

Family History Library. *Research Outline: Germany.*

Albert B. Faust and Gaius M. Brumbaugh. *List of Swiss Emigrants in the Eighteenth Century to the American Colonies.* Washington, DC: National Geographic Society. 1925. Reprinted, Baltimore: Genealogical Publishing Co. 1976.
> Contains descriptive lists of early emigrants from Zurich (1734-1744), Berne (1706-1795), and Basel (1734-1794), compiled from records in Swiss state archives. Indexed.

Heinz F. Friederichs. *How to Find My German Ancestors and Relatives.*

Institut grand-ducal, section de linguistique, de folklore et de toponomie. *Geschichte der Luxemburger Familiennamen* [*History of Luxembourger Family Names*]. Luxembourg: Imprimerie de Gasperich. 1989.
> Based on 1930 census. Indicates the number of bearers of each surname in Luxembourg and also in different towns and villages.

Ira A. Glazier and P. William Filby. *Germans to America: Lists of Passengers Arriving at United States Ports.*

Johann Glenzdorf. *Glenzdorfs Internationales Genealogen-Lexikon.* [*Glenzdorf's International Directory of Genealogists*].

Nicholas Gonner. *Luxembourgers in the New World.*

Charles M. Hall. *The Atlantic Bridge to Germany.*

Franz Heinzmann. *Bibliographie der Ortssippenbücher in Deutschland.* [*Bibliography of Village Lineage Books in Germany*].

Immigrant Genealogical Society. 1993 Updated Addresses to German Repositories.

Larry O. Jensen. *A Genealogical Handbook of German Research.*

Erich Dieter Linder and Günter Olzog. *Die deutschen Landkreise: Wappen, Geschichte, Struktur.* [*The German Counties: Their Coats-of-Arms, History and Structure*].

Herbert A. Mansfeld and Hans Burgauer. *Index Nominum Ex Libris Copulatorum Vindobonensibus*, 5 vols. Available in book form at the FHL, listed as the *Index to Paris Register Marriages*. Vienna: F. Bergmann. 1953.

MINERVA-Handbücher: Archive im deutschsprachigen Raum. [*MINERVA Handbooks: Archives in German-speaking Regions*].

Mario von Moos. *Bibliography of Swiss Genealogies.*

Jean-Claude Muller, ed. *Annuaire - Jahrbuch* [*Yearbook*]. Luxembourg City: Association Luxembourgeoise de Généalogique et d'Héraldique. Annually.
> Some yearbooks have been indexed and some have internal indexes. Some issues have chapter bibliographies.

Paul A. Nielsen. *Swiss Genealogical Research: An Introductory Guide.* Virginia Brach, VA: Donning Co. 1979.

Camille Perbal. *Fragments Généalogiques: Familles Luxembourgoises* [*Genealogical Fragments: Luxembourg Families*]. Brussels: Synthèse. 1990. 682 pp.
> Includes the Belgian province of Luxembourg. Has 13-page index with some unexpected entries, e.g., Baptists.

Horst A Reschke. *German Military Records as Genealogical Sources.*

Wolfgang Ribbe and Eckart Henning. *Taschenbuch für Familiengeschichtsforschung.* [*Handbook for Family History Research*].

G. Rusam. *Österreichische Exulanten in Franken und Schwaben.* [*Austrian Exiles in Franconia and Swabia*]. Neustadt/Aisch, Germany: Verlag Degener & Co. 1989. 171 pp.
> Protestant Austrian refugees in Franconia and Swabia.

Trudy Schenk, Ruth Froelke and Inge Bork. *The Wuerttemberg Emigration Index.*

Cornelia Schrader-Muggenthaler. *The Baden Emigration Book.* Apollo, PA: Closson Press. 1992. 193 pp.
> Lists emigrants, including some from Alsace, found in Karlsruhe archives.

Cornelia Schrader-Muggenthaler, comp. *The Swiss Emigration Book*, Vol. 1. Apollo, PA: Closson Press. 1993. 216 pp.
> Lists 18th and 19th century emigrants who migrated from or through Switzerland to America. Vol. 1 lists ca. 7,000 emigrants, with origins in Switzerland, Germany, Italy and France, recorded in the cantons of Solothurn, Basel and Aargau.

Karin Schulz, ed. *Hoffnung Amerika: Europäische Auswanderung in die Neu Welt.* [*The Hope of America: European Emigration to the New World*].

George K. Schweitzer. *German Genealogical Research.*

Dagmar Senekovic. *Handy Guide to Austrian Genealogical Records.*

Ronald Smelser, editor. *Preliminary Survey of the German Collection: Finding Aids to the Microfilmed Records of the Genealogical Society of Utah.*

Clifford Neal Smith and Anna Piszczan-Czaja Smith. *American Genealogical Resources in German Archives (AGRIGA): A Handbook.*

Clifford Neal Smith and Anna Piszczan-Czaja Smith. *Encyclopedia of German-American Genealogical Research.*

Kenneth L. Smith. *German Church Books: Beyond the Basics.*

Christa Stache. *Verzeichnis der Kirchenbücher im Evangelischen Zentral Archiv in Berlin [Inventory of Parish Registers in the Evangelical Central Archive in Berlin]*; Part I, *Die östlichen Kirchenprovinzen der evangelischen Kirche in der altpreussischen Union [The Eastern Bishoprics of the Evangelical Church in the Old Prussian Empire].*

Standesregister und Personenstandsbücher der Ostgebiete im Standesamt I in Berlin [Civil Registry and Civil Registration Books of the (German) Eastern Regions in the Civil Registration Office 1 in Berlin]. Frankfurt/Main: Verlag für Standesamtswesen.
> Lists the civil registers for the former German areas east of the Oder-Neisse which are in Berlin (only a minority of all such registers).

Adelreich Steinach. *Swiss Colonists in Nineteenth Century America.*

Ralph B. Strassburger and William J. Hinke, eds. *Pennsylvania German Pioneers.* 3 vols. Norristown, PA: Pennsylvania German Society. 1934.
> Transcript of original arrival lists at Philadelphia. Includes many Swiss immigrants.

Jared H. Suess. *Handy Guide to Swiss Genealogical Records.*

Ernest Thode. *Address Book for Germanic Genealogy*, 6th ed.

Heinrich Turler, Marcel Godet and Victor Attinger. *Historisch-biographisches Lexikon der Schweiz [Historical and Biographical Encyclopedia of Switzerland].* 7 vols. plus supplement. Neuenburg: Administration des Historisch-Biographisches Lexikons. 1921-34.
> Very useful set of biographical and genealogical articles on Swiss families and places, submitted by experts in the field, accompanied by good biographies for further consultation. Important activities, such as emigration, are covered by articles.

Verzeichnis der Postleitzahlen. [(Austrian) Postal Code Directory].

Verzeichnis der Postleitzahlen. [(Swiss) Postal Code Directory].

John Paul von Grueningen, ed. *The Swiss in the United States.* Madison, WI: Swiss American Historical Society. 1940.
> Contains information derived from census data explaining the distribution of the Swiss throughout the United States. Includes accounts of some prominent Swiss-Americans.

Maralyn A. Wellauer. *Family History Research in the German Democratic Republic.*

Maralyn A. Wellauer. *Tracing Your Swiss Roots.*

Martina Wermes. *Important Addresses and Telephone Numbers for Genealogical Research for the Five New (Eastern) States of the Federal Republic of Germany and Berlin.*

Martina Wermes, Renate Jude, Marion Bahr and Hans-Jürgen Voigt. *Bestandsverzeichnis der Deutschen Zentralstelle für Genealogie. [Index to the Holdings of the German Central Office for Genealogy].* Vol. III: *Die Kirchenbuchunterlagen der Länder und Provinzen des Deutschen Reiches. [Parish Registers of the States and Provinces of the German Empire].*

Gary J. Zimmerman and Marion Wolfert. *German Immigrants: Lists of Passengers Bound from Bremen to New York, with Places of Origin.*

Chapter XVIII

RESEARCHING GERMANIC ANCESTORS
IN EAST AND SOUTH EUROPEAN COUNTRIES

Few Americans realize how many German-speaking immigrants came to North and South America from non-Germanic countries, in addition to those from areas that were once Germanic. Two factors account for most of this:

- There was a large eastward migration of German-speakers in Europe over a period of a thousand years. Some of the medieval pioneers became assimilated Slavs. More Slavs became Germanicized. However, some of the medieval and nearly all of the modern migrants to German-speaking enclaves in Eastern Europe (many of them far from the Germanic core of Central Europe) retained their Germanic identity. In terms of the size of the population of those days, this eastward migration was of a magnitude almost comparable to the later, but overlapping, period of trans-oceanic migration.

- People whose ancestors or relatives had already migrated once were much more likely to migrate again than the descendants of those who stayed at home. Therefore, while a substantial majority of German-Americans have ancestors who emigrated from within the boundaries of the 1871-1918 German Empire (but with a rather large number from the former eastern provinces), several million North Americans are descended from East European Germans.

It is impossible to get very accurate figures on the number of German-speakers, or ethnic Germans, who lived in non-Germanic countries. However, Wilhelm Winkler has made a valiant effort in his *Statistisches Handbuch des gesamten Deutschtums* [*Statistical Handbook for Germans Throughout the World*]. So long as we keep in mind that there is a large possible margin of error, as he himself acknowledges, the following table will nevertheless give us some idea of the size of the Germanic population in non-Germanic Europe, based on data in the early 1920s, within the boundaries then existing:

Table 12: Germanic Population in Non-Germanic Europe, 1920s

Country	Population	Country	Population
Czechoslovakia	3,500,000	Belgium	150,000
France	1,700,000	Lithuania	131,000
Poland	1,350,000	Netherlands	80,000
Soviet Union	1,180,000	Latvia	75,000
Romania	800,000	Denmark	60,000
Yugoslavia	700,000	Great Britain	50,000
Hungary	600,000	Estonia	35,000
Italy	300,000	Turkey	25,500

Nearly all of those in Eastern Europe had previously been under German, Austro-Hungarian or Russian rule, but 3-4 million were nowhere close to a Germanic "homeland." On the other hand, the overwhelming majority of Germans in non-Germanic countries on the west, south and north lived in a border territory that had previously been under German or Austrian rule.

Clearly Winckler's estimates require both modification and explanation. For example, the 1897 census of the Russian Empire recorded 1,790,000 Germans. Despite the fact that about 750,000 of these Germans lived in former Russian territory which did not become part of the Soviet Union, according to Adam Giesinger, and despite emigration, wartime deaths, starvation and other factors which reduced the number of Germans, the figure recorded in the 1926 Soviet census was still somewhat higher than Winckler's estimate.

A greater complication stems from the concept of ethnic identity. We know that most Americans have ancestors who belonged to more than one ethnic group, although the first generation of German immigrants usually married other German-Americans.

The sense of ethnic identity was less ambiguous in Europe, especially Eastern Europe. Nevertheless, ethnic Germans did marry people of different ethnic origin, even though the number was considerably smaller than in the American "melting pot," the process of assimilation was much slower, and the ethnic self-identity of descendants of mixed marriages (who might well be bilingual) could just as easily increase as decrease the number of "Germans."

As an illustration, those Germans who had not yet fled in fear of the advancing Red Army were supposedly expelled pursuant to the 1945 Potsdam agreement. Nevertheless, when the border to the west opened up, a surprisingly large number of Poles with at least one provable German ancestor emigrated to Germany.

Nevertheless, the idea of das *Deutschtum* or *Volksdeutsche* (purporting to answer the question, "Who is a German?") was meaningful, though imprecise, in Europe, whereas it soon became impossible to define in non-European countries, where census data rarely recorded this information beyond those who had at least one parent born in a Germanic country.

Despite the imperfect figures, Winckler's data are nevertheless accurate enough to show that more Germans lived in non-Germanic countries during the interwar period than the combined population of Austria, Switzerland, Luxembourg, and Liechtenstein.

Those from non-Germanic eastern countries were particularly likely to migrate again. The number of North and South Americans descended from Germans in the diaspora is almost impossible to calculate, even without considering the complex question as to how many Jews were German-speakers, despite the growing interest in one's heritage.

The number of non-Jewish Americans and Canadians who have retained a sense of a Russian German heritage is probably between one and two million. However, because of the virtual irrelevance of ethnicity in marriage today, the number whose ancestors were all, or even nearly all, Germans who came from Russia is only a small fraction of this number, whereas those who have at least one German-speaking ancestor from the Russian Empire is probably in the range of 5-10 million and growing so rapidly that even rough estimates may well be both impossible and meaningless.

A key resource for researching German-speaking ancestors from Eastern Europe is the *Genealogical Guide to German Ancestors from East Germany and Eastern Europe*, prepared by the Arbeitsgemeinschaft ostdeutscher Familienforscher (AGoFF), i.e., the Working Group of Genealogists Concerned with Germans in the East (which is more accurate than a literal translation of the words). The second edition of this book, which contains maps showing all the German settlements in Eastern Europe, has been translated into English by Joachim O. R. Nuthack and Dr. Adalbert Goertz. It will be referred to in some places as the *AGoFF Guide*. Significant portions of the information in this book stem from that source. There is now a fourth German edition (scheduled to be translated into English). The fourth German edition will be referred to as the *AGoFF-Wegweiser*. (For further information on resources pertinent to East Europe, look under **GERMANY** and **AUSTRIA** earlier in this chapter.)

Many of the parish registers and other archival documents for Germanic areas in Eastern and Southern Europe are at the Deutsche Zentralstelle für Genealogie in Leipzig. Others are at Evangelisches Zentralarchiv in Berlin. See **GERMANY** for the addresses. The Leipzig records have been microfilmed by the Family History Library and are inventoried in an easy-to-use list form in Martina Wermes, Renate Jude, Marion Bahr, and Hans-Jürgen Voigt, *Bestandsverzeichnis der Deutschen Zentralstelle für Genealogie* [Index to the Holdings of the German Central Office for Genealogy], Vol. II: *Die archivalischen und Kirchenbuchunterlagen deutscher Siedlungsgebiete im Ausland: Bessarabien, Bukowina, Estland, Lettland und Litauen, Siebenbürgen, Sudetenland, Slowenien und Südtirol* [*The*

Parish Registers of the German Settlements in Other Areas: Bessarabia, Bukovina, Estonia, Latvia and Lithuania, Transylvania, the Sudetenland, Slovenia and South Tyrol] (see bibliography).

The *Ratgeber '92: Familienforschung GUS/Baltikum* [*Advisor '92: Family History Research in the CIS and Baltic Countries*] lists the names of a large number of individual researchers throughout the former Soviet Union (mostly in Russia, Belarus and the Baltics) who are willing to undertake private research. This article mentions the foreign language competence of the various researchers. Most of them know English, while all of the others know German, which simplifies the translation problem. The use of private researchers is complicated by the factors listed under **RUSSIA**, as well as by the slowness of mail service to the Commonwealth of Independent States (CIS). Irina and Rainer Zielke have compiled the *Ratgeber '95*, which has been published by the Verlag Degener & Co., Neustadt/Aisch.

For a good geographical sampling of CIS and Baltic researchers, see "Genealogical Spring in the Former Soviet Union" by Edward R. Brandt and David F. Schmidt, in the June 1993 issue of the *East European Genealogist*, published by the East European Branch of the Manitoba Genealogical Society (now the East European Genealogical Society).

For information on German-speaking Jews from Eastern Europe and elsewhere, see *Avotaynu* and *Dorot*, two of the leading Jewish genealogical periodicals, as well as the books listed in the bibliography.

There is also a lot of information pertaining to immigrants from East Europe, including the papers of the Jewish Archives Center, at:

> The Balch Institute of Ethnic Studies
> Temple University
> 18 S. 7th St.
> Philadelphia, PA 19106

The following institute also deals with East European Jewish genealogical research:

> YIVO Institute for Jewish Research
> 555 W. 57th St., Ste. 1100
> New York, NY 10019-2925

The leading American historical and genealogical expert on Germans who immigrated to southeastern Europe is:

> Robert Ward
> 21010 Mastick Rd.
> Fairview Park, OH 44126

The rapid increase in information about genealogical resources and researchers in Eastern Europe after the collapse of the Iron Curtain, and the fact that so many parts of Eastern Europe had ethnically mixed populations or significant minorities, led to the formation of the multi-ethnic Federation of East European Family History Societies (FEEFHS) in 1992. The first newsletter of that society was published in December 1992, in order to facilitate the rapid spread of such information. Both organizations and individuals may become members. Most East European-oriented ethnic genealogical societies are members, as are most Jewish Special Interest Groups for eastern Europe and a number of other Jewish genealogical societies. Most major German-American genealogical societies also belong to FEEFHS. The permanent address of FEEFHS is: P.O. Box 510898, Salt Lake City, UT 84151-0898, from where mail will be forwarded to officers, board members and others, as necessary. The area of interest of FEEFHS includes all of Germany and Austria, because of their historic links to Eastern Europe, but the focus is on the ex-Communist areas.

FEEFHS has published a *Resource Guide to East European Genealogy*, which is updated periodically. It includes information about all member societies and also provides information about professional genealogists and translators specializing in Eastern Europe (including the Germanic countries in Central Europe). To order a copy, write John D. Movius, P.O. Box 4327, Davis, CA 95616-4327.

Following American practice, the term "Eastern Europe" is used in this book to include what Europeans and historians refer to as East Central Europe and Southeast Europe.

THE SOVIET UNION: SUCCESSOR STATES

The migration of Germans to the Russian Empire is dealt with in Chapter X on **HISTORY**. The most authoritative history of the German settlements in the Russian Empire is Dr. Adam Giesinger, *From Catherine to Khrushchev: The Story of Russia's Germans*. The most comprehensive source of information as to the places of origin of these immigrants is Dr. Karl Stumpp, *The Emigration from Germany to Russia in the Years 1763 to 1862*. Robert and Margaret (Zimmerman) Freeman of the Glückstal Colony Research Association, prepared a place name index to Adam Giesinger's *From Catherine to Khrushchev* in 1986.

RESEARCH DIFFICULTIES AND POSSIBILITIES

The situation with respect to genealogical developments in the former Soviet Union (especially Russia, Ukraine, Belarus and Moldova) is changing so rapidly that a subscription to the *RAGAS Newsletter* is indispensable for anyone seeking, or contemplating seeking, information from those archives.

The best news is that more and more records are being found, the repositories where they are being kept are being identified (along with the exact archival numbers) and some material is being computerized.

However, many of these records are not readily available. Vladislav Soshnikov of the Genealogy and Family History Society (GFHS) in Moscow, a non-profit research service, states that the most serious barrier is the difficulty of gaining access.

Even though the governments in the CIS member states in which most Germanic ancestors lived have adopted laws providing for freedom of access to the archives and proclaiming genealogy to be a priority, the realities at the level of individual archival administration often do not reflect this. Some official regulations governing access do not even mention genealogists as users. In all too many cases, decisions are made arbitrarily and inconsistently. Favoritism is not unusual.

The old buddy mentality, as well as the lingering effects of attitudes produced by having become accustomed to the arbitrary decisions of the Soviet past, play a role. Genealogy (historically mostly for nobles) was frowned upon during the Communist era. Some archivists still have this attitude and are suspicious of genealogists.

Hence, a combination of severe financial difficulties and habits left over from the past account for most of the following problems:

(1) Some archives are being left unheated much of the time, due to a shortage of funds.
(2) Archivists in some places have not been paid for months.
(3) The low pay of archivists is not an inducement to recruiting professional staff.
(4) All of the above factors interfere with the efficiency of archival work, creating delays and sometimes leading to an unwillingness by the archives to cooperate with genealogical researchers.
(5) Often researchers are allowed to copy only single entries because of the belief that commercial and non-profit researchers, including those of the Russian-American Genealogical Archival Service (RAGAS), could get rich if such restrictions were not imposed, even though archives generally charge access fees to researchers searching records for clients.
(6) The funds generated by the archives go into the government's general fund, rather than to the archives, so there is little incentive for them to improve their services.
(7) Those in charge of some archives believe that they can get more money from research requests by individuals than by cooperating with North American (or West European)

organizations in providing entire sets of records, which, of course, seriously restricts access to these records by those genealogists who cannot afford to pay a large fee.

(8) Some archives have been closed for prolonged periods. Sometimes this is due to moves. More often it is because the archivists consider it necessary to prepare inventories of their holdings before granting access, partly because of pilfering and scandals.

(9) The danger of further deterioration of old and fragile records is also sometimes given as a reason for blocking access.

This does not mean that access to records is becoming more difficult in all cases, but it should serve as a precautionary warning that waiting to order desired information may not be a good idea.

On the positive side, some local authorities are willing to pitch in and provide the funds for the operation of archives where the national governments cannot do so. Furthermore, the attitudes of archivists vary a lot. Despite the foregoing problems, some archivists are extremely helpful. Those problems which stem from inadequate or obsolete equipment are remedial in nature.

It is because of these complications, with frequent and unpredictable changes of policy or practice, that the *RAGAS Newsletter*, which regularly provides the latest information, is so important. Most of the articles are written by Vladislav Soshnikov of Moscow, who has visited and spoken in the United States on several occasions; some are written by Patricia Eames, the newsletter editor, who works at the U.S. National Archives and knows what records are available there.

In no way does this decrease the importance of the journals of the various organizations of descendants of immigrants from the Russian Empire, or from adjacent territory which was later annexed by the Soviet Union.

Although the *RAGAS Newsletter* packs a lot of detail into each page, the larger periodicals for Jews and Germans from Russia carry articles which are more extensive in some respects. This is because many relevant records are already in the United States (or elsewhere in the Western world). The translation, coordination, computerization and indexing of these records to make them available to the public, either through publication or by sale, is very important.

Reports by genealogists who have traveled to the Commonwealth of Independent States and have done some research, or have arranged for it to be done, are very useful. Many of these have been published in one of the numerous relevant periodicals. Moreover, the increasing frequency of tours to the members of the CIS sometimes provide an opportunity for limited on-site research, or identification of sources, pertinent to the individual's personal research.

There are other difficulties besides those which can be attributed to a shortage of funds or problems with access.

(1) **Deciphering:** Some pre-revolutionary letters of the Russian alphabet no longer exist. The German *h* is usually rendered as *g* in Russian, the language used in most records (although not in Ukrainian or Belarussian, which lack the *g*). Deciphering the old Cyrillic script can be just as difficult as deciphering the Gothic script. For these reasons, people who are fluent in Russian (even native speakers) may have considerable difficulty with old records.

(2) **Privacy laws:** Members of the Commonwealth of Independent States, like other countries, generally have privacy laws that may permit access to records relating to your ancestors, but may impede access to quantities of documents for publication or filming. But the large number of articles which have been published show that at least the nature of various records can be printed, even though the explicit information contained in the records may be another matter.

(3) **Identifying records:** In this connection, it is important to understand the organization of archival collections. According to David Schmidt, co-author of "Genealogical

Spring on the Former Soviet Union" (East European Genealogist, June 1993), the largest unit in a Russian archive is a *fond*. Each *fond* (record group) is further subdivided into a collection called an *opis* (series). A *delo* is a still smaller unit, a file or storage unit. (Different terms are used in some other countries.) For example, the 1798 Volga lists are in the Russian State Historical Archive (RGIA) in St. Petersburg in *fond* 393, *opis* 19, with the *delo* varying according to the village. Without the exact archival record identification, it may take a researcher many hours just to find the records for which you are searching. Most archives don't have inventories or finding aids.

(4) **Sending money:** There is no secure way of sending money to CIS countries, except to Moscow. This makes it advisable to work through non-profit or commercial agencies which provide courier services, unless you have contacts with individuals traveling there who are willing to deliver your money to independent researchers.

(5) **Problems facing researchers:** There is a shortage of archivists in Russia (and even more so in other CIS countries) who are familiar with genealogy as we know it, the scattered records are often incomplete or in poor condition, and the field travel that is often required is complicated by weather, road conditions and various restrictions that may apply when researchers travel to other countries.

RECORDS OF THE FORMER RUSSIAN EMPIRE

For the above reasons, some of the specifics mentioned here may be out-of-date by the time this reaches the printer. That is one reason why we have avoided going into greater detail, even though much additional information is available to us.

For example, there are many as yet unfilmed religious and civil records for the Volga and Black Sea Catholics, as well as for a few Black Sea German villages, in the archives at Engels (formerly Pokrovsk) and in Saratov. Many records in the Russian State Historical Archive (RGIA) in St. Petersburg (the former capital) and the Russian State Archive of Ancient Acts (RGADA) in Moscow have not been filmed. The same is true of the numerous archives in Ukraine and other countries that were part of the Soviet Union.

Moreover, the archives at Samara have important information about the Germans who settled in mother and daughter settlements in this Upper Volga region in 1830-60, as well as about the exiles from the western regions of the Russian Empire (mostly Volhynia) who were deported to this area during World War I. They also have records of the Jewish community for 1864-1883. The St. George Evangelical Lutheran Church in Samara has a great deal of specific information, including vital events in other provinces (among them Russian Poland, Lithuania, Georgia and even Bavaria) for 1859-1923. For detailed information, including many family names, see the Winter 1996-97 issue of the *RAGAS Newsletter* (Vol. II, No. 4).

There are undoubtedly many records that have not even been found yet, in view of the secrecy of the Soviet era, the absence of adequate archival finding aids, and the shortage of researchers with a significant amount of genealogical experience.

A Handbook for Archival Research in the U.S.S.R. (1989) by Patricia Kennedy Grimsted, the leading American expert on Soviet archives, is the best introduction to this subject, dealing with archival organization, research strategies and general reference tools. Appendices list the major repositories in the former Soviet archives. The book is available from IREX (International Research & Exchanges Board), attn. Ann Robertson, 1616 H St. N.W., Washington, DC 20006. But it is of very limited value unless you know Russian and can read the Cyrillic script.

The territorial administrative structure during the Soviet and post-Soviet eras is quite different from that of the Czarist days. The Russian Empire was divided into *guberni(y)as* or *gubernii* (provinces), with roughly analogous regions known as *oblasts* or *oblasty* in Asia and the Caucasus. *Guberniyas* were divided into districts, each known as an *u(y)ezd*. (These terms are sometimes spelled with, and sometimes without, the *y*. We will use the *y* form, because it reflects the pronunciation and may therefore be less confusing to English-speakers.)

The number, boundaries and size of *guberniya*s changed frequently, beginning with 8 in 1709 and increasing to 11 in 1719. During the 1775-1914 period that is most relevant for Germanic research, the number of *guberniya*s increased from 40 (each comprised of about 10 *uyezd*s or *uyezdy*) to 78 (plus about 20 *oblast*s). In 1974 there were more than 125 Soviet *oblast*s. (Since English-speakers are accustomed to *s* as a plural, we will follow this practice, although it is contrary to Russian usage.)

Nineteenth-century imperial provinces in current Ukrainian or Moldovan territory included Kherson, Ekaterinoslav, Taurida, Bessarabia, Volhynia (*Zhitomir*), Podolia, Kiev and Kharkiv (Kharkov). Those in the Caucasus area included Kuban, Terek, and one for the trans-Caucasian province south of Terek.

Today an *oblast* serves roughly the same jurisdictional purpose as the former *guberniya* (a term no longer in use), with *uyezd* being the term still used for the sub-unit.

LUTHERAN, REFORMED, SEPARATIST AND MORAVIAN BRETHREN RECORDS

Slightly over three-fourths of the Germans in the Russian Empire at the time of the 1897 census were Lutherans, according to Giesinger. It is not clear whether this percentage includes the other non-Anabaptist Protestants, since Reformed and Lutherans alike prefixed their name with "Evangelical," the name of the merged church in Germany. Many of the Reformed churches (which had always constituted a minority) had become part of the Lutheran church organization by then, as had the smaller number of Separatists and Moravian Brethren.

The Family History Library has now microfilmed a collection of Lutheran parish registers of the Consistory of St. Petersburg. A total of 276 volumes of church books for over 199 parishes have been found in record group (*fond*) 828, series (*opis*) 14, at the Russian State Historical Archive in St. Petersburg. These records begin in 1833, when such vital registration became mandatory in the Russian Empire, with currently available films ending in 1885, although later registers are reported to have been discovered in the meantime. They are the duplicate copies that were sent yearly to the consistory office.

This consistory included the Black Sea region and Volhynia (i.e., all nineteenth-century settlements in Ukraine, except for those areas that belonged to the Austro-Hungarian Empire), as well as Belarus, western Russia and Moldova.

These records are mostly in the German language, are all in good shape, and are easy to read, but they have one drawback that makes them very difficult to use. Since they are the duplicate records that were sent yearly to the consistory office, they were filmed just that way, i.e., by year of receipt of the records in St. Petersburg (not always the year to which the records actually pertained), and without any geographic distinction. One roll of film can contain records from hundreds of different parishes. This means that a lot of time can be wasted in accessing these records.

Fortunately, Thomas Kent Edlund and a staff of volunteers at the Family History Library have spent over a year indexing these registers. The indexes contain the parish names, years covered, type of records, volume and page numbers, film numbers and item numbers on the film. In addition, Mr. Edlund details the historical background of German settlements in the Imperial Russian Empire. He also describes the history of the Lutheran Church and its jurisdictions.

The Germanic Genealogy Society published this index under the title *The Lutherans of Russia*, Vol. 1: *Parish Index to the Church Books of the Evangelical Lutheran Consistory of St. Petersburg, 1833-1885*, (ISBN 0-9644-337-1-0) in 1995. This is just the first step, we hope, in locating and microfilming other church records of the former Russian Empire.

Lists of a few of these film numbers, indicating which areas and dates are included, were published in an article on "German-Russian Church Records and Registers" (27 Oct. 1993), based on a compilation by Margaret Johnson and others, in the *Newsletter of the Puget Sound Chapter of GRHS* (reprinted by all other major American publications that focus on Russian Germans). "St. Petersburg Consistory Microfilms: 19th Century Lutheran Church Records" by Jerry Frank with the assistance of Howard Krushel (*Wandering Volhynians*, December 1994) lists the numbers for all Volhynian records.

Ewald Wuschke, publisher of *Wandering Volhynians*, is putting the film numbers for Volhynia on a computer database, a project expected to take several years.

The location of most records for churches that did not belong to parishes is unknown, but 24 registers for such churches are in the records of the Religious Council of the Evangelical Lutheran Church of St. Mary in *fond* 849 in the Saratov archive, according to Kahlile Mehr, "German-Russian Genealogical Records," in Vol. I, No. 22 (1994), of the *Genealogical Journal* published by the Utah Genealogical Association. The staff of the American Historical Society of Germans from Russia reports (in the Winter 1994 issue of its *Newsletter*) that *fond* 852 contains records for six Black Sea parishes. In the same issue, Russian archivist O. K. Pudovochkina, "Information About the Black Sea Records in Saratov," states that 80% of the records in this *fond* are in German. Some records may also be in the register of the St. George Evangelical Lutheran Church in Samara, which includes entries from places where there were few Germans.

Sparse samplings have also been found in the St. Petersburg City Archive (18 churches for 1712-1926), Minsk (Belarus) Central Historical Archive (record group 1952), Hrodna (Belarus) Central Historical Archive (record group 649 and others), and L'viv (Ukraine) Central Historical Archive (records group 427), as well as in local civil registry offices. Most of them, however, are believed to have been destroyed or lost. A few records from the Upper Volga area around Nizhny Novgorod, which became part of the St. Petersburg Consistory, have been microfilmed, but they include little, if any, information about Germans.

Gwen Pritzkau and Miriam Hall Hansen, Family History Library volunteers working with these records, have also compiled data for certain parishes. But there are gaps in the records for certain years and duplicate registers have not been found for all parishes. The filmed records for western Ukraine are more nearly complete than those for eastern Ukraine. Not all churches belonged to parishes because of the scattered German settlements in some areas.

The original parish registers for Ingria (*Ingermanland*, i.e., the St. Petersburg area) are known to be in Finland, which was also Lutheran and adjacent to St. Petersburg. This relatively small German settlement was older than the Volga colonies, but it is unknown whether these registers predate those of the other Germans.

A Lutheran consistory was opened in Saratov in 1819 and moved to Moscow in 1834, according to Pudovochkina. Some records for the Lutheran Consistory of Moscow have also been found in the Moscow City (formerly Regional) Archive, according to Mehr, who states that a 1961 description of this record group lists 62 items for 1803-1917.

Besides the consistories of St. Petersburg and Moscow, there were also six in the Baltics, viz., in Courland, Livonia, Estonia, Ösel (now Saaremaa), Riga and Reval (now Tallinn). There were 415 parishes in the Baltics, with a heavy concentration in Latvia, as contrasted with 87 in the St. Petersburg and 65 in the Volga river areas, in 1832. Lithuanian records are not included in this account, since most of the Lithuanian German parishes were in what was then East Prussia.

We are not aware of any published references to parish registers of the Reformed Church. However, Giesinger (on whose book we have relied for information about the Reformed, Separatist Lutherans, and Moravian Brethren) states that there were originally 3 Reformed parishes in the Volga area and that these were eventually absorbed into the Lutheran Church organization (apparently between 1810 and about 1840), although retaining their distinctive practices. In the early years, Catholic priests occasionally served the Reformed who were not close to one of the parish centers because of the antipathy between the major Protestant denominations. Somewhat less than one quarter of the Volga Protestants belonged to the Reformed Church in 1861.

In the Black Sea region, the pattern was somewhat different. Lutheran pastors served some of the Reformed living in scattered areas in the early years. Many of these became Lutherans. However, the remaining Reformed parishes never joined the Lutheran consistory.

Because of these complicated developments, the Lutheran parish registers may include data on members of the Reformed Church. For the early Volga years, Catholic records may also include data on Reformed Church members.

There were also fervent Separatists (dissident Lutherans from Württemberg) in the Black Sea region and the Caucasus. They were served by their own lay preachers, and later trained preachers, for decades, but they eventually returned to the Lutheran Church.

The missionary-minded Moravian Brethren established a Volga village in 1765. They became part of the Lutheran Church in 1894. However, some Germans who joined the Moravian Brethren before this date emigrated to Canada and retained that religious identity, according to an article in *Wandering Volhynians*.

ROMAN CATHOLIC RECORDS

About two-thirds of the Roman Catholics in the Russian Empire in the mid-nineteenth century were Germans, with Poles accounting for most of the rest (Giesinger). Presumably Russian Poland is excluded from this calculation.

The Tiraspol Consistory, established in 1847-50 (Giesinger), actually had its first seat in Kherson (Ukraine), then moved to Tiraspol (Ukraine) in 1852-53 (implied by Pudovochkina) and finally to Saratov (Volga area of Russia) in 1856-58 (Pudovochkina; Richard Rye of AHSGR). But it was generally known as the Tiraspol Consistory. There had been six Roman Catholic dioceses in the western *guberniya*s of the Russian Empire prior to this, but there were very few German Catholics in those areas.

According to Mehr, 647 Catholic parish register transcripts for the consistory located at Mogilev (Belarus) in 1783, and the Tiraspol Consistory, which assumed jurisdiction over the Black Sea and Volga Catholics, are in Saratov, specifically in *fond* 1166 ("Mogilev Roman Catholic Consistory") for 1801-1852 and in *fond* 365 ("Tiraspol Roman Catholic Consistory") for 1853-1918. The *fond* titles come from Pudovochkina, who also identifies the location more specifically as the State Archive of Saratov Oblast and specifies 513 files in *fond* 1166, *opis* 1, and 36 in an addendum thereto. About 500 of these files are registers, with the remainder devoted to other kinds of church business. (Magocsi lists the Belarussian spelling of Mogilev [Russian] or Mogilew [German] as "Mohiliou.")

Fond 1267 ("Kherson Roman Catholic Consistory") in Saratov also includes copies of church books for 1850-53 that were sent from Kherson to Tiraspol, per Pudovochkina.

One set of volumes includes the provinces of Saratov, Samara and Astrakhan, while the other part covers the Black Sea region (provinces of Kherson, Taurida, and Bessarabia), and the Caucasus, according to Mehr and Pudovochkina.

The address Mehr lists is:

Regional Government Archive
Kutyakova ul., Building 15
410710 Saratov
Russia

The Family History Library has not received permission to film these records. You can write to the archives for information, but no one in the reference section speaks English, so it would be best to write in Russian. Check the introductory material under the **COMMONWEALTH OF INDEPENDENT STATES** for contact channels.

An alternative is to work through private researchers, such as Dr. Igor R. Pleve, who has found some German Catholic parish registers for the Volga area, as well as some Lutheran registers, since the Volga area was not within the ecclesiastical jurisdiction of St. Petersburg.

According to a statement by Mehr at the May 1994 FEEFHS convention (confirmed by Pudovochkina), a Roman Catholic diocese also existed in Zhitomir, but very few of the Volhynian Germans were Catholics.

Catholic registers were mandated in the Russian Empire in 1826. Three copies were required: one for the church, one for the diaconate, and one for the consistory.

MENNONITE AND BAPTIST RECORDS

Until very recently there was only one significant Ukrainian or Russian source of information about Mennonite genealogy.

This was the 140,000-page Peter J. Braun Collection of records pertaining to the Molotschna (Molochna) colonies assembled during the Russian Civil War, which had long been lost and was discovered more or less accidentally in a building belonging to the Odessa archives which supposedly housed Jewish records. It includes, among other things, the very important 1835 revision records (in Russian) and the incomplete 1854-62 village pupil lists (in German).

The translated 1835 revision is available in Canada at the Mennonite Heritage Centre, Winnipeg; Conrad Grebel College, Waterloo, Ontario; and the University of Toronto. Presumably most Mennonite archives in the United States have copies by now. It can be purchased by contacting Alf Redekopp at the Mennonite Heritage Centre. The village pupil lists are now in the Provincial Archives of Manitoba.

A good description of the contents of the entire collection can be found in Ingrid I. Epp and Harvey L. Dyck, *The Peter J. Braun Russian Mennonite Archives, 1803-1920: A Research Guide*. The book includes various research aids: how to use the guide, chronology of Russian Mennonite history, list of microfilm reels and numbers, symbols, and glossaries.

Prior to the *glasnost* period, the only important European sources were in Germany, where numerous books and articles had been published. The most significant one was Benjamin Heinrich Unruh, *Die Hintergründe der mennonitischen Ostwanderungen im 16., 18. und 19. Jahrhundert* [*The Netherlandish-Low German Background of the Mennonite Eastward Migrations in the 16th, 18th and 19th Centuries*]. Besides a lot of historical material beginning with the sixteenth-century flight from the then Spanish Netherlands, mostly to West Prussia, it includes the Russian revision lists for 1795 and 1808, in addition to information from various (primarily West Prussian) archives which provides an almost complete list of emigrants from Prussia to what was then South Russia.

The 1808 revision list for Molotschna includes the village of origin in Prussia, the village of residence in Russia, and the names and ages of all household members. Similar but less complete information is provided in the emigrant lists, which are grouped by year of emigration. Unfortunately, there is considerably less detail for the Chortitza colony.

A huge card index collection of genealogical data on Prussian Mennonites and their descendants throughout the world is in the hands of:

> Hermann Thiessen
> Breslauer Str. 3
> D-31303 Burgdorf
> Germany

He has published quite a few massive histories of descendants with a common pre-1800 Prussian ancestral couple. Because of his age and his health, responses to queries are becoming uncertain. But copies of his books should be in most North American Mennonite resource centers.

However, a lot of additional information has been identified in, and sometimes obtained from, Ukrainian and Russian archives recently. For example, the Mennonite Heritage Centre has 30,000 pages of material from St. Petersburg. These are now on 24 reels of microfilms, with a somewhat detailed index for the first 20 reels and a more cursory one for the others.

These documents also include some Baptist records.

The Dnepropetrovsk archive has a lot of relevant information for both of the original colonies. Dmitry Y. Meshkov has compiled an inventory, *The Documents of the Dnepropetrovsk Archive as a Source on the History of the Mennonites, 1789-1944*. Copies of this unpublished material can be purchased by contacting Peter J. Klassen at the Center for Mennonite Brethren Studies in Fresno.

Many of the records in the Zaporozhye archives pertain to Mennonites.

Peter Rempel of Moscow is willing to accept Mennonite genealogical research assignments in Ukrainian and Russian archives. He reads and writes English, but prefers to speak German. He can be contacted by e-mail at borys@synapse.ru or by fax at 7-095-202-6934. It is also possible to contact him through his brother at:

> Box 37558
> 1030 AN Amsterdam
> Netherlands

Two articles by Brian J. Lenius, which include information about several Mennonite congregations in western Volhynia and eastern Galicia, are listed under **POLAND**.

The leading North American expert on the Galician Mennonites, who publishes the *Galician Grapevine*, is:

> Glen Linscheid
> Box 194
> Butterfield, MN 56120

Ewald Wuschke lists the records for four Mennonite congregations in Volhynia (1780-1940), as well as two in Poland (Warsaw, 1832-76; Gostynin, 1863-64), in *Protestant Parish Records on Microfilm for the Former Congress Poland*.

Almost all the sources of information about German Baptists from the Russian Empire are in North America. Addresses of pertinent resource centers are in Chapter XI.

Wuschke lists two Baptist church books for the 1870s in Central Poland. These may have some relevance for the Volhynian Baptists, since a majority of the Volhynian Germans came from Russian Poland.

A pioneering article by Charles Weisser, "The Baptist Movement Among the Germans in Russia," in the March 1992 issue of the *Heritage Review*, indicates that the Baptists began to gain ground in Russia between 1840 and 1860, and that by 1886 they had 12,000 members. For this reason, the Russian revision lists would be of only limited value for Baptist genealogy.

By and large, the Baptist church, which also had Orthodox converts, was not a church of the immigrants, but rather a church to which the Germans later flocked, although a few late immigrants to Volhynia were Baptists. It had a particular attraction for those affected by the Pietist movement, which influenced Lutherans, Mennonites and a few Catholics.

Several historical articles on German Baptists in or from the Russian Empire have been published in the *Journal of the American Historical Society of Germans from Russia*.

JEWISH RECORDS

Jewish registers were mandated in 1835, but are more complete after 1885. Duplicate copies were required, one for the government. Many of these records are in the rabbinates. There are 19 registers in Kiev. Records for some 70 localities in Galicia, which was formerly an Austrian crown province, are in L'viv (German: Lemberg). Some of these records are also in Warsaw. "What May be Learned from 19th-Century Czarist Jewish Birth Records and Revision Lists," by Harold Rhode, is one of the more recent of several detailed articles published in *Avotaynu* (Fall 1994) about Jewish records in the Russian Empire.

Those with Jewish ancestors from Ukraine (as well as Moldova and Poland) are in good luck. The following Jewish researcher spends half her time in these countries and has purchased an apartment in Ukraine to facilitate research:

> Miriam Weiner, C. G.
> 136 Sandpiper Key
> Secaucus, NJ 07904

A small number of Russian German immigrants, or their descendants, converted to Judaism, in addition to the Yiddish-speaking Jews who had been there for centuries in most cases.

Avotaynu regularly publishes articles about resources for Jewish genealogy from throughout the world, specifically including many from the former Pale of Settlement in the Russian Empire.

CIVIL REGISTRATION

Although universal civil registration did not exist until after the Czarist period, civil registers for certain groups apparently were mandated in 1879, with duplicate copies required, one going to the government. Members of smaller religious groups, like the Baptists, are included in these. Civil registration was mandated by Austria in Galicia (now partly in Ukraine) in 1874.

Civil records for the period after the Russian Revolution are in the *ZAGS* (Russian) or *ZAHS* (Ukrainian) offices, archival units of the ministries of justice. Many parish registers can also be found here.

REVISION LISTS

Besides the parish registers and rabbinical records, the most valuable sources of genealogical information appear to be the Russian revision lists, i.e., poll tax lists (also referred to as censuses). Every head of household, with certain largely irrelevant exceptions, had to pay a tax. Although there are some differences in the details provided by various revisions, they all include the names and ages of all members of the household. Some of them list the Russian patronymic form as the middle name, so that when you find a record of a male property owner, you automatically know the first name of his father. Unfortunately, the maiden names of the wives are usually not recorded.

These revisions generally show what happened to the owners since the previous revision, i.e., the date of death or the place to which the family had moved and when. Property was only infrequently listed as belonging to widows. Mothers, the families of unpropertied siblings or children, and others residing in the same household are recorded. Some of the early revisions record the village from which the immigrant came.

According to Kahlile Mehr, but expanding the range of years to include all those mentioned in various sources, the revisions pertaining to the Volga and Black Sea Germans (as well as the few pre-1860 Volhynian Germans) were as follows:

3rd (1761-69)	7th (1815-25)
4th (1775-88)	8th (1833-35)
5th (1794-1809)	9th (1849-52)
6th (1811-12; incomplete because of interruption by the Napoleonic War)	10th (1857-59)

Some records which have been received are inconsistent with this. There are two possible explanations: (1) errors by the recorder or (2) possible confusion which could have been caused by the many special poll tax lists prepared for certain areas from time to time.

Mehr states that the last six (5th-10th) revisions for the Volga Germans are in the Saratov archive. However, some lists are reported to be in the St. Petersburg Historical Archive or elsewhere.

There could have been two copies of each revision, since there are other discrepancies in reports as to whether various revisions were left in the central or provincial archives. In fact, in one known case, the revision, or a later transcription of it, was found in an entirely different location. For example, some revisions prior to 1850 are said to have been kept in local archives, i.e., in the *guberniya* capital, while later ones are supposed to be in the central archives, but this conflicts with information about the known contents of the local archives in the Volga area.

According to the *Ratgeber '92: Familienforschung GUS/Baltikum*, the 3rd, part of the 4th and the 5th revisions are at the Russian Central State Archive of Ancient Acts (RGADA) in Moscow. But David F. Schmidt believes that the records of the 4th revision for the Volga Germans have been destroyed. Soshnikov reported that the 8th, 9th and 10th revisions that have been found are incomplete, at least for the Volga area. The first three revisions are reported to be in the archives in Moscow. The 3rd revision was the first one to list females (but not maiden names), but the mass migrations to the Volga River, the Black Sea region and Volhynia did not occur prior to this.

The American Historical Society of Germans from Russia now has a complete set of the 1798 Volga German revision lists. These are being translated and most of them are available already.

The years when these revisions took place are usually not identical for the Volga and Black Sea areas. Therefore, it may be easier to find the records by specifying the revision list number than the year, once this is clearly established.

The 1st (1719-28), 2nd (1743) and 3rd (1761-69) revisions, as well as prior unnumbered revisions in 1646-48, 1676-78, 1710 and 1717, might be useful for the small number of Germans who were in St. Petersburg or Moscow by that time. Russia acquired the St. Petersburg area (Ingria) and the northern Baltics in 1721, adding Courland (southern and western Latvia) in 1795. Thus these early revisions could also be helpful for some Baltic Germans. However, the nobility and high-ranking public or church officials (to which class many of these Germans belonged) were exempt from taxation and thus are not listed.

Soshnikov reported that supplementary revisions were also made, but these are hard to find, since they are not indexed. A RAGAS flyer mentions local censuses, which may refer to the same kind of record. Richard Scheuermann suggests that there may have been a partial 1880 Volga revision. The Unruh book includes the entries for the Chortitza Mennonites in both 1795 and 1808 (which fall within the same revision period), suggesting that the first one may have been a special census for the recent (1789-1794) arrivals.

THE 1897 CENSUS

The only comprehensive census in the Russian Empire, which included everyone, was conducted in 1897.

According to Giesinger, the 1,790,489 Germans were broken down by area as follows:

Table 13: Germanic Population in the Russian Empire, 1897

Area	Germanic Population
Russian Poland	407,274
Volga region	390,864
Black Sea region	377,798
Volhynia	171,331
Baltics	165,627
St. Petersburg district	50,780
Caucasus and trans-Ural areas	71,027
Elsewhere in European Russia	155,788

By 1926 the number of Germans shrank to 1,238,549. This was due to relatively large-scale emigration after 1873, the severance of the Baltics, Russian Poland and half of Volhynia from the Soviet Union after World War I (areas that had about 750,000 Germans, per Giesinger), and the short-term consequences of the Russian Civil War. Despite flight from harsh Stalinist measures, famine, and the terroristic Stalinist purges, the total had climbed to 1,424,000 in 1939. The first post-Stalinist census in 1959 showed 1,619,000 and the 1970 census 1,846,000, despite the fact that German had been suppressed after Hitler's invasion of the Soviet Union (so that most young Russian Germans know little or no German) and talking about one's ancestors was a dangerous subject.

According to more recent published official figures, there are over 2 million Germans in the former Soviet Union, but a large number (known as *Aussiedler*) have since "resettled" in Germany.

The archives in Dnepropetrovsk (Ukraine) are known to have the complete 1897 census for that area. Some archives have only statistical reports.

NOBILITY AND BURGHER RECORDS

Genealogy is much more closely associated with heraldry in Europe, and especially Eastern Europe, than in the New World, which is one reason why it was suppressed by the Communists. Nobility records (many of which have been published, often in Germany for Russian German aristocrats) may be the best source of information for many Baltic Germans. Similar lists and published works exist for prominent burghers who did not belong to the aristocracy. According to Giesinger, there were about 25,000 German hereditary nobles and 17,000 non-hereditary nobles or officials in the Russian Empire in 1897, i.e., about 2% of the Germanic population.

Most of the Russian records pertaining to the Baltic German nobles are at the Russian State Historical Archive (RGIA) in St. Petersburg.

The *Ratgeber '92* lists researchers who have more research experience involving the nobility than in the tracing of non-aristocrats, with many of them in St. Petersburg or the Baltics. Even the archivists who work most closely with North American genealogical societies have often concentrated on this group in their graduate theses. However, the *Ratgeber '95: Familienforschung Mittel- und Osteuropa* has a longer list of genealogists in Russia and Ukraine who specialize in research Germans in the former Russian Empire, whose expertise is not limited to the Baltic nobility, and includes researchers with access to the KGB records.

OTHER RECORDS

Other records that may be particularly helpful for Volga German research include:

(1) the Ivan Kuhlberg lists of German settlers arriving in Oranienbaum, near St. Petersburg, in the 1760s; these are in Russian and at Saratov, with a second, less

detailed copy in Moscow; the birthplace of the head of household is included in the Saratov lists (David F. Schmidt)

(2) the list of 9,000 colonists transported to the Volga region (a small number were settled elsewhere); these are in German (David F. Schmidt)

(3) the 1767-68 list of settlers in the Saratov area (i.e., the original 1763-67 Volga settlement) compiled by the Saratov Office of Immigrant Affairs; a few villages are missing (David F. Schmidt)

(4) Volga family lists for 1798 (David F. Schmidt); similar lists were prepared for some early Black Sea settlements (Unruh)

Some of these records are described by Pleve in "Specific Genealogical Research Materials of Volga Germans" in the Fall 1993 issue of the *Journal of the American Historical Society of Germans from Russia.*

Dr. Alfred Eisfeld of Göttingen, Germany, plans to publish the original Volga settler lists and the American Historical Society of Germans from Russia has offered to assist him in marketing the book. He also intends to publish an inventory of the Odessa archives (Michael Miller).

Records mentioned in a RAGAS flyer that may be applicable to all Russian Germans include: (1) records of permission to emigrate (some of these are in Saratov, according to Jo Ann Kuhr of AHSGR); (2) military lists; (3) land and property records.

Those who are researching relatives, rather than ancestors, may be interested in knowing that the former KGB (secret police) records are now available for inspection, according to Prof. Borys Klein of the University of Hrodna (Russian: *Grodno*) in Belarus.

NORTH AMERICAN RESOURCES

The American Historical Society of Germans from Russia has extensive files, especially obituaries, as well as a library, relating to the Germans from throughout the former Russian Empire, except for the Baltics.

The Germans from Russia Heritage Society concentrates on Germans from the western Black Sea region, including Bessarabia and the Dobruja (which includes areas now part of Moldova, Romania and Bulgaria). GRHS has a large number of family, church or local histories, which may have useful background information on the German ancestors in the former Russian Empire, in its library.

The American Historical Society of Germans from Russia and the Germans from Russia Heritage Society have embarked upon a mammoth joint project to extract unfilmed records in the archives in the former Russian Empire (excluding the Baltics). Several hundred volunteer village coordinators are working on their respective ancestral areas. Although the project is expected to take many years, Ted J. Becker reports that he already has a great deal of material for Krasna and varying amounts of information are available from other coordinators. Contact AHSGR or GRHS to find out who the coordinators for your ancestral villages are.

The periodical, *Wandering Volhynians*, which publishes a surname index (as do the above), is the best source of information on Volhynia. Jerry Frank of Calgary has published this surname index in book form (*Research Helper for Germans from Poland and Volhynia*).

Various individuals, including Leona Janke of AHSGR, Tom Hoffman of GRHS, Ewald Wuschke of *Wandering Volhynians*, Margaret Freeman of the Glückstal Colony Research Association, and Evelyn Wolfer of Galizien German Descendants, have accumulated large quantities of published and unpublished information. These organizations may have the addresses of others with such private collections.

Records pertaining to North Americans who went back to the Russian Empire for a visit, applied for visas to do so, or had other contacts with Russian consulates were rediscovered following a lengthy disappearance after the Russian Civil War. The authoritative work for those in the United States is *Russian Consular Records Index and Catalog*, by Dr. Sallyann Amdur Sack and Suzan Wynne. Angus Baxter has a succinct treatment for such records for Canada in the 1994 edition of *In Search of Your German Roots*.

Check Chapter XIV, Section G, for information about American records concerning the interwar refugees who came to the Americas via China in 1929-32.

THE BALTIC COUNTRIES (ESTONIA, LATVIA, LITHUANIA)
(das Baltikum: Estland, Lettland, Litauen)

The history of the Germans in Estonia and Latvia is covered by Chapter X on **HISTORY**.

Germans in Lithuania are distinct from those in Estonia and Latvia in that the largest number of them lived in the Memel region, which belonged to East Prussia until after World War I and was thus contiguous to other Germanic territory. Much smaller numbers of Germans later moved to other parts of Lithuania, mostly to the area east of Memel, but with scattered later settlements in other areas. The Lithuanian Germans, for the most part, were not members of the nobility, but peasants, along with some burghers.

Lithuania also differed in that most of it was never conquered by the Teutonic Knights. It was part of the Commonwealth of Poland and Lithuania for several centuries and remained a Catholic country, except for the Germans.

Some German parish registers for the Baltic countries have been copied by the Family History Library (FHL) from the microfilms at the Deutsche Zentralstelle für Genealogie in Leipzig, Germany.

There are numerous German genealogical publications pertaining to the Baltic Germans, many of whom left after World War I, when they were deprived of their privileged status and most of their land.

See the section on **GERMANY** in Chapter XVII for additional pertinent genealogical information.

Since the Baltic countries were part of the Russian Empire for more than two centuries, you should also check the information on the **RECORDS OF THE FORMER RUSSIAN EMPIRE** and under **RUSSIA**.

ESTONIA (Estland)

There are microfilms of a few German parish registers at Leipzig, especially from the area of Dorpat (now Tartu), the site of the major university and seminary for the Germans in the Russian Empire. These have been copied by the FHL.

The other major German cities in Estonia were Tallinn (*Reval*) and Pärnu (*Pernau*).

Estonia became Lutheran in the early sixteenth century.

In addition to the few Estonian records in Leipzig, FHL crews are making rapid progress in filming the parish registers in Estonia. Some of these date back to the 1600s and continue through the 1940s.

The Estonian archives also cooperate with RAGAS. (See under **RUSSIA** for address.) Similarly, commercial firms with ties to the Russian State Historical Archive (RGIA) in St. Petersburg have also been successful in obtaining Estonian records.

The Estonian national archives are at:

> Eesti Ajaloo Arhiiv
> Tartu
> Estonia

LATVIA (Lettland)

A large number of Latvian German parish registers are on microfilm in Leipzig, as well at as the Family History Library.

There was a considerably larger urban element among the Germans in Latvia than in the other Baltic countries. Riga, Jelgava (*Mitau*), Liepäja (*Libau*) and Ventspils (*Windau*) were the major German urban settlements.

Latvia does not work with RAGAS. The Latvian State Historical Archive, which contains many records of births, marriages and deaths for the second half of the nineteenth and early twentieth centuries, is at:

> Latvijas Valsts Vestures Arhives
> 16 Slokaskiela
> Riga
> Latvia

However, most vital statistics records for the 1906-1940 period are stored at the Archive of Vital Records:

> Dzimtsaraktu Arhives
> 24 Kalku St.
> Riga
> Latvia

The latter archive is not open to private researchers, but written requests to the archives sometimes result in the receipt of documents.

Incidentally, many records for Jews, as well as German Christians, were kept in German, despite a Russian law to the contrary.

A useful article for all, although it focuses on Jewish research, is "Jewish Vital Statistic Records in the Latvian Archives," by Dr. Aleksandrs Feigmanis of the Museum and Documents Center of the Jews of Latvia in the Spring 1994 issue of *Avotaynu*. Some of the above information comes from this source.

The Family History Library has begun filming records in Riga.

LITHUANIA (Litauen)

The Lutheran records for the Memel area at the Evangelisches Zentralarchiv in Berlin are on microfilm at the Family History Library.

For the Memel (Klaipeda) area, where most of the Germans lived, try some of the books and addresses for East Prussia under **GERMANY**. For those parts of Lithuania that were part of interwar Poland, where there were a few scattered German settlements, see the information under **POLAND**.

The FHL has had little success in microfilming Lithuanian records to date. Lithuania has its own arrangements for genealogical research and does not participate in RAGAS.

The national archives of Lithuania are at:

> Lietuvos Valstybinis Istorijos Archyvas
> Gerosios Vilties 10
> 2015 Vilnius
> Lithuania

You can write to LVIA in English, but you must provide the town and the religion of the ancestors you are researching, according to:

Jessie L. Daraska, Department Chairperson
Immigration History & Genealogy Department
Balzekas Museum of Lithuanian Culture
6500 Pulaski Road
Chicago, IL 60629-5136

The museum can assist people in finding the right religious (Catholic, Jewish, Lutheran) records and especially in determining the correct town. This institution recently established the Lithuanian American Genealogy Society, which uses the above address.

Do not send money with your initial inquiry to LVIA. You will be informed of the cost, based on the available information. The archives will accept money orders or bank transfers from American Express, Bankers Trust Co., Citibank North America, and Midland plc (London), according to Bruce Kahn (*Avotaynu*, Fall 1994). Kahn reports that it costs $50 per family to initiate a search, $10 for extracts, and $20 for photocopies, including translation.

COMMONWEALTH OF INDEPENDENT STATES (CIS)
(Gemeinschaft unabhängiger Staaten/GUS)

Some of the addresses of former Soviet archives (listed above and below) are taken from "Archive Addresses: Lithuania, Belarus, Ukraine" in the Winter 1992 issue of *Pathways & Passages*, published by the Polish Genealogical Society of the Northeast. The addresses are also given in the Cyrillic alphabet to facilitate mail delivery.

You should note that the customary form of address in the CIS states is the opposite of what we are used to in the West, viz., the country is on the first line, then the city, then the street address or post office box, and lastly the individual. However, more and more articles by CIS archivists are being published in American periodicals, especially *Avotaynu*, which list addresses of archives in the Western order. Soshnikov suggests use of the Western order, since some CIS member states are apparently considering such a change for international mail.

By now, there are numerous channels for obtaining genealogical data from the CIS. Some are mentioned under the individual countries, while others can be discovered by reading relevant periodicals.

However, the Genealogy and Family History Society in Moscow, a non-profit research service which developed out of the binational Russian-American Genealogical Archival Service (RAGAS), is the only channel for doing non-Jewish research in all of the European CIS countries, especially Russia, Ukraine and Belarus. It has established good contacts with most of the archives in these countries, although field trips are sometimes necessary.

Moreover, many of the records for the entire former Russian Empire are in the Russian State Archives of Old Documents (RGADA) in Moscow or the Russian State Historical Archive (RGIA) in St. Petersburg, so that research performed there is important for other countries, too.

For bilingual forms for research requests, write to:

RAGAS
1929 - 18th St. N.W., Suite 1112
Washington, DC 20009

You can reach GFHS by e-mail at ragas02@infonet.ee or vladrag@glasnet.ru or by mail at:

Genealogy and Family History Society
P.O. Box 459
127349 Moscow
Russia

An initial non-refundable fee of $50 for a preliminary search of sources must be enclosed with each completed request. If the search is successful, there is an additional charge of $6 per hour for research, with a minimum deposit for 20 hours if you want a full genealogical profile, as contrasted with a request for a specific document. This deposit is refundable if the work takes less than 20 hours. (Prices are, of course, subject to change.)

A form is included for you to authorize expenditures up to a specified sum in addition to the minimum fee. Estimates, including all costs (record searches, copying and other archival fees, translation and compilation of reports, and travel expenses), will be provided for any research exceeding this amount. The $50 fee will be deducted from the total cost of the work.

The e-mail address of the RAGAS Newsletter is ragas@dgs.dgsys.com. Its mailing address is:

> RAGAS Newsletter
> Box 236
> Glen Echo, MD 20812

RUSSIA (Russland)

More progress has been made in getting records from the archives of Russia than from any of the other countries belonging to the Commonwealth.

The archives in Saratov, and especially Engels, are particularly useful for the records of the provinces of Saratov and of the *Wiesenseite*, which was separated from it in 1852 and included the Samara villages founded later farther north along the Volga River. (The *Wiesenseite* or "meadow side" referred to the flat land on the east side of the Volga, as contrasted with the *Bergseite* or "hilly side" on the west.) These records include incomplete revisions of 1834, 1850 and 1857, as well as parish registers and early settlement lists resembling revisions, and other post-1857 records. Soshnikov has a list of the Saratov records, and Igor R. Pleve has done extensive research in both archives. A revision was somewhat similar to a census.

With respect to the Volga region, very thorough reports (including all of the descendants of the Volga settlers, insofar as they are listed in the various records that have been preserved) have been received from the dean of the history faculty at Saratov State University, who has made several presentations in the United States and who receives substantial research assistance from his wife. Contact:

> Pleve, Dr. Igor R.
> B. Gornaja ul. 272, kv. 2
> 410 005 Saratov
> Russia

Pleve can also be reached by faxing 011-7-095-975-3273, with the notation, "for Pleve at Saratov" or through Internet e-mail at igor@pleve.saratov.su.

He has consulted many sources, not only in the Volga region, and has prepared a complete chart of all descendants of an ancestor who immigrated to the Volga, and who remained there for $450-$750. Sources include the Kuhlberg lists, revision lists and parish registers, when available. Not all parish registers have been preserved or found.

Numerous commercial channels for obtaining data from the Russian archives in Moscow and St. Petersburg also exist. Results vary from excellent to nil. The best service was rendered by Urbana Technologies, according to David F. Schmidt. This firm was sold in 1993, but the cooperative arrangement with MITEK Information Services in Moscow continues, through the following agent:

Julia Petrakis
United States Agent
Facts OnLine
812 Vista Drive
Camano Island, WA 98292

This company has also established contacts with researchers in other countries (Poland, Czech and Slovak Republics) and has access to TASS (government newspaper) files.

John Movius of FEEFHS is impressed by the amount of material put on the Internet by the following organization, which does searches only in the St. Petersburg archives:

Edward Nute
BLITZ
907 Mission Ave.
San Rafael, CA 94901

UKRAINE (Ukraine/Ukraina)

There were German settlements scattered throughout Ukraine, but none represented such a cohesive concentration as those in the Volga River region. Most of the Germans fell into one of two groups: the Black Sea Germans and the Volhynian Germans (in what is now northwestern Ukraine).

In addition, Ukraine includes three areas of German settlement in eastern parts of the former Austro-Hungarian Empire: East Galicia, North Bukovina, and Carpatho-Ukraine (which belonged to Czechoslovakia during the interwar period between World War I and World War II).

Most of the Bessarabian parish registers were microfilmed by the Family History Library in 1948, as a result of German access to this area when it still belonged to Romania.

For those parts of Ukraine that belonged to interwar Poland (i.e., western Volhynia and eastern Galicia), see the information under **POLAND**. For areas that belonged to **AUSTRIA**, **HUNGARY** or **ROMANIA** (i.e., the Bukovina, Bessarabia, Galicia and Carpatho-Ukraine (also known as Subcarpathian Rus'), check those countries, as well as **GERMANY** and **RUSSIA** for possible additional information. Records for Carpatho-Ukraine may also be in the **SLOVAK REPUBLIC** or possibly even in the **CZECH REPUBLIC**.

Soshnikov reported that the archives in Kharkiv and Poltava were largely destroyed in World War II, but there were only isolated German settlements in these areas. The archives in Odessa and Dnepropetrovsk are said to have lost between one third and one half of their German records as a result of removal of records during the German occupation or wartime damage or displacement. (Many records were evacuated to the Soviet East. It is possible that some of these records could have been lost or that they are still in some unknown locality.)

Nevertheless, North American scholars and tour groups report important successes in searching records in Odessa or asking archivists to help them. The Dnepropetrovsk archive is very cooperative and has an index of its German records, although some of the most important genealogical records are missing. The Stumpp squadron sent genealogical information about the Germans in Zaporozhye to Germany during World War II. It fell into the hands of the Western Allies, so some microfilms can be found in the U.S. National Archives. But most of its records are for the post-1917 period, so they would have direct genealogical relevance only for legal and illegal emigrants during the Communist era.

Many of the records formerly in L'viv (*Lemberg*) are now in Poland, but genealogically useful data have been obtained from L'viv.

The archives in Zhytomyr has an index for the early (1795-1858) revision lists of Germans in the Zhytomyr (Volhynia) *guberniya*, but substantial German migration to that area did not begin until the 1860s. However, a booklet with vital data for a later period has been found (although only for a small area around Zhytomyr) and its contents were published in *Wandering Volhynians* (September 1992).

The Crimean archives in Simferopol are believed to have records useful for Germanic genealogy, but we have not heard of any confirmation.

There are at least some revision lists in most of the larger Ukrainian archives, but there are no genealogically-oriented finding aids, except for Dnepropetrovsk and Zhytomyr.

Some of the revision lists for Germans in the Black Sea area have been published or microfilmed. Published lists, mostly for 1816 but including some earlier and later ones, can be found in Karl Stumpp, *The Emigration from Germany to Russia in the Years 1763 to 1862*, but there are no comprehensive lists which include all settlements.

The Kiev (German: *Kiew*; Ukrainian: *Kyyiv*) Central Historical Archive has Jewish rabbinical lists, including those for Volhynia.

The Russian archivists working with RAGAS have generally good relations with most of these archives, but Moscow-based field travel is sometimes necessary. The Odessa and Dnepropetrovsk archives are said to be very cooperative.

The two central state historical archives are:

Tsentralnyi derzhavnyi arkhiv Ukrainy
pl. Vozziednannia 3A
290 006 L'viv - 4
Ukraine

Tsentralnyi derzhavnyi arkhiv Ukrainy
u m. Kyievni
vul. Solomianska 24
252 601 Kyyiv - 1000
Ukraine

Incidentally, there are both central and *oblast* archives with genealogically significant records in both cities.

"Report on a Recent Trip to Ukrainian Archives" by Dr. George Bolotenko of the National Archives of Canada in the Spring 1994 issue of *Avotaynu* provides an extremely detailed description of the genealogically valuable contents of several archives in Western Ukraine, as well as the extremely difficult conditions under which these archivists are working. Topics covered by the article include the very complete 1785-88 Josephinian and the somewhat less accurate 1819-20 Franciscan revision lists (or land cadasters) for Galicia, as well as court records from 1372 to the end of the nineteenth century, found in the L'viv Central State Historical Archives. The Josephinian records are in German and Polish; the other records are mostly in Latin.

There are also metrical records (vital statistics books, including parish and synagogue registers), as well as various kinds of civil records, in L'viv.

The 37 *oblast* archives under the supervision of the Main Archival Directorate of Ukraine (MADU) also have valuable records.

Bolotenko reported that the procedure for written requests for information from these archives did not work very well in 1993, despite the willingness of local archivists to do research, because foreign requests had to be cleared by two national ministries, which rarely got around to dealing with these requests because of other priorities. However, *Avotaynu* editor, Dr. Sallyann Amdur Sack, says that top officials of the Archival Ministry of Ukraine stated, during a January 1994 visit to the National Archives of Canada, that the archives are now freely open to all foreigners on the same basis as they are to Ukrainians. This shows how rapidly policies can change. Other sources confirm this, but indicate that policy changes in CIS member countries are not necessarily irreversible.

In addition to the Bolotenko article, Brian J. Lenius has reported on the transfer of some East Galician Jewish and German Catholic records, respectively, from Ukraine to archives in Poland, viz., to Warsaw, Przemysl, and Lubaczów, in several articles in the *East European Genealogist*. The East European Genealogical Society in Manitoba also has the addresses of several North American researchers who accept genealogical assignments in Western Ukraine.

According to Paul Polansky of the Bukovina Society of the Americas (per letter from Roland Wagner), the last mayor of Rastadt (in the Odessa area) took the village archives with him when he left Ukraine, but he was detained in Poland, the material was confiscated and it somehow ended up in the archive in Poznan (*Posen*).

See Krushel, "Genealogical Research in Volhynia" (*Wandering Volhynians*, September 1994), for the most comprehensive treatment of that area. He is a representative of the MIR Corporation (USA and Ukraine) and often leads genealogical tours to Volhynia. He has done quite a bit of research in both Ukrainian and Polish archives concerning Volhynian Germans. Contact:

> Howard Krushel
> 136 Silver Springs Dr. N.W.
> Calgary, AB T3B 3G4
> Canada

The FHL has been less successful in gaining access to archival records in Ukraine than in Russia, but at least four film crews are now at work in that country. However, the records being filmed in L'viv and Kiev are not pertinent for Germanic research.

The archive in Uzhhorod has many records for Carpatho-Ukraine (historically part of Slovakia). However, it does not have any parish registers. There were Germanic enclaves around Mukachevo (*Munkatsch*) and in the *Theresienthal* (Theresa valley) around Deutsch-Mokra. This area is known variously as Carpatho-Ukraine, Sub-Carpathian Ukraine and Subcarpathian Rus'.

BELARUS (Weissrussland/Bjelorussland)

Except for the many Jews (who may or may not have had a close Germanic connection), there were comparatively few German settlers in Belarus, although there were German traders and business establishments there.

However, there were small settlements east of Bialystok, extending into Belorussian territory, and a few elsewhere along the Polish and Ukrainian borders. A Polish article received from Henryk Skrzypinski indicates that some of the Lutheran congregations near Brest had originally been Mennonite. These settlements date back, at least partly, to the seventeenth century when this area belonged to pre-Partition Poland-Lithuania.

The Narew area Germans, including all of those in interwar eastern Poland, were repatriated to Germany pursuant to the Hitler-Stalin Pact. The genealogical question-naires they filled out are in the German Federal Archives in Bonn.

Almost complete records for the Bialystok area in Northeastern Poland, which was briefly under Prussian rule in 1795-1806 and where there were a few German settlements, can be found in the following archive:

> Tsentralny dziarzhauny histarychny arkhiu Belarusi u h. Hrodne
> vul. Kozlova 26
> 230 023 Hrodna
> Belarus

The other major Belorussian archive is:

> Tsentralny dziarzhauny histarychny arkhiu Belarusi u h. Minsku
> pl. Lenina 2
> 220 038 Minsk
> Belarus

Some Belorussian records can be found in local archives.

Soshnikov, "Belorussian Archives Revisited" (*Avotaynu*, Fall 1994), provides a thorough report on records found there.

According to the embassy of Belarus in Washington, the following organizations in Belarus are engaged in genealogical research and would be interested in establishing contacts and cooperation with overseas societies:

Belarussian Genealogical Society
10, Kollectornaya St., Suite 208
220048 Minsk
Belarus

The Francysk Scarnyna Centre
15, Revalyucynaya St.
220050 Minsk
Belarus

If you are not successful in obtaining records from Belarus from RAGAS, the archives or the genealogical societies, try a history professor of Jewish origin who lived in the United States for a year or two and who is familiar with archival records and research:

Prof. Borys Klein
1 May St. 2/1, Apt. 8
Hrodna, 230023
Belarus

MOLDOVA (Moldau)

The northern part of the Bessarabian colonies and most of the Glückstal villages in the Odessa region are now in Moldova. Obtaining records from there has been difficult to date. The problem is complicated by the fact that the area east of the Dniester River (not part of Bessarabia) is not under the control of the Moldovan government.

However, Weiner has succeeded in getting Jewish records by going to the Moldovan archives in person.

THE CAUCASUS (Der Kaukasus)
(GEORGIA, AZERBAIJAN, ARMENIA, SOUTH RUSSIA)

Germans settled in the South Caucasus (southern Georgia and northern Azerbaijan, extending slightly into Armenia) in the early nineteenth century. Later, the Black Sea (and, to a lesser extent, the Volga) Germans established daughter colonies in the northern Caucasus. Most of this area is actually the southernmost part of European Russia, along the Georgian border, but it is partly in the autonomous regions of Ossetia, Chechnya, Ingushetia, Dagestan, Kabardino-Bulkaria, Adygea and Abkhazia (Abkhazia and the southern part of Ossetia being in northwestern Georgia), inhabited by distinct ethnic groups that have a degree of autonomy.

Although relatively few Germans appear to have emigrated from the Caucasus before World War I, they constituted an important share of the political refugees of the 1920s, partly because they were close to the Turkish and Iranian borders. At least one group escaped to Iran via the Caspian Sea, according to Arthur Flegel. But others were among those who moved to Eastern Siberia and then fled to Manchuria, finally ending up in North and South America.

Records from Azerbaijani archives have been obtained through RAGAS.

SIBERIA AND THE ASIAN MUSLIM REPUBLICS
(KAZAKHSTAN, TURKMENISTAN, KYRGYZSTAN, TAJIKISTAN)

Only a small number of Germans emigrated directly from Siberia or neighboring Muslim states, except for the *Aussiedler* (returnees) who have settled in Germany since the glasnost period. But one particular group is noteworthy. Germans from the European part of the Soviet Union moved to the Blagoveshchensk area in Eastern Siberia, beginning in 1926, to try to escape from collectivization. Because tax burdens soon became intolerable, many refugees crossed the frozen Amur River on winter nights, with at least a thousand reaching Harbin, Manchuria, by 1931. A majority were Mennonites. Most of the others were Lutherans (many from Volhynia), but there were also some Catholics. Church organizations representing 21 denominations from four continents helped them come to the Americas, with a large majority settling in Western Canada, Paraguay or the Brazilian state of Parana. But a few came to the United States (state of Washington) and other countries.

Look under **CHINA** in Chapter XIV, Section G, for more information about researching these refugees.

Although only a small number of Russian German emigrants came from Asia, any surviving relatives of immigrants are likely to be found there. Many of these people have become *Aussiedler* (resettlers who returned to Germany). The American Historical Society of Germans from Russia has an active program interviewing these "returnees." It has helped unite both *Aussiedler* and Germans remaining in CIS member states with relatives in North America.

Michael M. Miller, Bibliographer of the Germans from Russia Heritage Collection at the North Dakota Institute for Regional Studies (North Dakota State University) in Fargo, has also been very active in seeking to re-establish ties between the descendants of Germans from Russia in North America and the Germans remaining in the ex-Soviet Union, primarily in the Muslim republics and Siberia.

He is also the compiler of *Researching Germans from Russia*, an annotated bibliography of the Germans from Russia Heritage Collection (the largest of its kind in North America, although oriented more toward history than genealogy), as well as the holdings of the Germans from Russia Heritage Society library in Bismarck, which contains many family and village histories.

BULGARIA
(Bulgarien)

Only a very small number of ethnic Germans ever lived in what is now Bulgaria. Significant group migration of Russian Germans to the Dobruja began in 1842, with a second wave starting in 1873 or 1874. Paul Traeger, in *Die Deutschen der Dobrudscha* [*The Germans in the Dobruja*], mentions five older settlements in the interior of Bulgaria, but there is hardly any literature on these settlements.

The southern part of the Dobruja (*Dobrudza* in Bulgarian) region, known as Cadrilater, has fluctuated between Romanian and Bulgarian control since the Ottoman Turkish Empire lost it in 1878, but most of the time it has been under Bulgarian control. About 15,000 Dobruja Germans were resettled in German-ruled territory in 1940, but few lived in Bulgaria.

The *AGoFF Guide* and Thode's *Address Book* list the following village directory of those relocating as a source of information:

Heimatortskartei Südosteuropa-Umsiedler
Abteilung Deutsche aus Russland, Bessarabien, Bulgarien und Dobrudscha
Rosenbergstrasse 50
D-70176 Stuttgart
Germany

Check under **TURKEY** later in this chapter for potential governmental records.

CZECHOSLOVAKIA: SUCCESSOR STATES
(die Tschechoslowakei)

Czechoslovakia was formed as an independent state in 1918 from the Czech crownlands (Bohemia, Moravia and Austro-Silesia), Slovakia, and Subcarpathian Rus' (also known today as Carpatho-Ukraine). As a result of World War II, the Soviet Union assumed control over the last-mentioned area, formerly the eastern tip of the country. In 1993 Czechoslovakia split peacefully into the Czech and Slovak Republics.

The following publications and information apply to both the Czech and Slovak republics.

"Ethnic German Research in Czechoslovakia" by Michael Palmer (*German Genealogical Society of America Bulletin*, November 1989) represents the most thorough English-language genealogical article on this subject.

See Chapter XIII for a number of articles relating to Jewish research.

According to the *AGoFF-Wegweiser*, the Military Historical Institute in Prague (see Ernest Thode's *Address Book*), has all the military records of soldiers from the Czech Republic who served in the Austro-Hungarian army, including those who still had military obligations when Czechoslovakia was established. Those from the Slovak Republic were there also, but may have been moved to Bratislava. These records include the place of origin. However, you need to be able to identify the regiment.

There are also less detailed military registers at the Military Archives (*Kriegsarchiv*) in Vienna (listed earlier under **AUSTRIA**).

A Handbook of Czechoslovak Genealogical Research by Daniel M. Schlyter may also be helpful, although it may be hard to find since it is currently out of print.

Duncan B. Gardiner and Jiri Osanec are now working on a new guide, *Czech and Slovak Genealogy: A Practical Manual of Methods and Sources*, which is expected to be published in 1998. Gardiner, the leading American expert on the genealogy of Germans from these countries who provided most of the information in this section, and Osanec, one of the best genealogists in the Czech Republic are sure to write a book which will be more comprehensive and up-to-date than any English-language book now in print or out of print.

Gardiner, who knows German, Czech, Slovak, Russian and some Polish, makes frequent research trips to the various archives in the Czech and Slovak Republic (including archives in neighboring countries when appropriate). To obtain research services, contact:

> Dr. Duncan B. Gardiner, C.G.
> 12961 Lake Ave.
> Lakewood, OH 44107-1533

His gazetteer, *German Towns in Slovakia & Upper Hungary*, is the only major English-language book on this subject.

You no longer have to get advance permission to use the Czech or Slovak archives in person. But the records may be in Latin, as well as in German or Czech (in the Czech Republic) or in Hungarian or Slovak (in the Slovak Republic), so some knowledge of these languages is important if you want to do any substantial amount of research. Some archives are closed on Mondays and Fridays.

Since the Czech Republic was part of **AUSTRIA** and the Slovak Republic part of **HUNGARY** until World War I, check the information for those countries as well. In addition, look under **GERMANY**, since most of the Germans went there after World War II. Thus there are pertinent genealogical societies, archives, periodicals, etc., in Germany and, to a lesser extent, also in Austria. Some German socialists from the Czech area emigrated to **SWEDEN** and to other countries such as Canada after Hitler's annexation of the Sudetenland in 1938. They were joined by other immigrants after World War II. Therefore, there could possibly be some information on relatives, or conceivably even ancestors in rare cases, of Sudeten Germans who migrated to various non-European countries in Swedish records.

THE CZECH REPUBLIC
(die Tschechische Republik)

Germans comprised 37% of the population of Bohemia (the western Czech area), 28% of the population of Moravia (in the southeast) and 45% of the population of Austrian Silesia (in the northeast) around 1900. There were more Poles than Czechs in Austrian Silesia at that time; the eastern part of this territory now belongs to Poland.

The Jewish population (included among the German-speakers) was 1.5% in Bohemia and 1.8% in the other two territories. Almost all of the German Christians in Bohemia and Moravia were Catholics in 1900, with only 2-3% of the total population being Protestant. Some 13-14% of the people in Austrian Silesia were Protestant, but the percentage among Germans was much lower.

However, Prague was the birthplace of the pre-Luther Hussite movement that crossed ethnic lines, although John Huss seems to have had the strongest appeal to Czechs. The flight of Protestants began with the Austrian victory at White Mountain in 1620 and the subsequent coerced re-Catholicization of the area. The refugees included the Moravian Brethren, who are also known as the Czech Brethren, *Unitas Fratrum* in Latin, or *Herrnhuter*, after the place of refuge they found in southeastern Saxony in 1722, which led to their Germanicization, although some of the earliest records in Germany are in Czech. Others, especially Bohemian weavers, fled to the German-Polish linguistic border area and later migrated to Russian Poland.

PARISH RECORDS

The Deutsche Zentralstelle für Genealogie in Leipzig microfilmed about 70 parish registers, which can be obtained from the Family History Library. The Czech authorities plan to microfilm the remaining registers, but they will not be available from Salt Lake City. It is likely that visitors will be allowed to view only the films in order to avoid further wear and tear on the original registers.

All pre-1896 parish registers for all Christian denominations are in the regional archives, whose location is listed below. Later registers are in the local civil registry offices. According to the *AGoFF guide*, you can send written requests for birth, marriage and death certificates to these offices. In the past you could not visit them in person, but this may no longer be true.

Birth records since about 1830 have the following information: child's name; parents' names, occupations and addresses; all four grandparents' names, occupations and addresses; names of the godparents; name of the midwife; and name of the baptizing clergyman. The records for earlier years are less detailed. Angus Baxter states that a few registers go back to the 1500s. Marriage records include the names of the spouses and sometimes those of the parents. Death records indicate the name of the person, the date and place of death, and sometimes the cause of death.

From 1620 until 1781 all vital events were to be recorded in the Catholic registers, since Catholicism was the only legally permissible religion. Baxter states that thereafter Protestants could keep their own registers but were supposed to give copies to the Catholic priests for inclusion in the Catholic registers as well.

All or most parish registers for the Pilsen district are available, according to Robert Paulson. The 1780-1820 duplicate parish registers for those western Bohemian parishes which belonged to the Catholic diocese of Regensburg at the time are at the Catholic central archives there. See **GERMANY**. According to Angus Baxter, *In Search of Your European Roots*, the keeping of duplicate registers was instituted in 1799. These are very helpful in cases where the original registers have been lost, but they are less reliable because mistakes were made in transcribing the records

JEWISH RECORDS

Jewish communal records are at the following archive:

> Statní ústredni archiv
> Karmelitská 2
> 118 01 Praha 1 (Malá Strana)
> Czech Republic

CIVIL RECORDS

Mandatory civil registration was not introduced until shortly before World War II. But Baxter states that such registration was required for people who were not members of any church, beginning in 1918, and that a 1920 law authorized registration with the Central Statistics Office. These records are also in the regional archives.

LAND RECORDS

According to Duncan Gardiner, three different kinds of land records exist.

Among these are the land cadasters (German: *Kadaster*; Czech: *katastr*), which are the most well known and usually the most helpful for Germanic research. They include:

(1) Cadasters prepared by order of Empress Maria Theresia in 1748, with various revisions in 1749-56. They list each piece of property by community, and the owners (lessors, lessees), with additional information on each field and the amount of taxes due.

(2) Cadasters prepared while Franz Josef II was emperor, beginning in 1786. The Franciscan cadasters are similar to the Theresian cadasters, but they also define the obligations of serf and lord to each other.

(3) The "Stable Cadaster" of 1817, which is accompanied by "preliminary sketches" (*Indikaczi skice*). These are essentially plat maps which show the family name for each plot.

Dr. Milan Coupek of Brno wrote an article on "Old Cadastral Maps" for Bohemia, Moravia and Silesia, published in *Nase Rodina* (Winter 1992). He states that the oldest one of these land surveys dates back to 1653-56. Karen Hobbs has also published a small book on *The Tax Rolls of 1654 for Bischofteinitz and Taus*. These may refer to the same kinds of records and are believed to be available for other parts of Bohemia as well.

The second kind of record, somewhat similar in nature, is the urbarium (*urbár*), which also lists each piece of land, by community, and the name of the person farming it, with details as to type of plot, its value, feudal dues, etc.

But while the land cadasters were prepared by officials of the imperial government, the urbariums were compiled by the feudal landlords, at least in Bohemia, apparently as a result of imperial orders. The last urbariums for Bohemia were prepared in 1772-73.

The third kind of record, the land book (*pazemková kniha* or *gruntová*), was quite different in nature, but also undertaken by the feudal landlord. It records the parcel number and every transaction (sale, purchase, pay schedule, etc.) pertaining to each piece of property. Many of these books go back to the 1600s and end in 1848, when serfdom was officially fully abolished, the great estates broken up, and the land redistributed to the peasants. These are available in the regional archives, according to Gardiner, although the *AGoFF Guide* mentions the district archives.

ARCHIVES AND ARCHIVAL GUIDES

Palmer lists many German publications containing a description or inventory of registers for specific areas.

A comprehensive guide, which briefly describes the contents of each of the Czech and Slovak regional, district, city and special archives, is *Prehled archivu CSR* by Vladimír

Bystricky and Václav Hruby (Prague: Tisková. 1985), which is available from the Czech Central State Archives:

Archivní správá MV
Trída Milady Horákové 133
16 621 Praha 6
Czech Republic

The Czech archives will do research for you, but it is uncertain whether this service will continue. English-language mail can be handled. Fees for research by the Czech archives are no longer inexpensive, but neither are they excessive.

The other avenue of access is to hire a North American, Czech, Austrian or German researcher.

The regional archives (*Statní oblastní archiv*) are in Trebon for southern Bohemia, Plzen (*Pilsen*) for western Bohemia, Litomerice (*Leitmeritz*) for northern Bohemia, Zámrsk for eastern Bohemia, Prague (*Praha/Prag*) for central Bohemia, Opava (*Troppau*) and its branch for northern Moravia (including former Austro-Silesia), and Brno (*Brünn*) for southern Moravia. Actually most of the north Moravian records are at the branch archive in at Olomouc (*Olmütz*). Current addresses are available from several sources, including Duncan Gardiner's *German Towns in Slovakia (Upper Hungary)*, which also includes the addresses for the Czech Republic.

Felix Gundacker of the IHFF (address under Austria) has a very detailed list of Jewish records for the Opava area.

If you wish to write directly to a regional archive but are not sure which archive has records for your ancestral village, write to the Central State Archives in Prague. The Czech embassy no longer serves as a channel for research requests, but it will send you information about archival services. Write to the:

Embassy of the Czech Republic
3900 Spring of Freedom St., NW
Washington, DC 20008

Under Czech law, records which are at least fifty years old can be obtained from the civil registry offices. This would include the entire period prior to the expulsion of Germans from Czechoslovakia.

CONTACTS IN IMMIGRANT COUNTRIES

You may be able to obtain information about Germans, especially from western Bohemia, by contacting the following multi-purpose society:

German-Bohemian Heritage Society
P.O. Box 822
New Ulm, MN 56073

Border People: The Böhmisch (German-Bohemians) in America by Ken Meter and Robert J. Paulson contains many surnames of those who immigrated to Minnesota, Wisconsin and Michigan's Upper Peninsula.

Robert J. Paulson and Larry Jensen have published a smaller book, *The Parish Books of Kreis [County] Bischofteinitz in the Pilsen Archives, With Selected German-Bohemian Genealogical Research Information, Sources and Bibliography*. Karen Hobbs has also published the book on the 1654 tax rolls which has already been mentioned.

Societies or individuals in other countries with an interest in Sudeten German genealogy include:

Joachim Nuthack
11418 70th St.
Edmonton, AB T5B 1T4
Canada

Sudetendeutsche Landsmannschaft
   Argentinien
Warnes 95
1602 Florida-Buenos Aires
Argentina

Judith Williams
Puhoi, P.O.
New Zealand

THE SLOVAK REPUBLIC
(die Slowakische Republik)

The Slovak Republic was historically part of Hungary and was also known as Upper Hungary.

Since Austria and Hungary were separate administrative units centuries before the Dual Monarchy was established, the kinds of records which are available differ significantly from those in the Czech Republic.

PARISH AND METRICAL RECORDS

Parish registers in Slovak archives have been, or are being, microfilmed by the FHL, pursuant to an agreement with the Slovak government. Of particular interest to Americans with German-speaking ancestors is the filming that has been done, or is underway, at Levoca (*Leutschau*), Kosice (*Kaschau*) and Banská Bystrica (*Neusohl*), the latter in the *Hauerland* region.

Most of the Germans in the *Zips* area, with its historical connection to Transylvania, became Lutherans. Germans in the other Slovak settlements remained overwhelmingly Catholic.

The book by Jana Sarmányá, *Cirkevne matriky na Slovensku zo 16. - 19. storocia* [*Church Registers in Slovakia from the 16th to the 19th Centuries*], published in Bratislava in 1991, lists all the parish registers held in the Slovak regional archives.

Special Jewish registers were kept beginning in the 1830s, though actual records are very sparse before the 1860s.

The registers of all Christian denominations, as well as the records for the Jewish community, are in the regional archives listed below.

LAND RECORDS

The land records (*urbariums*), which also have considerable genealogical value, are not being microfilmed.

Duncan Gardiner reports that the earliest urbariums he has seen for Slovakia date back to about 1790. Apparently these records were compiled by each of the large estate owners, but on pre-printed forms supplied by the central imperial administration. They are now being cataloged by the Family History Library under **HUNGARY**.

The Slovakian regional archives also have the land redistribution records (*komasacné spisy*) for 1848 and 1849, along with maps of each community. However, these have not been cataloged in all the archives.

CENSUS RECORDS

The 1828 Hungarian land census, which has been microfilmed by the Family History Library, includes Slovakia. Its contents are similar to those of early American censuses, although their purpose, like that of many other kinds of records, was to serve as tax lists. They show the names of heads of households and the number of male and female members of the household in each age group. They are useful in identifying the localities where particular surnames appeared.

Some of these are now being transcribed, on a county-by-county basis, by Martha Remer Connor, but we are not aware of any volume on Slovak counties having been published to date.

ARCHIVES AND DIPLOMATIC ESTABLISHMENTS

The address of the Slovak Central State Archives is:

Archívná správa
Krizkova ulice 7
811 04 Bratislava
Slovak Republic

Both the central archives and the various regional ones (*Statní oblastní archiv*) at Banská Bystrica (*Neusohl*), Bytca, Kosice (*Kaschau*), Levoca (*Leutschau*), Nítra (*Neutra*), Presov (*Preschau*) and Bratislava (*Pressburg*) are equipped to respond to English-language requests for research.

The Slovak embassy no longer has any direct involvement as a research channel, but it may be able to provide information regarding archival research services. Its address is:

Embassy of the Slovak Republic
2201 Wisconsin Ave. NW, Suite 250
Washington, DC 20007

HUNGARY
(Ungarn)

In discussing Hungarian German genealogical records, we need to keep two important facts in mind.

The first one, which also applies to other countries in Southeast Europe, is that records concerning Germans in modern-day Hungary can be found in three European countries: Hungary, Austria and Germany. What became the Austro-Hungarian Empire in 1867 was the Austrian Empire before that. Consequently, some of the relevant public records are in the Austrian state archives, whose addresses are listed in Chapter XVII.

The Austrian national archives, especially the Haus-, Hof- und Staatsarchiv (the chief archives for governmental records), and the Kriegsarchiv (which has extensive military records for the whole empire, beginning in 1740), are most likely to have relevant information. The Burgenländisches Landesarchiv may also have some records, because this area belonged to Hungary until after World War I.

It is probable that some of the Catholic, Protestant and Jewish religious archives in Austria (*AGoFF Guide* and Thode's *Address Book*) also have records pertaining to Hungary. Prior to 1781, Catholic priests kept records for everyone, including Protestants and Jews. The voluntary or involuntary departure of most Germans from all Eastern European countries, including Hungary, in 1945 and the difficulty of obtaining records from there during the period of Communist rule, led to the assembling and reconstructing of a great deal of genealogical data by the refugees in Germany and Austria. The *AGoFF Guide* has a lengthy section on Southeast Europe, including the addresses of many organizations and institutions with a greater or lesser interest in genealogy. It also lists such resources as gazetteers and bibliographies. The major portion of this information is potentially relevant to Hungary.

The second important fact to keep in mind is that Hungarian records may also relate to Germans in the Slovak Republic, Croatia, the Serbian Vojvodina, Carpatho-Ukraine and Northwestern Romania. This is because Hungary historically included all or most of the territory surrounded by Austria, the Ottoman Turkish Empire, Poland-Lithuania and

Russia. This area has shrunk and expanded substantially over the last millennium, particularly with respect to the waxing and waning of Turkish fortunes in the Balkans.

The Transylvanian (*Siebenbürgen*) Saxons were invited by the king of Hungary to settle on his eastern frontier in the twelfth century for defensive reasons. They survived a long period of Turkish rule before becoming part of Hungary again in the late seventeenth century. The Germans in Slovakia were invited at the same time to defend the northern frontier. But this area was never under Turkish rule.

Nearly all of the other German colonies in the Balkans, except those near the Black Sea or close to Austria proper, were part of the large group usually referred to as the Danube Swabians, for they embarked in Swabia and sailed down the Danube River to Lower Hungary, although a much smaller settlement existed around Sathmar (now Satu Mare, Romania) which extended slightly into present-day Hungary. They were known as Hungarian-Germans until 1922, because the area in which they settled was on the Southern Hungarian frontier, where the Turkish forces had been pushed back. But Hungary lost most of this territory after World War I.

Thus these settlements were part of Hungary even before Hungary achieved co-equal imperial status with Austria in 1867, so that a few pertinent records for all of these groups may be found in the archives in Budapest (and possibly local Hungarian archives) for the period prior to 1919, when the map of Europe was drastically redrawn.

The address of the Hungarian national archives, which has a substantial amount of relevant information, is:

> Magyar Országos Levéltár
> Bécsikapu tér 4, Postafiók 3
> H-1250 Budapest 1
> Hungary

The archives provided the following information in December 1990 concerning German-American genealogical research:

(1) Archival contents include: church and synagogue registers (births, baptisms, marriages, deaths) that were created in the present territory of Hungary prior to October 1, 1895, when civil registration started; conscription records pertaining to nobles, serfs, etc.; socage contracts (*urbariums*); judicial archives; and military conscription records (for 1820-1910, according to Eva Liptak). About 95% of the parish registers are in good condition. There are some insufficiencies in the Jewish registers.

(2) The original church registers are kept by the parish. Copies of the registers (1828-95) are kept by the county archives. Civil registers have been kept by local administrative authorities since October 1, 1895. Requests for information may be sent to any of the three.

(3) Some of the above records date back to as early as the thirteenth century.

(4) The administrative language of Hungary historically was Latin, except for a short period toward the end of the eighteenth century, when German was used. However, local records in areas of German settlement were in German. This was also true for Jewish records, which began about 1830, according to Eva Liptak. She indicated that early Protestant records were in Latin.

(5) Dr. Ivan Bertenyi is the secretary of the Heraldic and Genealogical Society in Budapest, V. Pesti Barnabas u. 1., which is interested in all ethnic groups in Hungary, including Germans. He is primarily a heraldic specialist and speaks German, but not English.

(6) The national and regional or local archives do not undertake genealogical research assignments, but will provide information. However, their letter implies that some archivists may be willing to do private research, so a query may be worthwhile.

(7) For a response to a preliminary inquiry to the national archives of Hungary, enclose $20 (US) or the equivalent in any convertible currency by international money order or cash transfer to the archives' bank account.

(8) The national archives will respond to letters written in English and to queries specifying a locality if only limited research is required.

(9) Foreign genealogists have access to the archives in Hungary on the same basis as Hungarian researchers.

The *AGoFF Guide* states that an inventory catalog of the microfilm copies of pre-1895 ecclesiastical records was compiled by Margit Judak in 1977 as Volume 72 of the inventory of all the archives records. *Contents and Addresses of Hungarian Archives, with Supplementary Material for Research on German Ancestors from Hungary*, 2nd ed., by Edward Reimer Brandt, includes key information from an out-of-print English-language guide by the Hungarian Archives.

Thode reports that the synagogue registers in the Hungarian national archives also include those for the part of the Burgenland region that went to Austria in the boundary changes of 1919.

Martha Remer Connor is transcribing the microfilmed 1828 land records, with 5 volumes plus an index published to date. Eva Liptak reported that the Family History Library has filmed some tax records. Both kinds of records include counties that are no longer, or only partly, in Hungary.

The Family History Library has microfilmed all Hungarian parish registers up to 1895. Duncan Gardiner reports that the Family History Library is now microfilming other genealogically valuable records, including deed books (*Urbariums*).

ITALY
(Italien)

By far the largest concentration of Germans in present-day Italy is in the area around Bolzano (Bozen) and Merano (Meran), known to Germans as Südtirol (South Tyrol) and now called the Alto Adige region in Italy. (Adige is the Italian name for what Germans call the Etsch River, which flows through this Alpine region just south of the Brenner Pass.) The area around these two cities had a predominantly German-speaking population until recently. There were other pockets of German settlement farther south in the Trent (Trento/Trient) area. These areas were part of the same jurisdiction under both Austrian and Italian rule. This region was once part of Lombardy.

The following office, which includes the Staatsarchiv Bozen and the Südtiroler Landesarchiv, indicates that it has some relevant documents and welcomes visiting genealogists, but is not in a position to fulfill research requests:

> Abteilung III: Öffentlicher Unterricht und Kultur für die deutsche
>   und ladinische Volksgruppe
> Amt für Archivwesen, historische Bibliotheken und Volkskunde
> Autonome Provinz Bozen Südtirol
> Ansitz Rothenpuech
> Armando-Diaz-Strasse 8
> I-39100 Bozen
> Italy

Gundacker reports that seignorial records for South Tyrol are in the above-named Bozen (Bolzano) archives, as well as those in Trent (Trient). Some records pertaining to South Tyrol could also be in the Tyrolean state archives in Innsbruck, which was the capital for all of Tyrol.

The Trent State Archives (Archivio di Stato di Trento) has civil, land, and property tax records for various localities in the Trent area (south of Bolzano) where there were islands of German settlement. Parish registers may be found at the local parishes.

There were German-speaking residents in the Gorizia (*Görz*)-Gradisca area along the Slovenian border and near the Adriatic Sea. This area belonged to Austria until the end of World War I, although it was once part of Venice, and is now part of the Italian state of Friuli (*Friaul*)-Venezia Giulia. Much of northeastern and north central Italy belonged to the Hapsburgs until the eighteenth or nineteenth century, so there may have been a few people of Austrian origin elsewhere.

The Catholic church records of Venetia and Lombardy (which belonged to Austria until 1859 and 1866, respectively) have been partially microfilmed by the FHL. The remainder are divided between the individual parishes and the archives in Venice and Milan, according to Gundacker.

There were also small islands of German settlement in the Aosta River region in Piedmont bordering on Switzerland and France.

Anyone who succeeds in tracing ancestors back to the period of severe religious persecutions may find that the French Huguenots who fled to Germany included, or were closely related to, Waldensians from the Piedmont region in northwestern Italy. The FHL has microfilmed some rather old Waldensian parish registers from the Aosta region.

Also check under **AUSTRIA** for pertinent information.

POLAND
(Polen)

From the perspective of genealogical research, Poland's history is even more complex than that of Germany. For this reason and for the sake of cohesiveness (since Poland was divided among Prussia/Germany, Russia and Austria during the nineteenth century), we are including some historical material here, despite our efforts to incorporate historical information into Chapter X wherever feasible.

At the end of the Middle Ages, the union of Poland and Lithuania created the largest country in Europe, including most of what is now Belarus, Ukraine and Moldova. Poland offered a greater degree of religious freedom than any other European country, except for the Ottoman empire. Already in the Middle Ages, large numbers of Jews had fled to Poland, primarily from Germany, as Poland became the home to the world's largest Jewish community. In the sixteenth century, Mennonites, Socinians (Unitarians), Calvinists and various other religious dissidents found a refuge there. Many of these settled in the Danzig (Gdansk) area, whose residents were primarily Germans who had shaken off the rule of the autocratic Teutonic Knights.

However, a Poland weakened by internal dissension began to lose territory and power in 1648. Russia, Prussia and Austria took advantage of its weakness and divided the country among themselves in the three partitions of 1772, 1793 and 1795. Although Russia got over half of Poland's territory, the German residents lived primarily in the area of Poland that became part of Prussia. But an influx of Germans to previously Polish-populated areas, as well as to Austrian-ruled Galicia, followed, so that there were a significant number of Germans (although they constituted only a small percentage of the population of the areas ruled by Austria and Russia) in all of Poland, except for a few east central provinces.

Napoleon created the Grand Duchy of Warsaw in 1807. After he was defeated in 1815, Posen was given to Prussia, but the rest of the duchy, including the Polish core around Warsaw and Lublin, which had been controlled by Prussia and Austria, respectively, after 1795, became an autonomous Polish kingdom (Congress Poland) under the Russian czar. After the Polish Revolt of 1830-31, Russia assumed total control.

Poland was reestablished as an independent nation after World War I, with its western border approximating the dividing line between Polish and German residential majorities, but German-populated Danzig was made into a Free City in order to assure Poland access to the Baltic Sea. However, the Netze River region at the base of the Polish Corridor to the sea was incorporated into Poland, even though much of it had a German majority, since the Corridor would have had a very narrow bottleneck otherwise.

Germany attacked Poland on September 1, 1939, and Russia followed suit on September 17. When the war was over, Russia kept a large portion of Eastern Poland, which contained many Ukrainians and Belorussians. As compensation, the Polish border was pushed west to the Oder-Neisse.

Records pertaining to Germans in areas that belonged to Germany or the Free City of Danzig during the interwar period, but are now part of Poland, are scattered. Some (especially civil records) remained in Poland. In many cases (especially for Pomerania), it is unknown whether the records survived, although two recent publications have increased our knowledge about Pomeranian records substantially. These are Klaus-Dieter Kreplin, *Veröffentlichungen aus dem Genealogischen Archiv Kreplin: Bestandsverzeichnis Pommerscher Kirchenbücher in Zivilstandsregister (Pommern in den Grenzen von 1900)* [*Publications Based on the Kreplin Genealogical Archive: Inventory of Pomeranian Parish Registers in Civil Registers (Pomerania within the boundaries of 1900)*] and *Schnellüberblick Kirchenbuchbestand Greifswald: Pommersche Evangelische Kirche* [*Brief Overview of the Parish Register Holdings in the Archives of the Pomeranian Evangelical Church in Greifswald*]. For those that were taken west, see under **GERMANY**.

The best Polish-American genealogical guide (and the only one that is multi-ethnic) is Rosemary A. Chorzempa, *Korzenie Polskie: Polish Roots* (Baltimore: Genealogical Publishing Co., 1993). The Family History Library plans to publish a *Polish Research Guide*.

A shorter booklet, which also focuses on researching ethnic Poles, but with proportionately more material relevant for researching Germans, is Edward R. Brandt, *Resources for Polish-American Genealogy*, first published as an article in *Heritage Quest* in 1996.

EMIGRATION

Chorzempa lists the estimated number of immigrants in 1870-1914 from each partition as follows: Austrian (2 million); Russian (1.25 million); German (1.2 million).

Of course, there were far more Germans in the German Partition, which included some predominantly German-speaking areas, than in the other two partitions, so most of the Germans came from there.

However, the exceedingly heavy emigration from the least-populated Austrian Partition included a disproportionately large number of German and Jewish emigrants, compared to the other two partitions, even though the non-Jewish Germans accounted for only 1% of the total population, most of them living in what is now Ukraine.

On the other hand, most of the migratory Germans in the Russian Partition migrated eastward, predominantly to Volhynia (part of pre-partition Poland, with the western part belonging to interwar Poland). But some of the early emigrants went south to Bessarabia and some of the late ones north to the Balkan countries. Thus it is unlikely that many Germans migrated directly from Russian Poland to countries overseas.

The following genealogical society deals with Jewish ancestors from Galicia:

> Gesher Galicia
> 3128 Brooklawn Terrace
> Chevy Chase, MD 20815-3942

The following society is for those researching non-Jewish German ancestors from Galicia:

Galizien German Descendants
12637 South East 214th St.
Kent, WA 98031-2215

The multi-ethnic East European Genealogical Society in Winnipeg includes many members of German origin, especially from Galicia. A large percentage of articles in its journal, including many by Ukrainian-Canadians, are relevant for researching German ancestors.

CHURCH RECORDS

Although church records had already begun in some Polish areas in the 1400s, existing German parish records only date back to the 1700s, or occasionally to the 1600s. About 80% of the records in the Polish archives have reportedly been filmed by the Family History Library, but most Catholic registers are still in the parish offices. According to Adalbert Goertz, "Evangelische Familiennamen um Wladislawow in Mittelpolen zwischen 1776 und 1825" ["Evangelical Family Names around Wladislawow in Central Poland between 1776 and 1825"], in the April-June 1996 issue of the *Ostdeutsche Familienkunde*, a large number of predominantly German Evangelical parish registers for Kalisch (*Kalisz*), Kolo, Sompolno, Konin and Turek near the bend of the Warta River in the westernmost part of the former Congress Poland have been microfilmed. The authors have seen many other films of Evangelical and some Catholic parish registers for other parts of interwar Poland where Germans lived.

Of course, a substantial number of the parish registers from the pre-World War II German areas were taken to Germany. Many registers (or microfilms of them) are in Berlin, Leipzig and Greifswald, but others are scattered in various places.

As examples of what can be found on a trip to Poland, read the three articles under the overall title, "Research in German Areas Now in Poland," especially the one by Clarence Bittner on "Church Records in Niederschlesien," in the *German Genealogical Digest*, Vol. VI, No. 4 (4th quarter 1990). Names and addresses of several archivists and genealogists are listed.

A good example of a German-oriented article in a Polish-American periodical is "Expeditions to Several Catholic and Lutheran Parishes of Breslau (Wroclaw)" by Werner Freiherr von Zurek-Eichenau in the November 1993 issue of *Rodziny: The Journal of the Polish Genealogical Society of America*.

Virtually complete Roman Catholic registers for the 350 parishes, including German Catholic parishes, in the West Galician dioceses of Przemysl and Cracow have been preserved for the period after 1826. For Przemysl, they date back to 1786 and include some parishes in East (Ukrainian) Galicia. For information, write to:

Archiwum Diecezjalne
pl. Katedralny 4A
PL 37-700 Przemysl
Poland

For further information, see Brian J. Lenius, "German Catholics from Galizien [Galicia], Austria," in the September 1991 issue of the *East European Genealogist* and Edward A. Peckwas, *Register of Vital Records: Roman Catholic Parishes from the Region Beyond the Bug River* (Chicago: Polish Genealogical Society of America, 1984). In the meantime, Lenius has visited this archive and made copies of a large amount of material.

For the parts of Ukraine (mostly East Galicia and West Volhynia), Belarus and Lithuania that were part of Poland during the interwar period, vital records of many German parishes and churches for 1890-1945 can be found in the following archive, which is a part of the civil registry system, rather than the Polish state archival system:

Urzad Stanu Cywilnego
Warszawa Sródmiescie
Archiwum Akt Zabuzanskich
ul. Jezuicka 1-3
PL 00-281 Warszawa
Poland

Although there have been some difficulties and delays in getting records from this source, some genealogists have had success. These records have not been microfilmed by the FHL because of privacy laws and the recency of most of the records.

Pre-1890 records can be found at the following archive, which belongs to the Polish state archival system and can thus be accessed by writing to the National Directorate of State Archives (first address listed under **POLISH SOURCES** later in this section):

Archiwum Glówne Akt Dawnych w Warszawie
ul. Dluga 7
PL 00-950 Warszawa
Poland

For more details, see "The Zabuzanski Collection: New Information on Jewish, Lutheran, Mennonite and Catholic Genealogical Resources for Galicia and Volhynia" and "Accessible Records for Jews, Germans, Ukrainians and Poles in Galicia, Volhynia, Lithuania and Latvia: A Second Zabuzanski Collection (AGAD)" by Brian J. Lenius in the December 1992 and June 1995 issues respectively, of the *East European Genealogist*.

Lenius, who has now made two research trips to European archives with material on Galician Germans, reports that many of the Catholic records listed in Peckwas's book are now at the above archives in Warsaw.

The Roman Catholic archdiocese of L'viv in what is now Ukraine (formerly Polish: *Lwów*; earlier Austrian, bearing the German name, *Lemberg*; Russian *L'vov*) was moved to Lubaczów, Poland, as result of Soviet control over East Galicia due to World War II. Records can now be found at:

Kuria Arcybiskupia w Lubaczowie
ul. Mickiewicza 85
PL 37-600 Lubaczów
Poland

There is a list of current addresses of "Lutheran Churches Within Pre-1939 Borders of Poland" in the June 1991 issue of *Wandering Volhynians*. In addition, Ewald Wuschke, editor and publisher of *Wandering Volhynians*, has published a booklet, *Protestant Church Records on Microfilm for the Former Congress Poland (1815-1915) and Volhynia*, which covers Lutheran, Reformed, Mennonite and Baptist church records and includes references to a few parish registers that either have not been microfilmed or are not known to have survived World War II.

CIVIL RECORDS

Military and guild records began in the 1400s, but an inventory of what is available in the various archives is lacking. Civil registration in the Prussian-ruled area was instituted in 1874.

A form of civil registration, with the clergy acting as registrars, was introduced in the Grand Duchy of Warsaw, but few such registers have survived and civil registration was apparently discontinued after 1812.

In Galicia, as elsewhere in the Hapsburg monarchy, Austrian authorities declared all parish registers to be government property in the 1780s, so they were official governmental records, although not civil registers in the modern sense.

The most complete book on German genealogy in Poland is Alfred Lattermann's *Einführung in die deutsche Sippenforschung in Polen und dem preussischen Osten* [*Introduction to German Genealogy in Poland and the Prussian East*], originally published in 1938 and 1941 but reprinted in 1985 by Wilfried Melchior of Vaihingen, Germany. The *AGoFF Guide* provides relatively up-to-date information concerning available records and where they are located.

The Winter 1992 issue of *Pathways & Passages*, published by the Polish Genealogical Society of the Northeast, has an article on "The Keeping of Vital Statistics Records in the Austrian Partition" (of Poland, referring to Galicia). Also of great value for the Austrian land cadasters (land survey and maps) is the article by John D. Pihach, "Galician Land Cadastre Maps: Land Surveys of 1849 and 1874" in the *East European Genealogist* (June 1994). He found the records and very detailed maps (1:2,800) for the 1849 and 1874 land surveys, as well as a large book of records for the surveys of the 1780s and 1820, in the Central State Historical Archives in L'viv. He did not find the military maps accompanying the earlier land surveys, and suspects that they may be in Vienna. The East European Genealogical Society has the call numbers for the records in L'viv that pertain to each village.

Land records, developed for tax purposes, are also dealt with in some detail by Dr. John-Paul Himka in "A Neglected Source for Family History in Western Ukraine: The Josephinian and Franciscan Land Cadastres" (*East European Genealogist*, December 1992).

The early public records (1780s, 1812, 1820) were used as source material by Ludwig Schneider in his classic work on Galicia, *Das Kolonisationswerk Josefs II. in Galizien: Darstellung und Namenliste* [*The Colonization Activities of (Hapsburg Emperor) Joseph II in Galicia: Description and Lists of Names (of Settlers)*]. Schneider's book is based partly on the extensive research in the Austrian State Archives pertaining to the migration of the original German settlers to Galicia in the 1780s (as well as the Danube Swabians going to what was then southern Hungary in the second half of the 1700s and the early 1800s) done by Franz Wilhelm and Josef Kallbrunner and published by them in *Quellen zur deutschen Siedlungsgeschichte in Südosteuropa* [*Sourcebook for Histories of German Settlements in Southeast Europe*].

Both of these classics were recently reprinted by the Helmut Scherer Verlag in Berlin. The names are indexed in Bruce Brandt and Edward Reimer Brandt, *Where to Look For Hard-to-Find German-Speaking Ancestors in Eastern Europe*, 2nd ed.

JEWISH RECORDS

For information concerning Family History Library microfilms of Jewish records in various towns, see the Family History Library catalog. Other information may be available in *Avotaynu*.

NORTH AMERICAN SOURCES

Wandering Volhynians: A Magazine for the Descendants of Germans from Volhynia and Poland is compiling a rapidly expanding "Surname & Village Research List." The focus is on Volhynia, but there is also a fair amount of material on Germans from Russian Poland (i.e., Central and Eastern Poland), since most of the Volhynians came from there.

There are 12 Polish-American genealogical societies, devoting varying amounts of attention to the Germans in Poland. The following ones are known to have substantial periodicals:

Polish Genealogical Society of America
984 N. Milwaukee Ave.
Chicago, IL 60622-4199

Polish Genealogical Society of Michigan
c/o Burton Historical Collection
Detroit Public Library
5201 Woodward Ave.
Detroit, MI 48202-4007

Polish Genealogical Society of the Northeast
8 Lyle Rd.
New Britain, CT 06053-2104

Polish Genealogical Society of Texas
15917 Juneau Dr.
Houston, TX 77040-2155

There are also societies in California, Ohio, Maryland, Massachusetts, Minnesota, New York, and Wisconsin.

POLISH SOURCES

The best chance of obtaining genealogical information from Poland is to write to the Directorate of the Polish National Archives:

Naczelna Dyrekcja Archiwów Panstwowych
ul. Dluga 6 — skrytka pocztowa Nr. 1005
PL 00-950 Warszawa
Poland

As of early 1997, the fees are as follows, in U.S. dollars:

$30 for an initial search
$15 for each hour of research
$10 for xeroxing 1 or 2 pages of documents
$5 for xeroxing each additional page of documents
$2 for each microfilm frame

All payments for research should be sent to:

Naczelna Dyrekcja Archiwów Panstwowych
Powszechny Bank Kreditowy
III Oddziall w Warszawa
Warsaw
Poland
(Account # 370015-807885-3000-3-07)

Your research request will be processed more quickly and with less chance of confusion regarding the connection of the payment to the request if you send proof of payment simultaneously to the National Directorate of the Polish National Archives or to the archives which sent you the invoice.

It is now becoming acceptable to write to Polish regional and local archives. However, the National Archives in Warsaw will respond to English-language letters, although the reply will be in Polish. All other archives may have a problem with English-language queries. The National Archives will query the pertinent archives for the area you are researching.

The postal codes for other addresses, e.g., for use in writing to Polish civil registry or parish offices, are listed in the official postal code directory, subdivided by region: *Oficjalny Spis Pocztowych Numerów Adresowych* (Warsaw: Panstwowe Przedsiebiorstwo Uzytecznosci Publiczce, 1995).

Additional addresses of numerous Polish archives in former German territory can be found in the 6th edition of Ernest Thode's *Address Book for Germanic Genealogy* and George K. Schweitzer's *German Genealogical Research*. As far as English-language sources are concerned, the most comprehensive list of provincial and regional archives for all of contemporary Poland can be found in Chorzempa's book.

However, the most complete and most detailed information, including the most addresses and most detailed information (including hours when the archives is open and relevant publications), can be found in *Archiwa w Polsce: Informator Adresowy* [*Archives in Poland: Address Guide*], published by the National Directorate of the Polish National Archives in 1996, which includes religious and university archives, and other genealogically useful institutions like libraries.

It also lists addresses of Polish-oriented archives in 18 other countries, with the name of the country in Polish, but the names and addresses of the institutions in the language of the country.

The book is well organized, so that people who do not know Polish can still gain considerable information from it with minimal use of a Polish-English dictionary, but be sure to look at the list of symbols and abbreviations on page 11 of the book.

Inventories or other publications pertaining to the holdings of archives are available for 42 institutions, but many of them are outdated, incomplete, in-house finding aids, articles published in Polish periodicals, or rather general in nature.

However, revised, expanded, updated inventories or similar registers have been published since 1991 for Gdansk (*Danzig*), Kielce, Leszno (*Lissa*), Lublin, Piotrków Trybunalski (*Petrikau*), Plock (*Plozk*), Poznan (*Posen*), Przemysl, Radom, Rzeszów, Suwalki, the city of Warsaw, and the Main Archives of Old Documents in Warsaw.

The guide to resources up to 1945 in the Gdansk archives is particularly extensive (541 pp.). Joachim Zrdenka, "Das Staatsarchiv in Danzig: Führer durch den Bestand bis 1945" ["The State Archives in Danzig: Guide to the Holdings Until 1945"], in the *Ratgeber '95: Familienforschung Mittel- und Osteuropa* [*1995 Guide to Genealogical Research in Central and Eastern Europe*], briefly discusses this inventory, indicating that at least 30% of the records were lost as a result of World War II. Genealogical important holdings include parish registers since 1586, civil registers during the Napoleonic period (1809-12) and again after 1874 and the documents of the cities of Danzig (13th century-1815) and Elbing (13th century-1945). The guide also has information about nearly 500 local archives and indicates which records are where in Germany.

The largest other archival resource guides are for areas in which the number of Germans was modest. However, there are also post-Communist publications concerning the archives in Elblag (Elbing, but located in Malbork, formerly *Marienburg*), Katowice (*Kattowitz*), Koszalin (*Köslin*), Szczecin (*Stettin*) and Wroclaw (*Breslau*).

Branch archives for which recent publications exist include Raciborz (*Ratibor*), Sandomierz, Slupsk (*Stolp*), Chelm (*Cholm*), Tomaszów Mazowiecki, Lecycy (*Lentschütz*), Konin, Gniezno (*Gnesen*), Sanok and Pultusk.

Individuals ordering genealogical research about their family should provide, as far as possible, exact data concerning first names, surnames, dates and places of vital events (births or baptisms, marriages, deaths), religious affiliation, etc. Failure to do so can hamper research or be more time-consuming, hence also more expensive.

Members of genealogical societies doing on-site research for others must attach pertinent information, as listed above, with enclosed letters of authorization, which must be notarized at a Polish consular or other diplomatic establishment for the area where the party resides. This also applies to lawyers. Archival research is conducted only in cases where records are about 100 years old. More recent records are housed in local civil registry offices or in parish offices or archives.

Polish national, provincial and branch archives do not search for living relatives, since they do not have the necessary records.

One problem is that most archival inventories in Poland are incomplete, out-of-date and used only as in-house documents. The most comprehensive guide for all of Poland is the *Katalog Inwentarzy Archiwalnych* [*Catalog of the Inventory of the Archives*] by M. Pestkowska and H. Stebelska (Warsaw: Naczelna Dyrekcja Archiwów Panstwowych, 1971).

The recently established genealogical society in Poznan (*Posen*) is compiling inventories of archival sources and bibliographies, indexing vital registers, building up a genealogical library collection, and starting or coordinating other such research projects, but it does not offer research services at the present time. However, members will receive a *Genealogical Data Bank*, listing surnames being researched and updated semi-annually, as well as information sheets every 2-3 months about current events, new publications, etc. These will also be issued in English, as soon as the number of foreign members is sufficient. The society also publishes a quarterly, *GENS*, in Polish, with short summaries in English. Annual membership is $15 and subscription to *GENS* is $10, payable by postal money order or bank draft. Write to:

> Towarzystwo Genealogiczno-Heraldyczne
> Societas Genealogica AC Heraldica
> ul. Wodna 27 (Palac Górków)
> PL 61-781 Poznan
> Poland

An organized cluster of three genealogical and surname societies (specifically including German families from Galicia who stayed in Silesia), under the same leadership, was established in 1994. Its quarterly *Chronicle* is available in English, German, Polish or Esperanto for $25 per year (plus $7 fee for cashing U.S. money orders or bank drafts) from:

> Silesian Genealogical Society
> P.O. Box 312
> PL 50-950 Wroclaw
> Poland

The *Chronicle* is excellent for Germanic research, but the English version has not been published regularly because of the small number of English-speaking subscribers and the costs involved.

Recently the editor, Eduard Wojtakowski, has published two additional periodicals of interest to Germans, according to John C. Alleman (*FEEFHS Newsletter*, October 1996): *Cradle*, which is devoted to genealogy in western and northern Poland, including areas which were mostly Germanic until 1944-45; and *Galicia*, devoted to genealogy in Galicia and Bukovina.

Genealogical research services for all of Poland are provided by:

> Osradan Badan Genealogicznych
> (Piast Genealogical Research Centre)
> P.O. Box 9
> PL 00-957 Warszawa 36
> Poland

The center describes its services as: "The Center offers genealogical advice and information on the descent of the family name and the family itself. It works out the history of the family, genealogical tree and copies of the coats-of-arms. The Center collects and elaborates documentation concerning the history of Polish families since the earliest times to the present day. The materials cover families living in the historical territories of Poland, regardless of nationality, religion and social class. The Center has also established a Bank of Polish families which, being fully computerized, can admit all the data about Polish families."

Bear in mind that genealogy focused on the nobility. About 10% of the Polish people belonged to the *szlachta* (nobility), even though many of them were about as poor as the peasants. So don't expect too much in the way of results for families of German peasants.

The following multilingual historian, genealogical consultant and tour guide has been recommended for American genealogists visiting Poland to search for German ancestors:

> Henryk Skrzypinski
> ul. Grunwaldzka 10a/68
> PL 85-236 Bydgoszcz
> Poland

Also check the earlier section on **UKRAINE** in this chapter for information about Galicia.

ROMANIA
(Rumänien)

More Germans settled in Romania than in any other Balkan country. However, according to Hans Fehlinger, in 1911 there were only 32,000 Germans in Romania, half in the capital city of Bucharest, compared to about 900,000 after World War I. The explanation for this is that most of these Germans lived in Transylvania and the eastern Banat, which were transferred from Hungary to Romania after the war. The others lived chiefly in Bessarabia and the Bukovina, which had been under Russian or Austrian rule, and the Dobruja, which became part of Romania in 1878.

Nearly all of the Germans in Romania settled there when the territory in question belonged to Hungary, Austria, Russia, or Turkey. The ancestors of Germans who migrated to America from this region, with rare exceptions, never lived under Romanian rule or did so only briefly (as in the case of the Dobruja [Romanian: *Dobrogea*]).

However, Paul Traeger indicates that a significant number of Russian Germans migrated to Moldavia and Walachia in the 1840s and 1870s. But these apparently were not concentrated settlements, since little has been published on them. These two areas joined to form Romania in 1861, although its independence did not receive international recognition until 1878. An English translation of Traeger's German-language book, *Die Deutschen in der Dobrudscha* [*The Germans in the Dobruja*] was printed in serial installments in the *Heritage Review* (December 1985-December 1988).

The German-language book by Wilhelm and Kallbrunner lists the names, and often the villages of origin, of most of the Banat Germans, who settled around Timisoara and Arad. Complete surname index can be found in Bruce Brandt and Edward Reimer Brandt, *Where to Look For Hard-to-Find German-Speaking Ancestors in Eastern Europe*, 2nd ed.

Germans were granted considerable cultural freedom even under Communist rule and relations between German and Romanian ethnic groups have been relatively friendly.

The Romanian national archive contains both civil and parish registers of births, deaths and marriages. Also included are court records, land records, census records and guild records. Civil records are available 100 years after their creation and all other documents after 30 years. Access to documents is the same throughout the country. Contact the General Directorate to arrange a personal visit to the archive. Requests for genealogical information may be written in English and should be addressed to the General Directorate of the state archive:

> Directia Generala A Archivelor Statului
> B-dul M. Kogalniceanu 29
> R-70602 Bucuresti
> Romania

Felix Gundacker lists the addresses of 11 municipal archives in areas where there were a lot of Germans in Part IV of his article, "Research in the Former Austro-Hungarian Empire" (*Heritage Quest*, Nov.-Dec. 1996).

The addresses of the archives where the Germans were particularly numerous include:

> Primaria Municipiului Arad
> Bd. Revolutitiei 75
> R-2900 Arad
> Romania

> Primaria Municipiului Sibiu
> Bd. Victoriei 1-3
> R2400 Sibiu
> Romania
> (German: *Hermannstadt*)

Primaria Municipiului Brasov
Bd. Eroilor 8
R-2200 Brasov
Romania
(German: *Kronstadt*)

Primaria Municipiului Timisoara
Bd. C-Tin diaconovici Loga 1-3
R-2900 Timisoara
Romania
(German: *Temeschwar*)

Gundacker reports that while there are only a few FHL microfilms, the Romanian archives will now answer queries, although the response may be very slow. The archives in Arad, Timisoara, Bucharest, and possibly others, can be visited in person.

Thode's *Address Book* states that the archive has passport records for 1885 and 1890-1918 for several Transylvanian districts, as well as civil registers for Walachia and Moldavia since 1831-32. There are numerous sources of potentially helpful genealogical information in Germany listed in the *AGoFF Guide* and the Thode's *Address Book*.

Many Bukovina records have been filmed by the FHL. Paul J. Polansky has made several research trips to the Bukovina and photocopied civil records kept there. His address is:

Paul J. Polansky
104 Church St.
Spillville, IA 52168-0183

The Bukovina Society of the Americas also shares information with the following institute, which recently initiated shared historical research with the Czernowitz (Cernauti) University (now in Ukraine, but the administrative headquarters for the Bukovina, even though most of the Germans lived on the Romanian side of the current border):

Bukowina-Institut
Landsmannschaft der Buchenlanddeutschen e.V.
Alter Postweg 97a
D-86159 Augsburg
Germany

It was also through the Bukovina Society of the Americas that we learned of the Bukovina German Cultural Association in Brazil (address in chapter XV). The leading American Danube Swabian genealogist is Michael Stoeckl (address in earlier section on **GERMANY: Genealogical Resource Centers for Eastern Europe**).

The name of an English-speaking Romanian genealogist who is interested in founding a Romanian genealogical society follows. He would like to establish North American connections and may be able to provide helpful advice, although he says there are no professional genealogists in the country.

Ing. George Musat
Bucarest - 1, Str. B-dul 1 Mai
Nr. 111, Bloc 12 A, Sc. 1, Ap. 1
Romania

Check under **TURKEY** for census records that may be applicable to the Dobruja.

TURKEY
(die Türkei)

The modest number of Germans in modern Turkey were mostly business or professional people resident in cosmopolitan Istanbul, where a church served the international community from Christian Europe.

There may be some records in Turkey for the Transylvanian Saxons and Dobruja Germans who lived in vassal states of the Ottoman Empire at one time.

There are about 150 million documents, beginning in the fifteenth century and ending with the dissolution of the Ottoman Turkish Empire in 1922, in the Ottoman Archives.

However, only about 15% of these records have been classified to date and are thus accessible to researchers. Population records (censuses), taxes, military records and land registers constitute an important part of this vast collection.

Kahlile Mehr has confirmed that the 1876 Ottoman Nufüs census records include Bulgaria. It seems reasonable to believe that they include all of the Dobruja (including the much larger portion in Romania), since the whole area was under Ottoman rule until 1878. However, the 1884, 1905, 1911 and 1915 Nufüs records could be valuable for Germans in those areas that remained under Ottoman rule at the time.

The archive does not undertake research and knows of no private genealogists. However, you can request a copy of a specific document by filling out two Turkish forms, *Arastirma Talebinde Bulunanlar Için Müracaat Formu* [*Application Form for People Who Want to Search for Information*] and *Taahhütname* [*Agreement Form for Those Undertaking Research*], and enclosing two photographs. The forms are only in Turkish, so you will have to get a translator, unless you know the language. The first one is an application form for searching the files and the second one requests personal information, including your passport number. It may be that this applies only to census records. There is no charge, except for the cost of photocopies. Requests should be mailed to the Head of the Department of Ottoman Archives of the Prime Ministry's General Directorate of State Archives in Istanbul:

> Basbakanlik
> Devlet Arsivleri Genel Müdürlügü
> Osmanli Arsivi Daire Baskanligi
> Ticarethane Sokak
> Cagaloglu-Istanbul
> Turkey

Researchers may use the archives in person. Any published materials (which may include books or articles that are not in the Turkish language) are likely to be available at the Turkish State Library:

> Beyazit Devlet Kütüphanesi
> Imaret Sok. 18, Beyazit
> Istanbul
> Turkey

YUGOSLAVIA: SUCCESSOR STATES
(Jugoslawien)

Overview

Roughly the northwestern half of the former Yugoslavia was under Austro-Hungarian rule before World War I, although part of it was under Austria, part of it under Hungary, and Bosnia-Herzegovina was under the rule of the joint imperial government with its seat in Vienna.

There are five successor states to the former Yugoslav federation. The only one of these new states that had a negligible number of Germans is Macedonia, which thus is not covered below. The archival addresses listed below stem from the period when Yugoslavia was still united. It is possible that the postal code prefixes may change.

The Arbeitsgemeinschaft ostdeutscher Familienforscher (AGoFF), listed under **GERMANY**, has a research center for the former Yugoslavia, with a sub-center for Slovenia. In addition, some of the pertinent records may be in various Austrian or Hungarian archives.

BOSNIA-HERZEGOVINA

The Danube Swabian settlements in the Romania-Hungary-Vojvodina area eventually spilled over into northeastern Bosnia.

There were a number of German villages in the Banja Luka area of north central Bosnia, with one Lutheran and four Catholic churches in Windhorst and Rudolftal, which had a combined population of 4,500. Königsfeld and Schutzberg were a little farther west. The early Lutheran settlers came from the Batschka, while Catholics arrived from the Batschka and the Banat.

Settlers were recruited by the Mariastern Monastery, which sought farmers for the area. Most of them came from the Rhineland, Westphalia, Silesia and Alsace-Lorraine. Bismarck's *Kulturkampf* was an incentive for some of the settlers who came from mostly Catholic areas in the 1870s, although the shortage of land was also a factor. The Austro-Hungarian imperial government invited settlers from the Batscka and the Banat after Bosnia-Herzegovina fell under its administration in 1878, although it was not formally annexed until 1908.

The period of German settlement extended from the 1870s to the 1890s, with a few apparently arriving in the 1860s.

Friedrich G. Lamers published a revised and expanded version of a book which had originally been printed in 1928 to celebrate the 65th anniversary of the German settlement in Bosnia. The revised version updated the book to cover the period until 1944 and was published in Austria in 1970.

Genealogists who desire more information about Bosnian German ancestors are advised to contact:

> Joseph Lamers
> 23643 Granada Ave. N.
> Forest Lake, MN 55025

There has never been a permanent German settlement in Herzegovina, which is a small part of the hyphenated state in the south, along the border with Montenegro.

The address for the national archive is:

> The Archives of Bosnia and Herzegovina
> Save Kovacivica 6
> 71001 Sarajevo
> Bosnia-Herzegovina

CROATIA

There were quite a few Danube Swabian settlements in Eastern Croatia (essentially the territory occupied by the Serbs, as of early 1995), specifically a major part of the Baranya (German: *Baranja*) and East Slavonian villages.

A few Germans (primarily merchants, artisans and other middle-class non-peasant groups) lived in:

(1) Istria, which now forms the northwesternmost part of Croatia, but was ruled by Austria, instead of being part of pre-World War I Croatia, which was an autonomous part of Hungary;

(2) Dalmatia, the southern part of present-day Croatia, which also was under Austrian rule; and

(3) Zagreb, the capital city (*Agram* in German)

The first two areas are along the Adriatic coast. Any Germans who emigrated from there probably left from the port of Trieste (which may also have been the case for some of those leaving from other southern parts of the Austro-Hungarian Empire).

The Family History Library is making good progress in microfilming Croatian records and reportedly filmed some in eastern Croatia (where most of the Germans lived) prior to the Serbo-Croat fighting that destroyed the most significant archive.

The address of the national archive is:

> Arhiv Hrvatske
> Marulicev trg 21
> 41000 Zagreb
> Croatia

SLOVENIA

There were various German settlements in Carniola (German: *Krain*), south of the present-day Austrian border. Urbanites lived in the cities of Kranj (*Krainburg*), Ljubljana (*Laibach*) and Maribor (*Marburg/Drau*). Quite a few German Catholic parishes in Minnesota (and maybe elsewhere) were originally served by German-speaking Slovenian priests, whose ethnic origin is not always clear.

There were also some Germans in Gorizia and Gradisca, which is now divided between western Slovenia and northeastern Italy. The northern part of what was Istria is also in Slovenia today, but it is unlikely that there were many Germans there.

However, the agriculturists farther to the south, in the Kocevje (*Gottschee*) area, dating back to about 1330, retained their Germanic identity to a much greater degree. Large numbers of them were already in the United States by the 1920s. Another major wave of immigration occurred after World War II. They came from Germany, since the Gottscheers had already been forced to leave their home during the war as a result of a Hitler-Mussolini agreement about "spheres of influence," and thus they were considered "stateless persons." Others came after World War II. This group accounted for a disproportionately large number of emigrants, both to the United States and to Germany.

The Gottscheer Connection is published by:

> Gottscheer Research & Genealogy Association
> Elizabeth Nick, President
> 174 South Hoover Ave.
> Louisville, CO 80027

Elizabeth Nick (Liz Information Services) also publishes *The Gottschee Tree*.

Most of the key vital records for Slovenia have been microfilmed by the FHL recently. However, microfilms of Slovenian German parish registers and other archival records, chiefly for the *Gottschee* area, have already been in Leipzig for half a century. The FHL made copies of these before the current filming in Slovenia began.

The address of the national archives is:

> The Archives of Slovenia
> Krtov trg 4
> 61000 Ljubljana
> Slovenia

The 3-volume guide, *Vodnik po maticgah za obmocje s Slovenije*, published in 1972-74, lists all Catholic records which are still extant and the archives in which they are deposited. You can get a copy of this from the archives in Ljubljana.

YUGOSLAVIA (SERBIA-MONTENEGRO)

The "Yugoslav" rump state includes Serbia, with its formerly autonomous provinces of the Vojvodina and Kosovo, and Montenegro.

There were a very large number of Germans in the Vojvodina, which included Syrmia or Srem (*Syrmien* in German), most of the Backa (*Batschka*) and a significant portion of the Banat. This region, north of Belgrade, was ruled by Hungary before World War I and also has many Hungarian residents. Novi Sad (*Neusatz*) was the "Danube Swabian capital" of interwar Yugoslavia.

The Family History Library is now filming records in:

> The Archive of Vojvodina
> Dunavska 35
> 21000 Novi Sad
> Yugoslavia

The Banat and Batschka German settlers, who eventually spread into eastern Croatia and northeastern Bosnia, are listed by Wilhelm and Kallbrunner, whose book is included in the surname index in Bruce Brandt and Edward Reimer Brandt, *Where to Look For Hard-to-Find German-Speaking Ancestors in Eastern Europe*, 2nd ed.

As an alternative, it may be possible to obtain birth, marriage or death records through the Bureau of East European Affairs, U.S. Department of State, Washington, DC 20520, which will contact the American embassy in Belgrade, according to a communication received from the embassy of Yugoslavia before the country was dissolved.

There were very few Germans in Serbia proper, Kosovo or Montenegro.

MISCELLANEOUS OTHER COUNTRIES

A few Greek architects and artisans are known to have served at German royal courts, e.g., in Munich. Josef Vondra states that Templer families in Australia had family heirlooms from Cyprus in their homes. This was because of the temporary stay of Palestine Templers on the island after 1945. Nothing is known of any German family ties to Albania, Malta, or the mini-states of Monaco, Andorra and San Marino. Vatican City is a special case, since only high-ranking church officials, or their assistants and clerks, would have had any residential connection there.

BIBLIOGRAPHY (See ANNOTATED BIBLIOGRAPHY for full citations if not shown)

Almar Associates. *Bukowina Families: 200 Years*. Ellis, KS: authors. 1993. 247 pp.
> Contains the genealogy of many Catholic Bohemian families who emigrated to the Bukowina in 1799-1842 and later to the United States, Brazil and Germany, with references to emigrés to Canada.

Angus Baxter. *In Search of Your European Roots: A Complete Guide to Tracing Your Ancestors in Every Country in Europe.*

Bruce Brandt and Edward Reimer Brandt, compilers. *Where to Look For Hard-To-Find German-Speaking Ancestors in Eastern Europe: Index to 19,720 Surnames in 13 Books, with Historical Background on Each Settlement*, 2nd ed. Baltimore: Clearfield Co. 1993. 122 pp.
> Indexes nearly all major books on Germans in the eastern part of the Austro-Hungarian Empire and the Mennonite migrants to Ukraine, plus a few other books.

Edward Reimer Brandt. *Contents and Addresses of Hungarian Archives, with Supplementary Material for Research on German Ancestors from Hungary*, 2nd ed. Baltimore: Clearfield Co. 1993. Slightly revised 2nd printing 1995. 85 pp.
> Besides description of archival material, includes key historical dates, statistical tables relating to Germans, maps, bibliography, and names of selected localities in pre-1914 Hungary in Hungarian, German and other current languages.

Martha Remer Connor. *Germans & Hungarians — 1828 Hungarian Land Census*. Las Vegas: Author. Ongoing series. 5 vols. plus index to date.
> Extracts from the census now available for Bacs Bodrog, Baranya, Torontal and Tolna counties (parts of which are in Romania and the Serbian Vojvodina today), where there were many Danube Swabians. First four volumes include over 150,000 names.

Johann Christian Dressler. *Illischtie, a Rural Parish in Bukovina: Primary Source Records for Family History* [tr. by Irmgard Hein Ellingson]. Ossian, IA: translator. 1994. 517 pp.

> This compilation presents church, cemetery and school records; immigration lists; census and tax rolls; family letters; and personal interviews for 440 Bukovina families, covering the 1549-1949 period.

Cornelius J. Dyck. *An Introduction to Mennonite History: A Popular History of the Anabaptists and the Mennonites*, 3rd ed. Scottdale, PA/Waterloo, ON: Herald Press. 1993. 452 pp. Maps. Bibliography.

Thomas Kent Edlund. *The Lutherans of Russia.* Vol. 1: *Parish Index to the Church Books of the Evangelical Lutheran Consistory of St. Petersburg, 1833-1885.*

Ingrid I. Epp and Harvey L. Dyck. *The Peter J. Braun Russian Mennonite Archives, 1803-1920: A Research Guide.* Toronto/Buffalo/London: University of Toronto Press. 1996. 215 pp.

> Detailed account of the most important documents for Mennonite history and genealogy discovered in Ukraine.

Joseph S. Height. *Homesteaders on the Steppe: The Odyssey of a Pioneering People.* Bismarck, ND: North Dakota Historical Society of Germans from Russia. 1975. 431 pp.

> Deals with the cultural history of Lutheran colonies near Odessa, 1804-1945.

Joseph S. Height. *Paradise on the Steppe: The Odyssey of a Pioneering People.* Bismarck, ND: North Dakota Historical Society of Germans from Russia. 1973. 411 pp.

> Deals with the cultural history of three clusters of Catholic villages near Odessa, 1804-1972.

Karen Hobbs. *The Tax Rolls of 1654: Bischofteinitz and Taus.* St. Paul: Paulson. 1996. 45 pp. [Original German version: *Unser Heimatkreis Bischofteinitz: mit den deutschen Siedlungen im Bezirk Taus, 1883.* Eichstatt: Bronner und Daemtler KG, for Heimatkreis Bischofteinitz.]

> Has surnames in alphabetical order, showing the places and districts where each occurred and the status of the property owner, extracted by Hobbs.

Hermann Jantzen, "Mennonites in Turkestan: A 1923 Portrait," in the *Journal of the American Historical Society of Germans from Russia* (Summer 1996).

Friedrich G. Lamers. *65 Jahre Kolonien in Bosnien in Jugoslawien.* [*65 Years of Colonies in Bosnia in Yugoslavia*]. St. Gabriel/ Mödling, Austria: Mission Druckerei. 1970.

Erwin Massier, et al. *Fratautz and the Fratautzers: The Rise and Fall of a German Village Community in Bukovina* [tr. by Sophie A. Welisch]. Regina: Saskatchewan Genealogical Society. 1992. 231 pp.

> The book traces the history of Fratautz and discusses local customs, daily experience and the dialect spoken by the villagers.

Dmitry Y. Meshkov. *The Documents of the Dnepropetrovsk Archive as a Source on the History of the Mennonites, 1789-1944.* Unpublished. Available from Center for Mennonite Brethren Studies, Fresno.

Michael M. Miller. *Researching Germans from Russia.*

John D. Movius, comp. *1995 Resource Guide to East European Genealogy.*

Martha Müller. *Mecklenburger in Osteuropa: Ein Beitrag zu ihrer Auswanderung im 16. bis 19. Jahrhundert.* [*Mecklenburgers in East Europe: A Contribution to Their Emigration in the 16th to 19th Centuries*]. Marburg/Lahn, Germany: Johann Gottfried Herder Institut. 1972. 471 pp.

> Vital records on Mecklenburgers who migrated eastward, both within and outside the pre-World War I German Empire.

Friedrich Müller-Langenthal. *Die Geschichte unseres Volkes: Bilder aus der Vergangenheit und Gegenwart der Deutschen in Rumänien* [*The History of Our People: Portrayals of the Past and the Present of the Germans in Romania*]. Hermannstadt [now Sibiu], Romania: Verlag W. Krafft. Published during the interwar period. Over 170 pp.

> Good history of the Transylvanian Saxons, the Banat Swabians and other groups of Germans who migrated to that part of Romania which was former Hungarian territory.

Victoria M. Nied, "From Mokra to the Melting Pot: An Overview from 1775 to the Present of the Emigrations of Austrians Who Lived in Sub-Carpathian Ukraine (SCU) and Now Largely Reside in the United States," in the *Journal of the American Historical Society of Germans from Russia* (Summer 1996).

> Most detailed account of the double migrations of this group, including a Mokra migration timetable; towns of origin and present names in several languages; location of immigrants in specific areas in the United States, as well as in Argentina, Australia, Canada, and Germany, based on data about 3,600 families; and map of European homelands.

Michael P. Palmer. *Genealogical Resources in Eastern Germany (Poland)*. Claremont, CA: privately published. 1993. 12 pp.

> Lists historical bibliography, gazetteers, maps, genealogical societies and their publications, archives, and information about church registers (known information about survival, location, inventories and other relevant publications), with Family History Library film and book numbers, for the former German eastern provinces.

Edward A. Peckwas. *Register of Vital Records of Roman Catholic Parishes from the Region Beyond the Bug River*. Reprinted with an introduction by Edward A. Peckwas. Chicago: Polish Genealogical Society of America. 1984. 44 pp.

> Coverage includes German Catholic parish registers of East Galicia and West Volhynia.

Alfred Piwonka, comp. *The Parish Books from Kreis [County] Bischofteinitz in the Pilsen Archives, With Selected German-Bohemian Genealogical Research Information, Sources, and Bibliography*. With genealogical information, sources, and bibliography by Robert J. Paulson and Larry Jensen. St. Paul: Paulson. 1996. ca. 35 pp. plus map.

> Includes a complete list of parish records in the Plzen Archives (western Bohemia) and information on genealogical research. Most listed parish books reflect the status as of October 1992, a few as of 1983 or 1989.

Erich Quester (comp. for the Arbeitsgemeinschaft ostdeutscher Familienforscher), *Wegweiser für Forschung nach Vorfahren aus den ostdeutschen und sudetendeutschen Gebieten, sowie aus den deutschen Siedlungsräumen in Mittel-, Ost- und Südosteuropa (AGoFF-Wegweiser)*. English-language edition, *Genealogical Guide to German Ancestors from East Germany and Eastern Europe*.

Sallyann Amdur Sack and Suzan Fishl Wynne. *The Russian Consular Records Index and Catalog*. New York: Garland Publishing Co. 1987. 897 pp.

> Indexes records of Czarist Russia's consulates in the U.S., e.g., visa applications.

Daniel M. Schlyter. *A Handbook of Czechoslovak Genealogical Research.*

Josef Schmidt. *Die Banater Kirchenbücher.* [*The Parish Registers of the Banat*] Stuttgart: Institut für Auslandsbeziehungen. 1979. 67 pp.

> List of Banat parish registers (mostly pre-1860) in Stuttgart that were microfilmed in Romania and Yugoslavia during World War II (all of which are available from Salt Lake City). This book and a supplementary list of German parish registers in the Romanian archives in Timisoara and Arad are available from the Arbeitskreis donauschwäbischer Familienforscher.

Ludwig Schneider. *Das Kolonisationswerk Josefs II. in Galizien: Darstellung und Namenlisten.* [*The Colonization Activities of (Hapsburg Emperor) Joseph II in Galicia: Description and Lists of Names (of Settlers)*] Leipzig: Verlag von S. Hirzel for the Historische Gesellschaft für Posen, Poznan. Berlin: H. Scherer. 1939. 409 pp. Recently reprinted by the Helmut Scherer Verlag, Berlin.

> The authoritative book on Galicia, including genealogical data from the 1780s, 1812 and 1820.

Christa Stache. *Verzeichnis der Kirchenbücher im Evangelischen Zentral Archiv in Berlin* [*Inventory of Parish Registers in the Evangelical Central Archive in Berlin*]; Part I, *Die östlichen Kirchenprovinzen der evangelischen Kirche in der altpreussischen Union* [*The Eastern Bishoprics of the Evangelical Church in the Old Prussian Empire*].

Standesregister und Personenstandsbücher der Ostgebiete im Standesamt I in Berlin: Gesamtverzeichnis für die ehemaligen deutschen Ostgebiete, die besetzten Gebiete und das Generalgouvernement. [*Civil Regisers of the (Former) Eastern German Regions in the Civil Registry Office I in Berlin: Complete Directory of the Former German Eastern and Other Polish Territories*]. Frankfurt a.M., Germany: Verlag für Standesamtswesen. 1992.

Jacob Steigerwald. *Tracing Romania's Heterogeneous German Minority from Its Origins to the Diaspora.* Winona, MN: Translation and Interpretation Service. 1985. 61 pp. maps.

> Detailed history of the many German settlements in Romania, but excluding those in the eastern part of that country. Includes 7-page bibliography.

Karl Stumpp. *The Emigration from Germany to Russia in the Years 1763 to 1862.*

Jared H. Suess. *Handy Guide to Hungarian Genealogical Records.*

Anton Tafferner, Josef Schmidt and Josef Volkmar Senz. *Danube Swabians in the Pannonia Basin: A New German Ethnic Group.* Milwaukee: Danube Swabian Association. 1982. 24 pp.

> Historical overview and maps of Danube Swabian settlements.

Ernest Thode. *Address Book for Germanic Genealogy*, 6th ed.

Benjamin Heinrich Unruh. *Die niederländisch-niederdeutschen Hintergründe der mennonitischen Ostwanderungen im 16., 18. und 19. Jahrhundert.* [*The Netherlands and Northern Germany Background of Mennonite Migration to Eastern Europe in the 16th, 18th and 19th Centuries*] Karlsruhe: Author. 1955. 432 pp. May be available from the Mennonite Research Center, Weierdorf, Germany.

> The most comprehensive listing of Mennonite migrants from Prussia to the Russian Empire (Ukraine), with historical information on the Mennonite flight from the Spanish Netherlands to Polish Prussia during the Reformation era.

Ernst Wagner, et. al. *The Transylvanian Saxons: Historical Highlights.*

Diane J. Wandler and Prairie Heritage Chapter members, eds. *Handbook for Researching Family Roots, With Emphasis on German-Russian Heritage, Featuring a Step-By-Step Guide to Researching Family History.* Mandan, ND: Prairie Heritage Chapter (of Germans from Russia Heritage Society). 1992. 286 pp.

> Three books in one: good manual for beginners, regional directory for North Dakota and nearby areas, and several chapters on Russian (mostly Black Sea) Germans. Includes 4-page bibliography and index.

Charles Weisser, "The Baptist Movement Among the Germans in Russia," in *Heritage Review* (March 1992).

Sophie A. Welisch. *Bukovina Villages/Towns/Cities and Their Germans.* Ellis, KS: Bukovina Society of the Americas. 1990. 79 pp.

> Detailed history of 22 German villages in the Bukovina, with surnames of settlers, maps, places of origin and village names in all relevant languages.

Maralyn A. Wellauer. *Tracing Your Polish Roots.*

Martina Wermes, Renate Jude, Marion Bahr and Hans-Jürgen Voigt. *Bestandsverzeichnis der Deutschen Zentralstelle für Genealogie.* [*Index to the Holdings of the German Central Office for Genealogy*]. Vol. I: *Die Kirchenbuchunterlagen der östlichen Provinzen Posen, Ost- und Westpreussen, Pommern und Schlesien.* [*The Parish Registers of the Eastern Provinces of Posen, East and West Prussia, Pomerania and Silesia*]. Vol II: *Die archivalischen und Kirchenbuchunterlagen deutscher Siedlungsgebiete im Ausland: Bessarabien, Bukowina, Estland, Lettland und Litauen, Siebenbürgen, Sudetenland, Slowenien und Südtirol.* [*The Parish Registers of the German Settlements in Other Areas: Bessarabia, Bukovina, Estonia, Latvia and Lithuania, Transylvania, the Sudetenland, Slovenia and South Tyrol*].

Franz Wilhelm & Josef Kallbrunner. *Quellen zur deutschen Siedlungsgeschichte in Südosteuropa.* [*Sourcebook for Histories of German Settlements in Southeast Europe*].

Irina and Rainer Zielke, eds. *Ratgeber '92: Familienforschung GUS/Baltikum.* [*1992 Guide to Family History Research in the CIS and Baltic States*].

Irina and Rainer Zielke, eds. *Ratgeber '95: Familienforschung Mittel- und Osteuropa.* [*1995 Guide to Genealogical Research in Central and Eastern Europe*].

Chapter XIX

RESEARCHING GERMANIC ANCESTORS IN WEST AND NORTH EUROPEAN COUNTRIES

A large majority of the Germans from these countries came from ethnically-mixed border areas which had been part of the German Empire before World War I. This applies to Alsace-Lorraine in France, the Eupen-Malmedy region of eastern Belgium and the North Schleswig (Slesvig) area in southern Denmark.

The German-Dutch linguistic border was fluid until modern times and the current political boundary is also of relatively recent origin, although it has changed only slightly, mostly in the Rhine River region, in the last few centuries. This factor, combined with close linguistic affinity and commercial considerations, explains the presence of Germans in the Netherlands.

The number of people in the other northern and western countries who still have an identifiable German ancestor is small. The Germans in England (but not Ireland) are mostly nineteenth-century immigrants. In this respect, England resembles the trans-oceanic countries more than the continental European countries, even though the commercial considerations which played a prominent role in the small German emigration to the Scandinavian peninsula also applied to England. The fact that the United Kingdom and Hanover had the same monarch for a long time is also relevant.

There is no known German presence in Portugal or Iceland, although a few Germans must have gone to those countries for commercial reasons. Thus a rare birth, marriage or death may have been recorded there, even though it is more likely that it would have been registered by the consular section of the German embassy.

Ribbe and Henning's *Taschenbuch* has material (addresses, bibliographies) for all of Europe, although it is more likely that this will help you research Germans in the rimlands which once belonged to the German Empire than in other countries.

BELGIUM
(Belgien)

Like the Netherlands, Belgium experienced several rulers throughout its history. In 1815, after the fall of Napoleon, Belgium and Holland were merged into the Kingdom of the Netherlands. The area around Eupen and Malmedy became part of the Prussian province of Rhineland, only to be returned to Belgium one hundred years later. This area is now in the province of Liège. Church and civil records for the Eupen, Malmedy and Moresnet areas are at the Provincial Archives:

> Archives de l'État a Liège
> Rue Pouplin 8
> B-4000 Liège
> Belgium

Meyers Kleines Konversations-Lexikon [*Meyer's Small Encyclopedia of General Information*], a 6-volume "mini-encyclopedia," states that there were 11,000 Germans in the Belgian province of Luxembourg in 1900. This is not to be mistaken with the country by that name, although it belonged to Luxembourg until 1839.

Flanders was a highly developed and densely populated area in the late Middle Ages, so many people migrated eastward from it during that time. In the 16th century many Protestant refugees, both Flemings and Walloons, fled today's Belgium, which was under Spanish rule. Thus many Germans have historic roots in Belgium, but it is doubtful whether many families can be traced back directly to specific communities, where there might be some pertinent records.

There are two main languages in Belgium: French, spoken in the south, and Flemish, spoken in the north. These regions are known as Wallonia and Flanders. In addition, a small eastern area of Belgium has German-speaking people, because of the border changes with Prussia mentioned above.

CHURCH RECORDS

Belgium is predominantly Catholic, with church records beginning about 1600 written in Latin. Protestant Church records also begin about 1600 and are written in French or Flemish. Older records are found in the municipal archives and have been filmed by the FHL. From 1800 to present, church records can be found in the church office.

CIVIL RECORDS

The French occupation of 1795 brought about detailed civil registration. These population registers are cataloged by town name and have been filmed by the FHL. If you know the town of origin, you can also write directly to the town hall for information.

MISCELLANEOUS RECORDS

The FHL has filmed many of the military, notarial, and court records that are kept in the archives of Belgium. These records should be consulted first before writing to Belgium.

National Archives of Belgium:

Archives Generales du Royaume
Rue de Ruysbroeck 2-6
B-1000 Bruxelles/Brussels
Belgium

Belgian Archives for the Province of Luxembourg:

Archives de l'Etat à Arlon
Parc des Expositions
B-6700 Arlon
Belgium

Genealogical Society of Belgium:

Vlaamse Vereniging voor Familienkunde
Van Heybeeckstrat 3
B-2060 Antwerpen-Merksem
Belgium

DENMARK
(Dänemark)

The country of Denmark first appeared as an independent kingdom during the Middle Ages. At one time, the southern part of this country was part of Germany. The duchies of Schleswig and Holstein had long been the object of disagreement, and in 1864 Austria and Prussia forced Denmark to cede the two duchies. They remained German until after World War I, when the northern part of Schleswig was returned to Denmark while the southern part remained in Germany.

The Danes are a Scandinavian people and the majority of Danish records reflect this heritage. In the 1500s the Lutheran Church was established as a state church, and the populace has remained Protestant to this day. Beginning in 1646 the government required births, marriages and deaths to be recorded in the parishes. Among the oldest church books are those for the cities of Lauenburg and Ratzeburg. Duplicate copies were kept after 1812. The church records have not been filmed. The address of the Evangelical (Lutheran) Church archives and headquarters is:

Evangelisch-lutherische Landeskirche Schleswig-Holsteins
Dänische Strasse 27-35
D-24103 Kiel
Germany

The first Danish census was taken in 1787, and others have been taken at varying intervals since then. Those of Schleswig-Holstein for 1803-1860 are on microfilm, and are listed according to district (*Herred*). Also filmed are public, notarial, land and probate records as well as tax and military documents.

The Danish state archives contains records of the northern part of Schleswig that returned to Denmark in 1920. Its address is:

Landesarckivet for der sonderjyske Landesdele
45 Haderslevvej
DK-6200 Åbenrå
Denmark

FINLAND
(Finnland)

Finland has been influenced primarily by its two powerful neighbors: Sweden and Russia. For a time, Finland and a significant portion of the German coastal area were both under Swedish rule. Finland was part of the Swedish kingdom until 1809 when it was taken over by Russia. The Czar of Russia allowed Finland to have its own government as an autonomous grand duchy. Finland officially became an independent country in 1917.

Recent research has revealed that the number of Germans who settled in Finland was significantly greater than was previously known to us. The Teutonic Knights and the Hanseatic League had contacts with Finland which may have resulted in some Germans staying there. But most Germans came to Finland at a later date.

Where did the Germans originate and when did they arrive in Finland?

In the 1600s many merchants settled along the western and southern coast of Finland. Per Brahe, founder of the towns of Brahestad and Kristinestad, Finland, invited many Germans to settle in Finland in the 1600s. Many of the Germans came from Lübeck, Germany. Others came from Livonia, Danzig, Mecklenburg, Pomerania, and Westphalia. Some of the coastal towns where Germans settled are Uleaborg/Oulu and Brahestad/Raahe, Oululand; Wasa Stad, Nykarleby, Kristinestad, Jakobstad, and Gamlakarleby, Vasaland; Abo/Turku, Bjorneborg/Pori, and Rauma, Turku/Pori land; many towns near Helsingfors/Helsinki, Nyland; and Wiborg/Viipuri (now part of Russia) in the southeast.

Some Germans came to the coastal towns mentioned above and were employed in the trades, especially as *guldschmids* (gold smiths). Germans also came to Finland as military advisers.

During the Great Northern War between Sweden and Russia's Peter the Great, *Säxische fang* (German prisoners) were sent to the Jakobstad area. They are partially identified in the parish baptismal and marriage records. The Archives in Vaasa also has a list.

Genealogical data on quite a few German individuals or families, dating back as far as 1486, are listed by Martha Müller *Mecklenburger in Osteuropa: Ein Beitrag zu ihrer Auswanderung im 16. bis 19. Jahrhundert. [Mecklenburgers in East Europe: A Contribution to Their Emigration in the 16th to 19th Centuries]* (see Chapter XVIII bibliography).

It seems reasonable to believe that Germans also went to Finland from other areas along the Baltic coast, perhaps especially from West Pomerania which, like Finland, was ruled by Sweden for a considerable period of time.

The address of the Finnish national archives is:

Genealogiska Samfundet i Finland
Snellmaningatan 9-11
SF-00170 Helsingfors 17
Finland

Archives with a lot of material on Germans in Finland are:

Vaasan Maakunta-Arkisto	Vasa Landsarkiv
PL 240	PB 240
65101 Vaasa	65101 Vasa
Finland	Finland
(*Finnish*)	(*Swedish*)

These archives have most of the Finnish and Swedish language publications listed in this section. You can write to them in English and researchers will copy information for you.

One of the best channels for paid research at reasonable rates is the Genealogical Research Agency:

RADIX
P.O. Box 8
SF-20111 Turku
Finland

Numerous Swedish and Finnish-language books which include information of specific value for those researching Germanic ancestors in Finland are listed in the bibliography at the end of the chapter.

FRANCE
(Frankreich)

Nearly all of the German-speaking immigrants who came to the United States from what is now France came from Alsace-Lorraine. This area also provided a large number of German-speaking emigrants to Eastern Europe, mostly in the late eighteenth and early nineteenth centuries. A goodly number of their descendants emigrated to North America about a century later.

In the early years of the French Revolution (1789-94), all the French provinces were reorganized into a much larger number of departments. Alsace was divided into the departments of Haut-Rhin (Upper Rhine) and Bas-Rhin (Lower Rhine), while (German) Lorraine became the department of Moselle.

Old records in this area may be in French, German, or Latin. While some villages retained a clear-cut German ethnic identity until recent times, and others a French one, French-German marriages were not unusual.

Quite a few German-Americans may be able to trace their ancestry back to French-speaking Huguenots, who found refuge particularly in the Palatinate, Hesse, Franconia, Brandenburg, and Northwestern Germany, which had Reformed (Calvinist) rulers, in the sixteenth and seventeenth centuries. The largest number fled after the revocation of the Edict of Nantes (which had guaranteed religious tolerance) in 1685. Look under **GERMANY** for the address of the German Huguenot Society.

There are also some settlements of Mennonites of German-speaking Swiss origin in Montbéliard. For information, see articles in *Mennonite Family History*.

CHURCH RECORDS

The church records of German parishes in Alsace-Lorraine are listed in the *Mitteilungen der Zentralstelle für Deutsche Personen- und Familien-Geschichte* [*News from the Center for German Personal and Family History*], published by the H. A. Ludwig Degener Verlag shortly after World War I, when Alsace-Lorraine was part of the German Empire. Volume 9, titled *Die Kirchenbücher von Elsass-Lothringen* [*Church Books of Alsace-Lorraine*], lists the Lutheran parishes, while Volume 10, with a slightly different title, *Die Kirchenbücher des Reichslandes Elsass-Lothringen* [*Church Books of the Imperial Province of Alsace-Lorraine*], lists the Reformed and Catholic parishes. These publications may be hard to find, but the Family History Library has them. For further detail, see Larry O. Jensen, *A Genealogical Handbook of German Research*, Volume II.

Some Catholic records go back to the Middle Ages, with the Lutheran records beginning in 1525 and the Reformed Church records in 1559. The pre-1792 records can be found in the regional archives listed below. Later ones are probably still in the local parish office. Duplicate registers were required to be deposited with the town clerk and may still be available in the town hall.

CIVIL RECORDS

It was the French Revolution that started the whole business of civil registration in Europe. These records, beginning in 1792, are kept in the town hall, since the mayor or his designated representative serves as the registrar. The regional archives listed below have copies of these records up to 1870.

The French Revolutionary calendar was used for the most part between 1792 and 1805. To convert these dates to the Gregorian calendar that we use, see Chapter XXI and Larry O. Jensen, *A Genealogical Handbook of German Research*, Volume I.

EMIGRANT RECORDS

The 2-volume *Alsace Emigration Book* compiled by Cornelia Schrader-Muggenthaler provides detailed information, alphabetized for convenience, concerning 13,500 French and German emigrants who left Alsace during the 1817-69 period.

There are records of German emigrants in transit through Strasbourg to the French port of Le Havre, which have been microfilmed by the FHL. If your immigrant ancestor came from Southern Germany in the 1817-66 time period (and particularly if there is supposedly some Alsatian connection that you can't verify), try this. The earlier that people emigrated, the greater is the likelihood that they left via Le Havre or Rotterdam.

MISCELLANEOUS RECORDS

Other records include census, guild, notarial, and various public records. For information about these records or the Le Havre passenger records, write:

> Archives nationale de France
> 60 rue des Frances-Bourgeois
> F-75141 Paris
> France

For a more comprehensive list of relevant French records, see *In Search of Your European Roots*, by Angus Baxter.

REGIONAL ARCHIVES

The most extensive public and church records for the formerly German Alsace-Lorraine area can be found in the following regional archives (the records have been microfilmed by the FHL):

For Alsace:

Archives départementales du Haut-Rhin	Archives départementales du Bas-Rhin
rue Fleischauer	5-9 rue Fischart
F-68000 Colmar	F-67000 Strasbourg
France	France

For Lorraine:

Préfecture de la Moselle	Archives départementales de Meurthe-et-Moselle
9 place Préfecture	3 rue de la Monnaie
F-57000 Metz	F-54000 Nancy
France	France

For further information, see:

(1) The Church of Jesus Christ of Latter-day Saints, *French Records Extraction*.

(2) Francois J. Himly, "Genealogical Sources in Alsace-Lorraine (France)," a 12-page paper presented to the World Conference on Records and Genealogical Seminar.

(3) Hugh T. Law, "Locating the Ancestral Home in Elsass-Lothringen (Alsace-Lorraine)," an article in the *German Genealogical Digest*, 3rd quarter, 1990.

GENEALOGICAL SOCIETIES

There are genealogical societies concerned particularly with the Alsace and Lorraine areas. They can be reached by writing to the Cercle Genealogique de Alsace at the Strasbourg archives address above, or the Cercle Genealogique de Lorraine in care of the Nancy address above.

IRELAND
(Irland)

About 850 Palatine religious refugees landed in Dublin in 1709. Many of this same group of emigrants continued on to the mid-Atlantic states. However, some settled in Limerick and Kerry counties in Ireland, where surnames of German origin are still found.

Those searching for ancestors or collateral lines here should check *The Palatine Families of Ireland* by Henry Z. Jones for further information. This is a study of Palatine immigrants who came to Ireland about 1710, and lists 170 surnames of families with German ancestry, including some names that may have been modified or corrupted. Angus Baxter's book, *In Search of Your British & Irish Roots*, identifies the kinds of records that are available, but has no specific reference to the Palatine immigrants. The section on the **UNITED KINGDOM** later in this chapter contains additional references to German immigrants.

An Irish Palatine Association, which offers a genealogical research service regarding this group, has been recently established. It can be reached at:

> The Irish Palatine Information Office
> Rathkeale, Co. Limerick
> Ireland

This information comes from an article on "The Palatines of County Limerick" by Austin Bovenizer in the Winter 1990-91 issue of *The Palatine Immigrant*. The author details relevant historical and contemporary developments in Ireland and mentions a new book, *People Make Places: The Story of the Irish Palatines*, by Patrick O'Connor.

THE NETHERLANDS
(die Niederlande)

The Netherlands is often referred to as Holland, although the latter is properly only the name of the two most populous provinces in the northwest. Dutch and the Flemish spoken in Northern Belgium are essentially the same language. However, Frisian, still spoken in the province of Friesland, is a different language. At one time a Triple Frisia extended from Antwerp in the west to German Ostfriesland, on the Dutch border, and the islands and coastal areas of Schleswig-Holstein. Similarities in naming are still recognizable. Furthermore, Dutch linguistic and cultural influence extended up the Rhine beyond the current German-Dutch border until the Napoleonic Wars.

At the time of the Reformation, the Low Countries were under the control of the Spanish Hapsburg emperors, who were the harshest persecutors of the Protestants, the terror peaking under the Duke of Alva in 1568. This led to the declaration of a Dutch Republic in 1581. Although Spain did not recognize Dutch independence until 1648, the new nation soon prospered and became the world's greatest maritime power in the first half of the 1600s. Among other exploits, it established New Netherlands in the present-day Greater

New York area in 1624. Although the English captured New Netherlands in 1664, the area attracted German immigrants who felt an affinity for the closely related Dutch.

Meanwhile, many Dutch, Frisians and Flemings fled eastward by land and by sea, following earlier routes of traders and marshland-draining pioneers, before religious freedom had been won at home. Thus many Germans in Prussia, Pomerania, Brandenburg, Posen and Mecklenburg have historic roots in the Atlantic Lowlands.

The Mennonite migration from the Netherlands to West Prussia is thoroughly chronicled by Benjamin Heinrich Unruh in *Die niederländisch-niederdeutschen Hintergründe der mennonitischen Ostwanderungen im 16., 18. und 19. Jahrhundert* [*Background of the Mennonite Eastward Migration in the 16th, 18th and 19th Centuries from the Netherlands and Northern Germany*] (Karlsruhe: self-published, 1955). An article on "Hollanders in Germany" in the December 1988 issue of the *GGSA Bulletin* details information concerning the Dutch religious refugees in Mecklenburg.

Although many German emigrants, especially during the colonial period, embarked at Dutch ports, only fragments of these lists have been preserved. However, information about 17th century emigrants may be available in the chamber records and contracts of the Dutch East and West India Companies.

According to *Meyers Kleines Konversations-Lexikon* [*Meyer's Small Encyclopedia of General Information*], there were 32,000 Germans in the Netherlands in 1907. Also look under **Other Specialized Resource Centers** in the section on **GERMANY** for a Dutch-German genealogical society.

CHURCH RECORDS

The majority of the Dutch people are Protestant and church records have been kept since 1600. Most of the Protestants belong to the Dutch Reformed Church, but there are also some Mennonites, Lutherans, and members of other denominations. Over one third of the Dutch are Catholics, but these would be likely to have emigrated to Germany only in the Rhine area. The country had a larger percentage of Jews than Germany, but these are more likely to have come *from* Germany than vice versa. Early records are in the city and state archives. Later records are in church archives and many have been filmed by the Family History Library (FHL). The FHL has also filmed Mennonite parish registers, the oldest dating back to 1632, about half a century after mass migration to Prussia ended.

CIVIL REGISTRATION

Registration of births, marriages, and deaths began in the south in 1796, coinciding with the French occupation. In the north, registration began in 1811 and included population registers. Records are in the municipality and duplicates are in the state provincial archives. Registers after 1892 are not available to the public, but information can be obtained by writing to the city registry office.

CENSUS AND GUILD RECORDS

The first federal census was taken in 1829 and then every 10 years after that. Before that time, enumerations were taken locally for taxation purposes. Guild records have been kept since the 1500s and are generally found in the city archives. Some have been microfilmed by the FHL.

MILITARY RECORDS

Recruiting lists, service records, and national militia records began about 1700. These include the census of able-bodied men and those who died in the French service (1809-14). They are available at the state archives and some have been filmed by the FHL.

There are eleven provinces in the Netherlands, each with its own archive. The Central State Archive in the Netherlands is:

Algemeen Rijksarchief
Bleijenburg 7
NL-2500 's Gravenhage
Netherlands

Genealogical societies located in the Netherlands are:

Zentraal Bureau voor Genealogie
Prins Willem-Alexanderhof 22
Postbus 11755
NL-2595 BE 's Gravenhage
Netherlands

Nederlandse Genealogische Vereniging
Postbus 976
NL-1000 AZ Amsterdam
Netherlands

NORWAY
(Norwegen)

The Christian religion became important in Norway during the 10th century, with a national church being formed about 1070. Olaf II, called St. Olaf, was responsible for the forceful introduction of the Christian religion. The Reformation came to Norway at Bergen through the Hanseatic merchants from Germany. By 1536, Lutheranism had replaced the Catholic religion.

In 1250, Haakon IV granted trading privileges to the Hanseatic League, which controlled European trade during the 1300s and 1400s. By the late 1300s several German nobles had married into Norwegian royal families and the Norwegian crown had a strong German element. By the 1600s, many royal officials were imported from other countries, some being Germans from Holstein. Other German elements were refugees from war torn areas, especially South Jutland. Many German burghers with business experience and money moved into the towns of Norway about the same time. The German influence was stronger in the eastern part of Norway, with many of the wealthy in Christiania (Oslo) coming from South Jutland. There were also many German merchant families at Trondheim. Among other Germans in Norway were German glassblowers and priests.

Hanseatic League trade resulted in the settlement of a significant number of Germans in Norwegian ports, especially Bergen, as early as the fourteenth century. There were Hanseatic trading offices in Bergen, Oslo and Tønsberg. For more information, check publications about the Hanseatic League. Examples are Helen Zimmern, *The Hansa Towns*, 3rd ed. (1881. Reprinted, New York: G. P. Putnam's Sons, 1891; 389 pp. plus illus. and map) and John Allyne Gade, *The Hanseatic Control of Norwegian Commerce During the Late Middle Ages* (Leiden: E. J. Brill; 1951; 139 pp. plus 7-page bibliography).

In the 1600s a renewed interest in mining occurred throughout Europe, and in the 1620s King Christian IV of Norway formed several ironworks, with many of the miners being German. The Kongsberg silver mine opened in 1624 in the mountains west of Oslo. The copper mine at Kvikne opened in 1633, followed by several others, the most important being at Røros in 1644. Most of the miners in these mines were also German. *Beiträge zur Geschichte des Deutschtums in Norwegen: Die Deutsche Einwanderung in Kongsberg* [*Contributions to the History of the Germans in Norway: German Immigration to Kongsberg*], Dr. Alfred Hunhäuser, ed. (Oslo: Verlag Deutsche Zeitung in Norwegen A.S., 1944), details the history of silver mining by Germans in Kongsberg in the 1500s and 1600s.

Norway was controlled by the Danish monarchy from 1030 until 1814 when Sweden forced Denmark to cede Norway. After Norwegians refused to accept the Treaty of Kiel, the National Assembly convened and adopted its own Constitution on May 17 of that year. A Danish prince was elected King of Norway. But before the year ended, the king resigned and the National Assembly agreed to a union with Sweden. Norway became independent in 1905 when that union was dissolved.

LANGUAGE

There are two things you must know about the Norwegian language. First, there are three unique vowels (æ, ø and å) that are alphabetized after z in Norwegian publications (unlike the German practice) but as ae, oe, and aa in American publications. Second, there is a considerable variation in spelling since there are two official languages and dozens of dialects. The Norwegian language is part of the Germanic family of languages. In the mid-1800s, *nynorske* (new Norse) originated to create a distinctly Norwegian language that is based on many rural dialects. The old language, which is still used, is called *bokmål* (book language). *Bokmål* is closely related to Danish.

GEOGRAPHY

The basic geographical unit is the parish (*sogn* or *sokn*). This is often identical with the township or *herred*, although many townships contain several parishes. The townships are grouped into districts, the districts into counties (*fylke*). The simplest way to follow these subdivisions is in volumes 2 and 3 of *Norge* (Oslo: Cappelen, 1963. 4 vol.). In 1919, a major reorganization was made and the *amts* (counties) were changed to *fylke*. Norwegian reference sources are arranged by *fylke* in geographical order (southeast, central, south, west coast, north) rather than alphabetically.

NAMES

A Norwegian name generally consists of a first name, a patronymic, and a farm name. A person's farm name changed whenever that person moved to a different farm. Sharing a farm name does not mean that people were related. The first name was usually chosen according to a set pattern. The first son was named after the father's father, the second after the mother's father. The girls were named after their grandmothers. If a child died, the name was generally reused. Also children were often named after a deceased spouse of one of their parents.

To trace the farm name, you need to know the parish in which it is located since there are many common names for farms, e.g., *Dalen* - Dale; *Nygaard* - New farm, etc. There are two main resources for determining the possible location. The first is Oluf Rygh's *Norske gaardnavne* [*Norwegian Farm Names*] (Oslo, Fabritius, 1897-1936, 20 vols.) and the second is the postal guide, *Norsk stedfortegnelse* [*Norwegian Place-Lists*] (Oslo, Postdirektorastet).

Generally, when Germans immigrated to Norway they kept their German surnames but many also took on patronymic names, as was the Norwegian rule. Since few of them were farmers, they used the surname in lieu of a Norwegian farm name. They often had special names, such as Hoffman, Wöltzer, and Köster, and these names were kept through the generations, but the patronymics changed per Norwegian custom. If a German woman married a Norwegian man, their children generally took on the Norwegian style of name.

CHURCH RECORDS

The Lutheran Church is the state church in Norway, with records beginning in the 1600s. The early records are in Gothic script, although it differed slightly from German Gothic script. Samples of church records with their translations can be found in *Genealogical Guidebook & Atlas of Norway* by Frank Smith and Finn A. Thomsen (Logan, UT; Everton Publishers, Inc. 1979. 56 pp.). This source also contains sectional maps of Norway with an index to towns, a calendar of church feast days, a list of Norwegian counties and parishes and when records began in each parish, Gothic alphabet examples, a short Norwegian word list, and a short introduction to Norwegian records. The records of many Norwegian parishes have been microfilmed and are available through Family History Centers.

COMMUNITY HISTORY BOOKS (BYGDEBØKER)

Another important source for family information is the *bygdebok*. *Bygdebøker* are historical-genealogical books for a particular community in Norway. They will usually include a general history of the area with one or more volumes detailing the history of farm sites within the area. Stories will often include the genealogical heritage of the families residing on the farm sites. They are still being written for many parts of Norway. Also many communities are writing supplementary volumes to bring old volumes up to date. Excellent collections of *bygdebøker* can be found in the libraries at St. Olaf College (Northfield, MN), University of Wisconsin (Madison, WI), University of Minnesota (Minneapolis, MN), Concordia College (Moorhead, MN), Luther College (Decorah, IA), and the University of North Dakota (Grand Forks, ND).

CIVIL REGISTRATION

The 1664-66 tax list of Norway includes all men and boys who were over 12 years of age. In 1701, another list of males was made. In 1769, a census was taken that was mainly statistical, but some parishes listed complete families by name. The first national census was taken in 1801. It gives every person in each household and includes relationships, ages, occupations and status of marriage. The 1865 census includes the same information as the 1801 census plus the addition of the place of birth. The 1875 census includes the same information as the 1865 census except the year of birth is given in place of the age. The 1890 and 1900 census returns have similar information. Most of the tax and census information is available through the Family History Centers and the Vesterheim Genealogical Center, Madison, WI.

Probate records began around 1660 and were more universal after the passage of a probate law in 1685. Each county was divided into probate districts with some of the larger towns having their own probate jurisdiction. The probate matters of clergy and school teachers were handled through the ecclesiastical courts of the archdeaconries.

GENEALOGICAL SOCIETIES

Vesterheim Genealogical Center is a division of Vesterheim ("Western home"), The Norwegian-American Museum, Decorah, Iowa, and is designed to help and encourage genealogists with Norwegian and Norwegian-American research problems. A quarterly newsletter, *Norwegian Tracks*, is included with membership. An extensive collection of microfilmed church records owned by the Genealogical Center may be borrowed by members. Genealogical research in libraries, archives, and other resources is available at a reduced cost to members. Its address is:

> Vesterheim Genealogical Center and Naeseth Library
> 415 W. Main Street
> Madison, WI 53703

The documentation center of *Utvandrermuseet* (Norwegian Emigrant Museum) in Hamar includes a research library, a collection of letters written by Norwegian emigrants to their relatives at home, several private archives, a collection of photographs, microfilms of parish registers of 2,000 Norwegian Lutheran congregations in the United States, and lists of emigrants from various districts of Norway. The museum's Genealogical Society (NUSU) accepts genealogical inquiries concerning roots in Norway. The address is:

> Utvandrermuseet
> Strandveien 100
> Postboks 1053
> N-2301 Hamar
> Norway

The Norwegian Emigration Center was established in 1986 as a research and information center with the stated objective to develop contact between Norwegians around the world. It includes an extensive library of genealogical books and records, as well as providing a genealogical service. It has an excellent collection of *bygdebøker*, microfilmed Norwegian church records, national censuses of 1801 and 1865, and emigrant indexes. The minimum fee is $25 (in 1994) for answering written requests. Their yearbook, *Norse Heritage*, contains articles about Norse culture around the world. The address is:

Norwegian Emigration Center
Bergjelandsgate 30
N-4012 Stavanger
Norway

NATIONAL AND REGIONAL ARCHIVES

The Norwegian National Archives preserve the non-current records of government departments and other central offices. The Norwegian Regional Archives preserve documents from the regional and local branches of the state administration. As a rule, expect that records dating from before 1900 have been transferred to these central repositories. The archives are not obliged to make extensive searches, but you will receive some help. They will supply copies of baptismal, marriage, and death certificates, at fixed rates, and also photocopies, if accurate information is supplied. For extensive research they will help you find someone to hire. They have an informational booklet, *How to Trace Your Ancestors In Norway*, available through Norwegian consulates. The address of the consulate in Minnesota is:

Norwegian Consulate General
Foshay Tower
821 Marquette Ave.
Minneapolis, MN 55402

The addresses of the Norwegian national and regional archives are:

The National Archives:
Riksarkivet
Folke Bernadottesvei 21
Postboks 10 Kringsjå
N-0807 Oslo
Norway

Østfold, Akershus, Oslo:
Statsarkivet i Oslo
Folke Bernadottesvei 21
Postboks 8 Kringsjå
N-0807 Oslo
Norway

Buskerud, Vestfold, Telemark:
Statsarkivet i Kongsberg
Froggsveien 44
Postboks 384
N-3601 Kongsberg
Norway

Hedmark, Oppland:
Statsarkivet i Hamar
Strandgaten 71
N-2300 Hamar
Norway

Aust-Agder, Vest-Agder:
Statsarkivet i Kristiansand
Vesterveien 4
N-4600 Kristiansand
Norway

Rogaland:
Statsarkivet i Stavanger
Bergjelandsgate 30
N-4012 Stavanger
Norway

Hordaland, Bergen, Sogn og Fjordane:
Statsarkivet i Bergen
Årstadveien 22
N-5009 Bergen
Norway

Møre og Romsdal, Sør-Trøndelag, Nord-Trøndelag, Nordland:
Statsarkivet i Trondheim
Høgskoleveien 12
Postboks 2825 Elgesæter
N-7001 Trondheim
Norway

Troms and Finnmark:
Statsarkivet i Tromsø
Skippergaten 1C
N-9000 Tromsø
Norway

SPAIN
(Spanien)

Spain controlled the Netherlands and Belgium at the time of the Protestant Reformation and thus was primarily responsible for driving many religious dissidents out of this area into Germany. It ruled Belgium until 1830. Spanish soldiers fought on German soil during the Thirty Years' War. A small number of Spanish-German liaisons must have resulted. Whether anything of significance could be found in Spanish archives is unlikely.

SWEDEN
(Schweden)

Sweden as well as Norway was settled by Germanic tribes. Swedish sailors, along with their Norwegian and Danish counterparts, explored Europe to plunder, trade, and settle during the Viking era from 800 to 1050. By 1250 Sweden controlled part of Finland and had established the city of Visby as a military and trading base on the island of Gotland where many foreign merchants settled, especially those of the Hanseatic League. Having been attracted by Sweden's minerals, forests, and dairy products, the Hanseatic League was in control of Swedish trade by the 1300s.

Significant German migration to Sweden already occurred prior to the Hanseatic League. Germans at first migrated into southern Sweden, especially to Kalmar, giving it a German character. Later German migration from the middle of the 13th century onwards went more to central Sweden, with Germans apparently playing an important part in the founding of Stockholm about 1251. The Stockholm-Lübeck route was the vital artery of trade, being mostly controlled by Lübeck merchants and more by Stockholm merchants of German origin. The Hanseatic League developed the copper resources at Falun in the latter part of the 13th century, and miners from the Harz region of Germany settled around Falun. There were Hanseatic ports at Stockholm, Visby, Kalmar, and Falsterbo. The large cities attracted not only German merchants, but also artisans who founded guilds (German *Zunft* = Swedish *skrån*) similar to what they had in Germany.

In 1350, the bubonic plague (called the Black Plague in Sweden) devastated Sweden, killing about half of the Swedish population, and Sweden entered an economic decline through the 1400s. By the late 1300s, a German, Albrecht of Mecklenburg, succeeded to the throne of Sweden and there was a strong reaction against his efforts to decrease the power of the Swedish nobles. The Swedish ruling council turned to Norway's Queen Margareta to rule Sweden and by 1397 she had united Sweden, Norway and Denmark in the Union of Kalmar. Her successor and nephew, Erik of Pomerania, who taxed Swedish peasants heavily to fund Denmark's wars and forced the Hanseatic merchants to pay a toll, quickly lost popularity and was soon overthrown.

In the early 1500s, the Danes forcibly took over rule of Sweden, and Sweden's opposition to Danish rule increased until Gustav Vasa organized a peasant uprising and drove the Danes from Sweden. Gustav was elected king of Sweden in 1523. He stimulated mining, agriculture and commerce, and also allowed the government to seize the property of the Roman Catholic Church (which owned one-fifth of the country's land). Gustav encouraged Protestantism, to undermine the authority of the Catholic Church, and the Lutheran Church became Sweden's official religion in 1593. Gustav's grandson, Gustavus Adolphus, came to the throne in 1611.

During the latter part of the 16th century experienced craftsmen, particularly smiths, were brought to Sweden from Germany. Germans were brought into Sweden in the latter half of the 16th century for working iron ore to establish a domestic industry and were responsible for the so-called "German" method. Among the Walloon refugees from southern Belgium (then part of the Spanish Netherlands) in and after 1568, there were also immigrants with German names. In Sweden the term Walloon came to be used to describe workers, clerks, merchants and artisans who migrated and settled in Sweden during the 17th century. This group consisted mostly of people from the Wallonia area in Belgium, but also included others who migrated with them, including Germans, although these were in the distinct minority. Most of the migration to Sweden occurred within a relatively short time span, especially during the years 1620-1655.

Most of the officers of the Swedish army came from Germany. Although they had not belonged to the aristocracy in Germany, they became the foundation for the Swedish aristocracy.

About 1619, the Hapsburg Emperor, Ferdinand II, a militant supporter of the Counter-Reformation, and his Catholic allies in Germany fought their way north to Jutland and the Baltic coast. They forced the Danes to abandon their Protestant German allies with the Treaty of Lübeck of May 1629 and threatened annihilation of German Protestantism. King Gustavus Adolphus of Sweden did not want to see his country's domination of the Baltic challenged by the Catholic empire. Under his leadership the Swedes defeated the Hapsburgs at the Battle of Lützen in 1632, and after the end of the Thirty Years' War Sweden had extensive holdings in northern Germany, including most of the duchies of Bremen and Western Pomerania. In 1640, Sweden also occupied much of Brandenburg. However, Sweden's presence began declining after the mid 1600s and it lost much of its control of the Baltic to Russia.

Prussia gained part of Western Pomerania in 1720. Sweden lost all of its German territories by 1815. Sweden took control of Norway from Denmark as compensation for its loss of Pomerania and Finland. This control lasted until early in the twentieth century.

During the 18th century, some 4,000 foreign textile workers were recruited by Sweden from Germany, the Netherlands, and Denmark. At that time 85% of the industrial workers worked in this field, so there was an immense shortage, so recruiters were sent to Aachen, Wismar, Stettin, Frankfurt, Görlitz, Breslau, Danzig, Limburg, Westphalia, the Netherlands and Denmark in 1739.

This information and details about nearly 900 foreign textile workers (full names, place of origin, family status, date of arrival and the firm for which they worked) in 1759-63 were published by the Swedish Genealogical Society in 1992 as an article by Ann Hörsell in a book on the broader subject of migration, entitled, *Siden, sammet, trasa, lump: Importen av utländsk arbetskraft till Stockholms textilindustri 1759-1763* [*Silk, Velvet and Rags: The Import of Foreign Labor to Stockholm's Textile Industry, 1740-1763*]. The Aachen-Jülich area and Limburg ere especially prominent as places of origin; quite a few also came from Danzig or Hamburg.

For further information, contact:

> Mrs. Sonia Nippgen Holz
> Odens väg 10
> S-15534 Nukvarn
> Sweden

Before and after World War II, Sweden accepted Sudeten German refugees. Rudolf Tempsch, a son of these immigrants, published his doctoral dissertation, "Invandrare i Folkhemmet, Suddettyskar i Eskiluna, 1938-1988," in 1995. Tempsch's material was gathered with the assistance of the large Swedish Trade Unions Archives, which is open for public use:

> Arbetararrörelsens Arkiv & Bibliotek
> Box 1124
> S-11181 Stockholm
> Sweden

LANGUAGE

The Swedish language is part of the Germanic family of languages. The Swedish alphabet contains three additional letters (å, ä and ö), alphabetized at the end of the alphabet after the letter *z*, unlike the German practice. The Gothic script was also used in early Swedish records, although it differed slightly from German Gothic script.

NAMES

The patronymic method of naming was prevalent in Sweden, similar to Norway. A Swedish name generally consists of a first name and a patronymic. The first name was usually chosen according to a set pattern. The first son was named after the father's father, the second after the mother's father. The girls were named after their grandmothers. If a child died, the name was generally reused. Also, children were often named after a deceased spouse of one of their parents.

Surnames were also used, mainly by royalty and foreign immigrants to Sweden. Immigrants would tend to keep the surname they had before immigrating to Sweden. The Walloons as well as the Germans were examples of this pattern. Some 98% of the German commoners did not use the patronymic naming system. Spelling of German names also was not so much a problem in Sweden as much as it was with French names from Belgium, due to the closer similarity of the Swedish and German languages.

Swedish military names are another notable exception to the patronymic naming system. When Swedish men joined the military, they were issued a surname to be used while they were in the military. Military names tended to describe personal or military characteristics (Björn = bear, Modig = courageous, Svärd = sword), or were sometimes based on botanical names (Roth = root, Blom = flower, Ek = oak), or were derived from the area from which they came (Ekberg from Ekeby). Until the last few generations, the men usually dropped their military names upon leaving the military, but sometimes they or their descendants started using the military name again, sometimes with spelling changes, after the family emigrated to another country such as the United States.

Priests also took a surname, which tended to be a Latinized version of the Swedish name.

CHURCH RECORDS

The Lutheran Church became the state church in Sweden in 1593. Church ministers in Linköpings *stift* (diocese) were ordered to begin keeping church records beginning in 1596, with other church dioceses following suit at later times. The church law in 1686 made it mandatory for the minister in each parish to keep a record of every person living within the parish, as well as a record of all religious ordinances he performed. Records of marriages (*vigsellängd*) including residences and parents' names were also required to be kept, as well as births (*födelselängd*) and baptisms (*doplängd*) of all children, including names of parents, sponsors, birth date, christening date and place of birth. Also required were records of deaths (*dödslängd*) and burials (*begravningslängd*) and records of those people moving into (*inflyttningslängd*) or out of (*utflyttningslängd*) the parish. Records of confirmations (*konfirmationslängd*) and marriage banns (*lysningslängd*) were also kept, and later other secular records such as smallpox vaccinations were also kept.

A unique record kept by Swedish churches is the Clerical Survey, or House Examination Roll (*Husförhörslängd*). It is a record of a clerical religious examination of all members of the parish. Swedish church law prescribed these records to be kept starting in 1686, and many parishes kept these records starting at that time, although a few did not begin until about 1820. This record is a genealogical gold mine since it organizes people by place of residence and shows entire households together. In effect, it constitutes a running continuous census, with each particular record book covering a period of about five to ten years. Cross-outs and additions are indicated, and intermediate events are recorded, such as people moving within, into and out of the parish, where they came from and where they went. A person can usually be traced continuously from birth to death in this record. Do not miss using this record when doing genealogical research in Sweden.

Regional genealogical societies are preparing to publish the church records on CD-ROM and put this information on the Internet; access requires a monthly fee or a membership. Contact the regional archives or genealogical societies for further information.

If you have been informed that the parish registers were destroyed in a fire, contact the Federation of Swedish Genealogical Societies for further information (address below).

CIVIL REGISTRATION

Since 1991 the county and city tax offices (*Skatteförwaltningen*, *Personenregister*) have been responsible for the registration of all residents. Prior to that, the parish offices of the Swedish Lutheran Church kept such records, but only for the baptisms, marriages and burials of their members. You need to know the name of the parish.

GENEALOGICAL SOCIETIES

The following are two outstanding associations interested in Swedish genealogical research. Their mailing addresses are:

Sverige Släktforskarförbund
Box 30222
S-10425 Stockholm
Sweden
(*Federation of Swedish Genealogical Societies*)

Genealogiska Föreningen
Box 6442
S-11382 Stockholm
Sweden
(e-mail: f@mbox200.swipnet.se)

The following genealogical society may also be able to provide help:

Föreningen för Datorhjälp i Släktforskningen (DIS)
Gamla Linköping
S-58246 Linköping
Sweden
(Web site: http://www.dis.se/, e-mail: dis@dis.se)

Otherwise, genealogical societies in Sweden focus more on Swedes or American Swedes, not on Germans who came to Sweden. This is mainly because the early German immigrants to Sweden in the 13th to 18th centuries have become a part of the Swedish heritage.

Sweden's genealogical societies are establishing their own regional web sites. Because of the great interest in the United States, some of the information is in English.

The Federation of Swedish Genealogical Societies has its own newsletter, *Rötter* (*Roots*), on the Internet. Besides getting information about genealogy, you can publish queries. You can access this material on the Web at http://www.genealogi.se or by e-mail at hskogsjo@mailbox.aalnet.aland.fi.

NATIONAL AND REGIONAL ARCHIVES

Records of all Swedish parishes are available at Swedish archives and on microfilm through the Family History Centers. Other available records include emigration records from about 1865 (among the world's best), census and land records from about 1630, court records from the 1700s and military records from the 1600s. For those interested in genealogical research in Swedish records, *Cradled in Sweden: A Practical Help to Genealogical Research in Swedish Records*, by Carl-Erik Johansson, is an excellent and comprehensive guide.

The following archive, a section within the Swedish National Archives, is one of the most important in Sweden. Almost all of its older material is now available on microfilm or microfiche. It even has material which the FHL did not microfilm, since they did not obtain permission from all churches in Sweden. Microfiche copies may be purchased from:

Svensk Arkivinformation (SVAR)
Box 160
S-88040 Ramsele
Sweden

There is extensive material on Swedish Pomerania (part of which remained under Swedish rule until 1815) available at the following national archives. (For further information regarding the relevant contents, see the *AGoFF Guide*.) The Riksarkiv has a division called the Statens Utlänningskommissions arkiv (SUK), which has much information about foreigners in Sweden. The oldest documents (1540-1630) are kept here. They are property and ownership books.

Riksarkivet
Box 12541
S-10229 Stockholm
Sweden

Krigsarkivet
Banérgaten 64
S-11588 Stockholm
Sweden

The addresses of the Swedish regional and major city archives are:

Landesarkivet i Göteborg
Box 3009
S-40010 Göteborg
Sweden

Stockholms Stadsarkiv
Box 22063
S-10422 Stockholm
Sweden

Landesarkivet i Härnösand
Box 161
S-87124 Härnösand
Sweden

Landesarkivet i Uppsala
Box 135
S-75104 Uppsala
Sweden

Värmlamdsarkiv
Box 475
S-65111 Karlstad
Sweden

Landesarkivet i Vadstena
Box 126
S-59223 Vadstena
Sweden

Landesarkivet i Lund
Box 2016
S-22002 Lund
Sweden

Landesarkivet i Visby
Box 2142
S-62157 Visby
Sweden

Malmö Stadsarkiv
Stora Varvsgatan 11 N:4
S-21119 Malmö
Sweden

Landesarkivet i Östersund
Arkivvägen 1
S-83131 Östersund
Sweden

The city archives of the major cities (*Stadsarkiv*) have an immense amount of material of interest to genealogists, especially for the period since 1863.

The following archive has information about refugees from the German Third Reich:

Socielstyrelsen
Informationsenheten
S-10630 Stockholm
Sweden

Emigration records for 1852-1947 are kept at the Central Statistical Bureau:

Statistiska Centralbyrån (SCB)
Box 24300
S-10451 Stockholm
Sweden

The National Surveying Office has maps showing localities where ancestors lived:

Lantmäteriverket
Lantmäterigatan 2
S-80182 Gävle
Sweden

SPECIAL RESOURCES

Sweden has a unique institution known as the House of Genealogy, where you can get expert help or do your own research with modern equipment, located in Leksand in Dalom (Dalarna):

Släktforskarnas Hus
Box 175
S-79324 Leksand
Sweden

There is a similar House of Genealogy at Ramsele (for the northern part of Sweden and one in Kyrkhult (for the southern part of Sweden). These centers have no connection to the LDS Family History Centers.

THE UNITED KINGDOM OF GREAT BRITAIN AND NORTHERN IRELAND
(Grossbritannien/Nordirland)

The Angles and Saxons who settled in England in the fifth century were actually North German tribes. Even before that, Germanic soldiers served in the Roman army that occupied England for several centuries. Some must have had children and stayed there after being mustered out.

Early German immigration to England, after distinct German and English identities developed, was the product of trade relationships. The Hanseatic League's major non-German establishment was the Stahlhof (Stapelhof) in London, dating back to the league's origin in the thirteenth century (or perhaps even before the Hanseatic cities joined together). The Hansa dominated trade with England, pursuant to the Privilege of 1377. The Stahlhof was not actually liquidated until 1853. However, the Hanseatic League reached its peak of power in the fifteenth century and existed only in name after 1669.

These connections resulted in two-way migration between England/Scotland and northern German areas. The Hanseatic League comprised not only port cities on the North and Baltic Seas, but also cities extending inland as far as Cologne (*Köln*), Göttingen and Breslau.

Traders from England and Scotland settled in Mecklenburg, Pomerania and Prussia, as well as in western Germany. In most cases, their names became Germanicized (e.g., Piper became Pfeiffer), but in other cases the British spelling persisted (e.g., Howe is quite common in Westphalia). Danzig and Elbing had a number of Scottish and English council members.

Tens of thousands of Scottish mercenaries fought on the continent, since it was hard to sustain many people in the highlands. How many may have remained on German soil is unknown.

German businessmen and craftsmen helped rebuild London after the Great Fire of 1666. Tin miners were another early group of German immigrants.

England was often a temporary home for those who sailed onward. The Palatines of 1709, most of whom went on to the American colonies, are the best known example, but others followed this pattern, going to North America or Australasia. However, some who set out for the New World stayed in England, possibly due to lack of funds.

Royal connections also were conducive to an interchange of Germans and Britons. The British royal lineage has been of German origin since 1714, when the son of the Elector of Hanover became king of Great Britain. Queen Victoria married Prince Albert of Saxe-Coburg-Gotha, thus establishing that as the British royal house in 1901, although the name was changed to Windsor in 1917. The next king will begin the house of Mountbatten, which was originally Battenberg.

The Hanoverian kings brought many of their German subjects to England. Very informative records relating to the soldiers in the various regiments of the King's German Legion survive. Quite a few became Chelsea pensioners.

Britain fought numerous wars in alliance with various German states in the eighteenth and nineteenth centuries. This served as a backdrop for such events as the British hiring of Hessian soldiers to fight in the American Revolution.

However, the largest number of immigrants came to Britain (as well as to the New World) between the 1840s and World War I. Of course, a huge number merely traveled across England (from London, or more often Hull, to Liverpool) before embarking for their transoceanic destinations.

Most German peasants and craftsmen went to Britain for economic reasons. There was a large exodus in 1870-72 in order to avoid military service during or immediately after the Franco-Prussian War. There seem to have been at least a few at the time of Napoleon, although their objection may have been to Napoleon, rather than to military service per se.

The late nineteenth century immigrants already found a thriving German community in London, where German bakers, especially sugar bakers in the East End, had established a dominant position by the early nineteenth century. London had ten German churches (nine Protestant), a very large German hospital, German schools and German welfare institutions around 1880. At least ten German newspapers were published in London before 1914 (although not simultaneously). While the vast majority of Germans resided in London, there were German communities in many cities.

There seem to have been few Germans in Scotland, Wales or Northern Ireland. But there must have been some in the major Scottish cities. A small number of Germans of Huguenot origin settled in (mostly Northern) Ireland during the Plantations Era (1600s, early 1700s), according to Bill and Mary Durning, *The Scotch Irish*.

Immigrants came from all parts of Germany, but most seem to have come from the southwest, according to hospital records. Many apparently sailed on wine-laden small boats down the Rhine and all the way to London.

There is a Moravian Church, known as the Church of United Brethren, in England, but very few of its members are of Germanic origin.

The Anglo-German Family History Society publishes a periodical, the *Mitteilungsblatt* [*Communications Sheet, i.e., Newsletter*], and numerous booklets on specialized topics. Despite the absence of passenger arrival lists, it has compiled a master index listing more than 70,000 Germans who lived or worked in Britain, based on surviving parish registers, shipping lists and internment lists. There were about 100,000 Germans, including many seasonal workers, in England when World War I began. Nearly half that number were interned. For information, contact:

> Anglo-German Family History Society
> 14 River Reach
> Teddington, Middx.
> England TW11 9OL

Examples of articles of widespread interest are:

(1) Arthur Shadwell, "A History of the German Colony in London" (March 1996), which focuses on the Germans who emigrated to London during the thirteenth through sixteenth century as a result of commerce and the Reformation

(2) Jack D. Woods, "Colchester Garrison Church" (December 1996), which deals with the records of the church where marriages of members of the King's German Legion who opted to migrate to South Africa are listed

(3) Isobel Mordy, "The Mordy Collection of Jewish Genealogy" (March 1996), which deals with records of Jews born in England after 1600, but particularly during the nineteenth century, including some Jews from Germany

(4) Amanda Price's list of articles on Schleswig-Holstein which had previously appeared in *Mitteilungen* (December 1996), designed to be the first of a series of such indexes

and which includes such topics as Dutch and Negroes in that area, Germans in the Swedish army, and a Danish-German military parish register

Len Metzler is transcribing the records of several German churches in England, including the records in Hull, which begin in 1848. It would be interesting to find out whether these include any references to the many Germans who came to North America via Hull, since there were quite a few deaths en route (although most of them occurred while crossing the Atlantic) or whether they pertain exclusively to the resident German parishioners.

If you have ancestors among the Palatine immigrants of the early eighteenth century (or others who came to the New World via England), the following archive has unindexed Colonial Office records relating to them:

> Public Record Office
> Kew
> Richmond, Surrey
> England TW9 4DU

The largest Jewish library in England, which includes information about Jewish refugees from Hitler's regime, is the:

> Wiener Library
> 4 Devonshire Place
> London W 1

BIBLIOGRAPHY (See ANNOTATED BIBLIOGRAPHY for full citations if not shown)

GENERAL EUROPEAN:

Angus Baxter. *In Search of Your European Roots: A Complete Guide to Tracing Your Ancestors in Every Country in Europe.*

FINLAND

Herrick Emanuel Aspelin. *Wasa Stads Historia* [*History of the City of Wasa*]. Wasa/Vaasa, Finland: L. Holmberg. 1892. 757 pp.
> Gives a biographical sketch of some of the early merchants in Wasa Stad. A copy is located at the Vaasan Maakunta Arkisto.

Axel Bergholm. *Sukukirja Suomen Aatelittomia Sukuja* [*History of the Ministers for All of Sweden*]. 2 vols. Suomen Muinaismuistoyhdistyksen Puolesta Toimittanut Axel Bergholm. Helsingissa, Kustannusosakeyhtito Otava. 1901. Reprinted Helsinki: Suomen Sukutut-kimusseura. 1984.
> Lists prominent families and includes a background of the families and a detailed list of descendants. A copy is at the Family History Library and also at the Vaasan Maakunta Arkisto [Vaasan Archives]. This was a series of books published until the 1920s.

Tor Carpelan. *Attartavlor for de pa Finlands Riddarhus Inskrivna Efter 1809 Adlade, Naturaliserade Eller Adopterade Atterna. Enlight Riddarhusdirektionens Uppdrag.* Helsingfors, Finland. Frenckellska Tryckeri Aktiebolagets Förlag. 1942. 187 pp. Continued by *Attartavlor for de pa Finlands Riddarhus Inskrivna Atterna.* 1954-66. 4 vols.
> This is an excellent source for discovering German families in Finland. Included are detailed biographical sketches of the noble families, many of whom are of German origin. The early background of the families is also included. Written in Swedish and Finnish. FHL has a copy.

Tor Carpelan. *Finsk Biografisk Handbok. Under Medverkan af Fackman.* [*Finnish Biographical Handbook.* With the Assistance of Experts] Helsingfors/Helsinki: G. W. Edlunds Förlag. 1903. Several volumes.
> Genealogical information about the leading families of Finland. Many were of German origin. A copy is available at the Family History Library (Scand. 948.97 D36c).

Eero Kojonen. *Sursillin Suku. Genealogia Sursilliana [Sursill Genealogy]*. Helsinki: Weilin & Goos. 1971. 842 pp.

> This is a detailed genealogy of the Sursill family who came from the Umea area of northern Sweden and settled in Finland. Most of the early influential families, ministers, historians, politicians, etc., are connected to this family. A great many German names are included. Available on microfilm.

Vilhelm Lagus. *Abo Akademis Studentmatrikel. Forra Afdelningen 1640-1740*. Helsingfors/Helsinki. 1891.

> Contains a list of students and brief biographical information about them. Most of the students became ministers. Some were of German origin. The FHL has a copy.

Armas Luukko. *Vasa Stads Historia [History of the City of Vasa]*. Vol. 1: 1606-1721; vol. 2: 1766(i.e., 1712)-1808; vol. 3: 1809-1852. Translated to Swedish by Kurt Jern. Vasa, Finland: Vasa stad. 1972-87.

> On page 69 are identified early merchants in the Town of Vasa/Vaasa, who were of German background. A copy is located at the Vaasan Maakunta Arkisto.

Raimo Ranta. *Abo Stads Historia 1600-1721*, Vol. 1. Abo: Sydvastkusten. 5 vols. 1977-.

> This is a history of Abo/Turku, Finland, where many Germans who were merchants settled. It includes biographical sketches of some of the early influential residents. FHL has a copy.

Eino Rosten. *Vaasan Kaupungin Asulasluettelo 1600-1862 [History of the Merchants in Vaasa 1600-1862]*.

> Mentions the background of the prominent merchants in the town of Vasa/Vaasa, many of whom were of German origin. A copy is at the Vaasan Maakunta Arkisto.

Gunnar Soininen, Olavi Wanne, Yrjo Blomstedt, Ragnar Rosen, and Heikki Soininvaara, eds. *Uusi Sukukirja*. Vol. 20 of series *Suomen Sukututkimusseuran Julkaisuja* [Swedish: *Genealogiska Samfundets i Finland Skrifter*. English: *Genealogical Holdings of the National Archives of Finland*]. Helsingissa, Finland: Otava. 1943/46-1952/70. Several volumes in series.

> This genealogical study includes many Germans who settled in Finland. A copy is available at the Vaasan Maakunta Arkisto and the Family History Library.

Suomen Sukututkimusseuran Vuosikirja. [Swedish: *Genealogiska Samfundets i Finland Arsskrift*. English: *Genealogical Holdings of the National Archives of Finland*]. Helsinki/Helsingfors: Suomen Sukututkimusseura. Many volumes. 1927-.

> Many German families and their family backgrounds are included in this multi-volume work. A copy is available at the Vaasan Maakunta Arkisto and the Family History Library. Written in Swedish.

Arto Heikki Virkkunen, Aimo Halila, and Kustaa Hautala. *Oulun Kaupungin Historia [History of (Early) Merchants in Oulu]*. Vol. 1: *Kaupungin Alkuajoilta Isonvihan Loppuun*. Vol 2: 1721-1809; Vol 3: 1809-1856; Vol. 4: 1856-1918; Vol. 5: 1918-1945; Vol. 6: 1945-1990. Oulu, Finland: Kirjoittant Oulussa. 1919. Reprinted Oulu, Finland: Oulun Kaupunkti. 1953-95.

> Includes a list of the early residents of Uleaborg/Oulu(ssa) and some biographical information. Most were merchants involved in trade with Sweden, etc. Some German families are included. Includes bibliographies and indexes.

Oskar Wasastjerna, ed. *Attar-Taflor Ofven den pa Finland Riddarhus Introducerade Adeln*. Borga: Soderstroms Tryckeri. 1883. 369 pp. Several volumes.

> Deals with genealogy of nobility in Finland. Biographical sketches of leading families in Finland, many of whom were of German origin. A copy is available at the Family History Library.

Atle Wilskman. *Slaktbok*. Part of series: *Skrifter utgivna af Svenska Litteratursallskapet i Finland*. Helsingfors/Helsinki: Svenska Litteratursallskapet i Finland. 1912-33. Several volumes.

> Genealogical information about the leading families of Finland. Many were of German origin. A copy is available at the Family History Library (Scand. 948.97 D2 wa).

FRANCE:

The Church of Jesus Christ of Latter-day Saints. *French Records Extraction*. Salt Lake City: The Church of Jesus Christ of Latter-day Saints. No date but apparently early to mid-1970s. 171 pp.

> Shows examples of the form and content of French civil and parish registers. Includes terminology, symbols, old scripts, and dates.

Cornelia Schrader-Muggenthaler. *The Alsace Emigration Book*. Vol. 1, 277 pp.; Vol. 2, 203 pp. Apollo, PA: Closson Press. 1989-1991.

> Vol. 1 provides detailed information, in alphabetized form, on 13,500 German and French emigrants who left Alsace in 1817-69. Vol. 2 adds over 8,000 18th and 19th century emigrants and includes a list of all villages in Upper and Lower Alsace.

LUXEMBOURG:

Nicholas Gonner. *Luxembourgers in the New World*.

SWEDEN:

Carl-Erik Johansson. *Cradled in Sweden: A Practical Help to Genealogical Research in Swedish Records*, Revised Edition. Logan, UT: Everton Publishers, Inc. 1995. 345 pp.

> Comprehensive coverage of Swedish genealogical resources. Includes information on the Swedish language, naming patterns, archives, feast days, handwriting, emigration records, parish registers and clerical survey records, census and land records, court records, military records, probate records, genealogical associations, an index to all church parishes in Sweden, and other genealogical data pertinent to researching in Sweden.

Helmut Müssener. *Exil in Schweden: Politische und kulturelle Emigration* [*Exile in Sweden: Political and Cultural Emigration*]. Munich. 1974.

Rudolf Tempsch. *Invandrare i Folkhemmet: Sudettyskarna Eskilstuna, 1938-1988*. Eskilstuna, Sweden: Treuegemeinschaft sudetendeutscher Sozialdemokraten in Schweden. 1995. 159 pp.

> Comprehensive information, including 30 tables of data, about the Sudeten German Social Democrats who emigrated to Sweden after Hitler's annexation of the Sudetenland in 1938, the smaller number who escaped via various countries during the war and the renewed more extensive immigration after World War II, with peaks in 1938 and 1948 and on the number of those who left Sweden again after the war. Includes some reference to Germans, Austrians and Displaced Persons who went to Sweden primarily in 1946-50.

UNITED KINGDOM AND IRELAND:

Henry Z. Jones, Jr. *The Palatine Families of Ireland*, 2nd ed. Camden, ME: Picton Press. 1990. 166 pp.

> Lists Palatine families who went to Ireland in 1710. Shows Irish and German spellings of 172 surnames. Establishes German ancestry of 33 families.

Panikos Panayi. *German Immigrants in Britain during the Nineteenth Century*. Oxford: Berg. 1996

John Tribbeko and George Ruperti. *Lists of Germans from the Palatinate Who Came to England in 1709*. Baltimore: Clearfield Co. 1965; reprinted 1994. 44 pp.

> Detailed information on nearly 2,000 families, most of whom continued on to America, found in the British Museum and the New York Genealogical and Biographical Record.

Chapter XX

CORRESPONDING WITH EUROPEAN SOURCES

Some things to consider when corresponding with sources in Europe include determining the official language, how to send payment or money and where to find foreign language translators. This chapter discusses those items and also provides samples of genealogical letters written in the German language.

LANGUAGE OF CORRESPONDENCE

It is best to write in the current official language of the country involved. However, it is usually acceptable to write in English if you are writing to an archive with a paid professional staff that will charge you for its services. This applies to most Eastern European countries today because they are eager to get dollars.

If you are writing to a pastor or to some other person who is not engaged in making a living as a professional researcher, you should write in German or whatever the appropriate language for that country may be. You should expect that the chances of a reply will be reduced if you do not. Even if your letter is answered, there may be a long delay. If you must write in English, keep the letter short, simple and direct.

The following table lists the official languages of selected European countries.

Table 14: Official Languages of Selected European Countries

Country	Language(s)	Comments
Austria	German	
Belgium	French, Flemish	Includes Eupen, Malmedy
Czech Republic	Czech	Includes Bohemia, Moravia
Denmark	Danish	Includes North Schleswig
France	French	Includes Alsace, Lorraine
Germany	German	
Hungary	Hungarian	
Italy	Italian	Includes South Tyrol
Liechtenstein	German	
Luxembourg	French, German	
The Netherlands	Dutch	
Norway	Norwegian	
Poland	Polish	Includes Posen, East Pomerania, Silesia, East and West Prussia, East Brandenburg
Romania	Romanian	
Russia	Russian	
Slovak Republic	Slovak	
Switzerland	German, French, Italian, Romansh	Depends on the canton
Former Yugoslavia	Serbian, Croatian, Slovenian, Macedonian	Depends on the republic

SENDING MONEY TO FOREIGN COUNTRIES

You may want to send money to other countries to pay for research, order records or books, etc. Bear in mind that nearly all Western institutions, organizations and individuals want to be paid in their own currencies because of the bank charges they have to pay to cash checks made out in dollars.

By far the best, simplest and most economical way to get checks in German marks or other Western currencies is to obtain them from Ruesch International, 700 Eleventh St. N.W., Washington, DC 20001-4507. Call 1-800-424-2923 to order checks. The service charge is $3 per check. You will be given a confirmation number. The requested check will be mailed to you upon receipt of your payment. If you use this service frequently, you can get an account number and speed up the process a few days as the checks cross in the mail. Ruesch has branch offices in larger metropolitan areas like New York, Los Angeles and Chicago. If using these is more expedient for you, check the telephone directory.

For the benefit of Europeans who want to send funds in overseas western currencies, Ruesch International has two European offices with similar services:

18 Seville Row	Schipse
London W1X 2AD	CH-8023 Zürich
England	Switzerland

Since it is standard practice in Western Europe for people to transfer money from their own bank or postal account to an account anywhere in Western Europe for a minimal fee, the services of Ruesch presumably can be used by anyone in any West European country through this mechanism.

On the other hand, almost everybody in East Europe wants to be paid in dollars or other hard currencies, primarily because of the high inflation rates. However, the bank charges for dollars, checks or money orders are even higher (currently about $7 per check in Poland). International Reply Coupons are not very useful since they cost about double their value and post offices in smaller localities may be unfamiliar with them. So be sure to add $7 (or whatever other sum may be requested as policies change) to the amount you owe. It may be cheaper to get a money order in dollars from the post office than to get a bank draft.

WRITING LETTERS TO GERMANY

Local church parishes will have baptism, marriage and death records. If writing to a church pastor, you can offer to pay for the research and copying expenses. Whether or not payment is requested, it is courteous to enclose a donation to the church. Many church records are being transferred to regional church archives. These regional archives will be able to check multiple church parishes at the same time, but they may be more expensive and may not give you as much detailed attention as you would receive at the local level.

If you are writing to the local civil registry office (*Standesamt*), the local city archives (*Stadtarchiv*) or the state archives (*Staatsarchiv*), expect to be billed for any research they perform. Rates will probably be higher at the state archives. Send no money at first. In your letter include an ancestor chart, family group sheet or brief narrative of the facts related to your ancestor. German language charts and group sheets are available. If the person or place you write to cannot help, ask for a recommendation of someone who can.

Print or type your letters and write them as clearly and concisely as you can. Do not include too many requests in your letter. Write in German if possible. Include two International Reply Coupons for postage (available at any U.S. post office) and offer to pay for documents or research. Include more coupons if you expect to receive back more than a relatively simple letter. It may take quite a while, but you will get an answer from the archives. If a given archive cannot locate the information for you, write to another one nearby.

SAMPLE LETTERS

Four sample German letters and their translations follow. They are letters to a church pastor, a possible relative, a genealogical or historical society, and a mayor in charge of city archives.

These letters may be useful starting points. You probably will wish to add to them or interchange sentences between them. If you make modifications or additions to the letters, however, they should be proofread by a German speaker before sending them overseas.

Print or type your letter, since United States handwriting can be difficult for Germans to read. Remember to keep the letter short and to the point. You may wish to begin your letter with your name, address and date, then the name and address of whom you are writing to, as in the first sample. German nouns are always capitalized. It is a good idea to consult a German (or other) postal code book (*Postleitzahlenbuch*) in order to find the current postal code. Postal code directories for Germany, Austria, Switzerland and Liechtenstein are shown in the bibliography.

When requesting information from anyone in your own country, you should always enclosed a self-addressed, stamped envelope (SASE), unless you expect to pay for the services and information. Experts may get hundreds of requests for information.

When you are requesting information from any foreign country, you should always include one or more International (Postal) Reply Coupons (IRCs or IPRCs). Unless you expect only a brief letter in return, you should enclose two. If you are expecting actual documents as well, you should enclose three. These are available from any post office, although in small post offices where there is little demand for them, only the most senior employee may know where they are.

Of course, you should always offer to pay any expenses and fees in connection with research. Professional genealogists and archives will usually charge you, but many pastors and volunteer genealogists (who may be extremely knowledgeable) do not charge for their services. In such cases, enclose a donation to the church or for the promotion of further research.

Letter to a church pastor:

Your name
Street
City, State   ZIP Code
Date (day.month.year)

Herr Pfarrer _____
Street number
Postal-Code City
Country

Sehr verehrter Herr Pfarrer!

Anlässlich meiner Familienforschung ergab sich, dass mein Vorfahr _____*(name)*_____ aus _____*(city)*_____ stammte. Die Namen dieser Linie sind aus der hier beiliegenden Ahnentafel ersichtlich. Ich möchte die Linie gern weiter verfolgen und Sie bitten, mir Fotokopien über diesbezügliche Eintragungen zu machen und mir zuzusenden.

Für Ihre Bemühungen danke ich Ihnen im voraus und lege hier eine Teilzahlung von _____ DM bei.

Ihrer Antwort sehe ich mit Interesse entgegen.

Hochachtungsvoll

_____

Anliegend:
  1 Ahnentafel
  2 Antwortscheine
  __ DM Anzahlung

- -

Your name
Street
City, State   ZIP Code
Date (day.month.year)

Dear Reverend,

According to my research my ancestor _____*(name)*_____ came from _____*(city)*_____. I am enclosing an ancestor chart to show the names of those in that line. I would like to trace the line further and request that you send me copies of the relevant church records.

I thank you for your effort in advance and enclose a partial payment of __ Marks.

I look forward to your answer.

Respectfully,

_____

Enclosed:
  1 ancestor chart
  2 reply coupons
  __ German marks (advance payment)

Letter to a possible relative:

Your name
Street
City, State   ZIP Code
Date (day.month.year)

Herrn _____ Frau _____
Street number
Postal-Code City
Country

Sehr geehrter Herr _____! Sehr geehrte Frau _____!

Ihren Namen habe ich aus dem Telefonbuch entnommen. Mein Grossvater hatte den gleichen Familiennamen _____*(name)*_____ (wie auch ich). Meine Vorfahren stammten aus _____*(city)*_____ in _____*(state)*_____. Mein Urgrossvater kam im Jahre _____*(year)*_____ nach Amerika.

Könnte es sein, dass wir miteinander verwandt sind? Zu Ihrer Kenntnisnahme lege ich hier eine Ahnentafel bei, der Sie die Namen meiner Vorfahren entnehmen können. Stammt Ihre Familie eventuell aus der gleichen Gegend? Haben auch Sie Ihre Familie erforscht?

Ich würde mich freuen, von Ihnen eine Antwort zu bekommen. Zwei Antwortscheine, die gegen Rückporto beim Postamt eingelöst werden können, sind beigefügt.

Mit besten Grüssen

Anliegend:
  1 Ahnentafel
  2 Antwortscheine

_____

- -

Your name
Street
City, State   ZIP Code
Date (day.month.year)

Mr. _____ Mrs. _____
Recipient's name
Address

Dear Mr. _____, Dear Mrs. _____,

I found your name in a telephone book. My grandfather's surname was also _____*(name)*_____ (it is also my name). My ancestors came from _____*(city)*_____ in _____*(state)*_____. My great grandfather arrived in America in _____*(year)*_____.

Perhaps we're related? I am enclosing an ancestor chart to show who my ancestors were. Do you have any ancestors from the region? Have you traced your family?

I am looking forward to hearing from you. I have enclosed two international reply coupons that you can exchange for return postage at the post office.

Best wishes,

Enclosed:
  1 ancestor chart
  2 reply coupons

_____

Letter to genealogical or historical society:

Your name
Street
City, State   ZIP Code
Date (day.month.year)

Sehr geehrte Damen und Herren!

Wie ich bei verschiedenen Nachforschungen festgestellt habe, stammten meine Vorfahren aus _____(city)_____.

Ich lege einen Auszug meiner Ahnentafel hier bei, aus der Sie Einzelheiten ersehen können.

Würden Sie gewillt sein für mich weitere Sucharbeit durchzuführen? Wenn ja, bitte teilen Sie mir mit, welche Kosten für mich damit verbunden sind. Falls Sie selbst keine Forschungsarbeiten tun, wäre ich Ihnen dankbar, wenn Sie mir einen Ahnenforscher empfehlen könnten, der Zugang zu den Archiven und Bibliotheken hat.

Für Ihre Bemühungen danke ich im voraus.

Mit besten Grüssen

_____

Anliegend:
  1 Ahnentafel
  2 Antwortscheine

- -

Your name
Street
City, State   ZIP Code
Date (day.month.year)

Dear ladies and gentlemen,

Using various sources I have found that my ancestors came from _____(city)_____.

I am enclosing an ancestor chart to show who they were.

Would you be willing to conduct further research for me? Please tell me in advance what the expenses might be. If you don't do such research, could you suggest a researcher with access to the archives and libraries who might?

Thank you in advance for your effort.

Best wishes,

_____

Enclosed:
  1 ancestor chart
  2 reply coupons

Letter to a small town or local archive:

Your name
Street
City, State ZIP Code
Date (day.month.year)

Sehr geehrter Herr Bürgermeister!

Auf der Suche nach meiner Herkunft entdeckte ich, dass mein Vorfahr _____(name)_____
aus _____(city)_____ stammte. Ich möchte die Familie weiter zurück verfolgen und brauche
dazu Ihre Hilfe. Würden Sie die Sucharbeit für mich durchführen?

Bitte geben Sie mir die entstehenden Kosten bekannt, oder nennen Sie mir eine Person,
die gewillt wäre, Nachforschungen für mich durchzuführen.

Ich lege eine Ahnentafel und zwei Antwortscheine bei.

Ich danke Ihnen im voraus.

Mit besten Grüssen

_____

Anliegend:
  1 Ahnentafel
  2 Antwortscheine

- -

Your name
Street
City, State ZIP Code
Date (day.month.year)

Dear Mr. Mayor,

According to my research my ancestor _____(name)_____ came from _____(city)_____. I
want to trace the family further and need your help to do so. Would you conduct this
research for me?

Please tell me in advance what the expenses might be or give me the name of someone who
would be willing to do research for me.

I am enclosing an ancestor chart and two reply coupons.

Thank you in advance.

Best wishes,

_____

Enclosure:
  1 ancestor chart
  2 reply coupons

TRANSLATIONS

Sooner or later, you must deal with records and documents in another language. We all try to struggle through basic terms ourselves, but to learn the exact meaning in its context we may need to hire a translator.

The Germanic Genealogy Society has a list of people in Minnesota who will do professional translations for most European languages. So do some other German-oriented societies. *The Resource Guide to East European Genealogy*, published by FEEFHS, lists translators for nearly every European language. Always contact the translator and ask about fees. Also ask how well they know the language and how much experience they have translating it to and from English. Also ask the translators about their experience in doing Germanic genealogical research. Competent hands-on experience in translating genealogy-related documents is very helpful, and often necessary to get an accurate and thorough translation.

Request an estimate of possible costs if the project is a lengthy one; provide the details of your project and enclose a self-addressed stamped envelope (SASE). Language teachers in your local schools or at a university may also be willing to do translations. Many other genealogical organizations provide translation services or refer people to translators. Translation services found in the Yellow Pages are likely to be expensive since they concentrate on commercial work.

If your material is in the Gothic script, you need to check the experience of the translator in deciphering this script, since many translators cannot. Be aware that most Catholic church records are in Latin, not German. Written records vary greatly in clarity, so deciphering the script may take much longer than the translation itself. For this reason, the cost of translating the same number of pages or words may vary tremendously from document to document.

Part-time and full-time translators may differ considerably with respect to how long they take to complete an assignment. If you have a deadline or are willing to wait only a certain length of time, be sure you inform the translator of this.

Always send the translator a good copy of the material you have, unless the copy is so poor as to make deciphering it difficult. In that case, send the original to the translator and keep a copy for yourself, but be sure that there are always two copies as insurance against any possible loss or damage.

If the handwriting is hard to read, it may help to make an enlarged copy. In this case, you should send a copy of the whole page along with the enlarged copy of the key material.

In the case of parish registers, it may be helpful to send the translator a whole page or several pages, rather than just the entry you want translated. Then if the translator cannot decipher a personal or family name in which you are interested, seeing a larger sample of the handwriting may make deciphering possible.

FAMILY AND ANCESTOR CHARTS

The following Ancestor Charts and Family Group Sheets are helpful when corresponding with someone who reads the German, Polish or French language. These charts have a universal identity in format and are a great help in organizing the family information at a glance. In doing research on Germanic ancestry, any one of these may be useful since records are found in each of these languages.

Ahnentafel

Namen des Einsenders

Straße

Stadt   Staat

Datum

2
Geburtsdatum
Geburtsort
Heiratsdatum
Heiratsort
Sterbedatum
Sterbeort

1
Geburtsdatum
Geburtsort
Heiratsdatum
Heiratsort
Sterbedatum
Sterbeort

Namen des Ehemannes oder der Ehefrau

3
Geburtsdatum
Geburtsort
Sterbedatum
Sterbeort

4
Geburtsdatum
Geburtsort
Heiratsdatum
Heiratsort
Sterbedatum
Sterbeort

5
Geburtsdatum
Geburtsort
Sterbedatum
Sterbeort

6
Geburtsdatum
Geburtsort
Heiratsdatum
Heiratsort
Sterbedatum
Sterbeort

7
Geburtsdatum
Geburtsort
Sterbedatum
Sterbeort

8
Geburtsdatum
Geburtsort
Heiratsdatum
Heiratsort
Sterbedatum
Sterbeort

9
Geburtsdatum
Geburtsort
Sterbedatum
Sterbeort

10
Geburtsdatum
Geburtsort
Heiratsdatum
Heiratsort
Sterbedatum
Sterbeort

11
Geburtsdatum
Geburtsort
Sterbedatum
Sterbeort

12
Geburtsdatum
Geburtsort
Heiratsdatum
Heiratsort
Sterbedatum
Sterbeort

13
Geburtsdatum
Geburtsort
Sterbedatum
Sterbeort

14
Geburtsdatum
Geburtsort
Heiratsdatum
Heiratsort
Sterbedatum
Sterbeort

15
Geburtsdatum
Geburtsort
Sterbedatum
Sterbeort

Ehemann

	Tag	Monat	Jahr	Ort		Stadt	Kreis	Staat oder Land
Geburt				Ort				
Sterbe				Ort				
Beerdigung				Ort				
Heirat				Ort				

Vater

Mutter

Ehefrau

	Tag	Monat	Jahr	Ort		Stadt	Kreis	Staat oder Land
Geburt				Ort				
Sterbe				Ort				
Beerdigung				Ort				
Heirat			Religion					

Vater

Mutter

Kinder

	Geburtsdatum			Geburtsort			Heirat	Sterbedatum			Beerdigungsort		
	Tag	Monat	Jahr	Stadt	Kreis	Staat oder Land	datum / ort	Tag	Monat	Jahr	Stadt	Kreis	Staat oder Land
1													
Ehe.													
2													
Ehe.													
3													
Ehe.													
4													
Ehe.													
5													
Ehe.													
6													
Ehe.													
7													
Ehe.													
8													
Ehe.													
9													
Ehe.													
10													
Ehe.													

Name und Addresse des Einsenders des Bogens

Zakres Przodkow

Nazwisko _____

Adres _____

Miasto _____ Stan _____

Data _____

8
Data urodzenia
Miejsce
Data sluba
Miejsce
Data smierci
Miejsce

4
Data urodzenia
Miejsce
Data sluba
Miejsce
Data smierci
Miejsce

9
Data urodzenia
Miejsce
Data smierci
Miejsce

2
Data urodzenia
Miejsce
Data sluba
Miejsce
Data smierci
Miejsce

10
Data urodzenia
Miejsce
Data sluba
Miejsce
Data smierci
Miejsce

5
Data urodzenia
Miejsce
Data smierci
Miejsce

1
Data urodzenia
Miejsce
Data sluba
Miejsce
Data smierci
Miejsce

11
Data urodzenia
Miejsce
Data smierci
Miejsce

Maz lub zona

12
Data urodzenia
Miejsce
Data sluba
Miejsce
Data smierci
Miejsce

6
Data urodzenia
Miejsce
Data sluba
Miejsce
Data smierci
Miejsce

13
Data urodzenia
Miejsce
Data smierci
Miejsce

3
Data urodzenia
Miejsce
Data smierci
Miejsce

14
Data urodzenia
Miejsce
Data sluba
Miejsce
Data smierci
Miejsce

7
Data urodzenia
Miejsce
Data smierci
Miejsce

15
Data urodzenia
Miejsce
Data smierci
Miejsce

maz

	dzien	miesiac	rok	miasto	hrabstwo	stan lub kraj
urodzenie				miejsce		
smierci				miejsce		
pogrzeb				miejsce		
sluba				miejsce		

Ojciec

Matka

zona

	dzien	miesiac	rok	miasto	hrabstwo	stan lub kraj
urodzenie				miejsce		
smierci				miejsce		
pogrzeb				miejsce		
			religja			

Ojciec

Matka

dzieci	data urodzenie			miejsce urodzenie			data smierci			miejsce pogrzeb		
	dzien	miesiac	rok	miasto	hrabstwo	stan lub kraj	dzien	miesiac	rok	miasto	hrabstwo	stan lub kraj
sluba	data											
	miejsce											
1												
malzonka												
2												
malzonka												
3												
malzonka												
4												
malzonka												
5												
malzonka												
6												
malzonka												
7												
malzonka												
8												
malzonka												
9												
malzonka												
10												
malzonka												

tableau généalogique

nom _____

rue _____

ville _____ état _____

date _____

1

date de naissance

lieu

date de mariage

lieu

date du mort

lieu

époux / épouse

2

date de naissance

lieu

date de mariage

lieu

date du mort

lieu

3

date de naissance

lieu

date du mort

lieu

4

date de naissance

lieu

date de mariage

lieu

date du mort

lieu

5

date de naissance

lieu

date du mort

lieu

6

date de naissance

lieu

date de mariage

lieu

date du mort

lieu

7

date de naissance

lieu

date du mort

lieu

8

date de naissance

lieu

date de mariage

lieu

date du mort

lieu

9

date de naissance

lieu

date du mort

lieu

10

date de naissance

lieu

date de mariage

lieu

date du mort

lieu

11

date de naissance

lieu

date du mort

lieu

12

date de naissance

lieu

date de mariage

lieu

date du mort

lieu

13

date de naissance

lieu

date du mort

lieu

14

date de naissance

lieu

date de mariage

lieu

date du mort

lieu

15

date de naissance

lieu

date du mort

lieu

mari

	jour	mois	an	lieu	ville	comté	état ou pays
naissance				lieu			
mort				lieu			
enterrement				lieu			
mariage				lieu			

père

mère

femme

	jour	mois	an	lieu	ville	comté	état ou pays
naissance				lieu			
mort				lieu			
enterrement				lieu			
	religion						

père

mère

enfants	date de naissance			lieu de naissance			mariage			date du mort			lieu d'enterrement		
	jour	mois	an	ville	comté	état ou pays	jour	mois	an	jour	mois	an	ville	comté	état ou pays
1 date															
époux lieu															
épouse															
2															
époux															
épouse															
3															
époux															
épouse															
4															
époux															
épouse															
5															
époux															
épouse															
6															
époux															
épouse															
7															
époux															
épouse															
8															
époux															
épouse															
9															
époux															
épouse															
10															
époux															
épouse															

Chapter XXI

READING THE RECORDS

There are many obstacles that must be overcome in order to read the records of your Germanic ancestors. The records will most likely be written in German or some other non-English language, and will probably be written in Gothic script. This chapter provides both a brief introduction to the Gothic script and some German language notes, including lists of terms you will encounter in genealogically pertinent records. It also gives information regarding other languages you may encounter when reading the records.

THE GOTHIC SCRIPT

Gothic script, sometimes also known as German script, came into existence over a thousand years ago. It was used in many Germanic areas of Europe until the early 1800s, and persisted in Germany (as well as the United States) until World War II. It has been replaced with the script we use today, which is called Roman or Latin script. Whereas Latin cursive letters are based on rounded shapes, lowercase Gothic letters follow more of a straight line, giving the script an angular appearance.

A knowledge of the language in which the document is written is essential in trying to decipher it. The first step here is learning what words to expect in certain documents. Look for them first and then fill in the other words.

Reading Gothic script can be a complex task, since everyone has different handwriting and the handwriting of each individual also varies from time to time. However, you can use this variation to your advantage, since you may be able to read a letter, word or phrase in another portion of a document and then use that information to help read a difficult area.

Pick difficult words apart by letters or groups of letters. It helps a great deal to know common German words, and also which letter groups do and don't occur together in the German language. First, pick out the parts you can clearly read, and then work on the other parts. Ultimately with practice you can start to pick out whole words at a time.

When a given handwriting is particularly difficult to read, prepare a list of capital and small letters as you can make them out. Trace them if possible. You can use this list to help decipher other areas.

A mixture of both Gothic and Latin scripts is very common in church records. Names tend to be written in Latin script with the rest being in Gothic. Of course, exceptions are common.

A bar over a consonant indicates that it is doubled. The bar over the letter *n* is easy to confuse with the mark over the letter *u*.

There are two forms of the letter *s*. The first form (similar in appearance to *f*) is used in the middle of words (e.g., *deutsch*). The second form, known as the *Schluss-s* (final *s*), is used at the end of words (e.g., *das*), and within compound words (e.g., *Geburtstag*) when the component root ends in *s* (*Geburts* in this case).

The s-tset *β* (*sz*) looks similar to the English *B*. This is equivalent to *ss* at the end of a word or root of a compound word, and it is often written *ss* today.

Some words are occasionally abbreviated with an ending squiggle that looks like the Gothic letter *x*.

Common German word contractions are: *am = an dem, vom = von dem, zum = zu dem, ans = an das*. Apostrophes are not used in contractions.

Common abbreviations are: *ehel. = ehelich, u. = und, d. = den, M. = Mutter, V. = Vater, S. = Sohn, T. = Tochter, Taufz. = Taufzeugen, Fr. = Frau, Jgfr. = Jungfrau, ev. = evangelisch, kath. = katholisch*. An *X* is sometimes used to abbreviate certain names as in *Xan =*

Christian. Latin abbreviations sometimes also occur, such as: *ej.* = *ejusdem.* See the German vocabulary list later in this chapter for more examples.

German spelling has changed over the years. For example, *h* after *t* has been dropped, e.g., *verheirathet* is now *verheiratet.* About the only exceptions to this are in place names and surnames, although even these may have changed (especially place names). A synopsis of those changes in German spelling brought about through the government regulations of 1880 is given in *German Composition* by Hermann Lange (3rd. edition, Oxford: Clarendon Press, 1900).

European dates are generally given with day ahead of month, e.g., *den 17. Juni 1843* is June 17, 1843. A period after the day indicates the ordinal number, e.g., *17.* = "17th," so *den 17. Juni* literally means "the 17th of June."

Following is a chart of printed and written Gothic letters. Practice writing words from the genealogical word list using the written Gothic letters so you will have an idea what they should look like in Gothic before you get involved in trying to decipher a document.

Roman Type	German Type	German Script	Roman Type	German Type	German Script
A a	𝔘 𝔞		N n	𝔑 𝔫	
B b	𝔅 𝔟		O o	𝔒 𝔬	
C c	ℭ 𝔠		P p	𝔓 𝔭	
D d	𝔇 𝔡		Q q	𝔔 𝔮	
E e	𝔈 𝔢		R r	𝔑 𝔯	
F f	𝔉 𝔣		S s	𝔖 ſ 𝔰	
G g	𝔊 𝔤		T t	𝔗 𝔱	
H h	𝔥 𝔥		U u	𝔘 𝔲	
I i	𝔍 𝔦		V v	𝔙 𝔳	
J j	𝔍 𝔧		W w	𝔚 𝔴	
K k	𝔎 𝔨		X x	𝔛 𝔵	
L l	𝔏 𝔩		Y y	𝔜 𝔶	
M m	𝔐 𝔪		Z z	𝔷 𝔷	

Adapted from Beginning German by
Schinnerer, Otto P., 1935

GERMAN LANGUAGE NOTES

The German language uses three genders for its nouns. The gender for each German word must be learned.

(masculine)	*der Mann*	the man
(feminine)	*die Frau*	the woman; also wife
(neuter)	*das Kind*	the child

There are four different cases: nominative (subject), genitive (possessive), dative (to whom) and accusative (object). These cases are used to indicate the relationship of words within a sentence. Here is an example with the English translation:

Das Mädchen gab mir das Buch ihrer Mutter.
The girl gave me her mother's book.

(nominative case)	*das Mädchen*	the girl	(subject)
(genitive case)	*ihrer Mutter*	her mother's	(possession)
(dative case)	*mir*	(to) me	(to whom)
(accusative case)	*das Buch*	the book	(object)

This example illustrates some patterns in German. All German nouns are capitalized, although some writers may not always have been too careful about it. The gender and case of the noun changes the endings or forms of associated articles (a, the) and adjectives. Sometimes the noun itself will have a different ending. Prepositions belong to either dative, accusative or sometimes the genitive case.

Article changes:

(nominative case)	*der Mann*	*die Frau*	*das Kind*
(genitive case)	*des Mannes*	*der Frau*	*des Kindes*
(dative case)	*dem Mann*	*der Frau*	*dem Kind*
(accusative case)	*den Mann*	*die Frau*	*das Kind*

Article with adjective:

	(the old man)	(the young woman)	(the small child)
(nominative case)	*der alte Mann*	*die junge Frau*	*das kleine Kind*
(genitive case)	*des alten Mannes*	*der jungen Frau*	*des kleinen Kindes*
(dative case)	*dem alten Mann*	*der jungen Frau*	*dem kleinen Kind*
(accusative case)	*den alten Mann*	*die junge Frau*	*das kleine Kind*

The endings used when the article *ein* is present (*ein* is German for *a* or *an*):

	(an old man)	(a young woman)	(a small child)
(nominative case)	*ein alter Mann*	*eine junge Frau*	*ein kleines Kind*
(genitive case)	*eines alten Mannes*	*einer jungen Frau*	*eines kleinen Kindes*
(dative case)	*einem alten Mann*	*einer jungen Frau*	*einem kleinen Kind*
(accusative case)	*einen alten Mann*	*eine junge Frau*	*ein kleines Kind*

German plurals have a different article and the noun may have one of the following endings:

ending	singular	plural	English
-	*der Schüler*	*die Schüler*	pupil
-e (may add *Umlaut*)	*der Tisch*	*die Tische*	table
-er (may add *Umlaut*)	*das Buch*	*die Bücher*	book
-n	*die Lampe*	*die Lampen*	lamp
-en	*der Student*	*die Studenten*	student
-s	*das Auto*	*die Autos*	car

German verbs are often put at the end of sentences, e.g.,

Er ist am 17. Mai 1793 geboren. He was born on May 17, 1793.

German has many compound words built from simpler words.

Examples: *der Geburtstag* - birthday; *der Taufschein* - baptismal certificate.

German words are almost always spelled phonetically, i.e., the way they are pronounced. Spelling is much more consistent in German than in English, and without as many silent letters.

The sounds of the German vowels *a*, *o* and *u* are modified by putting an *Umlaut* over the vowel (i.e., *ä*, *ö* and *ü*). This changes the pronunciation and meaning of the word. Some German dictionaries alphabetize *Umlauted* vowels as if the vowel were followed by the letter *e*.

See Chapters VII and VIII, as well as the German vocabulary list in the next section, for more information regarding the spelling of German names and other German words.

For more information about the German language please refer to a German language textbook or a book on German grammar.

GERMAN VOCABULARY RELATED TO GENEALOGY

KINSHIP, JURISDICTIONAL AND OTHER TERMS

German	English	German	English
A.C. (Augsburger Confession)	Lutheran (creed)	ebenda	the same place
		Ehe, die	marriage
Ahn(e), der	male ancestor	Ehefrau, die	wife
Ahne, die	female ancestor	Ehegatte, der	husband
Ahnfrau, die	female ancestor	Ehegattin, die	wife
Ahnherr, der	male ancestor	ehelich (ehel.)	legitimate
Akte, die	public record, file	Ehemann, der	husband
Alter, das	age	einbürgern	naturalize
Ältere, der/die (d.Ä.)	senior	einwandern	immigrate
Amt, das (A.)	office	Einwilligung, die	consent
Amtsbezirk, der	lowest court	Einwohnermeldeamt, das	civil registration office
Amtsgericht, das (AG.)	local court house		
Amtsgerichtsbezirk, der	district court jurisdiction	ejusdem (ej.) (Latin)	the same
		Enkel, der	grandson/child
Amtshauptmannschaft, die	government district	Enkelin, die	granddaughter
		Enkelkind, das	grandchild
Anwohner, der	resident	Eltern, die	parents
Anzeige, die	notice	Erbe, das	inheritance
Aufgebot, das	publication/banns	Erbe, der	heir
ausgestorben	(line is) extinct	Erbschaft, die	inheritance
auswandern	emigrate	evangelisch (ev.)	Evangelical, Protestant (Lutheran-Reformed)
Band, der	volume		
Base, die	female cousin		
Base, die	aunt (in Switzerland)	Familienforschung, die	genealogy
Beerdigung, die	burial		
Begräbnis, das	burial	Familienname, der	surname
Bemerkungen, die	remarks, notes	Familienregister, das	family register
Berg, der	mountain, hill	Filiale, die	branch church
Beschneidung, die	circumcision	Fluss, der	river, stream
beziehungsweise (bzw.)	respectively, or	Frau, die (Fr.)	woman, wife
Bezirk, der	district	Fräulein, das	unmarried woman, miss
Bezirksamt, das	district office		
Bezirksgericht, das	district court		
Bezirkskommando, das (BKdo.)	district military office	Fürstentum, das	principality
		Gatte, der	husband
Braut, die	bride	Gattin, die	wife
Bräutigam, der	bridegroom	geboren (geb.)	born
Brief, der	letter, document	Geborene, die	the one who was born
Bruder, der	brother	Geburt, die	birth
Burg, die	fortress, castle	Geburtsort, der	birthplace
Confirmation, die	confirmation	Geburtstag, der	birthday
confirmiert	confirmed	Geburtsschein, der	birth certificate
Copulation, die	marriage	Gemeinde, die (Gem.)	community, parish, congregation
copuliert	married		
Cousin, der	male cousin	Gericht, das	court
Cousine, die	female cousin	Gerichtstag, der	day that court is in session
Departement, das	department (French unit of government)		
		geschieden	divorced
Diaspora, die	diaspora, dispersion (in foreign countries)	gestorben (gest.)	died
		Gestorbene, die	the decedent
Dorf, das (D.)	village	getauft (get.)	baptized
Drilling, der	triplet	getraut (getr.)	wed

German	English	German	English
getrennt	separated	Knabe, der	boy
Gevatter, der	godfather	Kreis, der (Kr.)	county
Gevatterin, die	godmother	Kusine, die	female cousin
Grafschaft, die	earldom	Land, das	land, country, state, province, rural area
Grosseltern, die	grandparents		
Grosskind, das	grandchild (Swiss/Mennonite)	Landgemeinde, die	rural parish, town(ship)
Grossmutter, die	grandmother	Landgericht, das	county court
Grosssohn, der	grandson	Landkreis, der (LKr.)	rural county
Grosstochter, die	granddaughter	Landratsamt, das	district office
Grossvater, der	grandfather	ledig	single, unmarried
Gut, das	estate, property	Leibeigene, der/die	serf (male/female)
H.C. (Helvetier Confession)	Reformed (creed) - Calvinist	lutherisch (luth.)	Lutheran
		Mädchen, das	girl
Halb(bruder)	half-(brother)	majorenn	of legal age
Hausmutter, die	mother	Mann, der	man, husband
Hausvater, der	father	männlich	masculine
hebräisch	Hebrew, Jewish	Matrikel, die	register
Heirat, die	marriage	Meer, das	sea, ocean
heiraten	to marry	mennonitisch	Mennonite
Herrschaft, die	domain, rule	minderjährig	underage
Herzogtum, das	duchy	minorenn	underage
hiesig	local	Mutter, die	mother
Hinterlassenen, die	survivors, heirs	nachgelassen	surviving
Hochzeit, die	wedding ceremony	Nachlass, der	legacy
Hof, der	farmstead	Name, der	name
hugenottisch	Huguenot	noch lebende	still living
israelitisch	Jewish, Hebrew	nota bene (NB) (Latin)	note well
Jahre, die (J.)	years	Obergericht, das	supreme court (Swiss)
jüdisch	Jewish		
Junge, der	boy	Oberlandesgericht, das	highest provincial court
Jüngere, der/die (d.J.)	junior		
Jungfer, die (Jgfr.)	unmarried woman	öffentlich	public(ly)
Jungfrau, die (Jgfr.)	unmarried woman	Onkel, der	uncle (also figurative)
Junggeselle, der	bachelor		
Jüngling, der	youth	Ort, der	place
Kaiserreich, das	empire	Ortschaft, die	locality
Kanton/Canton, der	canton	Pass, der	identification paper, passport
katholisch (kath.)	Catholic		
Kind, das	child	Pate/Pathe, der	godfather, or sometimes godson
Kinder, die	children		
Kirche, die	church	Paten/Pathen, die	godparents
Kirchenbuch, das	parish register	Patenkind/ Pathenkind, das	godchild
Kirchengemeinde, die	parish		
Kirchsprengel, der	diocese	Patensohn/ Pathensohn, der	godson
Knabe, der	boy		
Kolonie, die (Kol.)	colony	Patin/Pathin, die	godmother, or sometimes goddaughter
Kommunion, die	Communion		
Konfirmand, der	male confirmand		
Konfirmandin, die	female confirmand	Pfarramt, das	church office
Konfirmation, die	confirmation	Pfarrkirche, die (Pfk.)	parish church
konfirmiert (konf.)	confirmed	Pflege(kind)	foster-(child)
königliche und kaiserliche (k.u.k.)	royal and imperial	Predigt, die	sermon
		Protokoll, das	official record
Königreich, das	kingdom	reformiert	Reformed
Kopulation, die	marriage	Regierungsbezirk, der (RB.)	administrative area
kopuliert	married		

German	English	German	English
Reich, das	empire	Trauschein, der	marriage certificate
Reichsgericht, das	supreme court	Trauung, die	marriage (ceremony)
Rittergut, das (Rg.)	Nobleman's, knight's or Junker's estate	unehelich (unehel.)	illegitimate
		Untertan, der	subject, vassal
Schein, der	certificate	unverheiratet	single, unwed
Schwester, die	sister	Urkunde, die	document
Schwieger(mutter)	(mother-)in-law	Ursache, die	cause
Schwurgericht, das	juried court	Vater, der	father
See, der	lake	verehelichen	to marry, to give one's daughter in marriage
See, die	sea, ocean		
Seite, die	page	Verehelichung, die	marriage
Selbe, der/die (usually one word)	same (male or female)	verheirat(h)en	to marry, to be given in marriage
siehe (s.)	see	verheirat(h)et	married
Sohn, der (S.)	son	Verheirat(h)ung, die	marriage
Staat, der	state or province	verlobt	engaged
Staatsarchiv, das	regional archive	verstorben	deceased
Stadt, die	city	Verstorbene, der	(the) deceased
Stadtarchiv, das	city archive	Verwaltungsbezirk, der	administrative area
Stadtgemeinde, die	urban parish, urban community	verwandt	related
		verwitwet	widowed
Stadtkreis, der	urban county	Verzeichnis, das	register, index
Stand, der	position or occupation	Vetter, der	cousin, relative
		vide (Latin)	see
Standesamt, das (StdA.)	registry of vital statistics	volljährig	of legal age
		Vorname, der	given name
Sterbefall, der	case of death	Wahlkreis, der	voting ward
Stief(vater), der	step(father)	Waise, die	orphan
Synagoge, die	synagogue	Waisenkind, das	orphan
Tante, die	aunt (also figurative)	Weib, das	wife, woman
		weiblich	feminine
		weiland	deceased
Taufe, die	baptism	Weiler, der	hamlet
Taufpate, der	godfather	wie oben	as above, ditto
Taufpatin, die	godmother	wie vorher	as before, ditto
Taufschein, der	baptismal certificate	Wiedertäufer, der	Anabaptist
Taufzeuge, der	godfather	Witwe, die	widow
Taufzeugin, die	godmother	Witwer, der	widower
Tod, der	death	Wohnort, der	place of residence
Todesursache, die	cause of death	Zeuge, der	witness
totgeboren	stillborn	Zwilling, der	twin

GERMAN PREPOSITIONS

auf	on
an	on, to
aus	from, out of
bei	by, near
mit	with
nach	to, after
seit	since
um	about, in order to
über	over, above
unter	under, below
von	from, of
vor	before, in front of
zu	to, at

GERMAN GENEALOGICAL SYMBOLS

∗	born
+∗	stillborn
≈	christened
○	engaged
∞	married
†	died
▢	buried
++	line is extinct
○│○	divorced
✕	died in battle

OCCUPATIONS AND RELATED TERMS

German	English	German	English
Ackerer, der	farmer	Grützmüller, der	grain miller
Ackermann, der	farmer	Gutsbesitzer, der	estate owner
Ackerwirt(h), der	farmer	Häcker, der	vine grower
Älteste(r), der	elder	Hafner, der	potter
Altflicker, der	jobbing cobbler	Hakenbüdner, der	hook seller
Apotheker, der	pharmacist	Handarbeiter, der	manual laborer
Arbeiter, der	male worker	Handelsmann, der	merchant, trader
Arbeiterin, die	female worker	Handwerker, der	artisan, worker
Arbeitsfrau, die	female worker	Hausgenosse, der	household member
Arbeitsmann, der	male worker	Hebamme, die	midwife
Arzt, der	physician	Hirt, der	shepherd, cowherd
Bauer, der	farmer	Hofmann, der	courtier
Bäcker, der	baker	Holzflösser, der	raftsman
Beruf, der	occupation	Holzhändler, der	lumber dealer
Bierbrauer, der	beer brewer	Holzhauer, der	lumberjack
Bortenmacher, der	lacemaker	Honighändler, der	honey dealer
Brandweinbrenner, der	distiller	Hospitaler, der	nursing home resident
Brandweinschenker, der	liquor retailer	Hufschmied, der	farrier, blacksmith
		Kantor, der	choir leader, organist, lead singer
Brauer, der	brewer		
Brettschneider, der	sawyer	Kantorlehrer, der	lay minister, teacher
Briefträger, der	mailman	Kaufmann, der	shopkeeper
Büdner, der	stallkeeper	Kirschner, der	cherry brandy maker
Bürger, der	citizen		
Bürgermeister, der	mayor	Knecht, der	farmhand
Canonier, der	cannon gunner	Kolonist, der (Kol.)	settler, pioneer
Dienstbote, der	domestic servant	Kornmüller, der	grain miller
Dienstmädchen, das	maid	Krämer, der	shopkeeper
Distillateur, der	distiller	Krankenschwester, die	nurse
Dragoner, der	dragoon, soldier		
Eigengärtner, der	independent gardener	Krüger, der	innkeeper
		Künstler, der	artist
Eigenkätner, der	independent cottager	Küster, der	sexton
		Küsterlehrer, der	lay minister, teacher
Eigentümer, der	property owner	Kutscher, der	coachman
Einlieger, der	lodger, tenant farmer	Landfrau, die	female farmer
		Landmann, der	male farmer
Einwohner, der (E.)	inhabitant	Landwirt, der	farmer
Erbpächter, der	hereditary tenant	Lederhändler, der	leather dealer
Essigbrauer, der	vinegar maker	Lehrer, der	teacher
Färber, der	dyer	Leinenweber, der	linen-weaver
Fischer, der	fisherman	Magd, die	domestic servent, maid
Fleischer, der	butcher		
Fleischhacker, der	butcher	Mälzer, der	maltster
Förster, der	forester	Matrose, der	sailor
Füselier, der	light infantryman	Maurer, der	mason
Fusssoldat, der	foot soldier	Meister, der	master
Gärtner, der	gardener	Messner, der	sexton
Gastwirt, der	innkeeper	Metzger, der	butcher
Geselle, der	journeyman	Mietsfrau, die	female tenant
Gewerbe, das	occupation	Mietsgärtner, der	tenant gardener
Gewürzkrämer, der	spice trader	Mietsmann, der	male tenant
Grützer, der	grain miller	Milchträger, der	milkman

German	English	German	English
Mosquetier/ Musketier, der	musketeer	Soldat, der	soldier
		Spinner(mann), der	spinner
Müller, der	miller	Steinmetz, der	stone mason
Pfarrer, der	clergyman	Stellmacher, der	wheelwright
Posamentierer, der	haberdasher	Tagelöhner, der	day laborer
Postbeamte, der	postal worker	Tischler, der	cabinetmaker, carpenter
Posteleve, der	postal apprentice		
Posthalter, der	post-horse keeper	Töpfer, der	potter
Postillion, der	coachman	Tuchmacher, der	fabric maker
Tabbiner/Rabbi, der	rabbi	Uhrmacher, der	clockmaker
Rademacher, der	wheelwright	Unvermögende, der	pauper
Richter, der	judge, justice	Vormund, der	legal guardian
Rotgerber, der	tanner	Vorsänger(in), der (die)	choir leader, precentor, officiating minister
Schäfer, der	shepherd		
Schiffer, der	sailor		
Schmid/Schmied, der	blacksmith	Wagenmeister, der	wagonmaster
Schneider, der	tailor	Wagner, der	cartwright
Schuhflicker, der	cobbler	Wassermüller, der	watermill operator
Schuhmacher, der	shoemaker	Weber, der	weaver
Schulhalter, der	teacher	Weingärtner, der	vine-dresser
Schullehrer, der	male teacher	Weinschenker, der	waiter
Schullehrerin, die	female teacher	Winzer, der	vine-dresser
Schulmeister, der	schoolmaster (teacher)	Wirt, der	innkeeper
		Zeugkrämer, der	cloth merchant
Schulze, der	village mayor	Zeugmacher, der	fabric maker
Schuster, der	cobbler, shoe repairman	Ziegelbrenner, der	brickmaker
		Zimmermann, der	carpenter
Seifensieder, der	soapmaker	Zwirnmacher, der	thread or twine maker
Seidenkrämer, der	silk merchant		
Seiler, der	rope maker		

TIME

German	English	German	English
Abend, der	evening	tags	during the day
abends	p.m.	Uhr, die	hour
ejusdem anni (ej:a.) (Latin)	of the same year	Vormittag, der	forenoon
		vormittags	in the forenoon
ejusdem mensis (ej:m.) (Latin)	of the same month	weniger	less
		Woche, die	week
früh	early (a.m.)		
Jahr, das	year	7ber, 7bris	September
Jahrhundert, das	century	8ber, 8bris	October
Jahrzehnt, das	decade	9ber, 9bris	November
Mittag, der	noon	10ber, 10bris	December
mittags	at noon		
Monat, der	month	halb sechs	5:30 (half of six)
morgen	tomorrow	viertel vor sechs	5:45 (quarter to six)
Morgen, der	morning, tomorrow		
morgens	in the morning (a.m.)	viertel nach sechs	6:15 (quarter past six)
Nachmittag, der	afternoon	drei viertel sechs	5:45 (three quarters of six)
nachmittags	in the afternoon		
Nacht, die	night		
nachts	at night		
spät	late (p.m.)		
Stunde, die	hour		
Tag, der	day		

NUMBERS

German	Number	German	Number
eins, erste	1, first	zwölf, zwölfte	12, twelfth
zwei, zweite	2, second	dreizehn, dreizehnte	13, thirteenth
drei, dritte	3, third	vierzehn, vierzehnte	14, fourteenth
vier, vierte	4, fourth	fünfzehn, fünfzehnte	15, fifteenth
fünf, fünfte	5, fifth	sechzehn, sechzehnte	16, sixteenth
sechs, sechste	6, sixth	siebzehn, siebzehnte	17, seventeenth
sieben, sieb(en)te	7, seventh	achtzehn, achtzehnte	18, eighteenth
acht, achte	8, eighth	neunzehn, neunzehnte	19, nineteenth
neun, neunte	9, ninth	zwanzig, zwanzigste	20, twentieth
zehn, zehnte	10, tenth	ein und zwanzig,	21, twenty-one,
elf, elfte	11, eleventh	ein und zwanzigste	twenty-first

ILLNESSES, DISEASE, CAUSES OF DEATH

German	English	German	English
Abzehrung, die	consumption, emaciation	Krupp, der	croup
Alterentkräftung, die	debility of old age	Lungenentzündung, die	pneumonia
Altersschwäche, die	debility of old age	Mandelbräune, die	tonsillitis
Anfall, der	stroke	Mandelentzündung, die	tonsillitis
Angina, die	angina		
Auszehrung, die	consumption	Masern, die (plural)	measles
Blattern, die	smallpox	Mumps, der	mumps
Blutvergiftung, die	blood poisoning, toxemia	Pest, die	plague
		Pocken, die (plural)	smallpox
Bräune, die	angina	Rachenbräune, die	diphtheria
Cholera, die	cholera	rote Ruhr, die	dysentery
Diarrhöe, die	diarrhoea	Röteln, die (plural)	German measles
Diphtherie, die	diphtheria	Ruhr, die	dysentery
Durchfall, der	diarrhoea	ruhrartig	dysenteric
Ertränkung, die	drowning	ruhrkrank	suffering from dysentery
Fieber, das	fever		
Geschwulst, die	swelling, tumor	Scharlach, der	scarlet fever
Gift, das	poison	Scharlachfieber, das	scarlet fever
Halsentzündung, die	throat inflammation	Schlag(anfall), der	stroke
häutige Bräune, die	croup	Schwäche, die	debility, infirmity
Herzschlag, der	heart attack	Schwindsucht, die	consumption
Keuchhusten, der	whooping cough	Selbstmord, der	suicide
im Kinderbett gestorben	died while giving birth	Sumpfieber, das	swamp fever
		Tuberkulose, die	tuberculosis
Kindbettfieber, das	puerperal fever	Typhus, der	typhus
Kinderlähmung, die	infantile paralysis	unbekannt	unknown
Krampf, der	cramps, convulsions	Unfall, der	accident
in Krämpfen bewusstlos	convulsions while unconscious	Unterleibstyphus, der	typhoid fever
		Vergiftung, die	poisoning
krank	sick, ill	Wassersucht, die	dropsy
Krankheit, die	illness	weisse Ruhr, die	diarrhoea
Krebs, der	cancer	Ziegenpeter, der	mumps
Krebsgeschwür, das	cancer	Zuckung, die	cramps, convulsions

Ernest Thode's *German-English Genealogical Dictionary* is by far the most comprehensive book of its kind. It also includes many abbreviations and Latin terms.

If you cannot find the words you want in Thode or in a good modern German-English dictionary, look for an old one in a university library. A good one is the *Thieme-Preusser Wörterbuch der englischen und deutschen Sprache* [*Thieme-Preusser's Dictionary of the English and German Languages*], one edition of which was published in 1904. For specialized terms, consult the following:

- Larry O. Jensen, "Legal Terms Used in German Court Records," in *German Genealogical Digest*, Vol. V, No. 1 (1989), pp. 7-14.
- Maralyn A. Wellauer, *Tracing Your German Roots*, includes several lists of abbreviations (which may puzzle even Americans with a good knowledge of German), including one relating to maps, one relating to military terms and one that includes bibliographic citations.

RECORDS IN OTHER LANGUAGES

When searching for your German ancestors in Europe, records written in languages other than German may be encountered. This can happen with respect to records in what is now German-speaking Europe, as well as in border areas that may have changed hands and, of course, where there were larger or smaller islands of German settlement.

Latin was frequently used for Catholic Church records in all countries. During the Napoleonic period (1796-1815), records were sometimes kept in French in western Germany. Religious refugees who fled to Germany often kept their records in French or Dutch-Flemish for several generations.

The table at the top of the next page lists the languages that may have been used on documents and records (in addition to German or Latin) in various countries.

The Family History Centers have modest-sized Genealogical Word Lists for many languages, with more expected. Other sources that include genealogical terms in other languages, in addition to English and/or German, are listed at the end of the chapter.

CALENDARS AND DATE PROBLEMS

From the Roman Kalends came our methods of dividing time into hours, days, weeks, months and years. The solar day is based on daily rotation of the earth around the sun, the solar year on the cycle of seasons, the month on the phases of the moon: all natural divisions of time. The hour, week and civil month are conventional divisions.

Several calendars have been used over the centuries but the following two are of greatest importance to genealogists. The civil calendar of all European countries has been based on that of the Romans and the early church calendar. At the time of Julius Caesar, the year was fixed at 365¼ days. It was decreed that every fourth year have 366 days, otherwise 365 days. This calendar year was longer than the solar year by 11 minutes and 14 seconds, or one day in 128 years. By 1580 there were ten days too many. To correct this, a new calendar was proposed. The Gregorian calendar, named after Pope Gregory XIII, directed ten days to be excluded from the Julian calendar, retaining each fourth year as a leap year. Century years were also to be leap years only when divisible by 400, e.g., 2000 will be a leap year, but 1700, 1800 and 1900 were not. Accumulation of extra days was greatly reduced with this method. The Gregorian calendar is regulated partly by the solar and partly by the lunar cycles. It determines the dates of Easter and other church feast days.

The old Julian calendar was abolished in most Catholic countries of Europe in March 1582, with the new Gregorian calendar being adopted in 1582-85. The change was made in most European Protestant states in 1699-1701. Most German states fit the above pattern, each according to its religion. Prussia adopted the new calendar in 1612, Alsace and several small states in the 1600s, Lorraine in 1760, a few Swiss cantons between 1597 and 1812, and the Russian Empire/Soviet Union in 1918-20.

Table 15: Languages Used on Documents and Records

Country	Region(s)	Possible language(s)
Austria	Burgenland	Hungarian
Belgium	Eupen, Malmedy, Luxembourg province	French
Commonwealth of Independent States (CIS) (former U.S.S.R.)	European part	Russian, Ukrainian, Polish, Romanian, Belorussian
	Asian part	Russian, Kazakh, Uzbek, Tajiki, Turkmen
Czech Republic	Bohemia, Moravia	Czech
Denmark/Germany	Schleswig	Danish
Estonia		Estonian, Russian
France	Alsace, Lorraine	French
Hungary		Hungarian
Italy	South Tyrol	Italian
Latvia		Latvian, Russian
Lithuania	Memel region	Lithuanian
Luxembourg		French
Netherlands		Dutch
Norway		Norwegian
Poland		Polish, Russian
Poland/Germany	Pomerania	Swedish
Romania	Transylvania, Dobruja	Romanian, Hungarian, also Turkish
	Eastern areas	Russian, Ukrainian
Slovak Republic		Slovak, Hungarian
Switzerland	Western cantons	French
	Ticino canton	Italian
Former Yugoslavia		Serbian, Croatian, Slovenian, Hungarian

Table 16: Comparison of Julian and Gregorian Calendars

Julian (Old Style) (Replaced betweeen 1582 and 1920)	Month in Year	Gregorian (New Style)
March (25th, beginning of year)	1st month	January
April	2nd month	February
May	3rd month	March
June	4th month	April
July	5th month	May
August	6th month	June
September	7th month	July
October	8th month	August
November	9th month	September
December	10th month	October
January	11th month	November
February	12th month	December

References to "Old Style" and "New Style" were common during the 1583-1700 transition period to identify the calendar being used. Britain and its American colonies used double dating for the January 1-March 25 period, e.g., 1740/41, until 1782, because March 25 was the first day of the year.

In continental European countries, dates are written as day-month-year, e.g., 10.5.1860 means 10 May 1860.

The bottom table on the previous page shows a comparison of the Julian and Gregorian calendars and how to determine the month if only numbers were used.

Occasionally you may find other month names written in records. The following table shows old German names with variations, and Dutch month names, along with their modern German month name counterparts.

Table 17: Modern German, Old German and Dutch Month Names

Modern German Month Names	Old German Month Names	German Name Variations	Dutch Month Names
Januar, Jänner[1]	Hartung	Eismond	Louwmaand
Februar, Feber[1]	Hornung		Sprokkelmaand
März	Lenzing	Lenzmond	Lentemaand
April	Ostermond		Grasmaand
Mai	Wonnemond	Maien	Bloeimannd
Juni	Brachet	Brachmond	Zomermaand
Juli	Heuert	Heumond	Hooimaand
August	Ernting	Erntemond	Oogstmaand
September	Scheiding	Herbstmond	Herfstmaand
Oktober	Gilbhard	Weinmond	Wijnmaand
November	Nebelung, Nebelmond	Wintermond	Slachtmaand
Dezember	Christmond, Heilmond	Julmond	Wintermaand

[1] in Austria

The French Revolutionary calendar was used for civil records in western Germany during Napoleon's occupation of that region. In Ostfriesland, Dutch calendar months were used during this period. The French Revolutionary calendar for 1792-1805 had the following months, with the corresponding day of the Gregorian calendar for the first of each French month (varying slightly from year to year). Each month had 30 days. The additional 5 or 6 days each year were named complementary days and were added between the months of Fructidor and Vendémiaire. For exact dates each year, see Jensen's book.

Table 18: French Revolutionary Calendar

French Month	Gregorian Calendar	French Month	Gregorian Calendar
Vendémiaire	September 22-24	Germinal	March 21-22
Brumaire	October 22-24	Floréal	April 20-21
Frimaire	November 21-23	Prairial	May 20-21
Nivôse	December 21-23	Messidor	June 19-20
Pluviôse	January 20-22	Thermidor	July 19-20
Ventôse	February 19-21	Fructidor	August 18-19

The Christian BC (Before Christ) is known in Jewish circles as BCE (Before Common Era) and AD (Anno Domini) is known as CE (Common Era).

A great deal of valuable Jewish genealogical information is, however, based on the Hebrew calendar. This begins on October 7, 3761 BCE, considered by Jewish tradition to be the day of the Creation. Converting dates to the Gregorian calendar is complicated by the fact that the first month, Nisan, begins in March, but the new Hebrew year begins in September, so that the balance of the year, as counted today, belongs to a different year.

A similar problem exists with respect to the records of early American colonists, which used March 25 as the beginning of the new year until 1752, when England finally adopted the Gregorian calendar. Thus it can be confusing to determine the correct year to which events prior to that date belonged.

But the Hebrew calendar poses additional complications in converting dates to the Gregorian calendar in that the number of days per month follows the lunar month, alternating between 29 and 30 days, with 7 leap years during every 19-year cycle.

The most detailed information about converting a Hebrew date to the corresponding date in the Gregorian calendar can be found in Robert Schram, *Kalendariographische und chronologische Tafeln* [*Calendar and Chronological Timetables*] (Leipzig, 1908).

BIBLIOGRAPHY (See ANNOTATED BIBLIOGRAPHY for full citations if not shown)

Edna M. Bentz. *If I Can, You Can Decipher Germanic Records*.

Inger M. Bukke, Peter K. Kristensen and Finn A. Thomsen. *The Comprehensive Feast Day Calendar*. Bountiful, UT: Thomsen's Genealogical Center. 1983. 119 pp.
> Lists both fixed and movable feast days for both the Julian and the Gregorian calendar (1437-1837), as well as dates of calendar change in various countries, principalities and provinces. Also shows the 1792-1805 French revolutionary calendar.

The Classic Latin Dictionary: Latin-English, English-Latin. Chicago: Follett Publishing Co. 1938. 927 pp.

Reuben Epp. *The Story of Low German & Plautdietsch: Tracing a Language Across the Globe*. Hillsboro, KS: The Reader's Press. 1993. 133 pp.
> If you can trace your ancestors back to the late Middle Ages, the records could be in this dialect, which was a *lingua franca* along the coast from Flanders to Estonia and quite a way inland in northern Germany. Even for several centuries after the German language became standardized, you may still find references to names rendered phonetically according to the Low German pronunciation if your ancestors resided in the north.

Laraine Ferguson. *German Genealogical Digest*. [previously by Larry O. Jensen]

Judith R. Frazin. *A Translation Guide to 19th Century Polish-Language Civil Registration Documents*, 2nd ed. Northbrook, IL: Jewish Genealogical Society of Illinois. 1989. 311 pp,
> Numerous examples of Jewish and non-Jewish documents. Extensive English-Polish and Polish-English vocabulary lists.

Larry O. Jensen. *A Genealogical Handbook of German Research*, Vol I.
> Lists specific dates when various German political entities adopted the Gregorian calendar.

Karl H. Lampe, ed. *Latein II für den Sippenforscher*, 2nd ed. [*Latin II for Genealogists*].
> Latin to German (mostly names and occupations).

Frank Parise, ed. *The Book of Calendars*. New York: Facts on File. 1982. 350 pp.

Wolfgang Ribbe and Eckart Henning. *Taschenbuch für Familiengeschichtsforschung* [*Handbook for Family History Research*], 11th ed.
> See its section entitled "Zeitrechnung (Chronologie)" for computing dates.

Jonathan D. Shea. *Russian Language Documents from Russian Poland: A Translation Manual for Genealogists*. Orem, UT: Genun Publishers. 1989. 73 pp.
> All public records, including parish registers, had to be in Russian after about 1868. Many illustrations of documents, with short English-Russian glossary. Addresses of many Catholic and state archives.

Jonathan D. Shea and William F. Hoffman. *Following the Paper Trail: A Multilingual Translation Guide*. New Milford, CT: Language & Lineage Press. 1991. 240 pp. Hardcover reprint: Teaneck, NJ. Avotaynu. 1994. 256 pp.

>Provides genealogical terms, sample documents, written and cursive script, and diacritical marks in German, Swedish, French, Italian, Latin, Portuguese, Romanian, Spanish, Czech, Polish, Russian, Hungarian and Lithuanian.

Kenneth Smith. *German Church Books: Beyond the Basics*.

Jared H. Suess, *Central European Genealogical Terminology: German, French, Hungarian, Latin, Italian*.

Jared H. Suess, *Handy Guide to Swiss Genealogical Records: German and Swiss-German, French, Italian, Latin*.

Thieme-Preusser *Wörterbuch der englischen und deutschen Sprache* [*Thieme-Preusser's Dictionary of the English and German Languages*]. 1904.

Ernest Thode. *German-English Genealogical Dictionary*.

Fritz Verdenhalven, *Familienkundliches Wörterbuch*. [*Genealogical Dictionary*]. Neustadt an der Aisch: Verlag Degener. 1969. 137 pp.

>Latin and German, including abbreviations and archaic terms.

Maralyn A. Wellauer. *Tracing Your German Roots*.

Chapter XXII

ANNOTATED BIBLIOGRAPHY

Items shown here are included because of their broad applicability to German genealogical research. Gazetteers are listed in Chapter VIII, except for books that have a substantial amount of other information. References at the end of various chapters include books more specialized or less directly related to genealogy, as well as those that deal with non-European immigrant countries outside North America; many of those are not repeated here. Complete addresses of publishers are given in Chapter XXIII. Some of these books have been published in more than one country. Most of the following books are located in the Germanic Genealogy Society collection in the Buenger Memorial Library, Concordia College, Hamline Avenue & Marshall Street, St. Paul, MN 55104.

BOOKS

James Paul Allen and Eugene James Turner. *We the People: An Atlas of America's Ethnic Diversity*. New York: Macmillan Publishing Co. 1988. 315 pp., maps, indexes, 11-pg. bibl.
> Huge atlas. Could be considered geographic counterpart to the history in the Harvard Encyclopedia of America's Ethnic Groups.

A. Angermann. *Die Posener Kirche des Posener Landes seit 1772* [*The Posen Churches in the Area of Posen Since 1772*].

Karl J. R. Arndt and May E. Olson. *German-American Newspapers and Periodicals, 1732-1955*. Heidelberg, Germany: Quelle & Mayer. 1955. Revised and expanded 1961. Reprinted, New York: Johnson Reprint Corp. 1965.
> German-American newspapers are listed by state and county. Shows where existing copies may be found.

Ayer Directory of Publications. Philadelphia: Ayer Press. Published annually from 1869 until the 1980s. ca. 1,200 pp. (varies by year). Replaced by *IMS Directory of Publications: The Professionals's Reference of Print Media Published in the United States, Canada and Puerto Rico*. (See following.)
> Directory of print media (newspapers) published in the U.S. and Canada. Gives name of newspaper, place of publication and other information. Includes atlas of U.S. and Canada.

Fredrick H. Barth and Kenneth F. Thomsen, comps. *The Beginner's Guide to German Genealogical Research*. Bountiful, UT: Thomsen's Genealogical Center. 1988. 34 pp.
> Good short, simple starter for genealogical newcomers.

Angus Baxter. *In Search of Your European Roots: A Complete Guide to Tracing Your Ancestors in Every Country in Europe*, 2nd ed. Baltimore, MD: Genealogical Publishing Co., Inc. 1994. 304 pp.
> Specifies the kinds of records available in every European country, which is useful because ethnic Germans lived throughout almost all of Europe.

Angus Baxter. *In Search of Your German Roots: A Complete Guide to Tracing Your Ancestors in the Germanic Areas of Europe*, 3rd ed. Baltimore, MD: Genealogical Publishing Co., Inc. 1994. 114 pp. Map.
> Expansion of material on Germany in the author's book on European roots, but with added material on Germans who lived outside Germany.

Angus Baxter. *In Search of Your Roots: A Guide for Canadians Seeking Their Ancestors*, 2nd ed. Toronto, Canada: Macmillan of Canada. 1994. 368 pp.
> An overview of researching the Canadian records for your emigrant ancestor from other parts of the world. Includes sections on European countries as well as other major countries of the world.

Elizabeth Petty Bentley. *The Genealogist's Address Book*, 3rd ed. Baltimore: Genealogical Publishing Co. 1995. 653 pp.

> Sections on "Ethnic and Religious Organizations and Resource Centers" and numerous other valuable resources. Well-indexed. Has addresses of U.S. national and state archives.

Edna M. Bentz. *If I Can, You Can Decipher Germanic Records*. San Diego, CA: Self-published. 1982. Revised and corrected, 1987. 85 pp.

> A handbook of Germanic script, including English, German, Latin and Danish terminologies. Lists many feast days.

Gottlieb Beratz. *The Germans on the Lower Volga: Their Origin and Early Development*. Lincoln, NE: American Historical Society of Germans from Russia. 1991. 370 pp.

> History of the Volga Germans, but notes that settlers included French, Dutch, Swedes, Poles, Italians and South Slavic families.

Peter Brommer, Karl Heinz Debus and Hans-Walter Herrmann, comps. *Inventar der Quellen zur Geschichte der Auswanderungen in den staatlichen Archiven von Rheinland-Pfalz und dem Saarland* [*Inventory of Sources for the History of Emigration in the State Archives of Rhineland-Palatinate and the Saarland*]. Koblenz: Landesarchivverwaltung. 1976. 879 pp.

> Very detailed account of archival files, some even referring to a specific individual.

Inger M. Bukke, Peter K. Kristensen, and Finn A. Thomsen. *The Comprehensive Feast Day Calendar*. Bountiful, UT: Thomsen's Genealogical Center. 1983. 119 pp.

> Lists both fixed and movable feast days for both the Julian and the Gregorian calendar (1437-1837), as well as dates of calendar change in various countries, principalities and provinces. Also shows the 1792-1805 French revolutionary calendar.

Annette Kunselman Burgert. *18th Century Emigrants from German-Speaking Lands to North America*. Camden, ME: Picton Press.

> Vol. I: *The Northern Kraichgau* [area south of Heidelberg]. 1983. 485 pp.
> Vol. II: *The Western Palatinate*. 1985. 421 pp.
> Vol. III: *The Northern Alsace*. 1992. 714 pp.
> One of the classics on Pennsylvania German research by a leading expert on colonial-era immigration. Originally published by the Pennsylvania German Society in its Proceedings.

Annette Kunselman Burgert and Henry Z. Jones, Jr. *Westerwald to America: Some 18th Century German Immigrants*. Camden, ME: Picton Press. 1989. 284 pp.

> The most extensive work on immigrants from the area north of the Lahn River on both sides of the current boundary between western Hesse and northeastern Rhineland-Palatinate.

Bruce E. Burgoyne. *Waldeck (Germany) Soldiers of the American Revolutionary War*. Bowie, MD: Heritage Books. 1991. 182 pp.

> Contains brief biographies of every man who served in the 3rd British Waldeck Regiment, including date and place of birth, and who remained in America.

Eugene Camann. *Uprooted from Prussia—Transplanted in America*. Niagara Falls, NY: Self-published. 1992. 140 pp.

> Lists names and details about 800 "Old Lutherans" from the Ueckermark who settled in Wheatfield, New York, in 1843.

Johni Cerny. *A Guide to German Parish Registers in the Family History Library of the Church of Jesus Christ of Latter-day Saints*, Vol. I: Bavaria, Württemberg and Baden. Baltimore: Clearfield Co. 1988. 430 pp.

> Information on about 33,000 microfilmed parish registers.

Sanford Hoadley Cobb. *The Story of the Palatines: An Episode in Colonial History*. New York & London: G. P. Putnam's Sons. 1897. 319 pp. maps. Reprinted Bowie, MD: Heritage Books. 1988. 319 pp. maps.

> Covers Palatine communities along the Rhine River and migration in the early 1700s to the Carolinas, Virginia, New Jersey, Pennsylvania, and New York, with emphasis on New York.

Fay and Douglas Dearden. *The German Researcher: How to Get the Most Out of an LDS Family History Center*. 4th edition. Scottsdale, AZ (previously Minneapolis, MN): Family Tree Press. 1990. 72 pp. May be ordered from the authors at 8968 E. Gail Rd., Scottsdale, AZ 85260-6146.

> The author takes you step-by-step in finding and using the Family History Library's German microfilms. Sections include using the Hamburg passenger lists (with microfilm numbers and illustrations), library catalog, handwriting found in the German records (with illustrations), words and phrases found in German records (typed, in German script, and translation), terms and letter writing, translation of terms and abbreviations found in *Meyers Orts- und Verkehrs-Lexikon* (see Chapter V).

Deutsche Bundespost, Postdienst. *Das Postleitzahlenbuch.* [*The (German) Postal Code Book*] 1993. Distributed by Postamt Marburg, Dienststelle 113-21, Postfach 1100, D-35035 Marburg, Germany. 986 pp.

> Alphabetical postal code book shows codes for each town and for each street address in cities. Versions are also available in numerical postal code order, for post office boxes (no longer always the same as for street addresses), CD-ROM, BTZ, diskettes, and microfiche. Accompanying map of postal code districts (*Übersichtskarte der Postleiteinheiten*) also available.

Kenneth DeWall, comp. *Ost Friesen Roots: Obituaries in the Breda, Iowa, German Newspaper.* Indexed by Dale W. Wilken. Self published: Dale W. Wilken, 2005 Hillview Dr., Marion, IA 52302. 1996. 138 pp.

> Contains obituaries for Iowa, Illinois, Minnesota, and many more.

R. Dienst. *The German States*, Parts I and II. Hoddesdon, Herts, England: Anglo-German Family History Society. 1933. 44 and 48 pp., respectively.

> Has maps showing the approximate pre- and post-Napoleonic boundaries of dozens of states, with historic datelines of approximately one page for each.

June Drenning-Holmquist, ed. *They Chose Minnesota: A Survey of the State's Ethnic Groups.* Includes articles about Germans by Hildegard Binder Johnson, about Swiss by Louis de Gryse, and Jews by Hyman Berman. St. Paul, MN: Minnesota Historical Society Press. 1981. 613 pp.

> Chapters on German, Swiss and Jewish immigration to Minnesota by experts.

Mary Dunn. *Index to Pennsylvania's Colonial Records Series.* Baltimore: Genealogical Publishing Co. 1992, reprinted 1996. 228 pp.

> Consolidated index of 50,000 names appearing in the first 16 volumes of the *Pennsylvania Archives*, known as the *Colonial Records* series.

Thomas Kent Edlund. *Register to the Ahnenstammkartei des deutschen Volkes* [*Lineage Cards of the German People*]. St. Paul, MN: Germanic Genealogy Society. 1995. 133 pp.

> Shows how and where to find ancestral surnames in the collection of 2,700,000 lineage charts at the Deutsche Zentralstelle für Genealogie (German Central Office for Genealogy) in Leipzig, collected from 1922-1991, and now contained on Family History Library microfilms. Organized phonetically by surname, somewhat similar to, but not the same as, the U.S. census Soundex system (details of the system used are given at beginning of the book). Allows you to readily determine which microfilms may contain information about the surnames that interest you.

Thomas Kent Edlund. *The Lutherans of Russia*, Vol. 1: *Parish Index to the Church Books of the Evangelical Lutheran Consistory of St. Petersburg, 1833-1885.* St. Paul, MN: Germanic Genealogy Society. 1995. 370 pp. (ISBN 0-9644-337-1-0)

> This consistory included western Russia, Volhynia and the Black Sea settlements.

Wolfgang Eger, comp. *Verzeichnis der protestantischen Kirchenbücher der Pfalz* [*Inventory of the Protestant Parish Registers of the Palatinate*]. Improved, new version of the 1960 edition. Koblenz: Landesarchivverwaltung Rheinland-Pfalz. 1975. 171 pp.

Wolfgang Eger. *Verzeichnis der Militärkirchenbücher in der Bundesrepublik Deutschland (Stand vom 30. September 1990)* [*Inventory of Military Parish Registers in the Federal Republic of Germany, as of 30 September 1990)*]. Neustadt/Aisch: Verlag Degener & Co, 1993. 445 pp.

> Lists over 4,000 volumes of military parish registers in 152 archives, mostly for Protestants but with a few references to other groups. A large majority are at the Evangelical Central Office or the Prussian State Privy Archives, both in Berlin. Quite a few are in Koblenz and Bielefeld. Largest number of registers for Silesia, East Prussia and the 1870 Franco-German War, with a somewhat lesser number for Posen, Pomerania and Saxony.

Wolfgang Eger. *Verzeichnis der Militärkirchenbücher der Bundesrepublik Deutschland (neue Bundesländer - Römisch-Katholische Kirche)* [*Index of Military Parish Registers for the Federal Republic of Germany (New Federal States - Roman Catholic Church)*]. Neustadt/Aisch: Verlag Degener & Co. 1996. 218 pp.

> Lists over 1,100 military parish registers and over 1,000 filmed registers for more than 300 military units in 19 Catholic, 27 Protestant and 4 state or other public archives. The vast majority are in the church archives of the Catholic Military Bishop's Office in Bonn or at the German Central Office for Genealogy. The listed books are not limited to Catholic registers or to registers preserved in, or for units stationed in, the new eastern states, so this must be considered a general supplement. Both Eger military register books are indexed, with no apparent duplication, except where duplicate parish registers exist.

Erich Eisenberg, comp. *Kirchenbuchverzeichnis der Evangelischen Kirche von Kurhessen-Waldeck* [*Inventory of Parish Registers of the Evangelical Church of the Electorate of Hesse and Waldeck*]. Kassel: Evangelischer Pressverbund von Kurhessen-Waldeck. 1973. 80 pp.

Irmgard Hein Ellingson. *The Bukovina Germans in Kansas: A 200-Year History of the Lutheran Swabians*. Hays, KS: Fort Hays State University Ethnic Heritage Studies. 1987; reprinted 1993. 107 pp.

> Summarizes the history of German Lutheran settlement in the Bukovina and immigration to Kansas.

Family History Library. *Research Outline: Germany*. Salt Lake City: Family History Library. 1994. 52 pp.

> Very thorough coverage of pre-World War I German Empire, with some information on ethnic Germans elsewhere.

Albert B. Faust and Gaius M. Brumbaugh. *List of Swiss Emigrants in the Eighteenth Century to the American Colonies*. 2 vols. in 1; reprint of 1920-25 work with corrections from the *National Genealogical Society Quarterly* (March 1972). Baltimore: Genealogical Publishing Co. 1991. 429 pp. 201-page index.

> Indexed, authoritative work on immigrants from the canton of Zürich (1734-1744) in Vol. I, and of Berne (1706-1795) and Basel (1734-1794) in Vol. II.

P. William Filby and Mary K. Meyer, eds. *Passenger and Immigration Lists Bibliography, 1538-1900*. Detroit, MI: Gale Research Co. 1981. 5 volumes, ongoing.

> A guide to published arrival records of about 500,000 passengers who came to the United States and Canada in the 17th, 18th and 19th centuries.

Eckhart G. Franz, compiler. *Hessische Truppen im amerikanischen Unabhängigkeitskrieg (HETRINA).* [*Hessian Troops in the American Revolution (HETRINA project)*] Marburg, Germany: Archivshule. 1972. 4 vols. (Vol 4: 160 pp.)

> This series gives the full names, birth years, towns of origin, military units and other facts about 15,000 Hessian troops who fought in the American Revolutionary War 1776-1784. Volume 1 has a surname index of four Grenadier battalions. Most of these came from Hessen-Cassel but some were from the city of Frankfurt and other places to the south.

Dr. Heinz F. Friederichs. *How to Find My German Ancestors and Relatives*. (Send 5 International Reply Coupons to: Verlag Degener & Co., Postfach 1360, D-91403 Neustadt/ Aisch, Germany.) 2nd ed. 1985. 16 pp.

> Brief overview of German research opportunities and problems by a leading German genealogical authority.

Jürg Füchtner, et al. *Die Zivilstandsregister im Nordrhein-Westfälischen Personenstands-archiv: Eine Übersicht.* [*The Civil Registers in the Northrhine-Westphalian Civil Registration Archives: An Overview*]. Brühl, Germany: Nordrhein-Westphälisches Personenstandsarchiv. 1995. np.

> This archive has civil registers dating back to the Napoleonic period, but also has some parish registers not dealt with in this book.

Adam Giesinger. *From Catherine to Khrushchev: The Story of Russia's Germans*. Battleford, Saskatchewan, Canada: Marian Press. 1974. 443 pp. Reprinted 1993 by the American Historical Society of Germans from Russia.

> The most authoritative and comprehensive account of the German settlements in Russia.

Hugh F. Gingerich and Rachel W. Kreider. *Amish and Amish Mennonite Genealogies*. Gordonville, PA: Pequea Publishers. 1986. 858 pp.

> Comprehensive encyclopedia of Amish families up to 1850, including all known early settlements.

Montague S. Giuseppi. *Naturalization of Foreign Protestants in the American and West Indies Colonies*. Published by Huguenot Society of London, 1921; reprinted Baltimore: Genealogical Publishing Co., 1979. 196 pp.

> Records of 6,500 naturalizations (mostly of Germans), 1740-1722. Indexed.

Ira A. Glazier and P. William Filby. *Germans to America: Lists of Passengers Arriving at United States Ports*. Wilmington, DE: Scholarly Resources, Inc. 54 vol. covering January 1850 to mid-1887 published to date. Series is to continue through 1893.

> Information taken from the original ship manifests kept at Temple-Balch Institute for Immigration Research. Gives name, age, sex, occupation, date of arrival, and many times the former residence of each passenger. 1850-55 lists all passengers, but only on ships where at least 80% of the passengers were "German." 1856 and on includes all ships, but only passengers who called themselves Germans, including some from Switzerland, Luxembourg, and France. Includes some ships from Latin America and the Caribbean.

Johann Glenzdorf. *Glenzdorfs Internationales Genealogen-Lexikon.* [*Glenzdorf's International Directory of Genealogists*] Germany: Wilhelm Rost Verlag, D-31848 Bad Münder/ Deister. Vol. 1 - 1977, Vol. 2 - 1979, Vol. 3 - 1984. In German.

> Each volume contains an alphabetical list of genealogists submitting German genealogical information together with an individual biography, an index including surnames being researched and submitters, and an index to places the surnames are from. Volume 2 also includes genealogists who will do research by region. Volume 3 contains an alphabetical list of genealogists in all three volumes.

Nicholas Gonner. *Luxembourgers in the New World*. Edited and translated into English by Jean Ensch, Jean-Claude Muller and Robert E. Owen. Esch-sur-Alzette, Luxembourg: Editions-Reliures Schortgen. 1889. 2 Vols. New edition, 1987.

> Volume I contains Luxembourger emigration information between 1840-1890, Luxembourger settlements in the U.S. and aspects of the Luxembourger presence in the United States.
> Volume II contains a personal and place-name index to the *Luxemburger Gazette* newspapers (1871-1918). Volume II also contains a map of Luxembourg with superimposed grid, an alphabetical list of all place names, their postal codes and location on the map.

Felix Gundacker. "Research in the Former Austro-Hungarian Empire." Five-part series of articles in *Heritage Quest*, beginning in May/June 1996.

> Up-to-date information by the director of the Institut für historische Familienforschung Genealogie Gesellschaft in Vienna. Provides historical background and describes what kinds of records for what general periods are available where, and why it is difficult to get information from archives and parish offices. Includes information about successor states to the Hapsburg Empire.

Charles M. Hall. *The Atlantic Bridge to Germany*. 9 volumes. Vol. 1-7: Logan, UT: Everton Publishers, Inc. 1978-1989. Vol. 8-9: Monda Genealoga Ligo. 1993-1995.

> Each volume concentrates on a particular area or areas in Germany. Lists resources unique to the area, detailed maps showing small communities not included on other maps, and German records available at the Family History Library in Salt Lake City for each town.
>
> Vol. 1 - Baden-Württemberg
> Vol. 2 - Hessen, Rheinland-Pfalz (The Palatinate)
> Vol. 3 - Bavaria
> Vol. 4 - Alsace-Lorraine, Saarland and Switzerland
> Vol. 5 - Bremen, Hamburg and Schleswig-Holstein
> Vol. 6 - Mecklenburg (consisting of former East German districts of
>   Neubrandenburg, Rostock and Schwerin)
> Vol. 7 - Nordrhein-Westfalen (includes the Ruhr valley, Minden, Bielefeld,
>   Lippe-Detmold, Cologne and Bonn)
> Vol. 8 - Prussia (Brandenburg, East Prussia, West Prussia, Pomerania, Posen)
> Vol. 9 - Saxony

Charles R. Haller. *Across the Atlantic and Beyond: The Migration of German and Swiss Immigrants to America*. Bowie, MD: Heritage Books. 1993. 324 pp.

> Deals with changes of personal and place names, reasons for emigration, number and period (mostly 1727-1775) of colonial immigrants, the postwar whereabouts of Revolutionary War German conscripts, the rise of Protestantism, and quadripartite dialectic divisions, with maps of the Rhine valley, from where most early immigrants came.

Handy Guide to Italian Genealogical Research. Logan, UT: Everton Publishers. 1978. 30 pp

> Could be helpful for Waldensians and Germans along Italy's northern border area.

Werner Hegewaldt and Peter P. Rohrlach. *Berliner Adressbücher und Adressenverzeichnis 1704-1945*. [*Berlin City Directories and Address Lists, 1704-1945*]. Berlin: H. Scherer. 1990. 200 pp.

> An annotated bibliography for the whole of Berlin.

Otto Heike. *150 Jahren Schwabensiedlungen in Polen, 1795-1945*. [*150 Years of Swabian settlements in Poland, 1795-1945*]. 2nd. ed. Leverkusen, Germany: O. Heike. 1981. 364 pp.

> Lists the names of many settlers who came to Poland around 1800 and the community in Württemberg from which they came. Many of these Swabians migrated to Bessarabia in 1814 and the next few years. Others moved to Volhynia later, while some remained in Central Poland.

Franz Heinzmann. *Bibliographie der Ortssippenbücher in Deutschland*. [*Bibliography of Village Lineage Books in Germany*]. Dusseldorf: F. Heinzmann. 1991. 66 pp.

> Lists 6,486 books, including quite a few for villages outside Germany.

Eckart Henning and Christel Wegeleben. *Kirchenbücher: Bibliographie gedruckter Tauf-, Trau- und Totenregister sowie Bestandsverzeichnisse im deutschen Sprachgebiet*. [*Church Books: Bibliography of Published Baptismal, Marriage and Death Registers, as well as Inventories in German-Speaking Areas*]. Neustadt/Aisch: Verlag Degener & Co. 1991. 447 pp. and annotation.

Edward W. Hocker. *Genealogical Data Relating to the German Settlers of Pennsylvania and Adjacent Territory: From Advertisements in Newspapers Published in Philadelphia and Germantown, 1743-1800*. Baltimore: Genealogical Publishing Co. 1989. 242 pp.

Richard Hordern, ed./tr. *St. John's Evangelical Lutheran Church, 1890-1990*. Balgonie, SK: St. John's Lutheran Church, c/o Barbara Siebert. 1990. 138 pp.

> Translates the the parish registers of 1890-1927, as well as records of the work of early pastors in the districts of Assiniboia and Saskatchewan (Northwest Territories), later the province of Saskatchewan.

Immigrant Genealogical Society. *1993 Updated Addresses to German Repositories*. Burbank, CA: Immigrant Genealogical Society. 1994. 44 pp.

> Lists 1,224 German archives and 333 genealogical and historical societies, alphabetized by locality.

IMS Directory of Publications: The Professionals's Reference of Print Media Published in the United States, Canada and Puerto Rico. Fort Washington, PA: IMS Press. ca. 1,500 pp. (varies by year).

> Replacement for *Ayer Directory of Publications*. (See previous.)

Larry O. Jensen. *A Genealogical Handbook of German Research*. Pleasant Grove, UT: Jensen Publications. Vol. I: 1980 (209 pp.), Vol. II: 1983 (210 pp.), Vol. III: 1986 (np.).

> Guide to locating origins of German ancestors, maps and vital records. Includes information on naming practices of the Germans, Jewish genealogy, terminology and handwriting analysis of old records. Vol. 3 consists of maps and short histories for each area within the German Empire. Contains a listing of gazetteers for areas in Germany that were not Prussian provinces.

Arta F. Johnson, ed. *Bibliography and Source Materials for German-American Research*, Vol. 1. Columbus, OH: privately printed. 1982. 112 pp. Updated 1984.

> Comprehensive list of German genealogical books, materials and sources printed in the United States.

Arta F. Johnson. *A Guide to the Spelling and Pronunciation of German Names*. Columbus, OH: privately printed. 1981.

> Helps determine possible spelling variations of a German name.

Keith A. Johnson and Malcolm R. Sainty, eds. *Genealogical Research Directory (GRD)*. Published annually since 1984. North Sydney, Australia: Keith Johnson. 1996 edition has 1,248 pp.

> Lists genealogists researching particular German surnames on a worldwide basis. *GRD* for 1990-1996 is now available on CD-ROM. Addresses listed in Chapter XXIII.

Henry Z. Jones, Jr. *The Palatine Families of New York*. Camden, ME: Picton Press. 2 vols. 1985. 1,298 pp.

> Lists original Palatine families who came to New York state about 1710.

Henry Z. Jones, Jr. *More Palatine Families: Some Immigrants to the Middle Colonies, 1777-1776*. Universal City, CA: privately published. 1991. 592 pp.

> Majority of names listed are those who went to New Jersey. Every-name index.

Marion J. Kaminkow, ed. *Genealogies in the Library of Congress*. Magna Carta Book Co. 1987. 861 pp. Includes indexes.

> Series lists tens of thousands of genealogies in the Library of Congress through 1985. Continued by: Library of Congress, *Genealogies Cataloged by the Library of Congress*, since 1986.

Thomas Jay Kemp. *International Records Handbook*. 3rd ed. Baltimore: Genealogical Publishing Co. 1994. 417 pp.

> Consists chiefly of forms that can be photocopied for use in applying for information from various agencies.

Walter A. Knittle. *Early Eighteenth Century Palatine Emigration*. 1937. Reprinted Baltimore: Genealogical Publishing Co. 1989. 320 pp. Reissued 1997.

> Indexed list of about 12,000 Palatine immigrants to Pennsylvania, North Carolina and New York.

Københavnske Kirkebøger II. *Met et tillaeg omfattende diverse modtagne kirkebøger herunder kirkebøger fra Grønland og Dansk-Vestindien.* Forløbige arkivregistraturer udgived af Landesarckivet for Sjoelland m.m. Copenhagen. 1974.

Marek Konopka, ed. *Archiwa w Polsce: Informator Adresowy.* [*Archives in Poland: Address Guide*]. Warsaw: Naczelna Dyrekcja Archiwów Pañstwowych. 1996. 186 pp.

> Includes addresses of all central, provincial, branch, religious (also Lutheran and Reformed) and specialized archives in Poland, as well as key libraries, museums and other institutions, with very helpful place name and institutional indexes. The list of pertinent directories, inventories and other publications about the holdings of specific archives are very useful; the number of such publications is increasing rapidly, although they are not yet available for all archives. Many archives in foreign countries (France, Canada, Switzerland, Great Britain, Italy, Austria, Belarus, the Czech Republic, Estonia, Lithuania, Latvia, Germany, Russia, Slovakia, the United States, Sweden, Ukraine and Hungary) which could be helpful for Polish research are also listed. Phone numbers are given for all entries. The hours when each archive or other institution in Poland is open are also recorded. However, there seems to be no reference to when each of these closes for the vacation period. It is common practice in Europe to close for up to one month in summer — most often, but not always, in August.

Klaus-Dieter Kreplin. *Veröffentlichungen aus dem Genealogischen Archiv Kreplin.* [*Publications of the Kreplin Genealogical Archive*]. Vol. 1: *Bestandsverzeichnis Pommerscher Kirchenbücher in Zivilstandsregister (Pommern in den Grenzen von 1900).* [*Inventory of Pomeranian Parish Registers in Civil Registers (Pomerania within the borders of 1900)*]. Dortmund: Verein zur Förderung EDV-gestützter familienkundlicher Forschungen, Studienstelle Ostdeutsche Genealogie der Forschungsstelle Ostmitteleuropa an der Universität Dortmund. 1996.

Margrit B. Krewson. *The German-Speaking Countries of Europe: A Selective Bibliography*, 2nd ed. Washington, DC: Library of Congress. 1989. 318 pp.

> A highly diverse sampling of books in the Library of Congress, including many dealing with genealogy and migration history. For sale by Supt. of Docs., U.S. Govt. Printing Office.

Margrit B. Krewson. *Hidden Research Resources in the German Collections of the Library of Congress*. Washington, DC: Library of Congress. 1992. 170 pp.

> A selective bibliography of reference works in the German collection at the Library of Congress. For sale by Supt. of Docs., U.S. Govt. Printing Office.

Anton Krudewig, comp. *Neues Verzeichnis der Kirchenbücher der ehemaligen Rheinprovinz.* [*New Inventory of the Parish Registers of the Former Rhine Province*]. Köln: Westdeutsche Gesellschaft für Familienkunde. 1977. 84 pp. & annotation.

Arthur Kurzweil. *From Generation to Generation.* New York: Morrow. 1980. 353 pp. Revised and updated: Harper Collins. 1994. 388 pp.

Landeskirchlichesarchiv. *Schnellüberblick Kirchenbuchbestand Greifswald: Pommersche Evangelische Kirche.* [*Quick Overview of the Church Book Holdings of the Pomeranian Evangelical Church*]. 1995. 20 pp.

> Lists which Pomeranian church books are known to have been preserved, for what years and where they are now located. The parish registers for eastern Pomerania are in widely scattered places, but the largest number appear to be in Greifswald.

Heinz Lehmann. *The German Canadians, 1750-1937: Immigration, Settlement and Culture.* Translated by Gerhard P. Bassler. St. John's, Newfoundland: Jesperson Press. 1986. 541 pp.

> Incredibly detailed account of all German settlements in Canada, including place of emigration; maps; has few names of individuals.

Kate Everest Levi. *Geographical Origin of German Immigration to Wisconsin.* Originally published in Collections of the State Historical Society of Wisconsin. 1898. Reprinted Minneapolis: Edward R. Brandt. 1992. 28 pp.

> Detailed account of areas of origin of Germans who settled in various counties of Wisconsin.

Library of Congress. *Genealogies Cataloged by the Library of Congress Since 1986.* Washington, DC: Cataloging Distribution Service, Library of Congress. 1992. 1,349 pp.

> With a list of established forms of family names and a list of genealogies converted to microform since 1983. Continuation of series by Marion J. Kaminkow, which ended in 1985.

Glen E. Lich. *The German Texans.* San Antonio: University of Texas Institute of Texan Cultures at San Antonio. 1981. 240 pp.

Marilyn Lind. *Researching and Finding Your German Heritage.* Cloquet, MN: The Linden Tree. 1984. 132 pp. Updated 1988.

> A major strength of this book is its brief historical description of a large number of German states and provinces, with small maps showing their locations.

Erich Dieter Linder and Günter Olzog. *Die deutschen Landkreise: Wappen, Geschichte, Struktur.* [*The German Counties: Their Coats-of-Arms, History and Structure*] Munich: Günter Olzog Verlag. 1986. 280 pp

> Description of all 237 West German rural counties, including municipalities within each, state maps (showing intermediate district and county boundaries), historical development, tourist attractions and coats-of-arms. Excludes larger cities, each of which forms its own urban county (depicted on maps), and areas under Communist rule in 1986.

Stanislaw Litak. *The Latin Church in the Polish Commonwealth in 1772: A Map and Index of Localities.* Chicago: Polish Genealogical Society of America. 1990. 42 pp. + 24 maps.

> Useful for research on German Catholics in West Prussia, Posen and part of East Prussia.

Brent Allen Mai, "Researchers' Gold Mine: The 1798 Census of German Colonies on the Volga and Its Importance to Agronomists, Anthropologists, Demographers, Economists, Genealogists, Geographers, Religious Historians, and Sociologists, Among Others," in *Journal of the American Historical Society of Germans from Russia.* Winter 1996.

> Notes that the first Prussian census was conducted in 1719 and that the major Russian revisions in the Volga area were compiled in 1775, 1798, 1811, 1834, 1850 and 1857. Mentions the detailed genealogical information available in the 1798 revision, which has been translated by the American Historical Society of Germans from Russia. The 1775 revision is available for only a few villages.

Emil and Clothilde Meier, Fred D. Hänni, and Stephan and Claudia Mohr, eds. for the Schweizerische Gesellschaft für Familienforschung. *Swiss Surnames: A Complete Register, Commonly Known as Familienbuch der Schweiz.* 3 vols. Camden, ME: Picton Press. 1995. 2,084 pp. German-language Swiss editions: 1940, 1969-71. 1989.

> Swiss editions have a foreword, preface, instructions and index of abbreviations in the four official Swiss languages, as well as English.

Menschen im Exil: Eine Dokumentation der sudetendeutschen sozialdemokratischen Emigration von 1938 bis 1948. [*People in Exile: A Documentation of the Sudeten German Social Democratic Emigration from 1938-1948*]. Stuttgart: Seliger-Archiv e.V. 1974.

Brenda Dougall Merriman. *Genealogy in Ontario, Searching the Records.* Toronto, Ontario: Ontario Genealogical Society. 1988. 168 pp.

Ken Meter and Robert Paulson. *The Böhmisch (German-Bohemians) in America.* Minneapolis: Crossroads Resource Center, with the German-Bohemian Heritage Society, New Ulm. 1993. 32 pp.

> Packed with surnames of German immigrants from southwestern Bohemia to Wisconsin, Minnesota and Michigan's Upper Peninsula.

Mary K. Meyer, ed. *Meyer's Directory of Genealogical Societies in the U.S.A. and Canada,* 11th ed. Mt. Airy, MD: Mary Keysor Meyer. 1996. 135 pp.

> Also lists special interest organizations (ethnic, religious, geographic, adoptees).

Michael M. Miller. *Researching Germans from Russia*. Fargo: North Dakota State University, Institute for Regional Studies. 1987. 224 pp.

> Annotated bibliography of the Germans from Russia Heritage Collection at the North Dakota Institute for Regional Studies, North Dakota State University Library (mostly historical) and the library collection of the Germans from Russia Heritage Society in Bismarck, which includes family, local and church histories.

Olga K. Miller. *Migration, Emigration, Immigration: Principally to the United States and in the United States*. Logan, UT: Everton Publishers, Inc. Vol. 1: 1974. 278 pp. Vol. 2: 1981.

> Shows many routes and timetables of our emigrating ancestors. Has a large bibliography.

MINERVA-Handbücher: Archive im deutschsprachigen Raum. [*MINERVA Handbooks: Archives in German-speaking Regions*]. Berlin, Germany: de Gruyter. 2nd edition 1974. 2 volumes. 1418 pp.

> This valuable German work describes each German archive and what historical material may be found there.

Mario von Moos. *Bibliography of Swiss Genealogies*. Camden, ME: Picton Press. 1993. 848 pp.

> Includes registers of towns and names.

John D. Movius, comp. *Resource Guide to East European Genealogy*. Davis, CA: FEEFHS. 1995. Later versions available on the FEEFHS Home Page of Internet's World Wide Web.

> Lists names, addresses and periodicals of member societies of the Federation of East European Family History Societies, including member societies in North America, Europe and Australia. Also lists professional genealogists and translators specializing in Eastern Europe, including Germanic countries.

Paul Anthon Nielsen. "Swiss Genealogical Research: An Introductory Guide." (*Swiss American Historical Society Publications*, No. 5). Virginia Beach, VA: The Donning Co. 1979. 101 pp. Available from Picton Press.

Margaret Krug Palen. *Genealogical Guide to Tracing Ancestors in Germany*. Bowie, MD: Heritage Books. 1995. 159 pp.

> General guide on research in the United States and Germany, including what kinds of records are available in Germany, where to find them and how to access them.

Margaret Krug Palen. *German Settlers of Iowa, Their Descendants, and European Ancestors*. Bowie, MD: Heritage Books. 1994. 361 pp.

> Includes nearly 2,000 surnames. Alphabetical listing of entries, plus index of surnames buried in the text. Traces some families back to the 1600s.

Pennsylvania Archives. Series 1-9. 138 volumes. Phildephia: J. Severns & Co. 1852-56. Harrisburg. 1874-1935.

> An excellent genealogical source for early Pennsylvania and related areas. Has many lists of early Pennsylvania Germans, especially from the 18th century. (See *Genealogical Research in the Published Pennsylvania Archives* by Sally Weikel for a guide to the series.)

Pennsylvania German Church Records: Births, Baptisms, Marriages, Burials, Etc., with an introduction by Don Yoder, 3 vols. Baltimore: Genealogical Publishing Co. 1983. 2,371 pp.

> Some 125,000 persons are listed in the index. Includes all church records ever published in the *Proceedings and Addresses of the Pennsylvania German Society*.

G. Piepmeyer. *Findbuch zum Bestand Evangelisch-lutherischer Kirchenbücher des ehemaligen Herzogtums Braunschweig.* [*Finding Aid to the Evangelical-Lutheran Parish Registers of the Former Duchy of Brunswick*]. Göttingen: Staatsarchiv in Wolfenbüttel. 1978. 116 pp.

> Has a supplement on Lutheran and Reformed registers of the city of Brunswick compiled by Christoph Wilczek.

Karl Pisarczyk. *Slawische Ortsnamen, Personennamen: Entwicklung alter slawischer Ortsnamen zu germanisch-deutschen mit geschichtlichen Streifzügen.* [*Slavic Place and

Personal Names: Development of Old Slavic Places Names into Germanic-German Ones, with Historical Notes]. Uelzen, Germany: Becker-Verlag. 1986.

Brian A. Podoll. *Prussian Netzelanders and Other German Immigrants in Green Lake, Marquette & Waushara Counties, Wisconsin.* Bowie, MD: Heritage Books. 1994. 241 pp.
> Primarily marriage, naturalization and death records of Germans in these counties. Brief history of the Netze River area. Maps of various counties in Posen, Pomerania, West Prussia and the Neumark (Northeast Brandenburg), as well as in Wisconsin (and Minnesota, to which the Netzelanders went).

Erich Quester (comp. for the Arbeitsgemeinschaft ostdeutscher Familienforscher), *Wegweiser für Forschung nach Vorfahren aus den ostdeutschen und sudetendeutschen Gebieten, sowie aus den deutschen Siedlungsräumen in Mittel-, Ost- und Südosteuropa (AGoFF-Wegweiser).* 4th ed. Neustadt/Aisch: Verlag Degener & Co. 1995. 207 pp. 2nd English-language edition, *Genealogical Guide to German Ancestors from East Germany and Eastern Europe*, by the same publisher, scheduled for 1997; 1st English edition was a translation of the 2nd German edition by Joachim O. R. Nuthack and Adalbert Goertz.
> Most comprehensive list of sources of genealogical information for ethnic Germans in Eastern Europe. Gives information about former areas of Germany not in present-day Germany. These areas include East & West Prussia, Pomerania, Brandenburg (East), Silesia, Posen, Poland, Russia, Czechoslovakia, Hungary, Romania, Yugoslavia and Bulgaria. This major work includes maps, addresses of archives, bibliographies, etc. Referred to in this book as the *AGoFF Guide* (English edition) or *AGoFF-Wegweiser* (German edition).

Robert Rabe. *German Professions of the Eighteenth and Nineteenth Centuries.* Bainbridge Island, WA: Robert Rabe. (Order from Professor Robert Rabe, 14466 Sunrise Drive NE, Bainbridge, WA 98110.) 1995. 103 pp.
> Includes history and development of German guilds and discussions of guild life, discussions of common occupational terms, and facts relating to everyday life in the 18th and 19th centuries.

Ratgeber '92: Familienforschung GUS/Baltikum. [*Adviser '92: Family History Research in the CIS and Baltic States*]. Münster, Germany: Zielke-Verlag. 1992.
> Articles deal with new sources of information, including addresses of private researchers, in the former U.S.S.R. A 1993-94 edition with a slightly different title was due to be published in 1994.

Horst A. Reschke. *German Military Records as Genealogical Sources.* Salt Lake City: Author. 1990. 12 pp.
> Not all German military records were destroyed. This is a gold mine of information for those records that have been preserved (basically those of non-Prussian areas).

Horst A. Reschke, "Questions on Germanic Ancestry," regular column in *Heritage Quest.*
> Extremely thorough responses to genealogical queries by a native of Germany who lives in Salt Lake City. Selected queries and responses are published, while others are answered privately.

Wolfgang Ribbe and Eckart Henning. *Taschenbuch für Familiengeschichtsforschung.* [*Handbook for Family History Research*] Neustadt/Aisch, Germany: Verlag Degener & Co. 11th edition. 1995. 640 pp.
> Standard research guidebook for Germans. The six sections include:
> 1) German ancestor and family group sheets
> 2) social, biological and legal aspects of genealogy
> 3) source indexes for German research materials including: church registers, records of religious sects, funeral sermons, civil records, city directories, university student lists, entire village genealogies (200 plus), address books and bibliographies by region
> 4) handwriting, calendars, heraldry, meaning of names, using computers
> 5) genealogical terms, meaning of German first names, occupations, diseases, nobility titles

6) addresses for German city and state archives, libraries, genealogical and historical societies. Also contains information about and addresses for *Heimatortskarteien* (*HOK*), which is a special search service to locate people displaced by World War II. Combined catalogs list over 17 million people.

Shirley J. Riemer. *German Research Companion*. Lorelei Press. 1997. 646 pages. Indexed.
    Has many helpful hints for German genealogists. Covers a wide variety of topics.

La Vern J. Rippley and Robert J. Paulson. *The German-Bohemians: The Quiet Immigrants*. New Ulm, MN: German-Bohemian Society. 1995. 246 pp.
    History of German-Bohemian immigration to southern Minnesota in the 1800s.

Dan Rottenberg. *Finding Our Fathers: A Guidebook to Jewish Genealogy*. New York: Random House. 1977. Reprinted Baltimore, MD: Genealogical Publishing Co. 1986. Reprinted 1995. 400 pp.
    Guide showing how to trace Jewish families back many generations. Includes a guide to over 8,000 Jewish family names, giving their origins and a country-by-country guide to tracing Jewish ancestors abroad.

Israel Daniel Rupp. *A Collection of Upwards of 30,000 Names of German, Swiss, Dutch, French and Other Immigrants into Pennsylvania, 1727-1776*. Leipzig, 3rd ed., 1931. 2nd (English) rev. ed., with an index by Ernst Wecken from the Third Edition (1931) and added index to ships. Baltimore, MD: Genealogical Publishing Co. 1994. 583 pp.
    Passenger lists from 319 ships, giving name of ship and its origin arranged by date of arrival. Also included is a list of over 1,000 settlers who came to Pennsylvania from other states. Index to ships and surname index. Separately published index by Marvin Vastine Koger: *Index to the names of 30,000 Immigrants — German, Swiss, Dutch and French — into Pennsylvania, 1727-1776, Supplementing the I. Daniel Rupp, Ship Load Volume*, Pennington Gap, VA, 1935, 232 pp.

Trudy Schenk, Ruth Froelke and Inge Bork. *The Wuerttemberg Emigration Index*. Salt Lake City, UT: Ancestry, Inc. 1986. 5 volumes, ongoing.
    Each volume extracts a small area of Württemberg from German emigration records. Gives name, place and date of birth and often the destination of each emigrant.

Daniel M. Schlyter. *A Handbook of Czechoslovak Genealogical Research*. Buffalo Grove, IL: Genun Publishers. 1985. 131 pp.
    Written by the Eastern European specialist at the Family History Library in Salt Lake City. Currently out of print.

Schnellüberblick Kirchenbuchbestand Greifswald: Pommersche Evangelische Kirche. [*Preliminary Overview of the Parish Register Holdings in the Archives of the Pomeranian Evangelical Church in Greifswald*]. Greifswald, Germany: Landeskirchlichesarchiv. 1995. 20 pp.
    Lists about 70 East Pomeranian parishes for which this archive has partial original (1642-1946) or duplicate (1819-1874) registers, in addition to those in Western Pomerania, with a history of how it obtained these records, focusing mostly on those from present-day Poland.

George Schmucker. *The East Friesens in America: An Illustrated History of Their Colonies to the Present Time*. Translated by Pastor Kenneth DeWall from the original by Pastor George Schnucker. Topeka, KS: Jostens Printing and Publishing Div. 1986. 280 pp.

Karin Schulz, ed. *Hoffnung Amerika: Europäische Auswanderung in die Neu Welt*. [*The Hope of America: European Emigration to the New World*]. Bremerhaven Nordwestdeutsche Verlaggesellschaft. 1944. 293 pp.
    Deals with emigration from Germany and Eastern Europe through German ports. Heavy emphasis on Jewish migration to the United States.

Herrmann Schuricht. *The German Element in Virginia*. Originally published in 1898-1900; reprinted by the Clearfield Co., 1989. 2 vols. in 1. 1,433 pp.

>Examines early German settlements in a number of counties and the eventual concentration of Germans in the Shenandoah valley.

George K. Schweitzer. *German Genealogical Research*. Knoxville, TN: privately printed. 1992. 253 pp.

>German-American genealogical guide containing valuable information on geography, history, language, original and secondary records, location of records in Germany, and research procedures in the United States and Europe. Unindexed.

Dagmar Senekovic. *Handy Guide to Austrian Genealogical Records*. Logan, UT: Everton Publishers, Inc. 1979. 97 pp.

>Includes maps, addresses of Austrian archives and genealogical societies, lists of Jewish registers, Austrian Catholic and Lutheran parish names and dates of records.

Jonathan D. Shea and William F. Hoffman. *Following the Paper Trail: A Multilingual Translation Guide*. Teaneck, NJ: Avotaynu Press. 1994. 241 pp.

>A guide to translating vital statistic records in 13 European languages. Shows alphabets, word lists and sample vital statistic records for each language.

Ronald Smelser, editor. *Preliminary Survey of the German Collection: Finding Aids to the Microfilmed Records of the Genealogical Society of Utah*. Salt Lake City, UT: University of Utah Press. 1979. 580 pp.

>A comprehensive guide to the Family History Library's microfilm collection as of 1979. Listed by German state and province.

Clifford Neal Smith and Anna Piszczan-Czaja Smith. *Encyclopedia of German-American Genealogical Research*. New York, NY: R. R. Bowker Co. 1976. 273 pp.

>Contains in-depth study of German naming patterns and information on German churches in the United States, cites German history, describes German records, contains information about Jews in southwestern Germany, and lists manuscripts and source materials in the United States and Germany. Helpful sections include:
>
>(a) German religious organizations in the United States with a description of 18 groups and the location of German-speaking congregations throughout the United States by county as recorded in the 1906 religious census. (This census does not indicate German-speaking Catholic churches.)
>(b) Jews of Southwest Germany.
>(c) History and organization of the Holy Roman Empire which describes government levels and includes a place name gazetteer.
>(d) Chapter on genealogy in Germany with a detailed description of types of records found there.
>(e) List of German genealogical periodicals as referenced in *Der Schlüssel*.
>(f) Hints for evaluating German surnames and where they may have originated.
>(g) Chapter on German-American genealogical research.
>(h) Brief chapter on German heraldry.

Clifford Neal Smith. *German-American Research Monographs*. McNeal, AZ: Westland Publishers.

>Series of more than 20 monographs, each emigrants from specific regions, mostly from areas which are not very far from the Rhine River.

Clifford Neal Smith. *The Immigrant Ancestor: A Survey of Westland Monographs on Emigration from Germany, Great Britain, France, Switzerland and Eastern Europe*. 1994. 28 pp.

Clifford Neal Smith and Anna Piszczan-Czaja Smith. *American Genealogical Resources in German Archives (AGRIGA)*: A Handbook. New York, NY: R. R. Bowker Co. 1977. 336 pp.
> Has lists arranged alphabetically by village and individuals; also court records, emigration records, and other documents. Includes a bibliography of published emigration lists in German with English titles in brackets.

Kenneth L. Smith. *Confirming a Place of Origin*. Columbus, OH: privately printed. 1985. 28 pp.
> Gives many examples of how to find and confirm the place of origin, mostly for German ancestors.

Kenneth L. Smith. *German Church Books: Beyond the Basics*. Camden, ME: Picton Press. 1989. 224 pp.
> This excellent book for advanced genealogists provides detailed information about German church records: baptism, confirmation, marriage and death records. Other topics include German names, spelling, miscellaneous records and Gothic script handwriting examples.

Christa Stache. *Verzeichnis der Kirchenbücher im Evangelischen Zentral Archiv in Berlin* [*Inventory of Parish Registers in the Evangelical Central Archive in Berlin*]; Part I, *Die östlichen Kirchenprovinzen der evangelischen Kirche in der altpreussischen Union* [*The Eastern Bishoprics of the Evangelical Church in the Old Prussian Empire*], 2nd ed., 297 pp.; 1987); Part II, Berlin. Berlin: Evangelisches Zentralarchiv.
> Lists and dates of Protestant records for particular parishes in the former German eastern provinces in Vol. I. Vol. II includes Old Lutherans, French and other Reformed, and Moravian Brethren, with a few entries for Jews. A few records from the 1600s, most from 1700s or 1800s. Easy to use without knowledge of German.

Adelreich Steinach. *Swiss Colonists in Nineteenth Century America*, with four interpretive indexes by Urspeter Schelbert. Camden, ME: Picton Press. 1995 reprint of 1889 book. 512 pp.
> Highly recommended for post-colonial Swiss immigration.

Ralph B. Strassburger and William J. Hinke. *Pennsylvania German Pioneers, 1727-1808*. Pennsylvania German Society, Norristown, PA. Baltimore, MD: Genealogical Publishing Co., Inc. 3 volumes. 1934. Map. Reprinted in 2 volumes, 1966, 1980, 1992. 893 pp.
> Has all of the original lists of early Germans coming to the port of Philadelphia from 1727-1808. Includes 29,837 names in the index.

Karl Stumpp. *The Emigration from Germany to Russia in the Years 1763 to 1862*. Translation by Prof. Joseph S. Height and others. Lincoln, NE: American Historical Society of Germans from Russia. 1978 (1,018 pp.). 1982. Reprinted 1993.
> Most exhaustive lists of Germans who migrated to Russia, including places of emigration and immigration.

Jared H. Suess. *Central European Genealogical Terminology*. Logan, UT: Everton Publishers, Inc. 1978. 168 pp.
> Contains German, French, Hungarian, Latin and Italian genealogical terminology.

Jared H. Suess. *Handy Guide to Hungarian Genealogical Records*. Logan, UT: Everton Publishers, Inc. 1980. 100 pp. Maps.
> Includes Hungarian, German and Latin genealogical terms, Hungarian history, gazetteers, guide to genealogical records, sample parish records, and more.

Jared H. Suess. *Handy Guide to Swiss Genealogical Records*. Logan, UT: The Everton Publishers, Inc. 1978. 92 pp.
> This guide includes a brief history of Switzerland, guides to Swiss parish and civil records, terms in Swiss records given in four languages, religions, addresses and letter writing, maps and examples.

Maria Swiatlowska and Marek Budziarek. *Nekropolie lodzkie.* [*Lodz Cities of the Dead*]. Lodz: Muzeum Historii Miasta Lodzi. 1989. 32 pp.

> Has a brief history of Lodz, the largest center of German settlement in Russian Poland. Notes that there was a marked increase in Protestant and Jewish settlers in 1795-1806, when this area was ruled by Prussia, but that the large influx of post-1820 workers came from Saxony, Brandenburg, Bohemia, Moravia, Switzerland, Posen, Silesia, England and France. By 1850 mostly German Protestants outnumbered Catholics. Focuses on Protestant, Catholic, Jewish and Orthodox cemeteries. [The Old German Protestant cemetery dates back to the 1830s, with some gravestones still in excellent condition.]

Stephan Thernstrom, ed. *Harvard Encyclopedia of American Ethnic Groups.* Cambridge: MA: Belknap Press. 1980. 1,076 pp.

> Broad coverage. One of the few books dealing explicitly with Austrian immigration.

Ernest Thode. *Address Book for Germanic Genealogy*, 6th ed. Baltimore: Genealogical Publishing Co. 1996. 196 pp.

> Lists addresses of archives, genealogical societies (including religious societies), genealogists, publishers, libraries, *Heimatortskarteien*, German-language newspapers in North America, and other sources of information for German-American genealogical research in both Europe and North America. Latest edition includes the new German postal codes and quite a few additional East European addresses.

Ernest Thode. *Atlas for Germanic Genealogy.* 2nd rev. ed. Marietta, OH: E. Thode. 1983.

Ernest Thode. *German-English Genealogical Dictionary.* Baltimore, MD: Genealogical Publishing Co. 1992. 286 pp., plus 29 pp. introduction and map.

> Dictionary with genealogical emphasis. Contains at least 30,000 entries including historic place names, abbreviations, some Latin and French terms, and terms from bordering languages found in German research materials.

Don Heinrich Tolzmann, ed. *Americana Germanica: Paul Ben Baginsky's Bibliography of German Works Relating to America, 1493-1800.* 1942. Reprinted; Bowie, MD: Heritage Books, Inc. 1995. 219 pp.

> Especially useful for those with colonial ancestors.

Don Heinrich Tolzmann, ed. *The German-American Soldier in the Wars of the United States: J. G. Rosengarten's History.* 1890. Reprinted by Heritage Books, Bowie, MD, in 1996. 347 pp.

> Updated to cover the period from the Revolutionary War through the Gulf War.

Don Heinrich Tolzmann. *German-Americana: A Bibliography.* Metuchen, NJ: Scarecrow Press. 1975. Reprinted Bowie, MD: Heritage Books, Inc. 1994. 384 pp.

> About one third of the 5,300 listed sources relate to history. A survey of libraries, archives, and other institutions is also included.

Don Heinrich Tolzmann, ed. *German-Americans in the American Revolution: Henry Melchior Muhlenberg Richards' History.* 1908. Reprinted by Heritage Books, Bowie, MD, 1992. 552 pp.

> Definitive history of the involvement of Germans in Pennsylvania and neighboring colonies in the Revolutionary War. Extensive biographical information.

Don Heinrich Tolzmann, ed. *The German Element in Virginia: Herrmann Schuricht's History.* Original published in 1898; edited, expanded reprint: Bowie, MD: Heritage Books. 1992. 426 pp.

> Documents the history of Germans in Virginia, 1607-1898.

Don Heinrich Tolzmann. *German Immigration in America: The First Wave.* Bowie, MD: Heritage Books. 1993. 352 pp.

> Focuses on reasons for the first German wave of emigration to North America, beginning in 1708. Uses *The German Exodus to England in 1709* by Frank Ried Diffenderffer and *The German Emigration to America, 1709-1740* by Henry E. Jacobs.

Don Heinrich Tolzmann, ed. *John Andrew Russell's History of the German Influence in the Making of Michigan*. 1927. Reprinted: Bowie, MD: Heritage Books, Inc. 1995. 415 pp.

> The key book for researching Germanic ancestors in Michigan, where 29% of the population was Germanic in 1927.

Don Heinrich Tolzmann, ed. *Maryland's German Heritage: Daniel Wunderlich Nead's History*. 1913. Reprinted by Heritage Books, Bowie, MD. 304 pp.

> Standard text on the history of the Germans in Maryland and their close relationship with those in Pennsylvania.

Don Heinrich Tolzmann. *Ohio Valley Biographical Index*. Bowie, MD: Heritage Books. 1992. 78 pp.

> Alphabetical index of 3,754 names of German settlers in the tri-state Greater Cincinnati area, including some who migrated onward to other states, e.g., Iowa and Minnesota.

Don Heinrich Tolzmann. *Upper Midwest German Biographical Index*. Bowie, MD: Heritage Books. 1993. 125 pp.

United States Department of State. *Foreign Consular Offices in The United States*. Washington: U.S. Department of State, issued periodically. ca. 100 pp.

> Lists addresses of foreign chanceries (embassies, missions) and consular establishments in the United States. Cultural affairs attachés may be helpful in directing you to the proper archival and other genealogical sources in their countries. Especially helpful for countries that have split apart in recent years.

Verband deutscher Adressbuchverleger. *Offizielles Verzeichnis der bei den Mitgliedern des Verbandes erschienenen Adressbücher und Fernsprechbücher. [Official Catalog of City Directories and Phone Books Published by the Members of the Association (of Such Publishers)]*. Düsseldorf. 1972.

Verzeichnis der Postleitzahlen. [(Austrian) Postal Code Directory] Vienna, Austria. Published annually.

> Postal code directory for Austria. Can be ordered through Genealogy Unlimited.

Verzeichnis der Postleitzahlen. [(Swiss) Postal Code Directory] Baubedarf AG, Thunstrasse 5, Postfach, S-3000 Bern 22, Switzerland. Published annually.

> Postal code directory for Switzerland and Liechtenstein. Can be ordered through Genealogy Unlimited.

Edward von der Porten. "Hanseatic League," in *National Geographic* (October 1994, Vol. 186, No. 4, pp. 56-79).

> Story of the powerful Hanseatic League, an alliance of merchant cities, which controlled trade in the Baltic and North Sea from about 1200-1700.

Alexander von Lyncker. *Die altpreussischee Armee 1714-1806 und ihre Kirchenbücher. [The Old Prussian Army, 1714-1806, and Its Parish Registers]*. Berlin. 1937. Reprinted Neustadt/Aisch: Verlag Degener & Co. 1980. 326 pp.

Alexander von Lyncker. *Die preussische Armee 1807-1867 und ihre sippenkundliche Quellen. [The Prussian Army, 1807-1867, and Its Genealogical Sources]*. Berlin. 1939. Reprinted Neustadt/Aisch Verlag Degener & Co. 1981. 372 pp.

Ernst Wagner, et. al. *The Transylvanian Saxons: Historical Highlights*. Cleveland: Alliance of Transylvanian Saxons. 1982. 142 pp.

> History and maps pertaining to the Transylvanian Saxons in Europe and North America.

Jörg Walter. *Personengeschichtliche Quellen in den Militäria-Beständen des Niedersächsischen Hauptstaatsarchiv in Hannover. [Sources for Researching Individuals in the Military Holdings of the Chief State Archives of Lower Saxony in Hanover]*. Göttingen: Niedersächsische Archivverwaltung. 1979. 261 pp.

Sally A. Weikel. *Genealogical Research in the Published Pennsylvania Archives*. Harrisburg, PA: Pennsylvania Department of Education. 1978.

> This is a guide to the *Pennsylvania Archives* (see above).

Miriam Weiner. *Bridging the Generations: Researching Your Jewish Roots*. Secaucus, NJ: Self-published. 1987. 57 pp.

> A collection of genealogical columns, lists of resources and how-to information by a leading American Jewish genealogist.

Volkmar Weiss and Katja Münchow. *Bestandsverzeichnis der Deutschen Zentralstelle für Genealogie Leipzig, Part IV: Ortsfamilienbücher mit Standort Leipzig in Deutscher Bücherei und Deutsche Zentralstelle für Genealogie. [Village Family Books in Leipzig at the German Library and the German Central Office for Genealogy]*. Neustadt/Aisch: Verlag Degener & Co. 1996. 340 pp.

> Lists ca. 800 village lineage books and ca. 300 family parish registers. Information about 3,000 localities and nearly 1.8 million families in German-speaking areas in Europe. Over 100 village lineage books each for Rhineland-Palatinate, Baden-Württemberg, Hesse and Saarland; over 50 for Lower Saxony, Northrhine-Westphalia and Saxony.

Volkmar Weiss and Katja Münchow. *Ortsfamilienbücher mit Standort Leipzig in Deutscher Bücherei und Deutscher Zentralstelle für Genealogie. [Village Lineage Books Located in Leipzig in the German Library and the German Central Office for Genealogy]*. Leipzig: Deutsche Zentralstelle für Genealogie. 1994.

> Lists books which can be found in the two repositories in Leipzig.

Maralyn A. Wellauer. *Family History Research in the German Democratic Republic*. Milwaukee, WI: Roots International. 1987. 49 pp.

> A guide for doing research in the former German Democratic Republic. Somewhat dated, but still useful.

Maralyn A. Wellauer. *German Casualties of the Seven Weeks' War (1866) and the Franco-Prussian War (1870-1871)*. Milwaukee: Roots International. 1986. 80 pp.

> Lists names of 900 casualties in a regiment from Lower Saxony.

Maralyn A. Wellauer. *Tracing Your Polish Roots*. Milwaukee, WI: Private printing. 1991. 108 pp.

> Contains Polish history, sketches of former German territories, addresses in Poland and information about Polish genealogical sources in the United States.

Maralyn A. Wellauer. *Tracing Your Swiss Roots*. Milwaukee, WI: Private printing. 1979. 175 pp.

> Guide to tracing your Swiss-born ancestor back to Switzerland and extending this line in Switzerland. Many photo examples.

E. Welsch, J. Danyel and T. Kilton. *Archives and Libraries in a New Germany*. New York: Council for European Studies, Columbia University. 1994/5.

> Focuses on changes in the five new eastern states of Germany. Comprehensive subject matter.

Martina Wermes. *Important Addresses and Telephone Numbers for Genealogical Research for the Five New (Eastern) States of the Federal Republic of Germany and Berlin*, 3rd. ed. [partially translated, adapted and supplemented for English-language users by Edward Reimer Brandt]. Minneapolis: translator. 1996, 1997. 21 pp.

> Current addresses of religious institutions, archives (state, branch, city), libraries and genealogical organizations, with explanations and supplementary sources of information.

Martina Wermes, Renate Jude, Marion Bahr and Hans-Jürgen Voigt. *Bestandsverzeichnis der Deutschen Zentralstelle für Genealogie.* [*Index to the Holdings of the German Central Office for Genealogy*]. Vol. I: *Die Kirchenbuchunterlagen der östlichen Provinzen Posen, Ost- und Westpreussen, Pommern und Schlesien.* [*The Parish Registers of the Eastern Provinces of Posen, East and West Prussia, Pomerania and Silesia*]. Vol II: *Die archivalischen und Kirchenbuchunterlagen deutscher Siedlungsgebiete im Ausland: Bessarabien, Bukowina, Estland, Lettland und Litauen, Siebenbürgen, Sudetenland, Slowenien und Südtirol.* [*The Parish Registers of the German Settlements in Other Areas: Bessarabia, Bukovina, Estonia, Latvia and Lithuania, Transylvania, the Sudetenland, Slovenia and South Tyrol*]. Vol. III: *Die Kirchenbuchunterlagen der Länder und Provinzen des Deutschen Reiches.* [*The Parish Registers of the States and Provinces of the German Empire*]. Neustadt/Aisch: Verlag Degener & Co. 1991-94. Vol. I: 1991. 182 pp. Vol II: 1992. 189 pp. Vol. III: 1994. 217 pp.

> Bilingual introductory material. The rest is in list form.

> Volume I lists the archives' original or microfilmed parish registers for the German eastern provinces within the borders of 1905 but excluding East Brandenburg.

> Volume II lists microfilms of parish registers and other archival records for (1) North Bukovina (only those that arrived via Danzig, Bromberg, Posen and other places, since the 1940 Hitler-Stalin Pact prohibited the transfer of such registers); (2) South Bukovina (where Romania sanctioned the transfer of such records to Germany); (3) Bessarabia (from which the transfer of records was prohibited, but where all German repatriates received pedigree charts prior to their departure); (4) the Transylvanian districts of Mediasch, Schelk, Reps and Schässburg, which were in the archives at Kronstadt (Brasov), but not those for other districts; (5) the Baltic countries (but mostly Latvia); (6) South Tyrol (archival records in Bozen [Bolzano] and Brixen, plus a few Catholic parishes); and (7) Bohemia and Moravia, i.e., the Czech Republic (but the original microfilms suffered a loss of damage in World War II, so comparatively few records still exist).

> Volume III deals with Berlin, Schleswig-Holstein, Thuringia, Baden, Bavaria, Brandenburg (including the part now in Poland), Hamburg, Hanover, Hesse, Mecklenburg, the Rhine province, the Kingdom of Saxony, the Prussian Province of Saxony, Westphalia, Anhalt, Brunswick, Hesse-Nassau, Lippe, Oldenburg, the Saarland, Schaumburg-Lippe, and Württemberg.

Raymond Wiebe. *Hillsboro, The City on the Prairie.* Hillsboro, KS: Hillsboro Historical Society. 1985. 189 pp.

> Devotes considerable attention to the Mennonites, German Lutherans and Baptists who settled in an area with a heavy concentration of Germans from Russia.

Franz Wilhelm & Josef Kallbrunner. *Quellen zur deutschen Siedlungsgeschichte in Südost-europa.* [*Sourcebook for Histories of German Settlements in Southeast Europe*]. Part of the series: *Schriftenreihe der Deutschen Akademie* [*Series by the German Academy*]. Munich, Germany: Verlag von Ernst Reinhardt. 1932, 1934, 1938. 416 pp. Recently reprinted, Berlin: Helmut Scherer Verlag.

> Very extensive lists of Germans who migrated to Southeast Europe between 1749 and 1803, showing places of emigration and general area of immigration; maps and tables; has numerous errors, mostly with respect to two or more places having the same name.

Oren Windholz. *Bohemian Germans in Kansas: A Catholic Community from Bukovina.* Hays, KS: author. 1993. 50 pp.

> Illustrated history of the migration of Germans from the Bohemian Forest to the Bukovina and America.

Don Yoder, ed. *Rhineland Emigrants: Lists of German Settlers in Colonial America.* Baltimore: Genealogical Publishing Co. 1981; reprinted 1985. 170 pp.

> European origins of Pennsylvania Germans, with references to church, parish and provincial records in southwest German archives, and some corresponding Pennsylvanian records. Collection of 24 articles, most of them translated from the German originals. Extensive index.

Irina and Rainer Zielke, eds. *Ratgeber '95: Familienforschung Mittel- und Osteuropa. [1995 Guide to Genealogical Research in Central and Eastern Europe]*. Neustadt/Aish, Germany: Verlag Degener & Co. 1996. 228 pp.

> Articles by many leading German genealogists, as well as authors by authors from Austria, Switzerland, Ukraine, Poland, Russia, the United States and Canada. Includes list of genealogists, especially in Germany, but also in Austria, Switzerland, Russia, Belarus, Estonia, Poland and Hungary, most of whom are willing to undertake research for areas east of present-day Germany and Austria, and specifies their areas or fields of specialization.

Gary J. Zimmerman and Marion Wolfert. *German Immigrants: Lists of Passengers Bound from Bremen to New York, with Places of Origin*. Baltimore, MD: Genealogical Publishing Co., Inc. 1985-93 and ongoing. Volume 1: 1847-1854 (1985, 1993). 175 pp. Volume 2: 1855-1862 (1986, 1993). 167 pp. Volume 3: 1863-1867 (1988). 221 pp. Volume 4 (by Marion Wolfert after Zimmerman's death): 1868-1871 (1993). Continuation of series is uncertain, according to the publisher.

> The original lists of emigrants departing from the Bremen port were destroyed either by policy or remainder both before and during World War II. This series has reconstructed these records from official United States sources of arrival records rather than departure records. Only those passengers listing a specific place of origin are noted in the manifests. Immigrants' names are arranged in alphabetical order, with family members grouped together. Includes age, place of origin, date of arrival and name of ship, with citations to original source material.

Dieter Zwinger, comp. *Mitgliederverzeichnis 1996 der DAGV*. [1996 *Membership List of the German Federation of Genealogical Societies*]. Neustadt/Aisch: Verlag Degener & Co. 1996. 63 pp. Published annually.

> Descriptive list of members of the German genealogical umbrella organization, including addresses and telephone numbers of officers, scope of interest, membership dues, publications, and sometimes miscellaneous other information. Lists many details about each of the dozens of DAGV member societies, although few purely local societies are members.

PERIODICALS AND INDEXES TO PERIODICALS

This section contains an alphabetical list of periodicals which pertain only to specifically German-speaking groups or ancestors, or which are independent of any society. Check the section on **Multi-Ethnic and Non-Germanic Societies of Importance to Germanic Research** for other relevant periodicals. There are also pertinent entries in the text or bibliography for the various chapters. For more comprehensive information, check the Thode, Bentley and Meyer address books. Bentley lists organizations for adoptees.

Thode lists many Max Kade Institutes or Centers for German-American Studies. These are academic centers which devote a lot of attention to immigration, history and biography. Some of them also have genealogical resources, such as gazetteers, atlases and other publications. Thode also lists quite a number of societies devoted to people of Germanic origin in a particular state or local area, including some for Canada and Australia.

The Augustan Society Omnibus. P.O. Box P, Torrance, CA 90504-0210.
> Multi-ethnic, including German, coverage.

Sallyann Amdur Sack, ed. *Avotaynu: International Review of Jewish Genealogy.* 155 N. Washington Ave., Teaneck, NJ 07621.
> Independent Jewish periodical, with worldwide coverage.

California Mennonite Historical Society Bulletin. Published by the California Mennonite Historical Society, Mennonite Brethren Biblical Seminary, 4824 E. Butler Ave., Fresno, CA 93727-5097.

Jo Ann Kuhr, ed. *Clues.* Published by the American Historical Society of Germans from Russia.
> Annual 100-page publication comprised of a surname exchange list for Germans from Russia and supplementary genealogical data, such as passenger lists. Now also includes a chapter on Latin America.

Familienkundliche Nachrichten. [*Genealogical News*]. Neustadt (Aisch), Germany: Verlag Degener & Co. Often called FaNa. Six issues per year.
> Widely read German genealogical publication dealing with queries (see Chapter II).

Glen Linscheid, ed. *Galician Grapevine.* Box 194, Butterfield, MN 56120.
> Family history newsletter for Galician German Mennonites.

George B. Everton, Jr., ed. *The Genealogical Helper.* Published by The Everton Publishers, Inc., P.O. Box 368, Logan, UT 84321. Six issues per year.
> Contains general genealogical articles, queries and advertisements. Some German books, organizations and researchers are mentioned.

Laraine K. Ferguson and Gay P. Kowallis, eds. *German Genealogical Digest.* Published by German Genealogical Digest, 245 North Vine #106, Salt Lake City, UT 84103-1948.
> Quarterly publication with in-depth articles on German genealogical research and specialized areas. Ongoing indexes and specific help are available.

Elizabeth Nick, ed. and pub. *The Gottschee Tree.* c/o Liz Information Service, P.O. Box 725, Louisville, CO 80027-0725. Quarterly.
> Focuses on the former Gottschee German settlement (now Kocevje, Slovenia), 1330-1941.

Sophia Stalzer Wyant and Maria Wyant Cuzzo, eds. *The Gottscheer Connection.* Published by the Gottscheer Research & Genealogy Association, c/o Kate Loschke Pruente, 21534 American River Dr., Sonora, CA 95370-91112.

Heritage Quest. Historic Resources, Inc., P.O. Box 329, Bountiful, UT 84011-0329.
> Substantial number of articles on German-American genealogy by leading American and German experts. Edited by Leland K. Meitzler, Elbe, WA.

Gail Breitbard, ed. *The Lost Palatine.* Rt. 1, Box 1160, Estero, FL 33928-9801

Maajan—Die Quelle. [*Maajan—The Source*]. Published by the Schweizerische Vereinigung für jüdische Genealogie, Zurich, Switzerland.

Le Mar and Lois Zook Mast, eds. *Mennonite Family History*. 10 West Main St., Elverson, PA 19520-0171.

> Chief genealogical periodical in North America for Mennonites and closely related denominations, e.g., Amish and Brethren.

Mennonite Genealogist. Published by the California Mennonite Historical Society, Fresno Pacific College Archives, 4824 E. Butler Ave., Fresno, CA 93727

> Newsletter, started in 1995, of the Genealogical Project Committee.

Mennonite Historian. Published by the Mennonite Heritage Centre, 600 Shaftesbury Blvd., Winnipeg, MB R3P 0M4, Canada, and the Centre for Mennonite Brethren Studies, Winnipeg.

> Carries a substantial amount of genealogical information, especially for Mennonites in Western Canada.

Periodical Source Index (PERSI). Published by Allen County Public Library Foundation, 900 Webster St., Box 2270, Fort Wayne, IN 46801-2270.

> An index to 2000 genealogical and local history periodicals published in the United States, covering 1847 to 1985, with subsequent annual supplements. The index is arranged by locality, subject matter and surname. See "Using PERSI in German Genealogy" in *Der Blumenbaum*, April-May-June 1995, for instructions.

Myron E. Gruenwald, ed. and pub. *Die Pommerschen Leute*. [The Pomeranian People]. 1280 Westhaven Dr., Oshkosh, WI 54904.

> An English-language specialty newsletter offering articles and queries to Pomeranian researchers.

Praktische Forschungshilfe. [*Practical Research Help*]. Germany: C. A. Starke Verlag, Postfach 1310, D-65549 Limburg/Lahn. Often called PraFo.

> Quarterly genealogy supplement to the *Archiv für Sippenforschung* (see Chapter II).

Der Schlüssel. [*The Key*].

> A multi-volume index to German-Austrian-Swiss genealogical periodicals. Covers publications from 1870 to 1975 and includes the following registers: title index, place name register, register of subjects and surname index. The compilers, who devoted 40 years to this work, recently died, so the completion of the series beyond 1975 is in doubt. The Family History Library has the series, but not on microfilm.

Armand Bauer, ed. *Der Stammbaum*. [*The Family Tree*]. Published by the Germans from Russia Heritage Society, 1008 East Central Ave., Bismarck, ND 58501.

> Annual genealogical issue of the *Heritage Review*. Focuses especially on Germans who went from the western Black Sea region to the Dakotas. In English.

Bill Firestone, ed. *Stammbaum*. Published by Avotaynu, Inc. P.O. Box 900, Teaneck, NJ 07666.

> Genealogical periodical devoted to German Jews.

Maralyn A. Wellauer, ed. *The Swiss Connection*. 2845 North 72nd St., Milwaukee, WI 53120.

Ewald Wuschke, ed. and pub. *Wandering Volhynians: A Magazine for the Descendants of Germans from Volhynia and Poland*. Published by Ewald Wuschke, 3492 West 39th Ave., Vancouver, BC, Canada V6N 3A2.

> Chief publication concerning Volhynian Germans, with a Volhynia/Poland surname and village research list.

Chapter XXIII

USEFUL ADDRESSES

This section shows addresses of many publishers, booksellers, map sources, libraries, information centers and genealogical societies that can be of help to people doing Germanic genealogical research. To find other toll-free "800" numbers, call 800-555-1212 for information and ask the operator for the number of a specific company.

PUBLISHERS AND BOOKSELLERS

AKB Publications
691 Weavertown Rd.
Myerstown, PA 17067-2642
Phone: 717-866-2300
(refers to Annette K. Burgert, leading
author/publisher on colonial emigration
to Pennsylvania)

Alice's Ancestral Nostalgia
P.O. Box 510092
Salt Lake City, UT 84151
Phone: 801-575-6510

Ancestry, Inc.
P.O. Box 476
Salt Lake City, UT 84110-0476
Phone: 800-531-1790

Association of Professional Genealogists
3421 M St. N.W., Suite 236
Washington, DC 20007

Avotaynu, Inc.
Box 900
Teaneck, NJ 07666
Phone: 800-866-1525
(Book publishing address)

Avotaynu, Inc.
155 N. Washington Ave.
Bergenfield, NJ 07621
Phone: 800-AVO-TAYN(U)
        (800-286-8298)
(Jewish genealogy)

Robert Base, Publications Manager
Anglo-German Family History Society
15 Appleford Close
Hoddesdon, Herts
England EN11 9DE

Verlag C. H. Beck
Postfach 40 03 40
D-8000 München
Germany

Edna M. Bentz
13139 Old West Ave.
San Diego, CA 92129-2406
Phone: 619-484-1708

Böhlau Verlag GmbH & Co.
Theodor-Heuss-Str. 76
D-51149 Köln
Germany

R. R. Bowker & Co.
245 W. 17th St.
New York, NY 10011-5300
Phone: 800-521-8110 or 212-645-9700

Edward R. Brandt
13 - 27th Ave. S.E.
Minneapolis, MN 55414-3101

Calmar Publications
202 Wildwood Lane
Louisville, KY 40223
Phone: 502-425-0460
(Genealogies of German Turner gymnastic
group during Civil War)

Clearfield Company, Inc.
200 E. Eager St.
Baltimore, MD 21202-3761
Phone: 410-625-9004
(Branch of Genealogical Publishing Co.)

Closson Press
1935 Sampson Drive
Apollo, PA 15613

CMBC Publications
600 Shaftesbury Blvd.
Winnipeg, MB R3P 0M4
Canada
(Mennonite history)

Martha Remer Connor
7754 Pacement Ct.
Las Vegas, NV 89117-5122
(Hungarian German census transcripts)

Council for European Studies
Box 44, Schermerhorn Hall
Columbia University
New York, NY 10027

Crossway Publications
P. O. Box 1960
Steinbach, MB R0A 2A0
Canada

Alfred A. Curran
119 Sefton Dr.
New Britain, CT 06053-2550
Phone: 203-827-8023

Randy Daitch
820½ N. Detroit St.
Los Angeles, CA 90046
(*Shtetl gazetteer*)

Verlag Degener & Company
Nürnberger Strasse 27
Postfach 1360
D-91403 Neustadt/Aisch
Germany

DFP Publications
P.O. Box 669
Steinbach, MB R0A 2A0
Canada
(*Mennonite Kleine Gemeinde Historical
Series*)

Editions-Reliures Schortgen
43, rue Marie Muller-Tesch
L-4250 Esch-Alzette
Luxembourg
(*Luxemburgers in America*)

The Everton Publishers, Inc.
P.O. Box 368
Logan, UT 84323-0368
Phone: 800-443-6325 or 801-752-6022

Facts on File, Inc.
460 Park Ave. S.
New York, NY 10016-7382
Phone: 800-322-8755

The Family Album
RD 1, Box 42
Glen Rock, PA 17327
(*Rare old German books*)

The Family Historian
12961 Lake Ave.
Lakewood, OH 44107-1533
(*Slovak German gazetteer*)

Family Tree Press
8968 E. Gail Rd.
Scottsdale, AZ 85260-6146

Gale Research Inc.
835 Penobscot Bldg.
Detroit, MI 48226-4094
Phone: 800-521-0707 or 313-961-2242

Genealogical Publishing Co., Inc.
1001 N. Calvert St.
Baltimore, MD 21202-3897
Phone: 800-296-6687

Genealogists Bookshelf
Box 468
343 E. 85th St.
New York, NY 10028-4550

Genealogy House
3148 Kentucky Ave. S.
St. Louis Park, MN 55426-3471
Phone: 612-920-6990

Genealogy Unlimited, Inc.
(Genun Publishers)
P.O. Box 537
Orem, UT 84059-0537
Phone: 800-666-4363

Generation Press, Inc.
172 King Henry's Blvd.
Agincourt, Ontario, M1T 2V6
Canada

Germanic Genealogy Society
Branch of Minnesota Genealogical Society
P.O. Box 16312
St. Paul, MN 55116

Adalbert Goertz
12934 Buchanan Ave.
Waynesboro, PA 17261
(*Prussian Mennonite publications and
maps*)

Goodspeed's Book Shop
18 Beacon St.
Boston, MA 02108-3703

Groundworks
203 N. Genesee St.
Merrill, WI 54452
(*Specializes in genealogical forms*)

Otto Harrassowitz
Postfach 2929
D-65183 Wiesbaden
Germany

Hearthside Press
8405 Richmond Hwy., Suite H
Alexandria, VA 22309-2425
Phone: 703-360-6900
(*Genealogies of Shenandoah Valley,*
Virginia area Germans, Pennsylvania
Germans)

Hebert Publications
Rt. 2, Box 572
Church Point, LA 70525-9333
Phone: 318-873-6574
(*Genealogies of Louisiana Germans*)

Heimat Publishers
1 Lyme Regis Crescent
Scarborough, ON M1M 1E3
Canada
(*Danube Swabians*)

Heritage Books, Inc.
1540 Pointer Ridge Pl., Suite E
Bowie, MD 20716-1800
Phone: 800-398-7709

Heritage House
P.O. Box 39128
Indianapolis, IN 46239-0128
Phone: 317-862-3330

Heritage Quest
P.O. Box 40
Orting, WA 98360-0040
Phone: 800-442-2029

Hunterdon House
38 Swan St.
Lambertville, NJ 08530-1022
Phone: 609-397-2523
(*For Ontario, Canada, publications*)

Jensen Publications
c/o Larry O. Jensen
P.O. Box 441
Pleasant Grove, UT 84062-0441

Jesperson Press
26A Flavin St.
St. John's, Newfoundland A1C 3R9
Canada

Dr. Arta F. Johnson
153 Aldrich Rd.
Columbus, OH 43214-2625

J. Konrad
P.O. Box 222
Munroe Falls, OH 44262

Brian J. Lenius
Box 18, Grp. 4, R.R. 1
Anola, MB R0E 0A0
Canada
(*Galician gazetteer*)

The Linden Tree
1204 W. Prospect Ave.
Cloquet, MN 55720-1332
Phone: 218-879-5727

Macmillan of Canada
29 Birch Ave.
Toronto, Ontario M4V 1E2
Canada

Mennonite Heritage Centre
600 Shaftesbury Blvd.
Winnipeg, MB R3P 0M4
(*English and German books about*
Mennonites of North European origin in
the Americas and elsewhere)

Mary Keysor Meyer
5179 Perry Rd.
Mt. Airy, MD 21771

Monda Genealoga Ligo
P.O. Box 21346
Salt Lake City, UT 84121-0346

John D. Movius
P.O. Box 4327
Davis, CA 95617-4327
(*Resource Guide to East European*
Genealogy, and other FEEFHS
publications)

National Archives and Records Service
601 Penn. Ave. NW, Rm G9
Washington, DC 20004-2601
Phone: 202-724-0098
(*U.S. Government printing office for the*
Library of Congress)

Olde Springfield Shoppe
P.O. Box 171
Elverson, PA 19520-0171
(*Leading bookseller for Mennonite and*
Amish genealogy)

Oro Press
217 W. 1st Ave.
Denver, CO 80223-1507
Phone: 303-722-4425
(*Has tourist history of Germany and*
Austria)

Oxmoor House, Inc.
P.O. Box 2262
Birmingham, AL 35201-2262
Phone: 800-633-4712

Park Genealogical Books
P.O. Box 130968
Roseville, MN 55113-0968
E-mail:mbakeman@parkbooks.com

Robert J. Paulson
800 W. Idaho Ave.
St. Paul, MN 55117

Picton Press
P.O. Box 1111
Camden, ME 04843-1111
Phone: 203-236-6565

Prairie Heritage Chapter, GRHS
P.O. Box 328
Bismarck, ND 58502-0328

Helmut Preussler Verlag
Rothenburger Str. 25
D-90443 Nürnberg
Germany
(Sudeten Germans)

Verlag Rautenberg
Postfach 19 09
D-26789 Leer
Germany
(Specializes in former German eastern areas)

Horst Reschke
3083 W. 4900 S.
Salt Lake City, UT 84118-2527
(German military records)

Roots International
Maralyn A. Wellauer
3239 N. 58th St.
Milwaukee, WI 53216-3123
Phone: 414-871-7421

K. G. Saur
Subsidiary of R. R. Bowker Co.
121 Chanlon Rd.
New Providence, NJ 07974-1541
(American distributor for many German publishers)

Helmut Scherer Verlag
Boothstr. 21a
D-12207 Berlin
Germany

Scholarly Resources, Inc.
104 Greenhill Ave.
Wilmington, DE 19805-1897
Phone: 800-772-8937

George K. Schweitzer
Genealogical Sources, Unltd.
407 Ascot Court
Knoxvile, TN 37923-5807

Kenneth L. Smith
523 S. Weyant Ave.
Columbus, OH 43213-2275

C. A. Starke Verlag
Frankfurter Strasse 51-53
Postfach 1310
D-65549 Limburg/Lahn
Germany
(Publishes Archiv für Sippenforschung and Praktische Forschungshilfe - PraFo)

Dr. Jacob Steigerwald
355 West 4th St.
Winona, MN 55987-2805
(Romanian Germans)

Suhrkamp Publishers New York, Inc.
175 Fifth Ave.
New York, NY 10010-7703
Phone: 212-460-1653
(Distributor for German publishing houses)

Ernest Thode (Thode Translations)
RR 7, Box 306, Kern Rd.
Marietta, OH 45750-9437
Phone: 614-373-3728

Thomsen's Genealogical Center
P.O. Box 588
Bountiful, UT 84010

Charles E. Tuttle Co., Inc.
P.O. Box 541
28 S. Main St.
Rutland, VT 05701-0541
Phone: 800-526-2778 or 802-773-8229

University of Utah Press
University of Utah
101 University Services Bldg.
Salt Lake City, UT 84112
Phone: 800-444-8638

Miriam Weiner Routes to Roots
    Foundation, Inc.
136 Sandpiper Key
Secaucus, NJ 07094-2210
Phone: 201-601-9199

Westkreuz-Verlag Bonn/Berlin
Vühlenstr. 10-14
D-53902 Bad Münstereifel
Germany

Westland Publications
P.O. Box 117
McNeal, AZ 85617-0117
Phone: 602-642-3500

Who's Who in Genealogy & Heraldry
8944 Madison St.
Savage, MD 20763

Ye Olde Genealogie Shoppe
9605 Vandergriff Road
P.O. Box 39128
Indianapolis, IN 46239-0128
Phone: 317-862-3330

Zielke-Verlag
Stadtlohnweg 13 C407
D-48161 Münster
Germany
(*Current East European German
genealogy*)

MAP SOURCES

Genealogy House
3148 Kentucky Ave. S.
St. Louis Park, MN 55426-3471
Phone: 612-920-6990

Genealogy Unlimited, Inc.
P.O. Box 537
Orem, UT 84059-0537
Phone: 800-666-4363

International Maps
3930 - 69th St.
Des Moines, IA 50322-2608

Jensen Publications
P.O. Box 441
Pleasant Grove, UT 84062-0441

The Map Store
First Bank Place W.
120 S. 6th St.
Minneapolis, MN 55402-1800
Phone: 612-339-4117

The Map Store
World Trade Center
30 East 7th Street
St. Paul, MN 55101-4901
Phone: 612-227-6277

The Map Store
5821 Karric Square Drive
Dublin, OH 43017-4243
Phone: 800-332-7885

Jonathan Sheppard Books
Box 2020, Plaza Station
Albany, NY 12220-0020

Ernest Thode
RR 7, Box 306, Kern Rd.
Marietta, OH 45750-9437
Phone: 614-373-3728

Travel Genie
Books-Maps-Gifts
Lincoln Center
620 Lincoln Way
Ames, IA 50010-6900
Phone: 515-232-1070

Viking Penguin, Inc.
375 Hudson St., Floor #4
New York, NY 10014-3672
Phone: 800-631-3577

Ye Olde Genealogie Shoppe
9605 Vandergriff Road
P.O. Box 39128
Indianapolis, IN 46239-0128
Phone: 317-862-3330

LIBRARIES AND INFORMATION CENTERS

Allen County Public Library
900 Webster St.
P.O. Box 2270
Fort Wayne, IN 46802-2270
Phone: 219-424-7241

This library is second only to the LDS Family History Library for the extent of its genealogical holdings. Nationwide in scope with 128,000 volumes and 132,000 microtext items. *Publishes Periodical Source Index (PERSI).*

Austrian Cultural Institute
11 East 52nd St.
New York, NY 10022

Leo Baeck Institute
129 E. 73rd St.
New York, NY 10021

Leading archives for German Jews.

Balch Institute of Ethnic Studies
Temple University
18 S. 7th St.
Philadelphia, PA 19106

Has records used for *Germans to America* series and Jewish Historical Archives.

Bethel College
Mennonite Historical Library and
    Archives
300 E. 27th
North Newton, KS 67117-9989

Large library and archives, with many family history books.

Center for Austrian Studies
University of Minnesota
314 Social Sciences Bldg.
Minneapolis, MN 55455

Has one of the largest collections of books on the Hapsburg Empire in the United States.

Center for Mennonite Brethren Studies
4824 E. Butler Ave.
Fresno, CA 93727-5097

Large Mennonite library and archives.

Center for Mennonite Brethren Studies
Tabor College
Hillsboro, KS 67063-1799

Large library, including many family history books.

Centre for Mennonite Brethren Studies
1 - 169 Riverton Ave.
Winnipeg, MB R2L 2E5

Large library and archives. Resources not limited to the Mennonite Brethren.

Evangelical Lutheran Church of
    America Archives
5400 Milton Parkway
Chicago, IL 60018

Vast collection of materials, but not staffed to answer queries.

Family History Library
The Church of Jesus Christ of Latter-
    day Saints (Mormon)
35 North West Temple Street
Salt Lake City, UT 84150-1003

Main LDS library. See Chapter V referring to local branches (over 200 in the United States, others in Canada and Europe).

German Information Center
950 Third Avenue
New York, NY 10022

Publishes *The Week in Germany* and provides other informational services. Offers information, maps and posters.

Germans from Russia Heritage Collection North Dakota Institute for Regional Studies North Dakota State University Libraries Fargo, ND 58105-5599	Largest historical collection on Germans from Russia in the U.S.
Max Kade Institute for German-American Studies 2080 Wescoe Hall University of Kansas Lawrence, KS 66045-2127	
Max Kade Institute for German-American Studies University of Pennsylvania	
Max Kade Institute for German American Studies University of Wisconsin - Madison 901 University Bay Drive Madison, WI 53705-2269	German-American studies research center. Has a German gazetteer (prior to German unification in 1871) and other early historical works not readily available elsewhere.
Library of Congress 101 Independence Ave. S.E. Washington, DC 20003-1001	Contains over 80 million items in 470 languages.
Mennonite Heritage Centre 600 Shaftesbury Blvd. Winnipeg, MB R3P 0M4	1835 Russian revision list for the Molotschna Mennonite colonies, Prussian Mennonite microfilms and a large collection of genealogical, historical and other Mennonite books.
Mennonite Historical Library Goshen College Goshen, IN 46526-4794 *Phone: 219-535-7000*	History and index of names in Amish genealogies. Composite genealogy of all living married Amish persons.
National Archives & Records Administration General Services Administration Washington, DC 20004	Central repository for United States federal records. Also includes records of Nazi Germany and captured records.
Newberry Library 60 W. Walton St. Chicago, IL 60610-3380 *Phone: 312-943-9090*	Private, non-circulating reference library in history and humanities. Large collection of local history and genealogy, especially for the Midwest. Famous for *The Genealogical Index of the Newberry Library* (4 vols.), a surname index to most personal names found in the Newberry Library's local history and genealogy collection, prior to 1918. Has microfilms of registers of 444 Catholic parishes of Archdiocese of Chicago prior to 1910.
Swiss National Tourist Office 608 - 5th Avenue, Rm. #202 New York, NY 10020-2342	Offers information and maps.
University of Texas Barker Texas History Center Austin, TX 78712-1104	Records for German-Wendish settlement in Texas, also maps.

State Historical Society of Wisconsin
816 State St.
Madison, WI 53706-1488
Phone: 608-264-6535

One of the largest genealogical collections in the United States. The scope of the collection pertains to all parts of the United States and Canada. Contains over one million items. Has a complete microfilm collection of all available censuses of the United States and Canada; the largest newspaper collection in the United States outside the Library of Congress; an extensive city directory and telephone book collection; passenger lists on microfilm for major ports, including Quebec (1865-1900) and Halifax (1890-1900); and vital records, census and biographical indexes for Wisconsin.

University of Wisconsin - Eau Claire
McIntyre Library, Special Collection
Eau Claire, WI 54702-4004

Extensive map collection.

University of Wisconsin - Milwaukee
Golda Meir Library
2311 E. Hartford Ave.
P.O. Box 604
Milwaukee. WI 53201

Map Collection of the American Geographic Society.

YIVO Institute for Jewish Research
1048 Fifth Ave.
New York, NY 10028

Leading library and archives for Jews from Eastern Europe.

York County Historical Society
259 E. Market St.
York, PA 17403-2014

Has 10 volumes with indexes of Pennsylvania settlers, giving European origins.

LENDING LIBRARIES

Consult with your local library on the availability of interlibrary loans.

Genealogical libraries that have lending policies for their members are:

New England Historic Genealogical
  Society
101 Newbury St.
Boston, MA 02116-3087
Phone: 617-536-5740

Circulates 15,000 volumes. Specializes in historic New England, middle Atlantic states, the South, the Midwest, the West, Canada and Europe.

National Genealogical Society Library
4527 - 17th St. N.
Arlington, VA 22207-2399

Collection of published and non-published works.

American Genealogical Lending Library
P.O. Box 244
Bountiful, UT 84011-0244
Phone: 800-298-5358

Commercial lending library with microfilm and microfiche available for rental or for purchase. Covers United States and Canadian records.

SPECIAL RESOURCES IN AND NEAR MINNESOTA

"Selected Libraries for Germanic Genealogy (Twin Cities Area)" in the June 1995 issue of the *Germanic Genealogy Society Newsletter* lists 15 libraries with addresses, hours and phone numbers.

Brown County Historical Society Museum
415 Cherry St.
New Ulm, MN 56001

Has large collection of genealogically valuable material.

St. Paul Archdiocese
226 Summit Ave.
St. Paul, MN 55102

Contact person is Paul Anzelc, Assistant Archivist. Research hours 9 a.m. to 5 p.m. Tuesday and Wednesday by appointment. Available by phone 9 a.m. to 5 p.m. Monday through Friday. Research done in archive holdings for a fee.

The St. Paul Archdiocese encompasses a 12-county area in Minnesota including Anoka, Carver, Chisago, Dakota, Goodhue, Hennepin, LeSueur, Ramsey, Rice, Scott, Washington, and Wright counties.

Some of their holdings include:

U.S. Catholic Sources, A Diocesan Research Guide, compiled by Virginia Hemling (Ancestry Press, Slat Lake City, UT 84110);

Historical sketches of individual parishes in ND, SD, and MN.

4 volumes that include pictures of every parish in the Archdiocese. Copies are available for purchase. Many pictures are c. 1870-1880.

Supplement of Official Catholic Churches, a directory of Catholic churches worldwide. It provides addresses and phone numbers.

Microfilm records of all orphanages that the church operated. This includes St. Joseph's Home for Children.

Family History Centers in Minnesota

(*These are library locations, not mailing addresses.*)

2801 Douglas Drive, Crystal (612-544-2479) (largest in the area)

2140 Hadley Ave., Oakdale (612-770-3213)

2742 Yellowstone Blvd., Anoka (612-442-9679)

3033 NE Birchmont Dr., Bemidji (218-751-9129)

521 Upham Road, Duluth (218-722-9508)

1851 Marie Lane, North Mankato (507-625-8342)

1002 SE 16th St., Rochester (507-282-2382)

1420 - 29th Ave. N., St. Cloud (612-252-4355)

2006 Buffalo Hills Lane, Brainerd

Hwy. 25 N., Buffalo

Family History Centers in North Dakota *(These are library locations, not mailing addresses.)*	2502 - 17th Ave. SW, Fargo *(701-232-4003)* 2814 Cherry St., Grand Forks *(701-746-6126)* 1500 Country West Rd, Bismarck *(701-222-2794)* 2025 Ninth St. NW, Minot *(701-838-4486)*
Family History Centers in South Dakota *(These are library locations, not mailing addresses.)*	3900 S. Fairhall Ave., Sioux Falls (605-361-1070) 530 S. Mannston, Gettysburg (605-765-9270) LDS Church, Rosebud *(605-747-2818)* 2822 Canyon Ln. Dr., Rapid City *(605-341-8572)*
Family History Centers in Iowa *(These are library locations, not mailing addresses.)*	1201 West Clifton, Sioux City (712-255-9686) 2524 Hoover, Ames (515-232-3634) 4300 Trailridge Rd. SE, Cedar Rapids (319-363-9343) 3301 Ashworth Rd., West Des Moines *(515-225-0416)* 4929 Wisconsin Ave., Davenport *(319-386-7547)*
Family History Centers in Wisconsin *(These are library locations, not mailing addresses.)*	3335 Stein Blvd., Eau Claire (715-834-8271) 744 S. 6th, Barron 910 East Zingler, Shawano (715-526-2946) 1711 University Ave., Madison *(608-238-1071)* 9600 West Grange Ave., Hales Corner *(414-425-4182)*
Family History Centers in Manitoba and Western Ontario, Canada *(These are library locations, not mailing addresses.)*	45 Dalhousie Dr., Winnipeg, MB (204-261-4271) 700 Third St. W., Fort Frances, ON (807-274-9394) 2255 Ponderosa Dr., Thunder Bay, ON *(807-939-1451)*
Freeman Academy Heritage Archives 748 S. Main St. Freeman, SD 57029	Materials for Mennonites in South Dakota, who came from diverse places, including Galicia.
German Consulate 1100 First Bank Place West 120 S. 6th St. Minneapolis, MN 55402-1814 *Phone: 612-338-6559*	Will answer questions about Germany's current status, customs, history and mailing information. Check other major cities for other German consulates.
Germanic Genealogy Society Branch of Minnesota Genealogical Society P.O. Box 16312 St. Paul, MN 55116 *GGS library collection is located at:* Concordia College Buenger Memorial Library 275 N. Syndicate St. St. Paul, MN 55104	Collection of hundreds of genealogical materials useful to those researching German-speaking ancestors. Has gazetteers including *Meyers Orts- und Verkehrs-Lexikon* gazetteer and *Glenzdorfs*, maps, passenger list indexes, periodicals as well as general and specific reference works. The Concordia library itself contains an extensive German Lutheran collection. Library is at Hamline Ave. & Marshall Street *Phone: 612-641-8237*

Iron Range Resource Center
P.O. Box 392
Chisholm, MN 55719

Has a large multi-ethnic library collection. Many Finns, Germans, and Croats, Slovenes and other South Slavs migrated to this area (northern Minnesota)

Jewish Historical Society of the Upper
    Midwest
Hamline University Library
1536 Hewitt Ave.
St. Paul, MN 53104

Has an archives and library, with an increasing number of genealogical materials. Currently open only two mornings per week. Second largest Jewish group in Minneapolis came from Romania.

Jewish Historical Society of Western
    Canada
404 - 365 Hargrave St.
Winnipeg, MB R3B 2K3

Has a large collection of genealogical materials. Many Jews came to Western Canada from Galicia and nearby areas.

Minnesota Genealogical Society
P.O. Box 16069
St. Paul, MN 55116-0069
(*Library at 1650 Carroll Ave., St. Paul*)

Library has many books about Germans from Bohemia, mostly in the collection of the Czechoslovak Genealogical Society International, as well as maps, atlases and other general reference works. Many resources for Minnesota. Also has a list of newsletters and addresses for family associations.

Minneapolis Public Library
300 Nicollet Mall
Minneapolis, MN 55401-1992
Phone: 612-372-6500

Has special genealogy room in the history department. Contents include *Deutsche Geschlechterbücher* (dozens of volumes of biographies of nobles and prominent burghers).

Minnesota Historical Society
Research Center
345 W. Kellogg Blvd.
St. Paul, MN 55102-1906
Phone: 612-296-2143

Library collects published sources of Minnesota life and Minnesota people. Has an extensive collection of Minnesota newspapers, local histories, city directories, photographs and family histories. Also has a good collection of historical and genealogical material relating to many eastern states. Archives and manuscripts center houses state and federal census records, and town and county records of Minnesota. Some examples are military and pension records, naturalization records, alien registration records, school records, court records, vital records, burial permits, tax and election records, church records, business and railroad records.

National Huguenot Society
9033 Lyndale Ave. S., Suite 108
Bloomington, MN 55420-3535

Has publications relating to Huguenots who went to Germany. Library open only by appointment; call (612)885-9776.

North Star Chapter
American Historical Society of
    Germans from Russia
175 Spring Valley Drive
Bloomington, MN 55420-5537

Has good library of books and journals about Germans from Russia.

Stearns County Heritage Center
235 33rd Ave. S.
P.O. Box 702
St. Cloud, MN 56302-0702

Very extensive library and other resources.

Consulate of Switzerland
Mr. Schurt Schneider
15500 Wayzata Blvd.
Wayzata, MN 55391
Phone: 612-449-9767

Will answer questions about Swiss customs, history, postal codes and mailing problems. Check other major cities for other Swiss consulates.

University of Minnesota
Wilson Library, West Bank
309 - 19th Ave. S.
Minneapolis, MN 55455-0414
Phone: 612-624-0303 (reference)
Phone: 612-624-4549 (map library)

Has over two million volumes and 250,000 maps, several thousand newspapers and over a million government documents. Borchert Map Library has an extensive collection of historical and contemporary maps for European and other countries. Very strong collection of German materials, including biographical and language dictionaries of Germans and Austrians, local and church histories of German areas, many German gazetteers including *Müllers Grosses Deutsches Ortsbuch*, and works on Pennsylvania German pioneers. The University of Minnesota has a Center for Austrian Studies, and its Robert A. Kaan collection may be the largest American library collection of books on the Hapsburg Empire.

Wisconsin Area Resource Centers

Those closest to Minnesota are at:

Can access Wisconsin records, including vital statistics, local history books, county maps, etc., which can be found anywhere in the system.

Superior Public Library
1530 Tower Ave.
Superior, WI 54880
University of Wisconsin - La Crosse

Eugene W. Murphy Library
1631 Pine St.
La Crosse, WI 54601
University of Wisconsin - River Falls

Chalmer Davee Library
4th & Cascade
River Falls, WI 54022

University of St. Thomas
O'Shaughnessy-Frey Library
2115 Summit Ave.
St. Paul, MN 55105-1096

The Luxembourgiana Bach-Dunn Collection (Biblioteca Luxembourgiana) in the Department of Special Collections has over 1,000 items, many of interest to genealogists. Open afternoons, Monday-Friday, every 3rd Saturday of the month, and by appointment. Has a set of 30 sheets of very detailed maps of Luxembourg (1 inch = 1 mile).

GENEALOGY-RELATED GERMANIC SOCIETIES

A large number of German-American genealogical societies can be found in various directories. The most comprehensive one is probably Elizabeth Petty Bentley's, *The Genealogist's Address Book*, 3rd edition. In Part 3, listing "Ethnic and Religious Organizations and Research Centers," look under the Austrian, German, Luxembourg and Swiss categories, as well as under religious archives and organizations for groups that have retained a distinct religious identity (Jewish, Mennonite, Moravian), as well as for German mainstream churches. If your ancestors came from a non-Germanic country, look under that category, too, because many other societies (Czech, Hungarian, Polish, Slovak and Slovenian, for example) have a multi-ethnic scope.

The following is a selected list of the most prominent German-American genealogical societies, those specializing in certain particular areas, certain multi-purpose societies with relevant resources and the leading pertinent academic society. Many sell books.

For genealogy-related societies in countries outside the United States, check the chapters on the countries in question.

American Historical Society of Germans
   from Russia
631 D Street
Lincoln, NE 68502-1199
(*about 60 chapters, mostly in western U.S.
and Canada*)

American/Schleswig Holstein Heritage
   Society
P.O. Box 313
Davenport, IA 52805-0313

Association of German Nobility in North
   America
3571 E. Eighth St.
Los Angeles, CA 90023

Banat Listserver
c/o Bob Madler
1571 York Way
Sparks, NV 89431

Banat MajorDomo Genealogy Group
1571 York Way
Sparks, NV 89431-1939

The Bukovina Society of the Americas
P.O. Box 81
Ellis, KS 67637-0081

Danube Swabian Association
127 Route 156
Trenton, NJ 08620-1821

Emsland Heritage Society
4325 St. Lawrence Ave.
Cincinnati, OH 45205

Galizien German Descendants
12367 S.E. 214th St.
Kent, WA 98031-2215

German-Acadian Coast Historical and
   Genealogical Society
P.O. Box 517
Destrehan, LA 70047-0517

German-American Research and
   Document Center
University of Wisconsin Foundation
702 Langdon St.
Madison, WI 53706-1487

German-Bohemian Heritage Society
P.O. Box 822
New Ulm, MN 56073-0822

German Genealogical Society of America
P.O. Box 291818
Los Angeles, CA 90029-1818
(*Street address:
   2125 Wright Ave., Suite C-9
   La Verne, CA 91750-5814*)

German Interest Group
   of Chicago Genealogical Society
c/o Ronald Otto
16828 Willow Lane Dr.
Tinley Park, IL 60477-2948

German Interest Group of Southern
   Wisconsin
P.O. Box 2185
Janesville, WI 53547-2185

German Research Association, Inc.
P.O. Box 711600
San Diego, CA 92171-1600

German Society of Pennsylvania
611 Spring Garden St.
Philadelphia, PA 19123-3505

German-Texan Heritage Society
507 E. 10th St.
P.O. Box 684171
Austin, TX 78768-4171

Germanic Genealogy Society
Branch of Minnesota Genealogical Society
P.O. Box 16312
St. Paul, MN 55116-0312

Germans from Russia Heritage Society
1008 E. Central Ave.
Bismarck, ND 58501-1936
(*focuses on western Black Sea area; about
25 chapters in western U.S. and Canada,
about 2/3 in the Dakotas*)

Glückstal Colonies Research Association
1015 - 22nd St.
Santa Monica, CA 90403

Gottscheer Research & Genealogy
    Association
c/o Elizabeth Nick
174 S. Hoover Ave.
Louisville, CO 80027-2130

Illinois Mennonite Historical and
    Genealogical Society
P.O. Box 819
Metamora, IL 61548-0819

Immigrant Genealogical Society
P.O. Box 7369
Burbank, CA 91510-7369
(*major research service*)

Lancaster County Mennonite Historical
    Society
2215 Mainstream Road
Lancaster, PA 17602-1499

Luxembourger Society of Wisconsin
P.O. Box 328
Port Washington, WI 53074

Mid-Atlantic Germanic Society
P.O. Box 2642
Kensington, MD 20891-2642

Orangeburg-German-Swiss Genealogical
    Society
c/o Mrs. T.L. Ulmer
3415 Pine Belt Rd.
Columbia, SC 29204-3128

Ostfriesen Genealogical Society
c/o Rev. Kenneth De Wall
143 Virginia Ave.
Bethalo, IL 62010

Ostfriesian Genealogical Society
c/o Franklin Heibult, Pres.
R.R. 1
Ashton, IA 51232-9801

Palatines to America
Capital University, Box 101
Columbus, OH 43209-2394
(*focuses on colonial immigrants;
9 chapters, mostly between Illinois
and New York*)

Pennsylvania German Research Society
R.R. 1, Box 478
Sugarloaf, PA 18249-9735

Die Pommerschen Leute
c/o Myron E. Gruenwald
1280 Westhaven Drive
Oshkosh, WI 54904-8142
(*publishes Die Pommerschen Leute*)

Pommerscher Verein Freistadt
P.O. Box 204
Germantown, WI 53022-0204

Sacramento German Genealogical Society
P.O. Box 660061
Sacramento, CA 95866-0061

Johannes Schwalm Historical
    Association, Inc.
c/o Gratz Historical Society
P.O. Box 99
Pennsauken, NJ 08110
(*concerned with the descendants of
Hessian soldiers in the Revolutionary
War*)

Schwenkfeldian Exile Society
Pennsburg, PA 18073

Society of German-American Studies
c/o Professor La Vern J. Rippley
St. Olaf College
Northfield, MN 55057-1099

Swiss American Historical Society
6440 N. Bosworth Ave.
Chicago, IL 60626

Swiss American Historical Society
Old Dominion University
Norfolk, VA 23508

Transylvanian Saxon Genealogy and
    Heritage Society, Inc.
P.O. Box 3319
Youngstown, OH 55513-3319

MULTI-ETHNIC AND NON-GERMANIC SOCIETIES
OF IMPORTANCE TO GERMANIC RESEARCH

Germanic Genealogy and Research
   Committee
The Augustan Society, Inc.
P.O. Box P
Torrance, CA 90508-0219
(*Publishes The Augustan, multi-ethnic in
nature. From time to time also publishes
The Germanic Genealogist and The
Benelux Genealogist*)

Czechoslovak Genealogical Society
   International
P.O. Box 16225
St. Paul, MN 55116-0225
(*Publishes Rocenka*)

Patricia A. Eames, ed.
RAGAS Newsletter.
1929 18th St. NW, Suite 1112,
Washington, DC 20009-1710.
(*Latest developments regarding research
in the Commonwealth of Independent
States, with a lot of information relevant
for Germans and Jews. Useful for
researching Germans in eastern Galicia
and northern Bukovina*)

East European Genealogical Society
P.O. Box 2536
Winnipeg, Manitoba R3C 4A7
Canada
(*Publishes East European Genealogist*)

Federation of East European Family
   History Societies
P.O. Box 21346
Salt Lake City, UT 84121-0346
(*Multi-continental umbrella group,
publishes FEEFHS: Newsletter of the
Federation of East European Family
History Societies*)

Douglas P. Holmes, ed.
Hungarian/American Friendship Society
2701 Corabel Lane
Sacramento, CA 95821
(*Publishes Régí Magyarország [Old
Hungary] with genealogical articles from
all ethnic groups from pre-World War I
Hungary*)

Hungarian Genealogical Society of
   America
124 Esther St.
Toledo, OH 43605-1435

Association of Jewish Genealogical
   Societies
Robert Weiss, President
3916 Louis Road
Palo Alto, CA 94303-1622

Jewish Genealogical Society, Inc.
P.O. Box 6398
New York, NY 10128
(*Publishes Dorot*)

Jewish Genealogical Society of
   Greater Washington
P.O. Box 412
Vienna, VA 22183-0412
(*Publishes Mishpocha*)

Lithuanian American Genealogy Society
c/o Balzekas Museum of Lithuanian
   Culture
6500 Pulaski Road
Chicago, IL 60629-5136

Orphan Train Heritage Society of
   America
Route 4, Box 565
Springdale, AZ 72764

Polish Genealogical Society of America
984 N. Milwaukee Ave.
Chicago, IL 60622-4199
(*Publishes Rodziny and Bulletin of PGSA*)

Polish Genealogical Society of Michigan
c/o Burton Historical Collection
Detroit Public Library
5201 Woodward St.
Detroit, MI 48202-4007
(*Publishes The Eaglet*)

Polish Genealogical Society of the
   Northeast
8 Lyle Road
New Britain, CT 06053-2104
(*Publishes Pathways and Passages*)

Wisconsin State Genealogical Society
P.O. Box 5106
Madison, WI 53705-0106
(*Street address:
2109 - 20th Ave,.Monroe, WI 53566*)

DATELINE OF GERMANIC HISTORY

This dateline emphasizes events of genealogical importance or interest. *Items in italics refer mostly to non-European countries;* those in regular type refer to Europe.

321	First Jews settle in the Rhine River valley around Cologne
400-600	Angles and Saxons of Germany, and Jutes of Juteland in Denmark come to Britain. Angles and Saxons rule most of England after 600.
768-814	Charlemagne (Karl der Grosse) rules a large empire that becomes the Holy Roman Empire in 800. The empire includes today's France, Switzerland, Germany, Austria, the Benelux countries and northern Italy.
785	Saxons are the last German tribe to be Christianized.
9th-11th centuries	Jews settle in Mainz (800s), Worms, Magdeburg and Regensburg (900s), and Trier and Speyer (1000s), with freedom to engage in trade and finance until the Crusades, but barred from landownership as feudalism develops. Forced to wear distinctive yellow or orange hats since the 1100s.
943	Treaty of Verdun divides the Carolingian Empire of the Franks into three parts, with Louis (Ludwig) the German's Austrasia representing the beginning of a German ethnic identity separate from that of the French.
870-1648	Alsace is part of the Holy Roman Empire.
900-1350	Areas east of Hamburg-Halle-Northwest Czech line (including the Czech rimland), hitherto occupied by Slavs, become Germanicized through migration and assimilation. Lesser expansion since the Reformation, mostly in border areas east of the Oder River.
1000-1500	Most severe persecution of Jews in Germany and expulsion to Poland (1096-1391), caused initially by the animosity produced by the Crusades and ending with accusations that the Jews were to blame for the "Black Death" (1349-51) and further outbreaks of the bubonic plague in the decades that follow. Expulsion from Austria peaks in the 1400s. Jews are also expelled from all other Western countries, except for parts of Italy.
1100-1300	German colonization of eastern parts of Lorraine and the Netherlands.
1100-1600	German merchants form the Hanse, resulting in powerful trading alliances between the most important ports in the Baltic and North Seas. The Hanseatic League dominates the foreign trade of Scandinavia and northern Germany. Its influence fades in the late 1400s. Surnames become common in Germany during this period.
1141-1181	"Saxons" (mostly Franks) are invited to settle in Transylvania to defend Hungary's eastern border. Also to *Zips* region (northern or Upper Hungary, today the Slovak Republic) at the same time for the same reasons, but lasting till 1340 after Mongol devastation of the area in 1240-42 required resettlement.
1224	Hungarian king issues the Andreanum ("golden patent"), guaranteeing Germans on crownland personal freedom, right to own land and local autonomy.
1241-49	Founding of the Hanseatic League.
1291-1648	Growth and independence of Switzerland and formation of the Schwyz League by the original cantons of Switzerland. Switzerland slowly gains its

independence from the Holy Roman Empire and is officially recognized as independent in 1648.

1330	First settlement in Gottschee County, Slovenia, with immigration continuing until the 1790s.
1345-1918	Ottoman Empire of Turkey controls large portions of Europe, reaching its peak between 1400-1680. Gradually the Austrian Empire pushes it back. Modern-day European areas under Turkish rule at this time include Hungary, Serbia, Macedonia, Bulgaria, Romania, Greece and part of Ukraine.
1348-1365	Bubonic plague (also called the Black Death) threatens all of Europe. Over 25 million Europeans die in periodic outbreaks.
1419-36	Hussite wars for religious freedom in Bohemia. John Huss is leader of the reform movement. He is burned to death in 1415, causing his followers to demand more freedom.
1517	Martin Luther posts his theses disputing traditional religious doctrine of the Roman Catholic church.
1518-23	Ulrich Zwingli begins the Reformation in Switzerland, which leads to the formation of the Reformed (Calvinist) Church.
1524-25	Peasants' War, a mass uprising against secular authorities — inspired but repudiated by Luther — is crushed.
1526	Turkish defeat of Hungary at Battle of Mohacs soon leads to conquest of most of Hungary.
1530	Augsburg Confession (creed) adopted by Lutherans.
1530-1648	Non-Catholics subjected to extreme persecution during this period, including forcible conversion and expulsions and deaths in some areas. Areas dominated by Protestant rulers also persecute dissidents.
1545	Transylvanian Saxons and many Zipsers become Lutherans.
1555	Peace of Augsburg (between Catholics and Lutherans only) states subjects must adopt the religion of their local ruler.
1563	Catholic Counter-Reformation begins in Bavaria.
1568	Particularly notorious persecution of Protestants in the Spanish Netherlands (including Belgium) by the Duke of Alva. Large-scale flight of Walloon Calvinists, especially to the Palatinate, Hesse and Brandenburg, and Dutch-Flemish-Frisian Mennonites to the Danzig area, which is under the Polish crown (religious flight begins about 1530).
1582-85	Calendar reform is proposed by Pope Gregory XIII. The Gregorian calendar is adopted by most Catholic countries of Europe. It is adopted by Prussia in 1612, by most Protestant countries in 1700, by Great Britain in 1752 and by Russia in 1917.
1598	Edict of Nantes grants freedom of religion in France.
1600	Surnames are in common use throughout Germany (in some areas as early as 1100).
1617	John Calvin's works are published.
1618-48	Thirty Years' War. Many German areas are devastated and population drops from 15 million to 10 million. Peace of Westphalia grants Calvinists equal rights and gives subordinate German rulers more independence. Substantial migrations occur, especially Swiss to the Palatinate, to repopulate the most

ravaged areas. Restrictive emigration laws make it difficult and expensive to leave certain areas, e.g. Württemberg. Sweden gains control of Western Pomerania and parts of northwestern Germany. France gains control of most of Alsace.

1622	January 1 is declared to be the beginning of the year in Germany (previously it was March 25).
1650-1750	Introduction of church records (baptisms, marriages and deaths) in most German areas (about 1525 in Switzerland already).
1677	Changing of surnames is forbidden in Bavaria.
1678-79	Alsace acquired by France by the Treaty of Nijmegen.
1683	*Start of German group immigration to North America.*
1683	Turks are defeated at the gates of Vienna. Austria acquires substantial Turkish territories in the Balkans by 1699 treaty, which leads to heavy migration from western Germanic areas to repopulate devastated lands.
1685	King Louis XIV of France revokes the Edict of Nantes, which had granted freedom of religion. Persecution and forcible conversion of Huguenots (French Protestants) causes hundreds of thousands to flee to Switzerland, Germany, the Netherlands, Great Britain and North America. Friedrich Wilhelm, the Great Elector, helps many immigrate to Brandenburg.
1687-88	Transylvania reconquered by Austria (recognized by treaty, 1699). Later becomes haven for Austrian Protestants.
1689-97	War of the League of Augsburg results in French burning down many towns in the Palatinate and mass flight of the population.
1701	Brandenburg becomes the Kingdom of Prussia.
1710-11	*First relatively large-scale immigration of Swiss and Palatines to the American colonies.*
1718	The Banat (lower Danube) reconquered by Austria; is Austrian crownland, 1718-99.
1731-38	*Expulsion of Salzburger Protestants from the Austrian Empire, some of whom come to America, most going to East Prussia and other European areas. Schwenkfelders and Moravian Brethren also come to America in 1733-41.*
1740	Freedom of worship decreed in Prussia.
1740-48	War of the Austrian Succession involves much of Europe, with Prussia gaining most of Silesia.
1744-72	Second phase of "Great Swabian Migration" to the Lower Danube. (First wave, 1718-37, was largely wiped out by Turkish border raids.)
1749-53	*Peak of Germanic immigration to colonial America, mostly from near the Rhine valley.*
1750-52	*First Germans in Canada migrate to Nova Scotia.*
1750-1800	*Many German soldiers (mostly from North Germany) in the service of the Dutch East Indies Co. settle in South Africa (Cape Province).*
1756-63	Very destructive Seven Years' War, involving all major European powers, leads to prolonged Austrian-Prussian rivalry for German leadership.
1763	Catherine the Great's manifesto invites Germans to settle in Russia and grants them free land, freedom from military service and many special privileges.

1764-67	Heavy immigration of Germans to the Volga River region in Russia.
1767	Changing of surnames is forbidden in the Austrian Empire.
1768-1812	Three Russo-Turkish Wars open up newly acquired "South Russia" (Ukraine) to colonization.
1771	Decree ending use of patronymic surnames in Schleswig-Holstein.
1772-95	Partition of Poland by Russia, Prussia and Austria in three stages: 1772, 1793 and 1795. Poland disappears as an independent country until 1918.
1775	Austria gains the Bukovina from Turkey.
1775-83	*American Revolutionary War, with independence declared in 1776. Thirty thousand Hessians and other German mercenaries fight for Great Britain. Thousands remain in the United States and Canada after the war.*
1781	The Patent of Tolerance guarantees freedom of religion in Austria and opens the way for immigration of Protestants. Many medieval restrictions on Jews are removed in Austria, but they are not fully emancipated.
1781-1864	Serfdom is abolished in Northern Europe, but with steps toward it as early as 1718. Key dates: Austria (1781); France (1789); Prussia (1807); all German territory (by 1848); Hungary (1853-54); Russia (1861); Russian Poland and Romania (1864). The abolition of serfdom (personal bondage) was not identical with the abolition of all feudal relationships, such as various fees or services which the tenant peasant had to pay to, or perform for, the landowner or the lord's judicial jurisdiction over them. Moreover, abolition was not complete until 1848 because 1781 abolition was conditional.
1782-87	Third wave of Danube Swabian migration, accompanied by migration to Galicia and the Bukovina.
1784	The Hapsburg Emperor decrees that all parish registers are government property.
1785-1844	Jews required to adopt family names in all Austrian-ruled lands except Hungary (1785-87), in France and Germany (1808-12), and in Russia and Poland (1844).
1786	*German Mennonites from Pennsylvania begin to emigrate to Ontario, more heavily after 1807.*
1789-1824	Heaviest German immigration to the Black Sea region of Russia (now Ukraine).
1789-1917	Jewish people are emancipated granting them equality by law in France (1789), Prussia (1812-50), Austro-Hungarian Empire (1867), Baden, Hesse and Frankfurt (1808-1811) and all of Germany (1874), Switzerland (1874) and Russia (1917).
1792-1815	Wars against revolutionary France by Prussia, Austria and other countries. Napoleon forces the end of the Holy Roman Empire in 1806, with the Hapsburg family continuing to rule Austria, but no longer influential in Germany. Rhenish Confederation is founded in 1806. Civil registration is introduced in France and western Germany. In 1815, the Congress of Vienna establishes the German Confederation of 39 sovereign states, in which Prussia has considerable influence. Sweden loses the last of its territory in Germany.
1794	Changing of surnames is forbidden in Prussia.

1795-1835	Russia adopts laws establishing the Pale of Settlement (roughly Ukraine, Bessarabia, Belarus or White Russia, Poland and Lithuania), to which all new Jewish residents are restricted.
1798	Switzerland declares neutrality.
1810-24	*Most Latin American countries gain independence.*
1811	Decree ending use of patronymic surnames in Ostfriesland (East Frisia).
1814	*Cape Province ceded by the Netherlands to Great Britain.*
1816-17	*Crop failures and famine spark the first significant post-colonial immigration from Germany and Luxembourg to the United States.*
1817	Lutherans and Reformed Churches are ordered to merge into the Evangelical Church in Prussia and merge elsewhere about the same time. Religious groups are ordered to maintain vital records in what is now Romania.
1822-1889	*Independent Empire of Brazil; changed to a republic after the 1888 abolition of slavery.*
1824-29	*Heavy German immigration to Brazil, especially from Rhineland-Palatinate and Hesse.*
1830	*Gradually increasing German emigration to the United States and Canada, coinciding with the beginning of the Industrial Revolution at home and the failure of the 1830 revolution.*
1838-54	*Main wave of emigration of "Old Lutherans," who rejected the Evangelical merger, to New York, Wisconsin, Missouri, Michigan and Texas. About one third went to Australia (mostly South Australia) and some to Canada.*
1840-1890	*Period of heavy Jewish immigration from Germany to the United States, with most turning to Reform Judaism and spreading westward throughout the country.*
1843	Polish uprisings against Prussia and Austria fail.
1843-59	*First large wave of German emigrants to the United States (1846-1857), especially from the Palatinate and the Rhineland, but also from Luxembourg and some from Bohemia. This emigration peaks in 1854 and is largely stopped by the Panic of 1857. Most German immigration to Texas occurs during this period. German colonization societies spring up. Public subsidies and even coercion cause many German paupers to go to the United States, and Brazil (1846-59). Others go to Canada and Chile (1846-66, especially 1852-57). Some, including Swiss, go to New Zealand (1843-45) and assisted farm laborers go to Australia (mostly New South Wales). Many leave Europe after the crop failures of 1845-47, which affects most of Europe and are accompanied by famine and cholera epidemics. This coincides with a period of American boom.*
1848	Liberal revolutions occur in most of western and central Europe, with half of the approximately 30 revolutionary centers in the Hapsburg Empire. This leads to abolition of the last remaining feudal obligations of peasants to the landowners.
1848	*Ultimate failure of the revolution in Germany leads to emigration of many well-educated revolutionaries to the United States, where they become prominent leaders not only in the German-American community, but also in the country. Trans-Atlantic emigration exceeds migration to Eastern Europe after this time.*

1848	National civil registration is adopted in Switzerland (by religious denomination until 1876) after a brief civil war. Prior registration was at the cantonal level.
1851 ff.	*Australian Gold Rush, especially in Victoria, attracts many Germans from South Australia, New Zealand and elsewhere.*
1857-58	*Depression in the United States (Panic of 1857).*
1857-59	*Large wave of German military and civilian immigrants to South Africa (British Kaffraria, i.e., eastern Cape Province).*
1861-65	*American Civil War.*
1861-1900	Heaviest immigration of Germans to Volhynia, mostly from Poland, sparked mostly by abolition of Russian serfdom and rising Polish nationalism.
1861-86	*Relatively strong immigration from diverse Germanic areas (many from Hanover, Polish and Czech areas) to New Zealand, sparked partly by discovery of gold on West Coast of South Island.*
1861-91	*Rapid increase in German immigration to Queensland (especially from Mecklenburg to Silesia and east), making it the Australian state with the most Germans.*
1862	*Morrill Act makes free land available in the United States.*
1863-64	Second Polish uprising against Russia, followed by 1868 decree that all public records, including parish registers, must be in Russian. Prussian policies designed to forcibly Germanize the Poles under its rule leads to anti-German sentiment in Russian Poland, causing many Germans in Central Poland to migrate eastward to Volhynia and Eastern Poland.
1864	Austria and Prussia defeat Denmark.
1865	Changing of surnames is forbidden in Lippe.
1865-74	*Second large wave of German emigrants to the United States, peaking in 1873. Many people leave to avoid military service. Others emigrate because the Industrial Revolution destroys cottage industries.*
1866	*Prussia defeats Austria. As a result, Austria is forced to share power with Hungary as the Austro-Hungarian Empire is established in 1867. Magyarization policies lead to extensive German emigration from the Hungarian part of the Dual Monarchy.*
1867	*Dominion of Canada is created by the British North America Act as a self-governing confederation.*
1870-71	Prussia's victory over France leads to the creation of the (Second) German Empire, taking Alsace-Lorraine from France.
1871	Special privileges of Germans are revoked in Russia, sparking emigration to North and South America.
1871-85	*Heavy German and Swiss immigration to Argentina and Brazil.*
1871-1907	Over 500 killed and thousands made homeless in anti-Jewish pogroms in Russia, with a first serious wave in 1881-83 and a much worse one in 1903-07. This coincides with the forced relocation of all other Russian Jews to the Pale of Settlement in 1882-91, thus leading to emigration of half of the four million Jews, many of them to the United States. Jewish emigration resumes after World War I.
1873-79	*Depression in the United States (Panic of 1873).*

1874	An anti-Semitic movement develops in Germany and many other countries, triggering Zionism, but does not become acute in Germany until after World War I.
1874-76	Civil registration is required in Prussia (1874) and the rest of the German Empire (1876).
1874-1914	*Many Germans from Eastern Europe, especially Russia but also eastern parts of Austria-Hungary, immigrate to the Great Plains states, Canadian Prairie provinces and Argentina. Many Jews from the same areas emigrate, mostly to big eastern cities in the United States but also to Palestine and to Britain and its dominions, after the Russian pogroms begin in 1881 and as a result of starvation in Galicia.*
1878	Much of the Ottoman Turkish Empire is broken up, with international recognition of Romanian independence, Russian acquisition of Bessarabian and Caucasus territory, and Austro-Hungarian control over Bosnia and Herzegovina, among other changes.
1878-79	*Last large German immigration to South Africa.*
1880-90	*Largest number of Luxembourg emigrants come to the United States.*
1880-93	*Third wave of German emigrants to the United States, with all-time peak in 1882. Coincides with American economic boom, briefly interrupted by the Depression of 1884.*
1881-88	*Large numbers of Swiss emigrants come to the United States.*
1882-89	*Relatively heavy German (mostly Protestant) immigration to Chile.*
1884-86	*Establishment of German colonies and protectorates in Africa and the Southwest Pacific. Limited immigration, mostly to Namibia (German South-West Africa).*
1890-1914	Heavy migration of Russian Germans into Siberia.
1890	*American frontier officially declared closed. German-Americans start emigrating to Western Canada in considerable numbers.*
1892	*Ellis Island opens as immigration receiving center in New York. Immigrants previously were processed at Castle Garden.*
1893-96	*Economic crisis in the United States ends large-scale immigration from Germany.*
1895	Civil registration adopted in Hungary. Pre-1895 church records collected by the government after World War I.
1901	*Various Australian colonies form Commonwealth of Australia.*
1907	*New Zealand becomes a dominion (had a constitution since 1852.)*
1909-10	*Peak of Transylvanian Saxon immigration to the United States.*
1910	*Union of South Africa is established, following the 1899-1902 Boer War.*
1910-20	*Largest number of Swiss emigrants come to the United States during this period.*
1912-13	First and Second Balkan Wars.
1914-18	World War I, involving almost all of Europe. Bolshevik Revolution of 1917, followed by civil war, causes emigration from Russia. Internment of many German-born residents of the United States and Australia. Hostility toward Germans in Canada.

1917	*Severe discrimination against German-Americans begins with American entry into World War I.*
1919	Transformation of former German possessions into mandates of various Allied powers.
1919-23	Peace of Paris, including the Treaties of St. Germain (with Austria) and Trianon (with Hungary), breaks up the Austro-Hungarian Empire, while the Treaties of St. Germain and Versailles (with Germany) require cession of German and Austrian border territories with a sizable number of Germans to Czechoslovakia, Poland, Italy, France, Belgium and Denmark, creation of the Free City of Danzig, followed by transfer of the Memel region to Lithuania in 1923. German colonies and protectorates become Allied mandates, nominally under supervision of the League of Nations.
1921-23	Germany endures extreme inflation ($1 = 4 billion marks).
1921-24	*Immigration is severely curtailed by new American laws.*
1923-30	*Immigration of Mennonite refugees from the Bolshevik Revolution in Russia to Canada and Latin America. Simultaneous emigration of Western Canadian Mennonites to Mexico and Paraguay. Catholic and Lutheran refugees from the Soviet Union settle in southern Brazil.*
1924-41	Autonomous Soviet Socialist Republic of Volga Germans is formed.
1929	Beginning of worldwide Great Depression, ended by World War II.
1929-32	*Thousands of Germans, mostly Mennonites and Lutherans, flee from the Soviet Union via Manchuria, with most of them settling in South America and Canada.*
1932	Germany has 6 million unemployed.
1933-45	Adolf Hitler is the *Führer* (leader) of the Third Reich in Germany.
1933-39	*More than half of the Jews in Germany emigrate in 1933-39, with Austrian Jews following in 1938, settling in all countries willing to admit them. Many Jewish and political refugees are stranded in Shanghai during World War II. German socialists from the Czech lands settle in Sweden, beginning in 1938, with more Sudetenland Germans arriving after World War II. American immigration restrictions are eased somewhat to allow entry of political refugees from Nazi Germany.*
1938	Hitler annexes Austria and the Sudetenland region of Czechoslovakia. Civil registration begins in Austria and the Czech Republic.
1939-45	World War II, with German casualties of 3.8 million civilians and 4 million soldiers. Nazis kill 12 million civilians, half of them Jews. Total war deaths are about 25 million; Russia, Germany, Poland and Yugoslavia have the greatest losses.
1939	Hitler-Stalin Pact provides for repatriation of Germans in Stalin's sphere of influence in Eastern Europe (but not in the Soviet Union itself) to the "homeland," mostly the Warta River region in German-occupied Western Poland.
1941-42	Deportation of most Germans living east of the Dnieper River to the Asian portion of the Soviet Union and other remote areas (with most families split apart), after Hitler attacks Russia. Most of those west of the Dnieper River are saved by the rapid advance of the German armies.
1944-48	Mass flight of Germans from Eastern Europe before the advancing Soviet armies, with expulsion of most of the remainder after the end of the war (1945-48), pursuant to the Potsdam Agreement. Many are killed or returned

to Soviet control. Population of West Germany increases 25% as 14 million ethnic Germans arrive. Many displaced, stateless persons go on to North and South America and elsewhere.

1944-48	Many Romanian Germans sent to Russian slave labor camps (1944-45, some remaining until the 1950s); Germans in Yugoslavia in concentration camps there (1945-48).
1949	The democratic Federal Republic of Germany and the communist German Democratic Republic are formed.
1949 ff.	*Many Germans emigrate to the United States, Canada, Australia, and Latin America.*
1950s	*Heaviest immigration of Danube Swabians to the United States (Midwest, Northeast and California) and to many other countries, including Canada and Brazil. Many Sudeten Germans and other Displaced Persons also emigrate to various countries, including the United States, Canada, Australia, New Zealand, South America and Sweden.*
1953	Stalin dies. During the following thaw, Germans are released from slave labor camps, allowing families to re-unite, but not to return to their pre-war homes in the Volga and Black Sea regions. The new eastern German heartland is in Kazakhstan, other Muslim republics, and near the Trans-Siberian Railway.
1961	The Berlin Wall and other border barricades are built to prevent East Germans from fleeing the German Democratic Republic for the Federal Republic of Germany.
1980-85	Majority of Germans leave Romania for Germany, with many soon migrating all over the world (1983-85).
1987	*Glasnost* leads to emigration of many ethnic Germans and Jews from the Soviet Union, East Central Europe, and Southeast Europe. Those returning to Germany are known as *Aussiedler* (resettlers). Efforts to re-establish a Volga German homeland, return Germans to Ukraine, and resettle Germans in the Kaliningrad area (formerly northern East Prussia) produce minimal results, increasing the flow of Germans returning to Germany from the Asian parts of the Commonwealth of Independent States. This emigration is still continuing.
1989-1990	The Berlin Wall crumbles after East Germans flee to the West en masse. Democratic elections are held throughout East Central Europe, and Germany is reunified as the German Democratic Republic is dissolved and merges into the Federal Republic of Germany.
1991-92	Soviet Union collapses after failed coup. All non-Russian republics declare their independence. Loose Commonwealth of Independent States (excluding the Baltic countries and Georgia) is established.

MAPS

This selection of maps shows the major areas of German, Austrian and Swiss settlement in Europe throughout modern history. These maps have been selected or created to help locate hard-to-find regions or provinces (not individual towns). The historical maps show some of the many boundary changes that have occurred in Europe.

The following list identifies each map and the page where it appears.

		Page
1.	Modern Europe with Former German Areas, Present Day	452
2.	Central and Eastern Europe after World War II, 1955	453
3.	Central and Eastern Europe after World War I, 1924	454
4.	Central and Eastern Europe, 1815	455
5.	Central and Eastern Europe, 1721	456
6.	German dialects, High and Low German areas	457
7.	European Rivers, Showing Ports	458
8.	Federal Republic of Germany, Present Day	459
9.	Federal Republic of Germany (West Germany), 1949-1990	460
10.	German Democratic Republic (East Germany), 1949-1990	461
11.	German Empire, 1871-1918	462
12.	Growth of the Kingdom of Prussia, 1648, 1815, 1866	463
13.	Belgium, Netherlands and Luxembourg (Benelux) France, showing former Alsace and Lorraine	464
14.	Switzerland and Liechtenstein	465
15.	Czech Republic and Slovak Republic, Present Day	466
16.	Austria and Hungary, Present Day	467
16.	German Eastern Regions and the Sudetenland, 1918-1938 Denmark, showing North Schleswig	468
17.	German Settlements in the Austro-Hungarian Empire, 1867-1918	469
18.	Growth of the Austro-Hungarian Empire, 1282-1918	470
19.	Division of the Austro-Hungarian Empire after World War I, 1918-1923	471
20.	Poland, Present Day	472
21.	Partition of Poland, 1772-1795	473
22.	German Settlements: Volga River Region, Ukraine and Black Sea Areas	474
23.	The Pale of Settlement for Russian Jews, 1835-1917	475
24.	Successor States to Yugoslavia, Present Day	476
25.	South America and Central America Showing areas settled by Germans from Russia	477
26.	German Settlements in Australia and New Zealand	478

MODERN EUROPE

Present Day

WITH FORMER GERMAN AREAS

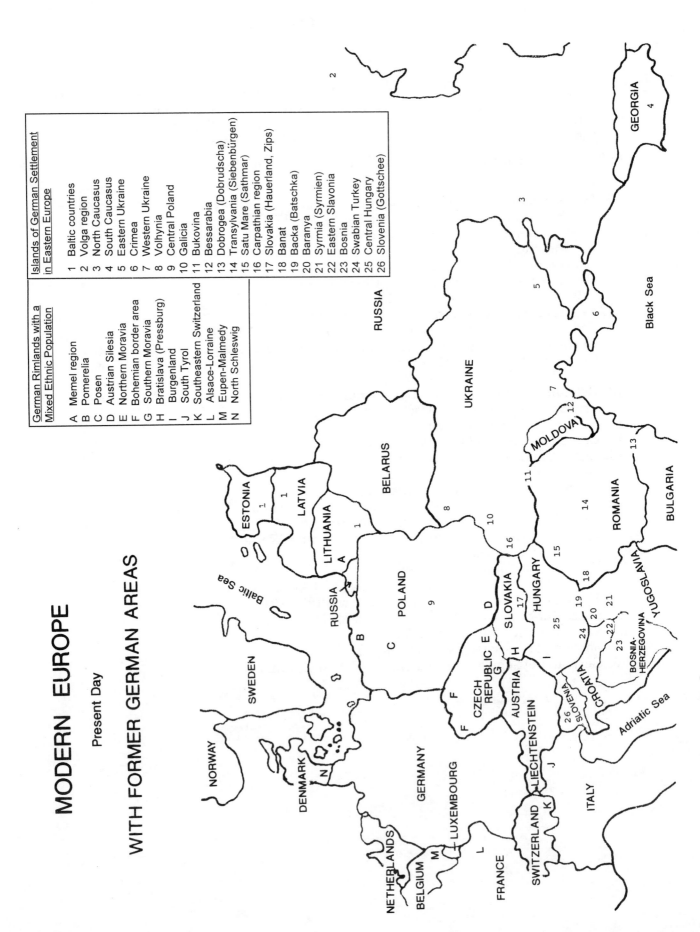

German Rimlands with a
Mixed Ethnic Population

A Memel region
B Pomerelia
C Posen
D Austrian Silesia
E Northern Moravia
F Bohemian border area
G Southern Moravia
H Bratislava (Pressburg)
I Burgenland
J South Tyrol
K Southeastern Switzerland
L Alsace-Lorraine
M Eupen-Malmedy
N North Schleswig

Islands of German Settlement
in Eastern Europe

1 Baltic countries
2 Volga region
3 North Caucasus
4 South Caucasus
5 Eastern Ukraine
6 Crimea
7 Western Ukraine
8 Volhynia
9 Central Poland
10 Galicia
11 Bukovina
12 Bessarabia
13 Dobrogea (Dobrudscha)
14 Transylvania (Siebenbürgen)
15 Satu Mare (Sathmar)
16 Carpathian region
17 Slovakia (Hauerland, Zips)
18 Banat
19 Backa (Batschka)
20 Baranya
21 Syrmia (Syrmien)
22 Eastern Slavonia
23 Bosnia
24 Swabian Turkey
25 Central Hungary
26 Slovenia (Gottschee)

CENTRAL and EASTERN EUROPE

After WW II - 1955

Germanic Genealogy: A Guide to Worldwide Sources and Migration Patterns   453

CENTRAL and EASTERN EUROPE

After WW I - 1924

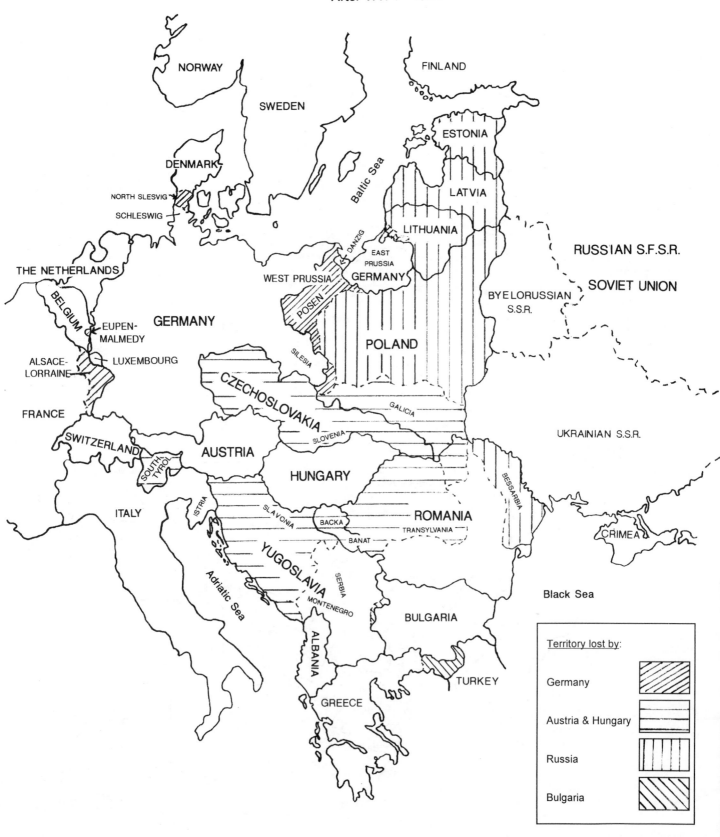

NORWAY

SWEDEN

FINLAND

DENMARK

Baltic Sea

ESTONIA

LATVIA

NORTH SLESVIG

SCHLESWIG

LITHUANIA

RUSSIAN S.F.S.R.

DANZIG

EAST PRUSSIA

THE NETHERLANDS

WEST PRUSSIA

GERMANY

SOVIET UNION

BELGIUM

POSEN

BYELORUSSIAN S.S.R.

EUPEN-MALMEDY

GERMANY

SILESIA

POLAND

ALSACE-LORRAINE

LUXEMBOURG

FRANCE

CZECHOSLOVAKIA

SWITZERLAND

SOUTH TYROL

AUSTRIA

GALICIA

UKRAINIAN S.S.R.

SLOVENIA

HUNGARY

ITALY

ISTRIA

SLAVONIA

BACKA

ROMANIA

BESSARBIA

BANAT

TRANSYLVANIA

CRIMEA

YUGOSLAVIA

SERBIA

Adriatic Sea

MONTENEGRO

BULGARIA

Black Sea

ALBANIA

TURKEY

GREECE

Territory lost by:

Germany

Austria & Hungary

Russia

Bulgaria

CENTRAL and EASTERN EUROPE - 1815

Showing Boundaries (Following Napoleon's Defeat)
of the Ottoman Empire, Austrian Empire, Russian Empire,
Germanic Confederation and the Prussian provinces outside
the Confederation (East Prussia, West Prussia, Posen).
(Historic Provincial Boundaries of Russia, 1815 to 1918, shown.)

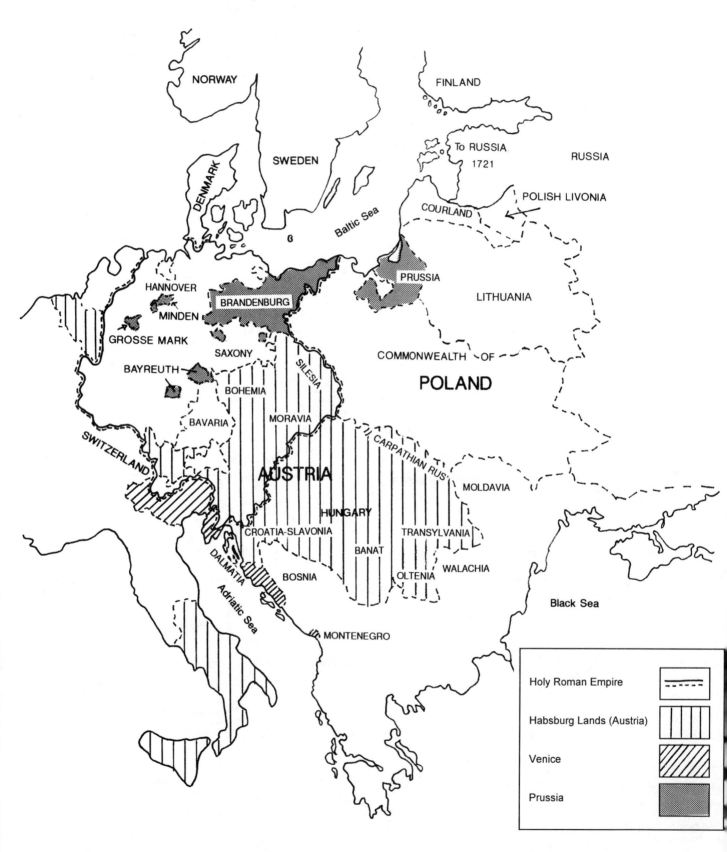

CENTRAL and EASTERN EUROPE – 1721

Showing the de facto Boundary of the Holy Roman Empire,
Habsburg Lands (Austria), Venice and Prussia

NORWAY

FINLAND

SWEDEN

DENMARK

To RUSSIA
1721

RUSSIA

POLISH LIVONIA

Baltic Sea

COURLAND

HANNOVER

BRANDENBURG

PRUSSIA

LITHUANIA

MINDEN

GROSSE MARK

SAXONY

COMMONWEALTH OF

BAYREUTH

SILESIA

POLAND

BOHEMIA

MORAVIA

BAVARIA

SWITZERLAND

AUSTRIA

CARPATHIAN RUS

MOLDAVIA

HUNGARY

CROATIA-SLAVONIA

TRANSYLVANIA

BANAT

DALMATIA

BOSNIA

OLTENIA

WALACHIA

Adriatic Sea

Black Sea

MONTENEGRO

Holy Roman Empire	
Habsburg Lands (Austria)	
Venice	
Prussia	

456

Germanic Genealogy Society

GERMAN DIALECTS

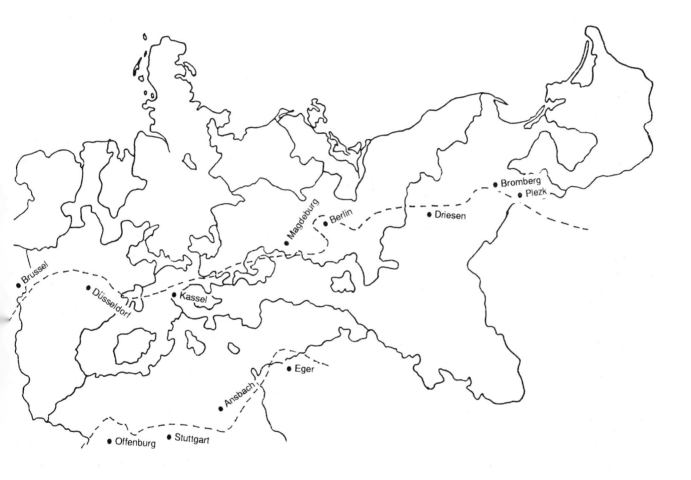

There was a fundamental difference between the German dialects spoken in the northern lowlands (hence the modifier "Low") where Low German served as a *lingua franea* from Flanders to the eastern Baltic, and the dialect spoken farther south. The distinction between the spoken German of Middle Germany and the High German dialects in the south was not as apparent. Since these lines were not entirely stable, depending upon which sounds are used as the criterion for drawing the lines, the map is only an approximation.

EUROPEAN RIVERS CONVERGING TO SEAPORTS

Used in Emigration

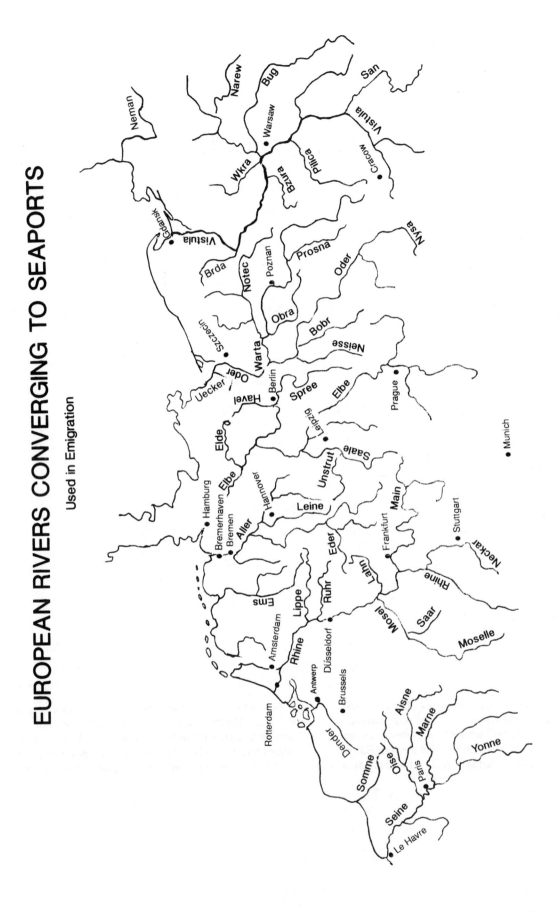

FEDERAL REPUBLIC OF GERMANY
(Present Day)

Kiel ●

SCHLESWIG-HOLSTEIN

Lübeck ●

Rostock ●

HAMBURG

MECKLENBURG-VORPOMMERN

Emden ●

Lüneburg ●

Wittenberge ●

Oldenburg ●

BREMEN

BRANDENBURG

LOWER SAXONY

BERLIN

Rheine ●

Osnabrück ●

Hannover ●

Branden-burg ●

Potsdam ●

Frankfurt (Oder) ●

Münster ●

Magdeburg ●

SAXONY-ANHALT

NORTHRHINE-WESTPHALIA

Kassel ●

Leipzig ●

Köln ●

Dresden ●

Aachen ●

Weimar ●

SAXONY

THURINGIA

HESSE

Koblenz ●

Frankfurt am Main ●

Trier ●

Mainz ●

Würzburg ●

RHINELAND-PALATINATE

Darmstadt ●

Nürnberg ●

SAARLAND

Heidelberg ●

Regensburg ●

Karlsruhe ●

BAVARIA

Stuttgart ●

BADEN-WÜRTTEMBERG

Augsburg ●

Freiburg im Breisgau ●

München ●

Rosenheim ●

Konstanz ●

FEDERAL REPUBLIC OF GERMANY

(West Germany)

1949-1990

SCHLESWIG-HOLSTEIN

BREMEN

Bremerhaven

HAMBURG

NIEDERSACHSEN (Lower Saxony)

WEST BERLIN

NORDRHEIN-WESTFALEN

(Northrhine-Westphalia)

HESSEN (Hesse)

RHEINLAND-PFALZ

(Rhineland-Palatinate)

SAARLAND

BAYERN (Bavaria)

BADEN-WÜRTTEMBERG

Germanic Genealogy Society

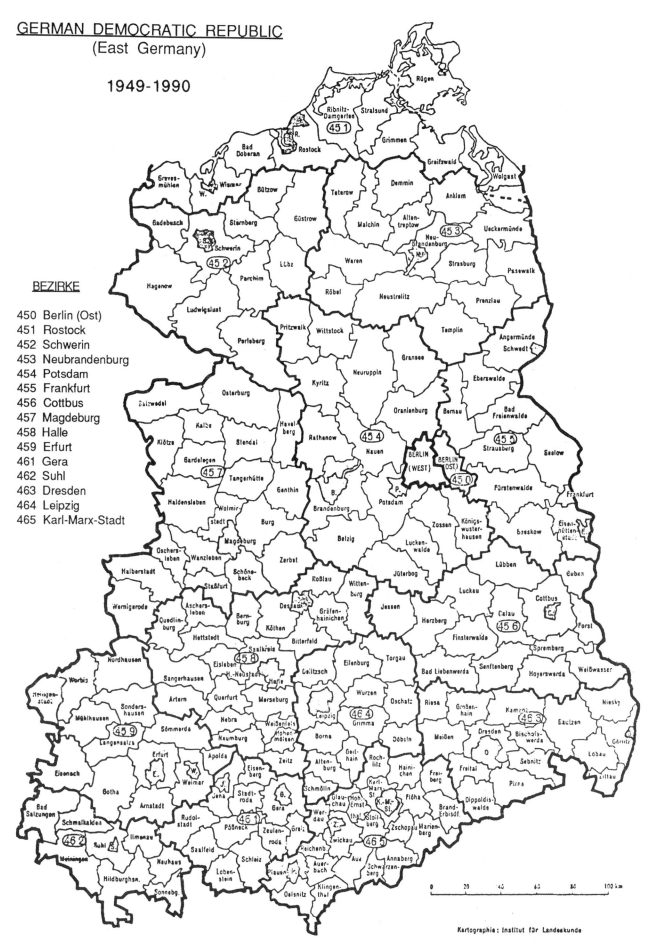

GERMAN DEMOCRATIC REPUBLIC
(East Germany)

1949-1990

BEZIRKE

- 450 Berlin (Ost)
- 451 Rostock
- 452 Schwerin
- 453 Neubrandenburg
- 454 Potsdam
- 455 Frankfurt
- 456 Cottbus
- 457 Magdeburg
- 458 Halle
- 459 Erfurt
- 461 Gera
- 462 Suhl
- 463 Dresden
- 464 Leipzig
- 465 Karl-Marx-Stadt

Kartographie: Institut für Landeskunde

Germanic Genealogy: A Guide to Worldwide Sources and Migration Patterns

461

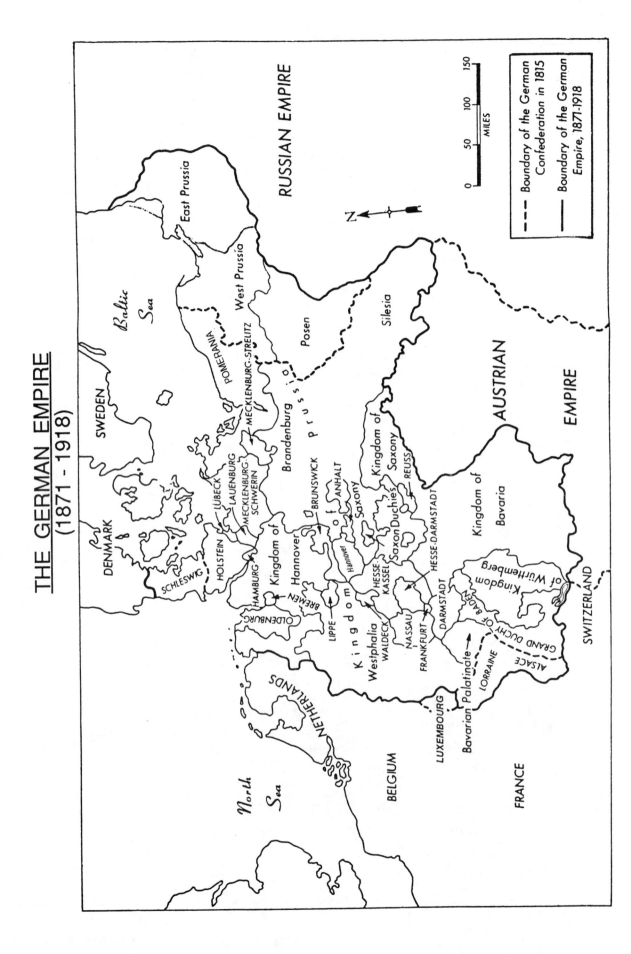

THE GERMAN EMPIRE
(1871 - 1918)

RUSSIAN EMPIRE

East Prussia

West Prussia

Posen

Silesia

AUSTRIAN

EMPIRE

Baltic Sea

SWEDEN

POMERANIA

MECKLENBURG-STRELITZ

Brandenburg

P r u s s i a

Kingdom of Saxony

REUSS

DENMARK

LÜBECK

LAUENBURG

MECKLENBURG-SCHWERIN

HOLSTEIN

SCHLESWIG

HAMBURG

Kingdom of Hannover

BRUNSWICK

ANHALT

Saxony

Hannover

Saxon Duchies

HESSE-DARMSTADT

Kingdom of Bavaria

SWITZERLAND

BREMEN

OLDENBURG

LIPPE

K i n g d o m o f

Westphalia

WALDECK

NASSAU

FRANKFURT

HESSE-KASSEL

DARMSTADT

Kingdom of Württemberg

GRAND DUCHY OF BADEN

ALSACE

LORRAINE

Bavarian Palatinate

LUXEMBOURG

NETHERLANDS

BELGIUM

FRANCE

North Sea

Boundary of the German Confederation in 1815

Boundary of the German Empire, 1871-1918

150

100

50

0

MILES

N

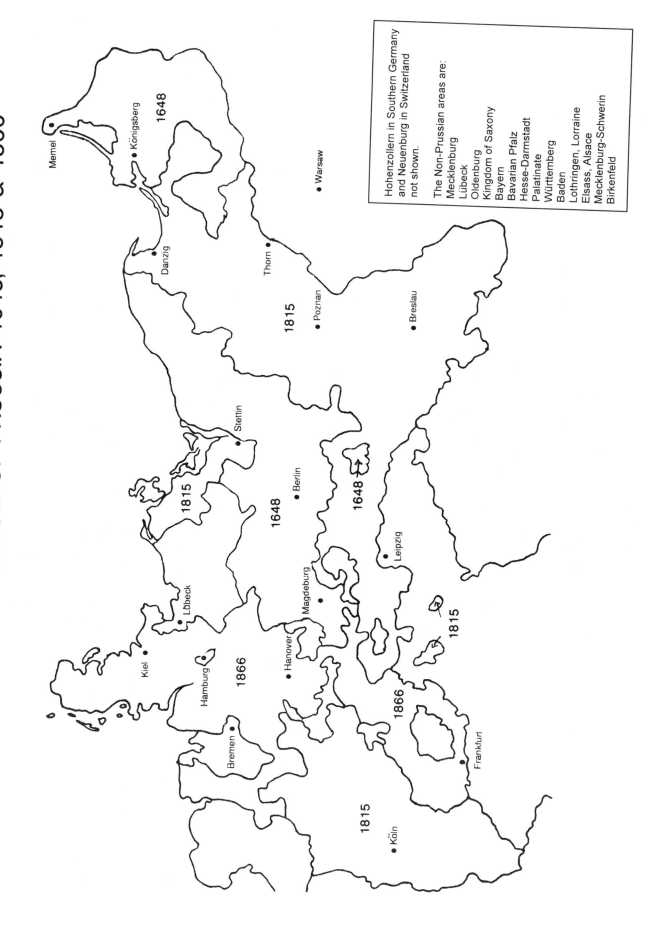

THE GROWTH OF THE KINGDOM OF PRUSSIA 1648, 1815 & 1866

Memel

1648

• Königsberg

• Warsaw

Danzig

Thorn

1815

• Poznan

• Breslau

Stettin

1815

1648

• Berlin

1648 →

• Leipzig

Magdeburg

1815

Lübeck

1866

• Hanover

Kiel

Hamburg

1866

Bremen

Frankfurt

1815

• Köln

Hohenzollern in Southern Germany
and Neuenburg in Switzerland
not shown.

The Non-Prussian areas are:
Mecklenburg
Lübeck
Oldenburg
Kingdom of Saxony
Bayern
Bavarian Pfalz
Hesse-Darmstadt
Palatinate
Württemberg
Baden
Lothringen, Lorraine
Elsass, Alsace
Mecklenburg-Schwerin
Birkenfeld

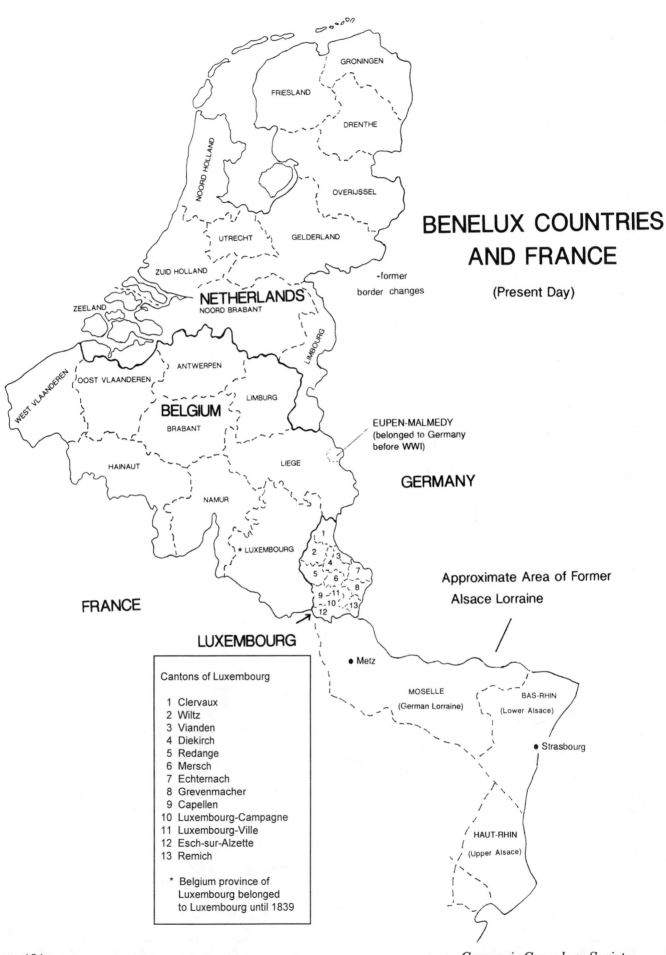

BENELUX COUNTRIES
AND FRANCE

(Present Day)

GRONINGEN

FRIESLAND

DRENTHE

NOORD HOLLAND

OVERIJSSEL

UTRECHT

GELDERLAND

ZUID HOLLAND

-former
border changes

NETHERLANDS

ZEELAND

NOORD BRABANT

LIMBURG

ANTWERPEN

WEST VLAANDEREN

OOST VLAANDEREN

LIMBURG

BELGIUM

BRABANT

EUPEN-MALMEDY
(belonged to Germany
before WWI)

HAINAUT

LIEGE

GERMANY

NAMUR

* LUXEMBOURG

Approximate Area of Former
Alsace Lorraine

FRANCE

LUXEMBOURG

● Metz

MOSELLE
(German Lorraine)

BAS-RHIN
(Lower Alsace)

● Strasbourg

Cantons of Luxembourg

1 Clervaux
2 Wiltz
3 Vianden
4 Diekirch
5 Redange
6 Mersch
7 Echternach
8 Grevenmacher
9 Capellen
10 Luxembourg-Campagne
11 Luxembourg-Ville
12 Esch-sur-Alzette
13 Remich

* Belgium province of
  Luxembourg belonged
  to Luxembourg until 1839

HAUT-RHIN
(Upper Alsace)

Germanic Genealogy Society

SWITZERLAND and LIECHTENSTEIN
(Present - Day)

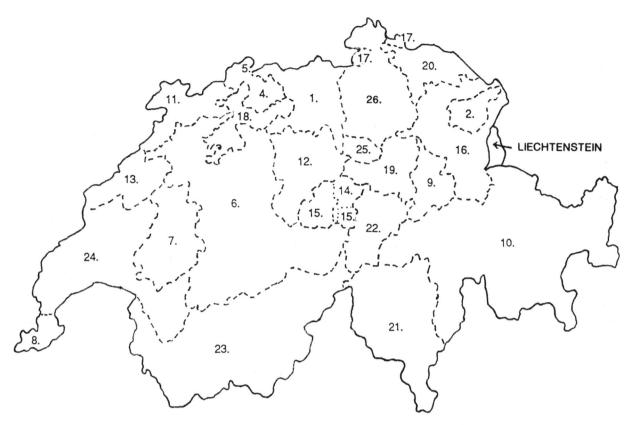

Cantons of Switzerland are listed below in 3 or 4 languages, the bold-faced ones indicating the principal language or languages spoken. Language is indicated by (Ger.) Swiss-German; (Fr.) French; (It.) Italian; and (Rom.) Romansch. Date indicates entry into Swiss Confederation.

1. **Aargau (Ger.)**, Argovie (Fr.), Argovia (It.)	1803
2. **Appenzell Inner-Rhoden (Ger.)**, Rhodes-Interieures (Fr.)	1513
3. **Appenzell Ausser-Rhoden (Ger.)**, Rhodes-Exterieures (Fr.)	1513
4. **Basel-Land (Ger.)**, Bâle-Campagne (Fr.), Basilea-Campagna (It.)	1501
5. **Basel-Stadt (Ger.)**, Bâle-Ville (Fr.), Basilea-Citta (It.)	1501
6. **Bern (Ger.)**, Berne (Fr.), Berna (It.)	1353
7. **Fribourg (Fr.), Freiburg (Ger.)**, Friborgo (It.)	1481
8. **Genève (Fr.)**, Genf (Ger.), Ginevra (It.)	1815
9. **Glarus (Ger.)**, Glaris (Fr.), Glarona (It.)	1352
10. **Graubünden (Ger.), Grischun (Rom.), Grigioni (It.)**, Grisons (Fr.)	1803
11. **Jura (Fr.)**, Jura (Ger.) *Separated from Bern Canton	*1974
12. **Luzern (Ger.)**, Lucerne (Fr.), Lucerna (It.)	1332
13. **Neuchâtel (Fr.)**, Neuenburg (Ger.), Neuchâtel (It.)	1815
14. **Nidwalden (Ger.)**, Nidwald (Fr.), Sottoselva (It.)	1291
15. **Obwalden (Ger.)**, Obwald (Fr.), Sopraselva (It.)	1291
16. **Sankt Gallen (Ger.)**, Saint Gall (Fr.), S. Gallo (It.)	1803
17. **Schaffhausen (Ger.)**, Schaffhouse (Fr.), Sciaffusa (It.)	1501
18. **Solothurn (Ger.)**, Soleure (Fr.), Soletta (It.)	1481
19. **Schwyz (Ger.)**, Schwyz (Fr.), Svitto (It.)	1291
20. **Thurgau (Ger.)**, Thurgovie (Fr.), Turgovia (It.)	1803
21. **Ticino (It.)**, Tessin (Ger., Fr.)	1803
22. **Uri (Ger., Fr., It.)**	1291
23. **Valais (Fr.), Wallis (Ger.)**, Vallese (It.)	1815
24. **Vaud (Fr.)**, Waadt (Ger.), Vaud (It.)	1803
25. **Zug (Ger.)**, Zoug (Fr.), Zugo (It.)	1352
26. **Zürich (Ger.)**, Zurich (Fr.), Zurigo (It.)	1351

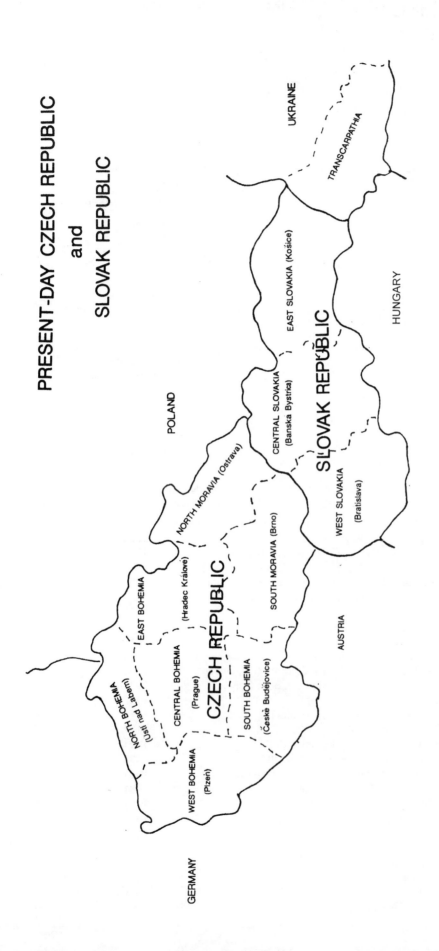

PRESENT-DAY CZECH REPUBLIC
and
SLOVAK REPUBLIC

GERMANY

POLAND

UKRAINE

TRANSCARPATHIA

EAST SLOVAKIA (Košice)

CENTRAL SLOVAKIA (Banska Bystrica)

SLOVAK REPUBLIC

WEST SLOVAKIA (Bratislava)

HUNGARY

AUSTRIA

NORTH MORAVIA (Ostrava)

SOUTH MORAVIA (Brno)

NORTH BOHEMIA (Ustí nad Labem)

EAST BOHEMIA (Hradec Králové)

CENTRAL BOHEMIA (Prague)

CZECH REPUBLIC

WEST BOHEMIA (Plzeň)

SOUTH BOHEMIA (České Budějovice)

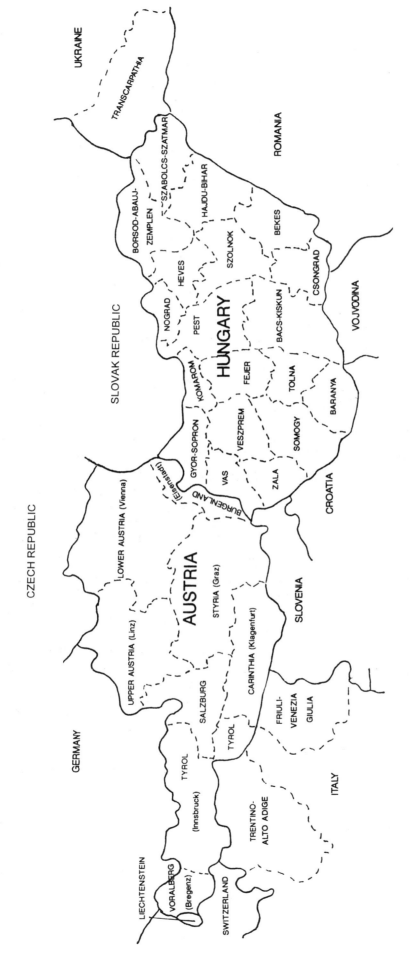

PRESENT-DAY
AUSTRIA and HUNGARY

GERMAN EASTERN REGIONS
and the Sudetenland 1918-1938

DENMARK AND NORTH SCHLESWIG

Legend:

- —— German border 1937
- —·—· Oder-Neisse-line and Polish-Soviet Demarcation line
- ········ German border until 1918
- Sudetenland 1938
- Teschener Silesia
- Province boundaries
- Other boundaries

DENMARK (Present Day)

Approximate Area of Former Schleswig

VEJLE

RIBE

HADERSLEV

TONDER

ABENRAA-SONDERBORG

SCHLESWIG-HOLSTEIN

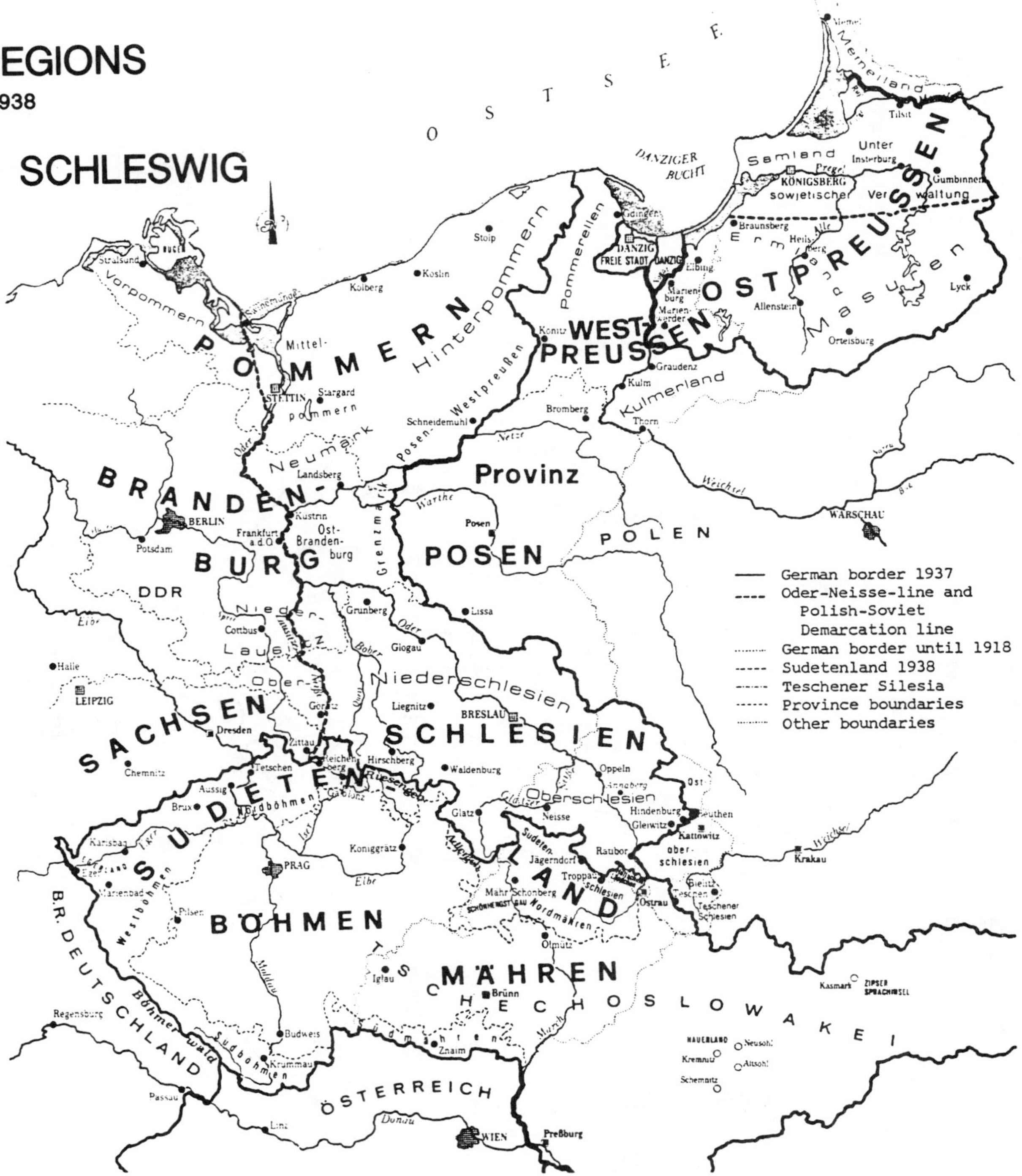

Major labels on map:

OSTSEE · MEMELLAND · OSTPREUSSEN · WESTPREUSSEN · POMMERN · Vorpommern · Hinterpommern · BRANDENBURG · Neumark · Ost-Brandenburg · Provinz POSEN · POLEN · Niederschlesien · SCHLESIEN · Oberschlesien · Ober-schlesien · SUDETEN-LAND · BÖHMEN · MÄHREN · TSCHECHOSLOWAKEI · SACHSEN · DDR · B.R. DEUTSCHLAND · ÖSTERREICH · Kulmerland · Ermland · Samland

DANZIGER BUCHT · FREIE STADT DANZIG · DANZIG

Cities: Memel · Tilsit · Gumbinnen · Insterburg · KÖNIGSBERG · Braunsberg · Heilsberg · Allenstein · Orteisburg · Lyck · Elbing · Marienwerder · Graudenz · Kulm · Thorn · Bromberg · Lissa · Posen · WARSCHAU · Stolp · Koslin · Kolberg · Stettin · Stargard · Schneidemühl · Landsberg · Küstrin · Frankfurt a.d.O. · BERLIN · Potsdam · Cottbus · Dresden · Chemnitz · Halle · LEIPZIG · Glogau · Grünberg · Guben · Görlitz · Liegnitz · BRESLAU · Waldenburg · Hirschberg · Glatz · Neisse · Oppeln · Gleiwitz · Hindenburg · Beuthen · Kattowitz · Ratibor · Troppau · Jägerndorf · Königgrätz · Aussig · Brüx · PRAG · Budweis · Krummau · Iglau · Znaim · Brünn · Olmütz · Pressburg · WIEN · Linz · Passau · Regensburg · Krakau

GERMAN SETTLEMENTS IN THE AUSTRO-HUNGARIAN EMPIRE

1867 to 1918

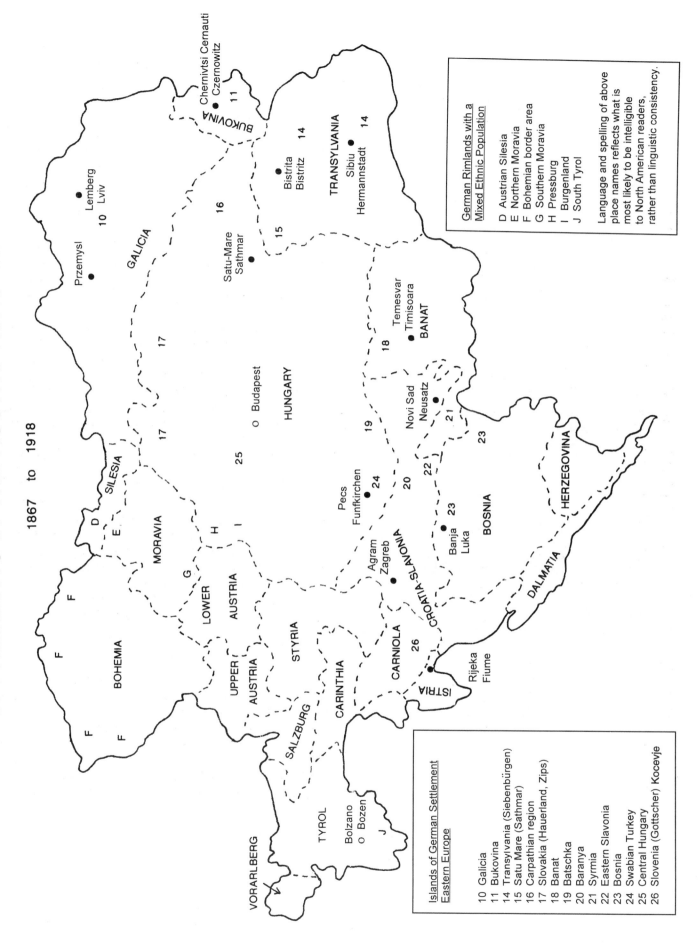

German Rimlands with a Mixed Ethnic Population

D Austrian Silesia
E Northern Moravia
F Bohemian border area
G Southern Moravia
H Pressburg
I Burgenland
J South Tyrol

Language and spelling of above place names reflects what is most likely to be intelligible to North American readers, rather than linguistic consistency.

Islands of German Settlement Eastern Europe

10 Galicia
11 Bukovina
14 Transylvania (Siebenbürgen)
15 Satu Mare (Sathmar)
16 Carpathian region
17 Slovakia (Hauerland, Zips)
18 Banat
19 Batschka
20 Baranya
21 Syrmia
22 Eastern Slavonia
23 Bosnia
24 Swabian Turkey
25 Central Hungary
26 Slovenia (Gottscher) Kocevje

Chernivtsi Cernauti Czernowitz 11
BUKOVINA

Lemberg Lviv 10
Przemysl
GALICIA
Satu-Mare Sathmar
16
15
17

Bistrita Bistritz 14
TRANSYLVANIA
Sibiu Hermannstadt 14

17
HUNGARY
Budapest
25

Temesvar Timisoara BANAT
18

Novi Sad Neusatz
19
21
23
22

Pecs Funfkirchen
24
20

Agram Zagreb CROATIA-SLAVONIA
Banja Luka 23
BOSNIA
HERZEGOVINA
DALMATIA

SILESIA
D
E
MORAVIA
G
LOWER AUSTRIA
H
I
F
F
BOHEMIA
F
UPPER AUSTRIA
STYRIA
CARINTHIA
SALZBURG
CARNIOLA 26
ISTRIA
Rijeka Fiume

TYROL
Bolzano Bozen J
VORARLBERG

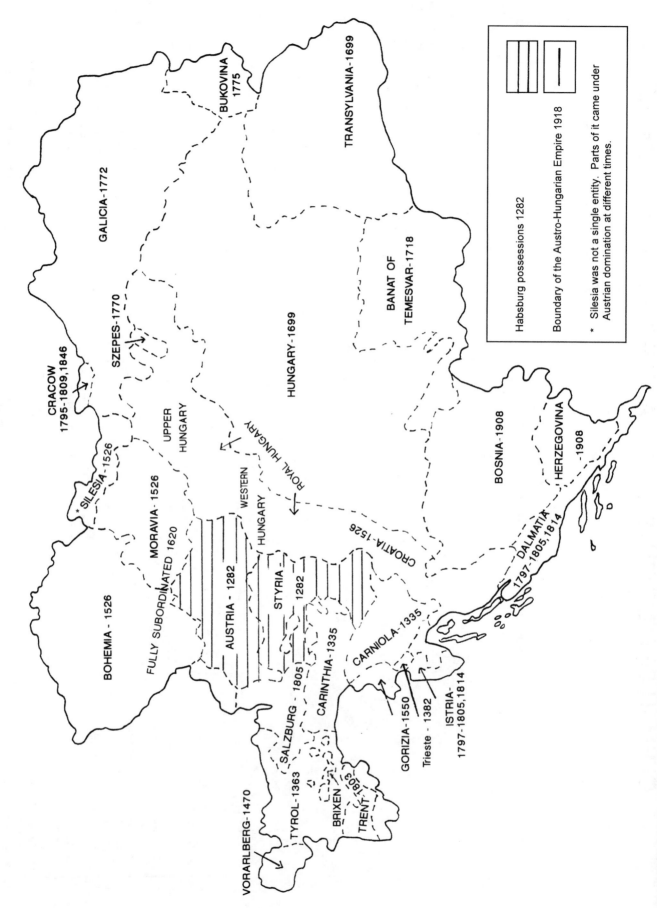

GROWTH OF THE AUSTRO-HUNGARIAN EMPIRE
with dates of annexation of various lands

Habsburg possessions 1282

Boundary of the Austro-Hungarian Empire 1918

* Silesia was not a single entity. Parts of it came under Austrian domination at different times.

BUKOVINA 1775

TRANSYLVANIA-1699

GALICIA-1772

SZEPES-1770

CRACOW 1795-1809,1846

BANAT OF TEMESVAR-1718

HUNGARY - 1699

UPPER HUNGARY

SILESIA-1526

ROYAL HUNGARY

WESTERN HUNGARY

MORAVIA - 1526

FULLY SUBORDINATED 1620

BOSNIA-1908

BOHEMIA - 1526

AUSTRIA - 1282

STYRIA - 1282

CROATIA-1526

HERZEGOVINA -1908

DALMATIA 1797-1805,1814

CARNIOLA-1335

CARINTHIA-1335

SALZBURG - 1805

GORIZIA-1550

Trieste - 1382

ISTRIA- 1797-1805,1814

VORARLBERG-1470

TYROL-1363

BRIXEN 1803

TRENT 1803

DIVISION OF AUSTRO-HUNGARIAN EMPIRE

after World War I. 1918-1923

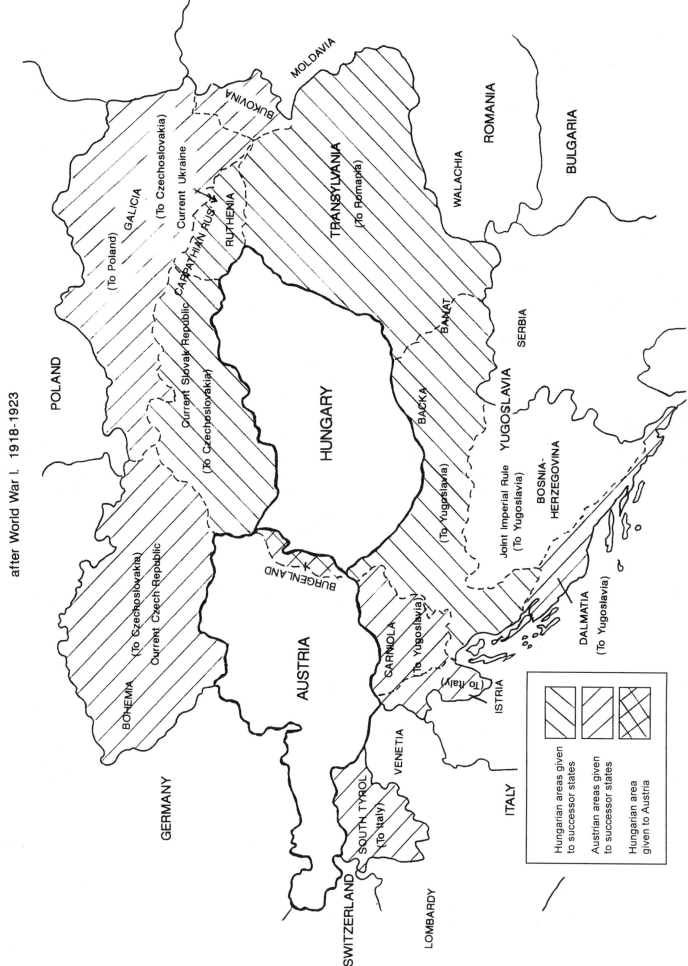

GERMANY

POLAND

MOLDAVIA

GALICIA
(To Poland)

(To Czechoslovakia)

Current Ukraine

BUKOVINA

CARPATHIAN RUS.

RUTHENIA

Current Slovak Republic

(To Czechoslovakia)

TRANSYLVANIA
(To Romania)

ROMANIA

WALACHIA

BULGARIA

BANAT

SERBIA

HUNGARY

BACKA

YUGOSLAVIA

BOHEMIA   (To Czechoslovakia)
Current Czech Republic

BURGENLAND

(To Yugoslavia)

Joint Imperial Rule
(To Yugoslavia)

BOSNIA-
HERZEGOVINA

AUSTRIA

CARNIOLA

(To Yugoslavia)

(To Italy)

ISTRIA

DALMATIA
(To Yugoslavia)

SWITZERLAND

SOUTH TYROL
(To Italy)

VENETIA

LOMBARDY

ITALY

Hungarian areas given
to successor states

Austrian areas given
to successor states

Hungarian area
given to Austria

POLAND
(Present Day)

Baltic Sea

RUSSIA

LITHUANIA

* SŁUPSK

* GDAŃSK

* ELBLĄG

SUWAŁKI

* KOSZALIN

* OLSZTYN

* SZCZECIN

× BYDGOSZCZ

* PIŁA

× TORUŃ

ŁOMŻA

OSTROŁĘKA

BIAŁYSTOK

* GORZÓW WIELKOPOLSKI

WŁOCŁAWEK

CIECHANÓW

× POZNAŃ

PŁOCK

WARSZAWA

SIEDLCE

BELARUS

KONIN

* ZIELONA GORA

SKIERNIEWICE

* LESZNO

× ŁÓDŹ

BIAŁA PODLASKA

KALISZ

SIERADZ

PIOTRKÓW TRYBUNALSKI

RADOM

LUBLIN

* JELENIA GORA

* LEGNICA

* WROCŁAW

CHEŁM

* WAŁBRZYCH

* OPOLE

CZĘSTOCHOWA

KIELCE

TARNOBRZEG

ZAMOŚĆ

× KATOWICE

CRACOW

TARNÓW

RZESZÓW

PRZEMYŚL

GERMANY

CZECH REPUBLIC

BIELSKO BIAŁA

NOWY SĄCZ

KROSNO

UKRAINE

SLOVAK REPUBLIC

* indicates the localities that belonged to Germany or the Free City of Danzig during the interwar period and having the largest number of Germans living in these areas.

+ considerable number of Germans in these places.

• capital of province, usually the same name as the province.

The northern, western and southwestern provinces (*voivodships*) of Poland once constituted parts of the German (Prussian) Provinces of East Prussia, West Prussia, Posen, Pomerania, Brandenburg and Silesia.

Germanic Genealogy Society

THE PARTITION OF POLAND
1772-1795

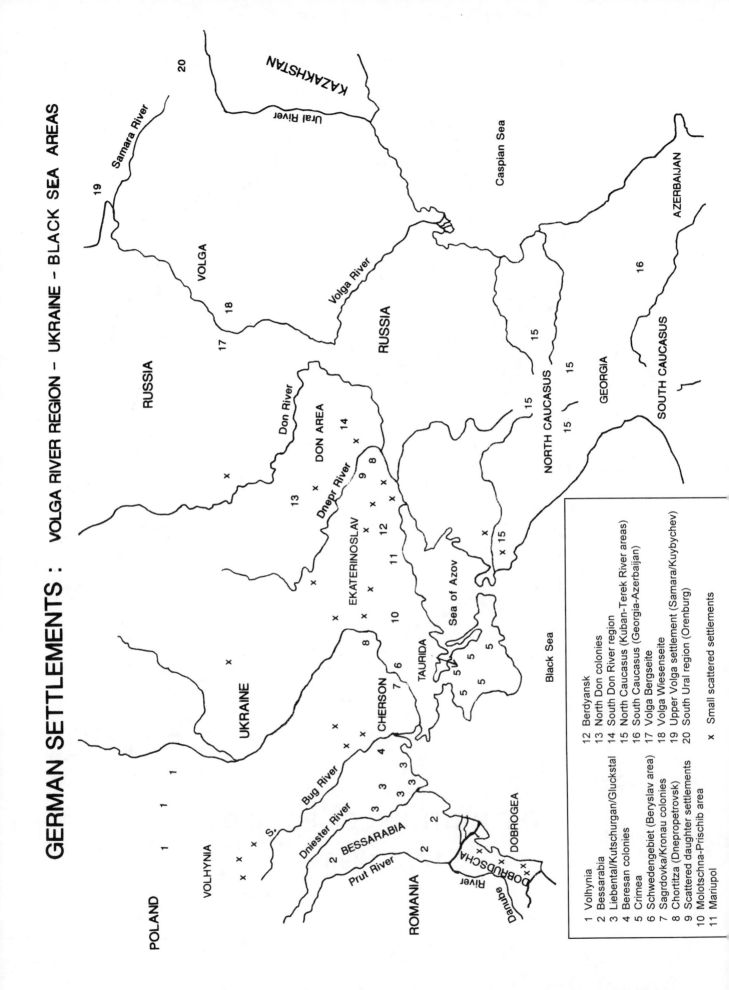

GERMAN SETTLEMENTS : VOLGA RIVER REGION – UKRAINE – BLACK SEA AREAS

POLAND

VOLHYNIA

UKRAINE

RUSSIA

RUSSIA

VOLGA

KAZAKHSTAN

Samara River

Ural River

Volga River

Caspian Sea

Don River

DON AREA

Dnepr River

EKATERINOSLAV

Sea of Azov

TAURIDA

CHERSON

Bug River

S.

Dniester River

BESSARABIA

Prut River

ROMANIA

DOBROGEA

DOBRUDSCHA

Danube River

Black Sea

NORTH CAUCASUS

GEORGIA

SOUTH CAUCASUS

AZERBAIJAN

1 Volhynia
2 Bessarabia
3 Liebental/Kutschurgan/Gluckstal
4 Beresan colonies
5 Crimea
6 Schwedengebiet (Beryslav area)
7 Sagrdovka/Kronau colonies
8 Chortitza (Dnepropetrovsk)
9 Scattered daughter settlements
10 Molotschna-Prischib area
11 Mariupol

12 Berdyansk
13 North Don colonies
14 South Don River region
15 North Caucasus (Kuban-Terek River areas)
16 South Caucasus (Georgia-Azerbaijan)
17 Volga Bergseite
18 Volga Wiesenseite
19 Upper Volga settlement (Samara/Kuybychev)
20 South Ural region (Orenburg)

x Small scattered settlements

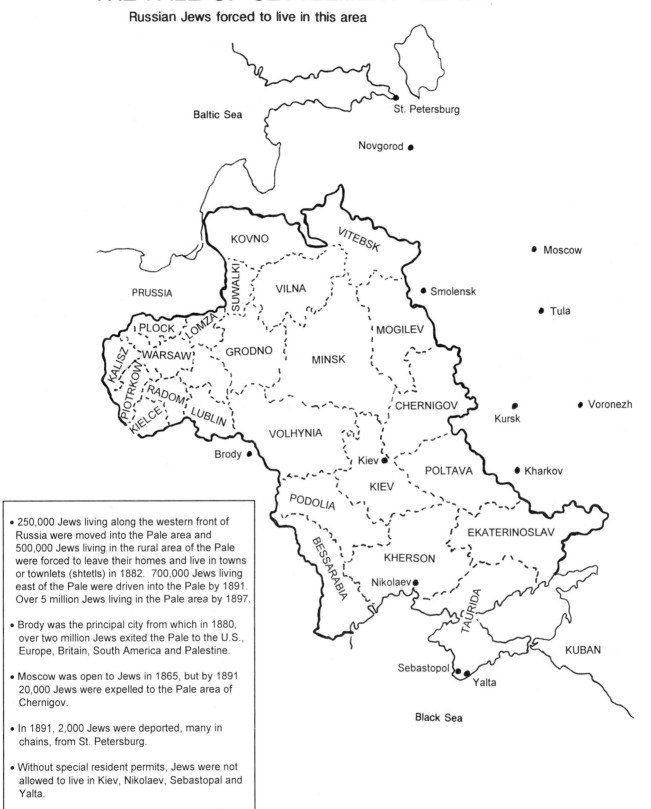

THE PALE OF SETTLEMENT 1835 -1917

Russian Jews forced to live in this area

Baltic Sea

St. Petersburg

Novgorod ●

KOVNO

VITEBSK

● Moscow

PRUSSIA

SUWALKI

VILNA

● Smolensk

● Tula

PLOCK

LOMZA

MOGILEV

KALISZ

WARSAW

GRODNO

MINSK

PIOTRKOW

RADOM

LUBLIN

KIELCE

CHERNIGOV

● Voronezh

Kursk ●

Brody ●

VOLHYNIA

Kiev ●

POLTAVA

● Kharkov

KIEV

PODOLIA

BESSARABIA

EKATERINOSLAV

KHERSON

Nikolaev ●

TAURIDA

KUBAN

Sebastopol ●

Yalta ●

Black Sea

- 250,000 Jews living along the western front of Russia were moved into the Pale area and 500,000 Jews living in the rural area of the Pale were forced to leave their homes and live in towns or townlets (shtetls) in 1882. 700,000 Jews living east of the Pale were driven into the Pale by 1891. Over 5 million Jews living in the Pale area by 1897.

- Brody was the principal city from which in 1880, over two million Jews exited the Pale to the U.S., Europe, Britain, South America and Palestine.

- Moscow was open to Jews in 1865, but by 1891 20,000 Jews were expelled to the Pale area of Chernigov.

- In 1891, 2,000 Jews were deported, many in chains, from St. Petersburg.

- Without special resident permits, Jews were not allowed to live in Kiev, Nikolaev, Sebastopal and Yalta.

SUCCESSOR STATES TO YUGOSLAVIA

(Present Day)

Vojvodina and Kosovo were autonomous provinces of Serbia. Slovenia, Croatia, Bosnia and Herzegovina, and Macedonia are now independent countries.

Map legend:
1 Belonged to the Austrian part of the Austro-Hungarian Empire.
2 Belonged to the Hungarian part of the Austro-Hungarian Empire.
3 Ruled by the Austro-Hungarian Empire after 1878 and annexed in 1908.
4 Independent prior to 1878.

SOUTH AMERICA AND CENTRAL AMERICA

Showing Areas Settled by Germans from Russia

BELIZE

HONDURAS

GUATEMALA

NICARAGUA

EL SALVADOR

COSTA RICA

PANAMA

VENEZUELA

GUYANA

SURINAM

Fr. GUIANA

COLOMBIA

ECUADOR

PERU

BRAZIL

Pacific Ocean

BOLIVIA

SANTA CRUZ

GRAND CHACO

PARAGUAY

PARANA

Ponta Grossa

Rio e Janeiro

Sao Paulo

Atlantic Ocean

Curitiba

MISIONES

SANTA CATARINA

CHILE

ARGENTINA

CORDOBA

SANTA FE

RIO GRANDE DO SUL

Porto Alegre

1

2

3

4

URUGUAY

Montevideo

Santiago

LA PAMPA

BUENOS
AIRES

Buenos Aires

Azul

1 Formosa
2 Chaco
3 Corrientes
4 Entre Rios

Valdivia

FALKLAND ISLANDS

ARGENTINA

AUSTRALIA

Showing Areas of German Settlement

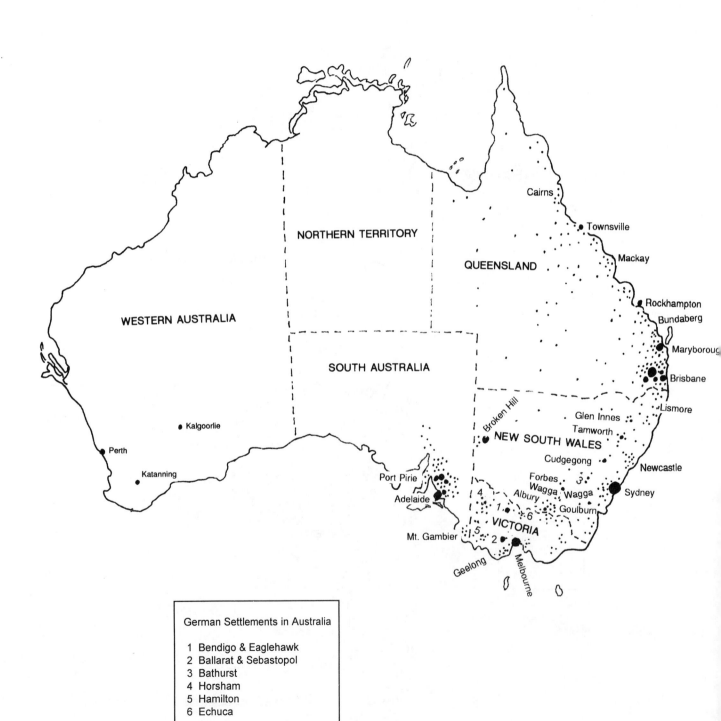

German Settlements in Australia

1 Bendigo & Eaglehawk
2 Ballarat & Sebastopol
3 Bathurst
4 Horsham
5 Hamilton
6 Echuca

— A —

Aachen, Germany, 79, 368

Aargau canton, Switzerland, 83, 146, 188, 225, 304

Abbreviations, 2, 59
  Information about, 9, 63, 64, 391, 400, 401, 405, 408, 420

Abella, Irving M., 232

Åbenrå, Denmark, 358

Abkhazia, 328

Abo, Finland, 358. *See also* Turku, Finland

Accredited Genealogists, 9

Acronyms, 2

Adamáua, 220. *See* Adamowa, Cameroon

Adamowa, Cameroon, 220

Adams, Willi Paul, 226

Address Abbreviations, 4

Address books, 269
  English, 420
  German, 263

Addresses
  Booksellers, 427
  Germanic genealogical societies, 439
  Lending libraries, 434
  Libraries and information centers, 432
  Map sources, 431
  Publishers, 427
  Special resources in and near Minnesota, 435

Adelaide, South Australia, 205, 209, 211, 244, 245, 247, 248, 249

Adler, H. G., 157

Adler, Reinhold, 174

Adriatic coast, 288, 338

Adventist Christian Church, 120

Adventists, 142, 194, 261
  In Latin America, 238

Adygea, 328

Africa. *See individual countries*

AGoFF, 77, 282, 283, 284, 286, 329, 330, 335, 337, 342, 347, 370, 416. *See also under* Genealogical societies: Arbeitsgemeinschaft ostdeutscher Familienforscher

Agram, 349. *See also* Zagreb, Croatia

Ahnenpässe. *See also* Pedigree charts

Ahnenstammkartei, 281, 303, 408

Ahnentafel. *See* Ancestor charts

AHSGR, 196, 234, 257, 314, 320. *See also* Genealogical societies: American Historical Society of Germans from Russia

Aicher, Manuel, 299

Aisch River, Germany, 81

Aitken, Kenneth G., 27, 28, 232

Alabama, 189

Alamanni tribe, 81, 104

Alb, 78

Albania, 351

Alberta, Canada, 192
  Civil records, 26
  Glenbow Archives, 22
  Homestead records, 22
  Land records, 22
  Provincial archives, 25
  Vital records, 27

Albion, Queensland, 246

Albrecht of Mecklenburg, 367

Albrich, Thomas, 222

Albright Evangelicals, 120, 121

Albury, New South Wales, 204, 244

Alderley, Queensland, 246

Alexandrovsk, Ukraine, 101. *See also* Zaporozhye, Ukraine

Alger (Algiers), Algeria, 256

Algeria, 212, 221, 256

Alien registrations, 16

Aliwal North, Africa, 217

Allanton, New Zealand, 210

Allegheny Mountains, 187

Alleman, John C., 345

Allen County Public Library, 426, 432

Allen, James Paul, 188, 226, 406

Allen, Walser H., 138

Allenstein, East Prussia (now Poland), 79

Almar Associates, 351

Alpen (Alps), 78

Alps Mountains, 78

Alsace, 79, 81, 82, 88, 89, 105, 119, 227, 407, 442, 444. *See also* France
  Census, 268
  Emigration, 225, 277, 360, 376
  Genealogical societies, 361
  German emigration, 102, 185, 213, 225, 278, 304, 360, 376
  History, 75, 88, 91, 115, 146, 359, 444
  Map of, 451
  Regional archive, 360
  Village genealogies, 268

Alsace-Lorraine, 76, 119, 152, 190, 411. *See also* France
  Church records, 359
  FHL cataloging, 44
  Gazetteers, 71
  German emigration, 349, 359
  History, 84, 86, 90, 186, 356, 447
  Place names, 66, 67

Altlutheraner, 261. *See also* Old Lutherans

Altmark, 78

Alto Adige, Italy, 84, 109, 337. *See also* South Tyrol, Italy

Altötting, Germany, 217

Amana Society, 111, 120
  Records, 137

American Civil War, 185, 447

American colonies, 403
  German immigration, 184, 227, 303, 372, 409, 444
  Naturalization, 223, 410

American Gathering of Holocaust Survivors, 169

American Genealogical Lending Library, 50, 434

American Geographic Society Map collection, 434

American Revolutionary War, 28, 183, 185, 187, 228, 409, 411, 420, 445

Amersfoort, Netherlands, 287

Amish, 115, 122, 133, 139, 140, 194, 410, 426, 433
  In Canada, 20

Ammann, Jacob, 115

Amsterdam, Netherlands, 363

Amur River region, 328

Anabaptists, 87, 143, 144
  History, 113, 114
  In Switzerland, 62, 105

Ancestor charts, 384. *See also* Pedigree charts

Ancestral File, 43

Andics, Hellmut, 153

Andorra, 351

André, Ken V., 214, 215, 237, 255

Andreanum ("golden patent"), 442

Andrews, Walter Scott, 228

Angermann, A., 406

Angles, 442

Anglicans
  In Canada, 20
  Records in Canada, 24

Anglo-Boer War, 254

Anhalt, 75, 76, 423
  FHL cataloging, 44
  Genealogical societies, 276
  History, 75
  State archives, 272

Anhalt-Dessau, 148

Ansbach, Bavaria, 79

Antin, Mary, 176

Antwerp, Belgium, 49, 186, 247, 266, 361
  Genealogical society, 357
  Passenger lists, 48, 49

Anzelc, Paul, 435

Aosta River region, Italy, 338

Apia, Samoa, 252

Apostolic Christian Church, 120, 124, 134

Appenzell-Ausser-Rhoden canton, Switzerland, 83

Appenzell-Inner-Rhoden canton, Switzerland, 83

Apprentice books, 263

Arad, Romania, 353

Archiv des Landeskirchenamts der Evangelischen Kirche von Westfalen, 282

Archival Ministry of Ukraine, 326
Archives of the Roman Catholic
     Central-Verein, St. Louis, MO, 126
Archshofen, Germany, 174
Area search, 9
Argentina, 118, 193, 196, 197, 207,
     233, 234, 238, 241, 447, 448
  Census records, 240
  Civil registers, 239
  Colonization, 193
  Genealogical societies, 243
  German immigration, 96, 103, 192,
     193
  German settlements, 192
  National archives, 242
  National library, 242
  Records at Family History Library,
     238
  Religions, 193
  Research helps, 238
Arlon, Belgium, 357
Armenia
  Records, 265
  Researching in, 328
Armgart, Martin, 284
Arndt, Karl J. R., 11, 16, 138, 139, 406
Arnsberg, Paul, 153
Arnstein, George E., 147, 153, 161,
     172, 174, 176
Aronius, Julius, 157
Asia, 101, 311
Asia Minor, 222
Asian Muslim Republics (CIS), 85, 104,
     328, 329, 450
  Researching in, 329
Aspelin, Herrick Emanuel, 374
Assemblies of God, 135
Assiniboia district, Northwest
     Territories, 232, 412
Assisted Immigration Scheme (New
     Zealand), 210
Assisted Passage Scheme (Australia),
     208
Astrakhan, Russia, 314
Asunción, Paraguay, 239, 242
Attinger, Victor, 305
Auckland, New Zealand, 51, 211, 249,
     250, 251
Auerbach, Berthold, 172
Auerbach, Rena R., 157
Auerbacher, Moses Baruch, 172
Aufhausen (Bopfingen), Germany, 174
Augsburg Confession, 443
Augsburg, Germany, 145, 217, 347
Aussiedler, 104, 319, 328, 329, 450.
     See also Resettlers
Australasia, 372
Australia, 235, 236, 448
  Archives, 248
  Austrians In, 259
  Church records, 246
  Civil registers, 245
  Colonies, 448
  Gazetteers, 248

Australia (*continued*)
  Genealogical societies, 244
  German immigration, 143, 195, 222,
     446, 450
  German language newspapers, 248
  German settlements, 202
  Jews In, 245
  Lutheran records, 247
  Map of, 451
  Marriage records, 247
  National library, 248
  Naturalization records, 248
  Newspapers, 248
  Other records, 248
  Passenger lists, 247
  State libraries, 249
  Swiss in, 105, 260
Australian Capital Territory, Australia,
     245
Austria, 75, 78, 109, 119, 148, 210,
     221, 240, 263, 289, 317, 330, 335,
     336, 337, 442, 444, 445, 446, 449
  Archives, 418
  Burgher books, 267
  Census records, 295
  Church records, 290, 418
  Civil records, 295, 335
  Emigration, 297
  Emigration records, 296
  Gazetteers, 63, 69, 71, 290
  Genealogical societies, 297, 418
  German emigration, 187, 188, 189,
     195, 199, 201, 207, 210, 211, 223
  History, 64, 76, 77, 84, 87, 89, 91–98,
     99, 105, 146, 150, 151, 152, 183,
     186, 196, 290, 335, 338, 346, 349,
     357, 444, 445, 447
  Institute for Historic Family Research
     (IHFF), 173
  Jewish museums, 173
  Land cadasters, 342
  Lutheran records, 293
  Map of, 451
  Microfilms, 41
  Military parish records, 266
  Military records, 295
  Miscellaneous records, 296
  National archives, 295, 296
  Old Catholics records, 293
  Periodicals, 426
  Postal codes, 73, 421
  Provinces, 290
  Religions, 119
  Research services, 173
  Researching in, 264, 288
  Seignorial Protocols, 294
  State archives, 294, 342
  States, 83
  Treaty of St. Germain, 74
Austrian Cultural Institute, 432
Austrian Empire, 443, 445
  Gazetteers, 71
  History, 75, 88, 90, 91–98, 115, 185,
     288, 335

Austrian Empire (*continued*)
  Religions, 444
  States, 75
Austrian Military Border, 106
Austrian Silesia, 71, 75, 77, 84, 85, 289.
     See also Austro-Silesia
  German emigration, 200
  History, 94, 331
Austrians
  In Australia, 208, 259, 296
  In Brazil, 195
  In Canada, 208
  In Chile, 199
  In New Zealand, 209
  In South Tyrol, 109
Austro-Hungarian Empire, 71, 190,
     293, 312, 325, 351, 448, 449
  Atlases, 72
  Emigration, 52, 191
  German emigration, 49, 193, 199, 211
  History, 76, 77, 84, 88, 91–98, 151,
     152, 185, 288, 290, 295, 306, 335,
     348, 447
  Map of, 451
  Military records, 330
  Rsearch in, 411
Austro-Silesia, 80, 333. *See also*
     Austrian Silesia
  History, 152, 329
Avignon, France, 146
Avni, Haim, 233
Azerbaijan, 84
  Researching in, 328

— B —

Baader, Heike, 154
Bach, Adolf, 57, 60
Backa, 78, 85, 350. *See also* Bácska,
     Yugoslavia. *See also* Batschka
Bacs Bodrog, Hungary, 351
Bácska, Yugoslavia, 78, 289. *See also*
     Batschka. *See also* Backa
  History, 85, 97
Bad Karlshofen, Germany, 286
Bade, James N., 182, 209, 235
Baden, 75, 76, 81, 89, 148, 152, 190,
     219, 262, 265, 423, 445
  Census, 267
  FHL cataloging, 44
  German emigration, 102, 185, 207,
     214, 225, 278, 304
  History, 97
  State archives, 270
Baden-Württemberg, 78, 80, 82, 411
  Genealogical societies, 274
  History, 91
  Religions, 119
  State archives, 270
  Tombstones, 163
  Village lineage books, 422
Baden-Württemberg (continued)
  Yizkor books, 168
Baginsky, Paul Ben, 420

Bahia, Brazil, 194
Bahlow, Hans, 59, 60
Bahr, Marion, 305, 307, 355, 423
Bailliere, F. F., 248
Bailyn, Bernard, 226
Bainton, Roland H., 139
Baker, Zachary M., 171, 176
Balch Institute of Ethnic Studies, 308, 432
Balkan region, 92, 109, 444
Balkan Wars, 448
Ballarat, Victoria, 206, 207
Baltic countries, 84, 98, 99, 103, 319, 450. *See also* Lithuania. *See also* Latvia. *See also* Estonia
  Burgher books, 267
  Genealogical societies, 284
  German colonization, 98
  Lutheran Consistories, 313
  Lutheran parishes, 313
  Microfilms, 41
  Researchers, 308
Baltic Sea, 80, 81
Baltimore, Maryland, 50
Balzekas Museum of Lithuanian Culture, Chicago, 323
Bamberg, Bavaria, 81
Bamberger, Naftali Bar-Giora, 163, 173, 176
Banat, 64, 78, 96, 97, 289, 296, 349, 350, 444
  Banat Listserver, 439
  Church registers, 353
  Emigration, 191
  Gazetteers, 64
  German emigration, 97
  History, 77, 85, 92
Bangladesh, 259
Banja Luka, Bosnia, 97, 116, 349
Banská Bystrica, Slovak Republic, 334, 335
Baptists, 120, 122, 124, 135, 261, 317
  In Alberta, 135
  In Argentina, 193
  In Australia, 207, 246
  In Brazil, 194
  In Canada, 20, 125, 191
  In Germany, 118
  In Great Plains states, 118
  In Iowa, 118
  In Kansas, 423
  In Latin America, 238
  In Luxembourg, 304
  In North Dakota, 118
  In Ostfriesland, 118
  In Russian Empire, 118
  In South Dakota, 118, 135
  In Switzerland, 298
  In Western Canada, 118
  Records, 135, 144
Baranja, 85, 97, 289, 349. *See also* Baranya, Yugoslavia
Baranya, Yugoslavia, 85, 97, 289, 349, 351

Barkai, Avraham, 226
Baron, Salo Wittmayer, 147
Barossa Valley, 235
Barrabool Hills, Victoria, 206
Barth, Frederick H., 5, 406
Barthel, Stephen, 68
Bartholdi, Albert, 302
Basel canton, Switzerland, 188, 225, 227, 304, 409
Basel City, Switzerland, 83, 89, 146. *See also* Basel-Stadt canton, Switzerland
Basel, Switzerland, 201
Basel-Land canton, Switzerland, 83
Basel-Stadt canton, Switzerland, 83
Bas-Rhin department, France, 359, 360. *See also* Alsace
Bassler, Gerhard, 190
Basutoland, South Africa, 218
Batowski, Henryk, 64, 68
Batschka, 78, 85, 97, 102, 289, 296, 349, 350. *See also* Bácska, Yugoslavia. *See also* Backa
  History, 77
Battle of Grunwald, 99. *See also* Battle of Tannenberg
Battle of Mohacs, 443
Battle of Tannenberg, 99
Battle of White Mountain, 94
Bauer, Armand, 230, 426
Bauer, E., 174
Bauer, Johannes, 154
Baum, Wilhelm, 107
Bavaria, 44, 75, 76, 78, 79, 81, 82, 148, 152, 190, 217, 219, 265, 311, 411, 423, 443, 444. *See also* Bayern
  Census, 267
  FHL cataloging, 44
  Genealogical societies, 274
  German emigration, 102, 207, 210, 211, 213, 214
  History, 75, 87, 91, 94, 95, 145, 146
  Religions, 119
  State archives, 270
  Yizkor books, 168
Bavarian Uplands, 78
Bavarian Woods, 196
Baviaanskloof, South Africa, 216
Baxter, Angus, 23, 25, 28, 222, 232, 264, 267, 268, 279, 282, 302, 303, 331, 332, 351, 360, 361, 374, 406
Bayerischer Wald, 78
Bayerisches Oberland, 78
Bayern, 76. *See also* Bavaria
  FHL cataloging, 44
Bayreuth, Bavaria, 78, 79
Bayswater, Western Australia, 244
Beck, Wolfgang, 160
Becker, Christian Ludwig, 222
Becker, Franziska, 176
Becker, Ted J., 320
Beckermann, Ruth, 153, 157
Beckert, Kurt Michael, 284
Bedell, Kenneth B., 125, 139

Beginning research, 1
Beider, Alexander, 59, 61, 161, 176
Beissel, Johann Konrad, 124
Belarus, 80, 81, 312
  Archives, 313, 327
  Atlases, 68
  Church records, 340
  History, 338, 446
  Microfilms, 41
  Researchers, 308
  Researching in, 327
  Yizkor books, 168
Belau, 212
Belgian Colonization Company, 198
Belgium, 79, 361, 442, 443, 449
  Church records, 357
  Civil records, 357
  Emigration, 287
  History, 76, 78, 84, 85, 87, 90, 92, 93, 106, 113, 356, 367
  Languages, 357
  Luxembourg province, 76, 84, 356
  Map of, 451
  Military parish records, 266
  Miscellaneous records, 357
  National archives, 357
  Place names, 65
  Provincial archives, 356
  Researching in, 356
Belgrade, Yugoslavia, 81, 96, 350
Beling, Eva, 222
Belize, 194, 199, 200, 234, 241. *See also* British Honduras
  Belize City, 239
  Civil registers, 239
  German emigration, 194
  German immigration, 240
Bell, W., 28
Beller, Steven, 153
Bellon, Eugen, 107
Belorussians, 339. *See also* Belarus
Bender, Harold S., 139
Bendigo, Victoria, 206, 207, 245
Bendix, Reinhard, 226
Bensheim, Germany, 288
Bentley, Elizabeth Petty, 16, 17, 53, 61, 125, 139, 165, 177, 407, 439
Bentz, Edna M., 404, 407
Benz, Wolfgang, 222
Beratz, Gottlieb, 407
Berdyansk, Ukraine, 102, 116
Berent, Irwin M., 164, 181
Beresan colonies, Ukraine, 102
Bergen, Norway, 363
Berghahn, Marion, 222
Bergholm, Axel, 374
Bergseite, Russian Volga, 324
Bergtheil, Jonas, 216
Bergtheil, South Africa, 216
Bering, Dietz, 157
Berlin Missionary Society, 216
Berlin, Germany, 82, 83, 90, 115, 152, 283, 340, 423
  Address lists, 411

Berlin, Germany (*continued*)
  Berlin Document Center, 270
  Berlin Wall, 450
  City directories, 411
  Genealogical societies, 274
  History, 146
  Weissensee Cemetery, 164
Berlin, Ontario, 190
Berman, Hyman, 228, 408
Bern, 83. *See also* Berne canton,
  Switzerland
Berne canton, Switzerland, 83, 105,
  188, 196, 227, 409
Berne, Switzerland, 89, 146
Bertenyi, Ivan, 336
Berwick, Victoria, 206
Bessarabia, 102, 103, 106, 116, 312,
  314, 320, 325, 328, 423, 448
  Church records, 325, 355, 423
  German immigration, 102
  History, 77, 102, 346, 446
  Swabian settlers, 411
  Yizkor books, 168
Bessarabien, 423. *See also* Bessarabia
Bethany, South Australia, 247
Bethlehem, South Africa, 217
Bettinger, Emmett, 134
Bialystok, Poland, 101, 327
Bielefeld, Germany, 282, 287, 411
Bienick, Helen, 72
Billeter, Julius, 299
Bilshausen-Lasalle, Ute, 286
Bingen, Germany, 79
Birkenfeld, 75
  FHL cataloging, 44
Birkett, P., 28
Birnstiel, Eckart, 155
Bismarck Archipelago, 212
Bismarck, North Dakota, 64, 329, 415
Bismarck, Otto von, 89, 90, 97, 147,
  219
Bistrita, Romania, 95
Bistritz. *See* Bistrita, Romania
Bistritz River, 97
Bittinger, Lucy Forney, 226
Bittner, Clarence, 340
Bjorneborg, Finland, 358. *See also* Pori,
  Finland
Black Death, 87, 95, 442, 443
Black Forest, 78
Black Sea region, 65, 79, 80, 81, 84,
  101, 102, 106, 109, 116, 152, 183,
  191, 192, 193, 230, 257, 285, 311,
  312, 313, 314, 318, 319, 320, 325,
  328, 336, 354, 408, 426, 445, 450
  Map of, 451
Blad, G., 174
Blagoveshchensk, Siberia, 328
Blakeney, Michael, 235
Blatt, Warren, 161, 167
Blevins, Scharlott A., 278, 303
Blinn, Dieter, 153
Bliss, Ruth, 283
Blodgett, Steven W., 296, 303

Bloemfontein, South Africa, 215, 216,
  253
Blom, D. von, 201
Blomstedt, Yrjo, 375
Blum, Martin, 301, 303
Blumenau, Brazil, 195, 197
Board for Certification of Genealogists,
  9
Bober River, 80
Bochinski, Cassie, 72
Boer War, 448
Boers, 212, 213, 215, 237, 254
Bohatec, M., 179
Bohemia, 75, 78, 79, 91, 93, 289, 423,
  443
  Archives, 162
  Cemeteries, 177
  Emigration, 208, 277, 297, 420
  German emigration, 186, 188, 196,
    198, 199, 200, 201, 209, 210, 213,
    229, 351, 414, 446
  History, 76, 77, 84, 87, 88, 90, 92, 94,
    97, 107, 112, 114, 146, 152, 186,
    329, 331
  Tax rolls, 297
  Urbariums, 332
Bohemian Forest, 79, 196, 232, 423
Bohemian Germans, 186
  In Brazil, 196
  In Bukovina, 95, 97, 144, 196, 232,
    423
  In Canada, 196
  In Cuba, 198
  In Czechoslovakia, 108
  In Hungary, 107
  In New Zealand, 209, 210, 211
  In Paraguay, 200
  In Romania, 196
  In Soviet Union, 108
  In United States, 144, 196, 229, 230,
    232, 414, 417, 423
  In Venezuela, 201
Bohemians
  In Michigan, 333
  In Minnesota, 333
  In Wisconsin, 333
Böhmen, 289. *See also* Bohemia. *See
  also* Bohemia
Böhmerwald, 79
Bohnke-Kollwitz, Jutta, 153
Bolivia, 200
  Civil registers, 239
  German immigration, 194, 240
  German settlements, 194
Bolotenko, George, 326
Bolshevik Revolution, 103, 183, 448,
  449
Bolzano, Italy, 95, 294, 337, 338, 423.
  See also Bozen, Italy
Bonjour, Edgar, 107
Bonn, Germany, 217, 411
Border crossing lists, 14
Border crossing records, 16
Bork, Inge, 225, 304, 417

Bornemann, Irma, 107
Borneo, 258
Borrie, W. D., 202, 203, 204, 205, 206,
  235, 248
Borussians, 98. *See also* Prussians
Bosnia, 93, 97, 108, 289, 349, 448
  History, 76, 77
Bosnia-Herzegovina, 289, 349
  History, 85, 348
  National archives, 349
  Researching in, 349
Bosnien, 108, 289. *See also* Bosnia
Boston, Massachusetts, 50, 124, 188
Botswana, 216, 218
Bounty land property, 13
Bovenizer, Austin, 361
Boyer, Carl, 50, 52
Boys Town (Nebraska), 11
Bozen, Italy, 95, 294, 337, 423. *See
  also* Bolzano, Italy
  Records, 297
Brachwitz, Heike, 282
Brahe, Per, 358
Brahestad, Finland, 358. *See also*
  Raahe, Finland
Brandenburg, 75, 76, 78, 80, 82, 89,
  204, 214, 219, 230, 362, 411, 416,
  423, 443, 444, 471
  Emigration, 420
  FHL cataloging, 44
  German emigration, 205, 210
  History, 77, 83, 88, 90, 91, 368
  Military parish records, 266
  Researchers, 284
  State archives, 271
Brandt, Bruce, 58, 342, 346, 351
Brandt, Edward Reimer, 58, 279, 296,
  308, 337, 339, 342, 346, 351
Brasov, Romania, 81, 423. *See also*
  Kronstadt
Bratislava, Slovak Republic, 85, 96,
  151, 335. *See also* Pressburg
Brauer, A., 247
Braun, Peter J., 352
Braunsberg, East Prussia, 79
Braunschweig, 76
  FHL cataloging, 44. *See also*
    Brunswick
  State archives, 271
Brazil, 118, 192, 193, 195, 196, 201,
  207, 233, 234, 238, 241, 347, 446,
  447
  Census records, 240
  Civil registers, 239
  Genealogical societies, 243
  German immigration, 95, 194, 195,
    196, 221, 240, 351
  German settlements, 194
  History, 240
  Immigration, 277
  Independent German Baptist Church,
    241
  Military records, 241
  National archives, 196, 242

Brazil (*continued*)
  National library, 242
  Records at Family History Library, 238
  Southern, 238
Brechenmacher, Josef Karlmann, 61
Brecht, Samuel, 133, 139
Bredstedt, Germany, 280
Bregenz, Austria, 294
Breimesser, H., 153
Breisgau, Germany, 79
Breitbard, Gail, 425
Bremen, Germany, 49, 50, 75, 76, 82, 90, 91, 115, 186, 208, 210, 224, 247, 411
  FHL cataloging, 44
  Genealogical societies, 274
  German emigration, 207
  History, 368
  Passenger lists, 48, 50, 424
  State archives, 271
Brenham, Texas, 188
Brenner Pass, Austria/Italy, 95, 337
Brenner, Michael, 158, 179
Breslau, Germany, 213, 344, 368, 372. *See* Wrozlaw, Poland
Brest Litovsk, Belarus, 80, 101, 327
Brethren, 261, 426
Brethren in Christ Church
  Records, 134
Breuer, Mordechai, 158
Bridgers, Frank E., 17
Brilling, Bernard, 171
Brisbane, Queensland, 51, 203, 205, 245, 246, 247
Britain, 78, 442. *See also* Great Britain. *See also* United Kingdom
  History, 146
British Columbia, Canada, 22
  Civil records, 26
  Homesteading in, 22
  Provincial archives, 25
British East Africa, 212, 215, 220, 226. *See also* Kenya
British East India Company, 258
British East Indies, 221
British Honduras, 194. *See also* Belize
British Kaffraria, Cape Province, South Africa, 214, 226, 237
Brixen, Italy, 423
Brno, Czech Republic, 94, 333. *See also* Brünn
Brody, 150
Broken Hill, New South Wales, 204, 244
Bromberg, 423. *See also* Bydgoszcz, Poland
  Researchers, 284
Brommer, Peter, 407
Bronsen, David, 157
Broome, Western Australia, 207
Brown County Historical Society Museum (Minnesota), 435
Brown, Michael G., 232

Bruce County, Ontario, 191
Bruell, Claire, 162, 177
Bruhn, Elmar, 284
Brumbaugh, Gaius Marcus, 227, 277, 280, 303, 409
Brumbaugh, Martin Grove, 139
Brunei, 259
Brünn, 94, 333. *See also* Brno, Czech Republic
Brunner, Gerhard, 217, 218, 219, 220
Brunswick, 75, 76, 423. *See also* Braunschweig
  Church records, 415
  FHL cataloging, 44
Brussels, Belgium, 113
  National archives, 357
Brym, Robert J., 232
Bubis, Ignatz, 157
Bubonic plague, 95, 367, 443
Bucharest, Romania, 346
Buchau, Germany, 174
Buchenland, 84, 85, 92. *See also* Bukovina
Bucuresti, Romania, 346
Budapest, Hungary, 85, 97, 150, 151, 288, 336
  Church records, 41
Budweis, 94. *See also* Cesky Budejovice, Czech Republic
Budziarek, Marek, 420
Buëa, 220. *See* Buea, Cameroon
Buea, Cameroon, 220
Buenos Aires, Argentina, 192, 193, 241, 242, 243
  Arrival lists, 52
Buffalo, New York, 188
Bug River, Ukraine, 82, 100, 101, 142, 353
Bühl (Baden), Germany, 174
Bukke, Inger M., 404, 407
Bukovina, 52, 107, 110, 140, 150, 163, 196, 197, 201, 223, 227, 289, 325, 352, 354, 409, 423, 445
  Church records, 355, 423
  Emigration, 191, 297
  German emigration, 186, 188, 196, 198, 200, 201, 233, 243
  German immigration, 97, 196, 351, 445
  History, 76, 77, 84, 85, 92, 95, 97, 98, 346
  Place names, 64
  Records, 347
  Research in, 345
  Researchers, 284
Bukowina, 84, 289. *See also* Bukovina. *See also* Bukovina
Bukowina-Institut, 347
Bulawayo, Zimbabwe, 219
Bulgaria, 79, 106, 109, 289, 320, 416, 443
  Census records, 348
  History, 77, 85, 329
  Microfilms, 41

Bulgaria (*continued*)
  Records, 265
  Researching in, 329
Bundaberg, Australia, 205
Burgauer, Hans, 291, 304
Burgenland, 83, 94, 119, 151, 289, 290
  Census records, 295
  German emigration, 186, 188, 197
  History, 77, 84, 288
  Jewish records, 337
  Lutheran records, 293
  Records, 292
Burgert, Annette Kunselman, 226, 227, 278, 407
Burgher books, 263, 266
Burgoyne, Bruce E., 227, 407
Burgundian tribe, 104
Burgundy, 92, 105
Burgwedel, Germany, 286
Burma, 259
Burrow, S., 28
Burstyn, Ruth, 177
Butler, Reg, 259
Bydgoszcz, Poland, 284, 345
Byler, John M., 139
Bystricky, Vladimír, 333
Bystrzycki, Tadeusz, 68
Bytca, Slovak Republic, 335

— C —

Cadrilater, Bulgaria, 329. *See also* Dobruja
Cahnman, Werner Jacob, 157
Cairo, Egypt, 256
Calendar, 407, 416
  French Revolutionary, 360, 403, 404, 407
  Gregorian, 360, 401, 404, 407, 443
  Hebrew, 403
  Julian, 401, 404, 407
Calgary, Alberta, 21, 22, 27, 192
California, 188, 189, 343, 450
Calvert, Albert F., 220, 237
Calvin, John, 105, 112, 443
Calvinists, 87, 88, 112, 114, 443
  In Canada, 20
  In Germany, 359
  In Poland, 338
  In Prussia, 261
  In Ukraine, 102
Calw, Germany, 286
Camann, Eugene, 227, 407
Cambodia, 45
Camden, New South Wales, 207
Cameroon, 212, 220, 256
Canada, 28, 106, 118, 260, 406, 413, 434, 444, 445, 446, 450
  Border crossing records, 27
  Canada East, 19
  Canada West, 19
  Census records, 21
  Church records, 19
  Civil records, 25

Canada (*continued*)
  Computerized Land Records Index, 19
  Court records, 27
  Genealogical societies, 21, 414
  German emigration, 194
  German immigration, 96, 103, 143, 185, 190, 196, 221, 223, 232, 351, 376, 409, 449, 450
  History, 447
  Immigration, 190–92
  Immigration records, 24
  Land grants, 24
  Li-Ra-Ma Collection, 23
  Lower Canada, 19
  National Archives, 23, 24, 50
  National Library, 23
  Naturalization records, 24
  Passenger arrival lists, 50
  Peter Robinson papers, 24
  Port cities, 186
  Prairie provinces, 103, 191, 448
  Probate records, 27
  Provincial archives, 22
  Provincial libraries, 25
  Researching in, 19, 406
  Special collections, 23
  Upper Canada, 19
  Wanka Collection, 23
  Western Canada, 22, 103, 426, 448
Canberra, Australian Capital Territory, 209, 248
Canterbury, New Zealand, 51, 210, 211, 249, 250
Cape Archives Depot, South Africa, 254
Cape Colony, South Africa, 213, 214, 237, 253
Cape of Good Hope, 258
Cape Province, South Africa, 214, 215, 226, 237, 253, 254, 444, 446, 447
Cape Town, South Africa, 52, 215, 253, 254, 255
Capellen canton, Luxembourg, 83
Card indexes, 269
Carinthia, 52, 75, 83, 92, 289, 290
  History, 76
  Lutheran records, 293
  Records, 292
Carniola, Slovenia, 75, 76, 85, 92, 96, 107, 109, 289, 350. *See also* Krain
Caroline Islands, 212
Carolingian Empire, 145, 442
Caron, Vicki, 153
Carpathia
  Yizkor books, 168
Carpatho-Ukraine, 96, 150, 289, 325, 327, 335
  Gazetteers, 68, 72
  History, 77, 84, 329
Carpelan, Tor, 374
Caspian Sea region, 82, 102, 152, 328
Cassubia, 100
Castle Garden, New York, 186, 448
Castlemaine, Victoria, 206

Catherine the Great, 81, 101, 223, 410, 444
Catholic Church. *See* Catholics
Catholic consistory
  Mogilev, Belarus, 314
  Saratov, Russia, 314
  Tiraspol, Ukraine, 314
Catholic Counter-Reformation. *See* Counter-Reformation
Catholics, 120, 183, 300, 321, 335, 443
  Ecclesiastical census records, 239
  History, 94, 95, 98, 295
  In Alsace-Lorraine, 359
  In Argentina, 193, 238
  In Australia, 207, 246
  In Austria, 418
  In Austrian Silesia, 200
  In Belgium, 357
  In Black Sea region, 192, 311, 314
  In Bohemia, 186, 331
  In Bosnia, 97
  In Brazil, 194, 196, 197, 238, 449
  In Bukovina, 97, 351
  In Cameroon, 220
  In Canada, 20, 191
  In Chile, 200
  In China, 221, 257
  In East Galicia, 326
  In East Prussia, 414
  In Eastern Europe, 282
  In France, 360
  In Galicia, 142, 340, 341, 353
  In Germany, 87
  In Latvia, 322
  In Liechtenstein, 302
  In Luxembourg, 106
  In Manchuria, 328
  In Minnesota, 350
  In Moravia, 186
  In Namibia, 218
  In Netherlands, 362
  In New Zealand, 211, 251
  In Norway, 363
  In Poland, 420
  In Posen, 414
  In Rhineland, 116
  In Russian Empire, 314
  In Silesia, 200
  In Slovak Republic, 334
  In South Africa, 217
  In Soviet Union, 449
  In Sweden, 367
  In Switzerland, 105, 298, 299
  In Tanzania, 220
  In Togo, 220
  In Ukraine, 102, 224, 314, 352
  In United States, 116
  In Volga River region, 311, 314
  In Volhynia, 142, 341, 353
  In West Prussia, 414
  In Westphalia, 200
  In Württemberg, 200
  Lansing (MI) Diocese, 126
  Naming practices, 59

Catholics (*continued*)
  Records, 10, 24, 41, 43, 126, 141, 240, 241, 261, 265, 282, 335
  Records in Canada, 126
  St. Joseph's Home for Children (MN), 435
  St. Paul (MN) Archdiocese, 435
  Writing to local churches, 265
Caucasus region, 102, 116, 311, 312, 314, 319, 328, 448
  History, 101
  Researching in, 328
CD-ROMs, 33, 408, 412
Celestino, Ayrton Gonçalves, 196, 198, 201, 233, 243
Celle, Germany, 285
Cemetery associations, 10
Cemetery records
  United States, 10
Census records, 263. *See also under each country*
  Latin America, 240
  State census, 16
  U. S. Soundex index, 15
  United States, 2, 14
Center for Mennonite Brethren Studies (Fresno, CA), 432
Center for Mennonite Brethren Studies (Hillsboro, KS), 432
Central America, 194, 226
  German settlements, 198
  Map of, 451
Central Archives for the History of the Jewish People, 171
Central Europe, 68
  Gazetteers, 68
Central Poland, 89, 98, 99, 100, 102, 286. *See also* Poland
  Genealogical societies, 285
  German emigration, 103, 447
  Researchers, 284
Centre for Mennonite Brethren Studies (Winnipeg, MB), 432
Cernauti, 97. *See* Czernowitz. *See also* Chernivsti, Ukraine
Cerny, Johni, 17, 18, 47, 407
Certified Genealogical Record Specialists, 9
Certified Genealogists, 9
Cesky Budejovice, Czech Republic, 94. *See also* Budweis
Ceylon, 218, 258
Chaco, Argentina, 193
Chamness, Leigh Ann, 139
Charbin, 221, 257. *See also* Harbin, China
Charlemagne, 82, 86, 87, 91, 442
Charlottetown, Prince Edward Island, 26
Chazan, Robert, 160
Chechnya, 82, 328
Chelm, Poland, 84, 100, 344
Chelmno, Poland, 80

Chernivtsi, Ukraine, 97. *See also*
Czernowitz
Cherson, Ukraine, 79. *See also*
Kherson, Ukraine
Chicago, Illinois, 126, 167, 188, 189
Chihuahua, Mexico, 200
Children's Aid Society, 11
Chile, 192, 199, 233, 234, 235, 238,
241, 446, 448
Census records, 240
Civil registers, 239
German immigration, 200
German settlements, 199
National archives, 242
National library, 242
Records at Family History Library,
238
Research helps, 238
Chiloé province, Chile, 199
China, 45, 221, 257, 321
German emigration, 197
Chlebowskiego, Bronislawa, 64, 72
Chmelar, Hans, 49, 52, 297
Cholm, Germany, 344. *See* Chelm,
Poland
Chortitza, Ukraine, 101, 318. *See also*
Chortitz, Ukraine
Chorzempa, Rosemary A., 339, 343
Chote, A. H., 235
Christchurch, New Zealand, 51, 210,
211, 249, 250
Christian Catholic Church in Zion, 120
Christian Reformed Church of North
America, 120, 124, 129
Christiania, 363. *See also* Oslo, Norway
Church of Christ, 120
Church of God, 118, 120, 121
Archives, 128
Church of Jesus Christ of Latter-day
Saints, 2, 40, 45, 120, 138, 361, 376
Church of Scotland. *See also*
Presbyterians
In Canada, 20
Church of the Brethren, 134
Church of the New Jerusalem, 138. *See
also* Swedenborgians
Church of United Brethren, 124, 373
Church records. Check under individual
countries and religions
Austria, 290
Churches, Genealogy of, 122
Chyet, Stanley F., 228
Cieszyn, Poland, 82, 84, 94
Cigler, Michael, 202, 203, 236, 259
Cilli, Slovenia, 85
Cincinnati, Ohio, 188, 232, 421
CIS. *See* Commonwealth of
Independent States (CIS)
Ciskei, South Africa, 214
Cis-Leithania, 93. *See also* Austria
City directories, 11, 263
Civic, Australian Capital Territory, 246
Civil records/civil registers, 262. *Check
under individual countries*

Clasen, Armin, 233
Clervaux canton, Luxembourg, 83
Cleugh, James, 109
Cleveland, Ohio, 188, 190
Cloos, Patricia, 235, 259
Cobb, Sanford Hoadley, 227, 407
Coburg, Germany, 76, 82
Coeckelberghe-Dutzele, Gerhard Robert
Walter von, 153
Cohen, Chester G., 68, 177
Cohen, Harvey A., 202, 235, 245
Cohn, Michael, 157
Colenbringer, H. T., 213, 237
Colket, Meredith B., Jr., 17
Colmar, France, 119, 360
Cologne, Germany, 217, 372, 411
History, 442
Colombia, 201
Colorado, 121, 188, 189, 190
German immigration, 103
Commonwealth of Independent States
(CIS), 257, 308, 326, 329, 441, 450
History, 104
Researching in, 323, 416
Commonwealth of Poland and
Lithuania, 99, 146, 321
Communist Manifesto, 90
Compromise of 1867, 93
Computers, 30–39, 43, 313, 345, 416
Bulletin board services, 34
CD-ROMs, 33
E-mail, 34
Family History Library, 42
GEDCOM, 30, 42
Genealogy software, 30, 42
GRANDMA database, 132
Mailing lists, 34
Newsgroups, 34
On line directories, 39
On line Jewish projects, 166
On line library catalogs, 37
On line services, 33, 34
Search engines, 39
Software, 30
World-Wide Web, 38
Concepcion, Chile, 199, 241
Congregational Christian Churches in
Canada
Headquarters, 130
Congregationalists, 117, 120, 124
Archives, 129
In Canada, 21, 124
In Latin America, 238
Congress of Vienna, 74, 99, 104, 445
Congress Poland, 82, 99, 338, 340. *See
also* Central Poland
Church records, 144, 341
Connecticut, 188
Connor, Martha Remer, 295, 335, 337,
351
Conolly, Gerald K., 235
Conrad Grebel College, 21

Conservative Congregational Christian
Conference
Headquarters, 130
Consistory of Moscow (Lutheran), 313
Consistory of Saint Petersburg
(Lutheran), 312
Consistory of Saratov (Lutheran), 313
Consolidated Jewish Surname Index,
167
Coolgardie, Western Australia, 207
Cope, J. P., 218, 237
Copenhagen, Denmark, 266
Church books, 413
Cordoba, Argentina, 193
Corkhill, Alan, 244, 259
Correspondence abroad, 377
Costa Rica, 199, 200
Civil registers, 239, 240
German immigration, 240
Cottbus, Germany, 83
Council of Local Union Churches, 124
Council of the Reformed Church in
Canada
Headquarters, 129
Counter-Reformation, 87, 92, 368, 443
County atlases, 11
County histories, 17
County plat books, 11
Coupek, Milan, 332
Courland, 80, 98, 99, 318
Lutheran consistory, 313
Court records, 11, 262
Cracow, Poland, 79, 80, 89, 340
Creglingen, Germany, 174
Crespo, Entre Rios, Argentina, 243
Crimean peninsula, 80, 81, 102, 116,
152
Yizkor books, 168
Crimean War, 102, 214, 259
Croatia, 78, 80, 85, 97, 108, 289, 349
Emigration, 211
German emigration, 209
History, 77, 98
Microfilms, 41
National Archives, 350
Researching in, 349
Croats, 93
Crop failures
Of 1816-17, 102, 105, 446
Of 1846-47, 105, 185, 446
Of 1880s, 105
Of 1932-33, 103
Crowe, Elizabeth Powell, 39
Crown Land, Canada Company, 24
Crusades, 146, 442
Crusius, Christian, 68
Cuba, 198
Curacao, 201
Curitiba, Brazil, 197, 241, 243
Cuxhaven, Germany, 208
Cuzzo, Maria Wyant, 425
Cyprus, 221, 351
Czech Brethren, 331

Czech Republic, 52, 71, 78, 79, 80, 81,
    82, 85, 86, 94, 119, 148, 187, 282,
    289, 298, 332, 333, 377, 402, 423,
    449
  Archives, 162, 330
  Burgher books, 267
  Church records, 331
  Civil records, 332
  Contacts, 333
  Embassy, 333
  German emigration, 199
  History, 84, 88, 94, 112, 152, 330,
    331
  Jewish records, 332
  Jews, 331
  Land records, 332
  Map of, 451
  Maps, 332
  Microfilms, 41
  Military parish records, 266
  Military records, 295, 330
  Regional archives, 333
  Research services, 173
  Researchers, 284
  Researching in, 331
  State Archives, 332
  Village genealogies, 268
Czechoslovakia, 150, 325, 416, 449.
    See also Slovak Republic. See also
    Czech Republic
  Gazetteers, 70
  Genealogical research, 417
  History, 76, 77, 87, 90, 91, 92, 96, 98,
    152, 186, 329
  Yizkor books, 168
Czechs, 93
Czernowitz, 97, 150. See also
    Chernivtsi, Ukraine
Czernowitz (Cernauti) University,
    Ukraine, 347

— D —

Dagestan, 82, 328
DAGV, 283, 424
Daitch, Randy, 68, 165
Daitch-Mokotoff Soundex system, 167
Dallas, Texas, 189
Dalmatia, 52, 289, 349
  Emigration, 211
  German emigration, 209
  History, 76, 77
Dalmatien, 289. See also Dalmatia
Danish East India Company, 258
Danner, Karl Heinz, 185
Danube River, 336
Danube River region, 77, 78, 79, 81, 96,
    146, 444, 445
Danube Swabians, 64, 71, 79, 80, 95,
    96, 97, 98, 109, 186, 190, 192, 197,
    201, 203, 286, 297, 336, 342, 347,
    349, 351, 354, 445. See also
    Hungarian Germans
  Genealogical societies, 285

Danube Swabians (continued)
  History, 109
  In Argentina, 64
  In Austria, 64
  In Brazil, 64, 450
  In Bulgaria, 64
  In Canada, 64, 450
  In France, 64
  In Germany, 64
  In Hungary, 64
  In Romania, 64
  In United States, 64, 450
  In Yugoslavia, 64
  Researchers, 284
Danyel, J., 422
Danzig, 49, 77, 81, 99, 143, 338, 344,
    358, 368, 372, 423, 443. See also
    Gdansk, Poland
  History, 76, 83, 339, 449
  Records, 339
Daraska, Jessie L., 323
Dar-es-Salaam, Tanzania, 220, 256
Darling Downs, Australia, 205
Darmstadt, Germany, 284
Darwin, Northern Territory, 246
Dateline of Germanic history, 442
Datikon, Switzerland, 299
Daugava River, Latvia, 81
Daum, Manfred, 284
Davenport, T. R. H., 214, 237
Davie, Maurice Rea, 227
Davies, Raymond Arthur, 232
Davis, Beverley, 202, 235
Daylesford, Victoria, 207
de Gruyter, Louis, 228
de Gryse, Louis, 408
de Guise, Jacques, 49
De Villiers, C. C., 260
De Wall, Kenneth, 440
Dearden, Douglas, 9, 47, 63, 408
Dearden, Fay, 9, 45, 47, 63, 408
Debus, Karl Heinz, 407
Decorah, Iowa, 365
Delaware, 121, 188
Delft, Heinz von, 215, 218
DeMarce, Virginia Easley, 28
Denmark, 280, 363, 368, 442, 449
  Census, 268
  Church records, 357
  Civil records, 357
  History, 75, 76, 84, 88, 89, 90, 357,
    368, 447
  Lutheran church archive, 357
  Map of, 451
  Place names, 65
  Researching in, 357
  State archive, 358
Denoon, Donald, 214, 218, 237
Depression of 1884, 448
der Porten, Edward von, 421
Detmold, Germany, 411
Detroit, Michigan, 188, 189
  Border crossing lists, 14

Deutsche Bundespost (German Post
    Office), 303, 408
Deutsche Geschlechterbücher, 62, 437
Deutsche Ostafrika Gesellschaft
    (DOAG), 219
Deutsche Zentralstelle fur Genealogie,
    Leipzig. See under Genealogical
    societies
Deutschenahnengemeinschaft, 281
Deutsch-Mokra, Ukraine, 327
Deutsch-Proben, 85, 96. See also
    Nitrianske Pravno, Slovak Republic
DeWall, Kenneth, 230, 408, 417
Diamant, Adolf, 153, 154
Diaspora, 203, 307
Dictionaries, 420
Die Zeitung (Australian newspaper),
    244, 246, 259
Dieckmann, Valerie, 244
Diekirch canton, Luxembourg, 83, 300
Dien, Albert, 258
Dienst, R., 278, 408
Diffenderffer, Frank Ried, 227, 231,
    420
Dimont, Max I., 160, 187
Disciples of Christ, 120
Displaced persons, 118, 182, 187, 197,
    203, 208, 376, 450
District of Columbia, 189
Dittrich, Kathinka, 177
Divack, Alan S., 178
Dnepropetrovsk, Ukraine, 79
  Archives, 319, 326
Dnieper River region, Ukraine, 104,
    449
Dniester River, Ukraine, 82, 328
DOAG, 219. See also Deutsche
    Ostafrika Gesellschaft (DOAG)
Dobrogea, 79, 85. See also Dobruja
  Emigration, 191
Dobrudscha, 79, 85, 289. See also
    Dobruja. See also Dobruja
Dobrudza, 329. See also Dobruja
Dobruja, 79, 106, 289, 320
  Census records, 348
  History, 85, 98, 329, 346
  Records, 347
Doerksen, Victor G., 143, 222, 247
Dollarhide, William, 1, 5, 17
Dominican Republic, 198, 240
Don River region, Russia, 79, 102
Don, Yehuda, 157
Donauschwaben, 79. See also Danube
    Swabians
Dongebiet, 79. See also Don River
    region, Russia
Dönnhoff, Marion, Gräfin, 157
Dorfsippenbücher, 273. See also
    Ortssippenbücher. See also Village
    genealogies
Dorpat, Estonia, 321
Dortmund, Germany, 286
Douala, Cameroon, 220
Doubek, F. A., 68

Doxford, Colin, 236, 260
Drabek, Anna M., 157
Draper, Paula, 177
Drenning-Holmquist, June, 408
Dresden, Germany, 83, 281
Dressler, Johann Christian, 223, 352
Drewenz River region, Poland, 100
Dual Monarchy, 150
    History, 297
Duala, 220. *See* Douala, Cameroon
Dublin, Ireland, 361
Dunbrody, South Africa, 217
Duncaster, Victoria, 206
Dundas County, Ontario, 190
Dunedin, New Zealand, 210, 211, 250
Dunkards, 116, 261
Dunkers, 116
Dunkirk, France, 195, 221
Dunn, Mary, 408
Durango, Mexico, 200
Durban, South Africa, 215, 216
Durnbaugh, Donald F., 139, 225
Durning, Bill, 373
Durning, Mary, 373
Durr, Volker, 157
Duss, John, 117
Dutch, 57
    Independence, 92, 361
    Language, 361
    People, 362
Dutch East India Company, 258, 362.
    See also Dutch East Indies Company
Dutch East Indies, 226
Dutch East Indies Company, 212, 213,
    215, 444. *See also* Dutch East India
    Company
Dutch people, 77, 99, 362
Dutch Reformed Church, 117, 253, 362
Dutch West India Company, 362
Dutch West Indies, 226
Dvina River, Latvia, 81. *See also*
    Daugava River, Latrvia
Dvorzág, János, 64, 68
Dyck, Cornelius J., 117, 139, 203, 223,
    352
Dyck, Harvey L., 352
Dyck, John P., 133

— E —

Eakle, Arlene, 17, 18
Eames, Patricia A., 310, 441
East Brandenburg, 247
East Central Europe, 74, 81, 285, 309,
    450. *See* Eastern Europe
    Atlases, 70
East Europe, 351
East Frankish Kingdom, 86
East Friesland, 207
East Frisia, 54, 55, 113, 446
East Galicia, 69, 97, 142, 325. *See also*
    Galicia
    History, 84

East Germany, 41, 91, 280, 284. *See
    also* Germany. *See also* German
    Democratic Republic
    Map of, 451
East India, 258
East India (or East Indies) Companies,
    258
East Indies, 258
East London, South Africa, 214, 215
East Netze River region, Poland, 284
East Prussia, 73, 75, 76, 79, 80, 89,
    141, 287, 321, 322, 411, 416, 471.
    See also Ostpreussen
    Burgher books, 267
    Church records, 355, 423
    FHL cataloging, 44
    Gazetteers, 68
    Genealogical societies, 285
    German emigration, 198, 210, 213
    History, 75, 76, 77, 83, 84, 90, 114,
    185
    Military parish records, 266
    Place names, 65, 66
    Religions, 119, 444
Eastern Europe, 41, 58, 63, 64, 67, 68,
    70, 71, 77, 82, 90, 94, 179, 182,
    199, 283, 308, 319, 377, 378, 417,
    448, 449
    Emigration, 230, 417, 418
    Gazetteers, 68
    Genealogical information, 416
    Genealogical societies, 280, 284
    Genealogists, 415
    German immigration, 359
    Maps, 65, 66, 72
    Translators, 415
Eastern Poland
    German immigration, 447
Eastman, Richard, 39
Ebenezer Society, 137. *See also* Amana
    Society
Echternach canton, Luxembourg, 83
Economic conditions, 182. *See also*
    Crop failures. *See also* Industrial
    Revolution
Ecuador, 201
Edenvale, South Africa, 253
Edict of Nantes, 89, 443
    Revocation, 359, 444
Edlund, Thomas Kent, 139, 170, 177,
    281, 303, 312, 352, 408
Edmonton, Alberta, 21, 22, 25, 26, 27,
    192
Educational Council for the German-
    Speaking Communities in South
    Australia, 249
Edwards, John, 160
Eger, Wolfgang, 266, 408, 409
Egerland, 211, 282
Egypt, 212, 221, 256
Ehl, Petr, 177
Ehrenbürgerbücher, 267
Eichhoff, Jürgen, 57
Eichholz, Alice, 17

Eichler, Evan, 133, 142
Eifel Mountains, 79, 194, 277
Eifel, Germany, 194
Eisenach, George J., 117, 140
Eisenach, Germany, 82
Eisenbach, Ulrich, 154
Eisenberg, Ellen, 227
Eisenberg, Erich, 409
Eisenstadt, Austria, 151, 294
Eisfeld, Alfred, 320
Ekaterinoslav, Ukraine, 79, 312. *See
    also* Jekaterinoslav, Ukraine
Elazar, Daniel Judah, 223
Elbe River, 57, 80, 86, 146, 183
Elbing, 99, 344, 372. *See also* Elblag,
    Poland
Elblag, Poland, 344
Elia, Christine, 72
Eliade, Mercia, 140
Elim Mission, Transvaal, South Africa,
    218
Eliov, Mordechai, 157
Ellenson, David Harry, 154
Ellingson, Irmgard Hein, 140, 223, 227,
    352, 409
Elliot, Wendy, 47
Ellis Island, New York, 186, 448
Ellman-Krüger, Angelika C., 174, 177
Ellwangen/Jagst, Germany, 217
Elmessiri, Abdelwahab, 237
Elsass-Lothringen, 76. *See also* Alsace-
    Lorraine
    FHL cataloging, 44
E-mail, 34
Emden, Germany, 114
Emigration
    Germanic Europe, 116
Emigration lists, 7, 52
Emigration records, 262
Endlich, Stefanie, 154
Engel, A., 176
Engels, Russia, 257, 311, 324
England, 184, 191, 208, 442
    Emigration, 420
    German immigration, 232, 376
    History, 78, 105, 258
Englander, David, 223
English East India Company, 258
Ensch, Jean, 301
Ensenada, Argentina
    Arrival lists, 52
Entre Rios, Argentina, 192, 193
Entre Rios, Brazil, 197
Ephrata Cloister, 124
Ephrata Society, 124
Epp, Ingrid I., 352
Epp, Reuben, 404
Erdély, Romania, 95. *See also*
    Siebenburgen. *See also* Transylvania
Erfurt, Germany, 83
Ermland, 79. *See also* Warmia, Poland
Erzgebirge, 79. *See also* Ore Mountains
Eschleman, H. Frank, 227

Esch-sur-Alzette canton, Luxembourg, 83
Eshleman, H. Frank, 140
Eskimos, 25
Espirito Santo, Brazil, 195, 226, 238
Estland, 98, 321. *See also* Estonia
Estonia, 79, 80, 84, 98, 99, 190, 423
  Church records, 282, 355, 423
  Genealogical societies, 285
  German colonization, 98
  Lutheran consistory, 313
  Microfilms, 41
  National archives, 321
  Researching in, 321
Ethiopia, 216
Etsch River, 337
Eugen, Duke Karl, 216
Eupen, Belgium, 71, 84, 90, 356
Europe, 434. Check individual countries
    and regions
  Atlases, 70
  Maps of, 451
European Rivers
  Map of, 451
Eutin, Germany, 76
Evangelical Association, 124
  Archives, 130
Evangelical Central Archives, 266
Evangelical Church, 111, 202
  In Germany, 116, 419
  In Poland, 141
  In Prussia, 261, 446
  Records, 261
Evangelical Congregational Church
    Archives, 130
Evangelical Lutheran Church in
    Canada, 21
  Archives, 128
Evangelical Lutheran Church of
    America (ELCA), 122
  Archives, 126, 127
Evangelical Lutheran Church of
    America Archives, 257, 432
Evangelical Lutheran Church of
    Australia, 248
Evangelical Synod, 128
Evangelical Synodical Conference of
    America, 128
Evangelical United Brethren
    Archives, 129
Evangelicals (Albright), 120, 121
Evangelisches Zentralarchiv in Berlin,
    144, 282, 305, 307, 322, 354, 419
Evans, Maurice C., 215
Everton, George B., Jr., 425
Everton, George B., Sr., 17
Expulsions
  Of Germans, 98, 449
  Of Salzburger Protestants, 142, 444
Exulanten, 115, 298

— F —

Falsterbo, Sweden, 367
Falun, Sweden, 367
Family group sheets, 384
Family histories, 11
Family History Centers, 2, 9, 19, 20, 23,
    24, 45, 46, 47, 50, 58, 63, 261, 364,
    365, 370, 401, 408
  In Iowa, 436
  in Manitoba and Western Ontario,
    436
  In Minnesota, 435
  In North Dakota, 436
  In South Dakota, 436
  In Wisconsin, 436
Family History Library, 2, 5, 8, 9, 17,
    23, 24, 27, 40–47, 48, 49, 50, 51,
    52, 61, 63, 64, 72, 238, 240, 241,
    242, 261, 264, 265, 266, 281, 282,
    286, 295, 297, 299, 300, 303, 307,
    312, 313, 314, 321, 322, 325, 327,
    331, 334, 337, 338, 339, 340, 341,
    342, 347, 350, 353, 357, 360, 362,
    408, 409, 411, 417, 418, 426, 432
  Accreditations Committee, 9
  Catalog, 33, 43
  FamilySearch Center, 42
  German parish registers, 407
  Germanic collection, 41
  Jewish records, 162
Family parish registers, 422
Family registers, 263
Family sources
  Family papers, 10
  Relatives, 10
FamilySearch, 42
Fangel, Kari, 186
Fassifern district, Queensland, 246
Father Flanagan's Boys Town
    (Nebraska), 11
Faust, Albert Bernhardt, 227, 231, 277,
    280, 303, 409
Federal Republic of Germany, 90, 450.
    See also Germany
  History, 91
  Länder (states), 82
  Map of, 451
Federation of Micronesia, 212
FEEFHS, 269. *See* Genealogical
    societies: Federation of East
    European Family History Societies
    (FEEFHS)
Fehlinger, Hans, 107, 346
Feigmanis, Aleksandrs, 322
Fellows, R., 28
Fellowship of Brethren Genealogists,
    134
Ferdinand II, 368
Ferguson, Laraine K., 279, 404, 425
FHL. *See* Family History Library
FHLC, 43, 44, 46. *See also under*
    Family History Library
Fichtner, R., 175

Fiedler, Jirí, 177
Filby, P. William, 9, 17, 18, 50, 52,
    223, 303, 409, 410
Finland, 367
  German immigration, 358
  History, 85, 358, 368
  Luheran records, 313
  National Archive, 358
  Researching in, 358
Firchau, Otto, 284
Firestone, Bill, 165, 426
Firth, Lester, 235
Fiti tribe (Tanzania), 219
Fiume, 289
Flanders, 113
Flanders, Belgium, 95, 357
  History, 95, 356
Flegel, Arthur, 328
Fleischmann, Konrad, 136
Flemings (Belgians), 57, 88, 356, 362
Flemish, 77. *See also* Flemings
    (Belgians)
Flemish language, 357, 361
Florey, Gerhard, 140, 228
Florianopolis, Brazil, 194
Florida, 117, 188, 189
Flynn, Oscar R., 228
Foisel, John, 107
Formosa, Argentina, 193
Forschungsstelle Niedersächsische
    Auswanderer in den USA (NAUSA),
    278
Forty-Eighters, 184
Foster, John, 235
France, 78, 79, 86, 89, 256, 442, 444,
    445, 449. *See also* Lorraine. *See also*
    Alsace
  Burgher books, 267
  Census, 268
  Church records, 359
  Civil records, 360
  Emigration, 418, 420
  Emigration records, 360
  Genealogical societies, 361
  German emigration, 50, 359
  History, 75, 76, 78, 84, 85, 87, 88, 89,
    90, 105, 146, 186, 443, 444, 445,
    447
  Map of, 451
  Military parish records, 266
  Miscellaneous records, 360
  National Archive, 360
  Place names, 65
  Records, 376
  Regional Archives, 360
  Religions, 119
  Researching in, 359
Franconia, 79, 89, 286, 304
  History, 87, 94, 95
Franco-Prussian War, 266, 373
  German casualties, 422
Frank, Jerry, 313, 320
Franken, 79. *See also* Franconia

Frankfurt am Main, Germany, 75, 89, 115, 145, 147, 148, 287, 409, 445
Frankfurt an der Oder, Germany, 83, 148
Frankfurt, Germany, 368
Frankl, Ludwig August, 177
Franklin district, Northwest Territories, 25
Franklin, Charles M., 140
Franklin, Karen, 170
Franks, 91, 442
Franschhoek, South Africa, 255
Franz Josef II (Emperor), 332
Franz, Eckhart G., 223, 277, 409
Franzheim, Liesel, 153
Fraser, Lynn, 25
Fratautz, Bukovina, 352
Frazin, Judith R., 177, 404
Fredericton, New Brunswick, 26
Free Christians, 138
Freeman Academy Heritage Archives (Freeman, South Dakota), 436
Freeman Junior College Library (SD), 133
Freeman, Margaret Zimmerman, 309, 320
Freeman, Robert, 309
Freiburg canton, Switzerland, 83, 196. *See also* Fribourg canton, Switzerland
Freiburg im Breisgau, Germany, 174
Freiburg, Germany, 79
Freiherr, Werner, 340
Fremantle, Western Australia, 51
French East India Company, 258
French Foreign Legion, 182, 212, 256
French language, 357
    Records, 359
French Reformed. *See* Huguenots
French Revolution, 195, 359, 360
Friaul, 92, 338. *See also* Friuli, Italy
Fribourg canton, Switzerland, 83
Friederichs, Heinz F., 261, 303, 410
Friedlander, Albert H., 158
Friedlander, Henry, 177
Friedlander, Saul, 160
Friedrichstadt, Germany, 287
Friends of Jerusalem, 117, 138
Friesen, Nick, 257
Friesland, 361. *See also* Frisia
Frisian language, 361
Frisians, 77, 362
Friuli, Italy, 92, 338
Frizzell, Robert W., 228
Froelke, Ruth, 225, 304, 417
Frötschl, Oswald, 284
Füchtner, Jürg, 410
Fulda River, Germany, 81
Fünfkirchen, 97. *See also* Pécs, Hungary
Funke, Alfred, 233
Furer, Howard B., 188, 228

— G —

Gade, John Allyne, 363
Galicia, 52, 64, 80, 98, 142, 150, 163, 289, 296, 317, 325, 341, 342. *See also* Western Galicia. *See also* East Galicia
    Catholic records, 340
    Church records, 340
    Civil records, 342
    Colonization, 354
    Emigration, 191, 297
    Gazetteers, 64, 70, 73
    German emigration, 186
    German immigration, 445
    Germans from, 22
    History, 75, 76, 77, 92, 97, 115, 150, 151, 338, 341, 342
    Land cadasters, 342
    Land records, 342
    Records, 285, 316
    Research in, 345
    Researchers, 284
    Yizkor books, 168
Galicja, 84. *See also* Galicia
Galizien, 80, 289. *See also* Galicia
Gallaland. *See* Somalia
Galveston, Texas, 50
Gamlakarleby, Finland, 358
Ganther, Heinz, 157
Gardiner, Duncan B., 68, 96, 330, 332, 333, 334, 337
Garnsey, Heather E., 245, 249
Gaudet, F., 28
Gay, Peter, 157
Gay, Ruth, 157
Gazetteers
    Australia, 248
    Austria, 63, 290
    Banat, 64
    Galicia, 64
    German Empire, 72
    Germany, 8, 63, 64, 72
    Hungary, 64
    Poland, 64, 72
    Prussia, 63
    Soviet Union, 65
    Switzerland, 63
Gdansk, Poland, 49, 338, 344. See also Danzig
    History, 83
Geburtsbrief, 267
GEDCOM. *See under* Computers
Geelong, Victoria, 206, 207
Geheimes Staatsarchiv Preussischer Kulturbesitz, 283. *See* Prussian State Privy Archives, Berlin
Geiger, Ludwig, 154
Gemeinschaft unabhängiger Staaten, 323. *See also* Commonwealth of Independent States
Genadendal, South Africa, 216
Genealogical documents, 180

Genealogical institutes. *See* Genealogical societies
Genealogical libraries, 432–38
Genealogical periodicals, 11
    Archiv für Sippenforschung, 7
    Avotaynu, 164
    Der Schlüssel, 418
    Die Pommerschen Leute, 282
    Familienkundliche Nachrichten (FaNa), 7, 8
    German, 263
    German Genealogical Digest, 8
    Heritage Quest, 416
    List of, 425–26
    Luxembourg News of America, 301
    Mennonite Genealogist, 426
    Newsletter of the Germanic Genealogy Society, 278
    Praktische Forschungshilfe (PraFo), 7, 8
    The Germanic Genealogist, 48
    The Gottschee Tree, 350
    The Gottscheer Connection, 350
    The Lost Palatine, 425
    The Palatine Immigrant, 279
Genealogical research, 425
Genealogical resources
    For religions in United States and Canada, 125
Genealogical societies, 7
    Akademie für Genealogie, Heraldik und verwandte Wissenschaften, 274
    Alberta Family History Societies, 21
    Alberta Genealogical Society, 21, 22
    Albury Family History Group, 244
    American Historical Society of Germans from Russia (AHSGR), 65, 66, 72, 193, 257, 313, 318, 320, 329, 410, 419, 425, 437, 439
    American/Schleswig Holstein Heritage Society, 439
    Anglo-German Family History Society, 373
    Arbeitsbund für österreichische Familienkunde, 297
    Arbeitsgemeinschaft für mitteldeutsche Familienforschung, 288
    Arbeitsgemeinschaft für Pfälzisch-Rheinische Familienkunde, 275
    Arbeitsgemeinschaft für Saarländische Familienkunde, 275
    Arbeitsgemeinschaft Genealogie, 276
    Arbeitsgemeinschaft ostdeutscher Familienforscher (AGoFF), 283, 307, 348, 353, 416
    Arbeitskreis donauschwäbischer Familienforscher, 285, 353
    Arbeitskreis für Familienforschung (Lübeck), 276
    Arbeitskreis für Familienforschung im Hagener Heimatbund, 275

Germanic Genealogy: A Guide to Worldwide Sources and Migration Patterns

Genealogical societies (continued)
Asociacion Argentina de los
Alemanes del Volga, 243
Associação Alema-Bucovina de
Cultura, 243
Association Luxembourgeoise de
Généalogie et d'Héraldique, 300
Association of German Nobility in
North America, 439
Association of Jewish Genealogical
Societies (AJGS), 165, 441
Augustan Society, 269, 279, 301, 425,
441
Australasian Federation of Family
History Organisations, 245, 249
Australian Institute of Genealogical
Studies, 244
Australian Jewish Genealogical
Society, 245
Banat Listserver, 439
Banat MajorDomo Genealogy Group,
439
Bayerischer Landesverein für
Familienkunde, 274
Belarussian Genealogical Society,
Belarus, 328
Bendigo Regional Genealogical
Society, Inc., 245
Bergischer Verein für Familienkunde,
275
Bohemian Association Originating in
Puhoi-Ohaupo, 251
British Columbia Genealogical
Society, 22
Broken Hill Family History Group,
244
Bukovina Society of the Americas,
107, 327, 347, 354, 439
Bund der Familienverbände, 288
Central Archives for the History of
the Jewish People, 162
Centre for Genealogical Research in
Grand Saconnex, Switzerland, 49
Centro Germano-Argentino de Entre
Rios, 243
Cercle Genealogique de Alsace, 361
Cercle Genealogique de Lorraine, 361
Conselho de Curadores da Fundação
Cultural de Pomerode, 243
Czechoslovak Genealogical Society
International, 96, 437, 441
Danube Swabian Association, 439
Deutsch-Baltische Genealogische
Gesellschaft, 284
Deutsche Arbeitsgemeinschaft
genealogischer Verbände
(DAGV), 273
Deutsche Zentralstelle für Genealogie,
280, 307, 321, 331
Deutsche-Hugenotten-Gesellschaft,
286
Deutsches Adelsarchiv, 288
Die Maus - Gesellschaft für
Familienforschung, 274

Genealogical societies (continued)
Directory of, 18
Directory of societies, 414
East European Genealogical Society,
308, 326, 340, 441
Emsland Heritage Society, 439
Familienkundliche Gesellschaft für
Nassau und Frankfurt, 274
Federacao dos Institutos Genealogicos
Latinos, 241
Federation of East European Family
History Societies (FEEFHS), 10,
265, 308, 315, 384, 415, 429, 441
Federation of Swedish Genealogical
Societies, 370
Föreningen för Datorhjälp I
Släktforskningen (DIS), 370
Francysk Scarnyna Centre, Belarus,
328
Friedrich-Wilhelm-Euler-Gesellschaft
für personengeschichtliche
Forschung, 288
Galizien German Descendants, 340,
439
Genealogical Association of English
Speaking Researchers in Europe,
287
Genealogical Association of Nova
Scotia, 21
Genealogical Society of Queensland,
244, 259, 260
Genealogical Society of South Africa,
255
Genealogical Society of Tasmania,
245
Genealogical Society of Utah, 305,
418
Genealogical Society of Victoria,
Australia, 244
Genealogische Gesellschaft,
Hamburg, 274
Genealogisch-Heraldische
Gesellschaft, Göttingen, 275
Genealogiska Föreningen, 370
Georgia Salzburger Society, GA, 128
German Central Office for Genealogy,
Leipzig, 268, 281. See also
Zentralstelle für Genealogie
German Genealogical Society of
America, 7, 330, 439
German Huguenot Society, 286, 359
German Interest Group of Chicago
Genealogical Society, 439
German Research Association, 58,
263, 439
German Research Group in
Queensland, 244
German Society of Pennsylvania, 439
German-Acadian Coast Historical and
Genealogical Society, 439
German-American Research and
Document Center, 439
German-Bohemian Heritage Society,
333, 439

Genealogical societies (continued)
Germanic Genealogy Society, 278,
312, 384, 406, 436, 440
Germans from Russia Heritage
Society (GRHS), 64, 70, 108, 109,
320, 329, 415, 426, 440
Prairie Heritage Chapter, 5, 354,
430
German-Texan Heritage Society, 440
Gesellschaft für Familienforschung in
Franken, 274
Gesellschaft für Familienkunde in
Kurhessen und Waldeck, 274
Gesellschaft für ostmitteleuropäische
Landeskunde und Kultur, 285
Gesher Galicia, 339
Glückstal Colony Research
Association, 309, 320, 440
Gottscheer Research and Genealogy
Association, 109, 350, 425, 440
Hamilton Family History Centre, 245
Heraldic and Genealogical Society in
Budapest, 336
Heraldisch-genealogische
Gesellschaft "Adler", 297
HEROLD, 273
Hessische Familiengeschichtliche
Vereinigung, 274
Hungarian Genealogical Society of
America, 441
Hungarian/American Friendship
Society, 441
Illinois Mennonite Historical and
Genealogical Society, 131, 440
Immigrant Genealogical Society, 9,
184, 261, 273, 279, 304, 412, 440
Institut für historische
Familienforschung Genealogie
Gesellschaft (Vienna), 411
Institut für pfälzische Geschichte und
Volkskunde, 240
Instituto Chileno de Investigaciones
Genealogicas, 243
Instituto Hans Staden, 243
Irish Palatine Information Office, 361
Jewish Genealogial Society of Greater
Washington (DC), 166
Jewish Genealogical Society of
Greater Washington (DC), 164,
178, 441
Jewish Genealogical Society, Inc.,
166, 441
Joseph Jacobs Organization, 178
Leo Baeck Institute, 162, 163, 170,
432
Liga Chileno-Alemana, 233
Lippischer Heimatsbund, 275
Lithuanian American Genealogy
Society, Chicago, 323, 441
Luxembourg Heritage, 302
Luxembourger Society of Wisconsin,
440
Manitoba Genealogical Society, 21,
22, 24

Genealogical societies (*continued*)
  Mid-Atlantic Germanic Society, 440
  Minnesota Genealogical Society, 437
  Mosaik: Familienkundliche
      Vereinigung für das Klever Land,
      275
  National Genealogical Society, 17,
      434
  National Huguenot Society, 130
  Nederlandse Genealogische
      Vereniging, 363
  New England Historic Genealogical
      Society, 434
  New South Wales Association of
      Family History Societies, 244
  New Zealand Society of Genealogists,
      249, 251
  Niederändische Ahnengemeinschaft,
      287
  Niedersächsischer Landesverein für
      Familienkunde, 274
  Nordfriisk Institut, 280
  Norwegian Emigrant Museum, 365
  Norwegian Emigration Center, 366
  Oldenburgische Gesellschaft für
      Familienkunde, 275
  Ontario Genealogical Society, 19, 21,
      22
  Orangeburg-German-Swiss
      Genealogical Society, 440
  Orphan Train Heritage Society of
      America, 11, 441
  Ostfriesen Genealogical Society (IL),
      440
  Ostfriesian Genealogical Society (IA),
      440
  Ostfriesische Landschaft
      Arbeitsgruppe Familienkunde, 275
  Palatines to America, 278, 440
  Pennsylvania German Research
      Society, 440
  Pennsylvania German Society, 231,
      419
  Piast Genealogical Research Centre,
      345
  Polish Genealogical Society of
      America, 61, 109, 142, 340, 342,
      353, 441
  Polish Genealogical Society of
      Michigan, 342, 441
  Polish Genealogical Society of Texas,
      343
  Polish Genealogical Society of the
      Northeast, 323, 342, 343, 441
  Pommerscher Verein Freistadt, 440
  Queensland Family History Society,
      Inc., 247
  Roland Society in Dresden, 281
  Roland zu Dortmund, 275
  Sacramento German Genealogical
      Society, 440
  Salzburger Verein, 287
  San Francisco Bay Area Jewish
      Genealogical Society, 166

Genealogical societies (*continued*)
  Saskatchewan Genealogical Society,
      22, 23
  Schleswig-Holsteinische Gesellschaft
      für Familienforschung und
      Wappenkunde, 276
  Schweitzerische Gesellschaft für
      Familienforschung, 299
  Schweitzerische Gesellschaft für
      jüdische Familienforschung, 173
  Schweizerische Vereinigung für
      jüdische Genealogie, 300, 426
  Schwenkfeldian Exile Society, 440
  Silesian Genealogical Society, 345
  Släktforskarnas Hus, 372
  Society of German-American Studies,
      440
  South Australian Genealogy and
      Heraldry Society, 244, 247
  Sudetendeutsche Landsmannschaft
      Argentinien, 243
  Sverige Släktforskarförbund, 370
  Swiss American Historical Society
      (IL), 440
  Swiss American Historical Society
      (VA), 440
  Swiss Genealogical Society, 299
  Towarzystwo Genealogiczno-
      Heraldyczne, 345
  Transylvanian Saxon Genealogy and
      Heritage Society, Inc., 440
  Utah Genealogical Association, 313
  Verein für Familien- und
      Wappenkunde in Württemberg
      und Baden, 274
  Verein für Familienforschung in Ost-
      und Westpreussen, 285
  Verein für Ost- und Westpreussen,
      285
  Verein zur Förderung der
      Zentralstelle für Personen- und
      Familiengeschichte, 273
  Vereinigung für Familien- und
      Wappenkunde zu Fulda, 274
  Vereinigung Sudetendeutscher
      Familienforscher und
      Sudetendeutsches Genealogisches
      Archiv, 285
  Vesterheim Genealogical Center, 365
  Vlaamse Vereniging voor
      Familiekunde, 357
  Werkgroep Genealogisch Onderzoek
      Duitsland, 287
  Westdeutsche Gesellschaft für
      Familienkunde, 275
  Western Australian Genealogical
      Society, 244
  Westfälische Gesellschaft für
      Genealogie und
      Familienforschung, 275
  Wimmera Association for Genealogy,
      245
  Wisconsin State Genealogical
      Society, 441

Genealogical societies (*continued*)
  YIVO Institute for Jewish Research,
      308
  Zentraal Bureau voor Genealogie, 363
  Zentralstelle für Genealogie, 423
  Zentralstelle für Personen- und
      Familiengeschichte, 273
Genealogical terminology, 405, 416,
      419
Genealogies
  In Library of Congress, 412, 414
  Switzerland, 415
Genealogists
  Accredited, 9
  Certified, 9
  Directory of German, 410
  Lists of European, 424
  Professional, 9, 17
Genee, Pierre, 177
General Convention of the New
      Jerusalem in the USA, 124
Generalgouvernement, Poland, 79, 354
Geneva, Switzerland, 79, 83, 89, 105,
      257. *See also* Genf canton,
      Switzerland
Genf canton, Switzerland, 83
Genoa, Italy, 208
Georgia (country), 84, 311, 328, 450
  Researching in, 328
Georgia (U.S. state), 141, 142, 188,
      189, 190, 287
  German immigration, 89, 116, 128,
      185, 187
Geppert, Karlheinz, 154
Gera, Germany, 83
German Baptist Brethren, 116, 120,
      121, 124
  Archives, 134
German Bohemians, 230, 417
German Central Office for Genealogy.
      See Genealogical societies: Deutsche
      Zentralstelle für Genealogie. *See*
      also Genealogical societies:Deutsche
      Zentralstelle für Genealogie
German colonies, 74, 95, 97, 98, 102,
      193, 197, 198, 200, 205, 211, 248,
      252, 255, 313, 328, 336, 448, 449.
      See also individual territories
German Confederation, 105, 106, 266,
      445
  States, 75
German Consulate, 436
German Customs Union, 90
  Census, 267
German Democratic Republic, 91, 279,
      422, 450
  Bezirke, 83
  Map of, 451
  Records, 270
German East Africa, 212, 219–20, 237,
      256. *See also* Tanzania
German East Africa Company, 219
German emigration. *See under*
      Germans. *See individual countries*

German Empire, 58, 71, 190, 264, 412, 447
  Atlases, 72
  Church records, 305, 423
  German emigration, 192, 193
  History, 74, 84, 86–91, 93, 183, 306, 352, 356, 359, 448
  Map of, 451
  Records, 270, 281
  Research, 409
  States, 76
German Evangelical Protestants, 120, 121, 128
German Evangelical Synod, 120, 121
German Federal Archives, Bonn, 327
German Information Center, 432
German Interest Group of Southern Wisconsin (Janesville, Wisconsin), 439
German language, 393
  Cases, 393
  Dialects, 56, 451
  Dictionary, 405
  Diseases, 400
  Gender, 393
  High German (Hochdeutsch), 56
  Interchangeable letters, 54, 66
  Jurisdictional terms, 395
  Kinship terms, 395
  Low German (Plattdeutsch), 56
  Newspapers abroad, 7, 259
  Nouns, 393
  Numbers, 400
  Occupations, 398
  Records, 359
  Time terminology, 399
  Umlauts, 67, 394
  Word list, 395
German Loyalists, 190
German Minority Census of 1939, 170
German names, 412, 418, 419
German Poland, 210
  German emigration, 210
German Reformed Church, 120, 121, 122
German script, 391. See also Gothic script
German Solomon Islands, 212
German South-West Africa, 52, 212, 215, 218, 255, 448. See also Namibia
German Temple, 117. See also Temple Society
German Wars of Unification, 183
German-American churches, 141
Germania Judaica (Library), 172
Germanic Emigrants Register, 280
Germans
  Aussiedler. See under Aussiedler
  Emigration of, 98
  Expellees (1945), 90, 100, 104
  Expulsions of, 98, 449
  In Africa, 448
  In Algeria, 182

Germans (continued)
  In Alsace-Lorraine, 359
  In Argentina, 182, 192, 199, 202
  In Armenia, 328
  In Asia, 101
  In Asian Muslim republics, 104, 328, 329
  In Australia, 51, 182, 202, 203, 259, 260
  In Austrian Empire, 93
  In Austro-Hungarian Empire, 91, 93, 190, 349, 351
  In Azerbaijan, 328
  In Balkan countries, 339
  In Baltic countries, 99, 318, 321
  In Banat, 70, 296
  In Belarus, 101, 327
  In Belgium, 306, 356
  In Bessarabia, 23, 102, 106, 307, 328, 339, 346
  In Black Sea region, 102, 285, 317, 325, 354, 426, 445
  In Bohemia, 73, 109, 188, 200, 201
  In Bosnia, 97, 98
  In Bosnia-Herzegovina, 349
  In Brandenburg, 284
  In Brazil, 182, 192, 195, 199, 202, 243, 329
  In Bukovina, 23, 73, 95, 98, 107, 140, 144, 188, 196, 197, 198, 200, 201, 227, 284, 307, 346, 352, 354, 409, 441
  In Bulgaria, 329
  In Canada, 50, 51, 182, 190–92, 199, 340, 413
  In Carpatho-Ukraine, 335
  In Caucasus, 101, 314, 328
  In Central America, 198
  In Central Poland, 284, 342
  In Chile, 182, 199, 200
  In China, 257
  In Commonwealth of Independent States, 323
  In Croatia, 335, 349
  In Czech Republic, 23, 284, 331
  In Czechoslovakia, 108, 306, 335
  In Denmark, 306, 356, 357
  In Dobruja, 106, 109, 329, 346
  In Dutch Guiana, 201
  In Eastern Europe, 109, 185, 196, 197, 264, 270, 281, 283, 306, 307, 335, 416
  In Eastern Poland, 342
  In Egypt, 182, 221
  In England, 356, 372, 374
  In Estonia, 306, 307, 321
  In France, 306, 338, 356, 359
  In French Foreign Legion, 182
  In Galicia, 23, 97, 98, 108, 284, 296, 340, 342, 345, 441
  In Georgia (country), 328
  In German Empire, 190
  In Great Britain, 306, 372
  In Guatemala, 238

Germans (continued)
  In Hungary, 110, 306, 335
  In Ireland, 361
  In Italy, 109, 306, 337, 411
  In Kenya, 220
  In Latin America, 52, 182
  In Latvia, 306, 307, 321, 322
  In Lithuania, 306, 307, 321, 322
  In London, England, 78, 373
  In Luxembourg, 106
  In Manchuria, 328
  In Maryland, 421
  In Mexico, 182, 200, 238, 241
  In Michigan, 231, 421
  In Moldova, 101, 328, 346
  In Moravia, 109
  In Morocco, 182
  In Namibia, 51, 182, 218
  In Netherlands, 306, 356, 361
  In Neumark, 284
  In New York, 362
  In New Zealand, 51, 182, 210, 259
  In Norway, 363
  In Ottoman Turkish Empire, 106
  In Paraguay, 182, 199, 200, 238, 329
  In Pennsylvania, 411, 421
  In Peru, 201
  In Poland, 89, 90, 100, 102, 103, 108, 284, 306, 338, 342
  In Pomerania, 284
  In Posen, 284
  In Romania, 97, 98, 109, 306, 335, 346, 354, 450
  In Russia, 58, 101, 102, 103, 104, 107, 109, 140, 189, 190, 223, 307, 318, 324, 354, 410, 419, 423, 425
  In Russian Empire, 49, 190, 311, 319
  In Russian Poland, 342
  In Satu Mare, Romania, 98
  In Scandinavia, 356
  In Serbia-Montenegro, 350
  In Siberia, 257, 328, 329
  In Siebenbürgen, 307
  In Silesia, 284, 345
  In Slovak Republic, 73, 334, 335
  In Slovakia, 96, 336
  In Slovenia, 96, 98, 109, 307, 338, 350
  In South Africa, 51, 182, 212
  In South Russia, 328
  In South Tyrol, 95, 98, 307
  In Southeast Europe, 110, 284, 423
  In Southwest Africa, 182
  In Soviet Union, 108, 183, 306
  In Subcarpathian Rus', 96
  In Sudetenland, 284, 307
  In Surinam, 201
  In Sweden, 367, 374
  In Switzerland, 338
  In Togo, 220
  In Transylvania, 296
  In Turkey, 182, 306, 347
  In Ukraine, 101, 102, 106, 325, 339, 340

Germans (*continued*)
In United Kingdom, 372
In United States, 49, 182, 199, 202, 223, 329, 410. *See individual states*
In Uruguay, 201
In Venezuela, 201
In Virginia, 418
In Vojvodina, 335
In Volga River region, 103, 182, 192, 193, 196, 243, 285, 317, 318, 319, 325, 407, 445, 449
In Volhynia, 100, 103, 108, 200, 241, 284, 311, 317, 325, 327, 339
In Walachia, 346
In West Indies, 198
In Western Australia, 207
In Western Canada, 329
In Yugoslavia, 306, 348, 350, 450
In Zimbabwe, 219
Of Dutch Descent, 287
Population statistics, 306
Repatriation of, 98, 107, 108, 449
Resettlers (1980s), 90, 100, 104. *See also* Resettlers
Turkish, 78, 107
Germans from Russia Heritage Collection, Fargo, 329, 415, 433
Germans of Dutch descent
Genealogical societies, 287
German-Speaking Catholic Community, South Africa, 217
Germantown, New Zealand, 210
Germantown, Pennsylvania, 141, 184
Germantown, Victoria, 206
German-Wendish settlement, 433
Germany, 107, 263, 330, 442, 444, 445, 450
Address books, 269
Archives, 412, 415, 422
Berlin Document Center, 270
Burgher books, 266
Card indexes, 269
Census, 267
Church book bibliography, 411
Church records, 141, 261, 265, 419, 444
City archives, 269, 378
Civil records, 265, 282, 335, 354
Civil registry offices, 378
Court house records, 269
Gazetteers, 8, 63, 64, 69, 71, 72
Genealogical helps, 231, 419
Genealogical societies, 273, 412
Geography, 74
German Central Office for Genealogy, 408
German emigration, 182, 185, 189, 193, 211, 213, 228, 230, 411, 417, 418, 446
German immigration, 351
Germans of Dutch descent, 287
Guild Records, 266
Guilds, 416

Germany (*continued*)
Historical societies, 412
History, 74, 84, 86, 87, 98, 338, 339, 445, 449
Land records, 283
Libraries, 422
Lineage card files, 281
Lineage societies, 288
Map books, 8
Microfilms, 41, 408, 418
Military parish records, 265, 374, 409
Military records, 265, 416
National archives, 270
Nobility, 288
Occupation zones, 90
Periodicals, 426
Phone books, 421
Postal code book, 71, 408
Postal codes, 264
Postal directories, 421
Professions, 416
Records, 265
Religions, 119
Research helps, 410, 411, 412, 414, 416, 422
Researchers, 283
Researching in, 264, 415
Researching specific areas, 277
Reunification, 91
Salzburger emigrés, 287
State archives, 270, 283, 378
Treaty of Versailles, 74
Use of surnames, 443
Village lineage books. *See also* Ortssippenbücher *and* Ortsfamilienbücher
Wars of Unification, 74
Gesamtarchiv der Deutschen Juden (Berlin), 162
Gidal, Nachum T., 157. *See also* Tim Gidal
Gidal, Tim, 157. *See also* Gidal, Nachum T.
Giesinger, Adam, 107, 117, 140, 190, 193, 223, 306, 309, 312, 313, 314, 319, 410
Giessen, Germany, 195, 198
Gilbert, Martin, 69, 145, 146, 149, 152, 157
Gilson, Miriam, 235, 248
Gingerich, Hugh F., 140, 410
Giovannini, Norbert, 154
Giuseppi, Montague S., 223, 277, 410
Glarus canton, Switzerland, 83, 196
Glasgow, Scotland, 48
Glasnost, 100, 104, 328, 450
Glatz, Silesia, 79
Researchers, 284
Glazier, Ira A., 50, 52, 177, 223, 228, 303, 410
Glenzdorf, Johann, 17, 304, 410
Glückstal colonies, Ukraine-Moldova, 84, 102, 328
Gnadenthal, South Africa, 216

Gnesen, Germany, 79, 344. *See* Gniezno, Poland. *See also* Gniezno, Poland
Gniezno, Poland, 79, 344
God, Dieter, 286
Godet, Marcel, 305
Goertz, Adalbert, 132, 307, 340
Goethe Institut, 235
Gold
Fields, 205, 206, 207, 210, 211
Miners, 202, 206
Rushes, 51, 206, 207, 210, 211, 214, 218, 250, 447
Gold, Hugo, 154, 177
"golden patent", 442
Goldner, Franz, 198, 223, 240
Goldstein, Jonathan, 257
Gonçalves Celestino, Ayrton, 196, 198, 201, 233, 243
Gonner, Nicholas, 223, 301, 302, 304, 376, 410
Göppingen, Germany, 163, 175
Gordon, Max, 235
Goren, Arthur A., 228
Gorizia, Italy, 85, 92, 289, 338, 350
Emigration, 208
Görlitz, Germany, 368
Gornberg, B., 228
Gorr, Shmuel, 59, 61
Görwihl, Germany, 175
Görz, 85, 289, 338. *See also* Gorizia, Italy
Gosnells, Western Australia, 206
Gostynin, Poland, 84
Gothic script, 364, 369, 391, 407, 419
Letter chart, 392
Goths, 86
Gotland Island, Sweden, 367
Göttingen, Germany, 372
Gottschald, Max, 61
Gottschee, 85, 96, 109, 192, 350, 425, 443. *See also* Kocevje, Slovania
German emigration, 186, 190, 350
Records, 350
Grab, Walter, 160
Gradisca, Slovenia, 85, 289, 338, 350. *See also* Gradiska
Gradiska, 85, 289. *See also* Gradisca, Slovenia
Graetz, Michael, 158
Gräf, H., 175
Grahamstown, South Africa, 217
Gran Chaco, Paraguay, 194, 200
Grand Duchy of Hesse, 75
Grand Duchy of Warsaw, 99, 102, 338
Civil registration, 341
Grand Forks, North Dakota, 365
Grassl, Peter, 107
Graubünden canton, Switzerland, 83, 188, 211. *See also* Grisons canton, Switzerland
Gravenhage, Netherlands, 363
Graz, Austria, 294, 295
Great Barbarian Migrations, 86

Great Britain, 444, 445, 446. *See also* United Kingdom. *See also* Britain
   Emigration, 418
   History, 85, 443
   Researching in, 372
Great Depression, 449
Great Dividing Range, Australia, 205
Great Lakes, 52
Great Nordic War, 99
Great Poland (early duchy), 79, 81
Grebel, Conrad, 113
Greece, 351, 443
Greenslopes, Queensland, 244
Greenstein, Ran, 237
Greenwood, Val D., 17
Greifswald, Germany, 282, 340
Grevenmacher canton, Luxembourg, 83
Grey County, Ontario, 191
Greytown, New Zealand, 210
GRHS, 313, 320. *See also* Genealogical societies: Germans from Russia Heritage Society
Grimm, J. A., 176
Grimsted, Patricia Kennedy, 311
Grisons canton, Switzerland, 83
Grodno, 80, 320. *See also* Hrodna, Belarus
Groß Tarna, 85. *See also* Tirna Mare, Romania
Grosspolen, 79. *See also* Great Poland
Grothe, Hugo, 107
Grovedale, Victoria, 206
Grubel, Fred, 178
Grueningen, John Paul von, 305
Gruenwald, Myron E., 426, 440
Grüner, Rolf, 216
Grunwald, Max, 154
Gruyter, Louis de, 228
Gryse, Louis de, 408
Guam, 212, 252
Guatemala, 198
   Civil registers, 239
   Records at Family History Library, 238
Guggenheimer, Eva H., 61, 161, 178
Guggenheimer, Heinrich W., 61, 161, 178
Guild records, 263, 266
Guilds, 367
Guise, Jacques de, 49
Gulf of Mexico, 52
Gundacker, Felix, 197, 224, 290, 294, 297, 333, 337, 411
GUS. *See also* Commonwealth of Independent States. *See also* Gemeinschaft unabhängiger Staaten
Gustavus Adolphus, 367, 368
Gut, B., 175
Guth, Hermann, 140
Guzik, Estelle M., 17, 178
Gypsies, 93

— H —

Haardt, 79, 81
Hacker, Werner, 224
Hagen, William W., 157
Hagin, Mathias, 196
Hahn, Joachim, 174
Hahndorf, South Australia, 205, 247, 259
Haigerloch, Germany, 173
Halifax, Nova Scotia, 21, 25, 26, 50, 186, 190, 191, 434
Halila, Aimo, 375
Hall, Charles M., 49, 69, 247, 278, 304, 411
Halle, Germany, 83, 442
Haller, Charles R., 228, 411
Halychyna, 84. *See also* East Galicia
Hamar, Norway, 365
Hamburg, Germany, 49, 75, 76, 82, 86, 90, 146, 152, 186, 191, 198, 199, 210, 214, 247, 259, 285, 368, 411, 423, 442
   Census, 267
   FHL cataloging, 44
   Genealogical societies, 274
   German emigration, 194, 207
   History, 91
   Indexes of transients, 49
   Names and occupations of workers, 49
   Passenger lists, 48, 240, 262, 408
   Passport records, 49
   State archives, 271
Hamilton, Ontario, 20
Hamilton, Victoria, 245
Hanau, Germany, 89
Hand, Dexter Learned, 231
Hande, D'Arcy, 28
Handwriting, 416
Hänni, Fred D., 62, 414
Hannover, 57, 76. *See also* Hanover
   FHL cataloging, 44
Hanover, 75, 76, 89, 215, 265, 372, 423. *See also* Hannover
   FHL cataloging, 44
   German emigration, 207, 210, 211, 214, 447
   History, 75, 78, 356
Hanover Lutheran Church, 217
Hanseatic League, 78, 86, 87, 109, 210, 358, 363, 367, 372, 421, 442
Hansen, Miriam Hall, 313
Hapsburg Empire, 68, 87, 94, 95, 98, 108, 150, 290, 354, 361, 445
   Book collections, 432
   Emigration, 208
   History, 88, 91, 115, 186, 295, 445, 446
Harbin, China, 221, 257, 258, 328
Harmonists, 117, 138
Harmony Society, 138
Harms, Kathy, 157
Harms, Wilmer, 257

Harmshope, South Africa, 216
Harmstorf, Ian, 202, 203, 236, 249, 259
Harris, James F., 154
Hartenstein, Johannes Georg, 154
Harz region, Germany, 367
Harzgebirge, 79
Hatz, Änder, 224, 301
Hauerland, Slovak Republic, 85, 96, 334
Hauländereien, 100
Hausler, Wolfgang, 154
Hautala, Kustaa, 375
Haut-Rhin department, France, 359, 360. *See also* Alsace
Hawaii, 189
Hawkes Bay province, New Zealand, 210
Haymarket, New South Wales. 245
Heebner, Balthasar, 142
Heese, J. A., 260
Hegewaldt, Werner, 411
Hehe tribe (Tanzania), 219
Heidelberg, Germany, 227, 407
Heider Index, 292
Height, Joseph S., 193, 224, 352, 419
Heike, Otto, 107, 411
Heilbronn-Sontheim, Germany, 175
Heilongjiang province, China, 221
Heimatarchiv der Deutschen aus Mittelpolen und Wolhynien, 286
Heimatortskarteien, 286, 329, 417, 420
Heineke, Thekla, 216
Heinemann, Hartmut, 154
Heintze, Albert, 61
Heinzmann, Franz, 8, 263, 269, 304, 411
Heise, Werner, 154
Helfert, Joseph Alexander, Freiherr von, 158
Heller, Fred, 233
Helmbold, F. Wilbur, 5
Helsingfors, Finland, 358. *See also* Helsinki, Finland
Helsinki, Finland, 358. *See also* Helsingfors, Finland
Hemling, Virginia, 435
Hemsbach, Germany, 175
Henning, Eckart, 8, 60, 62, 143, 241, 264, 267, 268, 279, 304, 356, 404, 411, 416
Henry Meyer Collection (Saskatchewan), 23
Hephzibah Faith Missionary Association, 120
Heraldry, 18, 416
Herdecke, Germany, 285
Herder-Institut, 283. *See also* Johann-Gottfried-Herder-Institut
Herman, Jan, 178
Hermannsburg Mission Society, 216
Hermannsburg, Hanover, 216
Hermannsburg, South Africa, 216
Hermannstadt, 81. *See also* Sibiu, Romania

Herrero tribe (Namibia), 218
Herrmann, Hans-Walter, 407
Herrnhut, Germany, 115
   Burials, 140
Herrnhuter, 112, 115, 213, 331
Herscher, Uri D., 228
Hertz, Joseph Herman, 237
Herzegovina, 93, 98, 289, 349, 448
   History, 76, 77
Herzegowina, 289. *See also*
   Herzegovina
Herzl, Theodor, 147
Herzog, Hertha, 186, 230
Hesse, 44, 76, 80, 81, 82, 89, 152, 194,
   195, 198, 214, 265, 286, 411, 423,
   443, 445, 446. *See also* Hessen
   Church records, 409
   FHL cataloging, 44
   German emigration, 102, 185, 210,
      407
   History, 75, 78, 88, 91, 115
   Religions, 119
   State archives, 271
   Village lineage books, 422
   Yizkor books, 168
Hesse-Cassel, 75, 409. *See also* Hesse-
   Kassel
   History, 75
Hesse-Darmstadt, 75, 190
Hesse-Kasse. *See also* Hesse-Cassel
Hesse-Kassel, 89
Hessen, 76. *See also* Hesse
   FHL cataloging, 44
   Genealogical societies, 274
Hesse-Nassau, 76, 152, 423. *See also*
   Hessen-Nassau
   FHL cataloging, 44
   History, 75, 97
   State archives, 271
Hessen-Nassau, 76. *See also* Hesse-
   Nassau
   FHL cataloging, 44
Hessian soldiers, 183, 223, 277, 373,
   440, 445
HETRINA, 223, 277
Heuberger, Rachel, 154
Heusser, J. Christian, 196, 201, 233
Hexel, Ernst, 285
High German (Hochdeutsch), 56
Higham, John, 228
Hill, Roscoe R., 242
Hiller, Georg, 193, 233
Hillman, T. A., 28
Hillsboro, Kansas, 423
Hilton, Sybil, 177
Himka, John-Paul, 342
Himly, Francois J., 361
Hinke, William John, 231, 277, 305,
   419
Hinterpommern, 79
Hirsch, Claus W., 171, 179
Historical dateline, 442

Historical societies
   Adams County Historical Society
      (PA), 128
   Amish Historical Society, 133
   California Mennonite Historical
      Society, 425
   Hanover/Steinbach Historical Society
      (MB), 131, 200
   Hillsboro Historical Society (KS), 423
   Historical Society of Tanzania, 220
   Institut für Geschichte der deutschen
      Juden, 172
   Institut für historische
      Familienforschung Genealogie
      Gesellschaft (Vienna), 290, 291,
      298
   Institut für pfälzische Geschichte und
      Volkskunde, 285
   Jewish Historical Institute (Warsaw,
      Poland), 181
   Jewish Historical Society of the Upper
      Midwest (St. Paul, MN), 437
   Jewish Historical Society of Western
      Canada (Winnipeg, MB), 437
   Johannes Schwalm Historical
      Association, Inc., 440
   Lancaster County Mennonite
      Historical Society, 131, 440
   Manitoba Mennonite Historical
      Society, 132
   Mennonite Historical Library (IN),
      433
   Mennonite Historical Library and
      Archives (KS), 432
   State Historical Society of Wisconsin,
      434
   York County Historical Society,
      Pennsylvania, 434
Hither Pomerania, 82
Hitler, Adolf, 76, 77, 79, 81, 87, 90, 94,
   98, 103, 109, 197, 198, 270, 319,
   350, 449
Hitler-Stalin Pact, 98, 103, 327, 423,
   449
Hlucín, Czech Republic. *See also*
   Hultschin
   History, 84
Hobart, Tasmania, 202, 209, 245, 246
Hobbs, Karen, 297, 332, 333, 352
Hocker, Edward W., 228, 411
Hodl, Klaus, 155, 228
Hoensch, Jörg K., 107
Hoerder, Dirk, 224
Hoffman, Marian, 17
Hoffman, Tom, 320
Hoffman, William F., 61, 180, 405
Hoffmann, Werner, 234
Hoffnungstal, South Australia, 247
Hoffnungstal, Ukraine, 102
Hofmayr, Jan H., 218, 237
Hoge, J., 213, 237, 254, 260
Hohenems, Austria, 152, 173, 174

Hohenzollern, 75, 76, 173
   FHL cataloging, 44
   State archives, 270
HOK, 417. *See also* Heimatortskarteien
Holendry, 77. *See also* Holländerein
Holland. *See also* Netherlands
   History, 356, 361
Holländereien, 77, 99
Hollenweger, Walter J., 135, 140
Holmes, Douglas P., 441
Holmquist, June Drenning, 228
Holstein, 75, 88, 190
   German emigration, 210
   History, 357, 363
Holy Roman Empire, 75, 79, 87, 88, 91,
   92, 104, 106, 107, 298, 418, 442,
   443, 445
Holz, Mrs. Sonia Nippgen, 368
Homestead Act (United States), 13
Homesteading, 183, 224, 352. *See also*
   Morrill Act
   In Canada, 22
   In United States, 13, 185, 447
Homolka, Walter, 158
Honduras, 198
Hong Kong, 221
Honigmann, Peter, 163, 164
Horb-Nordstetten, Germany, 172
Hordern, Richard, 232, 412
Hornad-Hnilec River, Slovak Republic,
   96
Horsch, John, 133, 140
Hörsell, Ann, 368
Horsham, Victoria, 206, 245
Horst, M. J., 259
Horyn River region, 101
Hössler, H., 175
Hostetler, John A., 113, 133, 140
Houghton, South Africa, 255
Hrebec, Czech Republic, 85, 94. *See
   also* Schönhengst
Hrodna, Belarus, 80, 320
   Archives, 313, 327
Hruby, Václav, 333
Hsia, R. Po-chia, 158
Hudson, Winthrop S., 141
Huebert, Helmut T., 200, 225
Huguenot Wars, 89
Huguenots, 88, 223, 373, 410
   French, 57, 105, 107, 338, 359, 444
   History, 112, 115, 143
   In Brandenburg, 115, 359
   In Canada, 143, 233
   In France, 89, 140, 143, 233
   In Franconia, 359
   In Germany, 140, 143, 233, 286, 359
   In Hesse, 359
   In Palatinate, 359
   In Saxony-Anhalt, 115
   In South Africa, 117, 143, 212, 233
   In Switzerland, 89, 115, 140, 298
   In United States, 143, 233
   Records, 130
   Resource centers, 286

Hull, England, 48, 186, 191, 373, 374
Hull, William, 136, 141
Hultschin. *See also* Hlucín, Czech
    Republic
    History, 84
Humboldt, Saskatchewan, 192
Humphrey, John T., 116, 141
Hundsnurscher, Franz, 155
Hungarian Germans, 64, 70, 79, 80, 96,
    108, 297, 336. *See also* Danube
    Swabians
Hungarians, 93, 97
Hungary, 78, 79, 80, 97, 102, 119, 150,
    289, 298, 330, 334, 416, 442, 443,
    445. *See also* Hapsburg Empire. *See
    also* Austro-Hungarian Empire
    1848 Census of Jews, 162
    Church records, 336, 337, 448
    Civil records, 335, 336, 448
    Danube Swabians, 109, 342
    Emigration, 208
    Gazetteers, 64, 68
    German emigration, 183, 186, 447
    History, 64, 75, 77, 84, 85, 87, 88, 91,
        92, 93, 94, 96, 114, 151, 186, 346,
        349, 350, 445, 447
    Land census, 295
    Map of, 451
    Microfilms, 41
    Miscellaneous records, 336
    National Archive, 336
    Records, 419
    Researching in, 335, 351
    Transylvanian Saxons, 95
    Treaty of Trianon, 74
Hunhäuser, Alfred, 363
Hunsrück, 79, 194, 195, 198, 221, 240,
    277
Hurtubise, Pierre, 126
Hury, Carlo, 301
Hus, Jan, 87. *See* John Huss
Huss, John, 87, 92, 112, 138, 331, 443
Hussite movement, 87, 112, 114, 331,
    443
Hussite wars, 94
Hussites, 140
Hutterian Brethren. *See* Hutterites
Hutterites, 122, 140, 143, 192
    History, 113, 114
    In Carinthia, 113
    In Moravia, 294
    In South Tyrol, 113
    In Tyrol, 294

— I —

Iceland, 356
Idaho, 121
Iggers, Wilma Abeles, 155
IGI. *See* International Genealogical
    Index
Iglau, 94

Illegal emigrants
    Germanic Emigrants Register, 280
    Swiss, 280
    Tracing, 280
Illegal emigration, 184
Illinois, 188, 189
Ilmenau, Germany, 288
Ilyana, Natalya, 258
Independent German Baptist Church in
    Brazil, 241
India, 214, 218, 221, 222, 258, 259
Indiana, 188, 189
Indlekofer, Sybille, 175
Indonesia, 221, 222, 258
Industrial Revolution, 73, 86, 90, 96,
    118, 152, 185, 195, 447
Ingermanland, 79, 313. *See also* Ingria,
    Russia
Ingria, Russia, 79, 318
    Lutheran records, 313
Ingushetia, 82, 328
Inn River, Austria, 291
Innsbruck, Asutria, 337
Inquisitions, 113
Institut für Auslandsbeziehungen
    (Stuttgart), 285
Institut für historische
    Familienforschung Genealogie
    Gesellschaft (Vienna), 224
Institute for Historical Family Research
    in Austria, 297
Insurance maps, 11
International Genealogical Index (IGI),
    33, 43, 58
International Reply Coupons, 378, 379,
    410
Internet, 34, 161, 181, 324. *See also*
    Computers. *See also* Electronic
    research
    Swedish information, 370
Inuit (Eskimos), 25
Iowa, 188, 189, 232, 415, 421
    Library collections, 436
Ireland, 356. *See also* Northern Ireland
    German immigration, 373
    History, 78, 85, 361
    Palatines, 376
    Researching in, 361
Iron Range Resource Center
    (Minnesota), 437
Irwin, Charlotte, 118, 141
Isaak, H. P., 260
Israelitisches Religionsgemeindeschaft
    Württemberg, 172
Istria, 92, 289, 349
    History, 76, 77
Istrien, 92, 289. *See also* Istria
Italians, 93
Italy, 78, 95, 107, 239, 289, 298, 337,
    350, 442, 449. *See also* South Tyrol
    History, 84, 87, 92, 94, 98
    Research in, 411
Iwan, Wilhelm, 143

— J —

Jabbour, George, 224
Jackson's Bay Special Settlement, New
    Zealand, 210
Jacobs, Henry E., 231, 420
Jacobs, Jens, 280
Jacobs, Noah Jonathan, 159
Jacquet, Constant H., Jr., 134, 139
Jakobeny, Bukovina, 97
Jakobstad, Finland, 358
Jamaica, 194
James, Edmund J., 228
James, Preston E., 195, 197, 198, 233
Jamestown, Virginia, 184
Janke, Leona, 320
Jannasch, Wilhelm, 143
Jansen, Norbert, 228
Jantzen, Hermann, 352
Japan, 221
Jaques, Heinrich, 158
Java, 258
Jebenhausen, Germany, 163, 175
Jekaterinoslav, Ukraine, 79. *See also*
    Ekaterinoslav, Ukraine
Jelgava, Latvia, 322. *See also* Mitau
Jenner, Margaret, 204, 234, 260
Jens, Walter, 158
Jensen, Larry O., 9, 45, 65, 69, 108,
    261, 264, 278, 304, 333, 353, 360,
    401, 403, 404, 412
Jersch-Wenzel, Stefi, 155
Jeske, Gerhard, 266
Jewish Historical Archives, 432
Jewish records, 41
Jews, 59, 70, 98, 183, 261, 335, 338,
    425, 441, 445, 446, 449, 450
    Anti-Semitism, 147
    Archives, 432, 434
    Ashkenazic, 145, 146, 187
    Bibliography, 153
    Cemetery records, 163
    Communal records, 161
    Computer genealogy, 166
    Demography, 152
    Early settlements, 145
    East European, 188
    Emancipation, 147
    Family histories, 164
    Family Name Laws, 148
    Family names, 61, 417
    From Persia, 152
    Genealogical research, 417
    Genealogical resources, 161–81
    Genealogical societies, 164, 245
    Germanic, 145
    History, 69, 93, 108, 145–60, 442,
        445, 446, 448, 449
    Holocaust research, 169
    In Alsace, 145
    In America, 187
    In Australia, 208, 209, 245
    In Austria, 145, 187, 418

Jews (*continued*)
  In Austro-Hungarian Empire, 445
  In Austro-Silesia, 145
  In Belarus, 61, 181
  In Bohemia, 108, 145, 331
  In Brazil, 194
  In Bukovina, 68, 98, 108, 150, 187
  In Canada, 20, 21
  In China, 257, 258
  In Czech Republic, 187, 331
  In East Galicia, 326
  In Eastern Europe, 67, 183, 185, 308
  In England, 187, 373, 374
  In France, 445
  In Galicia, 68, 98, 108, 150, 187, 339,
    341, 437
  In Germany, 143, 145, 184, 188, 418,
    442, 445
  In Hungary, 97, 108, 150
  In Italy, 178
  In Latin America, 240
  In Latvia, 61, 68, 322
  In Lithuania, 61, 68, 181
  In Luxembourg, 145
  In Minnesota, 437
  In Moldova, 61, 317, 328
  In Moravia, 145
  In Netherlands, 362
  In New Zealand, 211
  In North America, 185
  In Poland, 59, 61, 100, 181, 317, 338,
    420
  In Portugal, 187
  In Posen, 145
  In Prague, 179
  In Prussia, 445
  In Romania, 437
  In Russian Empire, 59, 61, 151, 187,
    193, 316, 445, 451
  In South Africa, 213, 216
  In Spain, 187
  In Switzerland, 145, 445
  In Trieste, Italy, 108
  In Ukraine, 61, 181, 317, 326
  In United States, 21, 188, 230, 417
  In Vienna, Austria, 108
  In Volhynia, 341
  In Western Canada, 437
  Libraries and archives, 170
  Massive expulsions, 146
  Naming practices, 161
  Periodicals, 164
  Pogroms, 447
  Records, 41, 332, 335
  Sephardic, 145, 187, 188
  Southwest Germanic areas, 172
  Surnames, 59, 61
  Yizkor books, 168
  Zionism, 148
Jiaozhou, China, 221, 258
Jiganoff, V. D., 258
Jihlava, Czech Republic, 94
Joachimová, Zoja, 177
Johannesburg, South Africa, 215

Johann-Gottfried-Herder-Institut, 282
Johansson, Carl-Erik, 370, 376
John, Barbara, 155
Johnson, Arta F., 58, 61, 125, 133, 134,
    137, 141, 412
Johnson, Hildegard Binder, 228, 408
Johnson, Keith A., 17, 412
Johnson, Margaret, 313
Jonasson, Eric, 28, 232
Jones, George Fenwick, 59, 61, 141
Jones, Henry Z., Jr., 184, 228, 229, 277,
    361, 376, 407, 412
Joseph, Samuel, 229
Judaism, 317
Judak, Margit, 337
Jude, Renate, 305, 307, 355, 423
Jüdisches Museum der Stadt Frankfurt
    am Main, 171
Jülich, 368
Junkers, 278
Jura canton, Switzerland, 79, 83
Jutland, 363, 368

— K —

Kabardino-Bulkaria, 328
Kaemmerer, M., 44, 69
Kaerger, K., 234
Kaffraria, 214, 215, 219, 220. *See also*
    British Kaffraria
Kagan, Joram, 178
Kaganoff, Benzion C., 161, 178
Kaganoff, Nathan M., 178
Kahn, Bruce, 166, 323
Kaiserslautern, Germany, 240, 285
    Village genealogies, 268
Kaiser-Wilhelms-Land, 212
Kalamazoo, Michigan, 129
Kalgoorlie, Western Australia, 207
Kaliningrad, Russia, 81, 99. *See also*
    Königsberg, East Prussia
Kalisch, 100, 340. *See also* Kalisz,
    Poland
Kalisz, Poland, 100, 340
Kallbrunner, Josef, 58, 110, 296, 342,
    346, 351, 355, 423
Kalmar, Sweden, 367
Kaminkow, Marion J., 17, 412, 414
Kamphoefner, Walter, 278
Kampmann, Wanda, 158
Kaniki, H. H. Y., 220, 237
Kann, Robert A., 108
Kannengieser, Alphonse, 158
Kansas, 140, 144, 188, 189, 190, 200,
    227, 232, 409, 423
Kaplan, Marion A., 158
Kaps, J., 141
Kap-Vlakte, South Africa, 217
Karady, Victor, 157
Karasek, A., 108
Karl der Grosse, 87, 91. *See also*
    Charlemagne

Karl Marx-Stadt, German Democratic
    Republic, 83. Same as Chemnitz,
    Germany
Karlsruhe, Germany, 225, 304
Kärnten, 83, 92, 289, 290. *See also*
    Carinthia
Karp, Abraham J., 229
Karpatalja, 168. *See also* Carpathia
Karpato-Ukraine, 84, 289. *See also*
    Carpatho-Ukraine
Kaschau, 96, 334, 335. *See also* Kosice,
    Slovak Republic
Kashubians, 191
Kashubs, 100
Käsmark, 96. *See also* Kezmarok,
    Slovak republic
Katanning, Western Australia, 207
Katowice, Poland, 344
Kattowitz, 344. *See also* Katowice,
    Poland
Kauder, Viktor, 108
Kaukasus, 328. *See also* Caucasus
    region
Kaunas, Lithuania, 80
Kavel, A. L. C., 247, 259
Kazakhstan, 84, 85, 102, 104, 328, 450
Kazmierczak, Wiktor, 109
Keeble, Jim, 201
Keel, William, 224
Keewatin district, Northwest Territories,
    25
Kei River, 214
Keiskama River, 214
Keller, Hanzheinz, 195, 234
Kemp, Thomas Jay, 18, 25, 238, 412
Kenawa, Western Australia, 207
Kenya, 212, 219, 220. *See also* British
    East Africa
Kerry county, Ireland, 361
Kessel, Martin, 169
Kessler, Gerhard, 141
Kessler, W., 108
Kestenberg-Gladstein, Ruth, 155
Ketsch, Germany, 176
Kezmarok, Slovak Republic, 96
KGB (Russian secret police), 320
Kharkiv, Ukraine, 312. *See also*
    Kharkov
Kharkov. *See* Kharkiv, Ukraine
Khazar kingdom, 152
Kherson, Ukraine, 79, 312, 314
Khmel'nyts'kyi, Ukraine, 80
Kiautschou, 221. *See* Jiaozhou, China
Kiefner, Theo, 286
Kiel, Germany, 357
Kielce, Poland, 344
Kiev, Ukraine, 312
    Archives, 326
    Records, 316, 327
Kieval, Hillel J., 155
Kiew. *See* Kiev, Ukraine
Killion, Martyn C. H., 245, 249
Kilton, T., 422
Kimball, Charlotte, 228

Kimberley, South Africa, 215, 217
King William's Town, South Africa, 215, 255
King, Susan, 166
King's German Legion (English), 214, 259, 372, 373
Kingston, Jamaica, 194
Kingston, Ontario, 190
Kinney, Miles, 27, 28, 224
Kinzig River, 81
Kirchenbuchverkartungen, 269
Kirchspielsippenbücher, 268
Kirkeby, Lucille L., 18
Kirkham, E. Kay, 18
Kirlibaba, Bukovina, 97
Kisch, Guido, 155
Kitchener, Ontario, 21, 22, 190
Klagenfurt, Austria, 294
Klaipeda, Lithuania, 322
Klaube, Manfred, 108
Klein, Borys, 320, 328
Kleinpolen, 80. See also Little Poland
Klemzig, South Australia, 205, 247
Klippenstein, Lawrence, 133, 141
Kneifel, Eduard, 141
Knittle, Walter Allen, 229, 277, 412
Kober, Bertram, 155
Koblenz, Germany, 82, 240
Kocevje, Slovenia, 85, 96, 350, 425
Koebner, Thomas, 224
Koger, Marvin Vastine, 230, 417
Kohl, Waltraut, 175
Kohn, Edith, 157
Kojonen, Eero, 375
Köln, Germany, 372
Kolo, Poland, 82, 84, 340
Kongsberg, Norway, 363
Königsberg, East Prussia, 79, 81, 99. See also Kaliningrad, Russia
Königsfeld, Bosnia, 349
Konin, Poland, 82, 84, 340, 344
Konopka, Marek, 413
Koop, Gerhard S., 194, 234
Kopittke, Eric, 51, 247
Kopittke, Rosemary, 51, 247
Korea, 45
Korean War, 45
Körner, Karl Wilhelm, 234
Kosice, Slovak Republic, 96, 334, 335
Kosiek, Rolf, 108
Köslin, Germany, 344. See Koszalin, Poland
Kosovo (Serbia), 350, 351, 476
Koss, David H., 112, 122, 125, 141
Kossmann, Oskar, 99, 100, 108
Koszalin, Poland, 344
Kotzian, Ruth Maria, 229
Kowallis, A. Les, 279
Kowallis, Gay P., 425
Kowallis, Otto K., 69, 278
Kowallis, Vera N., 69, 278
Kraichgau, Germany, 227, 407
Krain, 85, 92, 289, 350. See also Carniola, Slovenia

Krainburg, 350. See also Kranj, Slovenia
Krajnska, Slovenia, 85. See also Carniola, Slovenia
Krakow, 109. See Cracow, Poland
Krallert, Wilfried, 69
Kranj, Slovenia, 350
Krasna, Russia, 320
Krasnodar, Russia, 102
Krauss, Walter, 209, 236
Kraybill, Paul N., 141
Krebs, Edmund, 118, 129, 142
Kredel, Otto, 44, 64, 69
Krefeld, Germany, 114, 184
Kreider, Rachel W., 140, 410
Kremnica, Slovak Republic, 85, 96
Kremnitz, 85, 96. See also Kremnica, Slovak Republic
Kreplin, Klaus-Dieter, 339, 413
Kreplin, Pomerania
    Genealogical archives, 413
Krewson, Margrit Beran, 142, 229, 264, 413
Kriebel, Reuben, 142
Krippner, Mrs. C., 251
Kristallnacht, 148, 170
Kristensen, Peter K., 404, 407
Kristinestad, Finland, 358
Kroatien, 108, 289. See also Croatia
Kroeker, Irene Enns, 200, 234
Krohn, Helga, 154, 155
Kronstadt, 81, 423. See also Brasov, Romania
Kroonstad, South Africa, 217
Krudewig, Anton, 413
Krushel, Howard, 313, 327
Kuban River, 80
Kuban, Caucasus, 80, 312
Kubijovic, Wolodymyr, 69
Kucher, W., 175
Kuhlberg, Ivan
    Lists of settlers, 319, 324
Kuhling, Karl, 155
Kuhn, Heinrich, 70
Kuhn, Walter, 69
Kühner, J., 175
Kuhn-Rehfus, Maren, 155
Kuhns, Oscar, 229
Kuhr, Jo Ann, 320, 425
Kujawien, 80. See also Kuyavia, Poland
Kulischer, Eugene Michel, 224
Kulm, 80. See also Chelmno, Poland
Kulmerland, Poland, 80
Kulturkampf, 97, 116, 349
Kung, Hugo, 234
Künzel, Professor, 163
Kur-, 80
Kurhessen, Germany, 80
Kurland, 80, 98. See also Courland
Kurpfalz, Germany, 80
Kurrent (Gothic Script), 290
Kurzweil, Arthur, 178, 413
Kutschurgan, Ukraine, 102
Kuyavia, Poland, 80

Kuybyshev, 102. See also Samara, Russia
Kvikne, Norway, 363
Kyrgyzstan, 328
Kyrkhult, Sweden, 372
Kyyiv. See Kiev, Ukraine

—L—

L'viv, Ukraine, 79, 150. See also L'vov, Russia. See also Lemburg, Austria
    Archives, 313, 326, 342
    Records, 317, 327
    Roman Catholic archdiocese, 341
L'vov, Russia, 79. See also L'viv, Ukraine. See also Lemburg, Austria
La Frontera province, Chile, 199, 200
La Pampa, Argentina, 193
La Plata, Argentina
    Arrival lists, 52
Labadists, 117
Labrador, Canada, 26
Lackey, Richard S., 5
Lagus, Vilhelm, 375
Lahn River, Germany, 407
Laibach, 85, 96, 350. See also Ljubljana, Slovenia
Lainhart, Ann S., 18
Lake Erie, 190
Lake Llanquique (Chile), 199
Lake Nyasa (Tanzania), 220
Lake Peipus, 79
Lake Tanganyika, 220
Lamers, Friedrich G., 349, 352
Lamers, Joseph, 349
Lampe, Karl H., 404
Lancour, A. H., 52
Land cadasters, 326, 342
Land grants
    Canada, 24
Land records, 262
    United States, 12
Land, Gary, 142
Lande, Peter, 162, 171, 178
Landesarchiv Baden-Württemberg, 163
Landesverbund der Israelitischen Kultusgemeinde in Bayern, 171
Ländl, Austria, 80, 115
Landshut, Germany, 217
Lang, Betty, 22
Lange Hermann, 392
Lange, Bernd-Lutz, 155
Lange, Henry, 234
Lange, Hermann, 67
Lange, Peter, 288
Languages, 405
    Arabic, 256
    English, 241
    French, 256
    German, 241, 384
    Latin, 241, 384
    Portuguese, 241
    Spanish, 241
    Table of, 377, 401

Lantern: Journal of Knowledge and Culture, 215
Laos, 45
Latgalia, 80
Latin America, 103, 238, 241, 242, 425, 446, 450
  Atlases, 241
  Census records, 240
  Church and cemetery records, 238
  Civil registers, 239
  Family History Library holdings, 238
  Gazetteers, 241
  German immigration, 192–201, 221, 240
  German settlements, 192
  Land records, 240
  Language of records, 241
  Maps, 241
  Military records, 241
  Passenger lists, 52
  Probate and notarial records, 240
  Published records, 241
  Repositories, 241
  Useful addresses, 243
  Writing to, 242
"Latin farmers", 183
Latin language, 336
  Records, 359
Lattermann, Alfred, 342
Latvia, 79, 80, 81, 84, 190, 318, 341, 423
  Archive of Vital Records, 322
  Church records, 282, 355, 423
  German colonization, 98
  German emigration, 213
  Lutheran parishes, 313
  Researching in, 322
  State Historical Archive, 322
  Yizkor books, 168
Lauban County, Silesia
  Researchers, 284
Lauenburg, Germany, 357
Laupheim, Germany, 175
Laurentzsch, U., 174
Lausitz, Germany, 80. *See also* Lusatia
Law, Hugh T., 361
LDS, 2, 9, 47, 408, 432. *See also* Church of Jesus Christ of Latter-day Saints
LDS Library. *See* Family History Library
Le Havre, France, 186, 360
  Passenger lists, 48, 49, 360
League of Nations, 257
Lecycy, Poland, 344
Lehmann, Hartmut, 158
Lehmann, Heinz, 21, 28, 190, 191, 192, 232, 413
Leipzig, Germany, 83, 321, 322, 340, 350, 408
  Estonian records, 321
  German emigration, 213
Leitha River, 93

Leitmeritz, 333. *See also* Litomerice, Czech Republic
Leksand, Sweden, 371
Lemberg, Austria, 79, 108, 150, 317, 341. *See also* L'viv, Ukraine. *See also* L'vov, Russia
Lemieux, Victoria, 25
Leningrad. *See* Saint Petersburg, Russia
Lenius, Brian J., 24, 64, 70, 326, 340, 341
Lentschütz, Germany, 344. *See* Lecycy, Poland
Leo Baeck Institute. *See under* Genealogical societies
Leonard, David, 25
Lesotho, South Africa, 218
Less, Virginia, 235, 257
Lesser Antilles, 226
Lesser, Jeff, 234
Lesson, Daniel N., 178
Leszno, Poland, 344
Lettgallen. *See also* Latgalia
Lettland, 322. *See also* Latvia
Letzeburgesch dialect, 106
Leuschke, Arthur, 216
Leutschau, 96, 334, 335. *See also* Levoca, Slovak Republic
Levi, Kate Everest, 229, 413
Levinson, Nathan Peter, 154
Levoca, Slovak Republic, 96, 334, 335
Libau, 49, 322. *See also* Leipäja, Latvia
Libraries, 7
Library catalogs
  On line, 37
Library of Congress, 23
  Address, 433
  Bibliography of German sources, 229, 413
  Genealogies, 412, 414
  Local Histories, 17
  Polish consular records, 257
Lich, Glen E., 414
Liebental, Ukraine, 102
Liechtenstein, 83, 228
  Church records, 302
  Civil records, 302
  History, 106
  Map of, 451
  National archives, 302
  Postal codes, 73, 421
  Researching in, 264, 302
Liège, Belgium, 356
Liepäja, Latvia, 49, 322
Limburg, Germany, 217, 368
Limerick county, Ireland, 361
Lincoln, Nebraska, 257
Lind, Marilyn, 70, 75, 278, 414
Linder, Erich Dieter, 70, 304, 414
Lindi, Tanzania, 220
Lindner, Walter, 177
Lineage card files, 281
Lineage societies, 288. *See also* Genealogical societies
Linköping, Sweden, 369

Linscheid, Glen, 425
Linz, Austria, 294
Lipno, Poland, 84
Lippe, 54, 75, 76, 148, 411, 423
  FHL cataloging, 44
  Genealogical societies, 275
  History, 75, 447
  State archives, 272
  Surnames, 447
Lippe-Detmold
  Emigration, 278
Liptak, Eva, 336, 337
Li-Ra-Ma Collection (Canada), 23
Lissa. *See also* Leszno, Poland
Litak, Stanislaw, 414
Litauen, 99, 322. *See also* Lithuania
Lithuania, 81, 84, 89, 99, 190, 311, 341, 423, 449
  Atlases, 68
  Church records, 313, 322, 340, 355, 423
  German colonization, 98
  History, 65, 76, 90, 99, 114, 152, 335, 338, 446
  Memel River region, 84
  National archives (LVIA), 322
  Place names, 65
  Researching in, 322
  Yizkor books, 168
Litomerice, Czech Republic, 333. *See also* Leitmeritz
Little Poland, 80
Liverpool, England, 48, 186, 191, 247, 373
Livland, 80, 98. *See also* Livonia
Livonia, 80, 98, 99, 358
  Lutheran consistory, 313
Ljubljana, Slovenia, 85, 96, 350
Llanquique province, Chile, 199, 200
Lobethal, South Australia, 205, 247
Local histories, 11, 263
  In Library of Congress, 17
Locality index, 279
Lodewyckx, Augustin, 236
Lodge records, United States, 10
Lodomeria, 80, 92
Lodomerien, 80. *See* Lodomeria
Lodz, Poland, 80, 84, 89, 100, 152
  History, 420
Loeb, Rene, 300
Loewen, Abram J., 260
Lohrbächer, A., 176
Lombard, R. T. J., 51, 252, 260
Lombardy, 75, 337
Lome, Togo, 256
Lomza, Poland, 80
London Missionary Society, 217
London, England, 167, 372, 373
  Great Fire of 1666, 372
Lorenz, Dagmar C. G., 158
Lorenz, Ina Susanne, 155
Lorraine, 119, 442. *See also* France
  Census, 268
  Genealogical societies, 361

Lorraine (*continued*)
  German emigration, 96
  History, 75, 87, 88, 146, 359
  Map of, 451
  Regional archive, 360
Lorre, W. M., 28
Louis the German, 91
Louisiana, 189, 190
  German immigration, 187
Low German (Plattdeutsch), 56, 213
Low German surnames, 60
Lowenstein, Steven M., 155
Lower Austria, 83, 290
  Lutheran records, 293
  Records, 291
Lower Canada. *See also under* Canada
Lower Danube, 444
Lower Hungary, 336
Lower Hutt, New Zealand, 250
Lower Saxony, 79, 80, 82
  History, 91
  Military parish records, 421
  State archives, 271
  Village lineage books, 422
  War records, 422
Lower Silesia, 79
  German emigration, 143
Lubaczów, Poland, 326
  Roman Catholic archdiocese, 341
Lübeck, Germany, 75, 76, 358, 367
  FHL cataloging, 44
Lubetzky, R., 237
Lublin, Poland, 338, 344
Lucerne canton, Switzerland, 83, 146
Lück, K., 108
Ludwig the German, 86. *See also* Louis
  the German
Ludwigsburg, Germany, 175
Luebking, Sandra Hargreaves, 18, 52
Luft, Edward David, 70, 149, 162, 166,
  171, 178, 179
Luneburg Heath, 80
Lüneburg, Germany, 80, 216
Lüneburg, South Africa, 216
Lüneburger Heide, 80. *See* Luneburg
  Heath
Lunenburg, Nova Scotia, 190
Lunow, Germany, 210
Lusatia, 80, 86, 216. *See also* Lausitz,
  Germany
  German emigration, 205
Lütge, Wilhelm, 234
Luther, Martin, 57, 87, 92, 112, 147,
  443
Lutheran Church. *See* Lutherans
Lutheran Church of Australia, 246
Lutheran Church-Missouri Synod, 122,
  127, 142
  Archives, 126
Lutheran Consistory
  Moscow, Russia, 313
  Others in Russia, 313
  Saint Petersburg, Russia, 312
  Saratov, Russia, 313

Lutheran Theological Seminary,
  Gettysburg, PA, 128
Lutherans, 87, 99, 102, 120, 121, 122,
  261, 443. *See also* Old Lutherans
  Archives in Canada, 128
  Archives in United States, 432
  Buffalo Synod, 127
  Church records, 282, 312
  History, 98, 141, 312
  In Alsace-Lorraine, 359
  In Argentina, 193, 238
  In Australia, 202, 207, 208, 246, 248,
    259
  In Austria, 89, 293, 418
  In Belarus, 327
  In Black Sea region, 314, 408
  In Brazil, 194, 197, 238
  In Bukovina, 140
  In Canada, 20, 21, 125, 190, 191,
    232, 259, 412
  In Caucasus region, 314
  in Central Poland, 100
  In Chile, 238
  In China, 257
  In Denmark, 357
  In East Prussia, 89, 313
  In Estonia, 139, 321
  In Finland, 313
  In France, 360
  In Franconia, 89
  In Galicia, 192, 341
  In Germany, 116, 419
  In Kansas, 423
  In Latin America, 239
  In Latvia, 139, 322
  In Lithuania, 89
  In Lower Silesia, 259
  In Manchuria, 328
  In Michigan, 446
  In Missouri, 446
  In Netherlands, 362
  In New York, 446
  In New Zealand, 210, 251
  In North America, 140
  In Norway, 363, 364
  In Poland, 141
  In Pomerania, 259
  In Russia, 101
  In Russian Empire, 139, 312, 408
  In Saint Petersburg region, 313
  In Slovak Republic, 334
  In South Africa, 213, 214, 215, 252
  In South Australia, 247, 446
  In Soviet Union, 449
  In Swabia, 89
  In Sweden, 367, 369
  In Tanzania, 220
  In Texas, 446
  In Transylvania, 95
  In Ukraine, 224, 352
  In United States, 89, 116, 257, 259
  In Volga River region, 313
  In Volhynia, 192, 328, 341, 408

Lutherans (*continued*)
  In Wisconsin, 446
  In Württemberg, 314
  Merger with Reformed Church, 105,
    202, 261, 312, 446
  Missouri Synod, 127, 194
  Records, 10, 41, 43, 126, 144, 261,
    265
  Regional ELCA archives, 127
  Wisconsin Synod, 127
  Writing to local churches, 265
Lutz, Thomas, 154
Luukko, Armas, 375
Luxembourg, 75, 79, 442, 448
  Cantons, 83
  Census records, 300
  Church records, 300
  Civil records, 300
  Emigration, 185, 223, 277, 410, 446
  Gazetteers, 71
  German emigration, 50, 188, 446
  History, 76, 84, 87, 92, 93, 95, 105–6,
    185
  Language, 106
  Map of, 451
  Microfilms, 41
  Military parish records, 266
  National Library, 301
  Religions, 119
  Researching in, 300
  State archives, 300
Luxembourg province, Belgium, 356
  Archives, 357
Luxembourg-Campagne canton,
  Luxembourg, 83
Luxembourgers
  In United States, 302
Luxembourg-Ville canton,
  Luxembourg, 83
Luzern canton, Switzerland, 83, 188.
  See also Lucerne canton,
  Switzerland
LVIA, 322. *See* Lithuania: National
  archives
Lwów, Poland, 79, 150, 341
Lydenburg/Witbank, South Africa, 217
Lyncker, Alexander von, 421
Lyng, J., 202, 204, 205, 236, 248
Lynnwood Manor, South Africa, 255

— M —

Maas, Elaine, 229
Macartney, C. A., 93, 108
Macedonia, 443, 476
Mack, Alexander, 116
Mackay, Australia, 205
Mackenzie district, Northwest
  Territories, 25
Madison, Wisconsin, 188, 365
MADU, 326. *See* Main Archival
  Directorate of Ukraine
Mafra, Brazil, 196, 233

Magdeburg, Germany, 78, 83, 89, 115, 145, 442
  German emigration, 207
Magocsi, Paul Robert, 70, 149, 150, 152, 314
Magyarization, 151
Magyars, 88, 93, 96
Mähren, 289. *See also* Moravia. *See also* Moravia
Mährisch-Ostrau, 94. *See also* Ostrava, Czech Republic
Mährisch-Trübau, 94. *See also* Moravská Trebová, Czech Republic
Mai, Brent Allen, 414
Maier, Charles S., 158
Mailing lists, 34
Main Archival Directorate of Ukraine (MADU), 326
Main River, Germany, 80, 81, 146
Mainz, Germany, 44, 75, 76, 81, 97, 145, 217, 442
Maji Maji rebellion, Tanzania, 219
Makousková, Sylvia, 177
Malay Archipelago, 258
Malay Peninsula, 258
Malaysia, 259
Malbork, Poland, 99, 344. *See also* Marienburg
Mallee district, Victoria, 206
Mallersdorf, Germany, 217
Malmedy, Belgium, 71, 84, 90, 356
Malta, 351
Manchuria, 221, 257. *See also* Harbin and Charbin, China
Mändle, Max I., 162, 179
Manifesto of 1763 (Russian), 101
Manitoba, Canada, 192, 200
  Civil records, 26
  Homesteading in, 22
  Library collections, 436
  Provincial archives, 24, 25, 28
Mannheim, Germany, 97, 287
Mansfeld, Herbert A., 291, 304
Maps, 434, 451. *See also under individual countries*
  Europe, 451
  U.S. Army maps of Eastern Europe, 65
Maramures
  Yizkor books, 168
Marburg, Germany, 282, 288
Marburg, Queensland, 246
Marburg, Slovenia, 85, 96, 350. *See also* Maribor, Slovenia. *See also* Maribor, Slovenia
Marcus, Jacob Rader, 229
Maria Theresia (Empress), 332
Mariana Islands, 212, 252
Mariannhill, South Africa, 217
Mariastern Monastery (Bosnia), 349
Maribor, Slovenia, 85, 96, 350. *See also* Marburg, Slovenia
Marienburg, 99, 344. *See also* Malbork, Poland

Marinbach, Bernard, 229
Mariupol, Ukraine, 102
Marschalck, Peter, 224
Marseilles, France, 146
Marshall Islands, 212, 252
Marten, New Zealand, 210
Marx, Karl, 90, 195
Maryborough, Australia, 205
Maryland, 188, 189, 343
  German immigration, 184
Marzolf, Arnold H., 140
Masowien, 80. *See also* Mazovia, Poland
Massachusetts, 188, 343
Massier, Erwin, 352
Mast, Le Mar, 426
Mast, Lois Zook, 426
Masurien, 80. *See also* Mazuria, Poland
Mauelshausen, Carl, 142
Maurer, Trude, 158
Max Kade Institute for German-American Studies, 425, 433
Mayer, Egon, 159
Mayer, Sigmund, 155
Mazovia, Poland, 80
Mazuria, Poland, 80
McBride, Johanna, 202, 208, 209, 221, 236, 259, 296
McCagg, William O., Jr., 108, 149, 150, 151, 158
McEvedy, Colin, 70
Mecklenburg, 75, 81, 190, 263, 358, 362, 372, 411, 423
  Burgher books, 267
  FHL cataloging, 44
  Genealogical societies, 274
  German emigration, 210, 214, 352, 447
  History, 88, 114, 183, 362
  Records, 278
  State archives, 271
  Surnames, 60
Mecklenburg, Frank, 170, 171, 179
Mecklenburgica - Archival Research Service, 278
Mecklenburg-Schwerin, 76, 148, 198
  Census, 267
  German emigration, 194
Mecklenburg-Strelitz, 76, 148
Mecklenburg-Vorpommern, 82, 91, 204
Medessen, Germany, 283
Mediasch district, Transylvania, 423
Medicine Hat, 192
Meding, Peter, 223
Meed, Benjamin, 179
Mehr, Kahlile B., 313, 314, 315, 317, 348
Meier, Christian, 160
Meier, Clothilde, 62, 414
Meier, Emil, 62, 414
Meitzler, Leland K., 425
Melbourne, Victoria, 51, 203, 206, 207, 208, 209, 245, 247, 248
Melchior, Wilfried, 342

Meltzer, Milton, 229
Melville, Western Australia, 206
Memel River region, 65, 86, 90, 321, 322, 449
Memelland, 84, 108. *See* Memel River region
Menes Verlag (Switzerland), 173
Mennicken-Cooley, Mary, 206, 207, 236, 259
Mennists. *See* Mennonites
Menno Simons Historical Library and and Archives (VA), 131
Mennonists. *See* Mennonites
Mennonite Archives of Ontario (ON), 131
Mennonite Brethren, 432
  Archives, 132
Mennonite Family History (PA), 132
Mennonite Genealogy, Inc. (MB), 132
Mennonite Heritage Centre (MB), 131, 429, 433
Mennonite Historical Library (IN), 131
Mennonite Historical Library (OH), 131
Mennonite Historical Library and Archives of Eastern Pennsylvania, 131
Mennonite Library and Archives (KS), 131
Mennonite Templers, 117
Mennonites, 59, 102, 120, 121, 122, 138, 140, 141, 143, 183, 184, 222, 223, 225, 230, 234, 261, 263, 351, 354, 425, 426, 433. *See also* Templer Mennonites
  Archives, 432
  Dutch, 88, 99, 203, 443
  Flemish, 88, 115, 443
  Frisian, 88, 443
  German, 445
  History, 98, 113, 114, 139
  In Alberta, 194
  In Argentina, 193
  In Australia, 133, 203
  In Austria, 295
  In Belarus, 327
  In Belize, 194, 199, 200
  In Bolivia, 194, 200, 201
  In Brazil, 133, 197
  In California, 132
  In Canada, 21, 125, 133, 190, 191, 199, 200, 449
  In China, 197, 257
  In Costa Rica, 200
  In Danzig, 443
  In East Prussia, 143
  In France, 133, 359
  In Galicia, 341, 425, 436
  In Germany, 133, 140, 267
  In Holstein, 114
  In Illinois, 132
  In Kansas, 132, 200, 423
  In Latin America, 132, 449
  In Manchuria, 328
  In Manitoba, 132, 143, 200

Mennonites (*continued*)
In Mexico, 194, 199, 200, 201, 238, 241, 449
In Nebraska, 132, 143
In Netherlands, 115, 133, 199, 203, 362
In Oklahoma, 200
In Ostfriesland, 114
In Palestine, 203
In Paraguay, 133, 200, 238, 449
In Pennsylvania, 132, 140
In Poland, 338
In Prussia, 144, 199, 203
In Russia, 199
In Russian Empire, 101, 132, 144, 200, 203, 449
In Saskatchewan, 200
In South Dakota, 436
In Soviet Union, 197
In Spanish Netherlands, 144, 287
In Switzerland, 105, 115, 133, 298
In Ukraine, 116, 192, 318
In United Kingdom, 133
In United States, 133, 200, 201
In Uruguay, 133
In Volhynia, 341
In West Prussia, 114, 116, 132, 143, 362
In Western Canada, 132
Krefield, 116
Old Order, 194
Records, 131, 144
Split with Mennonites, 117
Split with Templers, 117
Mequon, Wisconsin, 126
Meran, 95, 337. *See also* Merano, Italy
Merano, Italy, 95, 337
Mercenaries, 185
Merriman, Brenda Dougall, 19, 28, 414
Mersch canton, Luxembourg, 83
Merseburg, Germany, 145, 270
Meshkov, Dmitry Y., 352
Meter, Ken, 229, 333, 414
Methodists, 120, 122, 124, 134, 137, 143, 261
Archives, 129
In Canada, 20, 21, 124, 190, 191
In Germany, 118, 122
In Switzerland, 118, 122
In United States, 118
Records, 137
Metz, France, 145, 360
Metzler, Len, 374
Mexico, 50, 52, 199, 200, 234, 241
Census records, 240
Civil registers, 239
German emigration, 194
German immigration, 240
German settlements, 200
México City, 242
National archives, 242
National library, 242
Records at Family History Library, 238

Mexico (*continued*)
Research helps, 238
Meyer, Mary Keysor, 9, 18, 142, 223, 409, 414
Meyer, Michael A., 158, 179
Meyer, Richard, 108
Meyerink, Kory, 18
Meyers Kleines Konversations-Lexikon, 118
Michalek, George C., 126, 139
Michels, John M., 64, 70, 108
Michigan, 188, 189, 333
German-Bohemians, 229, 414
Micronesia, 212, 252
Middle Ages, 87, 95, 105, 360
Migration to Eastern Europe, 77
Middle East, 152
Middle Kingdom, 86
Mies county, Czech Republic, 211
Military Death Index, 45
Military records, 263, 279
United States, 14
Military service, 183
Miller, Betty, 133, 142
Miller, J. Virgil, 133, 142
Miller, Michael M., 320, 329, 352, 415
Miller, Olga Katzin, 51, 229, 415
Miller, Russell E., 118, 142
Milwaukee, Wisconsin, 188
Minden, Germany, 411
Minert, Roger P., 290
MINERVA, 304
Minneapolis, Minnesota, 365
Public Library, 437
Minnesota, 188, 189, 230, 232, 333, 343, 416, 421
German-Bohemians, 229, 230, 414, 417
Library collections, 435, 437, 438
Minnesota Historical Society Research Center, 437
Minor, Ulrike, 155
Minsk, Belarus
Archives, 313, 327
Minson, Marian, 209, 210
Misiones, Argentina, 193
Missionary Church Association, 120
Mississippi, 188, 189
Mississippi River, 49
Missouri, 189
Mitau, 322. *See also* Jelgava, Latvia
MITEK Information Services, 324
Mittelmark, Germany, 80
Mittelpolen, 99. *See also* Congress Poland
Moeschler, Felix, 142
Mogilev, Belarus, 314
Catholic consistory, 314
Mogilew, Belarus. *See* Mogilev, Belarus
Mohiliou. *See* Mogilev, Belarus
Mohn, J., 174
Mohr, Claudia, 62, 414
Mohr, Stephan, 62, 414
Mohrer, Fruma, 171, 179

Mokotoff, Gary, 68, 70, 164, 166, 169, 179
Moldau, 80, 328. *See also* Moldova *and* Moldavia
Moldavia, 80, 92. *See also* Moldau *and* Moldova
Records, 347
Moldova, 80, 82, 84, 312, 320. *See also* Moldau *and* Moldavia
History, 92, 338
Researching in, 328
Möller, Hilde, 284
Möller, L. A., 218
Molochansk, Ukraine, 102
Molotschna, Ukraine, 102, 433. *See also* Molochna, Ukraine
Monaco, 351
Mönchengladbach, Germany, 286
Mongols, 95, 442
Montana, 189
Montbéliard, France, 115, 359
Montenegro, 77, 85, 349, 350, 351
Montevideo, Uruguay, 239, 242
Arrival lists, 52
Montreal, Quebec, 186
Moorhead, Minnesota, 365
Moors, 107
Moos, Mario von, 304, 415
Moravia, 71, 75, 78, 80, 85, 93, 289, 423
Archives, 162
Cemeteries, 177
Emigration, 208, 297, 420
Gazetteers, 72
German emigration, 186, 199, 210, 211
History, 76, 77, 84, 87, 90, 92, 94, 107, 112, 114, 152, 186, 329, 331
Moravian Brethren, 87, 112, 115, 120, 121, 140, 142, 143, 144, 194, 206, 213, 215, 220, 221, 312, 331, 419, 444
History, 138
In Argentina, 193
In Australia, 207
In Austria, 295
In Canada, 191, 314
In North Carolina, 116
In Pennsylvania, 116
In Russia, 314
In South Africa, 216
In Volga River region, 313, 314
Records, 137
Moravian Church, 112
In England, 373
Moravians, 261, 444
In Canada, 190, 191
Moravská Trebová, Czech Republic, 94
Mordy, Isobel, 373
Moresnet, Belgium, 356
Moreton Bay district, New South Wales, 204, 245
Moreton Bay, Queensland, 51
Morija, South Africa, 218

Moritz, Eduard, 237
Mormons. *See* Church of Jesus Christ of
    Latter-day Saints
Morocco, 212, 256
Morogoro, Tanzania, 220
Morrill Act of 1862 (Homestead Act),
    13, 185, 447
Morris, Pauline J., 209
Mortuary records, 10
Möschle, S., 175
Moscow, Russia, 102, 318
    "German Suburb", 101
    City archive, 313
    Lutheran Consistory, 313
Moselle department, France, 359, 360
Moselle River, 79, 95, 106, 146
Moshi, Tanzania, 220
Mosquito Coast. *See* Nicaragua *and*
    Honduras
Mosse, Werner E., 158
Movius, John D., 133, 142, 265, 269,
    309, 352, 415
Mozambique, 218
Mugdan, Joachim, 161
Mukachevo, Ukraine, 327. *See also*
    Munkatsch
Mulhall, Michael George, 234
Müller, Friedrich, 70, 71
Müller, Fritz Ferdinand, 219, 237
Muller, Jean-Claude, 301, 304
Müller, Martha, 352, 358
Müller, Sepp, 108
Müller-Langenthal, Friedrich, 353
Mumm, Hans-Martin, 154
Münchow, Katja, 269, 422
Muneles, Otto, 179
Munich Agreement of 1938, 94
Munk, Mary, 28
Munkatsch, 327. *See also* Mukachevo,
    Ukraine
Münster, Germany, 113
Münsterites, 113
Munz, G., 175
Murray River, Australia, 204
Musat, Ing. George, 347
Muscovy, 146
Museum and Documents Center of the
    Jews of Latvia, 322
Muslims, 295
Müssener, Helmut, 376
Mussolini, Benito, 350
Mutzelburg, Owen B., 249, 259
Myanmar, 221, 259

— N —

Nagler, Jörg, 224, 225
Nahe River, Germany, 79
Nama tribe (Namibia), 218
Names, 54–62
    Changes in English-speaking
        countries, 60
    Given, 59
    Meaning, 59

Names (*continued*)
    Surnames. *See under* Surnames
Namibia, 212, 218, 252, 255, 448
    Passenger lists, 51
Nancy, France, 360
Nanjing, China, 257
Nansen International Office for
    Refugees, 257
Napoleon, 89, 99, 102, 104, 338, 356,
    373, 445
Napoleonic Wars, 74, 92
Narew River region, Poland, 80, 101,
    327
Narewgebiet, Poland, 80. *See* Narew
    River region
Nassau, 75. *See also* Hesse-Nassau
    History, 75
Natal, South Africa, 214, 215, 216, 217,
    226
National archives, 50. Check under each
    country
National Archives and Records
    Administration, 433
National Archives of Canada, 23, 50,
    326
National libraries. Check under each
    country
National Library of Australia, 248
National Library of Canada, 23
Nationalism, 183
Naturalization records, 14
Naugard County, Pomerania, 282
Nead, Daniel Wunderlich, 232, 421
Nebraska, 188, 189, 190
Neckar River, Germany, 80
Neill, John, 279
Neisse River, 210
Nelson, New Zealand, 210, 211
Netherlands, 105, 113, 354, 368, 442,
    443, 444, 446
    Burgher books, 267
    Census records, 362
    Church records, 362
    Civil records, 362
    Emigration, 287
    Genealogical societies, 362, 363
    German emigration, 144, 184
    Guild records, 362
    History, 78, 85, 87, 88, 92, 105, 114,
        258, 356, 361, 367
    Map of, 451
    Military records, 362
    Researching in, 361
    State Archive, 362
Netze River region, 80, 81, 89, 100. *See*
    also Notec River region, Poland
Netze River region, Poland, 284, 339
Netzeland, 230, 416
Neubrandenburg, Germany, 83
Neuchâtel canton, Switzerland, 83, 146
Neuenburg, 83. *See also* Neuchâtel
    canton, Switzerland
Neufeld, Don F., 142
Neuman, Ron, 66

Neumark, 80, 191, 230, 416. *See also*
    East Brandenburg
    History, 100
    Researchers, 284
Neu-Ostpreussen, 80. *See also* New
    East Prussia
Neurussland, 80. *See also* New Russia.
    See also Black Sea region
Neusatz, 351. *See also* Novi Sad,
    Yugoslavia
Neusohl, 334, 335. *See also* Banská
    Bystrica, Slovak Republic
Neustadt/Main, Germany, 217
Neutra, 335. *See also* Nítra, Slovak
    Republic
New Apostolic Church, 120, 124
New Brunswick, Canada, 190
    Civil records, 26
New East Prussia, 80, 99
New Economic Policy (1921-28),
    Russian, 103
New Elsass Germanic Colony,
    Saskatchewan, 192
New England, 188, 189, 190, 434
"New Germany", 195, 199, 200
New Guinea, 212, 252
New Hampshire, 188
New Harmony, Indiana, 117
New Hermannsburg, South Africa, 216
New Jersey, 121, 188, 189, 227, 407
    German immigration, 229, 412
New Netherlands, 184, 361. *See also*
    New York
New Orleans, Louisiana, 49, 50, 186
New Russia, 80, 101. *See also* Black
    Sea region
New South Wales, Australia, 51, 202,
    203, 204, 205, 207, 208, 209, 235,
    245, 246, 259, 446
"new tribes", 86
New York, 121, 184, 188, 189, 227,
    343, 362, 407
    German immigration, 184, 228, 229,
        412
New York Children's Aid Society, 11
New York, New York, 49, 50, 51, 167,
    186, 189, 190, 191, 448
    Passenger arrival lists, 48
New Zealand, 51, 202, 204, 206, 235,
    447, 448
    Archives, 250
    Books and other publications, 251
    Church records, 251
    Civil registers, 249
    Genealogical societies, 249
    German immigration, 95, 446, 447,
        450
    German settlements, 209
    Land records, 251
    Map of, 451
    Passenger lists, 250
    Swiss in, 105
Newberry Library, 433
Newcastle, New South Wales, 51, 204

Newcomer, James, 108
Newfoundland, Canada, 26
  Civil records, 26
Newsgroups, 34
Newspapers, 11
  Directory of, 406
  German-language, 11
Nicaragua, 194
  Mosquito Coast, 198
Nick, Elizabeth, 350, 425, 440
Nidwalden canton, Switzerland, 83
Nied, Victoria M., 96, 108, 224, 353
Niederösterreich, 83, 290. *See also*
    Lower Austria
Niedersachsen
  Genealogical societies, 274
  State archives, 271
Nielsen, Paul Anthon, 299, 304, 415
Nigeria, 212, 220
Nítra, Slovak Republic, 335
Nitrianske Pravno, Slovak Republic, 85,
    96
Nizhny Novgorod, Russia, 313
Nonsectarian (Bible Faith), 120
Nord Slesvig, Denmark, 84. *See also*
    Schleswig
Nordrhein-Westfalen
  Genealogical societies, 275
  State archives, 272
Nordstetten, Germany, 172
Norst, Marlene J., 202, 208, 209, 221,
    236, 296
North Adelaide, South Australia, 246
North Africa, 107
North America, 444, 450
  German immigration, 49, 93, 103,
    185, 372, 444, 447
  Swiss immigration, 105
North Bukovina, 84, 325. *See also*
    Bukovina
North Carolina, 116, 188, 189, 227, 407
  German immigration, 185, 187, 229,
    412
North Caucasus, 80, 82, 84, 102, 328
North Dakota, 64, 70, 106, 108, 188,
    189, 190, 354, 426
  German immigration, 103
North Dakota Institute for Regional
    Studies, 230, 329, 415
North Friesland, 280
North Island, New Zealand, 210, 211
North Schleswig region, 356
North Sea, 80
North Sydney, Quebec, 50
Northern Baptist Conference, 135
Northern Bessarabia, 84
Northern Territory, Australia, 202, 203,
    209, 245
Northfield, Minnesota, 365
Northrhine-Westphalia, 79, 82, 95, 411
  Civil records, 410
  History, 91
  State archives, 272
  Village lineage books, 422

Northwest Territories, Canada, 25, 26,
    232, 412
  Civil records, 26
Norway
  Church records, 364
  Civil records, 365
  Community history books, 364
  Genealogical societies, 365
  Geography, 364
  German immigration, 363
  History, 85, 367, 368
  Language, 364
  Names, 364, 369
  National archives, 366
  Researching in, 363
Nösner Zipser, 95
Notec River region, Poland, 81. *See*
    also Netze River region
Nova Santa Rosa, Brazil, 243
Nova Scotia, Canada, 22, 190, 191, 192
  Civil records, 26
  Provincial archives, 25
Novi Sad, Serbia, 351
Nunavut, Canada, 25, 26
Nuremberg, Germany, 79. *See*
    Nürnberg, Germany
Nürnberg, Germany, 79
Nuthack, Joachim O. R., 307
Nyeko, Balan, 218, 237
Nykarleby, Finland, 358
Nyland, Finland, 358

— O —

O'Connor, Patrick, 361
Oberdorf (am Ipf, Bopfingen),
    Germany, 175
Oberhessen-Starkenburg, 148
Oberkassel, Germany, 217
Oberkirch, Valentin, 108
Oberösterreich, 83, 290. *See also* Upper
    Austria
Oberwihl nr. Waldshut, Germany, 175
Obwalden canton, Switzerland, 83
Odenwald, Germany, 80
Oder River, Germany-Poland, 80, 205,
    210, 442
Oder-Neisse River area, 216
Oder-Neisse River line, 74, 90, 186,
    339
Odessa, Ukraine, 79, 82, 102, 106, 116,
    224, 327, 328, 352
  Archives, 320, 326
  German immigration, 102
Offenburg, Germany, 175
Ohaupo, New Zealand, 251
Ohio, 188, 189, 343
Oklahoma, 121, 188, 190, 200
  German immigration, 103
Old Catholics, 126
  Records, 293
Old Economy, Pennsylvania, 117
Old Hungary, 151

Old Lutherans, 127, 143, 144, 183, 195,
    202, 227, 247, 259, 261, 407, 419,
    446. *See also* Lutherans
  In Australia, 117, 247
  In Canada, 117
  In Lower Silesia, 117
  In Pomerania, 117
  In United States, 117
Old Order Mennonites, 194, 201. *See*
    also Mennonites
Oldenburg, 44, 57, 75, 76, 148, 423
  FHL cataloging, 44
  Genealogical societies, 275
Oledry, 77. *See also* Holländerein
Olinyk, Dave, 66, 71
Olmütz, 85, 94, 333. *See also* Olomouc,
    Czech republic
Olomouc, Czech Republic, 94, 333. *See*
    also Ölmutz
Olson, May E., 11, 16, 406
Olzog, Günter, 70, 304, 414
On line directories, 39
On line services, 33, 34. *See also under*
    Computers
Ontario, Canada, 19, 190, 192, 445
  Abstract records, 24
  Civil records, 26
  Library collections, 436
  Provincial archives, 24, 25
  Research helps, 414
Opava, Czech Republic, 333. *See also*
    Troppau
Orange (Duchy), 89
Orange Free State, South Africa, 215,
    216, 217
Orange Walk, Belize, 194
Orangeois, 89
Oranien. *See also* Orange (Duchy)
Oranienbaum, Russia, 319
Ore Mountains, 79
Oregon, 188, 189
Orenburg, Russia, 84, 102, 103
Ornstein-Galicia, Jacob, 229
Orphanage records, 11
Orthodox Church
  In Poland, 420
Ortsfamilienbücher, 268
Ortssippenbücher, 8, 62, 268, 273, 304,
    411
Osanec, Jiri, 330
Ösel, Estonia
  Lutheran consistory, 313
Oslo, Norway, 363
Osnabrück, Germany, 216
Ossetia, 328
Österreich, 91, 289. *See also* Austria
Österreichisch-Schlesien, 85, 289. *See*
    also Austrian Silesia
Ostfriesland, 54, 55, 268, 361. *See also*
    East Frisia
  Genealogical societies, 275
  History, 446
  Research, 279
  State archives, 272

Ostgalizien, 84. *See also* East Galicia
Ostmark, 91. *See also* Austria
Ostow, Robin, 158
Ostpreussen, 76, 423. *See also* East Prussia
  FHL cataloging, 44
Ostrava, Czech Republic, 94
Ostsee, 80. *See also* Baltic Sea
Otago, New Zealand, 51, 210, 211
Ottawa, Ontario, 23, 191
Otto I, the Great, 87, 91
Ottoman Archives, 347, 348
Ottoman Nufüs census records, 348
Ottoman Turkish Empire, 347, 443, 448
  History, 78, 79, 91, 92, 106–7, 115, 329, 335, 338, 347
Oudtshoorn, South Africa, 217
Oulu, Finland, 358. *See also* Uleaborg, Finland
Oululand, Finland, 358
Our River, 106
Ovambo tribe (Namibia), 218
Owen, Robert E., 301

— P —

Pacific states, 187, 188, 190
Packer, D. R. G., 235
Paikert, Géza C., 109
Pakistan, 221, 259
Palatinate, 76, 81, 88, 89, 105, 190, 227, 277, 286, 407, 411, 443, 444. *See also* Pfalz
  Archives, 407
  Card index file, 285
  FHL cataloging, 44
  German emigration, 102, 184, 185, 201, 213, 232, 376, 444, 446
  History, 75, 78, 88, 97, 105, 114, 115, 182, 361
  Immigration, 443
  Parish registers, 408
  Rhenish, 76
  State archives, 272
Palatines, 184, 229, 361, 372, 374, 376, 412
Palau, 212
Pale of Settlement, 61, 68, 150, 152, 167, 176, 317, 446, 447
  Atlases, 68
  Map of, 451
Palen, Margaret Krug, 230, 415
Palestine, 117, 221, 222
Palmer, Michael P., 50, 107, 330, 332, 353
Palmerston North, New Zealand, 211
Pama, C., 260
Panama, 198
Panayi, Panikos, 376
Panic of 1857, 446, 447
Panic of 1873, 210, 447
Panic of 1893, 185
Pannonia, 80
Pannonien, 80. *See also* Pannonia

Panny, Rolf E., 209
Pape, Hinrich, 216
Papua New Guinea, 212, 252
Paraguay, 193, 197, 200, 201, 234, 241
  Census records, 240
  Civil registers, 239
  German immigration, 240
  German settlements, 200
  National library, 242
  Research helps, 238
Paramaribo, Surinam, 201
Parana River, 196, 197
Parana, Brazil, 194, 196, 197, 198, 329
Parík, Arno, 177
Paris, France, 360
Parise, Frank, 404
Pärnu, Estonia, 321
Partition of Poland, 342, 445. *See also* Poland
  Map of, 451
Passau, Austria, 291
Passenger lists, 14, 48, 262
  Antwerp, Belgium, 48, 49
  Arrival lists, 49–52
  Arrivals in United States, 52, 53, 223, 230, 231, 409, 410, 417, 419
  Bremen, Germany, 48, 424
  Departure lists, 48–49
  Hamburg, Germany, 48, 240, 262, 408
  Latin America, 52
  Le Havre, France, 48, 49, 360
  New York, New York, 48
  Rotterdam, Netherlands, 48, 49, 360
Patent of Tolerance (1781), 98, 151, 293, 445
Patronymics. *See* Surnames
Patton, Mrs. Simon N. Patton, 228
Paucker, Arnold, 158
Paulding, J. R., 228
Pauls, Peter, Jr., 197, 234
Paulson, Robert J., 229, 230, 331, 333, 353, 414, 417
Peace of Augsburg, 88, 114, 141, 443
Peace of Westphalia, 88, 92, 443
Peake, Andrew G., 51
Peasants' War of 1524-25, 87, 113, 443
Peckwas, Edward A., 109, 142, 340, 341, 353
Pécs, Hungary, 97
Pedigree charts, 263
Penn, William, 116
Penner, Horst, 143, 263
Pennsylvania, 116, 121, 187, 188, 189, 190, 227, 407, 434, 445
  Church records, 415
  Colonial records, 408
  German immigration, 184, 185, 229, 230, 412, 417
  Records, 422
Pennsylvania Archives, 408
Pennsylvania Dutch, 185, 226. *See also* Pennsylvania Germans

Pennsylvania Germans, 231, 415, 419, 420, 423
  Researching, 227, 407
Pentecostal Assemblies of Canada, 135
Pentecostals, 135, 140
Perbal, Camille, 301, 302, 304
Periodical Source Index (PERSI), 426
Perm, Russia, 84
Pernau, 321. *See also* Pärnu, Estonia
Personal names
  German, 54-62
  Slavic, 416
Perth County, Ontario, 191
Perth, Western Australia, 206, 207, 246
Peru, 201
Pestkowska, M., 344
Peter Robinson papers (Canada), 24
Peter the Great, 101
Peters, Anneliese, 216
Petersen, Carl, 109
Peterson, Wilhelm, 117
Petrakis, Julia, 325
Petrikau. *See also* Piotrków Trybunalski, Poland
Petropolis, Brazil, 195, 240
Pfaffendorf/Koblenz, Germany, 217
Pfalz, 76. *See also* Palatinate
  FHL cataloging, 44
  State archives, 272
Pfohl, Ernst, 71
Pforzheim, Germany, 285
Philadelphia, Pennsylvania, 50, 184, 188, 189, 231, 419
  Arrival lists, 52
Philippi, Bernhard-Eunom, 200
Phillips, Karen, 5
Phoenix, Arizona, 189
Piedmont region, Italy, 338
Pieges, H., 174
Piepmeyer, G., 415
Piet Relief, South Africa, 215
Pietermaritzburg, South Africa, 215, 253
Pietists, 116, 117, 140, 143, 144
  In North Dakota, 117
  In Pennsylvania, 117
  In South Dakota, 117
Pihach, John D., 342
Pilsen, 97, 333. *See also* Plzen, Czech Republic
Pinetown, South Africa, 217
Piotrków Trybunalski, Poland, 344
Pisarczyk, Karl, 415
Pitzer, Donald E., 139
Piwonka, Alfred, 353
Place names, 63
  Belgian, 65
  Danish, 65
  French, 65, 66
  Galician, 64
  German, 64, 65, 66
  Hungarian, 64
  Lithuanian, 65
  Misspelled, 66

Place names (*continued*)
  Polish, 64, 65, 66
  Romanian, 64
  Serbian, 64
  Slavic, 66, 416
  Soviet Union, 65
  Switzerland, 63
  Ukrainian, 64
Plauen, Germany, 82
Plett, Delbert F., 133, 143
Pleve, Igor R., 315, 320, 324
Plock, Poland, 80, 344
Plozk. *See also* Plock, Poland
Plymouth, England, 247
Plzen, Czech Republic, 97, 333
  Archives, 353. *See also* Pilsen
Podlachia, 80
Podlachien, 80. *See also* Podlachia
Podolia, 80, 312
Podolien, 80. *See also* Podolia
Podoll, Brian A., 230, 416
Poellnitz, G. von, 215
Pohl, Dieter, 284
Pohnpei, Micronesia, 212, 252
Pokrovsk, Russia, 311
Polackova-Henley, Kaca, 155
Polakoff, Eileen, 165
Poland, 69, 79, 80, 82, 84, 101, 118,
    176, 239, 284, 289, 311, 319, 325,
    326, 416, 423, 426, 443, 445, 446,
    447, 449, 471. *See also* Central
    Poland
  Archival inventories, 344
  Archives, 343, 413
  Atlases, 68
  Baptist records, 341
  Church records, 340, 341
  Civil records, 177, 282, 340, 341
  Consular log book, 257
  Emigration, 339
  FHL cataloging, 44
  Gazetteers, 64, 68, 72
  Genealogical periodicals, 345
  Genealogical resources, 353
  Genealogical services, 345
  Genealogical societies, 285
  German emigration, 103, 209, 210,
    211
  German genealogy, 342
  German immigration, 99
  History, 64, 74, 76, 77, 83, 84, 87, 90,
    91, 93, 94, 99, 114, 146, 152, 186,
    331, 335, 338, 445, 446, 449
  Jewish records, 342
  Jews, 59, 61
  Lutheran church addresses, 341
  Lutheran records, 341
  Map of, 451
  Mennonite records, 341
  Microfilms, 41
  National Archives, 343
  North American genealogical sources,
    342

Poland (*continued*)
  Partition of, 92, 99, 163, 267, 338,
    339
  Polish genealogical sources, 343
  Postal code directory, 343
  Records, 265, 339
  Reformed Church records, 341
  Religions, 119
  Research guides, 339, 422
  Researchers, 284
  Researching in, 338, 345
  State archives, 181, 341
  Swabian settlers, 411
  Zabuzanski Collection, 341
Polansky, Paul J., 327, 347
Polen, 99. *See also* Poland
Poles, 86, 89, 93
Polesie region, Belarus
  Yizkor books, 168
Police registers, 263
Polish Corridor, 76, 81, 339
Polish language
  Vocabulary lists, 177, 404
Polish Revolt of 1830-31, 338
Polish-American genealogical societies.
    See also under Genealogical
    societies
  List of, 342
Political freedom, 183
Political refugees, 449
Pomerania, 75, 76, 79, 81, 82, 100, 191,
    198, 216, 277, 339, 358, 362, 372,
    411, 416, 471. *See also* Pommern
  Burgher books, 267
  Church records, 355, 413, 423
  Civil records, 413
  Evangelical Church records, 417
  FHL cataloging, 44
  Genealogical societies, 285
  German emigration, 143, 195, 205,
    207, 210, 214, 358
  History, 77, 78, 83, 88, 90, 100, 114,
    183, 185, 368, 444
  Military parish records, 266
  Newsletter, 426
  Place names, 66
  Records, 282
  Researchers, 284
  Swedish, 370
Pomerelia, 81, 89
Pomerode, Santa Catarina, Brazil, 234,
    243
Pommerellen, 81. *See also* Pomerelia
Pommern, 76, 423. *See also* Pomerania
  FHL cataloging, 44
Pomorze, 83. *See also* Pomerania
Ponape, 212. *See* Pohnpei, Micronesia
Ponta Grossa, Brazil, 196
Poprad River, Slovak Republic, 96
Pori, Finland, 358. *See also* Bjorneborg,
    Finland
Port Adelaide, South Australia, 51, 247
Port Elizabeth, South Africa, 52, 215,
    217, 254

Port Philip, Victoria, 51, 206
Porten, Edward von der, 109, 421
Porto Alegre, Brazil
  Arrival lists, 52
Portugal, 356
Portuguese, 146, 213
Portuguese East India Company, 258
Posen, 75, 76, 79, 81, 82, 89, 95, 148,
    152, 327, 362, 411, 416, 423, 471.
    See also Poznan, Poland. *See also*
    Poznan, Poland
  Church records, 355, 423
  Emigration, 420
  FHL cataloging, 44
  Genealogical societies, 285, 344
  German emigration, 205, 247
  History, 75, 84, 90, 100, 102, 185,
    338
  Military parish records, 266
  Place names, 66
  Religions, 119
  Researchers, 284
Post, Bernhard, 155
Postal codes (German), 264
Postal Designations, 4
Postal Reply Coupons, 379. *See*
    International Reply Coupons
Potchefstroom, South Africa, 215, 253
Potsdam Conference/Agreement, 90,
    100, 307
Potsdam, Germany, 83, 170, 270
Poznan, Poland, 79, 84, 327, 344, 345.
    See also Posen
  Genealogical societies, 344
  Place names, 66
Prachatitz, Czech Republic, 97
Prag. *See* Prague, Czech Republic
Prague, Czech Republic, 94, 145, 146,
    152, 333. *See also* Praha, Czech
    Republic
  History, 331
  Jewish ceneteries, 179
  Jewish surnames, 176
  Military Historical Institute, 330
Praha, Czech Republic, 332, 333
Presbyterian and Reformed Church
    Historical Foundation
  Archives, 129
Presbyterian Church in America
  Archives, 129
Presbyterians, 105, 120, 122, 124
  Archives, 129
  In Australia, 208
  In Canada, 20, 21, 124, 191
Preschau. *See* Presov, Slovak Republic
Presov, Slovak Republic, 335
Pressburg, 85, 96, 151, 335. *See also*
    Bratislava, Slovak Republic
Pretoria, South Africa, 215, 216, 252,
    253, 254, 255
Preussen, 98. *See also* Prussia
Pribram, Alfred Francis, 156
Price, Amanda, 373
Price, Charles Archibald, 236

Prince Edward Island, Canada
 Civil records, 26
Printed family histories, 263
Printed genealogies, 11
Prischib, Ukraine, 102
Pritzkau, Gwen B., 313
Private school records, 10
Prochazkova, Sylvia, 179
Proeve, H. F. W., 247
Profesional genealogists, 9, 17
Professional associations, 11
Protestant Episcopal, 120
Protestant Reformation, 87, 367
Protestants, 87, 92, 106, 186, 228, 335,
 362, 411, 443, 444, 445
 Church records, 281
 History, 94, 98, 368
 In American colonies, 223, 410
 In Austria, 80, 304
 In Belgium, 357
 In Bohemia, 331
 In Brazil, 194
 In Bukovina, 97
 In Chile, 200
 In China, 221
 In Denmark, 357
 In Germany, 79
 In Hungary, 114
 In Poland, 114, 420
 In Romania, 114
 In Russian Empire, 312
 In Silesia, 331
 In South Africa, 213
 In Switzerland, 299
 Naming practices, 59
 Records, 10, 41, 144, 240, 335
Provence, France, 146
Prussia, 81, 148, 265, 354, 362, 372,
 411, 446
 Census records, 263, 267
 Evangelical Church, 446
 FHL cataloging, 44
 Gazetteers, 63, 68, 69, 73
 German emigration, 144, 201, 207,
 210, 259
 German immigration, 144
 History, 75, 88, 89, 90, 92, 93, 98, 99,
 102, 106, 183, 338, 357, 368, 443,
 444, 445, 447, 448
 Kingdom of, 444, 451
 Land records, 283
 Map of, 451
 Military parish records, 421
 Provinces, 75
Prussian State Privy Archives, Berlin,
 266, 283
Prussians, 98
Prypec River region, Belarus, 101
Przemysl, Poland, 326, 340, 344
Public records, 11
Publications listing names being
 researched, 7

Pudovochkina, O. K., 313, 314
Puhoi, New Zealand, 209, 211, 250,
 251
Pultusk, Poland, 344
Pulzer, Peter G. J., 159
Punch, Terrence, 28, 190, 232
Purin, Bernhard, 174

— Q —

Quakers, 136. *See also* Religious
 Society of Friends
 In Pennsylvania, 141
 Palatine, 116
Quebec, Canada, 19, 190
 Civil records, 27
Quebec, Quebec, 50, 186, 434
Queensland, Australia, 51, 202, 203,
 204, 205, 208, 209, 245, 447
Queenstown, South Africa, 217
Quester, Erich, 353, 416

— R —

Raahe, Finland, 358. *See* also
 Brahestad, Finland
Rabat, Morocco, 256
Rabe, Robert, 416
Rabinowitz, Dorothy, 179
Raciborz, Poland, 344
Radom, Poland, 344
Radspieler, Tony, 98, 109
RAGAS, 318, 320, 321, 322, 326, 328
Ramotswa, South Africa, 216
Ramsele, Sweden, 372
Rangitikei River, New Zealand, 210
Ranta, Raimo, 375
Rapp, George, 117
Rappists, 138
Rastadt, Ukraine, 327
Rastatt, Germany, 175
Rastede, Germany, 282
Rath, George, 230
Rathkeale, Ireland, 361
Ratibor, Germany, 344. *See* Raciborz,
 Poland
Ratisbon. *See* Regensburg, Germany
Ratzeburg, Germany, 357
Rauma, Finland, 358
Reaman, G. Elmore, 233
Reaman, George Elmore, 143, 233
Record sources
 Kinds available, 261
 Primary, 1
 Secondary, 1
Records handbook, 18
Redange canton, Luxembourg, 83
Reddig, Ken, 24
Reefton, New Zealand, 252
Reformation, 88, 92, 113, 114, 144,
 354, 361, 363, 442, 443. *See also*
 Protestant Reformation

Reformed Church, 88, 89, 121, 144,
 261, 419, 443. *See also* Calvinists.
 See also Dutch Reformed Church.
 See also Presbyterians
 History, 98
 In Alsace-Lorraine, 359
 In Argentina, 193
 In Austro-Hungarian Empire, 294
 In Belgium, 115
 In Black Sea region, 314
 In Brandenburg, 105
 In Canada, 125, 190
 In France, 112, 115, 360
 In Galicia, 294
 In Germany, 105, 116, 119, 359
 In Hesse, 105
 In Hungary, 294
 In Netherlands, 112, 362
 In Palatinate, 105
 In Russian Empire, 312
 In Scotland, 112
 In Slovakia, 294
 In South Africa, 213, 253
 In Switzerland, 105, 112, 298
 In Ukraine, 102
 In Volga River region, 313
 Merger with Lutherans, 105, 202,
 261, 312, 446
 Records, 126, 144, 261, 313
Reformed Church in America
 Headquarters, 129
Reformed Protestant Dutch Church, 129
Regensburg, Germany, 78, 145, 282,
 285, 442
Regenstein, Janice Mendenhall, 164,
 179
Regényi, Isabella, 71
Regina, Saskatchewan, 22, 23, 25, 27,
 192
Reichling, Gerhard, 71
Reichmann, Eberhard, 225
Rein, Kurt, 224
Reisinger, Joy, 28
Reiss, Marion, 222
Reiter, Josef, 186
Reith, Wolfgang, 216
Religion. *See also under each religious
 group*
 History, 87–89, 98, 111–44
Religions in United States, 120
Religious Demography
 German-Americans, 119
 Germanic Countries, 118
Religious freedom, 111–44, 183, 444.
 See also under each religious group
Religious Society of Friends, 136. *See
 also* Quakers
Remich canton, Luxembourg, 83
Renfrew County, Ontario, 191
Rennert, Udo, 158
Repatriation
 Of Germans, 98, 107, 108, 449
Reps district, Transylvania, 423
Reschke, Horst A., 265, 304, 416

Research Center on Religious History in Canada, Ottawa, Canada, 126
Research techniques, 1
Resettlers, 104, 329, 450. *See also* Aussiedler
Reuss-Gera, 76
Reuss-Greiz, 76
Reuter, Lutz R., 157
Reutlingen, Germany, 176
Reval, 321. *See also* Tallinn, Estonia
Lutheran consistory, 313
Revanchist movement, 95
Revision lists (Russian), 317, 318, 324, 326. *See also under* Russian Empire
Revolutions of 1830, 89, 99, 103, 105, 183
Revolutions of 1848, 89, 105, 183, 185, 190, 195, 199
RGADA, 311, 318. *See also* Russian State Archive of Ancient Acts
RGIA, 311, 319, 321. *See also* Russian State Historical Archive
Rheinhessen, Germany, 76, 81
FHL cataloging, 44
Rheinland, 76. *See also* Rhineland
FHL cataloging, 44
State archives, 272
Rheinland-Pfalz
Genealogical societies, 275
State archives, 272
Rhenish Confederation, 445
Rhenish Palatinate, 145
Rhine Province
Church records, 413
Rhine River, 79, 81, 82, 86, 95, 184, 227, 407
Rhineland, 75, 76, 86, 90, 113, 152, 190, 198, 277, 423. *See also* Rheinland
Archives, 407
FHL cataloging, 44
German emigration, 210, 221, 349, 446
History, 76, 87, 95, 106, 146, 356
Religions, 119
Rhineland-Palatinate, 79, 82, 95, 97, 194, 240, 411, 446
German emigration, 407
History, 91
Religions, 119
State archives, 272
Village lineage books, 422
Rhode, Harold, 180, 317
Rhodesia, 212, 215, 226. *See also* Zambia. *See also* Zimbabwe
Ribbe, Wolfgang, 8, 60, 62, 89, 143, 241, 264, 267, 268, 279, 304, 356, 404, 416
Riccards, Bishop, 217
Richards, Henry Melchior Muhlenberg, 420
Richarz, Monika, 159
Richmond, British Columbia, 22
Richmond, Surrey, England, 259, 374

Riemer, Shirley J., 264, 417
Riga, Latvia, 49, 80, 98, 99, 101, 322
Lutheran consistory, 313
Rijeka, Croatia, 289
Rio de Janeiro, Brazil, 52, 194, 195, 238, 242, 243
Arrival lists, 52
Rio Grande do Sul, Brazil, 194, 195, 197, 198, 233, 234
Rio Negro, Brazil, 196, 233
Rippley, La Vern J., 225, 230, 417, 440
Ristaino, Dr., 258
Rittmann, M., 176
River Brethren, 120, 124
Repository, 134
Roback, A. A., 149
Robinson, Jill, 252
Rochlin, S. A., 213
Roden, Oded, 180
Rohmeder, Wilhelm, 109
Rohold, S. B., 233
Rohrlach, Peter P., 411
Roman Empire, 86
Romania, 79, 80, 81, 82, 96, 97, 106, 109, 150, 193, 289, 297, 320, 325, 335, 346, 351, 354, 416, 423, 443, 448
Census records, 348
Danube Swabians, 109
Genealogists, 347
German immigration, 96
History, 64, 77, 85, 87, 92, 93, 98, 114, 196, 329, 346, 445, 446
Microfilms, 41
National Archive, 346
Researching in, 346
Village genealogies, 268
Romanians, 93
Romansch, 83, 211
Romantische Strasse, 81
Røros, Norway, 363
Rosario, Argentina, 241
Rose, Kenneth E., 137, 143
Rosen, Ragnar, 375
Rosenberg, Louis, 233
Rosenberg, Stuart E, 233
Rosengarten, J. G., 231, 420
Rosenkranz, Herbert, 225
Rosenthal, Odeda, 236
Ross, James Rodman, 235
Rosten, Eino, 375
Rosthern, Saskatchewan, 192
Rostock, Germany, 49, 83
Rostov, Russia, 79, 84, 102
Rottenberg, Dan, 161, 162, 165, 180, 417
Rotterdam, Netherlands, 186, 191
Passenger lists, 48, 49, 360
Rowe, Kenneth E., 126
Roy, Janine, 28
Rozenblit, Marsha L., 156
Rubinstein, Hilary L., 236
Rubinstein, W. D., 236
Rudolf, H., 63, 71

Rudolftal, Bosnia, 349
Rudolph I, of Hapsburg, 91
Ruf, Peter, 155
Rufiji River (Tanzania), 220
Ruhr River region, Germany, 81, 86, 217
Runcora, Queensland, 245
Ruperti, George, 232, 376
Rupp, Israel Daniel, 230, 277, 417
Rürup, Reinhard, 156, 159
Rusam, G., 304
Rusins, 93
Russell, John Andrew, 231, 421
Russia, 80, 81, 82, 89, 98, 99, 101, 103, 223, 284, 312, 324, 336, 353, 410, 416, 444, 445, 447, 448, 449
Gazetteers, 73
German emigration, 183, 193, 448
German immigration, 109, 419
History, 65, 74, 99, 101, 183, 338, 339, 346, 358, 368, 443, 445, 446, 447, 449
Microfilms, 41
Researchers, 308, 319
Researching in, 309, 324
Revision records, 414, 433
Russian Central State Archive of Ancient Acts, 318
Russian Civil War, 319, 320
Russian Empire, 71, 79, 81, 190, 257, 311, 315, 354
Atlases, 68
Census, 306, 318
Civil registration, 317
Emigration, 191
Emigration to Canada, 23
German emigration, 183
German immigration, 144
History, 77, 98–104, 185, 306
Jews, 59, 61
Lutheran records, 312
Moravian Brethren records, 312
Nobility and burgher records, 319
Records, 311, 312
Records extraction project, 320
Reformed Church records, 312
Revision lists, 317
Separatist records, 312
Russian Germans, 201, 222
Russian language
Documents, 404
Glossary, 404
Russian Poland, 82, 95
Russian Revolution, 317
Russian State Archive of Ancient Acts, 311
Russian State Historical Archive, 311, 312, 319
Russland, 324. *See also* Russia
Russo-Turkish Wars, 92, 101, 102, 106, 445
Rustenburg, South Africa, 215
Ruthenians, 93
Rutherglen, Victoria, 207

Ryder, Dorothy E., 19
Rye, Richard, 314
Rygh, Oluf, 364
Rypin, Poland, 84
Rzeszów, Poland, 344

— S —

Saale River, 81
Saarbrücken, Germany, 286
Saaremaa, Estonia
  Lutheran consistory, 313
Saarland, 76, 79, 82, 90, 411, 423
  Archives, 407
  Genealogical societies, 275
  Religions, 119
  State archives, 272
  Village genealogies, 268
  Village lineage books, 422
Sachs, Arlene, 164, 167
Sachsen, 76, 148. *See also* Saxony
  Province. *See also* Saxony Kingdom
  FHL cataloging, 44
  Genealogical societies, 275
  State archives, 272
Sachsen-Altenburg, 148
  FHL cataloging, 44
Sachsen-Anhalt
  Genealogical societies, 276
  State archives, 272
Sachsen-Coburg-Gotha
  FHL cataloging, 44
Sachsen-Meiningen
  FHL cataloging, 44
Sachsen-Weimar, 148
Sachsen-Weimar-Eisenach
  FHL cataloging, 44
Sack, Benjamin Gutelius, 233
Sack, Sallyann Amdur, 23, 70, 162,
  164, 179, 180, 321, 326, 353, 425
Saginaw, Michigan, 188
Saint Alban's, Vermont
  Border crossing lists, 14
Saint Augustine, Florida, 184
Saint Bartholomew's Day Massacre,
  115
Saint Gall canton, Switzerland, 83, 146
Saint John, Quebec, 50
Saint Lawrence River, 190
Saint Louis, Missouri, 126, 188
Saint Louis-Harrison, Lorraine, 28
Saint Petersburg, Russia, 79, 101, 103,
  311, 313, 318, 319, 352, 408
  City Archive, 313
  Historical Archive, 318
  Lutheran Consistory, 312
Sainte-Foy, Quebec, 27
Sainty, Malcolm R., 17, 412
Salaj, Romania
  Yizkor books, 168
Sallen, Herbert, 159
Sallet, Richard, 230
Salvador, Brazil
  Arrival lists, 52

Salvation Army, 120, 124, 135
Salzburg, Austria, 75, 80, 81, 83, 89,
  92, 115, 148, 289, 290, 294
  Archbishopric of, 115
  History, 76
  Lutheran records, 293
  Records, 292
Salzburger Protestants, 80, 116, 143,
  144, 298
  Expulsions of, 142, 444
  Genealogical societies, 287
  History, 140
  Name lists, 143
  Surnames, 141
Salzburgers, 128
  In Bavaria, 115
  In Brandenburg, 115
  In East Prussia, 115
  In Franconia, 115
Salzkammergut, Austria, 80, 81, 115,
  292
Samara, Russia, 102, 314, 324
  Archives, 311
  St. George Evangelical Lutheran
    Church, 311, 313
Samenhof, Ludwik, 152
Samoa, 211, 252
  Civil records, 252
Samogitia, 81
Samogitien, 81. *See also* Samogitia
Sample letters, 379
San Antonio, Texas, 188, 189
San Diego, California, 58
San Jose, Costa Rica, 240
San Marino, 351
Sandomierz, Poland, 344
Sankt Gallen, 83. *See also* Saint Gall
  canton, Switzerland
Sankt Ottilien, Germany, 217
Sanok, Poland, 344
Santa Catarina, Brazil, 194, 195, 196,
  197, 198
Santa Cruz, Bolivia, 194
Santa Fe, Argentina, 193
Santa Izabel, Brazil, 195
Santa Rosa, Brazil, 197
Sante, Georg Wilhelm, 109
Santiago de Chile, Chile, 199, 239, 241,
  242
  Genealogical societies, 243
Santo Tomas, Guatemala, 198
Santos, Brazil
  Arrival lists, 52
Sao Bento do Sul, Brazil, 196
Sao Leopoldo, Brazil, 194
Sao Paulo, Brazil, 194, 195, 196, 197,
  241, 243
Sapper, Karl, 198
Saratov, Russia, 102, 257, 311, 313,
  314, 319, 324
  Archives, 318
  Catholic consistory, 314
  Lutheran Consistory, 313
Sarmányá, Jana, 334

Sarna, Jonathan D., 178
Saron, Gustav, 237
Saskatchewan district, Northwest
  Territories, 232, 412
Saskatchewan, Canada, 191, 192, 200,
  232, 412
  Civil records, 27
  Henry Meyer Collection, 23
  Provincial archives, 25
Saskatoon, Saskatchewan, 21, 25, 192
Sathmar, 85, 97, 289, 336. *See also*
  Satu Mare, Romania
Satu Mare, Romania, 97, 289, 336
  History, 77, 85
Sauer, Paul, 143, 156, 170, 180, 236
Sauerland, Germany, 81, 275
Savoy, Italy, 89
Sawatzky, Harry Leonard, 200, 234
Sawatzky, Heinrich, 143
Saxe-Coburg-Gotha, 372
Saxonia, 148
Saxons, 97, 442
  History, 442
Saxony, 76, 79, 80, 82, 86, 138, 219,
  265, 411
  Burgher books, 267
  Emigration, 420
  Genealogical societies, 275
  German emigration, 201, 205, 207,
    210, 211
  History, 87, 91, 94, 95, 331
  State archives, 272
  Village lineage books, 422
Saxony Kingdom, 44, 75, 76, 423
  Place names, 66
Saxony Province, 75, 76, 423. *See also*
  Sachsen
  FHL cataloging, 44
  Military parish records, 266
Saxony-Altenburg, 76
Saxony-Anhalt, 78, 79, 82, 89
  History, 88, 91
  State archives, 272
Saxony-Coburg-Gotha, 76
Saxony-Meiningen, 76
Saxony-Weimar-Eisenach, 76
Scandinavia, 442
  History, 146
Schaab, Carl Anton, 156
Schaefer, Christina K., 18
Schäfer, D., 225
Schäfer, W., 173, 180
Schaffhausen canton, Switzerland, 83,
  146, 188
Schässburg district, Transylvania, 423
Schaumburg-Lippe, Germany, 75, 76,
  423
Scheel, Otto, 109
Schelbauer, Ignatz, 196, 197, 234
Schelbert, Leo, 225, 230
Schelbert, Urspeter, 419
Schelk district, Transylvania, 423
Schembs, Hans-Otto, 153
Schenk, Trudy, 225, 278, 279, 304, 417

Scherer, Anton, 64, 71
Scheuermann, Richard, 318
Scheurer, Kurt, 217, 218
Schlehdorf, Germany, 217
Schlesien, 423. *See also* Silesia
  FHL cataloging, 44
Schleswig, 280
  History, 75, 84, 90, 357
  Map of, 451
Schleswig-Holstein, 54, 55, 76, 82, 148,
  263, 279, 361, 373, 411, 423, 445
  Census records, 268, 357
  Emigration, 278
  FHL cataloging, 44
  Genealogical societies, 276
  German emigration, 207
  History, 75, 91
  Researching in, 303
  State archives, 273
  Village genealogies, 268
Schlyter, Daniel M., 330, 353, 417
Schmidl, Erwin A., 217
Schmidt, David F., 308, 310, 318, 320,
  324
Schmidt, Georg, 216
Schmidt, Josef, 109, 353, 354
Schmidt, Martin, 143
Schmidt-Pretoria, Werner, 212, 213,
  237
Schmiedehaus, Walter, 200, 234
Schmucker, George, 417
Schneider, Gertrude, 159
Schneider, Ludwig, 296, 342, 354
Schnell, E. L., 213, 214, 215, 237
Schnorbus, Ursula, 156
Schnucker, George, 230
Schoeps, Julius H., 160
Schön, Th., 176
Schönhengst, 85, 94. *See also* Hrebec,
  Czech Republic
Schrader-Muggenthaler, Cornelia, 225,
  278, 299, 304, 360, 376
Schram, Robert, 404
Schreiber, Hermann, 109
Schretzenmayr, Lore, 285
Schroeder, William, 200, 225
Schubert, David A., 259
Schubert, Franz, 267
Schubert, Kurt, 156, 177, 180
Schubert, Ursula, 156
Schulle, Diana, 241, 268
Schulz, Karin, 230, 304, 417
Schulz-Vobach, Klaus-Dieter, 109
Schuricht, Herrmann, 230, 231, 418,
  420
Schurz, Carl, 183
Schütz, Fritz, 141, 143
Schutzberg, Bosnia, 349
Schwaben. *See also* Swabia. *See also*
  Swabians. *See also* Alamanni
Schwäbisch Gmünd, Germany, 176
Schwäbische Türkei, 85, 289. *See also*
  Swabian Turkey
Schwabs, 100. *See* Swabians

Schwarz, Ernst, 69, 109
Schwarz, Richard W., 143
Schwarz, Stefan, 156
Schwarzburg-Rudolstadt, 76
  FHL cataloging, 44
Schwarzburg-Sondershausen, 76
  FHL cataloging, 44
Schweitzer, George Keene, 264, 279,
  304, 343, 418
Schwenkfeld, Caspar, 113
Schwenkfelder Historical Society
  Library (PA), 133
Schwenkfelders, 120, 142, 261, 444
  Archives, 133
  History, 113
  In Pennsylvania, 116
Schwerin, Germany, 83
Schwetzingen, Germany, 176
Schwierz, Israel, 174
Schwyz canton, Switzerland, 83
Scotland, 105, 191
  Germanicized Scots, 372
  History, 78
Scottish mercenaries, 372
Sea of Azov, 80, 84, 102
Search engines, 39
Seenplatte, 81
Seidel, Esther, 158
Seligmann, Rafael, 159
Semgallen, 81. *See also* Semgalia. *See*
  also Zemgalia
Semigalia, 81
Semipalatinsk, Russia, 103
Semland, 81
Sending money abroad, 378
Senekovic, Dagmar, 297, 304, 418
Senstius, Paul, 159
Senz, Josef Volkmar, 109, 354
Separatist (Lutherans), 312, 314
  In Volga River region, 313
Serbia, 289, 443
  History, 77, 85
  Researching in, 350
Serbs, 93
Seven Weeks' War, 93
  German casualties, 422
Seven Years' War, 92, 101, 182, 444
Seventh Day Baptists, 124
  Archives, 134
Seventh-day Adventists, 120, 136, 142,
  143, 261
  In Brazil, 194
  In Latin America, 238
Shadwell, Arthur, 373
Shaffir, William, 232
Shandong peninsula, China, 221
Shanghai, China, 221, 257, 258, 449
Shanghaiers, 208
Shea, Jonathan D., 180, 404, 405, 418
Sheehan, Colin Gordon, 259
Sherman, Ari Joshua, 225
Ship arrival lists, 14
Shipyard, Belize, 194
Shulvass, Moses Avigdor, 159

Siberia, 84, 102, 104, 109, 257, 328,
  329, 448
Sibiu, Romania, 81
Siebenbürgen, 81, 85, 95, 106, 289,
  336. *See also* Transylvania
Sieg River, Germany, 81
Silbermann, Alphons, 159
Silesia, 59, 69, 75, 76, 78, 79, 81, 82,
  219, 416, 471. *See also* Schlesien
  Church records, 355, 423
  Emigration, 420
  FHL cataloging, 44
  Gazetteers, 72
  Genealogical societies, 285
  German emigration, 142, 143, 200,
    205, 207, 214, 247, 349, 447
  History, 76, 77, 83, 84, 89, 90, 92, 94,
    100, 107, 331, 444
  Military parish records, 266
  Place names, 66
  Protestants, 331
  Religions, 119
  Researchers, 284
  Surnames, 60
  Yizkor books, 168
Simon Wiesenthal Center, 169
Simon, Hermann, 154
Simons, Menno, 113
Singapore, 259
Singerman, Robert, 161, 180
Sino-Judaic Archives of the Hoover
  Institution, 258
Skender, L. Edward, 96, 109
Skrzypinski, Henryk, 327, 345
Slask, 83, 84. *See also* Silesia
Slavonia, 97, 108, 289, 349
  History, 75, 77, 85
Slavs, 86, 93, 94, 306, 442
Slawonien, 85, 108, 289. *See also*
  Slavonia
Slesvig, Denmark, 356
Slovak Republic, 71, 92, 298, 335, 402,
  442. *See also* Slovakia
  Archives, 162, 330
  Census records, 334
  Church records, 334
  Embassy, 335
  Gazetteers, 68
  History, 96, 330
  Land records, 334
  Map of, 451
  Microfilms, 41
  Military records, 295, 330
  National archives, 335
  Regional archives, 335
  Researching in, 334
  Tax lists, 334
Slovakia, 163, 327. *See* Slovak
  Republic
  Gazetteers, 72, 330
  German emigration, 186
  History, 77, 95, 96, 329
Slovaks, 93, 96
Slovenes, 93

Slovenia, 78, 82, 85, 93, 94, 96, 289, 298, 350
  Church records, 355, 423
  Emigration, 208
  History, 77
  Microfilms, 41
  National Archive, 350
  Researching in, 350
Slupsk, Poland, 344
Smelser, Ronald, 305, 418
Smith, Anna Piszczan-Czaja, 119, 125, 143, 180, 231, 305, 418, 419
Smith, C. Henry, 139
Smith, Clifford Neal, 48, 117, 119, 125, 143, 180, 198, 205, 225, 231, 240, 247, 259, 278, 305, 418, 419
Smith, Frank, 364
Smith, Juliana Szucs, 18
Smith, Kenneth L., 62, 141, 262, 305, 405, 419
Smith, Leonard H., Jr., 29
Smith, Norma H., 29
Sobotik, Robert, 71
Social Security Death Index, 33, 45
Socinians, 114
  In Poland, 338
Sofala, South Africa, 213, 237
Soininen, Gunnar, 375
Soininvaara, Heikki, 375
Solomon Islands, 212, 252
Solothurn canton, Switzerland, 83, 146, 188, 225, 304
Somalia, 216
Sompolno, Poland, 340
Sondershausen, Germany, 288
Sorbs, 80. See also Lusatia
Sorin, Gerald, 225, 231
Sorkin, David Jan, 159
Soshnikov, Vladislav Yevgyenevich, 309, 310, 318, 323, 324, 325, 328
Soundex index to U. S. census records, 15
South Africa, 51, 117, 212, 213, 214, 218, 226, 237, 254, 258, 259, 260, 373, 444, 447, 448
  Archives, 255
  Boer War, 448
  Church records, 252
  Civil registers, 253
  Genealogical societies, 255
  German settlements, 212
  Immigration and naturalization records, 254
  King's German Legion. See King's German Legion (English)
  Land records, 254
  Military records, 254
  Other Records, 254
  Passenger lists, 51
  South African-German Cultural Association, 255
  Swiss in, 105
  Wills, probate and orphan records, 254

South African War
  Veterans records, 24
South America, 450
  Colonization, 233
  German immigration, 49, 103, 447, 449, 450
  Map of, 451
  Swiss in, 105
South Asia, 258
South Australia, 51, 202, 203, 204, 205, 206, 207, 208, 209, 211, 236, 245, 247, 249, 259, 260, 447
  German immigration, 259
  State library, 243
South Bessarabia
  History, 84
South Brazil, 234
South Bukovina, 423
South Carolina, 188, 227, 407
  German immigration, 185, 187
South Caucasus, 84, 102, 328
South Dakota, 189, 190, 426
  Library collections, 436
South Island, New Zealand, 206, 209, 210, 211, 249, 252, 447
South Prussia, 81
South Russia, 80, 81, 101, 260, 328, 445. See also New Russia. See also Südrussland. See also Ukraine
  Researching in, 328
South Saskatchewan River, 192
South Tyrol, Italy, 95, 109, 337, 423
  Archive, 337
  Church records, 355, 423
  History, 84, 95
Southeast Europe, 58, 108, 309, 335, 342, 450. See also Eastern Europe
  Genealogical societies, 285
  Researchers, 284
Southern Baptist Conference, 135
Southern Rhodesia, 219
Southern Trunk Railway (New Zealand), 210
Southhampton, England, 48
Southland, New Zealand, 210
South-West Africa, 218
Southwest Pacific
  German colonies, 448
Soviet Union, 49, 65, 90, 118, 257, 449, 450
  Gazetteers, 65
  German emigration, 197, 449
  History, 77, 83, 91, 96, 103, 104, 319, 329
  Maps of German settlements in, 65
  Place names, 65
  Researchers, 308
  Researching in former, 416. See under each country
Spain, 88, 361, 367
  History, 87, 92, 105, 146
Spalek, John M., 231, 264
Spanish Hapsburgs, 113
Spanish Inquisition, 113

Spanish Lookout, Belize, 194
Spanish Netherlands, 105, 140, 354, 367, 443
Spanuth, Johannes, 214, 237
Special Interest Groups (SIGs), 165
Spessart, Germany, 81
Speyer, Germany, 145, 442
Spis, Slovak Republic, 85, 96. See also Zips, Slovak Republic
Srem, Yugoslavia, 81, 85, 108, 289, 350. See also Syrmia. See also Syrmien
Sri Lanka, 218, 221, 222, 258
Staatsarchiv. See Germany:State archives
Stache, Christa, 144, 305, 354, 419
Stadtarchiv. See Germany:City Archives
Stalin, Josef, 65, 449, 450
Stalingrad, Battle of, 104
Standesamt. See Germany:Civil Registry Offices
Starbird, Ethel A., 192
State archives. Check under individual countries
State census records, 16
Stearns County Heritage Center (St. Cloud, Minnesota), 438
Stebelska, H., 344
Steel, Donald John, 180
Steel, Mrs. A. E. F., 180
Steiermark, 83, 289, 290. See also Styria
Steigerwald, Germany, 81
Steigerwald, Jacob, 97, 109, 193, 197, 201, 203, 225, 354
Stein, Neithard von, 284
Steinach, Adelreich, 299, 305, 419
Steinberg, Augusta, 159
Steinberg, Isaac Nachman, 236
Steinbruch, Karl-Heinz, 278
Steinherz, Samuel, 156
Stern, Malcolm H., 180
Stern, Maureen Joan, 260
Stern, Selma, 159
Stettin, Germany, 49, 344, 368. See also Szczecin, Poland
Stevens, Richard P., 237
Stiefvater, O., 175
Stirling, Western Australia, 206
Stobbe, Otto, 159
Stockholm, Sweden, 367, 371
Stoeckl, Michael, 285, 347
Stoeffer, F. Ernest, 144
Stoffel, Gertraut Maria, 209
Stoffel, Hans-Peter, 209
Stokes, K. R., 29
Stolp, Germany, 344. See Slupsk, Poland
Stormont County, Ontario, 190
Stourzh, Gerald, 157
Strasbourg, France, 114, 119, 360
Strassburger, Ralph Beaver, 231, 277, 305, 419
-strasse (suffix), 81

Strauss, Herbert A., 231
Strauss, Peter, 180
Strobel, Philip, 144, 231
Stucky, Solomon, 144
Studienstelle ostdeutsche Genealogie
    der Forschungsstelle
    Ostmitteleuropa, 286
Stumpp, Karl, 58, 62, 65, 72, 109, 354,
    419
Stutterheim, South Africa, 215
Stuttgart, Germany, 117, 163, 285, 329
    Deutsches Auslands-Institut, 48
Styria, 75, 83, 91, 94, 289, 290
    Census records, 295
    Emigration, 208
    History, 77
    Lutheran records, 294
    Records, 292
Subcarpathian Rus', 84, 163, 325, 327,
    329
    History, 77, 96
Sub-Carpathian Ukraine, 108, 327
Sub-Saharan Africa, 107
Suceava, Romania, 97
Sudauen, 81
Sudavia, 81
Süd-Bessarabien, 84. *See also* South
    Bessarabia
Suderman, Jim, 133, 141
Sudeten Germans, 94, 98, 330, 333,
    368, 414
Sudetengebirge, 81
Sudetenland, 81, 94, 119, 330, 449
    Church records, 355, 423
    Genealogical societies, 285
    German emigration, 449, 450
    History, 77, 84, 90, 186
    Map of, 451
    Researchers, 284
Sudhaus, Fritz, 234
Südpreussen, 81. *See also* South Prussia
Südrussland, 80, 81. *See also* South
    Russia. *See also* Ukraine. *See also*
    New Russia
Südtirol, 337. *See also* South Tyrol,
    Italy
    Records, 297
Suess, Jared H., 58, 63, 64, 299, 305,
    354, 405, 419
Suhl, Germany, 83
Sulimierskiego, Filipa, 64, 72
Sulz, Austria, 174
Sulzbach-Rosenberg, Germany, 173
Surnames
    Americanicized, 59
    Changes in English-speaking
        countries, 58
    Derived from locations, 55
    Descriptive, 56
    Dialectic, 56
    Double, 57
    French, 57
    German, 54
    Italian, 57

Surnames (*continued*)
    Lithuanian, 57
    Matronymic, 55
    Occupational, 55
    Patronymic, 54, 55, 317, 364, 369,
        445, 446
    Polish, 57
    Slavic, 57
    Spelling variations, 54
Sutschawa, Bukovina, 97. *See also*
    Suceava, Romania
Suwalki, Poland, 81, 344
Svitavy, Czech Republic, 94
Swabia, 89, 304, 336
    Danube Swabians, 96
    History, 87, 97
Swabian Turkey, 97, 110, 289
    History, 85
Swabians, 81, 102, 107, 191, 411, 444.
    See also Alamanni
Swakopmund, Namibia, 52
Swan River district, Western Australia,
    207
Sweden, 99, 281, 363
    Census records, 370
    Central Statistical Bureau, 371
    Church records, 369
    City archives, 371
    Civil registration, 370
    Court records, 370
    Emigration records, 370
    Genealogical resources, 376
    Genealogical societies, 370
    German immigration, 449, 450
    History, 78, 85, 88, 358, 367, 444
    House of Genealogy, 371
    Land records, 370
    Language, 368
    Lutherans, 369
    Military names, 369
    Military records, 370
    Names, 369
    National archives, 370
        Statens Utlänningskommissions
            arkiv (SUK), 371
        Svensk Arkivinformation
            (SVAR), 370
    National Surveying Office, 371
    Regional archives, 370, 371
    Researching in, 367
    Swedish Pomerania, 368, 370
Swedenborgians, 120, 124, 138
    In Canada, 191
Swedish East India Company, 258
Swiatlowska, Maria, 420
Swift Current, Saskatchewan, 192
Swiss, 78
    In America, 419
    In Argentina, 193
    In Australia, 105, 207, 260
    In Brazil, 194, 195, 201
    In Canada, 218
    In Chile, 199
    In Crimean peninsula, 102

Swiss (*continued*)
    In New Zealand, 105, 209, 211
    In North America, 105
    In South Africa, 105, 218
    In South America, 105
    In United States, 188
Swiss Brethren, 113
Swiss Confederation, 104
Swiss National Tourist Office, 299, 433
Switzerland, 78, 83, 106, 107, 116, 148,
    173, 185, 262, 263, 411, 442, 443,
    444, 447, 448
    Burgher rolls, 299
    Cantons, 83
    Census records, 299
    Central Office for Genealogical
        Information, 299
    Church records, 298, 444
    Civil records, 299
    Community of origin, 298
    Consulate, 438
    Emigration, 191, 225, 277, 304, 418,
        420, 443, 444, 446, 448
    Emigration records, 299
    Family records, 299
    Gazetteers, 63
    Genealogical societies, 299
    Genealogies, 415
    German emigration, 50, 102, 184,
        185, 188, 193, 195, 199, 207, 210,
        211, 213, 228, 411
    History, 75, 87, 88, 91, 92, 104–5,
        114, 146, 153, 446
    Languages, 298
    Map of, 451
    Microfilms, 41
    Military records, 299
    Miscellaneous records, 299
    Periodicals, 426
    Postal codes, 73, 421
    Records, 298, 419
    Religions, 119
    Research helps, 422, 426
    Researching in, 264, 298
    Surnames, 54, 61, 62
    Wills, 299
Sydney, New South Wales, 51, 203,
    204, 207, 208, 209, 245, 247, 248
Sydow, Rita, 284
Syrmia, 81, 97, 108, 289, 350. *See also*
    Srem, Yugoslavia. *See also* Syrmien
    History, 85
Syrmien, 81, 85, 97, 108, 289, 350. *See*
    also Srem, Yugoslavia. *See also*
    Syrmia
Szczecin, Poland, 344. *See also* Stettin,
    Germany
Szeged, Hungary, 78, 96
Szucs, Loretto Dennis, 18, 52

— T —

Tacitus (Roman historian), 86
Taddy, Gerhard, 155

Tafferner, Anton, 109, 354
Taiwan, 258
Tajikistan, 328
Tal, Uriel, 159
Talbot, Kathrine, 155
Tallagala, Queensland, 246
Tallinn, Estonia, 321
   Lutheran consistory, 313
Tampke, Jürgen, 235, 236, 259, 260
Tanganyika, 219, 237
Tanunda, Victoria, 205, 248
Tanzania, 212, 219–20, 237, 256
Tänzer, Aron, 173, 175
Tapper, Lawrence F., 29, 180, 181
Taranaki province, New Zealand, 210, 211
Tartu, Estonia, 321
   Records, 321
Tasmania, Australia, 51, 202, 203, 209, 245
Täufer, 116
Taunus, 81
Taurida, Russia, 79, 81, 312, 314
Taurien, 81. See also Taurida, Russia
Tax records, 262
   United States, 13
Taylor, Ryan, 29
Tbilisi, Georgia, 102, 116. See also Tiflis, Georgia
Te Awamatu, New Zealand, 251
Teddington, Middlesex, England, 373
Temeschburg, 96. See also Timisoara, Romania
Temeschwar, 96. See also Timisoara, Romania
Temora, South Australia, 204
Templars. See Templers
Temple Society, 111, 117, 120, 138, 222, 288. See also Templers
Temple-Balch Institute for Immigration Research, Philadelphia, 50, 223, 410
Templer Mennonites, 203, 221. See also Mennonites
   In Palestine, 221
Templer, William, 158
Templers, 117, 136, 139, 143. See also Temple Society
   In Australia, 246, 247
   In Canada, 138
   In Caucasus, 117
   In Germany, 222
   In Kansas, 138
   In New York, 138
   In Palestine, 117, 222, 247
   In Russia, 222
   In Russian Empire, 117, 247
   In United States, 117
   Information, 288
   Mennonite, 222, 247
Tempsch, Rudolf, 368, 376
Tennessee, 135
Tepper, Michael H., 52, 53
Terek River, 82
Terek, Caucasus, 82, 312

Teschen, 82, 84, 94. See also Cieszyn, Poland
Tesin, Czech Republic, 82
Tessin, 83. See also Ticino canton, Switzerland
Teutonic Knights, 86, 89, 98, 99, 298, 321, 338, 358
Texas, 189, 190, 414, 433, 446
   German immigration, 187
Thailand, 45
Theal, George McCall, 213, 237
Theilhaber, Felix A., 181
Theresienthal, Ukraine, 327
Thernstrom, Stephan, 231, 420
Thierfelder, Franz, 44, 64, 69, 213
Thirty Years' War, 56, 78, 88, 89, 92, 94, 105, 113, 114, 115, 118, 145, 182, 367, 368, 443
Thode, Ernest J., 57, 62, 66, 72, 78, 83, 125, 126, 137, 144, 181, 188, 231, 264, 265, 269, 273, 279, 290, 294, 295, 298, 305, 329, 330, 335, 337, 343, 347, 354, 400, 405, 420
Thomastown, Victoria, 206
Thompson, Kenneth F., 5, 406
Thomsen, Finn A., 72, 364, 404, 407
Thorn, 80, 84, 100, 143. See also Torun, Poland
Thurgau canton, Switzerland, 83
Thüringen, 76. See also Thuringia
   FHL cataloging, 44
   Genealogical societies, 276
Thüringerwald, 82
Thuringia, 75, 76, 79, 82, 88, 265, 423. See also Thüringen
   FHL cataloging, 44
   Genealogical societies, 276
   History, 75, 91
   State archives, 273
Thuringian Forest, 82
Ticino canton, Switzerland, 83, 211
Tiesenhausen, Berend von, 236
Tietze, Hans, 156
Tiflis, Georgia, 116. See also Tbilisi, Georgia
Timaru, New Zealand, 251
Timisoara, Romania, 78, 96, 353
Tiraspol, Ukraine, 314
   Catholic Consistory, 314
Tirna Mare, Romania, 85
Tirol, 83, 92, 289, 290. See also Tyrol
Tisza river region, 78
Togo, 212, 220, 256
Toleranzpatent, 98. See also Patent of Tolerance (1781)
Tolna, Hungary, 351
Tolzmann, Don Heinrich, 231, 232, 420, 421
Tomaszów Mazowiecki, Poland, 344
Tønsberg, Norway, 363
Toowoomba, Australia, 205
Torontal, Hungary, 351
Toronto, Ontario, 20, 21, 25, 26, 192
Torrensville, South Australia, 260

Torun, Poland, 80, 84, 100, 143
Toscano, Mario, 109
Tovar, Venezuela, 201
Traeger, Paul, 109, 329, 346
Traité de Paix, 74. See also Treaty of Versailles
Transkei, South Africa, 214
Translating records, 384, 418
Transnistria, 82
Transnistrien, 82. See also Transnistria
Trans-Siberian Railway, 84, 102, 450
Trans-Ural, Russian Empire (Asia), 319
Transvaal Archives Depot, 254
Transvaal, South Africa, 215, 216, 218
Transylvania, 81, 98, 289, 334, 423, 442, 444
   Church records, 282, 355, 423
   History, 77, 85, 114, 346
   Records, 347
   Yizkor books, 168
Transylvanian Saxons, 95, 97, 98, 106, 110, 115, 186, 190, 226, 336, 421, 443, 448
   Records, 347
Trappist Catholics, 215
Trappist monasteries, 217
Trappist monks, 217
Traverso, Enzo, 159
Trawnicek, Peter, 150
Treaty of Kiel, 363
Treaty of Lübeck, 368
Treaty of Nijmegen, 444
Treaty of St. Germain, 74, 449
Treaty of Trianon, 74, 449
Treaty of Verdun, 442
Treaty of Versailles, 74, 119, 449
Trebon, Czech Republic, 333
Trent, Italy, 95, 289, 294, 337
   History, 77
   State Archives, 338
Trentino, 294
Trento, 95, 337. See also Trent, Italy
Tribbeko, John, 232, 376
Trient, 95, 289, 294, 337. See also Trent, Italy
Trier, Germany, 145, 195, 198, 221, 240, 442
Triest, 289. See also Trieste, Italy
Trieste, Italy, 49, 92, 150, 208, 289, 349
   Emigration, 208
Triple Frisia, 361
Troper, Harold, 177, 232
Troppau, 333. See also Opava, Czech Republic
Tunkers, 116
Turek, Poland, 340
Turkey, 221, 222, 257, 258, 328, 445
   Archives, 348
   Census records, 348
   History, 85, 346
   Researching in, 347
   State library, 348
Turkish Wars, 96
Turkmenistan, 328

Turks, 80, 81, 88, 96, 107, 443, 444
Turku, 358. *See also* Abo, Finland
Turler, Heinrich, 305
Turner, Eugene James, 188, 226, 406
Tutzing, Germany, 217
Tvedt, Kevin, 57, 62
Twersky, Isadore, 156
Twigden, Liz, 202, 205, 236, 244, 260
Tyler, Elizabeth, 236
Tyrol, 75, 83, 148, 289, 290, 294, 337
   German emigration, 201
   History, 77, 92, 95, 96
   Lutheran records, 294
   Records, 292

— U —

Uecker River, 82
Ueckermark, Germany, 82, 204, 216,
   227, 407
Uetrecht, E., 63, 72
Ufa, Russia, 102
Uganda, 226
Ukraina, 325. *See also* Ukraine
Ukraine, 81, 82, 84, 89, 101, 103, 104,
   118, 163, 289, 311, 312, 317, 319,
   325, 326, 351, 354, 443, 445. *See*
   also Südrussland. *See also* South
   Russia. *See also* New Russia
   Archives, 313
   Atlases, 68
   Church records, 340
   Emigration, 191
   German immigration, 102, 144
   History, 64, 87, 101, 152, 338, 446
   Land records, 342
   Map of, 451
   Microfilms, 41
   Researching in, 325
   Yizkor books, 168
Ukrainians, 93, 339
Ulbrich, Heinz, 284
Uleaborg, Finland, 358. *See also* Oulu,
   Finland
Ullman, Robert, 94
Ulm, Germany, 96, 176
Ungarn, 289. *See also* Hungary
Union of Kalmar, 367
Union of South Africa, 448. *See also*
   South Africa
Unitarians, 114, 117, 136
   In Poland, 338
Unitas Fratrum, 112, 331
United Brethren in Christ, 120, 121
   Archives, 130
   In Canada, 21
United Church of Canada, 21, 124
   Archives, 129
United Church of Christ
   Archives, 128, 129
   In Latin America, 238
United Empire Loyalists, 24, 190
United Evangelical Church, 124
   Archives, 130

United Kingdom, 215. *See also*
   Northern Ireland. *See also* Britain.
   See also Great Britain
   History, 356
   Researching in, 372
United Protestant Ministers'
   Association and Conference, 124
United States, 89, 118, 445, 447, 448,
   450
   Atlantic states, 434
   Border crossing lists, 14
   Bounty land property, 13
   Cemetery associations, 10
   Cemetery records, 10
   Census records, 2, 14
   Church records, 10, 415
   Civil War, 191, 210
   Consulates, 353, 421
   County histories, 17
   Court records, 11
   Customs Service arrival records, 52
   Depression, 447
   Genealogical helps, 418
   Genealogical societies, 414
   German immigration, 50, 90, 95, 96,
     143, 184, 185, 187, 193, 196, 210,
     223, 227, 228, 229, 231, 232, 351,
     359, 376, 407, 409, 410, 411, 412,
     415, 420, 446, 448, 449, 450
   German settlements, 187
   German-American soldiers, 420
   German-language newspapers, 11
   Great Plains states, 103, 188, 190,
     448
   Homestead property, 13
   Immigration, 449
   Immigration and Naturalization
     Service, 52
   Land records, 12
   Library of Congress, 19, 70. *See also*
     Library of Congress
   Lodge records, 10
   Midwest states, 186, 187, 188, 421,
     433, 434
   Military Death Index, 45
   Military pension files, 14
   Military records, 14
   Mortuary records, 10
   National archives, 5, 17, 19, 50, 53
   Naturalization, 410
   Naturalization records, 14, 223
   Orphanage records, 11
   Port cities, 186
   Private school records, 10
   Professional associations, 11
   Reasons for immigration, 182
   Religions, 120
   Research helps, 412, 420
   Research in, 415
   Shenandoah valley, 418
   Ship arrival lists, 14
   Social Security Death Index, 45
   Southern states, 189, 434
   Tax records, 13

United States (*continued*)
   Upper Midwest, 191
   Vital records, 2, 13
   Western states, 434
United States Holocaust Memorial
   Museum and Archives, 169
United Zion Church, 134
Unity of Brethren, 112
Universalists, 118, 124, 136, 141, 142
University of Minnesota, 438
   Center for Austrian Studies, 432
University of St. Thomas (St. Paul,
   Minnesota), 301, 438
University of Texas, 433
University of Wisconsin, 434
University student lists, 263
Unruh, Benjamin Heinrich, 144, 318,
   320, 354, 362
Unterwalden canton, Switzerland, 83
Upper Austria, 83, 96, 290
   Lutheran records, 293
   Records, 291
Upper Canada. *See also under* Canada
Upper Hungary, 68, 92, 95, 334, 442.
   See also Slovak Republic
   Gazetteers, 330
Upper Silesia, 76
Ural Mountains, 84, 102
Uri canton, Switzerland, 83
Uruguay, 192, 197, 201, 239, 241
   Census records, 240
   Civil registers, 239
   National archives, 242
   National library, 242
   Research helps, 238
Usambara highlands, Tanzania, 220
Utah, 188
Uzhhorod, Ukraine
   Archives, 327

— V —

Vaasa, Finland, 358. *See also* Wasa,
   Finland
Vaduz, Liechtenstein, 302
Valais canton, Switzerland, 83
Valdivia province, Chile, 199
Vallendar/Rhein, Germany, 217
Valparaiso, Chile, 199
   Arrival lists, 52
Vancouver, British Columbia, 50, 192
Vanderhalven, F., 73
Varta River region, Poland, 104
Vasaland, Finland, 358
Vasmer, Max, 73
Vatican City, 351
Vaud canton, Switzerland, 83
Venetia, 75
Venezia Giulia, Italy, 338
Venezuela, 201
Venice, Italy, 338
Ventspils, Latvia, 322
Verdenhalven, Fritz, 405
Verdun, France, 145

Vesterheim Genealogical Center, Madison, WI, 365

Vianden canton, Luxembourg, 83

Victoria, Australia, 51, 202, 203, 204, 205, 206, 207, 209, 211, 245, 246, 447

Victoria, British Columbia, 25, 26, 50

Victoria, Cameroon, 220

Vienna, Austria, 83, 150, 152, 288, 290, 294, 295, 296, 297, 444. *See also* Wien

    "Lehmann" city directories, 295

    Alservorstadt, 291

    Archives, 291, 304

    Church records, 291

    City archives, 296

    Emigration, 290

    Erdberg, 291

    Marriage records, 291, 304

    Military Archives, 330

    Passports, 297

    Population explosion, 291

    Schottenfeld parish, 291

    St. Marx parish, 291

Vietnam, 45

Vietnam War, 45

Viipuri, Finland, 358. *See also* Wiborg, Finland

Village genealogies, 273. *See also* Dorfsippenbücher *and* Ortssippenbücher

Village lineage books, 422. *See also* Ortssippenbücher *and* Ortsfamilienbücher

Vilnius, Lithuania, 322

Vine Hill, Nick, 51, 243, 244, 246, 247, 248, 249, 252

Virginia, 121, 188, 189, 227, 231, 407, 420

    German immigration, 184, 187

Virkkunen, Arto Heikki, 375

Visby, Sweden, 367

Vistula River region, Poland, 80, 84, 100, 115, 143

Vistula-Nogat delta area

    History, 76

Vital records. *See under each country*

Vogel, Gudrun, 155

Vogesen, 82. *See* Vosges Mountains

Vogtland, Germany, 82

Voigt, Hans-Jürgen, 305, 307, 355, 423

Voigt, Karl, 63, 71

Vojvodina (Serbia), 78, 79, 81, 96, 297, 335, 350, 351, 476

    Archives, 351

    History, 77, 85, 289, 349

Volga German Republic, 103

Volga River region, Russia, 101, 102, 103, 191, 193, 196, 243, 257, 285, 318, 319, 324, 449, 450

    Map of, 451

    Records, 313

    Settlements, 84

    Settler lists, 320

Volhynia, 80, 89, 100, 103, 118, 142, 286, 312, 313, 315, 318, 319, 325, 326, 341, 426, 447. *See also* Zhitomir

    Church records, 144, 340

    Emigration, 191

    Genealogical societies, 285

    Genealogical sources, 342

    Genealogical tours, 327

    German emigration, 193, 200

    German immigration, 447

    Germans from, 22

    History, 77, 84, 115

    Researchers, 284

    Swabian settlers, 411

    Yizkor books, 168

Volhynian Germans, 197

Völkerwanderung, 86. *See also* Great Barbarian Migrations

Volkov, Shulamit, 159

von Blom, D., 201

von Delft, Heinz, 215, 218

von der Porten, Edward, 109

von Grueningen, John Paul, 305

von Helfert, Joseph Alexander, Freiherr, 158

von Lyncker, Alexander, 421

von Moos, Mario, 304, 415

von Poellnitz, G., 215

von Stein, Neithard, 284

von Tiesenhausen, Berend, 236

Vondra, Josef, 117, 144, 202, 208, 236, 246, 260

Vorarlberg, Austria, 83, 92, 148, 152, 174, 289, 290

    Emigration, 290

    History, 77

    Lutheran records, 294

    Records, 292

Vorpommern, 82

Vosges Mountains, 82

Vryheid, South Africa, 215, 217

Vysov, Czech Republic, 94

— W —

Waadt, 83. *See also* Vaud canton, Switzerland

Wachstein, Bernhard, 181

Wagemann, Ernst, 238

Wagenpfeil, H., 172, 181

Wagner, Ernst, 110, 226, 354, 421

Waibola Township, New Zealand, 210

Walachei, 82. *See also* Walachia

Walachia, 82

    Records, 347

Waldeck, 75, 76, 227, 279, 407

    Church records, 409

    FHL cataloging, 44

    History, 75

Waldensians, 87, 89, 112, 115, 140, 286, 411

    In Germany, 286

    In Italy, 338

Waldensians (*continued*)

    Records, 130

    Resource centers, 286

Waldner, Tony, 133, 144

Waldo, Peter, 87, 112

Waldus. *See* Waldo, Peter

Walker, Mack, 183, 194, 196, 198, 201, 226

Wall, Kenneth De, 440

Wallachia, Romania, 114

Wallis, 83. *See also* Valais canton, Switzerland

Wallonia, Belgium, 357

Walloons, 88, 356, 367, 369, 443

    History, 113

    In Germany, 286

    Records, 140

    Resource centers, 286

Walter, Jörg, 421

Walther, Suzanne, 154

Wandler, Diane J., 5, 354

Wanka Collection (Canada), 23

Wanne, Olavi, 375

Wanneroo, Western Australia, 206

Wappäus, Johann, 234

War of the League of Augsburg, 444

Ward, Robert, 263, 308

Wardale, Carol, 204, 234, 260

Warmia region, East Prussia, 119

Warmia, Poland, 79

Wars of Liberation (German), 89

Wars of Unification (German), 74, 90

Wars of Unification (Italian), 93

Warsaw, Poland, 79, 80, 81, 82, 89, 100, 109, 326, 338, 344, 345

    Archives, 344

    History, 99

    Records, 317

Warta River region, Poland, 82, 84, 98, 100, 340, 449

Warthe River, 84. *See also* Warta River region, Poland

Warthegau, 82, 98. *See also* Warta River region, Poland

Wasa, Finland, 358. *See also* Vaasa, Finland

Wasastjerna, Oskar, 375

Washington (state), 188, 189, 329

Washington, DC, 188, 189

Waterloo County, Ontario, 29, 190

Waterloo, Ontario, 21, 190

Web, Marek, 171, 179

Webster, J. B., 218, 237

Wecken, Ernst, 230, 417

Wegeleben, Christel, 269, 411

Wegemer, B., 175

Wegmann, Susanne, 202, 207, 237, 260

Weichsel River region, 84. *See also* Vistula River region, Poland

Weidlein, Johann, 110

Weikel, Sally A., 422

Weiman, Ralph, 159

Weimar Republic, 83

Weinberger, Gabriele, 158

Weiner, Miriam, 178, 181, 317, 328, 422
Weinfeld, Morton, 232
Weinstrasse, 81
Weiss, Bob, 166
Weiss, Volkmar, 269, 422
Weissbort, Daniel, 159
Weisser, Charles, 354
Welisch, Sophie A., 64, 73, 97, 110, 354
Wellauer, Maralyn A., 232, 299, 305, 354, 401, 405, 422, 426
Wellington County, Ontario, 29
Wellington, New Zealand, 51, 210, 211, 250, 251
Wellisch, Henry, 166
Welsch, E., 422
Welte, Thomas, 181
Wends, 80, 82
Wenzel, Reinhard, 285
Wermes, Martina, 279, 305, 307, 355, 422, 423
Werner, Manuel, 181
Werner, Michael, 160
Werner, Otto, 181
Werra River, 82
Wertheimer, Jack, 159
Weser River, 80
West Australia, 209
West Frankish Kingdom, 86
West Indies, 194, 223, 410
West Prussia, 75, 76, 191, 263, 411, 416, 471. *See also* Westpreussen
  Church records, 355, 423
  FHL cataloging, 44
  Gazetteers, 68
  Genealogical societies, 285
  German emigration, 102
  History, 75, 76, 77, 83, 84, 88, 89, 90, 100, 102, 114, 185, 200
  Military parish records, 266
  Name index files, 286
  Place names, 66
  Religions, 119
West Virginia, 121
West Volhynia, 142
Western Australia, 202, 203, 205, 206, 207, 208, 209, 235, 236, 244, 245, 259
Western Canada. *See under* Canada
Western Galicia, 84, 97, 340. *See also* Galicia
Western Pacific Islands, 212
Western Samoa, 211
Western Ukraine, 326
Westerwald, 82
Westfalen, 76. *See also* Westphalia
  FHL cataloging, 44
  Genealogical societies, 275
  State archives, 272
Westgalizien, 84. *See also* Western Galicia
Westland, New Zealand, 210, 250

Westphalia, 57, 75, 76, 148, 358, 368, 423. *See also* Westfalen
  Burgher books, 267
  FHL cataloging, 44
  German emigration, 200, 349
  History, 87
  Religions, 119
Westpreussen, 76, 423. *See also* West Prussia
  FHL cataloging, 44
Wheatfield, New York, 227, 407
White Russia, 446. *See also* Belarus
Whitehorse, Yukon Territory, 27
Whitoworth, Robert P., 248
Wiborg, Finland, 358. *See also* Viipuri, Finland
Wiebe, Raymond, 423
Wien, 83, 288, 290. *See also* Vienna, Austria
Wiesbaden, Germany, 81
Wiesenseite, Russian Volga, 324
Wilczek, Christoph, 415
Wilder-Okladek, F., 159
Wilhelm, Franz, 58, 110, 296, 342, 346, 351, 355, 423
Wilhelm, Peter, 156
Wilken, Dale W., 408
Williams, George H., 144
Williams, Judith, 209, 251
Wills, 262
Wilskman, Atle, 376
Wilson, Emily S., 19
Wilson, Lilian, 236
Wilson, Thomas B., 19
Wilson, Woodrow, 74
Wiltz canton, Luxembourg, 83
Wimmera, Victoria, 206
Winckler, Wilhelm, 306
Windau, 322. *See also* Ventspils, Latvia
Windhoek, Namibia, 255
Windholz, Oren, 144, 232, 423
Windhorst, Bosnia, 349
Windisch Mark, Slovenia, 82
Winebrenner church, 118
Winebrenner, John, 128
Winkler, Wilhelm, 182, 198, 200, 201, 212, 218, 219, 221, 226, 306
Winnipeg, Manitoba, 21, 22, 24, 25, 26, 27, 132, 192, 340, 426
Wintherthur, Switzerland, 146
Wischau, 94. *See also* Vysov, Czech Republic
Wisconsin, 187, 188, 189, 230, 333, 343, 416
  Area Resource Centers, 438
  German immigration, 229, 413
  German-Bohemians, 229, 414
  Library collections, 436
Wisconsin Lutheran Church, 126
Wisla River region, 84. *See also* Vistula River region, Poland
Wismar, Germany, 368
Wistrich, Robert S., 156, 160

Witwatersrand region, South Africa, 216, 218
Wlaschek, Rudolf M., 156
Wojtakowski, Eduard, 345
Wolf, Gerson, 157
Wolfert, Marion, 48, 53, 232, 305, 424
Wolga River region, 84. *See also* Volga River region, Russia
Wolhynien, 84. *See also* Volhynia
Woods, Jack D., 373
World War I, 58, 64, 65, 69, 77, 79, 80, 90, 94, 95, 99, 118, 148, 190, 212, 215, 218, 220, 241, 252, 256, 264, 266, 288, 319, 321, 325, 328, 330, 336, 339, 346, 348, 349, 350, 352, 356, 357, 373, 409, 447, 448, 449
World War II, 65, 74, 75, 77, 91, 96, 103, 108, 144, 183, 186, 189, 192, 197, 199, 201, 203, 207, 208, 220, 241, 248, 281, 325, 329, 330, 341, 344, 350, 368, 417, 449
World-Wide Web, 38
Worms, Germany, 79, 145, 442
Wörster, Peter, 73
Wroclaw, Poland, 344, 345
Württemberg, 75, 76, 79, 81, 88, 102, 148, 190, 217, 246, 263, 277, 423, 444
  Census, 267
  Danube Swabians, 96
  Emigration, 278
  Family registers, 263, 279
  FHL cataloging, 44
  German emigration, 102, 185, 200, 201, 213, 225, 417
  History, 97, 102, 115
  State archives, 270
  Swabians, 411
Württemberg Regiment, 216
Württemberg Separatists, 116
Würzburg, Germany, 145
Wurzner, Hans, 177
Wuschke, Ewald, 129, 142, 144, 193, 313, 320, 341, 426
Wyant, Sophia Stalzer, 425
Wycliffe, John, 112
Wynne, Suzan Fishl, 23, 73, 180, 181, 321, 353
Wyoming, 121, 189

—Y—

Yad Vashem Library, 169
Yaounde, Cameroon, 256
Yellowknife, Northwest Territories, 26
Yiddish language, 149
YIVO Institute for Jewish Research, 171, 434
Yizkor books, 168
Yoder, Don, 232, 277, 415, 423
Yorkton, Saskatchewan, 192
Young, George F. W., 199, 200, 201, 235
Young, Gordon, 235

Yugoslavia, 80, 297, 416
  Danube Swabians, 109
  History, 64, 77, 85, 87, 92, 93, 98, 348, 449
  Map of, 451
  Microfilms, 41
  Researching in, 348
  Village genealogies, 268
Yukon Territory, Canada, 25
  Civil records, 27

— Z —

Zabuzanski Collection, Poland, 341
Zagreb, Croatia, 349, 350
Zahm, Thomas R., 179
Zaleski, Jan Steven, 14, 18, 226
Zambesi River, 213, 237
Zambia, 212
Zámrsk, Czech Republic, 333
Zanzibar, 219, 237

Zaporozhye, Ukraine, 101
Zeitung. See Die Zeitung
Zelzer, Maria, 181
Zemgalia, 81
Zentralrat der Juden in Deutschland, 164
Zhdanov, 102. See also Mariupol, Ukraine
Zhitomir, 312, 315. See also Volhynia
Zielke, Irina, 308, 355, 424
Zielke, Rainer, 308, 355, 424
Zilk, Helmut, 177
Zimbabwe, 212, 219, 252
Zimmerman, Gary J., 48, 53, 232, 305, 424
Zimmern, Helen, 363
Zion Society, 148
Zionism, 448
Zips League, 96

Zips, Slovak Republic, 85, 95, 96, 97, 334, 442, 443. See also Spis, Slovak Republic
Zipser Bund, 96. See Zips League
Zmudz, 81
Zöllner, L., 260
Zrdenka, Joachim, 344
Zubatsky, David S., 164, 181
Zubrzycki, Jerzy, 235, 248
Zuellichau, East Brandenburg, 247
Zug canton, Switzerland, 83
Zululand, South Africa, 216, 217
Zurek-Eichenau, Werner Freiherr von, 340
Zürich canton, Switzerland, 83, 146, 188, 196, 227, 409
Zürich, Switzerland, 300
Zwinger, Dieter, 424
Zwingli, Ulrich, 87, 105, 112, 443
Zwittau, 94. See also Svitavy, Czech Republic

MEMBERSHIP COMMITTEE - keeps an updated list of the membership. The committee processes membership applications and renewals and prepares the address labels for the newsletter. A welcome packet will be sent to all new members.

PROGRAM COMMITTEE - obtains locations for meetings, arranges for speakers, prepares meeting sites and forwards this information to the newsletter.

SPRING CONFERENCE COMMITTEE - plans annual spring conference meeting, arranges for keynote speaker, location and luncheon.

RESEARCH COMMITTEE - provides information to members by writing or publishing genealogical research articles, answering queries, providing translators, and keeping a bibliography of resources and addresses to aid in Germanic research.

LIBRARY COMMITTEE - purchases and catalogs our group's books and materials, which are housed at the Concordia College Library in St. Paul. Also maintains clipping file, newsletter and quarterly collection.

REGIONAL RESOURCE COMMITTEE - gives ideas and assistance to various small study groups concentrating on a particular area. Plans Fall Workshop meeting which concentrates on specific Germanic regions.

NEWSLETTER COMMITTEE - issues an informative newsletter 4 times a year featuring German research hints, book reports, special articles, members' queries, as well as announcements and information about upcoming meetings. The committee writes, prints and mails this newsletter to Germanic Genealogy Society members. In addition, newsletters are exchanged with other genealogy groups.

SALES COMMITTEE - publishes various forms and research information helpful to Germanic Research.

In addition to the above Standing Committees, Special Committees are often established to carry out specific puirposes in the interest of the Society. Such committees might be:

By-Laws Review Committe   Telephone Committee
Cemetery Recording Committee   Auditing Committee
Nominating Committee   Archives Committee
Research Book Committee

All GGS members are eligible to serve on these committees and are encouraged to do so according to their interests.

HISTORY OF THE ORGANIZATION

The GERMAN INTEREST GROUP was started in December, 1979 and by-laws were officially adopted in September, 1980. The name GERMANIC GENEALOGY SOCIETY was officially adopted at the November 1992 Annual Meeting. It became a branch of the MINNESOTA GENEALOGICAL SOCIETY on January 10, 1981. On November 21, 1992 the name was officially changed to Germanic Genealogy Society

PURPOSES OF THE ORGANIZATION

The purposes are exclusively educational, more specifically to:
1) provide an association of those interested in genealogy;

2) provide opportunity for exchange of ideas relating to genealogical practices and experiences;

3) hold meetings for the instruction and interest of its members;

4) foster and increase an interest in Germanic genealogy;

5) collect, and when practicable, publish genealogical biographical and historical material relating to Minnesota families of German descent and their forbears;

6) encourage the establishment of German genealogical resources in genealogical departments in libraries throughout the State of Minnesota.

SALES MATERIAL

Germanic Genealogy: A Guide to Worldwide Sources & Migration Patterns.

The Lutherans of Russia, Vol. 1, Parish Index to Church Books of the Evangelical Lutheran Church of St. Petersburg, 1833-1885.

Die Ahnenstammkartei des Deutschen Volkes, An Introduction and Register. How to access a collection of pedigree charts and family group records & card index of 2.7 million names at the German Center for Genealogy in Leipzig.

A Translation of Abbreviations Found in *Müllers Grosses Deutsches Ortsbuch*

Using the *Meyers Orts - und Verkehrslexikon*

Guide to Pennsylvania Archives

Library Holdings of the Germanic Genealogy Society at Concordia Library

Blank Family Group Sheets & Ancestor Charts (English, German)

A complete list is available in the newsletter or on request with a S.A.S.E. from GGS.

GERMANIC GENEALOGY SOCIETY MEMBERSHIP

NAME _____

ADDRESS _____
_____

PHONE _____

APPLICATION _____ RENEWAL _____

MEMBERSHIP NUMBER _____

Membership is open to anyone interested in Germanic genealogy. A member is encouraged to become a member of the MINNESOTA GENEALOGICAL SOCIETY.

Dues are $8.00 per year payable in March.

Make check payable to Germanic Genealogy Society.

Mail to: GERMANIC GENEALOGY SOCIETY
         P.O. BOX 16312
         ST. PAUL, MN 55116-0312

5/97

* * * * * * * * * * * * * * * * * *

MINNESOTA GENEALOGICAL SOCIETY MEMBERSHIP

NAME _____

ADDRESS _____
_____

NATIONALITIES OF INTEREST _____

INDIVIDUAL $22 _____ FAMILY $28 _____

APPLICATION _____ RENEWAL _____

MEMBERSHIP NUMBER _____

Make check payable to Minnesota Genealogical Society.

Mail to: MINNESOTA GENEALOGICAL SOCIETY
         P.O. BOX 16069
         ST. PAUL, MN 55116

Germanic Genealogy Society Books

Germanic Genealogy:
A Guide to Worldwide Sources and Migration Patterns, Second Edition

by Edward R. Brandt, Ph.D., Mary Bellingham, Kent Cutkomp, Kermit Frye and Patricia A. Lowe
for the Germanic Genealogy Society, St. Paul, Minnesota

This comprehensive how-to handbook for the German family history researcher offers help for beginners through advanced. The book has been revised and greatly expanded especially chapters on research in Germany and Austria; computer genealogy; Germanic Jewish research and German religions.

Includes:
- Country by country guide to the sources
- Useful addresses of archives and societies
- Current German postal codes
- Worldwide Germanic migration patterns
- Jewish, Catholic, Lutheran, Mennonite history and sources
- Germanic history and geography
- Historical and modern maps, including boundary changes
- Annotated list of gazetteers
- German word list and language helps
- German naming patterns and place names
- Extensive, annotated bibliography

Tells how to:
- Get started on your research
- Find your ancestor's place of origin
- Use church and civil records
- Get the most from passenger departure and arrival lists
- Read German script
- Correspond abroad
- Use the resources of the Family History Library and its Centers and how to locate resources they haven't filmed yet

This well-indexed, up-to-date, easy-to-use book has 150 additional pages to what is already the best how-to book for Germanic research.
Softcover, Autobind, 520 pg., 1997. ISBN 0-9644337-3-7

Die Ahnenstammkartei des Deutschen Volkes: An Introduction and Register
by Thomas K. Edlund

The Deutsche Zentralstelle für Genealogie (German Central Office for Genealogy) has collected family histories of Germanic & Central European people since 1922. Their primary collection consists of "Ahnentafeln," or pedigree charts, and family group records, including an "Ahnenstammkartei," or card index, of 2.7 million names. These records have been microfilmed and are available at the Family History Library. However, the filming was not done in alphabetical sequence making the 1,200 rolls of microfilm difficult to use. This *Register* lists the grouping by family names including the spelling variations. It is not an every name index. This *Register* will help you identify the correct microfilm for each surname you are researching. A valuable finding aid for all German research facilities.
Paperbound, perfect binding, 133 pages, 1995. ISBN 0-9644337-2-9

Germanic Genealogy Society Books

	Price	Copies	Total
☐ Germanic Genealogy: A Guide to Worldwide Sources and Migration Patterns, Second Edition	$ 32.00	_____	$ _____
☐ Die Ahnenstammkartei des Deutschen Volkes: An Introduction and Register	20.00	_____	
Subtotal			_____
Minnesota Residents Add 6.5% Sales Tax			_____
S&H (US: $4.00 per book; Foreign Countries: $6.00 per book for Surface Mail)			_____
Total Due Books plus S & H			$ _____

Name _____ Phone (_____) _____

Address _____

City, State/Province, Zip/Postal Code _____

Enclose check or money order made out to GGS for total amount due for books plus shipping & handling.
Mail to: GGS, Sales Committee, PO Box 16312, St. Paul MN 55116-0312

HERE'S WHAT OTHERS ARE SAYING ABOUT
GERMANIC GENEALOGY!
Reviews of the First Edition

"When the *Research Guide to German-American Genealogy* was first published a few years ago, I was impressed with its scholarly, yet easy-to-use format. Now we are fortunate to have a new edition with the revised title *Germanic Genealogy: A Guide to Worldwide Source and Migration Patterns* and what I thought to be a near perfect handbook to the Germanic researcher, has yet been improved and expanded. This book answers a multitude of questions the beginner encounters in the struggle with the complexities of Germanic genealogy. But it also contains a wealth of information for the more seasoned researcher. We owe a debt of gratitude to the dedicated authors who created this great research tool."

Horst A. Reschke, Editor of the Q&A column,
"Questions on Germanic Ancestry," Heritage Quest Magazine

"While most guides to doing German research center on the present boundaries of Germany, this book deals with German speaking persons who emigrated throughout the world. ... This book is probably the most comprehensive guide available for persons doing research in German ancestry."

Immigrant Genealogical Society Newsletter

"Make space on your shelf for *Germanic Genealogy*. ... Loaded with useful information ... contains 130 more pages than the first version. ... German history buffs will discover sections of the book that are especially intriguing to them. ... the 32-page index makes this vast pool of information readily useful to the researcher. ... Definitely a book to keep at one's side."

Der Blumenbaum, Sacramento German Genealogy Society

"This is an excellent resource for beginners and more advanced researchers, with a well-presented format showing the procedure to find those German-speaking ancestors. ... This book is highly recommended to all who are engaged in research for German-speaking ancestors."

The Palatine Immigrant, Palatines to America

"The 370 page book is indexed and is the first ever published which deals with the genealogy of German-speakers and their descendants in about sixty countries."

Olmsted County [Minnesota] Genealogical Society

"Retitled and dramatically enlarged since its 1991 debut ... contains a wealth of information for genealogical researchers at all levels. ... This guide is of value to people with European and Eastern European roots and extends itself to Asians, South Africans, and other ethnicities which may have been affected by Germany. The first few chapters are devoted to novice genealogists. ... The remainder of the book is invaluable to the more sophisticated genealogist. ... All in all, *Germanic Genealogy* will be a welcome addition to the most popular genealogy collections ... Public libraries may want to consider purchasing reference and circulating copies, since the price is right."

Booklist, American Library Association